FROM COLONY TO SAR

From Colony to SAR

Hong Kong's Challenges Ahead

Edited by

Joseph Y. S. Cheng

and

Sonny S. H. Lo

The Chinese University Press

ISBN 962–201–671–5

The Chinese University Press
The Chinese University of Hong Kong
Sha Tin, New Territories
Hong Kong

Printed in Hong Kong by Nam Fung Printing Co., Ltd.

Contents

Preface

The recent Sino-British agreement on the Court of Final Appeal may have signalled renewed efforts in cooperation in the last two years of the transition period. It cannot be denied, however, that the diplomatic impasse between Beijing and London since the autumn of 1992 had caused much delay in negotiations and agreements on the necessary arrangements for the transfer of power in 1997. The recent economic slow-down has prompted the community to examine more closely the territory's problems and challenges at the present stage of economic development. While the progress in representative government has served to highlight issues in public housing, education, medical care, transport, and so on, neither the British administration nor the political parties have impressed the public with far-sighted policy proposals. It is not surprising that many people now say they wish 1997 could come sooner, so that all could concentrate on their daily work after the political uncertainty had passed away.

This book intends to contribute to a meaningful discussion of the issues facing Hong Kong in various policy areas in the transition era. A team of academics from the local tertiary institutions would like to offer their thoughts on the identification of the problems, outlining the options available, and assessing their merits. The emphasis is on what needs to be done by the government in the mid-1990s so as to ensure Hong Kong's continued development and prosperity. The team involves scholars with expertise covering the spectrum of major policy areas. The general consensus is that it will be unfortunate if the political uncertainty and the Sino-British diplomatic impasse pose serious obstacles to the formation and implementation of long-term policy programmes. It is perhaps relatively easy for academics to initiate discussions. Cultivating a consensus and mustering the political will to secure the endorsement of the policy programmes by the public and legislature will be much more arduous tasks.

Finally, the Editors would like to take this opportunity to thank the authors for their cooperation in keeping deadlines, etc. We are also most grateful for the good work and support rendered by Mr. Fung Wai-kit and other staff members of The Chinese University Press in the publication of this book. Obviously we have to assume responsibility for the errors and omissions.

Joseph Y. S. Cheng
Sonny S. H. Lo
5 July 1995

Contributors

Mark BRAY holds the post of Reader in the Department of Education, The University of Hong Kong. He is a specialist in comparative education, and has written extensively on the financing of education and on aspects of education and social change.

Johannes M. M. CHAN is Senior Lecturer in Law at The University of Hong Kong and a practising barrister in Hong Kong. He has published widely, and is one of the founding editors of the *Hong Kong Public Law Reports* and the *Bill of Rights Bulletin*.

Joseph Y. S. CHENG is Professor at the Contemporary China Research Centre, City University of Hong Kong, and is the founding editor of the *Hong Kong Journal of Social Sciences*.

Leonard K. CHENG is Associate Dean and Professor of Economics at the School of Business and Management, Hong Kong University of Science and Technology. His research interests include international economics, applied game theory, and economic development of China and Hong Kong.

Nelson W. S. CHOW is Professor of Social Work and Social Administration at The University of Hong Kong. He is specializing in comparative study of social security systems in East and Southeast Asian countries. He has also carried out research in the issue of community support for the Chinese elderly.

Robert T. Y. CHUNG is Research Officer in charge of the Public Opinion Programme at the Social Sciences Research Centre, The University of Hong Kong. He is also the developer of exit polls in Hong Kong and currently a part-time member of the Central Policy Unit of the Hong Kong government.

Peter K. W. FONG is Studies Director at the Senior Staff Course Centre in Hong Kong and Visiting Professor at Tongji University in Shanghai. He was formerly a Consultant of the World Bank and taught urban planning and housing at The University of Hong Kong.

John D. HO is Associate Professor in the Department of Law, City University of Hong Kong. He has a Ph.D. from the University of Minnesota and a J.D. from the University of California at Davies. He is also a member of the State Bar of California.

HUNG Ching-tin is Managing Director of Polling Business Research Co. He graduated from The University of Hong Kong and received his M.A. in translation from The Chinese University of Hong Kong. He is also a pollster, a political analyst and a cross-cultural socio-political commentator.

Jane C. Y. LEE is Chief Executive Officer of Hong Kong Policy Research Institute. She is also Honorary Research Fellow of the City University of Hong Kong. Her most recent publication is on *Public Sector Reform in Hong Kong* published by The Chinese University Press.

LEE Wing-on is Director of Comparative Education Research Centre at The University of Hong Kong. He is the author of *Social Change and Educational Problems in Japan, Singapore and Hong Kong*, and co-editor of *Social Change and Educational Development in Mainland China, Taiwan and Hong Kong.*

LI Yuet-wah is Assignment Editor of *Ming Pao*. She served as chairman of the Hong Kong Journalists Association for three terms and is currently an executive committee member of the Association.

LO Chi-kin is Managing Director of C. K. Lo & S. Lam Limited, a public affairs consultant firm. He contributes regularly to local dailies in Hong Kong and has published a number of books on politics of Hong Kong and China.

Sonny S. H. LO is Assistant Professor in the Division of Social Science, Hong Kong University of Science and Technology. His research focus is on the politics of Hong Kong and Macau.

LUI Yu-hon is Associate Professor in the Department of Economics and Finance, City University of Hong Kong. He is also an associate member of the Association of Cost and Executive Accountants, the Institute of Chartered Secretaries and Administrators, and the Hong Kong Institute of Company Secretaries.

MAN Si-wai is Lecturer in the Department of Educational Administration and Policy, The Chinese University of Hong Kong. She has written books and articles on social and political philosophy, applied ethics, and technology and society.

NG Mee-kam is Lecturer at the Centre of Urban Planning and Environmental Management, The University of Hong Kong. She is also a member of the Hong Kong Institute of Planners and the Royal Town Planning Institute.

NG Sek-hong is Lecturer in Management Studies at The University of Hong Kong. He has published several books and articles about labour and industrial relations in Hong Kong.

Stephen M. H. SZE is Lecturer in the Division of General Education at Lingnan College. His research interests consist of aesthetics, critical theory, mass culture and media criticism, and he has several publications on these topics.

TANG Shu-hung is Head and Reader of the Department of Economics, Hong Kong Baptist University.

John URE is Director of the Telecommunications Research Project at the Centre of Asian Studies, The University of Hong Kong. He is a member of the Hong Kong Consumer Council Steering Group on Telecommunications Policy, and was a member of the Hong Kong delegation to the APEC Telecommunications Working Group in 1994.

Anthony G. O. YEH is Assistant Director and Reader of the Centre of Urban Planning and Environmental Management and Director of the Geographical/Land Information System Research Centre, The University of Hong Kong. He is Fellow of the Hong Kong Institute of Planners and the Royal Australian Planning Institute.

Peter P. YUEN is Head of the Department of Management, Hong Kong Polytechnic University. He was President of the Hong Kong Public Administration Association for the year 1992–1993 and he sits on a number of statutory committees on health policies.

Introduction

Sonny S. H. Lo & Joseph Y. S. Cheng

The secret visit to China by the Chief Secretary of the Hong Kong government, Anson Chan Fang On-sang, in July 1995 marked another phase in the development of Sino-British relations over Hong Kong. The tense Sino-British relations since the Tiananmen incident in the People's Republic of China (P.R.C.) in June 1989, and particularly since the arrival of Governor Patten in Hong Kong, are now taking a turn for the better. While it is premature to jump to a conclusion that Britain and China will be able to cooperate smoothly and easily on all the baffling problems in the run-up to 1997, the entire political transition can be viewed as turbulent, controversial and heavily politicized. The politicization of this decolonization period is unprecedented in Hong Kong, and such politicization can be seen in almost all the political, legal, economic, social and cultural issues discussed in this book.

The contributors in this book adopt a trend scenario; they not only analyse the political, legal, economic, social and cultural issues during the twilight of the British colonial rule, but also attempt to make some predictions about the post-1997 circumstances through analysing the current developments. It is the trend scenario which constitutes the most prominent and significant theme in this book. Indeed, the predictions made by our contributors will be tested as events gradually unfold after 1997. Some contributors seek to propose solutions to solve the problems that they discuss, whereas some adopt a critical perspective to analyse the roots of the problems. The amalgamation of the trend scenario with a critical or imaginative perspective is arguably a reasonable approach to comprehend Hong Kong's political transition from a colony to a Special Administrative Region.

Chapters 1 to 4 discuss the changing political arena of Hong Kong. Joseph Cheng analyses the development of the Sino-British negotiations in his chapter, concluding that Hong Kong's political future may have to rely on international or external forces. He points out that the Hong Kong model will set an example for Taiwan. Moreover, maintaining the rule of law and protecting press freedom are, according to Cheng, probably more significant than the development of representative government. In fact, in July 1995, Governor Patten also told the media that his future policy priorities would include liberalization, i.e., the revision of ordinances concerning press freedom, individual rights, and human rights.

Whether the adaptation of laws in Hong Kong will be acceptable to P.R.C. officials remains to be seen. Not all the reforms implemented by the colonial administration will be allowed to survive after 1997. Lo Chi-kin in Chapter 2 adopts a critical perspective, contending that the plan of establishing the "second stove" will not only exacerbate the "lame-duck" image of the Patten administration, but will also mean the P.R.C.'s control over Hong Kong's polity after 1997. According to Lo, both Britain and China are responsible for the political uncertainties and instability in post-1997 Hong Kong.

While it is relatively difficult to predict the shape and the make-up of the post-1997 political institutions of Hong Kong, Jane Lee believes that the civil service is evolving and will evolve in a more predictable manner. She highlights the fact that in contrast to a democratic British system, the ruling regime of the P.R.C. is an authoritarian one. As a result, Hong Kong's civil servants will become both "servants" of Hong Kong people and "subordinates" of the authoritarian regime. This political situation will, according to Lee, put Hong Kong civil servants in a dilemma. She also predicts that the political system after 1997 will be "executive-dominated" in which bureaucrats will face enormous pressure and numerous challenges. In order to ease the anxiety of civil servants and help them understand China better than ever before, Lee suggests that they should have a mechanism to keep in touch with P.R.C. officials. In fact, recent discussions in Hong Kong about whether and how civil servants should assist the future Preparatory Committee for the formation of the post-1997 government underscores the inevitability of strengthening cooperation between P.R.C. authorities and them. The crux of the problem is to solve the issue of how to ensure that civil servants helping the Preparatory Committee will not encounter role conflicts.

While the conflicting role of civil servants is a foremost concern of the Patten administration in cooperating with China, political conflicts have become ever more apparent since the transition period began in 1984, when the Sino-British Joint Declaration was reached. Sonny Lo argues in his chapter that some political parties are, strictly speaking, either legislative cliques or political groupings without tight organization at the central and grassroots levels. He anticipates that the Democratic Alliance for Betterment of Hong Kong will sooner or later become the most influential political party after 1997, and that any attempt to restructure the current electoral system may likely constitute a move towards political underdevelopment. In other words, time seems to be running out for political development.

Johannes Chan asserts that time is definitely running out in terms of legal development. He concludes that the legal system is endangered by the fact that P.R.C. officials refuse to admit the lack of confidence on the part of Hong Kong people towards China, and that there is a huge gap between Hong Kong and China with regard to the perception of the rule of law.

In fact, the entire debate concerning the Court of Final Appeal in Hong Kong proves that many Hong Kong lawyers, who were trained in the Common Law system and who are accustomed to it, and the P.R.C. authorities have different constitutional traditions. While these varying traditions may lead to debates, conflicts and confrontations in the short run, they may hopefully generate constitutional conventions between Hong Kong and China in the long run. Viewed from this vantage point, although time is no doubt running out for Hong Kong's legal system, as Chan maintains, the political will of both Hong Kong people and the P.R.C. authorities to reconcile their constitutional differences requires the test of time.

The time factor, according to Hung Ching-tin in his chapter, is probably relatively insignificant in the sense that the P.R.C.'s view of Hong Kong is actually attributable to the Chinese culture. Adopting a critical perspective, Hung contends that China should alter its perception of Hong Kong "from the realm of historical hate to modern miracle." He also highlights the perpetual problem of the Chinese leadership dealing with Hong Kong affairs: "The more it attempts to solve problems, the more it creates problems; the more it creates problems, the more it says it is solving problems" (p. 114). Hung's observations are thought-provocative, saying that the ultimate solution of cultivating better understandings between Hong Kong and China is to change the Chinese character — a difficult if not impracticable solution.

Economically speaking, Hong Kong's economic future may not be so problematic and perhaps pessimistic than its political prospects. Tang

Shu-hung discusses the economy of Hong Kong during the political transition, and he asserts that the conservative fiscal policy adopted by the Hong Kong government is becoming outdated. Tang also observes that the fiscal conservatism of the Hong Kong government is approved and promoted by the P.R.C. authorities. While Tang questions the wisdom of maintaining fiscal conservatism in Hong Kong, Lui Yu-hon observes that the developments of the banking industry, monetary sector and financial markets have already laid a foundation for Hong Kong to meet the challenges after 1997. However, Lui emphasizes that in order to maintain Hong Kong as an international financial centre, some key principles must be observed, including accountability to the public, depoliticization of financial systems and markets, and notably avoidance of favouritism and privileges. While favouritism and privileges appear to become the hallmarks of the developing Mainland Chinese economic system, Hong Kong has to maintain its own character and to prevent the possibility of being Sinified or "China-ized."

Leonard Cheng adopts a trend scenario and prediction-oriented approach, analysing Hong Kong's trade and industry beyond 1997. He points out that Hong Kong's "greatest comparative advantage" is its acquaintance with Chinese and foreign values, practices and systems. According to Cheng, in order to retain the territory's comparative advantage, Hong Kong people have to improve their command of Putonghua and to maintain or enhance their English standard. Cheng's observations are important as the English standard of many Hong Kong students, according to some members of the public, appears to have declined considerably. In addition, Cheng believes Hong Kong will not follow the footsteps of post-liberation Shanghai. He argues for a moderate approach to improve Hong Kong's social welfare, which according to him "must be based on need and should never become entitlements" like some Western countries where welfare payments undermine individual initiative and incentive to work (p. 194). As a matter of fact, recent developments suggest that the Hong Kong government, politicians and business people tend to opt for a moderate approach to cope with the demand for improvement of social welfare on the one hand and the maintenance of Hong Kong's economic prosperity and competitiveness on the other.

The economic prosperity of Hong Kong has long been attributable to not only the business sector, but also the labourers. Ng Sek-hong discusses Hong Kong's labour movement, which is often subordinated to the government and capitalists. It has been politically co-opted by the colonial government through representation to political institutions, and is internally split along right-wing, independent and left-wing lines. According to Ng, the post-1997 government may inherit the relative lack of legislation to protect working-class interests, and the weaknesses of the current consultative mechanisms linking labour with the administration. The solution that Ng proposes is to institutionalize and regularize the dialogue between labour and management, and to reform the existing bodies for genuine "tripartite" participation, particularly the Labour Advisory Board. Undoubtedly, whether the working-class interests can be further promoted depends not only on the political will of the parties concerned, but also on a long-term governmental plan to strike a balance between the interests of capital and those of labour.

Town planning is emerging as an indispensable ingredient of the Hong Kong government during the political transition. Ng Mee-kam observes that Hong Kong's land use planners have encountered new challenges and problems since the 1980s. Striking a balance between urban planning and environmental concerns, according to Ng, is becoming a necessity. Moreover, town planning is impracticable without the support of China. Ng concludes that the authorities of Hong Kong and China should strengthen their dialogue and cooperation regarding urban and regional planning.

Ng's view is also shared by Anthony Yeh, whose chapter provides an in-depth analysis of planning and management of Hong Kong's border. As Hong Kong is economically integrated with the Pearl River Delta, including Shenzhen, Zhuhai and Macau, better regional planning and coordination become necessary and urgent. The recent establishment of the Sino-British Infrastructure Coordinating Committee, Yeh says, provides a good example of how local governments in South China should and can cooperate in the development of their infrastructural projects. After 1997 and 1999, when Hong Kong and Macau will become Special Administrative Regions of China respectively, a similar coordinating committee should also be set up to tackle any conflicting interests between Hong Kong, Macau, Shenzhen and Zhuhai. Yeh points out that in the planning for Hong Kong's infrastructural development, the environmental impact on its neighbours should be taken into consideration — a situation necessitated by economic and political integration in South China.

Planning should not be confined to land use, but should include housing as well. Peter Fong elaborates the goals and priorities that the Hong

Kong government should adopt with a view to tackle macro and micro issues concerning housing. He emphasizes that an appropriate strategy is to concentrate on the provision of housing to households who cannot afford to secure their own accommodation in the private property market. Fong also discusses the roles that should be played by the Housing Branch, Housing Society and Housing Authority, and the micro-strategies that should be adopted to address the problems of housing.

The search for solutions to cope with thorny issues during the political transition also encompasses the environment. Man Si-wai adopts a critical perspective to explore the roots of the environmental problems in Hong Kong. She argues that Hong Kong should define its own identity in terms of environmental development, and that the underprivileged and under-represented people have often been marginalized. To tackle environmental problems in the long run, the government and the people should critically reconsider their often-held assumptions concerning Hong Kong's environmental development.

Utilizing the critical perspective, Lee Wing-on and Mark Bray raise an interesting question whether Hong Kong's education is actually being decolonized or recolonized. They observe that while it is relatively easy to alter textbooks and syllabi, changing "the values of those who operate the system" is by no means an easy task. Lee and Bray also make a noteworthy point that international schools which have moved to set up branches in China not only have educational functions, but also entails commercial as well as political implications for the Mainland. As with other political and economic issues, local education is increasingly integrated into China and its adaptation to the changing political circumstances can be regarded as a persistent theme in Hong Kong beyond 1997.

Another policy area that requires adaptation and reform is health care. Peter Yuen analyses the development of the health care system in the transition period, and he believes that 1997 provides both opportunities and problems to the providers and consumers of Hong Kong's health care services. Some of the problems, according to Yuen, will be inherited by the post-1997 government, for the current Patten administration still fails to provide imaginative solutions. In other words, the legacy of the colonial administration with regard to health care will be felt after 1997.

The legacies of the colonial era can also be seen in the realm of social welfare. Nelson Chow identifies these legacies in Hong Kong, including (1) the inputs provided by non-governmental agencies in social policy-making; (2) the social and political influence of social workers; and (3) the increasing popularity of adopting social welfare as the objectives of various political parties. Nevertheless, owing to the Basic Law's constraint on government expenditure, Chow predicts that there will not be "radical changes" in social welfare after 1997. He concludes that social welfare in Hong Kong "has never lacked an ideological basis" (p. 408), and that it will have some room for further development after 1997 even though there are constraints set by the Basic Law.

While Chow's predictions tend to be cautiously optimistic, John Ho is sceptical about the prospects of law and order in post-1997 Hong Kong. He identifies two opposing tendencies that affect law and order in the political transition: one emphasizing the differences in the "two systems" and the other stressing the importance of "one country." Specifically, according to Ho, these tendencies can be manifested in the debate over a suitable balance between the protection of civil liberties and the maintenance of state power. As long as P.R.C. officials adopt a conspiratorial perspective in assessing legal reforms in Hong Kong, any attempt to liberalize the system will be seen as having hidden motives. Ho concludes that China should exercise its authority and power to maintain law and order in post-1997 Hong Kong with caution, wisdom and restraint. Otherwise, Hong Kong's international status may be affected.

The challenges that Hong Kong encounters must include telecommunications. John Ure discusses three scenarios concerning the development of telecommunications, and he notes that Hong Kong is well-positioned to serve the market in China while at the same time acting as "an information gateway" between the P.R.C. and the outside world. Ure maintains that Hong Kong can provide a regional centre for storing, retrieving, processing and relaying data or information. In the long run, according to Ure, China will find Hong Kong's skills in telecommunications useful. But in the short run, Hong Kong must continue to improve its telecommunication technologies and networks. In his chapter, Ure offers some interesting insights on how Hong Kong can develop its telecommunications sector further so that it will be beneficial and valuable to China's telecommunications development after 1997.

While telecommunications development in Hong Kong is an obviously depoliticized issue during the transition period, freedom of the press becomes a heavily politicized one. Li Yuet-wah discusses the development of press freedom in Hong Kong. She predicts that although the future for press freedom may be gloomy, it is by no means a hopeless scenario. The journalism profession, according to Li, is facing the challenge of maintaining Hong Kong as "an oasis of press freedom" under Chinese sovereignty after 1997. Li acknowledges that there is no easy solution to retain this oasis, but she vows to "keep eternal vigilance in safeguarding [the] basic human right" of providing a free flow of information in China. In the event that journalists in Hong Kong are imbued with Li's idea of safeguarding their rights, press freedom may have to rely more on the initiative and determination of journalists at the grassroots level than on the mercy and tolerance of political elites at the ruling stratum.

In practice, public opinion at the grassroots level is increasingly becoming a concern of Hong Kong's policy-makers. Robert Chung summarizes his major findings from various public opinion polls conducted in the political transition period. He observes that Hong Kong people are still not confident of the "one country, two systems" scenario. If so, it is necessary and urgent for the policy-makers of Hong Kong before as well as after 1997 to comprehend the feelings of the populace.

Finally, Stephen Sze discusses the cultural "crisis" in Hong Kong. He observes that in the capitalistic and individualistic society of Hong Kong, there is a polarization of cultures, "the elite forms of high culture" and "the vulgar forms of mass culture." Sze also observes little development of an indigenous identity and cultural awareness. If the cultural "crisis" in Hong Kong exists, as Sze maintains, China is probably encountering a similar problem as the Mainland's society and culture are increasingly "Hongkongized."

Overall, Hong Kong encounters enormous challenges and problems in the current political transition or decolonization period. It remains to be seen whether Hong Kong's political system will be decolonized or recolonized after 1997, whether its legal system will adapt to the different constitutional tradition in the Mainland, whether its society will be able to retain and develop its pluralistic character, whether its economy will continue to prosper and to balance the interests of capitalists and workers, and whether its culture will be able to undergo meaningful and fruitful transformations. While all these developments will soon be unfolded, analysing them from the trend scenario and critical perspective is perhaps the most viable approach to understand the evolution of Hong Kong from a British colony to a Special Administrative Region under Chinese sovereignty.

1

Sino-British Negotiations and Problems of the British Administration[1]

Joseph Y. S. Cheng

INTRODUCTION

On 23 October 1994, the *Sunday Morning Post* published an opinion poll which indicated that 34% of the respondents supported the establishment of a provisional legislature in 1997 to fill the possible legislative vacuum upon the creation of the Special Administrative Region (SAR) in July 1997. In the same survey, 32% of the respondents opposed the idea, while 34% expressed no opinion. The surprise findings shocked political observers and the pro-democracy politicians, who previously believed that the public had been overwhelmingly opposed to the proposal of the Preliminary Working Committee (PWC)'s sub-group on government and administration.

The opinion survey is perhaps a good illustration of the state of Sino-British negotiations on Hong Kong and the current problems enforced by the British administration. The Sino-British diplomatic confrontation roused by Chris Patten's political reform package prompted the Chinese authorities to abandon their plan of cooperation with the British administration in jointly cultivating the leaders of the future SAR government. In the wake of Chris Patten's visit to Beijing in October 1992, Lu Ping, head of the Chinese State Council's Hong Kong and Macau Affairs Office, warned that the Chinese authorities would "set up another stove," i.e., organize a group of pro-Beijing community leaders in the territory to advise on the planning of the transfer of power. This set-up would likely amount to a "shadow government" in Hong Kong threatening the legitimacy and effective rule of the British administration. It was reported that the statement, "set up another stove," came from Deng Xiaoping himself. In contemporary Chinese politics, when the supreme leader has spoken, the policy will be implemented at all cost until he is ready to review the situation and change his policy.

When Chris Patten's political reform package was finally endorsed by the Legislative Council (Legco) on 29 June 1994 by a margin of 32 to 24 votes, the Chinese authorities' threat to "set up another stove" was further interpreted as a plan to replace the colony's political institutions that have been evolving in accordance with the Governor's political reform package with new ones defined in accordance with the Chinese authorities' version of implementing the Basic Law. The threat had caused considerable fear and worry that without some measure of political continuity — the "through train" arrangements which would straddle the transfer of power — Hong Kong's political and economic life could be seriously disrupted. Many had maintained the hope that, while Beijing might make bellicose threats in the run-up to 1997, its actual behaviour would be dictated by a pragmatic desire to keep Hong Kong functioning smoothly. In early September 1994, however, the National People's Congress (NPC) passed a resolution "to abolish the political structure based on Governor Chris Patten's electoral reform package," and this was followed by the provisional legislature proposal.

After the Chinese authorities had threatened the abolition of the "through train" arrangements in view of Patten's political reform package, some pro-Beijing politicians argued that it would be unnecessary and undesirable to hold fresh elections immediately after 1997 at the District Board and Urban/Regional Council levels. In the discussions on the monitoring process associated with the "through train" arrangements before and after the Tiananmen incident, friends and opponents of the pro-Beijing united front all pointed out the technical difficulties of kicking politicians such as Martin Lee and Szeto Wah off the train. They cited the examples of *dangwai* politicians (the forerunners of the Democratic Progressive Party) in Taiwan in the late 1970s and early 1980s. When they were thrown into prison, their wives stood in their places as candidates and usually won landslide victories in the elections. Such a scenario would only embarrass the Preparatory Committee for the Hong Kong SAR which has been given the "monitoring" authority by the Basic Law in the formation of the first legislature of the SAR. Apparently, even the leaders of the pro-Beijing Democratic Alliance for Betterment of Hong Kong had questioned the provisional legislature proposal. It is significant that all these appeals for moderation have failed to make an impact. Furthermore, the respectable performance of the pro-Beijing political groups in the District Board elections in September 1994 has not much alleviated the Chinese authorities' sense of insecurity.

In their eagerness to mobilize Hong Kong people against the British administration, the Chinese authorities have fully exploited the appeal of nationalism and patriotism, which in turn have reinforced the spread of suspicions and "conspiracy theories." It is paradoxical but typical of the present stage of development in Beijing's united front strategy to concentrate on the former supporters of the British administration. That was why Dorothy Liu shed tears in public for sharing the same position as Sir S. Y. Chung as PWC members. In the initial years of the People's Republic of China, there was a saying: "Old revolutionaries are not as treasured as new revolutionaries, new revolutionaries are not as treasured as those who have not participated in the revolution, and the latter are not as treasured as the counter-revolutionaries." After the former counter-revolutionaries have been absorbed into the united front, they are certainly under pressure to demonstrate their loyalty to the Chinese leaders and their spite for the colonial regime.

SINO-BRITISH COOPERATION IN THE FINAL STAGE OF THE TRANSITION

On 30 June 1994, the day after Chris Patten's political reform package had gone through the Legco, China and Britain agreed to release twenty-five military sites to the Hong Kong government, while China would retain fourteen sites for its future garrison. On 8 July, legislators approved the HK$4 billion funding for the reprovisioning of defence facilities which was part of the agreement, thus ending the seven-year Sino-British dispute over the disposal of military sites. At the same time, Chinese officials indicated that agreement on the financial package for the new airport could soon be reached, as long as both parties would follow the 1991 Memorandum of Understanding on Port and Airport Development Strategy. They emphasized that the crucial issue was the cost-effectiveness of the project. Beijing and London appeared to be moving firmly towards an agreement on the Container Terminal No. 9 project too which had been discussed by the Sino-British Joint Liaison Group (JLG). Finally, the Chinese authorities promised to pursue negotiations with Britain on the promotion of the Hong Kong SAR passports to overseas countries amid growing fears that Hong Kong residents would lose their visa-free access to dozens of countries after the transfer of sovereignty, in contrast to their previous position that passports were a sovereignty issue and that the British government would not be involved.

There was thus considerable optimism when the British Foreign Office minister responsible for Hong Kong, Alastair Goodlad, visited Beijing in mid-July 1994. There were hopes that the Chinese Foreign Minister, Qian Qichen, would visit the United Kingdom in return for the visit of the British foreign secretary, Douglas Hurd, to Beijing in July last year. It seemed that Qian had turned down the invitation, and insisted that China was looking forward to "comprehensive cooperation in all areas," refusing to accept, as Alastair Goodlad had suggested, that the row over the constitutional reform in Hong Kong should be put aside.

The cool reception of Goodlad serves as a good indicator of the present state of Sino-British relations on the Hong Kong question. Strong suspicions remain, but both sides are adopting a damage-control strategy, attempting to avoid total diplomatic confrontation. While both parties understand that there can be no more cooperation concerning the political system and "through train" arrangements, it is in their mutual interest to maintain cooperation in other areas. On both sides, new factors have emerged pushing for a softening of their respective positions. John Major's government certainly felt the pressure when the Clinton administration dissociated human rights issues in China from the Sino-American most-favoured-nation (MFN) negotiations. Australia and Canada, which had openly supported Britain's Hong Kong policy, gradually shifted and fol-lowed the broad trend of Western countries eager to expand economic exchanges with China. Chris Patten is acutely aware of John Major's difficulties at home and that the British business community has shown some uneasiness over the fact that it is being surpassed by the Germans and the French in the China market. Hong Kong people's enthusiasm for political reforms has obviously been in decline, and local business leaders are openly complaining. The Major government and the British administra-tion in Hong Kong are therefore under pressure to demonstrate that they can maintain cooperation with the Chinese authorities to safeguard Hong Kong's economic interests.

Beijing too appreciates that British cooperation is essential to a smooth transition. After all, Beijing will have to bear responsibility for Hong Kong after 1997 and its credibility will suffer should Hong Kong encounter major problems during the transfer of sovereignty. The business community has been lobbying hard for the Chinese authorities' green light for various infrastructural projects straddling beyond 1997 because any delays will be costly and will adversely affect the territory's economic development. The Chinese authorities want to win the hearts of Hong Kong people, and they understand that their "another stove" is far from popular and effective. So there is some flexibility on the Chinese side as well.

It was in this kind of context that there were some expectations of the Governor's policy speech in October 1994 regarding proposals to improve the atmosphere and re-establish a dialogue for cooperation between Beijing and London on Hong Kong. But Hong Kong people were disappointed again. Chris Patten indicated that the PWC was only an advisory body of the NPC, hence there could be no formal relationship between the PWC and the Hong Kong government. The latter's position is that civil servants can neither join the PWC nor attend its meetings, including those of its sub-groups. They too cannot pass on to the PWC information which has not been released to the public. On the other hand, the Governor indicated that he had not forbidden contacts between civil servants and the PWC, and civil servants in fact had been supplying information to the PWC. The only concrete proposal offered by the Governor at this stage was that PWC members could take part in the JLG meetings as experts of the Chinese team.

The reaction from the Chinese authorities was predictably negative. Their distrust for the British side had prompted them to demand information on the assets of the Hong Kong government, the profile of its civil servants, and an outline of its 1997–1998 budget. They certainly perceived the willingness to cooperate with the PWC as the test of the British administration's sincerity to improve relations in the final years of the transition. They considered the Governor's promise to assist the Preparatory Committee for the Hong Kong SAR only a delaying tactic to gain time to complete his strategic planning in order to force a *fait accompli* on Beijing.

Under such circumstances, one certainly cannot expect smooth co-operation even outside the political system and "through train" arrangements. The prevalence of conspiracy theories mean that both sides will take special care to scrutinize each other's proposals and suggestions, and lower-level bureaucrats will often hesitate to assume responsibility and declare the other side's position acceptable. Worse still, both parties may often be tempted to score political points off the other in negotiations of a purely technical nature, e.g., the tendering process of Container Terminal No. 9. As a result, negotiations at the JLG would be slow and painful, while agreements are to be reached on a piecemeal basis. In the autumn of 1994, Hong Kong people had a glimpse of what was to come. While the agreement on overall airport financing had been concluded, new controversies emerged concerning Container Terminal No. 9 and the proposed sewerage system.

Conspiracy theories can easily allow minor incidents to develop into major controversies. In November 1994, the Hong Kong government indicated its readiness to allow an amendment proposed in a private member's bill by Legislative Councillor Martin Lee to drop the "good relations" clause from the Film Censorship Ordinance. Local New China News Agency (Xinhua) officials immediately responded that this was a "major policy matter" which should only be determined by the JLG after discussion. Earlier, permission given to pro-Kuomintang groups to celebrate the Double Tenth anniversary at the Hong Kong Cultural Centre even attracted a protest from the Chinese foreign ministry. The Chinese authorities believe that these are not individual incidents, but part of a British strategy to create trouble in the final years of its colonial rule.

All parties concerned are aware of the slow progress in the JLG meetings. The general worry is that in view of the limited achievements secured in the past years, the chance of completing the daunting list of agenda items in the remaining years of the transition will be slim indeed. This worry will be exacerbated as one approaches 1997, and more and more people will discover problems emerging because of lack of appropriate arrangements made on the basis of Sino-British agreements.

In turn, the pro-Beijing united front becomes increasingly assertive. In various attempts to avoid any "vacuum" at the end of the transition period, the PWC acts as a shadow government and unilaterally plans for the future SAR government. Apparently, the confidence of Hong Kong people which has risen and fallen rapidly in response to events has been further damaged. The Political Confidence Index released by the *South China Morning Post* based on telephone interviews by Survey Research Hong Kong started with a score of 91 in January 1994, fell to 88 in April, rose to 91 in July and then declined to 88 in November.

DIFFICULTIES OF THE BRITISH ADMINISTRATION

❑ *Support from the People*

The deterioration of Sino-British relations on Hong Kong has now been seen as a failure on the part of the British administration, and especially the Governor himself. An opinion poll held after Chris Patten's policy speech in October 1994 showed that the respondents gave Patten only 3.7 on a scale of 10 for his handling of relations with China in the policy speech. Many senior civil servants are acutely aware of the pragmatism and volatility in Hong Kong people's attitudes towards relations with China. They also understand that the local community wants the British administration and local politicians to take a strong and critical stand *vis-à-vis* Beijing. But when such a stand encounters severe retaliatory measures from the Chinese leaders, the British administration and local politicians concerned will get the blame. It appears that Patten has been adversely evaluated exactly because he has antagonized Beijing and thus has failed to promote Hong Kong people's interests.

❑ *New Policy Initiatives*

Before Governor's third policy speech, the Hong Kong government had been eager to search for policy proposals to demonstrate its commitment to the improvement of the livelihood of the people in its last one thousand days. This was probably the best way to dispel the perception of a lame-duck government, especially in view of the recent deterioration in Sino-British cooperation on Hong Kong. After all, in almost every major policy area, new approaches and new policy programmes are called for. In public housing, for example, the government has promised a new initiative to satisfy the demand of the sandwiched income class. What is the responsibility of the government or the Housing Authority in meeting the demand for home ownership of the young middle-class families? How should the Housing Authority limit the subsidies to public housing tenants who already possess their own flats or whose incomes have been steadily improving since their initial years of tenancy? In the field of medical care, some kind of medical insurance scheme is called for to ensure the long-term standards of medical and hospital care. How should this scheme be introduced so as to protect those who may not be covered, namely, the old and the underprivileged? In education, the territory now has an oversupply of places in tertiary institutions but the government has very limited responsibility in child-care and kindergarten education. Meanwhile, the community has become more concerned with the quality of education and the morale of teachers in our primary and secondary schools.

In the early 1990s, the worry was that if the top civil servants and the political groups could not find time from their daily work to turn to these long-term policy issues, Hong Kong people would have to wait till the next century for appropriate solutions. The concerned public realized that if concrete policy proposals could not be formulated by 1994 or so for thorough discussions and planning, the British administration might no longer have the political will to initiate important policy reforms and steer them through the legislature. The year 1995 will be Hong Kong's election year and policy issues are bound to be over-politicized. From 1995 to 1999, the British administration and its successor, the SAR government, will be preoccupied with the transfer of power and measures to guarantee stability and prosperity in the transition period.

The Governor apparently had failed to convince the community of the British administration's commitment to raise its living standards. The above-mentioned survey held after Patten's third policy speech revealed that the Governor attained only average marks for improvements in social welfare and government accountability, scoring 5.2 and 5.4 respectively on a 10-point scale. Further, only 30% of the respondents had taken note of the speech via the mass media, compared with 60% in 1993 and 49% in 1992. Most observers believe that Hong Kong people are turning away from the political scene. They have lost interest in local politics including the Governor's policy speech. The survey results thus have demonstrated a low level of expectation and satisfaction regarding the policy speech, the basic ingredients for the perception of a caretaker government. The Sino-British confrontation over Hong Kong has certainly reinforced such perception, as people cast doubt on the continuity of major policy programmes of the British administration in the absence of explicit support from the Chinese authorities.

The old-age pension scheme proposal is a good example. The Hong Kong government promised that it would make a decision by the end of 1994. In view of the opposition from the business sector and the academic community, it is doubtful whether the British administration can get a majority support in the Legco before it adjourns for the election in September 1995.

Political groups and politicians will be eager to score points off the government, and few would prefer to be seen as a total supporter of the British administration. If the bill is delayed till after the elections, it is likely that the government will face a majority in the Legco consisting of legislators from the pro-democracy groups and their sympathizers. It will be very difficult for the government to satisfy their even higher demands then.

❑ *Support in the Legco*

The British administration's situation in the legislature has become increasingly difficult since the 1991 elections. It has been counting on the support of three official members and a majority of the eighteen appointed unofficials. Then it forms shifting majorities with either the pro-democracy groups or the conservative Liberal Party, depending on the issues at stake. The small number of elected independents are prime targets of the government's lobbying efforts too. Senior civil servants complain that they now spend up to one-third of their time in the Legco, trying to explain the government's policy positions and lobbying for support. This calls not only for commitment and dedication, but also an enthusiasm to adapt to the changing political environment and cultivate new political skills. The situation will worsen after the 1995 elections when there will be no more appointed seats in the Legco. Beijing's direct and indirect influence in the legislature, especially on the conservative legislators, will certainly be on the ascent. In the crucial votes on the political reform packages in late June 1994, it was reported that Beijing officials had contacted a few legislators who were also Hong Kong Affairs Advisers in an attempt to influence their voting behaviour.

The British administration, like any other democratic government, requires a stable majority support in the Legco in order to function smoothly. After the 1995 elections, on issues relating to relations with China and the pace of political reforms, the British administration may have to count on the support of the pro-democracy groups and their sympathizers as the pro-business legislators will be most reluctant to antagonize Beijing. Under such circumstances, the dangers are that the government may be forced into a more radical position than appropriate, and that this in turn will reinforce the Chinese authorities' suspicion of collusion between the British administration and the pro-democracy groups to confront Beijing in the final years of the transition. On social service issues, the British administration will encounter considerable pressure from the pro-democracy groups so much so that its basic political philosophy will be threatened. Its position may well become more untenable because of the reluctance of the pro-business legislators to compromise. The latter will be eager to establish their credentials in the eyes of Beijing, and will be unwilling to engage in serious bargaining with the Hong Kong government and the pro-democracy groups because the Chinese leaders are only too eager to discredit them.

In general, the British administration will have even weaker bargaining power compared to that of the United States President facing a Congress controlled by the opposition party. The President often has sufficient carrots and sticks to be used for bargaining, and he can also exploit his personal political appeal. The Governor and the senior civil servants do not have such political assets. They do not have any influence on the next election, and the traditional honours they bestow on politicians are more shunned than favoured. Now few community leaders want their knighthoods to be publicly acknowledged, and some have quietly dropped their CBEs and OBEs from their name cards. Severe criticisms of the Hong Kong government, on the other hand, remain popular among the media and Hong Kong people, and politicians will not hesitate to score points off the British administration. Self-censorship certainly does not apply to this category of criticisms. In fact, they may become more intense as self-censorship prevails in criticisms of the Chinese leadership.

❏ *The Consultative System*

In view of the Sino-British confrontation, the British administration will find it increasingly difficult to co-opt respectable community leaders into the consultative system. This will weaken the appeal of the administration. At the same time, senior civil servants may be tempted to appoint more compliant figures into their advisory committees. This will make their job easier as they have to spend more time on the Legco and the media. Members of many advisory committees also complain about an absence of important papers to discuss, reflecting the lack of initiatives and the difficulties of the senior civil servants at the last stage of the transition. Serious members (and often severe critics) in some advisory committees may feel that they have little to contribute, and a few have resigned in their frustration. To a large extent, advisory committees cannot compete with the Legco for the limelight. But the British administration earlier had a strategy: to choose a group of prominent non-politician business persons, professionals, academics, etc. to fill the advisory committees so that they can offer the civil servants valuable advice and support. Apparently, the emphasis has been too much on support. As a result, while the system of advisory committees has not caused trouble to the Hong Kong government, it has gradually lost its previous important function.

Complacency and neglect also wasted an important opportunity for the civil service to establish an effective dialogue with the pro-Beijing united front. Beijing's most-trusted community leaders in Hong Kong had suffered injustice under the British administration. Leaders of the pro-Beijing Chinese General Chamber of Commerce, for example, were barred from the Hong Kong Trade Development Council membership until after the conclusion of the Sino-British Joint Declaration. Another example related to pro-Beijing educators in Hong Kong. Their primary and secondary schools began to receive government subsidies only in recent years. Such community leaders' perception of the British administration naturally would not be favourable, and this perception in turn coloured the assessment of the Chinese officials responsible for Hong Kong affairs.

The British administration had the foresight to alter the situation since the Joint Declaration. The intention was to improve relations with Beijing and its united front; to educate the united front so that it would have a better understanding of the operations of the Hong Kong government; and thereby to facilitate agreements on the arrangements for the transfer of power. But the British administration had not done enough in the decade after 1984 to achieve the above objectives. Deterioration in Sino-British relations on Hong Kong in recent years has certainly destroyed the chance for a smooth transition, but apparently the senior civil servants could not claim to have succeeded in cultivating the pro-Beijing united front before the arrival of Chris Patten nor prior to the Tiananmen incident.

❏ *The Civil Service*

In 1994, the Chinese authorities' hawkish stand on "through train" arrangements and the setting up of "another stove" has served to highlight the difficult situation of the civil service. Most threatening to the effectiveness of the British administration in its final years will be the loyalty of senior civil servants. For those who will remain faithful, the likelihood is that they have sought British passports and will leave before 1997. A small minority will be eager to please the Chinese authorities. A vast majority, however, will choose to adopt a low profile exactly when the British administration can no longer control a majority in the Legco and needs the senior civil servants to play an active role in defence of its policies. A survey of the directorate grade officers by the author and Jane Lee in 1993 showed that 36.8% of the respondents said they were worried about their careers in the civil service after 1997. Some 68.1% of the respondents said they were concerned about the involvement of Beijing officials in Hong Kong's important political decisions. Early retirement and resignation from the civil service may be the ways by which the bureaucrats express their negative feelings towards the future political system. Our study found that 64.3% of the respondents held British passports, another 10.9% held other foreign passports, and that 33.4% did not plan to remain in their positions after 1997.

The same survey revealed that the senior civil servants were not too certain of their role in the development of representative government. A total of 59.9% of the respondents believed that they should be accountable to the Legco, while 24% considered that they should not and 16% felt unsure. Moreover, 40.1% of the respondents thought that the Legco was fairly unrepresentative of the interests of Hong Kong people and 7.1% indicated that it was "not at all representative." Consequently, 47.7% of the respondents felt that they were "fairly dissatisfied" with the performance of the Legco while only 37.9% felt that they were "fairly satisfied." Furthermore, 54.7% and 23.7% of the respondents respectively felt that the Legco was "too politicized" and "immature" after the 1991 direct elections. Only 17.6% commented positively that it had become "more open and democratic." During the in-depth interviews, the interviewees generally felt that members of the Legco were "irrational" and "opportunistic," and they only aimed at pleasing the voters or the Chinese government. When asked who should decide on the major policies of the Hong Kong government before 1997, 64.7% of the respondents indicated the Governor in Council, 16.2% indicated senior government officials, 22.5% the Legco, 8.2% Hong Kong citizens themselves and 6.3% the Chinese government.

Both the Hong Kong government and the Beijing officials responsible for Hong Kong affairs attempted to play down the findings of the survey when they were released in early 1994. But their subsequent actions certainly reflect their serious concern. It is no secret that the pro-Beijing united front has been actively approaching senior civil servants. Further, civil service trade unions, especially those of the disciplinary forces, have been encouraged to send delegations to Beijing; and retired senior civil servants have been prime targets in appointments to the PWC and those of Hong Kong Affairs Advisers. The latter have been encouraged to get organized to advise the Chinese authorities on the transition, and they have been given prestigious receptions in Beijing. The PWC has also set up a special working group to discuss issues relating to the civil service, chaired by a former civil servant. On the part of the British administration, the Civil Service Branch announced in early November 1994 that it would attempt to determine civil servants' intentions to stay beyond 1997 in its performance evaluation exercises.

Understandably, the Hong Kong civil service has encountered many new challenges in recent years. The development of representative government has brought considerable pressure on civil servants. They now encounter many more queries and criticisms from members of the District Boards, municipal councils and the Legco. Many civil servants consider such queries and criticisms a nuisance and a waste of their precious time. As Hong Kong's civil servants are accustomed to be accountable only to their superiors, they have not yet developed a sense of accountability to the public which they regard as ignorant of the government's work. Civil servants have to appreciate that the pro-democracy political parties and pressure groups are also their clients. The attitude called for is one of "constructive engagement." All clients offer invaluable inputs which contribute to the administration's effectiveness. Civil servants should be willing to listen, to learn and to improve their work. At the same time, they should be proud of their performance, and should not be afraid to defend the government's policies. The priorities are to explain and win over the people, and not just fend off criticisms or expose the ignorance of the public.

The engagement between our senior civil servants and the Legislative Councillors since the introduction of direct elections to the legislature in 1991, however, has not been a very constructive one. Legislative Councillors from the pro-democracy camp have been eager to exert pressure on the government to demonstrate the value of direct elections as well as their accountability to the electorate. Naturally, there are obvious attempts to attract the media's attention, and causing embarrassment to top civil servants is counted as an indicator of parliamentary skill. Considerations of establishing an effective dialogue with the administration and maximizing inputs into the government's policy-making process are apparently not priority items in the agenda of the pro-democracy camp.

Most of the senior civil servants have been ill-prepared for the challenges of the development of representative government. At best, the limited goodwill and dedication have not been backed up by resources and clear-cut guidelines from above. At worst, there is strong resentment against "the harassment by radical social workers and teachers" whose salaries were only in the middle range of the Government Master Pay Scale. (Senior civil servants generally regard pay and rank as indicators of competence and achievement.)

Top civil servants' relations with the pro-Establishment legislators also deteriorated sharply in the first six months of the Legco session beginning in October 1991. The latter soon formed the Cooperative Resources Centre which then evolved into the Liberal Party. Its members were eager to show their independence *vis-à-vis* the Hong Kong government and to cultivate their popularity in the community. The separation of the Legislative and Executive Councils by Chris Patten in the autumn of 1992 meant that the core members of the Cooperative Resources Centre had to withdraw from the Executive Council, thus depriving them of their special status and privilege. As a result, they felt they had no obligation to defend the British administration and their motivation to cultivate Beijing was much strengthened. In sum, the civil servants have failed to establish a meaningful and constructive dialogue with the politicians based on mutual trust and respect in which both parties can exchange information and opinions in confidence with a view to arrive at agreements to serve the public.

Perhaps our senior civil servants may have something to learn from their counterparts in Taiwan in terms of their relations with the community. Senior civil servants in Taiwan are much more active in cultivating good relations with the media and the public, and they are much more willing to establish personal ties with journalists, pressure group activists, politicians and community leaders. Hong Kong civil servants have been much too passive in these areas. They are often seen as arrogant, shy and afraid to mix with the people. Our senior civil servants' work schedule and lifestyle are such that few of them understand how a family with a household income of less than $10,000 per month living in Wong Tai Sin makes its ends meet. Criticisms by the media, pressure groups and the opposition may result in the downfall of top civil servants in Taipei and Seoul. Top civil servants of the Hong Kong government are not yet threatened by such termination of their careers. But changes are inevitable. Hong Kong civil servants have to be more active in defending the government's policies to the people and to secure their support. From September 1991 onwards, the administration can no longer count on a stable majority support in the Legco. The situation after the September 1995 elections will be even more difficult. Smooth passage of its policy programmes through the legislature will depend on the administration's ability to explain its stance, to lobby the legislators and to secure the community's support. Every civil servant counts in this campaign. But how many are dedicated to deliver their very best?

In times of deteriorating Sino-British relations on Hong Kong, it is easy for our civil servants to put the blame on the Chinese authorities. But it has to be admitted that most of our senior civil servants do not understand China. This should not be surprising because in their early careers, they were under pressure not to show an interest in China. Seminars organized by the Civil Service Training Centre help, but the impact remains limited. Understanding China requires conscious and continuous efforts, yet few senior civil servants even take an initiative to spend their holidays in China. Cynics have argued that close encounters with China may well be harmful to civil service morale because those who know China well tend to have less confidence in its future. However, there is no alternative. A willingness to study China, to learn Putonghua and to improve Chinese language skills are obvious signs of commitment to a career in Hong Kong after 1997. Such efforts must be encouraged and rewarded, and they should be seen to be rewarded too. This incidentally will please the Chinese authorities. However, Chinese language skills are still not recognized as an important qualification in career development in the civil service. Instead, the general public's perception is that those top civil servants who have been enthusiastic in toeing Chris Patten's line to confront Beijing in public have been rewarded with promotions.

In his policy speech in October 1994, the Governor promised to enhance the China Studies Programme for the civil service, as well as courses on Putonghua and Chinese language skills. The Governor indicated that the number of civil servants attending these courses would increase from 7,000 to 45,000 per annum in 1995. While such efforts are laudable, the figures also show that much remains to be done.

Many criticisms of the Hong Kong government are due to ignorance of its plans. A proactive publicity strategy anticipating criticisms will help to reduce their impact and damage. If the policy branches in policy areas like education and transport are enthusiastic in informing and consulting with the public of their future plans, the problems they are studying, and the difficulties they have encountered, it will not be easy for critics to make an impact.

In many ways, top civil servants will have to act like cabinet members of a minority government, eager to defend the Hong Kong government *vis-à-vis* the political groups and the pro-Beijing united front. This contest takes place everyday, and it will become a daily responsibility of the top civil servants. Because of their access to information and the mass media, civil servants tend to have a distinct edge if they are well-prepared. If the government attaches sufficient importance to this contest, civil servants should have a much better resource base in their publicity campaign than the political groups and the pro-Beijing united front.

Advisory committees of the Hong Kong government should be de-politicized. This should be an explicit policy to be firmly implemented. Advisory committees therefore should become committees of respected experts serving the policy branches. They should be more relied upon to explain to the community the policy options available and the rationale behind their preferences. In view of Hong Kong people's respect for exper-tise and neutrality, and the confusion created by the debates among political groups and the government, the media too have a considerable respon-sibility to seek out the experts, present their ideas to the community in a simplified manner, and help Hong Kong people form their opinions.

Senior civil servants in general maintain good relations with interest groups which are regarded as pro-Establishment or part of the Estab-lishment. On the other hand, labour unions, grassroots pressure groups, etc. often feel that they have been neglected or slighted by government officials. These groups often attempt to influence government policies by means of petitions and demonstrations, and these tactics are regarded as embarrass-ments to the administration and detrimental to its image. Nevertheless, these groups well understand the limits to their actions. They normally have a sophisticated assessment of the degree of tolerance of the community, and they appreciate that their relationships with the government departments concerned are long-term ones. Civil servants have a long way to go to develop cordial, and even personal, ties with pressure group activists to facilitate dialogue and avoid unnecessary confrontation. The latter usually show respect for those civil servants who have demonstrated sincerity to help them.

Some efforts had been made in this regard in the 1980s. But the emphasis then turned to the legislature after 1985 and especially after 1991. The British administration, however, has to appreciate that political groups and politicians in the Legco together have limited mobilization power in the community. A significant segment of Hong Kong people and grassroots pressure groups treat political groups and politicians with suspicion, and are of the opinion that they are only interested in publicity. The priority accorded to the legislature is only natural given the urgency to secure its consent to legislation and requests for appropriations. But grassroots pressure groups must not be neglected. To some extent, this neglect has been part of the cause for the decline of public support for the Governor, the British administration and its policies in recent years.

Since the latter half of the 1980s, there are considerable complaints against the District Officers. They are often criticized for being too young, immature, unable to speak good Cantonese, and insensitive to traditions and customs. They stay in their posts for two to three years only, and do not have sufficient time to establish strong ties with the community leaders of their respective districts. In contrast, the local New China News Agency has been active in cultivating the district-based community leaders, voluntary bodies and interest groups. It normally sends high-ranking officials to attend the latter's functions, and these officials are usually experts in united front tactics. The Hong Kong government apparently does not see this as a threat and has been reducing funding for the Home Affairs Branch (previously known as the City and New Territories Administration) since the early 1990s. This reduction in funding seems to be related in some ways to the performance of the two successive policy secretaries concerned.

Chris Patten has obviously done an excellent job in ~~~~~ ~~~~~ government service for the public. Government de sector agencies have been asked to establish perfo enhancing their accountability to the community. (in direct contact with people have a great imp perception of the government. They therefore re incentives for good performance, i.e., better p into consideration all the fringe benefits, the between our top civil servants and their most the greatest in the world. Promotions for routine exercises where seniority and avai most significant determinants. This mean by junior civil servants and nurses to the public has vastly improved in the past two decades, there has been no improvement in their promotion prospects that are commensurate with a better performance. The Hospital Authority, for example, rewards its chief executive for satisfactory performance with a handsome bonus, but the nurses in the wards do not get such rewards and still suffer from a manpower shortage. In sum, despite the recent efforts put into changing the mentality of the civil service as well as staff appraisal, promotions within the civil service, especially in the lower and middle echelons, are far too rigid to offer attractive inducements to better performance.

THE POLITICAL SCENE AND PEOPLE'S POLITICAL APATHY

Hong Kong people apparently adopt a highly utilitarian attitude towards democracy. Chris Patten's political reform package was obviously in line with Hong Kong people's aspiration for more rapid development of representative government as a guarantee for their liberty, their lifestyle and the rule of law. In an opinion survey conducted immediately after the Governor's policy speech, 73% of the respondents claimed to agree with the Governor's plan for Hong Kong, while 60% agreed that he had gone far enough to meet the aspirations for democracy in the territory. Some 48.8% of the respondents believed that the Hong Kong government should proceed with the Governor's political reform package even if the Chinese authorities rejected it. In another survey held after Chris Patten's return from his subsequent futile trip to Beijing, 59% of the respondents still considered that Hong Kong should go ahead with the political reform proposals despite China's objections.

In the subsequent Sino-British diplomatic confrontation, the Hong Kong community, however, became further polarized. In the eyes of the Chinese authorities, Hong Kong people were either pro-China or pro-British. Demand for the development of democracy was thus interpreted as support for the British administration, and the Chinese government's position on this was defined in terms of defence for national sovereignty. This had been effective in intimidating Hong Kong people and deterring articulation for a faster pace of the development of representative Hong Kong people realized that democracy had lost its in view of the strong opposition from Beijing, and they prepared to sacrifice for the cause.

The sad thing was, by the time Chris Patten's political reform package was finally endorsed by the Legco, the community had become amazingly apathetic. An opinion poll indicated that over 90% of the respondents did not understand or were not aware of the competing major political reform packages being debated in the legislature. Various opinion surveys also revealed declining support for all major political groups in the territory. In the intense competition for support before the crucial votes in the Legco on the political reform packages, the ugly aspects of lobbying were reported by the media with severe criticisms of the political deals behind closed doors. The subsequent mutual accusations among politicians and political groups certainly caused further damage to their image.

It appears that the political parties have not been able to broaden their respective bases of support. None of them have more than one thousand active members. Even the United Democrats of Hong Kong (UDHK), Meeting Point (MP) and the Hong Kong Association for Democracy and People's Livelihood (ADPL) failed to expand after their spectacular electoral victories in 1991. Before the amalgamation of the UDHK and MP to form the Democratic Party, the Chinese authorities attempted to cultivate MP and ADPL and isolate the UDHK. In fact, leaders of MP and ADPL were appointed Hong Kong Affairs Advisers. These "divide and rule" tactics, together with the policy of isolating the major enemy, will continue to 1997 and beyond. The easy absorption of politicians into the pro-Beijing united front, however, has contributed much to the community's cynicism of politicians and its general apathy.

The limited mobilization power of the political parties means that they have to depend heavily on the mass media to win the support of Hong Kong people. They are therefore often tempted to adopt radical postures to attract attention. The price is that it makes it very difficult to establish a constructive dialogue with the government, and mutual trust hardly exists. Political posturing on the part of the pro-democracy groups apparently has cost them dearly among the intellectuals, whose support for them has been in decline.

Almost all political parties have little human and financial resources at their disposal. As a result, they can only concentrate on parliamentary politics on a weekly basis, and neglect long-term policy planning. On the arrangements relating to the transfer of power, for example, political groups have not been able to contribute in any significant way. At this stage, they tend to limit themselves to just responding to the British administration's policy proposals. Even in this area of activity, they still seem to be handicapped. In the first place, seeking publicity remains a very important consideration. Secondly, they have not been able to develop high-powered think-tanks. Finally, they do not have time and manpower to consult their respective grassroots networks, often resulting in frictions between the parliamentary parties and their respective organs at the district level.

Despite the satisfactory turnout at the District Board elections in September 1994, a number of phenomena should cause alarm to the political parties. A poll conducted early in the month showed that up to 70% of the respondents remained undecided on how to vote in the elections. This meant that the political parties had failed to attract many dedicated followers. It also reaffirmed the previous pattern that most voters went to vote to fulfil a civil obligation, and that they usually did not bother to study the candidates carefully to make a considered choice. Another survey held at the same time revealed that about half of the respondents indicated that they could not trust any of the political parties; and another 23% could not identify a political party which they could trust. It was small wonder that some candidates with party affiliations chose to pose themselves as independents in the District Board elections.

By the end of 1994, many Hong Kong people demonstrated a district political apathy or fatigue. They were tired of the Sino-British quarrels, and believed that both parties would not accord priority to Hong Kong people's interests. They considered that they were the ultimate victims of the disputes, and were concerned if the final stage of transition would be a period of chaos and uncertainty. It seems that both the British administration and the political parties have failed to show them the direction. Hong Kong people often find themselves in a contradictory position too. They despise politicians who have been eager to please the Chinese authorities, and appreciate those who boldly criticize Beijing. That is why Emily Lau is even more popular than all Democratic Party legislators. However, they shun confrontation with the Chinese leaders, because they know that a deteriorating relationship with Beijing will hurt the Hong Kong economy. Such dilemmas easily prompt them to "exit" from politics. Incidentally, a survey in October 1994 indicated that 60% of the respondents believed that freedom of speech would be more restricted in the coming three years.

There is of course the more obvious form of "exit." From 1981–1986, around 20,000 people emigrated from the territory each year. The figure jumped to 30,000 in 1987, and further to 45,800 in 1988, 42,000 in 1989, 62,000 in 1990, 60,000 in 1991, 66,000 in 1992 and then fell to 53,000 in 1993.

The economic difficulties in the West probably have generated some disincentive among the local professionals. In early 1994, consulates general of Western countries in Hong Kong reported a decline in the numbers of emigration visas granted. For example, the United States Consulate General indicated that only 13,142 people were granted emigration visa in 1993, down from 14,882 people in 1992 and 18,880 in 1991. There were also signs that an increasing number of people who had emigrated are returning to Hong Kong. The Hong Kong government estimated that at least 12% of persons who emigrated in the ten years before 1992 have returned to Hong Kong.

In October 1994, however, the media noted an unexpectedly high number of people applying to emigrate. In the past two months, applications to settle in Canada and Australia had risen considerably; and immigration consultants also reported an upsurge of business by about 20%. The Deputy Secretary for Security, Patrick Hayes, had to admit that if trends of the past two months continued, the brain drain statistics would be back to 62,000 for 1994. Middle-class families again are getting indications from many of their relatives and friends who are planning to leave the territory in the coming two years.

The business community, on the other hand, has been firmly supporting the Chinese government in the Sino-British conflict. It has confidence in China's economic reforms and opening up to the outside world. Such momentum has picked up so soon after the Tiananmen crackdown. Business persons believe that the trend is irreversible. Hence they have been very bullish about the economic future of China and Hong Kong's role in China's development. Seen in this context, the Sino-British confrontation was a temporary phenomenon which would become irrelevant as the territory approaches 1997. Such business confidence explains the continuing boom in the real estate and stock markets in the past years, though mild adjustments took place in the property market since the second quarter of 1994 and in the stock market since the beginning of 1995. Undeniably, there has been a lot of money flowing from China into the markets too. It is not surprising that the business community has been most critical of Chris Patten's·China policy.

The above may help to explain why the community treasures the status quo and is unwilling to rock the boat by challenging the Chinese authorities. It did not even bother to react to the confirmation that the People's Liberation Army would station in the urban areas of the territory nor to the establishment of a provisional legislature in 1997. Some people feel that they are so fed up with the present impasse that they even wish 1997 could come sooner.

CONCLUSION

In the final analysis, Hong Kong people may have to count not so much on the Joint Declaration and the Basic Law but on the following domestic and international factors to ensure that the Chinese leadership lives up to its promises made during the Sino-British negotiations for the Joint Declaration. In the first place, the Chinese leadership has been assuring the international community in recent years that its economic reforms and open door policy will remain unchanged. Its policy towards Hong Kong has been looked upon as a litmus test of its economic reforms and open door policy. Any violation of the spirit and the terms of its promises to Hong Kong would hurt the world's confidence in China's modernization process. Second, as an SAR under China's sovereignty, Hong Kong will set a significant example for Taiwan, and the rising mood for independence in the island has certainly been worrying Beijing. Third, a change in China's policy towards Hong Kong might have a signalling effect on its domestic reforms too. Various liberal economic policies and foreign investments in China would most likely be affected. Finally, as long as the Chinese leadership values Hong Kong's contributions to its modernization programme, this capitalist enclave may continue to be tolerated. All these factors, however, do not constitute an absolute guarantee that Hong Kong will remain unchanged up to the year 2047. Moreover, these factors may be more effective in ensuring that Hong Kong's "previous capitalist system and way of life shall remain unchanged for 50 years" than in guaranteeing the "high degree of autonomy" and "self-administration" promised.

If Hong Kong people accept this, and it seems they do, then the role of the British administration in the final years of the transition will be limited indeed. All parties concerned no longer believe that Beijing and London can fully cooperate to secure a smooth transition by 1997. Regarding the political system, each will go its own way. Both sides have been preparing for the worst, and various contingency plans, once set in motion, will gather momentum of their own. There are vested interests in both camps who would like to see an escalation of confrontation.

Hong Kong people have all heard of this praise of their territory: Shenzhen learns from Hong Kong, Guangdong learns from Shenzhen, and the whole country learns from Guangdong. (Hong Kong's media have been wise not to play up this slogan.) What must be borne in mind is that the Hong Kong model is an integrated whole. This recognition is all the more important in the approach to 1997. While foreigners come and admire the territory's public housing achievements and the work of the Independent Commission Against Corruption, it is the entire nexus of its political, economic, social and cultural values and attitudes that lays the foundation of its success. Hong Kong people therefore have a responsibility to inform and convince the Chinese authorities that the maintenance of Hong Kong's stability and prosperity depends on the preservation of such values and attitudes. This recognition and responsibility are even more significant when the community becomes increasingly politicized and polarized.

This task of preservation demands the understanding of the Chinese authorities, and the strengthening of the dialogue between Hong Kong and Beijing. In the foreseeable future, maintenance of the rule of law and freedom of the media is perhaps more important than the further development of representative government. It is important to enlist the business community, at least its enlightened segment, to support such an objective; and the best way to secure this support is to demonstrate that it is in the interest of the business community to do so. For example, business leaders in the territory are interested in the burgeoning telecommunications market in the Asia-Pacific region. Hong Kong already has an early start, and it must try its best to maintain this advantage. This privileged position can only be secured if the existing freedom of the media can be guaranteed after 1997. This in turn means that the business leaders have an important stake in safeguarding the Hong Kong SAR's freedom of the media. In sum, Hong Kong people must strengthen their consensus based on the highest common factor of enlightened self-interests in persuading the Chinese leaders to maintain the territory as it is. There appears to have no other alternatives.

Note

1. For background information, please refer to: (a) *The Other Hong Kong Report*
    series published by The Chinese University Press; (b) *The Basic Law of the
    Hong Kong Special Administrative Region of the People's Republic of China*
    (Hong Kong: The Consultative Committee for the Basic Law of the Hong
    Kong Special Administrative Region, April 1990); and (c) Mark Roberti, *The
    Fall of Hong Kong: Britain's Betrayal and China's Triumph* (New York: John
    Wiley & Sons, 1994).

2

From "Through Train" to "Second Stove"

Lo Chi-kin

THE CONCEPT OF "THROUGH TRAIN"

"Through train" is a political metaphor in Hong Kong. For the past four decades, the on and off of through train service has marked the up and down of Sino-Hong Kong relations. For the sovereignty transition in 1997, "through train" stands for continuity and stability.

In its literal sense, through train means uninterrupted train service between Hong Kong and Mainland China without interruption at the border. For about three decades before 1979, through train service was suspended due to the closed door policy of the Chinese government. At that time, all the passengers going by train to Mainland China from Hong Kong had to get off at the border and go through customs check at Lo Wu–Shenzhen.

Through train service was resumed in 1979 as a result of the Chinese government switching to the open door policy. The frequency of the service has gradually increased since then and it is still always fully booked. The thousands of passengers commuting between Hong Kong and Mainland China everyday provide one of the best indicators for the economic and social integration of the two territories.

"Through train" entered Hong Kong's political vocabulary during the drafting of the Basic Law in the late 1980s. It was used to symbolize a proposal to allow sitting members of the last Legislative Council (Legco) under British rule to serve as members of the first legislature of Hong Kong Special Administrative Region (SAR) under China's sovereignty without new elections. "Through train" was a graphic presentation of the hope that political institutions in Hong Kong could cross the "border" of 1997 without interruption of service.

The concept of "through train" was accepted by the Chinese government and incorporated into the Basic Law. On 4 April 1990, China's National People's Congress (NPC) adopted the Decision on the method for the formation of the first government and the first legislature of the SAR as an integral part of the Basic Law. This Decision defines the term of office of the first SAR legislature as two years (1997–1999), instead of the normal term of four years for subsequent legislatures. These two years can fit in nicely as the latter half of the term of office of the last legislature under British rule, which commences in 1995, and this should be the intent of China's lawmakers. This is because the Decision also provides that:

> If the composition of the last Hong Kong Legislative Council before the establishment of the Hong Kong Special Administrative Region is in conformity with the relevant provisions of this Decision and the Basic Law of the Hong Kong Special Administrative Region, those of its members who uphold the Basic Law of the Hong Kong Special Administrative Region of the People's Republic of China and pledge allegiance to the Hong Kong Special Administrative Region of the People's Republic of China, and who meet the requirements set forth in the Basic Law of the Region may, upon confirmation by the Preparatory Committee, become members of the first Legislative Council of the Region.

Although the concept of "through train" has been mainly used to describe the transitional arrangement for the legislature, the concept is in fact embedded in many parts of the Basic Law. For example, Article 8 of the Basic Law provides that:

> The laws previously in force in Hong Kong, that is, the common law, rules of equity, ordinances, subordinate legislation and customary law shall be maintained, except for any that contravene this Law, and subject to any amendment by the legislature of the Hong Kong Special Administrative Region.

Article 93 provides that:

> Judges and other members of the judiciary serving in Hong Kong before the establishment of the Hong Kong Special Administrative Region may all remain in employment and retain their seniority with pay, allowances, benefits and conditions of service no less favourable than before.

Article 100 provides that:

> Public servants serving in all Hong Kong government departments, including the police department, before the establishment of the Hong Kong Special

Administrative Region, may all remain in employment and retain their seniority with pay, allowances, benefits and conditions of service no less favourable than before.

The above list of examples is not exhaustive. There are more similar examples in the Basic Law.

The "through train" was a very popular concept. It was seen as an effective mechanism ensuring continuity and stability during sovereignty transition in 1997. Perhaps because of its popularity, the concept's viability had not been seriously examined. There were a few dissenting voices, which expressed concern about the viability of the concept, but they were rapidly brushed aside.

The key to the viability of "through train" concept is Sino-British cooperation. The physical through train cannot be operational without close cooperation between rail management on both sides of the border. Similarly, the political "through train" requires close cooperation between the two sovereign powers, China and Britain.

At the time the Basic Law was drafted, China and Britain had in general maintained a good cooperative relationship over Hong Kong matters. However, things began to change in 1992. A new Governor, Chris Patten, arrived in Hong Kong in July 1992. Patten proposed a package of constitutional proposals in his first policy address in October 1992, without seeking prior consent of the Chinese government. This set off a furious row between China and Britain. The "through train" was derailed.

PATTEN'S CONSTITUTIONAL PROPOSALS

By the standards of full democracy, the constitutional proposals put forward by Patten in 1992 are far from radical. They merely exploit the grey area of the Basic Law, maximizing the room for popular elections within the boundaries of its provisions.

According to the Basic Law,

The first Legislative Council of the Hong Kong Special Administrative Region shall be composed of 60 members, with 20 members returned by geographical constituencies through direct elections, 10 members returned by an election committee, and 30 members returned by functional constituencies.

The Legco during the term of 1991–1995 is composed of 60 members, with three government officials, 18 members appointed by the Governor,

18 members returned by geographical constituencies through direct elections, 21 members returned by functional constituencies. For the composition of the Legco which commences its term in 1995 to be in conformity with the first SAR legislature, the three officials' seats have to be abolished, two seats for the geographical constituencies have to be added, nine new functional constituencies have to be created, and an election committee has to be formed to return ten members.

The key elements of the Patten proposals are: the election committee is to be composed of all the directly elected members of the District Boards (total number being 346); and every member of the working population will be entitled to vote in one of the nine new functional constituencies which will be created along the lines of occupational classification. By these proposals, the election committee will have an indirect electoral base of universal franchise and the functional constituencies will have an electoral base of the size of the workforce in Hong Kong, about 2.7 million.

For many years after the signing of the Sino-British Joint Declaration on the future of Hong Kong, the British government had always deferred to the wish of the Chinese government on the issue of constitutional development. In 1987, the Hong Kong government undertook a review of future development of representative government. The Chinese government voiced strong objection to introduction of direct election to the Legco in 1988, on the ground that such a move would pre-empt the drafting of the Basic Law. At the end, the Chinese government's wish prevailed despite strong local support for direct election in 1988.

In the aftermath of the Tiananmen incident in 1989, there was a surge in popular demand in Hong Kong for a faster pace of democratization. Members of the Executive and Legislative Councils agreed on a compromise formula on constitutional developments known as the "OMELCO consensus." The "OMELCO consensus" called for 50% of the Legco seats to be returned by direct election in 1995. The members also urged the Hong Kong government to convince the Chinese government of the need to allow for greater democracy in the Basic Law in line with the "OMELCO consensus." However, the Hong Kong government merely managed to get the Chinese government's consent to introduction of 18 directly elected seats to the Legco in 1991. As described above, the Basic Law provides for only 20 directly elected seats in the first SAR legislature, 10 less than what the "OMELCO consensus" proposed. At that time, the British government did not raise strong objection to the Basic Law.

Patten's constitutional proposals did not violate the letters of the Basic Law. Nonetheless, the way Patten handled the constitutional issues clearly departed from the previous policy of the British government. He was prepared to implement the proposals without the Chinese government's consent. As a matter of fact, seventeen rounds of Sino-British negotiations on constitutional issues in 1993 failed to resolve the differences between the two governments. Patten then tabled his 1992 proposals to the Legco and all of the proposals' major elements were carried.

The British government has not explained the change in its policy. The Chinese government has perceived the policy change as part of a wider international conspiracy to isolate and subvert China as a result of the Western powers' reaction to the 1989 Tiananmen incident. However, the timing of the policy change renders the Chinese government's interpretation unconvincing. In early 1990, more than half a year after the Tiananmen incident, when the Western powers' hostility to China was at the peak, the British government was actually adopting a compromising attitude in negotiation with the Chinese government over Hong Kong's constitutional issues.

The British government's policy change should therefore be related to events more recent to Patten's arrival in Hong Kong. Three of them provide the most plausible explanations and they are not incompatible.

The first is the protracted Sino-British negotiations over the new airport projects during 1990–1991, which culminated in British Prime Minister John Major's visit to Beijing in September 1991. The new airport projects were proposed by Governor David Wilson in 1989 as a confidence boosting measure to counter the gloom in Hong Kong caused by the Tiananmen incident. However, the massive infrastructure projects could not take off without the Chinese government's expressed approval which was essential for any financing deals. Taking advantage of the Hong Kong government's weak position on the issue, the Chinese government had managed to force the British government to concede to its authority on major infrastructure projects straddling 1997. On top of that, Major was forced to go to Beijing to sign the Sino-British memorandum on the new airport projects, becoming the first Western government leader to visit China after the Tiananmen incident. Major's displeasure with the visit was well known. The event might have prompted him to review the "appeasement" policy towards China over Hong Kong matters.

The second is the first ever direct election to the Legco held in September 1991. Of the 18 seats contested, candidates advocating faster pace of democracy ("democrats") won 16. This was a strong, unambiguous popular mandate. Although the "democrats" were still a minority in the Legco (the majority being conservatives composed of government appointees and functional constituency representatives), the voice of the voters could hardly be ignored. If the Hong Kong government put forward too conservative a proposal for constitutional development in 1995, it could face strong public opposition.

The third is the change in political loyalty of the conservative camp in the Legco. The conservatives, mainly composed of government appointees, used to be loyal supporters of government policies. After the 1991 election, the conservatives formed the Cooperative Resources Centre (CRC) to counter the growing democrats force in the Legco. A number of CRC members were appointed to the Executive Council by Governor Wilson. With the number of officials in the Legco reduced from ten to three in 1991, the Hong Kong government probably hoped that the conservatives could help it command majority support in the Legco.

However, before long, the conservatives failed to deliver the votes in the Legco on an important issue: the Court of Final Appeal. During a Legco motion debate in December 1991, many CRC members voted alongside the democrats to oppose the Sino-British agreement on the establishment of the Court of Final Appeal before 1997. At the same time, the conservatives started wooing the Chinese government. They shifted gradually to a pro-China, anti-British stance.

By early 1992, it became obvious to the Hong Kong government that a conservative package for constitutional development in 1995 would not guarantee stability of its rule. By the same logic, the impact of enlarging the franchise and promoting the status of the Legco on its authority would only be marginal.

CHINA'S "SECOND STOVE"

Patten's constitutional proposals aroused strong reaction from the Chinese government. The ferocity of the reaction was perhaps beyond the British government's expectation. In fact, the Chinese government's concern is not only about the contents of the proposals *per se*. It is more concerned about the wider implications of the Patten proposals: the British government's departure from the path of cooperation; the collaboration between the Hong Kong government and the democrats; the ascendancy of the Legco and the weakening of the executive-led government. All these are seen as developments which can destabilize sovereignty transition in 1997.

During the years 1984–1992, the Chinese government had banked on cooperation with the British to prepare for the 1997 transition. Despite minor altercations from time to time, cooperation between the two governments had been generally smooth. When Patten put forward his constitutional proposals in 1992, the Chinese government was apparently caught by surprise. Its initial response was furious but it probably still wished resumption of cooperation. Hence, after a few months of war of words, the Chinese and British governments managed to agree in April 1993 to hold talks on constitutional development in Hong Kong.

However, the Chinese government soon realized that, unlike previous negotiations, the British government was taking a much less compromising stance for the current one. At the same time when the Sino-British talks kicked off, the Chinese government began to review its strategy on transitional matters in response to British policy change. During 1993–1994, the new strategy gradually took shape.

The cornerstone of the new strategy is to prepare for the 1997 transition single-handedly, that is, without British cooperation or participation. As far as the constitutional issues are concerned, the Chinese government has taken a number of steps to make sure that the "destabilizing" factors introduced by the Patten proposals will be completely removed.

First, soon after the passage of the Patten proposals in the Legco in June 1994, the NPC Standing Committee adopted a resolution on terminating the terms of office of all the three tiers of representative assemblies (District Boards, municipal councils, Legco) by 30 June 1997. This was a formal burial of the "through train" concept, and was a clear signal to the British government that, with the end of cooperation on constitutional issues, influence of the political institutions under British rule would not be allowed to extend into the era of Chinese sovereignty.

Secondly, the Chinese government has declared the establishment of a "second stove" to dilute the impact of the Patten proposals. There are two different interpretations of the "second stove." The first, which is the official one put forward by the Chinese government, is that a new set of political institutions need to be set up on 1 July 1997 as the old ones under British rule will not be in conformity with the Basic Law and have to be dismantled. The second, which is the conventional wisdom, is that the "second stove" operates before 1997. It is a "shadow government" in the form of the Preliminary Working Committee (PWC), and later, the Preparatory Committee.

Judging from the behaviour of the PWC, it is close to a shadow government. In fact, there is no provision in the Basic Law for the establishment of the PWC. It was borne as the consequence of the Sino-British row over the constitutional issues.

It is the NPC Decision on the method for the formation of the first government and the first Legco, adopted in April 1990, where the establishment of a Preparatory Committee for the SAR has a legal basis. According to the Decision, the Preparatory Committee will be set up within the year 1996 but its terms of reference are rather limited. The Preparatory Committee "shall be responsible for preparing the establishment of the Region," "shall prescribe the specific method for forming the first Government and the first Legislative Council," and "shall be responsible for preparing the establishment of the Selection Committee for the First Government" of the SAR.

As explained above, the Basic Law was drafted and adopted when Sino-British relations were still on relatively good terms. Most of the transitional matters were expected to be dealt with by the Sino-British Joint Liaison Group (JLG), that is, bilaterally rather than unilaterally. That explains why the Preparatory Committee had been designed to be operational only at a date near to 1997 and with limited responsibilities. When the Chinese government decided upon the strategy of unilateral preparation for the 1997 transition, it found such a design for the Preparatory Committee rather inconvenient, hence the establishment of the PWC, which is not mentioned by the Basic Law and the related NPC Decisions.

Since its inception, the PWC has concerned itself with a variety of topics, which go far beyond the scope of responsibilities of the Preparatory Committee as defined by the NPC Decision. It has been virtually writing the policy programme for the first SAR government. It has commented on many Hong Kong government policies of the day. It behaves like a shadow government.

Most importantly, the PWC has drawn up the timetable for forming the first SAR government. The Preparatory Committee will be established in early 1996 so that it can implement the task of forming the Selection Committee for the first SAR Chief Executive as early as possible. The Chief Executive is scheduled to be selected within the second half of 1996.

The advanced announcement of the above timetable has a significant psychological effect on Hong Kong society. People are made to be aware of the existence of the future "political master." While the British are still in charge before 1997, the gravity of political authority will no doubt gradually shift towards China. The Legco elected in 1995 will be constituted according to the Patten proposals but its authority will be undermined by the Preparatory Committee and the Chief Executive designate.

Thirdly, the PWC has proposed the establishment of a provisional Legco to start functioning on 1 July 1997. Details concerning the provisional Legco are yet to be clearly defined. The main points of the PWC proposals are: the provisional Legco will be formed by the end of 1996 or early 1997; and it will exist for a year after 1 July 1997, with powers and functions similar to those of a normal Legco as defined by the Basic Law.

The PWC's justification for the provisional Legco is that it is the best solution to the problem of "legislative vacuum" on 1 July 1997. The problem of "legislative vacuum" is in fact a direct consequence of the derailing of the "through train." Without the "through train," the first SAR Legco has to be elected before 1 July 1997 if it is to start functioning on that date. However, in view of the poor state of Sino-British relations, holding elections to the SAR political institutions while Hong Kong is still under British rule is just impossible. If elections to the Legco are held after 1 July 1997, there will be a period, no matter how short it is, when there is a lack of institution responsible for legislation ("legislative vacuum"). The PWC has examined four possible candidates for filling such a vacuum: (1) the Preparatory Committee; (2) the NPC; (3) the first SAR Chief Executive; and (4) a provisional Legco. In the end, the PWC picked the provisional Legco as the preferred option.

However, if the sole purpose of the provisional Legco is to serve as a stop-gap legislature, it does not need a term of office of one year. Also, it should not have powers similar to those of a normal Legco. Some critics in Hong Kong had suggested that the function of the provisional Legco should be limited to drafting the electoral law for the first SAR Legco. The suggestion had not been accepted by the PWC.

It is therefore reasonable to guess that the provisional Legco will serve other purposes. One obvious purpose is to ensure political stability. In this regard, establishment of the provisional Legco can put off fresh elections which are regarded as a factor of political instability or challenge to the authority of the SAR government. Also, as the composition of an unelected provisional Legco will be under total control of the Chinese government, it can easily prevent some "undesirable elements" from getting into the Legco. Even before the latest Sino-British row over constitutional issues erupted, the Chinese government had already made it clear that it would not allow some of the democrats (like Martin Lee, Szeto Wah) to become members of the post-1997 Legco.

Fourthly, the Chinese government has called the applicability of the "through train" concept for other political institutions into question.

For example, the PWC put forward a proposal that all civil servants should be asked to indicate if they are willing to work for the SAR government. The proposal was received by the civil servants with uproar. It is viewed both as a contradiction to Article 100 of the Basic Law and as a significant departure from existing practice where civil servants could leave their jobs by giving notice according to their contracts. Upon strong objection from the civil servants, the PWC members clarified that their proposal only meant to take stock of the staffing situation of the Hong Kong government by 1997.

Another example is a comment made by senior Chinese officials towards the end of 1994. Lu Ping, the Director of Hong Kong and Macau Affairs Office under China's State Council, said that there was no guarantee for the judges of the pre-1997 Court of Final Appeal to sit on the post-1997 Court. This is a clear contradiction to Article 93 of the Basic Law.

Therefore, to the Chinese government, the "through train" concept applies not only to the Legco but to other political institutions as well. As the "death certificate" for the "through train" concept is signed, not only the composition of the Legco will be affected by the 1997 transition, personnel of other political institutions will be affected as well. On 1 July 1997, passengers on the political "train," no matter which carriage (executive, legislative, judicial) they are in, will have to undergo customs check.

In a way, the derailing of the "through train" has given the Chinese government the pretext to arrange the post-1997 political order at its will. The "second stove" to be set up after 1997 will be political institutions with "Chinese characteristics." The pre-1997 institutions will be dismantled. The Patten proposals will be reversed. The "undesirable elements" will be eliminated. The authority of the executive-led government will be upheld.

JOURNEY INTO THE UNCERTAINTY

By having formulated the master plan for the post-1997 "second stove," the Chinese government probably believes that political stability in Hong Kong will be maintained during the sovereignty transition in 1997. By the end of 1994, the Chinese officials exuded confidence which was lacking about a year ago.

The current plan of "second stove" will no doubt give the Chinese government the chance to exercise control over the post-1997 political institutions. However, whether this can translate into political stability is debatable. In fact, to a certain extent, the plan will aggravate the political uncertainty in Hong Kong rather than eliminate it.

First of all, as the mandate of the existing political institutions will end on 30 June 1997, the ability of their decisions to survive that date is now in question. The issue has been exacerbated by the Chinese government's tendency to view any new policy initiative by the Hong Kong government with suspicion. For example, the Chinese officials and the PWC have already declared their plan to reverse many recent amendments to the laws in Hong Kong. They have labelled new social welfare and infrastructure spending as extra burden for the future SAR government. They have attacked measures to enhance the transparency and accountability of the government as conspiracy to change the system of executive-led government. Under the watchful eye of the Chinese government and the PWC, the lame-duck syndrome of the Hong Kong government is becoming more and more serious.

On the other hand, the democrats, who expect having a hard time after the 1997 transition, probably feel that they are in a hurry. As a result of democratic reform introduced by the Patten proposals, the democrats look forward to making substantial gains in the Legco elections in September 1995. With only twenty-one months left before the 1997 transition, the democrats will attempt to maximize their influence in existing political institutions. Caught between the pressure from the Chinese government and the democrats, the Hong Kong government requires a very fine balancing act to be able to govern coherently and rationally during 1995–1997.

The political uncertainty is unlikely to end with the "second stove" beginning to function in 1997. This is because neither the first SAR Chief Executive nor the provisional Legco will have a strong popular mandate. The SAR Chief Executive will be chosen by a Selection Committee composed of 400 members, the majority of whom are likely to be appointed by the Chinese government. Members of the provisional Legco will probably be nominated by the same Selection Committee.

In recent years, the Chinese government has been gradually building up quite an extensive consultation network in Hong Kong. By the beginning of 1995, the Chinese government had appointed 37 Hong Kong people to the PWC, about 150 Hong Kong Affairs Advisers, 537 District Affairs Advisers, on top of the original circle of the Deputies to the NPC and Members of the Chinese People's Political Consultative Conference. In the spring of 1995, the Chinese government is likely to appoint another new batch of Hong Kong Affairs Advisers. It is highly probable that the 400 members of the Selection Committee for the first SAR Chief Executive and provisional Legco will be chosen from this network.

So far, the Chinese government has excluded the mainstream democrats from this network. In April 1994, Cheung Bing-leung, then Chairman of a democrat group Meeting Point and later Vice-Chairman of the Democratic Party, was appointed as a Hong Kong Affairs Adviser. That was before the announcement of the merger of Meeting Point and the United Democrats of Hong Kong to form the Democratic Party. After the announcement, the Chinese government withdrew Cheung's appointment. The message was clear: the Chinese government's policy is to excommunicate the Democratic Party which has "subversive" elements in its leadership.

The results of the District Board election in 1994 showed that the democrats were still the most popular political force in the territory. If they remain popular at the time of sovereignty transition in 1997 but are excluded from the political institutions, the legitimacy of these institutions can easily come under challenge. That popular politicians are exiled to political wilderness can be a potent source of conflict and instability.

Another area of uncertainty is the appointment of principal government officials. According to the Basic Law, they will be nominated by the Chief Executive and approved by the Chinese government. If the Chinese government is keen about removing anything tainted with British colonialism after 1997, it is not impossible that symbolic changes to the principal official positions will be effected.

In fact, as the Chinese government is still pondering its move in 1997, some senior civil servants may have already lost their heart. Early retirement has become more frequent in recent years. The longer the

Sino-British row goes on, the more likely the number of early retirees will increase.

In sum, the years of 1995–1997 will be riddled with political uncertainties. Only one thing is certain. That is, frequent and major changes in the political structures will take place: Legco elections with a new set of rules in 1995; selection of the first SAR Chief Executive in 1996; stepping down of the incumbent members of the Legco and other representative assemblies and establishment of the provisional Legco; concurrent changes in the line-up at the top level of the executive branch of the government; fresh elections to the Legco with another set of rules in 1998. In the next two to three years, political figures will go up and down the stage through a revolving door.

Such a scenario is certainly far from ideal. The transition period is 13 years long. The Hong Kong public have the right to question why, with so much time for planning, the 1997 transition is still a matter of uncertainty and confusion. And both the British and Chinese governments owe the Hong Kong public an answer.

3

The Civil Service

Jane C. Y. Lee

Introduction

For the first 125 years of the British rule, the Hong Kong civil service has never been a subject of academic interest. Prior to the early 1980s, the civil service was small, colonial and bureaucratic which was largely insulated from the life of the Chinese population. In recent years, the subject began to arouse public attention. Since 1984, the civil service has been politicized to an unprecedented degree by the processes of decolonization and development of representative government. Moreover, the civil service is directly affected by any changes relating to the transfer of government. Similar to most local people in Hong Kong, the 180,000-strong civil service is overshadowed by a sense of uncertainty and anxiety. Needless to say, the effective functioning of the civil service is essential to the maintenance of prosperity and stability in society. The fundamental concern is whether civil servants can successfully accommodate themselves from serving the colonial administration to serving the Special Administrative Region (SAR) government.

This chapter analyses the challenges confronted with the civil service in the run-up to 1997 and beyond. After discussing the major issues affecting its transition, the chapter pays attention to discussing possible scenarios in the post-1997 period.

The Civil Service in Transition

Analysis of the Hong Kong civil service is founded upon the "executive" nature of the colonial administration. Prior to 1985, the civil service

constituted the backbone of the Hong Kong government. It was un-
democratic and authoritarian, but was largely able to make policies without
interference from politics. The civil service was said to be enjoying a high
degree of autonomy in this period. At that time, Hong Kong society was
predominantly apathetic and passive, posing little challenge to whatever
policies were implemented by the government. Organized groups were
weak which could not threaten the effectiveness of the governing process.
The Legislative Council (Legco) was not constituted by any form of elected
members, who rarely disagreed with government's legislation. China, too,
virtually had no involvement in the governing process of Hong Kong. The
Hong Kong government might be criticized as not enjoying any popular
sovereignty. Its legitimacy, however, vested with continued economic performance and administrative efficiency. By the early 1980s, the civil service
has been managing a wide range of public services, including nine years
of compulsory education, public housing for the lower-income groups,
and free hospital services. The civil service did play an important role in
improving the quality of life of the ordinary people.

Under the colonial administration, civil servants gradually emerged as
a distinguished class of ruling elite, who were not merely "public servants"
but also "political masters." Since there was no politics in the conventional
sense, civil servants performed dual functions both as policy-makers as
well as policy-executors. Civil servants were fundamentally concerned with:
(1) administrative rationality; (2) minimum political conflicts and controversies; and (3) organizational procedures and bureaucratic regulations
in the making of policies. By regarding themselves as professionals and
technocrats, they consciously claimed themselves as making decisions
according to "public interest" rather than "political interests." Prior to the
Sino-British negotiation on the future of Hong Kong, civil servants have
already established as a powerful, but conservative, force in society. Civil
servants were fundamentally status quo-oriented who were reluctant to see
any major changes affecting their social status and fringe benefits that they
have been enjoying.

Both the British and Chinese governments recognized the importance
of preserving the satisfaction of the civil service to a smooth transfer of
government. The 1984 Sino-British Joint Declaration had provided a
framework for maintaining the continuity and stability of the civil service.
As stipulated in Annex 1 (Section IV), the Chinese government recognized
the continuation of any impartial, stable and effective public service as an

essential factor to ensuring Hong Kong's future stability and prosperity. Under the provisions of this section of the Annex, it ascertained that serving officers would be able to continue in employment with the Hong Kong SAR government on terms and conditions no less favourable than before 1 July 1997. Special commissions dealing with pay and conditions of services would be retained. All pension and other benefits due to those officers leaving the public service before or after 1 July 1997 or to their dependants would also be paid by the Hong Kong SAR government.

Apart from promising the preservation of the civil service's fringe benefits and conditions of service, the Chinese government quickly emphasized in the post-1984 period the importance of maintaining the executive-dominated nature of the political system. This virtually meant to preserve the superior policy-making role which the civil servants had been possessing in the 125 years of colonial rule. Strategically it also enabled the Chinese government to have better control over a non-elected executive government, hence downplaying the importance of the elected legislature.

All these careful designs to cushion the civil service from the impact of power transfer, however, did not totally alleviate the problems confronting it in the course of decolonization. Challenges to the transitional administration came from a variety of sources.

CHALLENGE OF LOCALIZATION

Localization has been an issue which divided the civil service. According to the Joint Declaration, serving foreign nationals could remain in employment after 1997, except at the highest "principal official" levels, which had to be occupied by Chinese nationals, who were permanent residents of Hong Kong SAR, having no right of abode in any foreign countries. By 1994, expatriate staff in the Hong Kong government only constituted about a tiny proportion of 1.2%, yet most of them were occupying senior posts at point 45 or above of the Government Master Pay Scale. It was thus desirable on the part of the Hong Kong administration to identify suitable local candidates to replace as many expatriate staff as possible. These candidates should also be senior and "young" enough to remain in posts after 1997. The primary rationale was to ensure a degree of continuity, hence confidence in the workforce. Localization policy was implemented through two separate arrangements respectively for the principal official level posts and non-principal official level posts.

According to Article 101 of the Basic Law, principal official level posts included the posts of Chief Secretary, Financial Secretary, Attorney General, fourteen policy secretaries, Director of Audit, Director of Immigration, Commissioner of Independent Commission Against Corruption, Commissioner of Police, and Commissioner of Customs and Excise. Since 1993, the government had taken active steps to move up prominent locals to take up senior posts. Anson Chan, for example, became the first local to fill the post of Secretary for Civil Service in mid-1993 and then promoted to become the Chief Secretary a few months later. Li Kwan-ha was the first Chinese Commissioner of Police and was replaced by Hui Ki-on when he retired in July 1994. In November 1994, the Hong Kong government made some more changes by announcing Peter Lai to take over from Alistair Asprey as Secretary for Security, and Bowen Leung to become Secretary for Planning, Environment and Lands. By early 1995, 16 of the top 23 posts[1] have been filled by ethnic Chinese. It was expected that further steps would be taken in 1995 to replace the Financial Secretary and the Attorney General with locals. For those who have reached the retirement age, their posts would definitely be filled by locals. Those who were required to leave the civil service before their retirement age were offered attractive compensations for early retirement.

Localization at the principal official levels aroused a lot of public attention in recent years. The major issue was whether suitable locals with good quality and experience could be identified for succeeding the senior posts occupied by expatriates. The case of Bowen Leung, who had been promoted from a relatively junior post, was justified by the government as "promotion by performance and merits," but the government had in fact broken the civil service tradition of promoting staff primarily by seniority. Bowen Leung's unprecedented promotion basically revealed that the succession plans might be confronted with tremendous problems.

The succession plan was handicapped by the British government's earlier policy to grant British nationality to 50,000 households in Hong Kong. The British nationality package was introduced in 1990 which aimed to help retain those people in position within the government and the private sector who were considered indispensable to the continued prosperity of the territory. The government claimed that by providing these people with an option to leave Hong Kong, they would not emigrate overseas. The nationality package was partly designed to hold the civil service in place after the Tiananmen incident happened in Beijing in June

1989. Consequently, about one-third of the quota (i.e. approximately 15,000–18,000 households) were used up by civil service families, who either belonged to disciplinary forces or sensitive posts like Administrative Officers or other long-serving senior staff.[2] Whether these officers would remain in the civil service after 1997 depended very much on their confidence towards the future SAR government. My recent survey with the directorate officers (the 1,000 most senior government staff) showed that about 36% of them were worried about their career in the civil service after 1997. Moreover 64.3% of them had held British passports, while another 10.9% held other kinds of foreign passports. More significantly, irrespective of whether or not they were holding foreign passport, about 34.7% of them claimed that they would not remain in the civil service after 1997.[3]

As shown in Table 1, the number of civil service staff choosing early retirement in the three years between 1991 and 1994 had been on a steady increase. In the first five months of 1994, 493 had already applied for early retirement, accounting for 28% of all the retirement cases.

In October 1994, the Secretary for Civil Service, Michael Sze, admitted that he was worried about the number of staff retiring from the civil service in the run-up to 1997.[4] Then in a Legco briefing, Michael Sze stated that, "much will depend on developments in the next 12–18 months (i.e. 1995–1996)."[5] This shows that the government was quite worried about possible exodus of senior local staff, hence constituting potentially a leadership vacuum in 1997.

By 1994–1995, public scepticism towards the civil service succession plan was aroused. Much questions remained unanswered. Would there be enough local candidates qualified for promotion to principal official level posts? Did the government have enough choice? Would the senior officers

Table 1: Staff Opted for Early Retirement, 1991–1994

Year	Number
1991–1992	542
1992–1993	582
1993–1994	543
Jan.–May 1994	493

Source: *South China Morning Post*, 2 November 1994, p. 2.

committed to the well-being of the local community? More importantly, would they be accepted by the Chinese government? Would they be seen by the Chinese government as loyal to the Hong Kong SAR or the British government? All these were related to the criteria essential to good administrative leadership, namely quality, experience, sense of loyalty to the national government and sense of commitment to the local community.

More controversies were even aroused from localization of the non-principal official level posts. In this case, the government became confronted with conflicts between local and expatriate staff.

There were no stipulations in the Basic Law as to which types of non-principal official level expatriate staff could remain in employment. The government had wanted to preserve the status quo as much as it possibly could. Prior to 1993, the government basically regarded localization as naturalization of overseas officers to permanent resident status and transferring them from expatriate to local terms of service. The government also assumed that overseas contractual officers had an understanding that their contracts would not be renewed unless no local staff was available. Expatriate staff quickly used the newly enacted Bill of Rights to criticize the government as violating their right to have equal access to the civil service. The government was equally bombarded by local staff associations for blocking the promotion opportunities of the aspiring locals. After much debates and consultation with the Legco, the government had decided in mid-1994 to open 600 contract posts for competition. The policy encouraged local officers hired on contract terms to transfer to permanent position, but barred expatriates from doing the same. The government also made arrangements to give overseas officers with permanent resident status the right to apply for transfer to local terms. But the transfer was subject to several conditions. If the applicant was occupying a promotion rank, a board would be convened to determine whether there was a local officer suitable to replace him. If there was no such replacement, the officer could continue to serve his present rank. If there was a replacement, he would have to take a step down to the rank below but continued to receive a personal salary and local conditions of service based on his original rank. Under this new policy, over 130 overseas officers had applied and by September 1994, over 70 had been approved for transfer to local agreements under the new arrangement.[6] The new policy was meant to be a compromise which opened more promotion opportunities for locals while retaining the original salary of the expatriates.

The new arrangement was obviously an extremely unsatisfactory one, especially for the expatriate staff. Expatriate staff association immediately applied to the court to sue the government for consciously violating the Bill of Rights. The issue remained unresolved at the time of writing. The controversy over localization has no doubt affected the morale and credibility of the civil service. The problems are most serious among senior level staff.

CHALLENGE TO THE EXECUTIVE-DOMINATED SYSTEM

Apart from the troubles of localization, senior civil servants were also confronted with increased attacks from various political forces in the course of political transition. The preservation of the executive-dominated system did not prevent the emerging politicians from criticizing the administration. The Chinese authorities also began to exercise increasing influence over public opinion on individual policy issues. Consequently, the executive-dominated political system remained but the degree of autonomy which the civil servants had previously enjoyed has been heavily eroded.

The gradual introduction of direct and indirect elections had facilitated the growth of a new generation of politicians who were elected to different levels of the government machinery without actually exercising any political power. What the politicians could do was to make use of their elected positions to exercise a stronger monitoring role towards the administration. This basically forced the introverted civil servants to speak up openly and answered criticisms. Practically speaking, civil servants were required to become more open and responsive to public wishes, but their policy-making role were subject to serious challenge.

My recent survey with the directorate officers revealed that senior civil servants have changed from their apolitical attitude and were more prepared to win public opinion through persuasion.[7] Nevertheless, they were dissatisfied with the Legco, considering the legislators as too politicized and immature. The data indicated that civil servants were ambivalent in their attitude towards the process of democratization. On the one hand, they agreed that the executive government should be accountable to the elected Legco, and on the other, they resented the interference of the elected politicians, regarding them as incompetent, senseless and sometimes even against public interest. Only a minority of the senior officers were genuine supporters of open government. Civil servants were prepared to openly explain their policy proposals but reiterated their neutrality and impartiality in politics.

In fact, civil servants had to engage increasingly in high-profile lobbying and campaigning in order to win the support of the legislators, relevant professionals and public opinion. Failure to do so would result in the voting down of government policy by the three readings of the Legco. Still there was always a possibility that the civil service policy-makers could not arrive at compromise with the legislators, hence leading to an open confrontational situation.

The resignation of Lau Chin-shek from the Legco in December 1994 has provoked a constitutional crisis in Hong Kong's executive-dominated political system. An Employment (Amendment) Bill was submitted to the Legco by Michael Leung, Secretary for Education and Manpower, for three readings. The bill was a result of the compromise and negotiations between the government and the labour representatives in the government-appointed Labour Advisory Board. Lau, the labour representative in the Legco, considered the amendment too mild and inadequate to protect the interests of the labouring class. His amendment was successfully passed in the second reading. Leung, however, immediately withdrew the bill before the third reading began, claiming that the Legco was against the wishes of the representatives of the Labour Advisory Board. Lau therefore protested and resigned immediately from the Legco.[8] This was possibly the first instance in Hong Kong's colonial history in which the government officials openly confronted with the elected legislators. While Leung's move aimed at preserving the dominant role of the executive government, he was heavily criticized for not respecting the decision of the elected Legco and acting against public interest.

Civil servants equally resented interference from the Chinese government. Civil servants had not felt strongly that the Chinese government was interfering into their day-to-day operation. Nevertheless, my survey showed that they were worried about the possibility of "Beijing governing Hong Kong." On many occasions, senior government officials said that they would not consult the Chinese government on most policy issues. But by 1994–1995, there were signs showing that the Hong Kong government needed to obtain approval from the Chinese government to ensure policy continuity, hence the smooth transfer of government.

The controversy over old age pension scheme in 1993–1994 was an example. While opinions in Hong Kong society were divided, the

Chinese government had criticized the Hong Kong administration for mixing up social security with retirement benefits. Recently, the Hong Kong government had indicated that if the Chinese government strongly objected to it, they might drop the proposal and raised it in the Sino-British Joint Liaison Group (JLG) for discussion.

Controversy over the setting up of the Court of Final Appeal in late 1994 was another example. The Hong Kong government wished to set up the Court of Final Appeal before 1997. Yet it had received strong criticisms from both the legal profession and local politicians. China, too, criticized the Hong Kong government for not honouring its promise to set up the Court of Final Appeal in 1993 and therefore the issue should be handled by the future SAR government rather than by the British government in the two years prior to 1997.

The two examples suggested that the policy-making role of the Hong Kong civil service was subject to increasing challenge. Their autonomy has been undermined by the combined efforts of the politicians and the Chinese authorities. Civil servants were losing the degree of confidence they had once developed. They wanted minimum interference from China as well as from the politicians. Both attitudes were however inconsistent with their commitment to serving the well-being of the local community.

IMPLICATIONS FOR THE POST-1997 CIVIL SERVICE

What are the scenarios in the post-1997 period? What will be the executive-dominated political system like under China's sovereignty?

Table 2 shows the characteristics of the evolving civil service from the pre-1985 period to the post-1997 period. It suggests that Hong Kong's civil service has been transforming from an authoritarian regime to a more open executive-dominated system.

Developments in the post-1985 period suggests that the civil service has to adapt to two parallel changes, namely democratization of the political process and decolonization and power transfer from a British colony to an SAR under China's sovereignty. The two processes of democratization and decolonization often occurred simultaneously in many ex-colonial societies in the post-war period. The basic issue in these countries was: who should take over from the colonial government and form a new political leadership? In Hong Kong, the issue is complicated by the transfer of sovereignty

Table 2: The Evolving Civil Service

Pre-1985	Post-1985	Post-1997
Authoritarian executive-dominated system under colonial rule	A more open executive-dominated system during decolonization	Executive-dominated system under China's sovereignty
Autonomous, non-interference from politics	Less autonomy and less authority in policy-making; increased interference from politics	Less autonomy and authority in policy-making; strong interference from politics
Minimum criticism from a non-elected legislature	Stronger monitoring role exercised by an elected legislature	Strong monitoring role of the elected legislature
No interference from the Chinese government	Increasing influence from and coordination with the Chinese government	More interference from and coordination with the Chinese government
Legitimacy vested with economic performance and administrative efficiency	Legitimacy vested with economic performance and political accountability	Legitimacy vested with economic performance, Chinese endorsement and political accountability

from one political power to another. The introduction of direct elections to the Legco is not aimed to cultivate local political leaders to take over the government. Elected politicians only serve to play a quasi-representative role, having no genuine political power. Thus civil servants are not obliged to conform with the demand of the elected legislature, or by implications public opinion. Civil servants should fundamentally be accountable to the sovereign master(s) — the British government before 1997 and the Central People's Government in Beijing after 1997. But unlike a British system which has a democratic tradition, the Chinese government is an authoritarian regime. Hence civil servants are both "servants" of the Hong Kong public, as well as "subordinates" of an authoritarian government. These two roles are in conflict with each other. Civil servants are sandwiched between (1) the elected politicians who force the civil servants to be responsive to public needs, and (2) the Chinese authorities who require civil servants to comply with the command of the central government. Structurally speaking, it is obvious that the commands of the Chinese government should be supreme and, in case of conflicts, override the wishes of the Hong Kong public or the elected legislature.

The ultimate question is how civil servants accommodate themselves within such a "sandwiched executive-dominated" political system. In the pre-1997 period, uncertainty remains. Since Sino-British relations have deteriorated in the second half of the transition, the Chinese government is making unilateral arrangements for most of the crucial issues affecting the transition. By early 1995, civil servants are totally detached, for example, from the preparation of the provisional legislature (but Hong Kong government officials were major actors steering the development of the representative government between 1985–1991). Moreover, civil servants are required by the colonial government to remain loyal, hence accountable, to the British administration before 1997. Therefore they are banned from having any official contact with the Chinese Preliminary Working Committee (PWC). The British government insists that the PWC is not a formal organization within the Chinese political structure. Some senior officials in Hong Kong also openly claimed this as evidences of preserving Hong Kong's local autonomy. Yet it practically means that civil servants are not allowed to have any direct contact with the Chinese side, except through the JLG. On some occasions, Hong Kong officials even have to defend the British position in case of disagreement with the Chinese authorities. The same group of senior officials however expect to remain in employment and will report to the Chinese government after 1997. Lack of a comprehensive plan for the transfer of government means that civil servants are not able to achieve better understanding and coordination with the Chinese authorities and vice versa. Consequently, resentments towards the interference of the Chinese government become intensified.

Civil servants have to accept an erosion of the degree of autonomy they have enjoyed in the pre-1985 period. They should be prepared to compromise with the Legco and respect the legitimacy of the popularly elected legislators. Moreover, they should develop a mechanism whereby they can have formal, but open, contact with the Chinese authorities so that a better mutual understanding and mutual respect should be developed.

Ultimately legitimacy of the civil service vests with its "publicness." Fruitful cooperation with the legislature as well as the Chinese government is most crucial to Hong Kong's continued prosperity and stability.

Notes

1. The government originally estimated that there were 22 posts equivalent to the principal official level. Since November 1994, the post of Secretary for Housing was resumed, thus increasing the number of principal official posts to 23. For an earlier discussion, see Jane C. Y. Lee, "Civil Servants," in *The Other Hong Kong Report 1994*, edited by Donald H. McMillen and Man Si-wai (Hong Kong: The Chinese University Press, 1994), p. 57.
2. See Anthony B. L. Cheung, "The Civil Service," in *The Other Hong Kong Report 1990*, edited by Richard Y. C. Wong and Joseph Y. S. Cheng (Hong Kong: The Chinese University Press, 1990), p. 91.
3. Joseph Y. S. Cheng, and Jane C. Y. Lee, *A Study of the Bureaucrat-Politician Relationships in Hong Kong's Transition* (Hong Kong: City Polytechnic of Hong Kong, February 1994).
4. *South China Morning Post*, 28 October 1994, p. 2.
5. Michael Sze's response to a question raised at the briefing session on the Governor's Policy Address on 15 October, Daily Information Bulletin (Hong Kong: Hong Kong Government, 9 November 1994).
6. *South China Morning Post*, 2 November 1994, p. 9.
7. See Note 5. See also Jane C. Y. Lee, "Civil Servants," in *The Other Hong Kong Report 1994*, p. 43.
8. *Eastern Express*, 15 December 1994, p. 2.

4

Legislative Cliques, Political Parties, Political Groupings and Electoral System

Sonny S. H. Lo

DEFINITIONS OF POLITICAL PARTIES, GROUPINGS AND LEGISLATIVE CLIQUES

Since the Tiananmen incident in China in June 1989, political parties have rapidly emerged in Hong Kong. Although it can be said that those officially recognized political parties, such as the Reform Club and the Civic Association, existed in Hong Kong long before the initialling of the Sino-British Joint Declaration in 1984, they only fielded candidates in municipal elections and failed to obtain substantial political power.[1] While Western democracies are characterized by a rotation of political party in power, this does not exist in Hong Kong's colonial polity in which the bureaucracy constantly wields far more policy-making power than any political party.

If political parties are defined as organizations acquiring political office and power through elections, all the existing "political parties" in Hong Kong do not fit this definition because they participate in elections without gaining either political office or power. Yet, if political parties are loosely defined as organizations that participate in elections with the aim of only influencing government policy, all the groups that are claiming themselves as parties can really be viewed as political parties.

This chapter rejects both the narrow and broad definitions of political parties; instead it adopts a moderate definition, namely parties as groups that have organization, attain local bases of support and participate in elections so as to influence government policy-making. As Huntington points out, the essence of political parties are "continuing organization and social support."[2] Another political scientist argues that the presence of "local bases of support" distinguishes political parties from legislative cliques.[3] A legislative clique is "a factional group whose relationships depended upon a family, a commanding individual, or a close coterie of personal associates: generally the demise or retirement of the focal personal led to the collapse of the clique."[4] With the demise of the "focal personal," the clique may lose its political influence in the legislature. Even if the clique may still survive, it becomes a loosely organized grouping without sufficient grassroots-level support in various districts. According to Huntington, legislative cliques

> are parliamentary not electoral organizations. Typically they are formed within the legislature by successful candidates after they are elected rather than in the constituency by aspiring candidates in order to get elected. Candidates are elected as individuals on the basis of their social or economic status and appeal. The legislative faction or clique then becomes a means of linking them to other political activists, not a means of linking political activists to the masses.... The legislative clique is thus one form of preparty faction typical of the early phases of modernization.[5]

In short, legislative cliques are political factions within the legislature, trying to organize themselves among friends and supporters of some identified leaders. Above all, such cliques tend to lack organization and local bases of support. One can argue that it is not easy to come up with the criteria of absence or presence of organization and local support. Nonetheless, one important indicator of organization and local support can be seen in election results. The poorer the performance in local elections, the more difficult a legislative clique in transforming itself into a political party. Another indicator of organization and local support is the degree of loyalty among clique members. The larger the number of members withdrawing from the clique, the more difficult for it to evolve into party organization with tight discipline.

Political "groupings" are similar to legislative cliques in the sense that they all represent "preparty factions," to borrow from Huntington. Political groupings

> have little durability and no structure. They are typically projections of individual ambitions in the context of personal rivalries and affiliations.[6]

Strictly speaking, groupings do not necessarily have members elected or appointed to the legislature and they are usually formed among like-minded people outside the law-making body. However, legislative cliques must originate from the law-making body in which political elites attempt to enhance their influence and power. Using these criteria of distinguishing between political groupings, legislative cliques and parties, this chapter will offer a critique of the emergence and development of political "parties" in Hong Kong.

THE EMERGENCE AND DEVELOPMENT OF LEGISLATIVE CLIQUES AND POLITICAL PARTIES IN HONG KONG

It can be argued that both the Democratic Party (DP, and formerly called the United Democrats of Hong Kong or UDHK) and the pro-business Liberal Party (LP) were originally legislative cliques. But the most important difference in the development of the DP and LP is that while the former eventually succeeds in transforming itself from a clique into a political party, the latter so far fails to do so.

❏ *The Liberal Party: A Legislative Clique without Grassroots Support*

From a critical perspective, although the LP claims itself as a "political party," it actually remains a legislative clique organized around a group of experienced legislators. It can be recalled that the major organizers of the LP were also the former members of the Cooperative Resources Centre (CRC), a group established by some members of the Legislative Council (Legco) towards the end of the governorship of David Wilson. Four members of the CRC — Allen Lee Peng-fei, Rita Fan Hsu Lai-tai, Selina Chow Liang Shuk-yee, and Edward Ho Sing-tin — were at one time members of both the Executive Council (Exco) and the Legco. Nonetheless, all the CRC members lacked public support as none of them was directly elected by ordinary citizens.

This absence of a local base or grassroots-level support provided an impetus for the CRC to organize itself in a more coherent manner, particularly in view of the UDHK's formation and resounding success in Legco's direct elections in 1991.[7] While CRC leaders were determined to compete politically with the UDHK more effectively than ever before, they made several strategic errors in the process of forming the LP. First, while the LP is a pro-business group, its leaders have constantly refused to use the name of Conservative Party; instead, they opted for the name Liberal Party. The crux of the problem is that ideologically speaking, the LP is actually conservative in terms of its pro-business and slightly anti-social welfare orientations. The word "Liberal" in fact becomes a political burden to the LP, which only arouses the suspicion and perhaps distrust among some voters. It is therefore not surprising that the LP did poorly in the 1994 District Board elections, and that to improve the public image the "party" eventually only fielded three candidates in the 1995 Urban and Regional Council elections.

In comparison with the DP, the LP lacks local bases of support. Although many business people have reportedly contributed financial support to the LP since it was founded, the "party" completely lacks popular support from the grassroots level. Instead of recruiting more politicians from non-business and upper-middle-class background, the LP tended to solicit support from mostly conservative-minded and middle-class members of District Boards. This was understandable given the political ideology of the "party." But the price of such recruitment strategy was not only to reinforce the upper-class image of the "party," but also to deprive the "party" of any substantial grassroots support. The LP leaders claimed that the "party" had hundreds of members, yet they failed to realize that some politicians only harboured the motive of acquiring financial support from the LP in local elections.[8] The continual withdrawal of numerous members from the LP prior to the 1994 District Board elections corroborated that "party" discipline left much to be desired, and that "party" leadership was questionable. The withdrawal of two election strategists, Ada Wong and Cheung Wing-sum, from the LP after the 1994 District Board elections again exposed serious internal differences and split. Cheung openly told the media that he was unhappy about some LP leaders who gave their views on policy issues without discussion with other members beforehand. Undoubtedly, the LP encounters a leadership problem as its members have reservations about the style, competence and consistency of leaders at the top level.

In addition, the LP's lack of effective coordination between the central leadership and local branches had a devastating blow to its performance in the 1994 District Board elections. One informant, who was a LP candidate defeated in the district elections, told the author that the central leadership failed to consult the opinions of candidates before it designed and planned the election campaign.[9] He criticized the standardized campaign leaflets of all LP candidates as "idiotic" and accused a minority of top leaders for monopolizing power and making "party" decisions without listening to the views of "party" candidates. The informant regarded the LP as "a poison of the box office" and he decided not to run in elections by using the name of the LP at least in the short run. He went so far as to suggest that the LP should better change its name into "Industrial and Business Party" so as to project a clearer image to the voters.

Such remarks testified the complete failure of the LP in consulting the opinions of "party" branches. The LP's decision not to field any candidate in the Tai Po district during the 1995 Regional Council election was reportedly a deliberate compromise made with other political parties so that its leader, Allen Lee, would secure district support to participate in the 1995 Legco elections. But such compromise aroused the anger of some LP members in Tai Po, who called upon Lee to go to their district to explain the decision. Clearly, such open disagreement voiced by members revealed that the LP remained a legislative clique without support from some local branches. "Party" decisions appeared to be imposed upon the locality and, if this phenomenon were not ameliorated urgently, the prospects of the LP in direct elections held for various political institutions would be gloomy.

However, it can be anticipated that the LP will still have a role to play in Hong Kong politics particularly after 1997. As long as Hong Kong's electoral system does not allow for complete direct elections, the LP will still have its members elected to the Legco through functional constituencies and the future Election Committee. The recent proposal of the Preliminary Working Committee (PWC), a body set up by China in 1993 to counter Governor Patten's political reform package, to consider the idea of implementing proportional representation in future Legco elections will no doubt have the unintended consequence of giving more room for the LP to survive.

❏ *The Democratic Party: A Learning Political Party Transformed from a Legislative Clique*

This does not mean that the DP is perfect in terms of organization, local bases of support, party discipline and party leadership. Objectively speaking, the DP occasionally also has members withdrawing from the party, and its leaders' handling of the resignation of member Lau Chin-shek from the

Legco in 1994 also exposed the immature leadership of the pro-democracy party.[10] However, the DP is so far more successful in transforming its character from a legislative clique into a political party, and in consolidating the party organization internally as well as externally. The DP grew out of the Legco after some liberal-minded professionals, like lawyer Martin Lee and educationalist Szeto Wah, were elected by functional constituencies (like law and education) to the legislature in 1985. Frustrated by the policies of the executive-dominated administration, especially the postponement of the introduction of direct elections to the Legco in 1988 due to the opposition from China,[11] and then later alienated by the Tiananmen incident in China in 1989, Lee and Szeto decided to organize a political party named the United Democrats of Hong Kong (UDHK) in preparation for the 1991 Legco elections.

What distinguished the DP from the LP at the inception of their formation was the former's strategies of developing itself from a legislative clique to a political party. First, the DP is a product of the merger between the UDHK and Meeting Point (MP), a political grouping that often made comments on government policies and supported candidates to run in local elections in the latter half of the 1980s. The merger could be regarded as a marriage of convenience partly because MP needed the popularity of UDHK's core members to rescue its relatively lacklustre performance in local elections, and partly due to the UDHK's desire to cooperate with those MP leaders who were acceptable to China.[12] Whatever the motives of the merger, it apparently consolidates the strength of the liberal democrats, who can now pool their manpower and financial resources to compete with political foes in local elections. Although Chinese officials were unhappy about MP's merger with the UDHK and then decided to withdraw the appointment of former MP chairman, Anthony Cheung Bing-leung, as one of China's Hong Kong Affairs Advisers, this had no impact on the appeal of liberals to voters. China's political exclusion of Anthony Cheung might even have the unintended consequence of sharpening the liberal and pro-democracy images of the newly formed DP.

Another DP's strategy of organizing itself into an effective political machinery in elections is to recruit hard-working liberals at the grassroots level in various districts. Although the DP was unable to field candidates to compete in all geographical constituencies during the 1994 District Board and 1995 Urban and Regional Council elections, the party did recruit numerous energetic activists whose pro-democracy ideals served as a powerful momentum in election campaigns.[13] Most candidates and campaign managers of the DP worked very hard in their constituencies long before the election.[14] Moreover, the way in which DP candidates answered questions from voters during the forums held for the 1994 District Board elections showed that their quality was in general much higher than the LP candidates. In fact, many LP candidates were either absent from the candidates' forums or failed to answer questions from ordinary citizens.[15]

The third strategy that the DP adopts in transforming itself into a party organization is to constantly emphasize party discipline and to forbid members to join other political parties, except for pro-democracy and liberal-minded "political commentary groups" (a term used by the media) like the Hong Kong Affairs Society.[16] The emphasis of the DP on party discipline and loyalty was markedly different from the LP. In the wake of the 1991 Legco elections, one UDHK member who had supported a non-UDHK candidate in the Sha Tin constituency was expelled from the party. After the 1994 District Board elections, another DP member who was criticized for making compromise with political opponents in the selection of a chairperson of the Tuen Mun District Board had to formally withdraw from the party. Such consistent implementation of strict party discipline is the most prominent feature distinguishing the DP from other political parties and cliques in Hong Kong.

Finally, the DP has been recruiting members from all strata of Hong Kong society. Unlike the LP which is more an aristocratic legislative clique than a populist political party, the DP has co-opted some unionists and working-class members at the grassroots level. Ideologically speaking, the DP is the champion of the interests of middle-lower classes. It advocates the establishment of a Central Provident Fund, the provision of more social welfare to the poor and the elderly, and the provision of more housing to members of the "sandwich class." The populist appeal of the DP is a far cry from the upper-class and conservative images of the LP, a difference that could explain the former's success and the latter's fiasco in the 1994 District Board elections.[17]

Nonetheless, the DP encounters a number of problems in its future development. First, as long as the seats in the Legco are not entirely directly elected, the DP's populist appeal cannot and will not lead to its control of the legislature. In other words, the electoral system severely constrains the political influence of the DP. In the event that the proportional representation system were adopted in the Legco's direct elections after 1997, the ability of the DP to win most directly elected seats would be reduced.[18] Strategically speaking, the DP will have to make compromises with like-minded political groupings so that liberal candidates will not compete among themselves in elections. These strategic compromises are becoming more urgent than ever before, partly because the conservative and "pro-China" forces are cooperating among themselves to counter the democrats, and partly because the electoral system will most probably be changed to maintain a relatively weak legislature in which the power of liberal democrats to check the executive branch will be restricted.

Nevertheless, it can also be argued that even if the proportional representation system were adopted in the Legco's direct elections after 1997, this does not necessarily undermine the overall strength of the liberals. For one thing, as long as the liberal democrats are not homogeneous in terms of their attitude towards China (some do not exclude the possibility of confronting with Chinese officials, and some stress mutual dialogue and communication with China), there will be at least two liberal-minded political "parties" in Hong Kong. At present, in addition to the DP, the Hong Kong Association for Democracy and People's Livelihood (ADPL) can be regarded as a small political grouping with limited local bases of support. The ADPL's power base is traditionally located at Shum Shui Po district, and its relatively "pro-China" attitude has been criticized by some members of the DP. Given varying attitude towards China, it is unlikely that the DP and the ADPL will merge together as a united front against conservative and nationalist forces in the foreseeable future. Therefore, it is and will be essential for the DP to make compromise with the ADPL with a view to minimizing the political impact of the emerging nationalist or "pro-China" party, namely the Democratic Alliance for Betterment of Hong Kong (DAB). It can also be anticipated that if any proportional representation system parallel to Macau's electoral method were introduced to the Legco's direct elections, the beneficiaries would be not only the small conservative political parties or cliques, but also the ADPL which is ideologically pro-social welfare and pro-democracy.

One danger that the DP faces is the possibility of an internal split due to opinion differences. A DP member told the author that during the inauguration convention of the party, one member accused the former MP members as "pro-communist," an indication that a minority of former UDHK members had a misperception of MP. Such misperception stemmed partly from slightly different attitudes between MP and the UDHK towards

China, and partly from the hyperpoliticization of Hong Kong polity particularly after the Sino-British dispute over Governor Patten's political reform proposals. It can be recalled that some MP members, who emphasized communication with China and whose nationalist sentiment was relatively strong, withdrew from the grouping as it publicly supported Patten's reform blueprint in 1993. Clearly, even within MP itself there were opinion differences towards Hong Kong's political reforms. Any opinion difference within the DP, if not handled in a skilful manner, would probably lead to a split that could undermine the solidarity of liberal democrats in the future.

Another challenge faced by the DP is the apparent difficulty of striking a balance between having dialogue with China and advocating democratization. Since the political exclusion of Anthony Cheung, the current vice-chairman of the DP, from China's batch of advisers, it is no longer necessary and urgent to discuss the question of how to strike such a balance, especially when Chinese officials refuse to communicate directly with all the "subversive" elements of the DP. Yet, in the event that Chinese officials adopt a more softline policy towards the DP and initiate a dialogue with some DP members, whose views are politically acceptable to China, it is very likely that other DP members may view such dialogue as a co-optation attempt by China to stifle or control the demands for democratization. Hence, there is an irony that while the hardline policy of China actually has the unintended consequence of enhancing the internal unity of the DP, any softline policy to co-opt moderate DP members will most probably generate or exacerbate some potential tensions and policy disputes within the party.

Overall, the DP realizes the necessity of learning how to maximize its political power within the confines of Hong Kong's colonial polity. Although the Patten administration is decolonizing and democratizing the polity, the DP leaders appear to be psychologically prepared for any attempt by the post-1997 government to recolonize the local institutions, especially the Legco in which the democrats have, since the introduction of elected seats in 1985, been quite successful in limiting the power of the executive. Given the Basic Law's constraints on the ability of individual Legco member to initiate a bill in the post-1997 legislature,[19] and given the temptation of post-1997 government to manipulate the electoral system, the DP will face a formidable challenge to adapt to the changing rules of the game in Hong Kong politics.

❑ *The Democratic Alliance for Betterment of Hong Kong:* *A Newly Emerging Political Party with Increasing Political Power*

Contrary to the LP and DP, the Democratic Alliance for Betterment of Hong Kong (DAB) is a political party not emerging in the form of a legislative clique. Like the DP, the DAB has become a party acquiring popular support at the grassroots level. When the DAB was founded in 1992, most of its organizers were members of District Boards, leaders of the "left-wing" Federation of Trade Unions (FTU), and Hong Kong delegates to China's political institutions such as the Guangdong People's Political Consultative Conference. Only one DAB organizer, Tam Yiu-chung, was a Legco member in 1992. This bottom-up recruitment strategy eventually showed its success when the DAB had 37 of the 89 candidates won the 1994 District Board elections.

The DAB adopted a number of strategies that contributed to its success in the 1994 district-level elections. First, its candidates were successful in mobilizing employees and staff members of numerous "pro-Beijing" or nationalist organizations in their election campaign. Such mobilization could be seen in many constituencies where DAB candidates solicited political support by utilizing a list of names, telephone numbers and address of those voters who worked in such organizations as the Bank of China and Overseas Chinese Commercial Bank.[20] The door-to-door campaign of DAB candidates was generally no different from DP candidates, who all lobbied very hard for popular support. One DAB candidate who was not a resident in a constituency spent much time in communicating with individual voters during her campaign, and eventually she was able to defeat two opponents, one from the DP and the other representing the LP.[21]

Second, DAB candidates used different methods of explaining their political platforms and views to voters, and this pluralistic campaign strategy was a far cry from LP candidates who adopted standardized campaign leaflets. While DAB candidates cherished their campaign leaflets and ensured that each leaflet describing their platforms reached the hands or mailboxes of voters, some campaign supporters of LP candidates appeared to be amateur and distributed leaflets to voters in an unorganized and aimless manner. Specifically, on the election day, several LP campaign supporters in one constituency in Sha Tin kept on giving leaflets to all those people who went into a restaurant. Yet, when some of these people threw the leaflets away, the LP campaign supporters continued to hand out the candidate's leaflets to others aimlessly. This reckless campaign strategy of some LP candidates was no match for the relatively cautious and organized manner of DAB campaign. While the quantity of campaign leaflets of some LP candidates was much larger than that of DAB candidates, the election campaign of the latter was generally far more organized and effective than the former.[22]

Third, the DAB tended to build its local bases by utilizing district networks, such as the branches of the FTU, *kaifong* associations and some Mutual Aid Associations (MACs). Those MACs supportive of any DAB candidates were mobilized as a political machine to contact individual voters in a constituency. This did not necessarily mean that such MACs were controlled by the DAB, but they were skilfully utilized by party candidates in the process of political mobilization. It can be anticipated that if DAB members continue to cultivate such grassroots support, they will become a more powerful force in future direct elections held for the District Boards, Urban and Regional Councils, and the Legco.

While the DAB becomes quite successful in formally participating in local elections, it is fully supported by Chinese officials. The appointment of numerous DAB members as China's Hong Kong Affairs Advisers and local District Affairs Advisers proves that Chinese officials are trying to legitimize the DAB's position in Hong Kong politics. Arguably, even if China does not co-opt the DAB members, the party has already succeeded to project an image as a local organization fighting for the interests of Hong Kong people at the grassroots level. Indeed, the official Chinese endorsement and support serve to strengthen the DAB's current and future status in the Hong Kong polity.

There are grounds for believing that the DAB will be increasingly powerful in Hong Kong's polity after 1997. First, through the Chinese strategy of political appointment,[23] the DAB will probably play an influential role in the Election Committee that will select the future Chief Executive of the Hong Kong Special Administrative Region. In addition, DAB members will have more say in many consultative and policy-making bodies in the foreseeable future. These bodies include, for example, the committees that often give advice to the government on educational and health policies, and the institutions (such as the National People's Congress) that link Hong Kong people with the Chinese government. In the event that the future Chief Executive wants to appoint some DAB members, who may be directly elected by citizens to the Legco, into the top policy-making Exco, such overlapping appointment will no doubt elevate the political status and influence of the DAB to an unprecedented degree. Since politics is "the art of the possible," as Bismark said, the possibility of appointing some DAB legislators into the Exco after 1997 cannot be excluded. In a nutshell, the DAB may have the opportunity of becoming the political party with much power and influence on the post-1997 administration, just like the former CRC which had several members sitting in the Exco under the administration of Governor Wilson.

Second, in the event that the direct elections held for the Legco adopt the proportional representation system, this will probably be beneficial to some DAB candidates who are relatively weak in some constituencies. In terms of charisma and political prestige, the DAB leaders appear to lag behind the DP counterparts. Any change in the current electoral system for the Legco's direct elections will not only compensate for the relatively weak political appeal and charisma of some DAB leaders, but also strengthen the power of the DAB to check the liberal democrats in future elections.

Third, given the relatively harmonious relationship between the DAB and China, the party is in a more advantaged position than either the LP or the DP to influence Chinese policies towards Hong Kong. The AIDS test that was once implemented in 1993 by the Guangdong authorities on Hong Kong travellers was eventually shelved because of the opposition from many Hong Kong people. The DAB also joined the opposition to the AIDS test, indirectly or directly contributing to the abandonment of the Guangdong policy. While critics may argue that the DAB's action to lobby against the AIDS test was either a political show or a coincidence with the eventual policy change of China, one cannot turn a blind eye to the fact that the DAB at least succeeded in portraying itself as the party fighting for the interests of Hong Kong people. The DAB's contact with Chinese authorities over the AIDS test showed that this nationalistic party enjoyed a direct access to Chinese policy-makers, an advantage that makes it potentially more powerful than the DP to influence Chinese policies towards Hong Kong. In the event that the DAB realizes this political advantage, its determination to speak and fight for the interests of Hong Kong people will to some extent protect and enhance Hong Kong's autonomy *vis-à-vis* the central government in Beijing after 1997.

However, the DAB encounters two major problems in its future development. First, its middle-lower-class image and pro-social welfare orientation clash with the interests of Hong Kong's capitalist class. While China is trying to forge an alliance between the capitalists and the DAB to govern post-1997 Hong Kong, the alliance itself has internal contradictions. It remains to be seen how the DAB reconciles its political positions with the interests of capitalists over such issues as the import of workers from China, and the establishment of the Central Provident Fund. Another problem of the DAB is its relatively "pro-China" attitude without adopting a critical perspective. During the 1994 District Board elections, some voters told a DAB candidate in public that they would vote for him in the event that he withdrew from the DAB, which in the minds of them is too "pro-Beijing."[24] Clearly, at least a portion of middle-class voters are deeply concerned about the image of the DAB, whose leaders are sometimes uncritical of Chinese policies towards Hong Kong. The decision of the DAB's vice-chairman and Legco member, Tam Yiu-chung, to abstain from voting on the Employment (Amendment) Bill was accused by critics of not fighting for the interests of the working class. While Tam wanted to distance himself from the action of DP member Lau Chin-shek who amended the Bill, it was apparently unwise for him to put political differences between the DAB and the DP before the common objective of protecting the welfare of workers. To acquire the wholehearted support of more voters and workers, the DAB will have to strike a balance between partisan struggle and the protection of working-class interests.

❏ *The Other Legislative Cliques and Political Groupings: Problems and Prospects*

In addition to the LP, a legislative clique, and the two political parties, the DP and the DAB, there are a number of small legislative cliques and political groupings in Hong Kong. One legislative clique whose future political influence in the legislature will be questionable is the Hong Kong Democratic Foundation (HKDF), which was founded by some Legco members in 1990. The withdrawal of chairman Leong Che-hung from the party, and the recent retirement of core member J. D. McGregor from participation in the Legco's functional constituency election showed that the clique's longevity is in doubt. Without local bases of support, the HKDF remains politically very weak. Strategically speaking, the recent HKDF's decision not to merge with the DP might be a strategic error. Unless the

HKDF retains its appeal and influence through the Legco's functional constituency elections, it is unlikely that the clique can and will exert significant influence on the government's policy-making process. The fact that McGregor's voting behaviour was usually consistent with the former UDHK members in the Legco proved that a political alliance between the HKDF and the DP would by no means be harmful to the clique's long-term development. Overall, the departure of McGregor from the political arena probably signalled the "collapse" of the HKDF, a feature of any legislative clique as discussed by Huntington.

One small political grouping with limited local bases of support is the ADPL. The ADPL does not have an internal structure as with the DP and the DAB, which have committees studying various government policies, implementing party discipline and connecting with local party branches. The ADPL leader, Fung Kin-kee, had relatively strong local bases of support in the 1991 Legco's direct elections and he was eventually elected to the legislature. However, in the event that the future electoral system for the Legco's direct election were changed, the ADPL would probably face an uphill battle to retain one or two seats in the legislature. Strategically, the ADPL will still realize the necessity of pooling the manpower and resources with the larger and better-organized DP in future Legco elections, while at the same time making some compromises with independents and even "pro-China" candidates in municipal and district elections. The ADPL will persist as long as its unique character is accepted by both China, the DP, the LP and also the DAB. Yet, its political influence alone remains generally minimal.

The other small political "party" — the Liberal Democratic Federation (LDF) — is also, strictly speaking, a political grouping with loose organization and relatively weak leadership. The LDF's influence concentrated on the Kowloon City district. It fielded 28 candidates in the 1994 District Board elections and 11 of them were elected (39%), a result slightly better than the LP. Both the LDF and the LP are pro-business in political outlook, but the LDF tends to be a grouping that tries to consolidate its power base at the district level first instead of establishing a base inside the legislature in the first place as with the LP. The LDF is influential in a few relatively old districts like Kowloon City and Hung Hom, where urban development is comparatively slow and where traditional *kaifong* associations and MACs are strong. It can be anticipated that if urban development proceeds more quickly in these districts, the LDF will encounter a problem of how to retain its political appeal to younger and new residents. In the mean time, as with the ADPL, the LDF remains a district-based political grouping which has little influence on the government's policy-making inside and outside the Legco.

Indeed, there are other small and district-based political "parties," such as the pro-Taiwan One Two Three Alliance, the "pro-Beijing" Hong Kong Progressive Alliance, the nationalistic Kwun Tong Residents Alliance, the Sha Tin-based Civic Force, and the relatively liberal-minded Kowloon City Observers.[25] But all these self-proclaimed parties are actually political groupings in which their organization is loose, political platforms vague, leaders relatively either unpopular or not charismatic, and members comparatively inexperienced in politics. As long as the larger political parties, like the DP and the DAB, and such legislative clique as the LP find it difficult to field sufficient members to compete in all the constituencies in Hong Kong's elections at legislative, municipal and district levels, these small political groupings will still possess plenty of opportunities to make strategic compromises. Compromises between political groupings, like the DAB and the LP, to avoid having their candidates compete against each other could be seen in the 1995 Urban and Regional Council elections.[26] The relative weaknesses of the larger political organizations, which are constrained by either the electoral system or their flawed developmental strategies, not only help to sustain the existence of small groupings but also make strategic compromises a political culture in Hong Kong's future elections. Moreover, in the event that some appointed seats were reintroduced into District Boards after 1997, members of some "pro-China" political groupings will most probably be appointed by the government to serve various districts. In other words, any move to recolonize or decelerate the democratization of District Boards will consolidate the strength of small political groupings which are supportive of China's policies towards Hong Kong.

CONCLUSION

It is crucial to distinguish between legislative cliques, political parties and groupings in Hong Kong. The introduction of elections to the Legco in 1985 facilitated the rise of legislative cliques, including the CRC and the liberal democrats. The liberals have been successful in transforming their clique (called the "democratic faction" by the media) into political party, firstly the UDHK and later the DP. On the other hand, it remains to be seen whether the LP leaders will also be able to transform their clique into a genuine political party. Among the major political organizations in Hong Kong, the LP encounters the most difficult problem of how to organize and manage a "party" effectively.

Although the DP remains the party that gains a majority of popular support in direct elections held for the District Boards, Urban and Regional Councils and the Legco, its popularity will be sooner or later eroded particularly when the existing electoral system undergoes a process of adjustment, if not manipulation. With the support from China and given its hard work at the grassroots level, the DAB will sooner or later become the most influential political party in Hong Kong after 1997.

The colonial electoral system in Hong Kong, where the most powerful political institutions like the Legco and the Exco are not composed of all directly elected members, generates some peculiar phenomena. While such legislative clique as the LP is without popular support, it could become a powerful force in policy-making, such as its predecessor the CRC. Political parties that gain popular support, like the former UDHK and the present DP, could have little influence upon policy-making at the top level. Although Governor Patten has implemented his political reform proposals under which the most members of District Boards are directly elected, the relatively popular DP found it difficult to field enough talents in all constituencies. As a result, democratization of District Boards does not necessarily lead to the political preponderance of liberal democrats. On the other hand, the rapid emergence of the DAB has become an effective check against the liberal democrats in local elections.

The lateness of party formation and transformation in Hong Kong, and the inevitable change of electoral system in the Legco's direct elections after 1997, imply that "pro-Beijing" political parties and a minority of legislative cliques with relatively weak local bases will have far more policy-making influence than the currently most popular party, the DP. This situation will become more obvious in post-1997 Hong Kong than ever before. In conclusion, while the present decolonization and democratization period is characterized by the relative success and increasing influence of the popularly supported DP, the post-1997 Hong Kong polity will be at least for some time characterized by the inevitable dominance of the DAB, the rejuvenation of the LP under political patronage, and the continual survival of numerous political groupings. If political development entails the introduction of directly elected seats to political institutions and the emergence of popularly supported parties, the current transition period in Hong Kong does display some degree of development. Nevertheless, there will most probably be a retrogressive movement towards political under-development in post-1997 Hong Kong if the electoral system is reshaped in such a way to check the power of any popularly supported party.

NOTES

1. Norman Miners, *The Government and Politics of Hong Kong* (Fifth edition; Hong Kong: Oxford University Press, 1991), p. 197.
2. Samuel P. Huntington, *Political Order in Changing Societies* (New Haven: Yale University Press, 1968), p. 413.
3. Alan R. Ball, *Modern Politics and Government* (Second edition; London: MacMillan Press, 1982), p. 75.
4. William N. Chambers, *Political Parties in a New Nation* (New York: Oxford University Press, 1963), p. 26, cited in Huntington, *Political Order in Changing Societies*, p. 413.
5. See Note 2, p. 414.
6. Ibid., p. 413. Huntington does not distinguish between "groupings" and "groups," a distinction that has been made by some political scientists. This chapter applies Huntington's concepts of "legislative cliques" and "political groupings" into the case of Hong Kong, and therefore the finer distinction between "groupings" and "groups" is not discussed and used here. For the distinction between "groupings" and "groups," see H. Gordon Skilling, "Groups in Soviet Politics: Some Hypotheses," in *Interest Groups in Soviet Politics*, edited by H. Gordon Skilling and Franklyn Griffiths (New Jersey: Princeton University Press, 1971), pp. 29–31. It can be argued that any distinction between "groupings" and "groups" tends to be arbitrary, and that perhaps Huntington himself perceives the two terms as more or less the same. In this chapter, the term "groupings" instead of "groups" is used although the author regard them as basically the same.
7. For the results of the 1991 Legco's direct elections, see Rowena Kwok, Joan Leung and Ian Scott, *Votes without Power: The Hong Kong Legislative Council Elections 1991* (Hong Kong: Hong Kong University Press, 1992), Appendix A, pp. 212–19.
8. Personal discussion with a former LP member.
9. Interview with a LP member, 1 October 1994.
10. In December 1994, Lau resigned from the Legco in protest against the government's withdrawal of the Employment (Amendment) Bill after it was

successfully amended by Legco members. Lau's resignation prompted the DP chairman, Martin Lee, to order him not to resign or face expulsion from the party. Lee's order was criticized by some DP members. This incident reflected the internal differences of opinion between Lau and Lee, both men of principles. For a review of the Lau Chin-shek incident, see Chris Yeung and Catherine Ng, "The Martyr Who Is Coming Out on Top," *South China Morning Post*, 19 January 1995, p. 17.

11. For details of the politics of postponing the introduction of direct elections to the Legco in 1988, see Lo Shiu-hing, "Colonial Policy-makers, Capitalist Class and China: Determinants of Electoral Reform in Hong Kong's and Macau's Legislatures," *Pacific Affairs*, Vol. 62, No. 2 (Summer 1989), pp. 204–18.

12. Before the merger, a candidate supported by Meeting Point performed poorly in a by-election held for the Regional Council in Sai Kung district in August 1993. See *South China Morning Post*, 10 August 1993, p. 5.

13. This was the result of the author's participant observation when the author followed some candidates of the DP and the "left-wing" Democratic Alliance for Betterment of Hong Kong (DAB) in their election campaigns during the 1994 District Board elections.

14. This was the author's observation of a DP candidate's campaign in a constituency in Kwun Tong during the 1994 District Board elections. He eventually defeated his opponent easily.

15. Result from the author's observation of a candidates' forum of District Board elections in the Eastern district on 3 September 1994. One LP candidate arrogantly refused to answer questions from voters about his lifestyle. On the other hand, one DP candidate in another constituency performed poorly in the same forum, failing to prepare his speech beforehand and to deliver it in a fluent manner. This DP candidate was eventually defeated by a candidate of the DAB. Of course, not all LP candidates performed poorly in forums; some did quite well in projecting their image as competent politicians. For example, Jennifer Chow Kit-ping appeared to be successful in answering questions from voters in a poorly attended forum held on 11 September 1994. She was eventually re-elected to the Eastern District Board.

16. All these "political commentary groups" are not influential in the government's policy-making process. The Hong Kong Affairs Society is largely inactive particularly after its leaders have joined the UDHK and then the DP since their formation.

17. The DP fielded 133 candidates and 75 of them (56.4%) were elected in the 1994 District Board elections. But the LP had only 18 of its 89 candidates elected (20.2%).

18. Macau's elections are using the proportional representation system which, if implemented in Hong Kong, will benefit those political groupings or

legislative cliques with relatively weak local bases of support. See Lo Shiu-hing, "Political Mobilization in Macau: The 1992 Legislative Assembly Elections," *Issues and Studies*, Vol. 29, No. 5 (May 1993), pp. 89–122.

19. Article 74 of the Basic Law states that "Bills which do not relate to public expenditure or political structure or the operation of the government may be introduced individually or jointly by members of the [Legislative] Council. The written consent of the Chief Executive shall be required before bills relating to government policies are introduced." See *The Basic Law of the Hong Kong Special Administrative Region of the People's Republic of China* (Hong Kong: The Consultative Committee for the Basic Law of the Hong Kong Special Administrative Region of the People's Republic of China, April 1990), p. 29.

20. Result of the author's participant observation of how a DAB candidate campaigned in a constituency on 16 September 1994.

21. Result of the author's participant observation of this DAB candidate in her constituency in the District Board elections, and personal interview with her after the election on 23 September 1994.

22. On the election day on 18 September 1994, the author was surprised to see that LP candidates had far more campaign workers than all the opponents in several constituencies. These campaign workers used banners to attract for voters' attention, but many voters had probably made their voting decisions before they went to the polling stations. If so, the last-minute campaign strategy of some LP candidates was probably ineffective at all.

23. Political appointment is one of the most important strategies of co-optation used by China. See Lo Shiu-hing, "The Politics of Co-optation in Hong Kong: A Study of the Basic Law Drafting Process," *Asian Journal of Public Administration*, Vol. 14, No. 1 (June 1992), pp. 3–24.

24. This was the author's observation of a conversation between these voters and a DAB candidate in an election forum held on 11 September 1994.

25. The One Two Three Alliance has members who formerly studied in Taiwan. The Kwun Tong Residents Alliance is a "pro-China" grouping that competes with the emerging liberal democrats in Kwun Tong district. The Civic Force is led by District Board member Lau Kong-wah, who was a former member of the UDHK and who has been criticized for becoming more "pro-China" than ever before. The Kowloon City Observers (KCO) also has some former members of the UDHK and DP, such as Chiang Sai-cheong, and it constantly competes with the LDF. One KCO member told the author that the KCO tried to "make the red light district greener," meaning that Kowloon City was politically dominated by "pro-China" people, who made the district "red" or "pro-communist." Another KCO member complained that when he publicly collected donations from Kowloon City residents for the flood relief in China,

a LDF member called the police to interfere with his public donation activity. Owing to mutual distrust and dispute over district affairs, the relations between the KCO and the LDF have been strained. Interview with KCO members, 10 September 1994.

26. In the 1994 District Board elections, the LP alienated some DAB members as the former sent candidates to compete with the latter in many districts, such as the Eastern District. The intention of the LP to make compromises with the DAB in the 1995 Urban and Regional Council elections was clearly a strategic move by the clique to improve its relations with the "pro-China" party.

5

Time Is Running Out:
The Endangered Legal System

Johannes M. M. Chan

In late 1994, two clock towers were respectively erected in Beijing and Shenzhen counting down to 1997. While some people in Hong Kong resented such an expression of eagerness of the resumption of sovereignty over Hong Kong, the clock towers do convey an important message: time is running out. The Sino-British Joint Declaration promised that the legal system in Hong Kong before 1997 would remain basically unchanged after 1997. This is a deceptively simplified statement: numerous changes will have to be made in order to reflect the change in sovereignty and to ensure that the present legal system could be maintained after 1997. Yet with less than 900 days before the resumption of sovereignty, one would be amazed by the number of outstanding items which have to be resolved before the midnight of 30 June 1997. This chapter will look at two issues only, namely the continuation of legislation and treaties applicable to Hong Kong, and the Court of Final Appeal.

CONTINUATION OF LOCAL STATUTES

Article 18 of the Basic Law provides that the law in force in the Hong Kong Special Administrative Region (SAR) shall be the Basic Law, the laws previously in force in Hong Kong, and the laws enacted by the legislature of the SAR. "The laws previously in force in Hong Kong" is defined in Article 8 as a reference to "common law, rules of equity, ordinances, subordinate legislation and customary law." This formulation deliberately leaves out any reference to imperial or prerogative legislation, the preservation of which is considered to be inconsistent with the resumption of sovereignty. Further, only those previous laws which do not contravene the Basic Law will be preserved. Upon the establishment of the SAR, the Standing Committee of the National People's Congress (NPC) will declare whether any particular piece of previous legislation contravenes the Basic Law.

The consequences of these provisions are these: first, the Letters Patent and the Royal Instructions will not be preserved after 1997. Indeed, they will be replaced by the Basic Law itself, which will be the constitution of the Hong Kong SAR. Second, imperial legislation extended to Hong Kong will not be retained after 1997. At present, there are about 300 English Acts which are applicable to Hong Kong, mainly in the areas of civil aviation, shipping and admiralty, and intellectual property. Unless these English Acts are re-enacted into local laws before 1997, there will be a vacuum in these areas. Third, of the 600 odd principal ordinances and about 1,000 pieces of subsidiary legislation in Hong Kong, only those which are not inconsistent with the Basic Law will be preserved. It will be necessary to determine which of them are not inconsistent with the Basic Law before 1997.

The problem of ensuring the continuance of local laws has long been identified by the government. A Localization and Adaptation of Laws Unit has been set up within the Legal Department to review the situation since 1986. This Unit liaises with the relevant government departments on the legislation concerned and decides what changes are required. It is monitored by a steering committee chaired by the Law Draftsman. Both the Solicitor-General and the Law Officer (International Law Division) are members of this committee.

❑ *Local Statutes*

Statutory provisions which have to be amended in order to bring them in line with the Basic Law are of vastly diverging nature and can roughly be grouped into different overlapping categories. The first category includes those legislation which are uncontroversial and require technical changes only. Some may require only a change in terminology. For example, there are some 21,000 pages of laws full of the words "Crown," "Royal" and "Commonwealth," such as the Crown Land Resumption Ordinance. The terms "Governor" and "Governor in Council" appear numerous times in local statutes; they may have to be replaced by "Chief Executive" and "Chief Executive in Council." Other changes may require considerable technical amendments or even sometimes outright repeal. For example, the Supreme Court Ordinance provides that the High Court shall exercise jurisdiction and adopt practices of a like nature and extent as that exercised and adopted by the High Court of Justice in England. While the Hong Kong courts have developed its own practice over the years in its case law, such practice has never been clearly spelt out in local legislation. To set them out requires detailed study of the current jurisdiction and practice in both Hong Kong and the United Kingdom (U.K.). Another example is the Application of English Law Ordinance, which provides that English Acts of Parliament may apply to Hong Kong by Order in Council or by incorporation, and that English common law shall be applied in Hong Kong subject to applicability to the local circumstances and to local modification. The Interpretation and General Clauses Ordinance sets out the definitions of various terms and expressions which will be adopted in the interpretation of statutes in Hong Kong unless such definitions are clearly inapplicable. Many of these terms and expressions will have to be repealed (e.g. Order in Council, Secretary of State), or modified (e.g. alien, common law, enactment, statutory declaration). Even public holidays as defined in the Holidays Ordinance will have to be amended: obvious deletions include Birthday of the Queen, whereas obvious additions include the National Day of the People's Republic of China (P.R.C.)!

The second category of legislation is those which require amendments but the amendments cannot take effect for one reason or another until after the change of sovereignty. One interesting example involves non-governmental bodies such as charitable organizations. The Hong Kong Red Cross, which is incorporated by statute, is a branch of the British Red Cross. The affiliation is set out in the British Red Cross (Hong Kong Branch) Ordinance. It will become a branch of the Chinese Red Cross after 1997. Under the Statute of International Red Cross Movement, the Hong Kong Red Cross, being a regional branch, must affiliate to its national branch and cannot exist independently. However, any statutory amendment to give effect to the change in affiliation can only take effect upon the change of sovereignty. The present government cannot pass a law before 30 June 1997 to change the affiliation of the Hong Kong Red Cross, yet such law has to exist on the very day of 1 July 1997!

A third category is those involving highly controversial issues which have not been resolved. As a result, no amendment can yet be made. The definition of "Hong Kong permanent resident" as contained in the present

Immigration Ordinance is not the same as that appeared in the Joint Declaration or the Basic Law. The right of abode in Hong Kong, which carries the inherent right to leave and to return to Hong Kong, depends on the concept of "Hong Kong permanent resident," which in turn is related, under the Joint Declaration and the Basic Law, to one's nationality. The definition in the Basic Law distinguishes between Chinese and non-Chinese persons. Nationality itself is a very complicated subject. Dual nationality is recognized under the English law but not the Chinese law. The problem is exacerbated by the presence of a large number of local Hong Kong residents who have acquired foreign passports in the last few years. Are they Chinese nationals? That might depend on the means they obtain their foreign nationality, as Chinese nationality may be lost by operation of law if they have acquired a foreign nationality and settled overseas. Those who acquire their foreign nationality by investment without settling abroad may still be considered as Chinese nationals, and those who have obtained British nationality by the British Nationality Scheme may not be recognized as foreign nationals. Non-Chinese persons will become Hong Kong permanent residents only if they have ordinarily resided in Hong Kong for a continuous period of seven years and have taken Hong Kong as their place of permanent residence. It is still unclear whether the requirement of taking Hong Kong as their place of permanent residence can be fulfilled by a simple declaration or whether there are other additional requirements. It is also unclear whether former Hong Kong permanent residents who have emigrated and returned to Hong Kong after 1990 would lose their permanent residence and have to satisfy the seven years' residence requirement. All such details have to be set out in the Immigration Ordinance, but this cannot be done until there is an agreement on these issues.

The large number of local Hong Kong Chinese residents returning to China to get married in recent years poses another problem. Their children born in China will be "Hong Kong permanent resident" under the Basic Law, but not so regarded under the present Immigration Ordinance. It is estimated that there are about 300,000 such children, who can only come to Hong Kong at present under the one-way permit system pursuant to an agreement between Hong Kong and China. All of them will have a right of abode in Hong Kong after 1997, and their number is ever increasing.

The last category covers those which are so controversial and political that it is likely that they will not survive the change of sovereignty. The most obvious one is that reflecting political development in Hong Kong, and in particular, the composition of the Legislative Council (Legco) in 1995, which is set out in the Legislative Council (Electoral Provisions) Ordinance. Equally obvious is Part 1 of the Crimes Ordinance dealing with treason and seditious libel against the Crown, which will be inconsistent with the resumption of sovereignty. Indeed, Article 23 of the Basic Law specifically requires the Hong Kong SAR to enact laws "to prohibit any act of treason, secession, sedition, subversion against the Central People's Government." The concept of secession does not exist under the common law, and it is inappropriate simply to adopt the current law on treason and seditious libel by changing the subject from the Crown to the Central People's Government.

It is clear that a lot of work has to be done in order to ensure that the present legislation can survive the change of sovereignty. There is of course no guarantee that the amended legislation will be consistent with the Basic Law and can therefore be preserved after 1997. As a result, the government decided that the best way to proceed is to consult China through the Joint Liaison Group (JLG) on each and every of these amendments. Unfortunately, partly due to the tense Sino-British relationship, very little progress has been made in this area. The Chinese government, who is forever suspicious of the British government, has even stated that amendments to domestic statutes is a matter of sovereignty and will be dealt with by the Chinese government. It would not be bound by whatever amendments made by the Hong Kong government before 1997.

In mid-1993, China set up a Preliminary Working Committee (PWC) to prepare for the establishment of the SAR. Their work was speeded up after the breakdown of the Sino-British negotiation on the electoral arrangement for the Legco in 1995. In early 1994, a legal subgroup of the PWC has commenced their examination of the compatibility of local legislation with the Basic Law. Its task is extremely onerous. The subgroup comprises a few Hong Kong lawyers and a retired Court of Appeal judge who are known of their pro-China attitude. Apart from the lack of credibility of its membership, the proceedings of the PWC lack transparency. Its agenda has not been made public, and it is unclear what criteria they have adopted in scrutinizing existing legislation. In mid-1994, the subgroup was reported to have said that the amendments to the Societies Ordinance and the Public Order Ordinance made in 1992 and 1993 respectively in order to bring them in line with the Bill of Rights were inconsistent with the Basic Law. They proposed to restore the pre-amended version of the Public Order Ordinance, which imposed stringent control on public meetings and processions, and of the Societies Ordinance, which had been described by an eminent constitutional scholar as one of the most draconian laws in the entire Commonwealth.

Given the current pace of progress, it is doubtful if the exercise of bringing local statutes in line with the Basic Law can be completed before 1997. As 80% of the necessary amendments are of a technical nature, there is no reason why those amendments cannot be made without consultation with the Chinese government. In view of the time constraint and the large number of amendments that are required, the government has decided to introduce in three batches all necessary amendments unilaterally. The first batch of legislative amendments, most of which would be uncontroversial, was scheduled to be introduced to the Legco in 1995.

❑ *Imperial Legislation*

While there may be disagreement on which statutory provisions of local ordinances have to be amended, no such problem exists for imperial legislation because all of them have to be replaced. Such imperial legislation can be divided into two groups: pre-1843 and post-1843 English Acts. For historical reasons all English Acts which existed in England on 5 April 1843, the date when Hong Kong obtained its first legislature, formed part of Hong Kong law. A major reform was carried out in 1966, resulting in the enactment of the Application of English Law Ordinance. It was provided that only those pre-1843 English Acts which were set out in the Schedule to the Ordinance would be preserved. About 70 had been preserved, and over the years the number has been cut down to about 20 through various amendments to the Schedule. Some of these Acts could be traced back to 1385 (Justice of the Peace Act), while most of them were enacted in the nineteenth century. Despite their ancient origin, some of them are still of great importance, such as the Habeas Corpus Acts 1679 and 1816.

The second group includes all post-1843 English Acts applicable to Hong Kong. Most of them apply to Hong Kong through Order in Council. They fall mainly in the areas of merchant shipping, maritime law and intellectual property. The reasons why they have to be extended to Hong Kong are that they have extraterritorial application and most of them are either directly or indirectly related to international treaties. Being a colonial legislature, the Hong Kong legislature was not, until 1986, competent to enact legislation with extraterritorial application. There are also others of a more political/constitutional nature, such as the Colonial Laws Validity Act and the Official Secrets Act.

The government has embarked on a "localization" project of these English Acts since 1988, that is, converting and re-enacting these laws into Hong Kong statutes. To facilitate this project, an amendment has been made to the Letters Patent to empower the Hong Kong legislature to enact legislation with extraterritorial effect. Since 1988, the government has decided that about 150 of the 300 odd English Acts are outdated and should be repealed. The British side has prepared about 80 papers on those remaining English Acts for consideration by the Chinese side, with 11 more consultation papers in preparation. By early 1995, 35 of these Acts have been localized and agreement has been reached on another 32 English Acts, which will be localized and the new bills will soon be introduced to the Legco. About 68 English Acts are still under consideration by the Chinese team. The slow progress is partly because of the complexity of some of these legislation (particularly in admiralty law), partly because some of these Acts are related to international treaties to which the P.R.C. is not a party, partly because the Chinese side has been slow in responding to some of the proposed amendments tabled at the JLG and has not accorded priority to these matters, partly because the British side of the JLG has failed to identify the priority of localization among this group of legislation, and partly because of the strenuous Sino-British relationship in the last few years. It is unfortunate that the government has decided to consult the Chinese government through the JLG on every piece of these legislation. This seems unnecessary. For example, there is no reason why repeal of outdated Acts or localization of Habeas Corpus Acts or the Prescription Act 1832 requires any discussion at the JLG.

CONTINUED APPLICATION OF INTERNATIONAL TREATIES

Another problem of preserving the existing legal system arises from the lapse of international treaties applicable to Hong Kong at the moment. By the end of 1992, Hong Kong is a party to about 180 bilateral and over 250 multilateral international treaties. The issue basically is how to ensure that all the rights and obligations enjoyed by Hong Kong before 1997 can continue to be enjoyed by the Hong Kong SAR after 1997. The situation is slightly more complicated here, as in many cases it involves other foreign governments. As a result, the cooperation of the P.R.C. government is essential.

❏ *Multilateral Treaties*

In the cases of multilateral treaties, they have been classified into 22 major categories covering almost every kind of human and business activities such as civil aviation, conservation, human rights, economic and financial affairs, international crime, intellectual property, nationality and telecommunication.

These treaties can be further classified into two major categories. The first category includes those to which both the P.R.C. and the U.K. are signatories, such as some of the International Labour Conventions, the Convention Against Torture 1984 and the New York Convention on the Enforcement of Arbitration Awards 1958. Convention on the Elimination of All Forms of Discrimination Against Women (CEDAW) falls into this category as well, although it has not been extended to Hong Kong yet.

The second category includes those treaties to which the P.R.C. is not a signatory. This represents about 60% of all treaties applicable to Hong Kong at the moment. Whether Hong Kong can continue to be a member to these treaties after 1997 depends to a large extent on the provisions and nature of each treaty, and whether other signatories are prepared to accept Hong Kong as a party to the treaty.

Since 1985, the British side of the JLG has prepared over 200 papers, one on each of these multilateral treaties. By late 1994, agreement on how to proceed has been reached in about 110 treaties. Out of these 110 treaties, Hong Kong's continued participation after 1997 has been confirmed in only 29 of them, most of which deal with participation in international organizations such as the Asian Development Bank and United Nations (UN) Specialized Agencies.

The overall picture is rather complicated. In some cases, it is possible for Hong Kong to join the treaties in its own right, such as the General Agreement on Tariffs and Trade (GATT) which Hong Kong is eligible to join as an independent customs zone. In other cases, this may not be possible, especially if the treaties are only open to ratification by a sovereign state, such as the International Covenant on Civil and Political Rights (ICCPR). In some cases, it is possible for the P.R.C. to ratify a treaty on behalf of Hong Kong, and the treaty will have effect in the Hong Kong

SAR only. For example, the U.K. has extended some of the International Labour Conventions, including Convention No. 87 on Freedom of Association and No. 98 on Right to Collective Bargaining, to Hong Kong under the relevant articles of the International Labour Organization (ILO) Constitution concerning "non-metropolitan territories." These Conventions do not apply to China. Agreement has been reached that they will continue to apply to Hong Kong after 1997, and that Hong Kong will continue its participation in the ILO. This is made possible by way of analogy under the same articles of the ILO Constitution governing non-metropolitan territories. As the relevant Chinese Declaration pointed out, the Hong Kong SAR, though not a "non-metropolitan territory," will be an autonomous region and will be autonomous in the enactment of its labour legislation and its administration of labour affairs. In some other cases, difficulties may arise if the relevant treaty contains an express federal clause, such as Article 50 of the ICCPR, that is, the treaty must apply to every part of the state.

The ICCPR and the International Covenant on Economic, Social and Cultural Rights (ICESCR) require special consideration, as they have been expressly referred to in the Joint Declaration. These two international Bill of Rights, as they have been called, were ratified and extended by the U.K. to Hong Kong in 1976. Under these Covenants, the British government is required to submit periodic reports respectively to the Human Rights Committee and the Economic, Social and Cultural Rights Committee, which the British government has done. The reports will then be examined by the respective UN bodies. In the examination of the 2nd and 3rd Periodic Reports on Hong Kong under the ICCPR in 1988 and 1991, and the 2nd Periodic Report on Hong Kong under the ICESCR in 1994, the British government has sent a delegation to appear before the respective Committees to defend its reports.

The Joint Declaration expressly said that these two international Bill of Rights as applied to Hong Kong shall remain in force after 1997. As soon as the Joint Declaration was published, critics and academics had queried the meaning of "shall remain in force." It is not possible to recapture the discussions here because of space constraint, but the main arguments run as follows: The two Covenants are not part of Hong Kong domestic law, and unless they are so incorporated, they have no legal effect in the Hong Kong domestic legal system. While the U.K. is under an obligation to report to the UN bodies under the Covenants, the P.R.C. is not a party to either Covenant and has no such legal obligations. If this is the case, the phrase "shall remain in force" is an empty promise, at least in the international plane. The P.R.C. government took the view that "shall remain in force" simply means that the Hong Kong SAR government shall implement the provisions of the Covenants through domestic enactments, such as giving effect to the right to life by prohibiting murder, without having to give legal effect to the Covenants in the domestic legal system. This is the way, argued the P.R.C. government, how an international treaty is "enforced" in domestic law under the English legal system, and this will be the manner the Covenants will "remain in force" in Hong Kong after 1997.

Continued applicability of the Covenants has been the concern of the respective UN bodies. The question has been raised by the Human Rights Committee during its examination of the U.K. Periodic Reports on Hong Kong in 1988 and 1991, and by the Economic, Social and Cultural Rights Committee in 1994. No satisfactory solution has been proposed. The British reply is that this is a matter essentially for the P.R.C. government. As a result, unless the P.R.C. government ratifies the two Covenants, they will lapse after 1997. However, in October 1994, the Governor of Hong Kong argued that the provision in the Joint Declaration means that the P.R.C. government was bound to submit periodic reports to the respective UN bodies after 1997. This has provoked strong rebuke from the P.R.C. In a highly emotive tone, the P.R.C. officials stated categorically that the P.R.C. was not bound by the two Covenants. It would not submit reports on Hong Kong to the UN bodies after 1997 and the British government should not attempt to internationalize the Hong Kong issues.

❏ Bilateral Treaties

In so far as bilateral treaties are concerned, it requires negotiation of new treaties with the other contracting states. These treaties cover vastly diverse issues, such as aviation, extradition, civil procedure, enforcement of judgments and orders and so on.

Aviation is the only area where substantial progress has been made. By the end of 1993, Hong Kong has initialled 19 agreements and signed another 9. The initialled agreements are still pending the approval of the P.R.C. government.

Less progress has been made in extradition treaties, which involve about 80 different countries. It has been agreed by the JLG that the British government may proceed with negotiation with foreign governments on extradition arrangement on the basis of a standard model agreement adopted by the JLG. However, approval from China is required for initiating formal discussion with each country. By February 1994, only 6 agreements made respectively with Australia, the Netherlands, Canada, Malaysia, the Philippines and India have been initialled. Among them only the agreements with Australia, the Netherlands and Canada have been approved by the Chinese side. Negotiation is still taking place with the United States, Singapore and New Zealand, whereas informal discussions have been made with 7 other countries. The problem of a lapse of these extradition treaties by 1997 is obvious: the SAR government cannot request extradition of fugitives from other jurisdictions, and cannot extradite criminals in Hong Kong to other countries for trial. Extradition is, of course, of great importance these days in relation to cross-border crimes, drug-trafficking and money-laundering. Hong Kong has received about 70 extradition requests in 1993. Without a proper extradition arrangement, Hong Kong can easily be turned into a safe haven for international criminals.

Another area concerns mutual legal assistance. This will cover not only the enforcement of judgments and orders, and in particular, Anton Pillar Order and Mareva injunction, in foreign jurisdictions, but also matters such as taking of evidence, provision of information on companies and witnesses, recognition of foreign marriages, service of pleadings outside jurisdiction. Very little progress has been made in this area.

Also related is the problem of recognition and mutual judicial enforcement of judgments in other parts of the P.R.C., such as service of judicial documents and orders, enforcement of maintenance orders, probate, divorces and adoptions. In some cases, bilateral agreement has been made, such as service of judicial documents. Interestingly, mutual enforcement of arbitral awards is possible at present because both the U.K. and the P.R.C. are parties to the New York Convention on the Enforcement of Arbitration Awards 1958, but this will no longer be possible after 1997 when Hong Kong becomes part of the P.R.C. Again, little progress has been made in this area.

Another area of concern relates to agreements on visa exemption. Under the Joint Declaration, the P.R.C. has permitted the British Dependent Territories Citizens (BDTC) in Hong Kong to continue to use British travel documents after 1997. This travel document is the British National (Overseas) (BNO) passport, which must be applied for before 1997 as the BDTC passport will expire by 1997. At present, BDTC and BNO passport holders are exempted entry visas by about 70 countries. In contrast, holders of P.R.C. passports are exempted entry visas by only a handful of countries. The British government is trying to obtain as many visa exemption agreements as possible with respect to BNO passport after 1997. The difficulty is, of course, that the British government is not in a position to guarantee that the Chinese government would receive a BNO passport holder from the Hong Kong SAR after 1997 should he be refused entry or deported by a visiting country. While the Chinese government has generally been cooperative in this area, progress has been rather slow. This is partly because the Chinese government is understandably not too keen to promote the BNO passport, whereas the British government is reluctant to promote the P.R.C. passport. The slow progress is also partly due to the time required to negotiate an agreement with foreign states, which may be sceptical about the position after 1997.

More progress has been made with respect to investment protection, covering subjects such as dispute resolution, expropriation and the grant of the most-favoured-nation status. Investment protection agreements have been signed with the Netherlands, Canada, Australia and Sweden. Agreements have also been initialled with Denmark, France, Germany, Italy and Switzerland, and negotiation is being carried on with the United States, Singapore, New Zealand and Japan.

❑ *Conclusion*

The overall picture is rather gloomy. As far as local ordinances are concerned, none of these have been amended in order to bring them in line with the Basic Law. Although the government intends to introduce amendments to the first batch of legislation which are regarded as uncontroversial in early 1995, the prospect of being able to introduce amendments to the more controversial issues, such as treason, sedition or official secrets, before 1997 is rather pessimistic. The picture is even more gloomy when we come to the continuation of international treaties. In the past ten years, the JLG manages to agree on less than half of the multilateral treaties, and less than a quarter of all bilateral treaties. According to the Hong Kong government, they have prepared a paper on each of these treaties to the JLG, explaining the background of the treaties, their importance to Hong Kong and their proposals. Some of these papers have been before the JLG for years. One of the reasons of the slow progress is the lack of expertise in international law on the Chinese side. At the same time, mutual distrust and the strained Sino-British relationship render the Chinese side reluctant to rely just on the papers put forward by the British team. As a result, some of these papers are simply left idle for years.

An early resolution of these problems will benefit not only Hong Kong, but the P.R.C. government as well. To turn Hong Kong into a safe haven for criminals because of the lack of extradition treaties is likely to affect adversely the P.R.C. interests. Unfortunately, the Chinese government does not perceive the same degree of urgency of, or attach the same importance to, these matters as the people in Hong Kong do. After all, they have run the country without law for forty years. This problem also highlights the different perceptions of the notion of the rule of law between Hong Kong and China, and the difficulties of integrating a highly sophisticated modern legal system of Hong Kong into the relatively rudimentary legal system of China. Given the importance of these issues to Hong Kong, and given their complexity and the tight time schedule before 1997, it is rather pessimistic that these treaties can be continued after 1997.

COURT OF FINAL APPEAL

The present court of final appeal of Hong Kong is the Judicial Committee of the Privy Council. Members of the Judicial Committee of the Privy Council include the Lord Chancellor and the Lords of Appeal in Ordinary, that is, the judges sitting on the House of Lords in Britain. Membership has also been extended from time to time to distinguished judges of the Supreme Court of the Commonwealth countries. Because of the eminence of its membership, the decisions of the Privy Council enjoy high authority throughout the common law world. Appeal to the Privy Council requires leave granted either by the Hong Kong Court of Appeal or by the Privy Council itself. On average, the Privy Council hears about 5 appeals from Hong Kong each year. Decisions of the Privy Council are binding on the Hong Kong courts.

While many former British dependent territories retain the Privy Council as their court of final appeal upon independence, this option is obviously politically unacceptable in so far as Hong Kong is concerned. Thus, both the Joint Declaration and the Basic Law stipulate that the Hong Kong SAR will have to set up its own Court of Final Appeal.

❏ *The JLG Agreement*

Sino-British discussions on the Court of Final Appeal began in 1988. It was agreed that the court should comprise 5 judges. The British proposal was that there should be 3 local and 2 overseas judges. The Chinese disagreed. It took the view that to allow an overseas judge to sit on the Court of Final Appeal was already a major concession. The British wished to have the Court of Final Appeal set up as soon as possible, and the question of having 1 or 2 overseas judges on the Court of Final Appeal was not a matter of major concern. Accordingly, in 1991, the JLG reached an agreement (the JLG agreement) that the Court of Final Appeal should comprise 5 judges, namely the Chief Justice, who must be a Chinese national with no right of abode elsewhere, 3 permanent Hong Kong judges and 1 non-permanent judge drawn from either a list of serving or retired local Judges of Appeal or from a list of judges from other common law jurisdictions. This agreement was reached without any prior consultation with the legal profession or the judiciary, except the Chief Justice.

The agreement, which has never been published, received strong opposition when it was made known to the public. The legal profession argued that this agreement was inconsistent with the Joint Declaration and the Basic Law. Article 82 of the Basic Law provides:

> The power of final adjudication of the Hong Kong Special Administrative Region shall be vested in the Court of Final Appeal of the Region, *which may as required invite judges* from other common law jurisdictions to sit on the Court of Final Appeal. [emphasis added]

Under Article 82, argued the legal profession, the power to decide when and how many overseas judges are required to sit on the Court of Final Appeal lies in the Court of Final Appeal itself. The JLG agreement is an attempt to interfere with the discretionary power vested in the Court of Final Appeal. It damages the real and perceived independence of the Court of Final Appeal and therefore the judiciary as a whole. To the legal profession, it is not just a question of one or two overseas judges, but a matter of principle that a discretionary power clearly granted by the Basic Law cannot and should not be fettered or taken away by an inter-governmental agreement reached at the JLG.

The agreement was also scathingly attacked by the Legco. It agreed with the legal profession that the statutory power of the court should not be limited by an executive agreement, and that the agreement did not allow any flexibility in the composition of the Court of Final Appeal. In a motion debate on 4 December 1991 calling for greater flexibility in the composition of the Court of Final Appeal, the Legco rejected the JLG agreement by a vote of 34 to 11 (with all the government members voting against). This was the first time that a Sino-British agreement was rejected by the Legco. The clear message to the government was that any bill implementing the JLG agreement would likely be defeated. On the following day, China vehemently attacked the Hong Kong legislature as having no power to veto an agreement reached between two sovereign states. Both the British and Hong Kong governments maintained that the agreement was still valid. However, in light of the strong opposition from the Legco and in order to avoid a possible constitutional crisis, the matter was held in abeyance for almost three years.

❏ *The Court of Final Appeal Bill 1994*

The matter was raised again by the Chief Justice in early 1994. The argument is that although the agreement is imperfect, it is important to set up the Court of Final Appeal well before 1997. The leap time for taking a case to the Privy Council is about a year. Therefore, the Court of Final Appeal has to be in place at the latest by mid-1996. The legislative process and the process of appointment of qualified judges may take another year. Time is running short, and litigants have a right to know where their cases will finally be decided. The government also pointed out that, apart from the composition, there are many other important issues that deserve close examination, such as its jurisdiction, the appeal procedures, the qualifications and even the retirement age of judges on the Court of Final Appeal. It is far better to decide these issues, to set up the Court of Final Appeal and to appoint the best-qualified judges while the government is still in control. This is an attractive pragmatic argument which does sway some of the former opposition groups to the JLG agreement. The government's assessment is that the attitude of the Legco as well as some of the former opposition groups such as the Law Society may change with the passage of time. In April 1994, the government announced its intention to introduce a bill along the line of the 1991 JLG agreement to the Legco.

A draft Court of Final Appeal Bill was prepared. In November 1994, the government sought the view of the legal profession on the draft Bill.

On 8 December 1994, the Bar Association, by an overwhelming majority, rejected the Bill as drafted, but maintained that it would be desirable to set up a Court of Final Appeal before 1997 provided that any legislation setting up the court is consistent with the Basic Law and the Joint Declaration. It reaffirmed its view that the 1991 JLG agreement was in breach of the Basic Law, and maintained that it could not, as a matter of law, support a Bill which was a clear violation of the Basic Law. Whether the Bill should be accepted on grounds of expediency is a matter for the politicians, not the legal profession. The Bar Association also rejected the draft Bill on the ground that it was poorly drafted, and a list of recommendations on improvement on technical issues were suggested.

The Law Society Council at first maintained its stance in 1991 and opposed the Bill, but later changed its view without any adequate or satisfactory explanation. It also refused to hold any general meeting with its members on this matter. This has provoked the criticisms of some of its members, who successfully requested an Extraordinary General Meeting (EGM). Extensive lobbying was done by both camps. Eventually, in an adjourned EGM held on 15 January 1995, the Law Society Council, armed with more than twice as many proxy votes as the opposition camp, narrowly defeated the motions opposing the Bill by a margin of about 100 votes.

❑ *An Assessment*

There were three unusual features in the consultation with the legal profession. First, it was done in a high profile. Extensive publicity was given that the government was consulting the legal profession. Second, the content of the Bill was made known by the Attorney General to the general public. However, the government refused to disclose the full text of the draft Bill to the general public on the ground that the matter was still before the JLG. Third, the draft Bill itself was marked confidential and a duty of confidentiality was imposed on the legal profession. The "consultation" put the legal profession in a catch-22 position. If they maintained their 1991 stance and opposed the Bill, they would be blamed for having obstructed the establishment of the Court of Final Appeal before 1997. On the other hand, if they changed their stance and supported the Bill, they would be the target of criticisms by the democratic parties in the Legco who opposed the Bill. In either case, the legal profession rather than the government would be blamed. This tactic is successful to a large extent, as the government has successfully shifted the media attention to the legal profession. The government's lack of sincerity in consultation is further demonstrated by its active lobbying for support to the draft Bill. It has been reported that the Solicitor General has requested all Crown Counsels who are members of the Law Society to vote in favour of the draft Bill in the EGM, and if they cannot do so, they are probably not fit to remain in the government!

Is the JLG agreement a violation of the Basic Law? It seems to be so. Article 82 of the Basic Law clearly vests in the Court of Final Appeal itself a discretion to invite overseas judges "as required." The discretion of course has to be exercised objectively, but how can one say objectively that in any circumstances no more than one overseas judge will be required? Yet this will be the result of the government's argument. The government also argued that under the Vienna Convention on the Interpretation of Treaties, the Joint Declaration is subject to subsequent agreement of the two governments. This argument overlooks the fundamental principle that all international treaties must be interpreted in good faith in accordance with the ordinary meaning to be given to the terms of the treaty in the light of its object and purpose, which is to confer a high degree of autonomy on the Hong Kong SAR. Besides, it is fundamentally wrong that the clear provisions in the Basic Law can be overridden by a secret agreement between the two governments. Once executive arrangement is permitted to override the clear language of the law, the rule of law is endangered.

There is also a practical dimension. The practical effect of the JLG agreement would be that the 4 local judges on the Court of Final Appeal would have to be chosen from either existing or retired Court of Appeal judges. If the Court of Final Appeal is nothing more than the present Court of Appeal, what is the point of having the Court of Final Appeal? Would a renamed Court of Appeal as Court of Final Appeal improve the quality of justice? Besides, five senior judges on the Court of Appeal had retired between 1993 and 1995, and there have been difficulties in finding suitable replacement. What impact would it make on the legal system if there are insufficient qualified judges to sit on the Court of Appeal, let alone the Court of Final Appeal?

It would be politically naive to think that the government would have control on the appointment of judges on the Court of Final Appeal if it were to be set up before 1997. History shows that the P.R.C. is much more concerned with personnel than structural matters. Thus, even if the Court of Final Appeal Bill were to be adopted without any amendment, the P.R.C.

government would no doubt argue that it would have a legitimate interest (on behalf of the future SAR) in the appointment of judges on the Court of Final Appeal if they were to remain as judges of the Court of Final Appeal after 1997. Otherwise, as the Chinese government has already stated, no judges on the Court of Final Appeal can continue their service after the change of sovereignty. In the absence of judicial "through train," the Chinese government will, on behalf of the Hong Kong SAR, "appoint" judges on the Court of Final Appeal after 1997 in accordance with the provisions of the Basic Law. This is a matter of sovereignty, so it argued. Interference with the independence of the judiciary (in terms of judicial appointment on the Court of Final Appeal) seems inevitable in any event.

From the "two systems" perspective, it is perfectly reasonable for the legal profession to demand that the Court of Final Appeal be staffed by the best-qualified judges. The JLG agreement, by limiting the choice of the majority of judges to local talents, is obviously not conducive to the attainment of this objective. Yet from the "one country" perspective, it is, to say the very least, awkward to allow a provincial court of final appeal to be staffed by internationally renounced judges who enjoy higher prestige and reputation than even the judges of the national supreme court. Viewed from these perspectives, the argument is more than just one between idealism and pragmatism, as the British government portrays, but one testing the limit of the dividing line between "one country" and "two systems."

There is an aspect of the Court of Final Appeal which has escaped attention so far. Any Court of Final Appeal Ordinance enacted before 1997 has to be amended after the change of sovereignty. The reason is that Article 158 of the Basic Law provides that, if an appeal involves the interpretation of certain provisions of the Basic Law, the Court of Final Appeal must, before making a final judgment, seek the interpretation of the Standing Committee of the NPC, whose interpretation will be binding on the Hong Kong courts. Details of such referral procedure has to be set out in any legislation governing the jurisdiction of the Court of Final Appeal, but such provisions cannot be included before 1997. The referral procedure may involve many complicated constitutional issues which have not been resolved. For example, will the parties to the appeal proceedings be allowed to make representation to the Standing Committee of the NPC on the interpretation of the relevant provisions of the Basic Law? Such interpretation may be crucial to the resolution of the appeal, and it would be a clear violation of the right to a fair hearing if the parties concerned are denied the opportunity to make representation on what may be the most crucial stage of the appeal. The NPC Standing Committee has to consult the Basic Law Committee before it makes any authoritative interpretation. What would be the role of the Court of Final Appeal *vis-à-vis* the Basic Law Committee? These burning issues have to be dealt with and provided for in any Court of Appeal Ordinance after 1997.

On 23 January 1995, the Executive Council decided to make some amendments along the suggestions made by the legal profession before the Bill is sent to the JLG for comments by the Chinese side. It was also made clear that the composition of the Court of Final Appeal as set out in the draft Bill would remain unchanged. At the same time, Martin Lee has publicly declared his intention to propose amendments to the Bill once it is introduced to the Legco.

By early March, the Chinese side of the JLG has still not indicated its approval of the amended Bill. Given the time constraint, the Hong Kong government has stated that it may have to introduce the Bill to the Legco without the Chinese approval. This will make the case for amending the composition of the Court of Final Appeal even stronger, as the whole object of complying with the JLG agreement will be defeated if there is not even the slightest assurance from the P.R.C. of any judiciary "through train" on the Court of Final Appeal.

Whatever may happen to the Bill, doubt has been cast on the independence of the judiciary after 1997. Many senior lawyers who are qualified to be appointed to the bench are hesitated to go to the bench partly because of their worry of the lack of independence of the judiciary after 1997. The message that there will be no "through train" for the judiciary simply reinforces such concern, namely, China is going to pick and choose the judges it favours. Once independence of the judiciary is eroded, the collapse of the rule of law will not be far away.

The Prospect

This chapter has only dealt with two particular aspects of the legal system. There are many other burning issues which have to be resolved before the transfer of sovereignty, such as the continuing validity of Certificate of Identity, a travel document held by over 2.5 million people in Hong Kong, and their acceptance by foreign states as a valid travel document after 1997; the repatriation of the Vietnamese boat people; the shortage of good quality judges at all levels of the judicial system; the uprising trend of corruption; the prospect of the Bill of Rights and other human rights legislation after 1997; the detailed mechanism governing referral of questions on the interpretation of the Basic Law by the Court of Final Appeal to the Standing Committee of the NPC and so on. The last part of the journey from a colony to an SAR is bound to be rough and bumpy. Whether the journey can be made less bumpy may depend on two important factors. The first is the persistent refusal of the P.R.C. officials to acknowledge that people in Hong Kong generally do not have confidence in the Beijing government. Its insensitivity to the concern of the people in Hong Kong and its rhetorical, and sometimes rude, emphasis on sovereignty could only weaken the already fragile confidence over the future. It is not what one says but what one does which would instil confidence. Some of what the Chinese government has done may be out of good intention, but that is no excuse if damaging consequences have been the outcome. China would still have a lot to learn to manage a modern, open and pluralistic society.

The second obstacle is the increasingly diverging gap between Hong Kong and the Mainland on the perception of the rule of law. The rule of law is more than the preservation of legislation and the establishment of a Court of Final Appeal. At the end of the day, any legal system rests on a number of fundamental ideological principles. The legal system will be radically different if one does not believe that it is better to acquit ten guilty persons than to wrongfully convict an innocent person. There will then be no presumption of innocence, no right against self-incrimination, no right to silence, or even no right to personal liberty and security. If one does not believe in an open, democratic and pluralistic society, there will be no freedom of expression or right to peaceful assembly. All these fundamental values make up the rule of law, which Hong Kong society has cherished for more than a century. Unfortunately, these fundamental values have a fragile root in our community. Professor Joseph Y. S. Cheng is right in pointing out that in the next few years, the maintenance of the rule of law and the protection of human rights may be of far greater importance than further development of representative government. If these values are not rooted in the hearts of the average citizens, the Hong Kong SAR will soon be a society very different from what we know of it today, and any promise of "one country, two systems" in the Basic Law will soon become illusory. Unfortunately, time is running out.

6

Historical Hate vs. Modern Miracle: The Hong Kong Case and Philosophic Roots of China's Reverse-convergence Policy on Hong Kong — An Interpretation

Hung Ching-tin

This chapter begins with an interpretative account of Hong Kong's past fifteen years, then goes on to trace the philosophic roots of China's policies towards Hong Kong, and finally surmises possible scenarios awaiting Hong Kong in the run-up to and beyond 1997.

The sovereignty transition of Hong Kong in 1997 is not only an enormous economic and political project, but a social and philosophic convergence of two cultural blocks centuries apart. The gulf that divides Hong Kong and China comprises two defining dimensions:

1. Historical grudges that poison the relations firstly between Britain and China and secondly between Hong Kong people and the Chinese central government;
2. Contemporary modernization that separates the ways of life, economics, world-views, value systems and ideals of Hong Kong and China.

Interdependent and interwoven, these two perception systems have been fighting for pre-eminence. The situation is further complicated by the fact that each of them is intrinsically linked to its own deep-seated philosophic mentality, both in Hong Kong and China.

PARADIGM SHIFTS

Sometimes, the Hong Kong case to China is more a historical hate than a modern miracle; sometimes it is the other way round. Hong Kong's vicissitudes have been incidental to how Hong Kong is perceived. This little capitalistic enclave has been rocked around by these conflicting perceptions of Beijing. To a lesser extent, these conflicting perceptions are also found in Hong Kong.

China's perception of the Hong Kong case (i.e. either as a historical hate or as a modern miracle) determines its policies, strategies and sentiments towards Hong Kong and Britain. Hong Kong's fate has been rocked by the shifts from one perception to the other.

Right now, Beijing sees Hong Kong as a historical hate to be redressed. Invoking nationalistic fervour and philosophic forces, it is embarking on a soft hate campaign against Britain and Hong Kong.

During the 40 years from the founding of the People's Republic of China in 1949 to 1989, Beijing was ill at easy dealing with Hong Kong. It tried extremely hard to forget the unforgettable historical grudges and made good use of Hong Kong as its sole window to the world economically, financially and diplomatically.

Rather unconsciously, Hong Kong had demonstrated to China the direction, standards and workings of a modern society. And even more unconsciously, and unwillingly, China had more than once corrected its own mistakes by looking up to Hong Kong. In terms of modern ideals and values, it had been China converging with Hong Kong, rather than the other way round.

CHINA'S POLICY U-TURN

During the past four years since 1990, Beijing has been U-turning. It adopted a completely opposite course of action: to drag Hong Kong to conform with China's values and philosophic constructs.

All for a mission in life, China has been taking Hong Kong's 1997 transition to Chinese rule into its own hands. Beijing has been methodically edging the current British Hong Kong government and legislature comprising vocal pro-democracy critics of China out of the scene.

China is overwhelmed by an urge to redress the 150-year insult. It is remoulding Hong Kong according to its own wishes, even risking wrecking Hong Kong's modern miracle.

In the late 1970s, Deng Xiaoping was caught unprepared by the British to face the 1997 issue. China was then fully preoccupied with the internal reforms and struggles. Historical hate was put aside for the time being. Suddenly awakening from the day-dreams of the Great Cultural Revolution idealism to face the stark reality of economic reconstruction, Beijing looked up to Hong Kong as a modern economic miracle awash with money and management know-how.

Nevertheless, China stuck to its guns. It is after all an idealistic, holistic and moralistic culture-state willing to pay all prices, and against all odds, to safeguard its pride, soul and identity. And it feeds on outside pressure and adversity. In 1982, it went into the Sino-British negotiations over Hong Kong's future with two apparently irreconcilable goals: to reclaim sovereignty and to maintain Hong Kong's prosperity, stability and way of life, which includes pluralism, freedom and openness.

Meanwhile, Beijing formed a team to study Hong Kong's mode of operations and to decode the success formula so that China would not only maintain under its sovereignty a Hong Kong of what it had been, but even to build many Hong Kongs in China.

Shenzhen, a small village bordering Hong Kong, was turned into a sprawling city with a population of 3.5 million in fifteen years.

Single-minded on the sovereignty issue and backed up by the newly gained partial knowledge about Hong Kong's success, Beijing almost dictated the terms in the Sino-British Joint Declaration on Hong Kong's post-1997 future. It was signed in 1984.

A Decade of Conflicts, Cooperations and Mutual Penetration

The past fifteen years that preceded and followed the signing of the Joint Declaration witnessed what could be the longest, peaceful transfer of sovereign power in history.

In the early 1980s, China primarily viewed Hong Kong as a modern miracle to be studied and protected, and secondly as a historical account to be set straight. On the one hand, it emulated Hong Kong; on the other, it forced the British to relinquish control.

In the five years after 1984, a multifold of convulsive conflicts and cooperations characterized relations between the United Kingdom and China, between Hong Kong and China, between Britain and Hong Kong, and among Hong Kong's pro-democracy and pro-Beijing sectors.

By and large, however, the process smacked of a give-and-take, live-and-let-live bargaining. No one got completely what one wants. There were no total losers nor absolute winners. Emerging from the unprecedented turbulences, all parties involved in these five years' interactions obtained mixed results.

The greatest winner is obviously China. It regained sovereignty and received a flourishing Hong Kong which immediately gave much-needed financial and managerial input to China's start-up modernizations. For that, Beijing forsook much of its pride and bowed low to Hong Kong's views and way of doing things. Both in a positive sense and in a negative sense, China has been "Hongkongized."

Hong Kong's ledger, though, was only better than the doomsday scenario that had been widely anticipated in the early 1970s. Its gradual, grudging return to China in the past decade broke the social and economic walls in between and brought about an economic synergy seldom seen in human history.

While the manufacturing sector moved northward to benefit from the cheap land and labour there, Hong Kong prospered as China's only world-class financial and service centre, thus reasserting its position as a sea and air entrepôt linking China and Taiwan with the rest of the world. The resultant economic growth in the late 1980s was the envy of the world.

Unfortunately, only the rich and the adventurous risk-takers benefited from the unexpected boom. The man in the street, especially manufacturing workers, was subjected to economic hardship and socio-political pressure.

As if a consolation for Hong Kong people's sufferings from the jitters and decline in freedom and other modern values, Hong Kong people were promised continuity of their way of life and a small fresh dose of democracy in the Basic Law, a mini-constitution for Hong Kong after 1997 which was drafted by China with the participation of Hong Kong people and Britain from 1985 to 1990.

Despite being "China-ized," Hong Kong survived and prospered, although lopsided.

SINO-HONG KONG AND SINO-BRITISH INTERACTIONS AFTER 4 JUNE 1989

The June 4 massacre in Beijing in 1989 was a turning point in the relationships and interactions between Britain and China, and between China and Hong Kong. More than once, millions of Hong Kong people took to the streets to condemn the massacre and ridiculous Deng Xiaoping, Li Peng and Yang Shangkun. The spontaneous pro-democracy demonstrations were mainly led by Szeto Wah, Lau Chin-shek, Martin Lee and Yeung Sum, who later formed the political party the United Democrats of Hong Kong (UDHK). Riding high on the anti-Beijing central government sentiments, they routed the pro-Beijing candidates and won 12 out of the 18 directly elected seats in the territory's first-ever direct elections to the 60-member Legislative Council (Legco) in 1991. None of the pro-Beijing candidates was elected.

Around 1991 and 1993, a stunned China threw thinly veiled demands on Britain to bar some of the UDHK legislators from riding the political "through train" which both Britain and China seemingly agreed upon to let all the legislators elected in 1995 cross the 1997 transition automatically.

Unable to fend off China's pressure, Hong Kong Governor David Wilson was kicked upstairs to the House of Lords and replaced by a heavy-weight politician, former Chairman of the Conservative Party, Chris Patten. The new governor's "strong man" style and fresh political culture, a far cry from David Wilson's timidity and indecisiveness, enthralled the Hong Kong populace.

His highly imaginative and creative proposal on the unresolved electoral arrangements for the Legco redefined the functional constituency and the election committee, and widely expanded the electorate base for the 1995 elections. It was hailed as a long-awaited present to the Hong Kong people.

Patten said it was a proposal to be discussed with China. But Beijing never counter-offered on the basis of Patten's framework, denouncing it as contradicting the Basic Law as well as the agreement and understanding reached in the seven letters exchanged between the foreign ministers of the two countries in the early 1990s.

Both sides went into the seventeenth-round negotiation on 1995 elec-toral arrangements half-heartedly, but concurrently preparing to go their own ways.

China's Soft Take-over of Hong Kong before 1997

Upon the collapse of the negotiations, Patten pushed ahead with his full package of electoral arrangements. China retaliated by gearing up the working of the Preliminary Working Committee (PWC), a forerunner of the

Preparatory Committee of the future Hong Kong Special Administrative Region (SAR), which was formed nominally to advise Beijing on the 1997 transition and preparations, but virtually to softly take over Hong Kong before 1997.

Together with other suggestions, the PWC recommended, and Beijing accepted, the overthrow of all the three-tier representative bodies constituted before 1997, and the creation of a new Provisional Legislative Council (PLC) on 1 July 1997, wiping out all traces of democracy that had been in place even before Chris Patten's coming to Hong Kong.

Deeming Chris Patten to have contravened the Joint Declaration and the Basic Law, China has been counter-attacking with a vengeance. It is virtually redrafting and redefining the Joint Declaration and the Basic Law, barring Britain and Hong Kong's pro-democracy camp from involving in the transition works. Calling Chris Patten's name without salutations and reasserting itself as the supreme master of Hong Kong, China goes on the offensive now. It is poking its nose into nearly all the decisions on major policies and issues the Hong Kong government and the legislature made.

Long before the prescribed hand-over on 1 July 1997, Beijing has been coming down on Hong Kong like Mao Zedong towering over China. Gone are the traces of give-and-take, live-and-let-live in the "constructive engagement" that existed in the 1980s.

FROM "CONSTRUCTIVE ENGAGEMENT" TO "DESTRUCTIVE ISOLATION"

China's current policy towards Patten and the pro-democracy camp is "destructive isolation" and strategic assault. In the name of sacred sovereignty, nationalism and patriotism, all means are justified by the end, much as all doings are justified for the sake of Maoist socialism and world revolution during the Cultural Revolution. Due procedures, processes, a sense of proportion, and calculation of gains and losses are all trivialities.

China is giving Hong Kong people a taste of what sovereign power with Chinese philosophic ingredients is like.

Power is total, absolute, organized brutality. All objectives are defined and redefined in accordance with bureaucratic organizational logic. The target post is always moving. Once reached, it moves ahead. Blundering policies, often the outgrowth of the stupidity of the mammoth control-minded bureaucratic machinery, are propagated as holy sermons to be received by the people with different degrees of zeal.

Not the slightest dissent. No minute deviance. No room for the opposition. Dissent, deviance, difference and opposition are all defined as belligerence. Friends are defined as yes-men. Some yes-men are recruited to put up a façade of widespread support.

Mao's rule is a paragon of Chinese rulers' blending philosophic tenets with mundane despotism. Philosophic precepts provide the sacred principles and justifications for all crimes against humanity, as well as the inspiration for heinous gambits to destroy all enemies, big or small, real or imagined. The brutality in turn invigorates the philosophic sainthood on earth.

Chinese history over the past two thousand years was trapped many times in the vicious circle of philosophic and moral supremacy, and, Machiavellian gambits which reinforced each other and caused periods of self-suffocation. This vicious circle could only be stopped and reversed when all the absolute absurdity exhausted the human imagination, as in the case of the Cultural Revolution.

Hong Kong is right now savouring this vicious circle of "the rule of philosophic and moral despotism," and *"realpolitik* brutality and stupidity."

If this interpretative analysis is not too far from reality, China's hardline policies towards Hong Kong in the past four years are merely the beginning of an end that was suggested in the early 1980s. Hong Kong's challenge now is how to break this historical strait-jacket.

CHINA'S CONFLICTING ROADS TO MODERNIZATION

Over the past two hundred years, the Chinese people have been wobbling between two different paths of modernization.

One is to make the Chinese cultural value system and sense of being imbued with individualism and pluralism, and to reform the traditional static world-view into a new order of dynamic equilibrium. This school of thought deems the creation of individualism and pluralism as a way of reconstructing China's senile, rigid collectivism, monism and holism.

Another school of thought rigidly regards everything Chinese, such as the nation, culture and people, as an inalienable whole. Individualism and pluralism are separatism that will tear apart the holism of the Chinese spirit, being and identity. Followers of this school of thought advocate unreserved selflessness and sacrifice as the way to national salvation and to the regaining of a position in the contemporary world stage.

These two schools have been at odds with each other over the past two hundred years. China's modernization has been swerving along these two roads.

The young Mao Zedong was a proponent of individualism, pluralism and anti-conservative revolution when he was not in power. But Chairman Mao, once in total power, was a self-styled "absolute free man" who allowed only himself to practise poetic individualism and freedom, even romanticism and nihilism. At the height of the Great Cultural Revolution, only Mao did the thinking and the writing; the whole Chinese people are reduced to nobodies, blindly yet creatively, following the Great Helmsman to the historic absurdities of mankind.

Central to Mao's magic is the Chinese people's fear of the cleavage of the Chinese being. In the existential arena, the Chinese people have no religion to fall back on. They can only rely on the earthly wiseman to provide them with a harmonious social order, a holistic meaning of life and a sense of conniving identity and gratification. Daily chores are readily elevated to existential importance of the highest order. Once the total Chinese being is punctuated or fractured, a spiritual vacuum will appear and all the people will feel lost in the existential vacuum.

In different historic periods and by different sectors over the past two hundred years, the Chinese people sometimes viewed the West as a destroyer of collective tradition and identity, and sometimes as a mentor of modern individualism and new social order. They were always torn between hate and adulation towards the West. However, portraying the Westerners as a destroyer is always much easier than as a mentor.

MAOIST TOTALITARIANISM AND CHINESE HOLISM

Mao is an epitome of a "philosophic and moral despot" with Chinese characteristics. Tapping the fundamentals of these Chinese philosophic tenets and sentiments, he defined, spearheaded and dominated Chinese politics and total social life for nearly half a century. He pre-set a multi-century agenda for China and probably for the world community.

Mao could be the only one in China's past two thousand years who had a supernatural understanding of the structure and components of Chinese philosophic mentality and utilized it, consciously and unconsciously, in Machiavellian *realpolitik* both on a day-to-day basis and megatrends.

In every life-and-death struggle, he seemed to be way ahead of the intellectuals and politicians around him. With real-time speed and supernatural touch, he always pre-empted his dissenting foes and friends both within and without the Party or the country, and swung a billion people into happy self-destruction.

In total subservience to Mao as an embodiment of China's total being, the Chinese people might believe that a person is nothing in comparison to the collective self, that the present life is secondary to the after-life destiny. Every inch is an embodiment of collectivism and holism, Mao after 1949 was simply unstoppable. Disaster after disaster, the whole country up and down was motivated and elevated by him to new heights of ecstasy and absurdity. The Chinese people, together with some from the West and the Third World countries, joined Mao in a mass orgiasm of self-destruction and self-creation.

DENG XIAOPING'S HISTORICAL FEAT AND LIMITATIONS

After Mao's death, his anointed successor, the mediocre Hua Guofeng, resumed the title of the Great Helmsman. Mao's ideological followers, later called the Gang of Four, stretched their utmost in vain to carry forward the revolution forever at a time when the country "had been" at the brink of total collapse. They were replaced by Deng Xiaoping in 1987.

Deng Xiaoping will go down in history as the main architect and engineer who halted and reversed the 10-year-long historical vicious circle of philosophic and moral idealism, and earthly absurdity and brutality which influenced one billion people.

However, China's totalitarian absolutism and absurdity disappear only from the internal political domain. No top-down nationwide political movements were undertaken in Deng's reign. Yet, the mode and mechanisms of the vicious circle are alive and kicking. Deng has not shed China's century-old political and philosophic strait-jackets in other domains of the public's life.

In the realm of economic development, totalitarian absolutism spawns implementation stupidities which in turn are forged ahead in the name of totalitarian absolutism. The policy-formulating and decision-making processes are more like philosophic and moral wishful thinking than get-things-done pragmatism. Fanatic upheavals still poison China's economic reform. China still has decades, if not centuries, to go before it can build up social, legal and cultural infrastructures commensurate with its economic development and management.

The problem is: China is not aware of the need for these infrastructures and is even more ignorant of the cultural and philosophic prices it has to pay if it wants to institutionalize these infrastructures.

China is still blind to a modern, pluralistic world in which each individual is an entity in his own right, interacting with others for his own interest in accordance with values and rules agreed by the interactors who constantly review the rules of the game as times change.

When it comes to the ultimacy of collective identity and meaning of life, the Chinese mind simply cannot accept that all things are relative and temporary. Realization of life in Chinese cultural context is the attainment of a holistic, indivisible, non-relative, static, harmonious and eternal meaning and identity, not the mastering of the ever-going, dynamic processes of change as in the West.

PROMISE AS JUSTIFICATION FOR SUPPRESSION

The Confucian ideal statehood is one in which Chinese rulers earn their legitimacy by the achievement of, and the provision to the subjects with, this holistic life and meaning. In practice, over two thousand years, rulers only made the promise and equated the promise with actual achievement and delivery, that in turn justifies all brutalities said to be needed for the "further" fulfilment of the promise.

This inverted circular logic can also be seen in the argument that since Confucians demand all emperors to be saints, therefore all emperors are saints.

With regard to Hong Kong, China's centuries-old vicious circle of "philosophic and moral principles" and "*realpolitik* brutalities and bureaucratic absurdities" reinforcing each other has been revived. Central to China's doings to Hong Kong in the past four years is to bring the philosophic and moral ferocity, and earthly brutalities and bureaucratic absurdities upon Hong Kong to bear. In the name of something sacred, all means are justifiable.

Since the early 1980s, China has been promising Hong Kong a paradise after 1997. However, it has been more inclined to make use of the promise to suppress dissents and propagate China's philosophic dictatorship over Hong Kong than to deliver, in a get-things-done manner, what are actually needed to make Hong Kong tick as it does.

The main thrust of China's policy towards Hong Kong now is dictated by the pre-reform totalitarian mentality. Deng has transformed China's one billion people from political fundamentalism and futile fanaticism to economic pragmatism, but he did not reform his perception of Hong Kong. China's hardline stand towards Hong Kong is a reflection of Deng's pre-reform cultural and philosophic mentality. He is the fountain head of China's hardline policy towards Hong Kong.

Especially in the past four years, Deng still indulged in absolutism, subjectivism, sheer will power and inverted circular logic that characterized the ultra-Leftism of the Great Cultural Revolution.

His understanding of Hong Kong's mode of existence and operations could well just be based on his personal feeling of Shanghai in its 1930s. Hong Kong's post-modern systems and workings, cultural values and ideals, and philosophic implications are totally beyond him or any of the Chinese officials in power. In China, there are an increasing number of intellectuals who are able to appreciate Hong Kong from these post-modern perspectives, but they are not in power yet. In Taiwan, such intellectuals and officials abound, but there is a gap of different nature that separates Hong Kong and Taiwan. In the past two or three years, the gap has been somehow bridged.

Hong Kong's Modernity: A Chinese Culture Reborn

Hong Kong is a place which thrives on doubts, queries, criticism, dissent, new ideas and challenges.

Hong Kong's modern miracle is not confined to economics. What Hong Kong has achieved is a total modern miracle with cultural and philosophic constructs.

The ultimate problem of China over the past two hundred years is the restructuring of the philosophic planks and pillars of its self-contained system. That involves the opening up of the closed system to alien objects, the secularization of politics and morality, the division of holism, the decentralization of power and values, the pluralization and relativization of concepts and tenets, the individualization of existential modes, self-rule and liabilities, and the liberalization of control.

China is like a single-cell jellyfish. Its modernization requires cell differentiation and organ formation.

A philosophic reorientation of these ideals and values is a prerequisite for the institutionalization of social, legal and political infrastructures for a viable existence and effective operation of a modern society.

Yet, all these ideals and values are anathemas to China. It takes China two hundred years to change. China is still hesitating whether to plunge into the modern age or not.

CULTURE AS A FORM

In Hong Kong, all these modern ideals and values are in daily practice. Hong Kong did not disintegrate as China feared. Hong Kong becomes the only Chinese community in the world that has restructured its philosophic mentality from bottom up so successfully and peacefully.

Drawing on the East and the West and participating wholeheartedly in the interactions in every aspect of daily routines, Hong Kong has built individualism and pluralism into Chinese culture. A working balance between vibrancy and stability has been attained on the individual and social levels. Hong Kong has resolved the hate-and-adulation complex towards the West as well as many other problems and contradictions which have plagued China for two thousand years.

In China, the form and the substances are integral to each other. In Hong Kong, culture is a form rather than substances. The cultural form constitutes a public space for free, open and fair meritocracy, business level ground and a modern way of life.

The reconstruction of Chinese culture with Hong Kong characteristics has brought Hong Kong to the forefront of the modern times, boasting a new social and cultural order based on pluralism, individual freedom and free-flowing interactions. Individualism with Oriental characteristics has been incorporated into Hong Kong culture. Western and Chinese cultural attributes have been deconstructed and reconstructed to forge a new relationship between the individual and society. In short, Chinese culture with Hong Kong characteristics has been reinforced with infrastructures and systems, processes and procedures.

In tandem with this development, Hong Kong attained quality administration and rule of law, efficiency and clean governance, fairness and entrepreneurship, stability and vibrancy, drive and resilience, economic growth and social equity. The formless fears, dreads, anxieties and anguishes of the modern age have been converted into positive energies in Hong Kong.

While Hong Kong thrives on the free-flowing interactions of pluralistic contradictions, China suppresses contradictions. Patten's political reforms and interactions with China over the past three years have given these ideals and values sturdier formal structures and fuller play. China not only fears that if Hong Kong adopts these ideals and values, it will collapse, but also believes that Hong Kong will collapse if these ideals and values are institutionalized and given fuller play.

China cannot benefit from the modern mode of social and cultural operations, and it forbids Hong Kong from doing so. China has been woefully consumed in its suppression of contradictions, it is forcing Hong Kong into this predicament. Hong Kong has resolved many problems of the Chinese culture, yet China is forcing these old problems on to Hong Kong.

Hong Kong represents a Chinese culture reborn. The philosophic gulf between Hong Kong and China is one between a small, rudimentary modern Chinese culture and a mammoth, senile Chinese culture.

HONG KONG'S INADEQUACY AND PATTEN'S LIMITATIONS

It is no exaggeration to say that Hong Kong has broken the spell of Chinese holism and monism, and has constructed a dynamic pluralism within its territory.

What Hong Kong fails so sadly is the systematization, intellectualization, institutionalization and operationalization of this Hong Kong culture. Hong Kong has all the raw materials for the abstraction of a new culture. But these invaluable materials have been squandered for over fifteen years. Despite its strengths, the Hong Kong culture is miserably limited by its shallow utilitarianism. It is solely utility-oriented and application-driven. The cultural attributes are only skin-deep and thrown away right after use.

Hong Kong is a place known for its cultural diversity, not for its intellectual ferocity. Research along the cultural significance of its mode of existence and workings, if any, is all piecemeal. Despite its rich material, Hong Kong has not grown fully-fledged in terms of philosophic constructs and cultural knowledge. Over the past 150 years, Hong Kong did not require philosophic support, and the society was void of cultural knowledge.

What was useless before the surfacing of the 1997 issue is now essential for the survival of Hong Kong after 1997. Hong Kong's cultural value system and philosophic tenets have not much use before 1997, but now they are the lifeline of Hong Kong. China is forcing its philosophic tenets on Hong Kong, but Hong Kong has no counteracting power on the same level. Over the decade and especially in the past four years, China has absolute monopoly of the philosophic precepts in Sino-Hong Kong interactions. In the debate on the pros and cons of Patten's political proposal, Hong Kong manifested sheer poverty of knowledge of the subject and its implications.

The visit to Hong Kong by Lu Ping, Beijing's Hong Kong and Macau Affairs Office Director, was a showcase of China's imperial, fluid cultural values and ideas. But what Patten could only do was to counteract with concrete administrative problems and transition arrangements.

Hong Kong detests being dragged into the senile Chinese culture, but it has failed to argue its own case in terms of cultural values and ideals. It simply cannot tell the Chinese that Hong Kong is essentially a modern miracle, no longer a historical hate.

Over the past fifteen years, Hong Kong failed to convey to China that it has been through China's gruelling road to modernization with such an impressive success, and to show China the cultural significance of Hong Kong's mode of existence and operations as an example for China's modernization.

What Hong Kong did was to stress its economic value to China. Economic achievements were completely dissociated from their social, cultural and philosophic roots.

Partly because of this, and more importantly because of China's own limitations, China only centred its study on Hong Kong in the 1980s on the economic aspect, thus viewing Hong Kong as just a physical outfit devoid of any cultural meaning and significance.

China does not understand that the economy of Hong Kong and the society as a whole survive on pluralism, relativism, freedom, dynamic interactions, level ground, and on the separation and cooperation of the individual and the group. Nevertheless, Hong Kong fails to convey these messages in a way comprehensible to China.

In the early 1980s, Hong Kong wanted its own system and way of life to be prolonged for 50 years, but regrettably Hong Kong itself did not understand comprehensively what the system is, how it works and how to safeguard it. Furthermore, Hong Kong people did not anticipate what and how China would tinker with the system in the run-up to 1997.

Hong Kong's case has been told as if it was devoid of philosophic and cultural significance, thus China is imposing its philosophic and cultural world-view on Hong Kong with ease.

PHILOSOPHIC LANDSCAPE SHIFT AND CULTURAL CONFLICTS

Both China and Hong Kong are paying dearly for the ignorance and negligence.

China is plucking Hong Kong away from its own cultural and philosophic milieu, wishfully and mindlessly transplanting it into the Chinese absolutism, monism and static closed system. China is not prepared to let Hong Kong live as a total society in its own cultural and philosophic environment.

China's overwhelming intuitive urge for a harmonious order and a collective existence rules out all detraction and deviance, innovation and things alien, regardless of the prices of underdevelopment and retardation. All things are tightly sealed in a self-contained system of philosophic ideals.

Hong Kong is now in a very dismal and weird situation: China wants it to survive only as an economic entity in the context of Chinese philosophic, social, political and cultural parameters. In case of clash, China might be more likely to opt for principles and sentiments than for economic interests and rationality.

China has no modern values and ideals for its own use, not to say to lead Hong Kong with. It can only invoke the unreformed, unmodernized nationalism, patriotism, cultural link and historical hate. In the name of all these sacred values and principles, China is throwing Hong Kong back to the fold of its 2,000-year history.

Hong Kong resists, but only with not much self-awareness, ingenuity and strategy. Both Hong Kong and China have been probing in the dark to find what the other party is up to and really wants.

Before 1980, China saw Hong Kong as an outcast wasteland, a decadent capitalistic backdrop yearning for redemption by the superior mother country.

Invoking historical hate as a driving force, China is remaking Hong Kong into an object it can feel comfortable with. Arbitrarily branding nearly anything it dislikes as colonial, China has begun a cultural cleansing policy to rid Hong Kong of the heritage of pluralism and openness that are

alien and apprehensive to China, yet so essential to Hong Kong. Historical
hate can only explain the past, but cannot build a future.

LEARNER DRIVING ALONE: PRE-1997 TAKE-OVER OF HONG KONG

A primitive capitalist China taking back an advanced capitalist Hong Kong
is a daunting task. On the cultural and philosophic level, nearly all things
cherished in Hong Kong are anathemas to the Chinese mind in Beijing,
especially to those in power. Even Hong Kong's economic affairs, once
elevated to cultural and philosophic meanings, would not be that easy to
accommodate.

In the fifteen years of learning from the British about how to rule Hong
Kong, China has bent a lot both to accommodate and remould Hong Kong.
The interactions between a feeble, free and secular Hong Kong and an
overpowering, dogmatic and archaic China has overstretched the endurance
and tolerance of all parties concerned.

Learner China was at the wheel soon after the arrival of Chris
Patten. Beijing snatched the driving wheel from Chris Patten upon
the breakdown of the negotiations on the 1995 election arrangements. With newly gained self-confidence, Beijing is slamming hard on
the accelerator.

Beijing is now being coached by a selected few of Hong Kong Chinese
who were previously close associates of the Hong Kong government. They
are more on the Beijing side of the philosophic gulf than on the Hong Kong
side. In fact, they had been the forces that opposed Hong Kong's social
rationalization and political modernization movements over the past quarter
of this century.

An "appointed-by-consultation" PLC, expected to be formed by people
of this background, will replace the planned first SAR legislature. The PLC
is to be constituted by 60 members "elected" by a 400-member Selection
Committee, members of which are in turn to be appointed by China, i.e.
not by open and fair one-man-one-vote election as now in practice and
generally accepted in Hong Kong.

Procedure-wise, the PLC members will not obtain their mandate from
the Hong Kong electorate, but from the Selection Committee which in turn
will be empowered by China. The electoral link that ties legislators to Hong

Kong people, a procedural imperative in the principle of "Hong Kong people rule Hong Kong," will be cut off by the PLC.

Membership-wise, China has lined up a pool of like-minded politicians to fill the Selection Committee and the PLC. They are mainly (1) the conservative, pro-nineteenth-century-capitalism leftovers from the British administration, and (2) the pro-socialism-with-Chinese-characteristics ideologues nurtured by grassroots organizations of the Chinese Communist Party (CCP) in Hong Kong over the decades.

One thing typically in common about them is their ignorance and disdain for Hong Kong's new politics developed in tandem with its social and economic rationalization over the last two decades.

The pro-democracy group, which has been at the centre of Hong Kong's social and political development over the last two decades, canvassed the majority popular mandate and are expected to spearhead the political momentum in the years up to 1997, will be barred from the PLC.

Right on 1 July 1997, China's first "present" to Hong Kong will be a PLC with dubious credibility and calibre.

The make-shift legislature is expected to enact laws that would have an impact on many aspects of the way of life of Hong Kong beyond its imagination. It is expected to target its "dictatorial rule," albeit mellowed by Hong Kong's "one country, two system," at the pro-democracy group and electoral base. The first legislature after the 1997 transition which is stipulated in the Basic Law to be constituted by elections will be postponed for at least one year, and upstaged after that.

REVERSE CONVERGENCE

According to the Basic Law, most of the matters the PWC has been discussing are within the terms of reference of the future SAR government. But now, long before the establishment of the SAR, China has dealt with these matters through the workings of the PWC and built in many reinterpretations.

Beijing is all decided and determined to quash the promised "Hong Kong people rule Hong Kong" autonomy. As mechanisms of resolving Hong Kong's internal matters through Hong Kong's practising and respected system and procedures have been interfered, the autonomy is being eroded. Hong Kong's way of life and the quality of life, which are strongly linked to its autonomy, have also been deteriorating in the past few years.

For China, freedom is uncertainty, individual entity is independence, difference is separation, giving freedom to the individual is irresponsibility.

For Hong Kong, freedom is the very essence of success for a place devoid of any natural resources. Freedom (and quality administration) reigns supreme, giving all parties concerned a trust and absolute guarantee that both person and money can flow in and out of the place without censorship or being tracked. Because of the proven freedom of moving out any time, talents and money are willing to flow in any time.

In the Chinese world-view, such freedom is an invitation to anarchy. Freedom is tantamount to loss of control and power, and moral irresponsibility. Those in power are entrusted by a sense of eternal, all-encompassing responsibility to history and the people. Conscientious rulers must keep everything under control, give the people a heavenly peace and harmony. Failure to fulfil this ultimate goal is an eternal moral sin. In the endeavour to bring peace and harmony to their subjects, nothing is prohibited.

In China, the greatest crime against humanity is the destruction of social order. To maintain social order and to bring a heavenly peace, crime against humanity in the Western sense can be fully justified or even commended.

The accelerating contraction of Hong Kong's political, journalistic and social freedom since 1989 has been somehow compensated by the expansion of economic activities offered by China's phenomenal economic growth.

Hong Kong, being an outlying island for business and bare-bone survival, sought comfort in the economic benefits over the past five years. After all, political and social ideals and values have been inhibited over the 150 years of British rule. It is widely accepted that Hong Kong is not in a bargaining position *vis-à-vis* China. The prevailing mood is that Hong Kong can only get what China is ready to give. Other than waiting for miracle, there is not much Hong Kong can do. Hong Kong is now at wit's end in a dead alley.

China is reversing Hong Kong to converge with the old Chinese mode of existence and operations:

1. from open system to closed system,
2. from international centre to inland regional centre,
3. from the threshold of the twenty-first century to the late nineteenth century,

4. from dynamic equilibrium to static stability,
5. from individual entity to non-entity,
6. from mass participation to power to a chosen few,
7. from bottom-up popular mandate to top-down appointment,
8. from institutionalized procedures and standards to arbitrariness,
9. from sense of proportion to over-reacting,
10. from pluralism to monism,
11. from interactional to one-directional,
12. from equality to subservience,
13. from competition to privileges,
14. from level ground to skewed rules,
15. from modern rationality to ancient rationale,
16. from earned authority, morality and legitimacy to heaven-sent authority, morality and legitimacy,
17. from limited government ability and liability to government omnipotence,
18. from restricted responsibleness to all-responsibleness,
19. from real autonomy to empty autonomy,
20. from contractual social and political relationships to patriarchal social and political relationships,
21. from trust in system to trust in person,
22. from high speed to low speed,
23. from temporariness to externality,
24. From secularism to quasi-religious idealism,
25. From relativism to absolutism,
26. From pragmatism to perfectionism,
27. From youthful meritocracy to senile autocracy,
28. From advanced capitalism to primitive capitalism.

PATTERN OF DISASTER: FROM POLITICAL TO ECONOMIC DICTATORSHIP

Less than 800 days into the 1 July 1997, China's Middle-Age philosophic dictatorship has been spreading from social, cultural and political domains to the economic domain.

The past four years witnessed China's different ways of pre-1997 take-over of Hong Kong:

1. Beijing's central government participated in the decisions on major issues straddling 1997 through the Sino-British Joint Liaison Group (JLG), as provided by the Joint Declaration.
2. Many of the responsibilities were transferred to the PWC. Its reinterpretations of the Joint Declaration and the Basic Law were pronounced by China as standards for the British Hong Kong government to comply with.
3. China's newly emancipated official-turned-businessmen over-zealously cooperated with the central government to come down on Hong Kong in force, turning Hong Kong into lumpen-capitalism.
4. China's regional governments and self-serving ruling functionaries took the initiatives to encroach on Hong Kong's autonomy and even territorial integrity. They do not necessarily have the ap-proval of the central government, but Beijing's hardline stands on Hong Kong definitely gave them, rather inadvertently, the neces-sary self-rationalization.

In the name of contributing to Hong Kong's prosperity and stability, the Chinese central and local governments have been swarming Hong Kong. The danger may come in two ways:

1. The multifarious Chinese interests in Hong Kong, affiliated with various sectors and cliques in Beijing, might form political-cum-business oligarchies, jockeying for positions and privileges in Hong Kong, making a mockery of Hong Kong's level ground and fair competition.
2. The central government might stop the free flow of capital and destroy Hong Kong's status as a financial centre.

For China, all these doings can easily be proclaimed as for the good of Hong Kong. China cannot afford to let Hong Kong go down the drain, so it must do everything it can to shore up Hong Kong in the transition period. What Beijing know is to put everything under its own brute control. It will be excused if it screws things up in the process of doing what it knows to save the world, but will be condemned to eternal sin if it does nothing in the first place.

Leaving nothing to chance, China will be dictated by the logic that controlled stability is the only preventive medicine for all possible disasters. Interference by the leaders' iron fist is China's usual answer to things beyond its comprehension and tolerance. Non-interference is irresponsible. Tolerance is immoral.

China's century-old philosophic dictatorship takes on a pattern like this: It dreams up looming disasters to give it a chance to show off its omnipotence and all-inclusive moral responsibility.

Signs are that China is now turning its control-minded attention from social and political freedom to the economic and financial front.

Its oppression of the political and social freedom has been gaining enormous ground and eradicated a great source of possible unrest and disorder. The logic and reflexes used in the suppression of social and political freedom can easily be transferred to the suppression of economic and financial freedom.

In a fit of financial crisis when money is flowing out of Hong Kong rather erratically, it would be reflexively logical to the Chinese mind to halt the free flow of money.

THE DANGER IN AN INFORMATION AGE

China is error-prone but interference-bent. The need to interfere comes from China's hyper-zeal, hyper-fear, hyper-confidence and hyper-sensitivity, or any combination of these.

To be "a master of all," China might do anything within its power no matter how destructive to itself or to others, or both.

Culturally, check and balance to power is a taboo in the Chinese tradition. Nor are there institutionalized rethink and feedback mechanisms. Mistakes are detected and corrected only after a long long time when staggering prices have been paid. Even after mistakes are corrected, the Chinese seems to be unable to benefit fully from the lessons. The selfsame mistakes have been repeated and repeated over the decades by the CCP, just as by dynastic despots over the centuries.

However, the CCP ruling block now faces an even greater risk its predecessors had never witnessed. It might be precipitated into unprecedented blunder in split second.

In this post-modern age, information is power, knowledge is power. Information and knowledge are flying in all directions, multi-point-to-multi-point. Hong Kong's pluralistic and interactive mode of existence and operations is in line with this form of information and knowledge power structure. Decisions are made on the basis of information and knowledge, not so much on coercion or moral pressure.

Change has become an accelerating factor in life. Judgement, decision and action are more a learned probability than a substantive certainty. Risks and the consequences are a fact of life to be weighed and taken rationally and quickly.

Decisions and their consequences are usually determined in split second. Time is the top-most defining factor. Hong Kong prospers in its race against time. The Chinese agrarian mentality is not accustomed to this mode of decision-making. In this time-first mode of decision-making and under such time pressure, China is more error-prone.

In this age of globalization, world financial syndicates and hot money are chasing around, from the mature markets to the feeble, small markets of newly industrializing economies. Hong Kong's state-of-the-art liquidity mechanism and post-1997 uncertainty could be a formula for disaster. It is awash with valid reasons to feed China's fear and paranoia.

In a fit, China will make decisions without judgement and take action without consideration. China's only way to deal with international conspiracy is to shut itself off from the outside world and retract to its century-old logic and reflexes.

In an ever-changing environment, China still holds dear its self-righteous moralism and perfectionistic rigidity.

China lacks Britain's experience in handling grave financial crises, and the Sino-British relationship has completely turned sour. Beijing has been accusing Patten as a source of conspiracies. In time of crisis, to protect Hong Kong from the onslaught of the scheming international financial monsters in a split second, what else would China most likely do than to shut Hong Kong off from the outside world?

CHINA'S BRAVE OLD WORLD

Consequences? China thinks it is immune to all consequences. Even if they come, they are to be dealt with later.

Beijing's way of decision-making is not that rational, weighing the consequences against the choices, especially when they elevate the issue to moral and political levels.

For the Chinese mind, time is infinite. There are bound to be some way out of the consequences no matter how grave they may be for the time being. All Chinese leaders want to be the master of time and fate, not the hostage of consequences. Ultimately, their behaviours are conditioned by unconditional and infinite idealism. A hard decision that disregards consequences provides the leaders with self-gratification, even a chance of becoming an all-mighty god.

All Chinese, be they high-ranking officials or the man in the street, want to play the role of god. Old Mao never dies.

The argument for the establishment of the PLC is a case in point. China maintained that the PLC is precipitated by Patten's refusal to cooperate with China on the political "through train." The PLC, one of the four possible options, was chosen to fill in the legal and constitutional vacuum.

Whether the move creates more problems than it sets out to solve has never been addressed. The consequences seemingly were not taken into account in the decision-making process. Even if they were, China would not have budged.

The Chinese usually seek refuge in, and comfort from, the heavenly meaning and the past history. They are not forward-looking in gauging possible consequences.

Over the past two thousand years, every Chinese sought the ultimate gratification for a good cause to dictate the course of events and others' lives without regard to the consequences. This is a euphoria of absolute freedom.

Ultimately, what matters most to the Chinese mind is the past and the philosophic high order, not the future or the earthly rationality. When the leadership extols the people to sacrifice for the future, it is virtually urging the people to be the slaves of past history and the heavenly ideals.

To emulate the paragon of the past is the Confucian ideal type of state politics and the holy, unavoidable obligation of both the ruler and the subjects. Himself a perpetual revolutionary, Mao is no exception. He consciously set off the Great Cultural Revolution to propel the whole country forward into the post-capitalistic socialism, only to fall victim to the feudalism of the "Brave Old World."

CHINA'S INVERTED LOGIC AND THE HONG KONG PARADOX

Starting from this idealism, China has often stood on its head over the past two hundred years, hence the modern world being completely inverted to the Chinese eye.

A modern society makes decisions mostly on the basis of bottom-up reality and weighs possible consequences rationally, but the Chinese mind has a habit of making decisions from top-down idealism.

The ideal type of Chinese leadership confesses, and is expected by its subjects, to perform the moral functions of a deity. But when it comes to actualization and maintenance of the ideals, it lacks the pragmatic get-things-done systems and procedures. It has a long history of meticulous methods of wishful thinking and the dictatorship of a traditional, static, harmonious and moral social order, but has little experience in the systems and procedures of the modern amoral administration of a changing social order.

The more it attempts to solve problems, the more it creates problems; the more it creates problems, the more it says it is solving problems.

The more it interferes, the more it errs; the more it errs, the more it says it needs to interfere.

The more it does not to fail, the more it does to fail; the more it does to fail, the more it says it does to achieve.

The more it does to safeguard Hong Kong's prosperity, stability and way of life, the more it wrecks them; the more it wrecks them, the more it says Hong Kong needs its safeguard of these properties.

China does not know that the best way to safeguard Hong Kong's prosperity, stability and way of life is for China to lay back and relax, and let Hong Kong people rule themselves in accordance with the current norms, procedures, values and ideals.

International money flows into Hong Kong because it can freely flow out. Hong Kong has a working social order because all the constituents are so dynamic. Policies proclaimed are followed because they have been debated, dissected and criticized. Public authority is upheld because it is open to the public. Government power is effective and responsibility manageable because they are kept to the minimal.

China has been stymied by this Hong Kong paradox. It does not know where, when, what and how to and not to do.

Hong Kong treasures people's relative freedom and power to tackle problems and shoulder the consequences themselves as the beauty of autonomy.

China treasures the rulers' absolute freedom and power to solve all the problems for the people as a moral obligation.

The paradox that a government's best policy is doing as little as possible is beyond China's comprehension and acceptance.

WHAT NEXT: SUPER-IMAGINATION, SUPER-COMMUNICATION AND SUPER-LUCK

China is reversing Hong Kong to converge with China. Patterns of disaster and inverted logic are everywhere to be seen. Hong Kong is not counteracting, nor is Governor Chris Patten.

What Hong Kong needs is a cultural self-awakening and social self-salvation to:

1. probe the scope, depth, gravity and nature of the problems straddling the boundary between Hong Kong and China;
2. abstract convincing theorems on Hong Kong's mode of existence and operations, workings and vulnerability;
3. link daily issues with Hong Kong's mode of existence and operations, workings and vulnerability;
4. integrate daily operational and administrative routines and cultural and philosophic implications;
5. communicate to China the grave consequences of imposing China's world-view and mode of operations on Hong Kong;
6. decode daily issues and disputes, systems and practices along the philosophic and cultural dimensions;
7. convey to China the cultural and philosophic significance of Hong Kong's modernity;
8. divert China's perception of Hong Kong from the realm of historical hate to modern miracle;
9. construct common grounds and norms, values and ideals acceptable to both Hong Kong and China.
10. argue convincingly that the Hong Kong case is a modern miracle rather than a historical hate.

That means we have to deconstruct and reconstruct the Chinese culture and the whole Chinese people.

If there is still any hope, it may lie in the super-imagination and super-communication of each and every Hong Kong people, especially the new generation who in the past quarter of the century have been on the forefront of Hong Kong's social rationalization and democratization.

Above all, Hong Kong needs super-luck.

7

The Economy

Tang Shu-hung

INCREASING ECONOMIC RELATIONSHIP BETWEEN CHINA AND HONG KONG

On 1 July 1997, China will resume its sovereignty over Hong Kong. The 1984 Sino-British Joint Declaration and the 1990 Basic Law guarantee that Hong Kong, as a Special Administrative Region (SAR) of China, will adopt the model of "one country, two systems" that Hong Kong will preserve its capitalist economic system for 50 years. The Basic Law also stipulates clauses on various aspects of Hong Kong's economic system and policies to achieve this noble objective.

Hong Kong entered into the transition period after the signing of the Joint Declaration in December 1984. The Sino-British negotiation was started in 1982, a year when the world economy was suffering from recession. The Hong Kong economy was hardest hit because of not only its high degree of openness and dependence on overseas markets, but also its extreme political uncertainty at that time undermining investors' confidence. The conclusion of Sino-British negotiation thus cleared most of political uncertainties, at least for the intermediate term. The property market rebounded, the capital investment increased and the budget deficits of the Hong Kong government since 1982–1983 gradually eliminated. All these reflected that in the early 1980s when political reform had not been instituted by the colonial administration, the Hong Kong economy was very sensitive to internal social unrest and external political confrontation, in addition to economic recession of overseas markets.

Table 1 gives the real growth rate of the Hong Kong economy, i.e. the gross domestic product (GDP), since 1967. The Hong Kong economy took

Table 1: Real Growth of Hong Kong Economy, 1967–1994

Year	GDP real growth (%) Before Aug. 94 adjustment	After Aug. 94 adjustment	Year	GDP real growth (%) Before Aug. 94 adjustment	After Aug. 94 adjustment	Year	GDP real growth (%) Before Aug. 94 adjustment	After Aug. 94 adjustment	Year	GDP real growth (%) Before Aug. 94 adjustment	After Aug. 94 adjustment
			1970	9.5		1980	10.4		1990	3.2	3.4
			1971	7.4		1981	9.4		1991	4.1	5.1
			1972	11.0		1982	2.7		1992	5.6	6.0
			1973	12.7		1983	6.3		1993	5.6	5.9
			1974	2.1		1984	9.8		1994*	5.5	5.7
			1975	0.4		1985	0.2				
			1976	17.2		1986	11.1				
1967	2.0		1977	12.0		1987	14.5				
1968	3.2		1978	8.8		1988	8.3				
1969	12.0		1979	11.8		1989	2.8				
Average	5.7			9.3			7.6			4.8	5.2

* In line with an established international practice to introduce major improvements to the compilation of GDP estimates once every few years, the Census and Statistics Department has undertaken in August 1994 a non-routine revision of the GDP estimates over the past years up to 1993. In so doing, structural change in the economy can be better reflected and new or more reliable data incorporated to enhance the quality of the GDP estimates. As a result of this round of revision, both the level and the growth rate of the GDP estimates in the more recent years are revised upwards. The revised GDP estimates before 1990, if there is any, should be published in March 1995 on the Budget day.

Sources: Various issues of *The Gross Domestic Product Estimates*, and *Economic Report*.

off in 1966. The average real growth in the 1970s and 1980s were 9.3% and 7.6% respectively. This is a remarkable achievement by any standard. It is quite interesting to observe that prior and after the Sino-British negotiation, the Hong Kong economy suffered from two recessions, one in 1982 and the other in 1985. Unlike 1982, the almost zero growth in 1985 was exclusively due to world economic recession. The growth of total exports dropped drastically from 21.9% in 1984 to just 5.7% in 1985.

The China factor has long been regarded as one of the most contributing factors to Hong Kong's economic growth. For example, China was the most important market for Hong Kong's re-export trade before the 1950s; the influx of capital, entrepreneurs, skilled and unskilled labours in 1950 provided the needed factors of production to develop Hong Kong's light manufacturing industries; the continuous and uninterrupted supply of foodstuff, water and materials at relatively low cost helped maintaining low production cost and inflation in Hong Kong. On the other hand, Hong Kong was fortunate to be immunized from China's political campaigns and disturbances, a national policy that Beijing firmly adhered to, except in the early years of the Cultural Revolution. With China's adoption of open door policy and economic reform since 1979 and the signing of the Joint Declaration in 1984, the China factor takes on a new dimension.

Because of geographical proximity as well as racial and cultural affinity, Hong Kong benefits very much from China's economic reform which oriented towards marketization and privatization. As early as in 1980, Hong Kong business persons started moving manufacturing production processes into the Pearl River Delta to cut production costs. These outward-processing activities expanded rapidly in the mid-1980s. The Hong Kong economy rebounded markedly in 1986 after the 1985 recession and peaked in 1987 at a growth rate of 14.5%, only next to the historical climax 17.2% of 1976. This growth impetus was reinforced by deepening ties between the Chinese and Hong Kong economies. But such close economic relationship also subjects the Hong Kong economy increasingly to influence of the economic and political development in China. This happened in 1989 when China adopted macroeconomic readjustment policy after political disturbance in June. The Hong Kong economy suffered badly, achieving only a 2.8% real growth rate, down from 8.3% in 1988. The real growth rate of total exports plummeted from 26.4% in 1988 to 10.2% in 1989.

THE POTENTIAL GROWTH OF THE HONG KONG ECONOMY

After a decade of open door policy and economic reform since 1979, the cycle of Chinese economy becomes gradually synchronized with the Western economic cycle. This happened in 1989 when Organization for Economic Cooperation and Development (OECD) economies also experienced economic downturn. A synchronized Chinese and Western economic cycle would increase the amplitude of economic fluctuation in Hong Kong. George Shen has long been advocating that the Hong Kong government should recognize the importance of adopting active industrial policy to enhance productivity and to fine-tune the economic cycle.[1] This active Keynesian anti-cyclical policy has been rejected by the Hong Kong government simply because it would generate fiscal deficits, a policy which is contradictory to prudential financial management imposed onto the colonial administration by Britain. The average growth rate of the economy in the 1980s amounted to 7.6%, which was much lower than the 9.3% achieved in the 1970s. This indicates that as the Hong Kong economy becomes more mature, the growth potential will be stabilized. A research conducted by Hang Seng Bank found that for the 1991–1995 period, the growth potential of the Hong Kong economy ranged from 4.7–5.7%. Table 2 gives detailed breakdown of the sources of growth potential for this projection.

This projection has been supported by the official forecast as indicated by the trend growth rate of the economy stipulated in the Medium Range Forecast of the Hong Kong financial budgets. It ranged from 5.0–5.5% for this period. But the official forecast gave neither the detailed breakdown of sources of growth nor the way in which the forecast value was arrived at. Nevertheless, these projections all reflected that the Hong Kong economy entered into a state of slow growth and high inflation. Table 3 shows the actual growth rates of the GDP components since 1990. The average growth rate of GDP for 1991–1994 is 5.2% and 5.7% before and after the non-routine revision of the GDP estimating method respectively. It falls within the projection range of Hang Seng Bank.

Hang Seng Bank argued that declining growth in labour force and capital investment were the two factors contributing to the slow economic growth in the 1990s.[2] For example, Hong Kong's labour force grew by 4.2% annually in the 1970s, but it fell to 1.7% in the 1980s, and further declined to 1.1% in the 1990–1993 period. On the other hand, the gross

Table 2: Sources of Potential GDP Growth (%)

	1981–1989		1991–1995	
	Annual growth	Contribution	Annual growth	Contribution
Labour force	2.0	1.0	0.8	0.4
Factor productivity	5.6	5.6	4.3/5.3	4.3/5.3
Capital stock*	7.7	3.7	5.0/7.0	2.5/3.5
Technical progress*	1.2	1.2	1.2	1.2
Restructuring	0.7	0.7	0.6	0.6
Average annual growth for potential GDP		6.6		4.7/5.7

* Includes buildings and construction, and plant, machinery and equipment. The projected growth rate of capital stock is based on its range of the past five years.
Source: "The Growth Potential of the Hong Kong Economy and Its Inflation Implication," *Hang Seng Economic Monthly* (September 1990).

domestic fixed capital formation grew at 13.4%, 4.4% and 8.0% respectively for the above corresponding periods. Table 3 also gives similar result of gross domestic fixed capital formation, which grew at an average 7.6% for the 1991–1994 period. This is the upper range of Hang Seng Bank's projection for the 1991–1995 period.

The projection of growth potential for the second half of the 1990s would encounter more uncertainties. The change of sovereignty on 1 July 1997 does not necessarily follow that political uncertainty would be eliminated or reduced completely. On the contrary, the Sino-British row over Hong Kong's optimal or acceptable stage of democratic development at the end of the transition period may be intensified, and be extended beyond 1997 over human right issues and the so-called British's moral obligation to monitor and protect Hong Kong people's interest according to the spirit of the Joint Declaration. Domestically, the success of experimenting "one country, two systems" model hinges on whether mutual understanding and willingness to adapt, adjust and compromise could be achieved. It has been and will be Beijing's policy to rely heavily on local business community to shape and implement its policy on Hong Kong.

Table 3: Real Growth Rate of the GDP and Its Main Components, 1990–1994

GDP components		1990	1991	1992	1993	1994*	91–94 average
Private consumption expenditure	Revised	5.7	8.6	7.6	7.4	7.0	7.7
	(Before revision)	(6.3)	(9.2)	(8.3)	(7.7)	(7.0)	
Government consumption expenditure	Revised	5.5	7.7	6.8	1.5	4.4	5.1
	(Before revision)	(6.0)	(6.9)	(7.1)	(0.9)	(3.5)	
Gross domestic fixed capital formation	Revised	8.1	9.3	9.0	4.1	7.8	7.6
	(Before revision)	(8.0)	(9.0)	(9.6)	(4.7)	(5.2)	
Total exports of goods	Revised	9.6	17.3	19.8	13.5	11.0	15.4
	(Before revision)	(9.2)	(16.6)	(19.2)	(13.1)	(16.5)	
Imports of goods	Revised	11.4	19.0	22.2	12.7	12.5	16.6
	(Before revision)	(11.4)	(19.0)	(22.3)	(12.8)	(16.7)	
Exports of services	Revised	3.6	4.7	11.6	8.2	9.0	8.4
	(Before revision)	(5.9)	(3.6)	(11.0)	(7.8)	(9.0)	
Imports of services	Revised	12.1	11.3	9.1	7.8	8.0	9.1
	(Before revision)	(10.7)	(8.1)	(7.0)	(6.9)	(8.0)	
Gross domestic product	Revised	3.4	5.1	6.0	5.9	5.7	5.7
	(Before revision)	(3.2)	(4.1)	(5.6)	(5.6)	(5.5)	(5.2)

* The revised forecast values were announced by Census and Statistics Department on 26 August 1994.
Sources: *Quarterly Economic Report*, various issues.

Such approach would undoubtedly enhance the business community's political clout and dominance. However, it may not necessarily increase their confidence and investment in Hong Kong because the general public, once nourished by gradual democratization, accountability and transparency of the government, may be very critical, if not confrontational, to the SAR government, which may be interpreted by the business community as an inherent and growing source of social unrest. In other words, the business community would be very cautious — sometimes over-cautious — in capital investment in years around 1997. Sluggish capital investment in machine and equipment is detrimental to productivity growth. The growth of capital investment in the second half of the 1990s will again depend heavily on the public sector's investment in infrastructure.

One of the sources of growth potential mentioned in the Hang Seng Bank analysis was economic restructuring.[3] That analysis assigned 0.6% as the contribution from economic restructuring to economic growth for both the 1981–1989 and 1991–1995 periods. Starting from the early 1980s, many industrialists moved their production lines into the Pearl River Delta as a strategy to reduce labour and other production costs. At present, more than four million workers in the Pearl River Delta work for Hong Kong firms. Such a massive exodus of manufacturing jobs creates problems for domestic unskilled manufacturing workers. On the other hand, the expansion of service sector in the process of economic restructuring absorbs surplus manufacturing workers. The expansion of higher value-added service industries also explains Hong Kong's high labour productivity growth since the mid-1980s. The share of manufacturing sector to the whole economy has continuously dropped from 22.3% in 1986 to 13.7% in 1992 (see Table 4).

Virtually the process of moving manufacturing production northward has almost completed in 1994. Economic restructuring should take on a new dimension of upgrading the technology scale of services and manufacturing industries. Recent development in capital investment and technological upgrading does not move in this direction. The contribution of economic restructuring to economic growth for the 1996–2000 period would not be significant, if not minimal, probably at 0.4%, taking also into account the recent non-routine GDP revision of raising the contribution of export of services to China. Moreover, the contribution of technical progress will also be reduced to 1.0%.

The accuracy of the projected labour force growth in the 1996–2000

Table 4: Percentage Distribution of GDP at Current Factor Cost by Economic Activity, 1980–1992 (%)

	1980	1981	1982	1983	1984	1985	1986	1987	1988	1989	1990	1991	1992
Agriculture and fishing	0.8	0.7	0.7	0.6	0.5	0.5	0.5	0.4	0.3	0.3	0.3	0.2	0.2
Mining and quarrying	0.2	0.2	0.2	0.2	0.1	0.2	0.1	0.1	0.1	@	@	@	@
Manufacturing	23.8	22.8	20.7	22.8	24.1	21.9	22.3	21.7	20.1	18.9	17.2	15.2	13.7
Electricity, gas and water	1.3	1.4	1.8	2.4	2.5	2.7	3.0	2.8	2.5	2.3	2.3	2.2	2.2
Construction	6.7	7.5	7.3	6.3	5.3	5.0	4.8	4.7	4.8	5.3	5.6	5.6	5.1
Wholesale, retail and import/export trades, restaurants and hotels	20.4	19.5	19.1	19.5	22.2	21.8	21.3	23.2	23.8	24.0	24.3	25.5	26.2
Transport, storage and communication	7.5	7.5	7.7	8.2	7.8	8.1	8.1	8.7	9.2	8.9	9.4	9.5	9.7
Financing, insurance, real estate and business services	22.8	23.8	22.6	17.9	15.9	16.3	17.3	18.2	19.2	19.8	20.8	22.7	24.5
Community, social and personal services	12.5	13.3	15.6	16.4	15.9	17.3	16.6	15.0	14.6	14.6	15.0	15.5	15.2
Ownership of premises	9.6	9.8	10.8	11.8	10.8	11.0	10.7	10.3	10.5	10.9	10.8	10.9	10.7
Less imputed bank service charge	5.6	6.5	6.5	6.1	5.1	4.8	4.7	5.1	5.1	5.0	5.7	7.3	7.6
Gross domestic product at factor cost	100.0	100.0	100.0	100.0	100.0	100.0	100.0	100.0	100.0	100.0	100.0	100.0	100.0

Notes: The estimates are subject to revisions later on as more data become available.

@ Less than 0.05.

Sources: *Estimates of Gross Domestic Product: 1966 to 1993* (Census and Statistics Department, March 1994), p. 41.
Third Quarterly Economic Report 1994 (Economic Analysis Division, Financial Services Branch, November 1994), p. 125.

period depends on the following factors: the number of outgoing and returning emigrants, the magnitude of quota increase of daily immigrants from China, and the changing ceiling of imported labour. It is expected that the quota for Chinese immigrants and imported labour would gradually be increased, while the number of outgoing and returning emigrants depends on the economic conditions overseas and the smoothness of sovereignty transition in 1997. Considering all these factors, it would not be too unrealistic to assume a 1.2% average annual growth of labour force in the 1996–2000 period.

Summing all these sources of potential growth for the 1996–2000 period, we arrive at an average annual growth rate ranging from 5.1–6.1%. After discounting the upward adjustment of the recent non-routine GDP revision, the potential GDP growth for the 1996–2000 period is not much different from the previous 1991–1995 period, except for changing importance of the components of sources of growth. For the whole 1990s, the potential growth of the Hong Kong economy ranges from 5–6%.

Strategy for Hong Kong's Economic Development

Comparing with the actual average annual growth rates of the 1970s and the 1980s, the downward trend of the growth potential of the economy is very obvious. We may argue that it is a natural development of a mature economy. However, one must not ignore the fact that either the actual or potential growth of the Hong Kong economy is the lowest among the four newly industrializing economies (NIEs) in Asia, the so-called "four little dragons."[4] This is a direct result of different development strategies adopted.

In the early 1980s, Singapore, South Korea and Taiwan devoted more resources in research and development (R & D) to raise their technological level in order to maintain and improve their competitiveness in overseas markets. They followed the traditional path of development by transforming their production activities from factor-driven to technology-driven. On the other hand, Hong Kong shifted emphasis from manufacturing industries to financial services in the early 1980s and service industries in the 1990s. Tax incentives were granted to develop Hong Kong as an international financial centre in the 1980s. Recommendations from the Advisory Committee on Industrial Diversification in the late 1970s were either rejected or downplayed. China's economic reform and open door policy in 1979 offered Hong Kong industrialists a golden opportunity to move their labour-intensive production processes into China to utilize its cheap labour and land. The outward-processing activities continued to expand in the 1980s. The Census and Statistics Department started compiling data on outward-processing activities in 1989. In the first half of 1994, about 72% of Hong Kong's domestic exports to China and about 40% re-exports to China were for outward-processing activities. About 76% of Hong Kong's imports from China was related to outward-processing purposes. With regard to Hong Kong's re-exports to overseas markets which were of China origin, about 81% was related to outward-processing activities commissioned from Hong Kong. These labour-intensive processing activities have little impact on technological improvement of Hong Kong's manufacturing industries. Hong Kong's economic development in the 1990s continues to be factor-driven instead of technology-driven.

The Hong Kong government is not keen at pursuing economic development planning or strategy. Its "positive non-interventionism" philosophy favours market-orientation of economic development. The Hong Kong government prefers to refer its industrial policy in a much broader sense, embracing from infrastructural to educational areas. Teresa Wong referred this as a diffusion-oriented industrial policy, which does not cater for promoting a specific industry.[5] The prudential financial management policy of the Hong Kong government emphasizes "living within our means," which avoids budget deficits and does not involve the Hong Kong government on risky private sector's manufacturing endeavours. This explains why spending on economic services is not more than 6% of total public expenditure, even in the 1990s when virtually all developed and developing countries put more emphasis on promoting R & D. This conservative fiscal policy, however, explains the Hong Kong government's promotion of financial industry in the early 1980s because it required neither massive infrastructure investments nor subsidies. Thus both internal and external forces promote the expansion of service industries in Hong Kong.

Striking a proper balance between manufacturing and service industries is very important not only for economic growth but also for employment purposes. It is generally accepted that as an economy matures, its service sector will grow and the manufacturing sector will decline gradually. The manufacturing share of the economy ranges from 20% (the United States) to 40% (Japan), with other NIEs and developed countries in between. These developed countries usually move their labour-intensive and less technological manufacturing industries to developing countries, and strive to upgrade their high-technology industries. Hong Kong adopts a complete different development path, moving labour-intensive manufacturing industries up north without correspondingly upgrading technological content of the remaining industries or introducing high-technology industries. The prominence of the service sector in Hong Kong's economy is a result of passive development strategy rather than a planned outcome of an active industrial policy. Many expanded service industries such as retailing and restaurants, etc. create only low value-added and low-paid jobs.

In the early 1990s, the business community expressed concern that a too drastic reduction of the share of manufacturing sector would cause disastrous effect on employment and growth potential. In its agenda for analysing economic development strategy for the 1990s, the Business and Professionals Federation of Hong Kong (BPF) addressed the questions such as "Can Hong Kong lose its manufacturing base without affecting macroeconomic performance?" and "Is there a macroeconomic limit to becoming a service and service export/re-export economy?".[6] At the time such questions were addressed, the latest statistic on manufacturing share of the economy was 16.7% for 1990. This was a preliminary estimate and was subsequently revised upward to 17.2%. The business community's concern was warranted because a shrinking manufacturing base would deteriorate trade balance which would have unfavourable impact on the stability of the linked $US–$HK exchange rate. All these are valid concerns and should be carefully studied, especially for the Hong Kong government, so that appropriate fiscal and monetary policies could be formulated. Unfortunately, the 1992 BPF research report, *Hong Kong 21: A Ten Year Visit and Agenda for Hong Kong's Economy*, addressed none of the above issues.

The *Hong Kong 21* instead put heavy emphasis on maintaining Hong Kong as an international financial and operating centre as the main source of economic growth. The role of manufacturing industries was neither mentioned nor discussed. This is in complete contrast with the recommendations of a previous research report, *Building Prosperity: A Five-Part Economic Strategy for Hong Kong's Future*, published in September 1989, which was also funded by prominent business persons. The *Building Prosperity* gave a balance emphasis on improving competitiveness of manufacturing, finance and entrepôt services. As far as manufacturing was concerned, it proposed that the Hong Kong government should set up an Industrial Training Challenge Grants (ITCG) to retrain and upgrade manufacturing workers. The cost of ITCG should be shared equally by the Hong Kong government and the private sector, with a target level amounted to 1.0% of GDP. Similarly, total public and private spending on R & D should also target at 1.0% of GDP. These recommendations gave manufacturing industries a prominent role in Hong Kong's long-term economic development. The industrialists also committed to investing in industrial training and R & D.[7]

Unfortunately, the business community's initiatives and recommendations received no public response and support from the Hong Kong government. The main reason, one may argue, is the reluctance of the Hong Kong government in committing substantial and recurrent financial resources on manufacturing industries. The Hong Kong government's passive attitude, though in conformity with its prevailing "positive non-interventionism" philosophy, discouraged the business community's enthusiasm in developing high value-added manufacturing industries. Thus in the subsequent report *Tasks for the 1990s* which was published in June 1990 to formulate implementing strategy for *Building Prosperity*, the above 1.0% of GDP target on industrial training and on R & D was covertly discarded, retaining only recommendations to establish the Economic Development Board, the Science and Technology Council, and Technology Department.[8] The Hong Kong government was quite cautious in responding to the business community's demand to involve in formulating economic development policy. It was a conspiracy theory subscribed by the officials that such demand, if entertained, would not just change the Hong Kong government's philosophy of managing the economy, but would also undermine the authority of the executive-led colonial administration. The Hong Kong government was very tactful and careful in handling this high-profile demand for sharing powers in economic policy setting. Instead of setting up an Economic Development Board, an Economic Advisory Committee was established. The Science Technology Committee was also established. But the terms of reference of these two Committees were circumscribed to have only an advisory role, rather than the executive role proposed by *Tasks for the 1990s*.

It would be unfair to say that the Hong Kong government did not have a developmental policy for the 1990s. In fact, it did. The 1989 Governor's policy speech described a macro plan of physical infrastructure development for the 1990s, in particular the building of the new airport. The deficiency of such a development plan is its over-reliance on infrastructure investment as an engine of growth, without giving proper recognition to the importance of maintaining and improving the comparative advantages of our manufacturing and service industries before the potential gains from these large-scale, long-term infrastructure investment could be realized. The announcement of pursuing competition policy in the 1992 Governor's policy speech as a new development strategy was in essence a response to criticism on deficiency of the 1989 overall development policy. However, competition policy at best can remedy the undesirable allocative effect caused by the existing monopolistic market structure, and cannot be, or should not be, regarded as a substitute for an active industrial policy on manufacturing and services. Moreover, details of objectives and implementing schedules and mechanisms of the official competition policy have never been well defined. So long as the Hong Kong government is not seriously pursuing competition policy, it becomes a public relation exercise rather than a genuine policy for economic development. Incidentally, the business community also asked the Hong Kong government to clarify its stance on competition policy.[9] The Hong Kong government's passive and conservative approach to long-term development of Hong Kong's economy explained the business community's abandonment of the target of 1.0% GDP spending on industrial training and on R & D.

The Hong Kong government is very experienced and sophisticated in handling demands which are not in line with the official stance. Instead of complete rejection of the demand, the Hong Kong government in general modifies the demand to such an extent that the new version would not much deviate from the official stance. The handling of the business community's request to invest in R & D is a typical example of this approach. Instead of agreeing on the proposal to spend the amount equivalent to 0.5% of GDP on industrial training and on R & D respectively (i.e. the government's share), the Hong Kong government set up the New Technology Training Scheme (NTTS) in June 1991, and the Industry and Technology Development Council (ITDC) in early 1993. For the NTTS, the Hong Kong government provided financial support to employers to send their managers and technicians aboard to learn advanced technologies. The Hong Kong government also set aside $200 million to the ITDC to assist applied R & D. Total commitment for these two schemes was about 0.03% of GDP in 1992, which was far less than the 1.0% GDP target. The business community was not very enthusiastic about these two schemes; for example, up to the end of 1994, only about $36 million matching grant on R & D was spent. The $200 million appropriation to the ITDC in 1993 was a one-off grant. Starting from 1994–1995, the Industry Department allocates $200 million additional support for funding industrial assistance services. This is a recurrent appropriation. In other words, the policy of public funding support for R & D and industrial upgrading remains piecemeal and insignificant.

The Hong Kong government's lukewarm support for manufacturing R & D was widely criticized except those academic economists who sub-scribed to the doctrine of marketism of the Chicago School. A majority of academic economists in Hong Kong either graduated from or subscribed to that School. They argued that the Hong Kong government should not involve in supporting R & D, because it not only unnecessarily subsidizes industrialists with public money, but also distorts the market price signals such that resources are inefficiently allocated. Their criticism in fact be-came the rationale for the Hong Kong government's minimal or notional support for R & D. The academic scientists, on the other hand, adopted a different approach. In 1991, the academic scientists of the five tertiary institutions in Hong Kong, under the coordination of Professor Kao, Vice-Chancellor of The Chinese University of Hong Kong, conducted an in-depth analysis of the strengths and weaknesses of Hong Kong's manufacturing industries, and identified the technology areas (or industries) that Hong Kong should develop and they could assist. Their research report, *Technology Road Maps for Hong Kong*, gave a clear direction where Hong Kong manufacturing industries should move forward to.[10] Again, the Hong Kong government did not respond to these recommendations because the official policy was not to select any industry for funding assistance.

The academic scientists knew beforehand that it was extremely dif-ficult to convince the Hong Kong government to amend its passive stance on industrial policy. Without public funding support, it would be too risky for industrialists to engage in those large-scale and long-term investments. After publishing the report, these academic scientists neither pressed hard the Hong Kong government for adoption, nor offered themselves as a linkage between the private and public sectors on possible cooperation in developing new industries. They may consider that political lobbying is beyond the domain of academic pursuit and should be refrained from.

On the other hand, the Beijing–Hong Kong Academic Exchange Centre (BHKAEC) adopts a different approach to promote industrial development in Hong Kong. The BHKAEC is based in Hong Kong, with funding support from the China Academy of Science in Beijing. The BHKAEC initiated a long-term research project on "The Hong Kong Manufacturing Industries in Year 2000" in the early 1990s with an objective to study in what way and to what extent the Chinese enterprises in Hong Kong, especially those in manufacturing and financial businesses, could help the development of Hong Kong's manufacturing industries in the year 2000 and beyond. This is a noble objective. The research project is privately funded and is being conducted by a group of scientists and economists from China. The BHKAEC has so far published many case studies of this project. Since the Chinese enterprises in Hong Kong invest only a small proportion on manufacturing, their contribution to Hong Kong's future manufacturing development would be minimal. Nevertheless, the BHKAEC has long been advocating the proposition of utilizing China's advanced science and technology capacity to assist Hong Kong's manufacturing upgrading and adapting to new and high technology. Some Hong Kong firms did invite Chinese scientists on short-term contract basis to involve in R & D in Hong Kong. But it was only until late 1994 that the Hong Kong Productivity Council has eventually formalized with the China Academy of Science on research cooperation, which is on project basis.[11] The positive effect of such cooperation on upgrading the technological content of Hong Kong's manufacturing industries is quite obvious. However, as funding support to the Hong Kong Productivity Council from the Industry Department is very small, it would be expecting too much from such cooperation if there is no corresponding adjustment of official stance on funding manufacturing development.

The continuous declining trend of manufacturing seems inevitable. The growth momentum shifts to service industries. Service export at current market prices exceeded that of export of domestic product for the first time in 1993. In spite of the dominance of service sector in Hong Kong's economy, a consistent policy on services has yet to be formulated. A notable example was the latest GATT (General Agreement on Tariffs and Trade) Uruguay Round Negotiation in which service industry was for the first time being included. Delegations from member countries of GATT participating in the multilateral negotiations were exclusively government officials of relevant departments. The Hong Kong delegation was composed of officers of Trading Department and Industry Department. They had been very successful in previous negotiations because Hong Kong, as a

free port economy imposing no tariff on imports except for a few commodities and no non-tariff restrictions on trade, was in a better position to
gain from negotiation. But the Hong Kong delegation faced difficulties and
challenges at the Uruguay Round Negotiation because they knew very little
about service sector. They solicited support from the Hong Kong General
Chamber of Commerce (HKGCC). Under the auspices of the HKGCC, the
Hong Kong Coalition of Service Industries (HKCSI) was formed in 1990.
The HKCSI studied the strengths and weaknesses of the important service
industries in Hong Kong, and examined to what extent domestic and
foreign policies hampering free trade of these services. The HKCSI came
up with a list of Initial Commitment on these important service industries.
The list was then adopted by the Hong Kong government and subsequently
became Hong Kong's official stance on the negotiation table.

This incidence reflected that for an advanced economy like Hong
Kong, also an important international trading and financial centre, surprisingly there lacks a consistent and coordinated economic policy on service
industries. This is not an unfair observation. Service sector needs more
regulation, supervision and monitoring than manufacturing sector, because
many services are non-traded goods which do not subject to the same
degree of international competition as many internationally traded
manufacturing goods. In the past, the Hong Kong government only regulated the financial industry and public utility. Even this limited scope of
regulation was far from success. For example, there were frequent bank
runs and crashes in the securities markets in the 1970s and 1980s, which
reflected mismanagement of the banking and securities industries. The
Schemes of Control for public utilities has been constantly criticized for its
guarantee of high rates of return for investments. The recent announcement
of pursuing an overall competition policy in October 1992 Governor's
policy speech and the continuous improving regulation and monitoring of
many important services and public utilities represent a move in the right
direction, but it is far less than a comprehensive policy on service industries. Paradoxically, the proposal to establish a Fair Trade Commission
moved by a Legislative Councillor in a motion debate at the legislature was
rejected by the Hong Kong government, of course, with the support from
Councillors representing the business's interests.[12]

As the Hong Kong economy is dominated by the service sector, and the
Uruguay Round Negotiation still left several important items of service
industries unsettled at the conclusion of the talks in late 1994 and subject

to further negotiations, it is imperative for the Hong Kong government to place proper attention to service industries. As far as administration hierarchy is concerned, the Hong Kong government should split the Industry Department into the Department of Manufacturing Industries and the Department of Service Industries. The corresponding policy branch of Government Secretariat should be entrusted with the responsibility to draft an overall economic development strategy, including service industries.

EXTERNAL FACTORS AFFECTING GROWTH OF THE HONG KONG ECONOMY

As a small open economy, the performance of Hong Kong's economy depends also on its economic relationship with, and the state of economy of, overseas countries. China is now Hong Kong's second largest trading partner, after adjusting for outward-processing activities. But China is the largest foreign investor in Hong Kong. Moreover, Hong Kong is also China's second largest trading partner after Japan. Hong Kong's economic relationship with the Pearl River Delta is particularly close as there are more than four to five million workers producing for Hong Kong manufacturing firms. The cooperation in manufacturing has gradually been expanded to all other sectors. The degree of integration between these two economies is unprecedented. The China factor has become a dominant force of economic growth in Hong Kong. It was estimated by Hang Seng Bank that 25.7% of Hong Kong's GDP in 1990 could be attributed to the China factor.[13] Economic integration with China is much deeper in 1994 than in 1990. It would not be unfounded to suggest that over 30% of Hong Kong's GDP in the mid-1990s is attributed to the China factor. Thus, China's economic cycle would have a huge impact on Hong Kong's economic performance. After macroeconomic adjustment in the early 1990s, the Chinese economy took on a "high growth, high inflation" path, especially since Deng Xiaoping's southern tour in early 1992. The over 20% inflation rate and uncontrollable growth of capital formation in 1994 has overheated the Chinese economy to such a dangerous state at which macroeconomic adjustment becomes imperative. The slowdown of the Chinese economy would have an adverse effect on the growth of the Hong Kong economy too.

After adjusting for effects of outward-processing activities in China on trade flows, the United States (U.S.) is still Hong Kong's biggest trading partner. The U.S. economy was in a tough position two years ago and is now reviving. With ever intense overseas competition especially from the Asia-Pacific Rim, and struggling through internal economic restructuring, the amplitude of fluctuation of U.S. business cycle is increasing. For example, the present tough period is larger than previous cycles. It is expected that another recession will come in the 1997–1998 period. If the slowdown of the Chinese economy is followed by U.S. economic recession, Hong Kong's economy would be hardest hit in the second half of the 1990s.

The China–U.S. trade relationship would also be an important determinant of Hong Kong's economic growth. For example, when China was encountering the possibility of losing the most-favoured-nation (MFN) status, Hong Kong investors were hesitated in expanding their investments in Hong Kong and in China. Hong Kong would lose 2–2.5% growth of GDP if China's MFN status were not granted continuously by the U.S. When MFN is no longer an issue on China–U.S. trading agenda, the China negotiation with GATT to resuming its membership becomes another delicate issue. The U.S. requested China to resume its GATT membership as a developed country and to observe all obligations on market access, national treatment, MFN, protection of intellectual property rights, and so on. It is assumed that the successful conclusion of the GATT Uruguay Round Negotiation and the subsequent establishment of the World Trade Organization (WTO) would increase world trade, and Hong Kong's GDP would be increased by 0.5%. China successfully becoming a founding member of the WTO would also enlarge Hong Kong's gain, especially those financial and trading service industries which would gain access to the vast Chinese market. On the other hand, China's huge trade surplus with the U.S. would continuously be a negative factor in China–U.S. trade normalization. China will be constantly accused of violating the protection of intellectual property rights, practising trade discrimination, dumpling, etc., even after it becomes a founding member of the WTO. Hong Kong, as an operating centre for China–U.S. re-exports, would be gravely affected if its two largest trading partners are at trade war.

In addition to these conflicting factors, Hong Kong is also subject to increasing competition from neighbouring economies. A new emerging competitor would be Guangdong province, which has been the production base for the Hong Kong manufacturing firms since 1979. Over half of Hong

Kong's investment in China is in that province. After ten years uninterrupted high growth, the Guangdong economy is now entering into the second stage of development for sustained growth. Guangdong Provincial Legislature has recently revolved to adopt a development strategy which gave greater emphasis on heavy and high-technology industries such as petrochemical, automobile, electronics, construction material, pharmaceutical industry, and so on. Hong Kong has apparently little technical know-how and experience on these industries. In other words, Hong Kong's involvement in Guangdong's future economic development would be much less than its dominant role in the 1980s. Consequently, gains to the Hong Kong economy would be reduced. Moreover, as Guangdong's transportation and communication facilities improve in the coming years, especially the build-up of airports and container ports, some of the re-export trade previously through Hong Kong will inevitably be diverted to Chinese ports.

Singapore is Hong Kong's traditional competitor, especially in the financial services area. In the 1970s, Singapore competed with Hong Kong in developing Asia's U.S. dollar market. In the 1980s and 1990s, Singapore offered tax incentives to attract foreign financial institutions to set up their regional headquarters there. Recently, Singapore has relaxed restrictions on provident funds' portfolio investments, with an intention to overtake Hong Kong as an Asia centre of fund management after 1997. Moreover, Taipei and Shanghai also have intentions to develop as international financial centres, and are in the process of pursuing financial liberalization, drafting appropriate legislation and establishing operating institutions. They all aim to compete with Hong Kong. At present, Hong Kong still enjoys its comparative advantages in good legal framework, effective administration, stable fiscal policy, good communication facilities and management. But Hong Kong should not be complacent about its financial status because the maintenance of an independent legal and judiciary system free from executive interference is a prerequisite for an international financial centre. Although the Joint Declaration and the Basic Law have already provided double guarantees for such independence, interpretation and implementation of the Basic Law is a delicate business because of the divergent political and legal backgrounds between Beijing and Hong Kong. If the quality of monitoring and regulating financial sector declines, and the independence of legal and judiciary system cannot be upheld after 1997, Hong Kong's comparative advantages as an international financial centre will greatly be diminished.

Hong Kong is an important international trading centre and serves as a trade intermediary between China and Taiwan. Recently, Taiwan has been advocating to become an operating centre of the Asia-Pacific region as its crucial strategy for economic restructuring and development. A more ambitious plan is to bypass its self-imposing policy of direct trade restriction between the Taiwan Strait. At present, over 90% of China–Taiwan trade is through Hong Kong. The new Director of Mainland Committee of Executive Yuan in Taiwan, Vincent C. Siew, has been pondering on innovative ideas of setting up an operating centre physically in Taiwan, but making it outside Taiwan in legal terms, to achieve the above twin objectives of political separation and economic integration. With ever-growing Taiwanese investments in China and increasing trade flows between these two economies, merely cost consideration would render it desirable to have direct trade between China and Taiwan. When Hong Kong becomes an SAR of China after 1997, it would become unjustifiable that Hong Kong remains a third party to handle China–Taiwan trade. This adds to the urgency for Taiwan to find an alternative place or method to replace Hong Kong as its trade intermediary. It was estimated that the China–Taiwan direct trade would be reduced about 12.6% of Hong Kong's total re-export trade in 1993.[14] This is a very heavy, though not fatal, blow on Hong Kong's re-export business. Moreover, if Taiwan were successful in developing as an operating centre of the Asia-Pacific region, some businesses must be diverted from Hong Kong to Taiwan. Although foreign trade competition is not a zero-sum game, and a growing Asian economy will generate more trade, one should not underestimate the potential threat from Taiwan's drastic change of trading policy on Hong Kong's economic growth.

The above upcoming potential competition from neighbouring economies on financial and service sectors makes it imperative for Hong Kong to arrest the trend of deindustrialization and to increase the share of manufacturing sector in the economy. Maintaining a target share of 18–20% of manufacturing to GDP would be a viable option for Hong Kong's future economic development. In other words, the Hong Kong government should assist the development of more skill and technology-oriented industries. These high value-added industries provide better growth potential for Hong Kong's economy, and also assist in solving current problems such as inflation, underemployment, and income inequality.

HONG KONG'S CURRENT ECONOMIC PROBLEMS

❑ *Inflation*

Hong Kong enjoyed a very low inflation rate of 2.8% in 1986. Since then, inflation rate gradually rose and it reached 10.1% in 1989. Double-digit inflation rates maintained for several years before it dropped to single-digit. The downward trend started in 1992 and inflation rate is expected to remain at 8% level for the next few years. A high inflation rate raises cost of living, reduces purchasing power of fixed income, lessens international competitiveness of domestic product, and eventually hampers growth of the economy.

Inflation is one of the most delicate economic and social issues. Its causes are complex and it affects social classes differently. Before introducing functional constituency representation in the legislature in 1985, the Hong Kong government did not pay much attention to control inflation. Of course, no pressure groups at that time had sufficient political clout to influence economic policy and administrative priority. The gradual democratization of the Hong Kong legislature changes the Hong Kong government's attitude towards controlling inflation. When the inflation rate, which is represented by the Consumer Price Index (A) [CPI(A)], reached 13.4% in April 1991, the Hong Kong government considered that it had already surpassed the society's tolerance level. Immediate and effective actions must be taken, otherwise inflationary expectation would be formed which would be difficult to eradicate. The Hong Kong government at that time applied fiscal, monetary and wage policies to combat inflation. All sectors and classes were affected, though of different degree. The BPF apparently did not favour this "attacking at all fronts" approach in fighting inflation. The BPF commissioned a group of academic economists to study the underlying forces of inflation. They concluded that economic restructuring towards service industries, coupled with labour shortage, were the main reasons for Hong Kong's double-digit inflation. They suggested that Hong Kong should control wage rate increase and should import overseas workers.[15]

While agreeing economic restructuring towards service industries was the main reason for higher inflation in Hong Kong, Tsang Shu-ki argued that it was inconclusive in the causality of wage rate growth and inflation, if real payroll per person instead of nominal wage rate growth were used.[16]

Tsang suggested that profit-driven inflation, a special phenomenon of the Hong Kong government's assurance of rates of return for public utilities, should need to be investigated. Tsang's interpretation of the relationship between structural transformation and inflation deserves more discussion. Tsang pointed out that the transformation of the Hong Kong economy towards more services orientation was not prompted by productivity enhancement of manufacturing industries, but occurred as a result of increasing outward-processing manufacturing activities in the Pearl River Delta. Surplus manufacturing workers, especially those unskilled aged workers, either were absorbed in the low-paid service industries or become unemployed or underemployed. Service industries are characterized in general as high labour-intensive, low-productivity and costly. Detailed analysis of CPI components confirmed that services were the most contributing factor for high inflation in Hong Kong. The profitability of outward-processing activities in the Pearl River Delta released the pressure and incentive for technological upgrading of manufacturing industries in Hong Kong. When output and manpower of these outward-processing activities were included, Hong Kong's manufacturing productivity growth lags behind the other three NIEs.[17] Tsang was concerned of its adverse effect on the long-term efficiency of Hong Kong's economy. Tsang's recommendation was to pursue technological upgrading and to maintain a viable industrial base, which would bring long-term benefits. It was different from those proposed by the BPF which depended on wage growth restraint and labour importation. Unfortunately, the Hong Kong government considered technological upgrading only as an industry policy issue, rather than as one of the options tackling inflation.

❑ *Underemployment and Income Inequality*

Slow growth of labour force in the past five years and the recent structural transformation to labour-intensive service industries both cause acute labour shortage problem in Hong Kong. The Hong Kong government started to import overseas workers in 1989. On the other hand, unskilled and old-aged workers, especially in the manufacturing industries, are either unemployed or underemployed, or moved to low-paid service industries. Table 5 shows the employment situation since 1990. The total number of unemployed and underemployed workers surpasses the 100,000 threshold since the second quarter of 1991, which is much larger than the 25,000

Table 5: The Labour Force and Employment Situation, 1990–1994

Year	Quarter	Labour force	Persons unemployed	Persons underemployed	Seasonally adjusted unemployment rate (%)	Underemployment rate (%)	Seasonally adjusted unemployment rate + underemployment rate (%)
1990	Q1	2,743,500	37,900	18,100	1.7	0.7	2.4
	Q2	2,737,700	36,000	25,800	1.6	0.9	2.5
	Q3	2,736,400	41,100	28,500	1.7	1.0	2.7
	Q4	2,774,700	31,200	21,400	1.4	0.8	2.2
1991	Q1	2,782,500	41,100	43,000	1.8	1.5	3.3
	Q2	2,790,600	58,300	46,700	2.4	1.7	4.1
	Q3	2,796,100	54,300	43,200	2.1	1.5	3.6
	Q4	2,825,900	47,600	45,100	1.8	1.6	3.4
1992	Q1	2,779,800	58,200	61,900	2.4	2.2	4.6
	Q2	2,803,600	57,500	62,000	2.3	2.2	4.5
	Q3	2,768,200	46,500	52,600	1.9	1.9	3.8
	Q4	2,820,400	56,500	56,700	2.1	2.0	4.1
1993	Q1	2,844,800	61,400	46,100	2.3	1.6	3.9
	Q2	2,848,100	57,600	57,000	2.2	2.0	4.2
	Q3	2,870,100	54,400	37,900	2.0	1.3	3.3
	Q4	2,929,000	54,300	43,600	2.0	1.5	3.5
1994	Q1	2,933,000	56,900	50,100	2.2	1.7	3.9
	Q2	2,958,400	47,900	38,600	1.9	1.3	3.2
	Q3	2,974,000	67,400	32,600	2.3	1.1	3.4

Sources: *General Household Survey*, Census and Statistics Department, various issues.

quota of imported workers. If the Hong Kong government and the industrialists were genuinely pursuing industrial training and occupation
retraining programmes, at least the underemployment problem could be
alleviated somewhat and there is no need to import overseas workers. But
the Hong Kong government and the employers choose a different route
by importing overseas workers to keep the local wage rate from rising,
and many employers even replace high-paid local workers with overseas workers. Many surplus manufacturing workers, after completing the
occupation retraining course, still cannot find even low-paid jobs in the
service sector. The real income of manufacturing workers rose at a lower
average rate than per capita real GDP for the 1982–1991 period.

The 1991 Population Census reflected the summary result of the effects
of structural transformation, stagflation, ageing population, and labour
importation on the livelihood of ordinary people. Table 6 gives the
decile distribution of household incomes in Hong Kong since the 1971
Population Census. The Gini Coefficient is at 0.48 in 1991, which is the
highest since 1971, indicating a widening income inequality. The 1991
result was so daunting because not just the lowest-income group suffered
from reducing share of total income, all the income groups up to the seventh
decile suffered, though of different degree. This had never happened
before. In contrast, the highest-income group gained tremendously, taking
37.3% of total income.

Hong Kong's income inequality is the worst among the NIEs in Asia.
Many reasons are proposed to explain the increasing trend of income
disparity. One of them is structural transformation of the economy, a
phenomenon which had not been experienced in the 1970s and early 1980s.
We understand that outward-processing activities not only maintain Hong
Kong's international competitiveness, but also enable many Hong Kong
investors reaping huge profits. For example, it was estimated about at least
three million workers producing for Hong Kong firms in the Pearl River
Delta in 1992. The wage rate in China was about one-tenth of Hong Kong's
standard. The saving in labour cost alone amounted to around $12,000–
15,000 million per month, i.e. $140–180 billion per year, which was over
10% of Hong Kong's GDP in 1992. These huge profits somehow escaped
the China and Hong Kong tax net. Many of these profits repatriating to
Hong Kong were mainly for asset acquisition, in securities and property.
The high rates of return in these markets increases their wealth substantially. Asset inflation also squeezes middle-income class that they have to

Table 6: Decile Distribution of Household Income and Gini Coefficients in Hong Kong, 1971, 1976, 1981, 1986 and 1991

Decile of households	1971		1976		1981		1986		1991	
	%	Cum. %	%	Cum. %	%	Cum. %	%	Cum. %	%	Cum. %
1st	2.3	2.3	1.9	1.9	1.4	1.4	1.6	1.6	1.3	1.3
2nd	3.9	6.2	3.5	5.4	3.2	4.6	3.4	5.0	3.0	4.3
3rd	5.1	11.3	4.6	10.0	4.4	9.0	4.4	9.4	4.0	8.3
4th	5.1	16.4	5.5	15.5	5.4	14.4	5.4	14.8	5.0	13.3
5th	7.0	23.4	6.8	22.3	6.5	20.9	6.4	21.2	6.1	19.4
6th	7.3	30.7	8.1	30.4	7.8	28.7	7.6	28.8	7.4	26.8
7th	9.0	39.7	8.8	39.2	9.4	38.1	9.1	37.9	9.0	35.8
8th	11.0	50.7	11.3	50.5	11.5	49.6	11.4	49.3	11.4	47.2
9th	14.7	65.4	15.9	66.4	15.2	64.8	15.2	64.5	15.5	62.7
10th	34.6	100.0	33.6	100.0	35.2	100.0	35.5	100.0	37.3	100.0
Gini Coefficient	0.43		0.43		0.45		0.45		0.48	

Note: The Gini Coefficient falls by definition within the range of 0.0 to 1.0, with 0.0 representing absolute equality and 1.0 absolute inequality. The larger the coefficient, the more unequal is the income distribution.

Source: *Main Report, Volume 1, Hong Kong 1981, 1991 Census* (Hong Kong: Census and Statistics Department).

pay a higher proportion of their income for housing mortgages. The wage restraint policy adopted since the early 1990s to combat inflation affects all salary and wage earners.

The Hong Kong government realizes the grave implication of widening income inequality to social stability. To avoid the discussion of the underlying reasons for this worsening trend, the Hong Kong government argues that the Gini Coefficient is only one of the measurements of income distribution, which has its own deficiency, and points out that improving living standard as reflected by the cumulative real growth rate of per capita income should be more relevant. Pushing aside the income disparity issue is not what a responsible government should pursue. The Hong Kong government should conduct a genuine and impartial analysis, with all its manpower and resources at the Economics and Financial Services Branch, on the relationship between economic restructuring and income disparity in Hong Kong. Equity should assume an equal, if not heavier, weight as economic growth in the Hong Kong government's objective domain. The Hong Kong government should amend its industrial and wage policies and introduce redistributive income policy to accommodate for this added objective.

CONSERVATIVE FISCAL POLICY IN THE TRANSITION PERIOD

Adopting an active industrial policy and pursuing redistributive income policy implies a Keynesian-type anticyclical policy. Hong Kong as a British colony must adhere to the prudential financial management policy laid down in the Colonial Regulations. The Hong Kong government was granted financial autonomy in 1958, but it still adheres consistently to this conservative fiscal policy. Simply put, the Hong Kong government avoids Keynesian deficit financing and subscribes to the "living within our means" principle. Successive Financial Secretaries have developed budgetary guidelines to control expenditure growth, size of the public sector and to minimize budget deficit, if it is unavoidable. The primary purpose of taxation policy is to generate sufficient recurrent revenue so as to finance a major portion of government programmes and to maintain fiscal reserves at a satisfactory level.[18]

The famous philosophy of positive non-interventionism, the doctrine of economic management practised by government officials, is a natural outcome developed from such conservative fiscal policy. It is argued that resource allocation is more efficient if left to the operation of market mechanism. Government intervention in general causes more harm than good in the long run, according to this doctrine. The Hong Kong government's role is to provide a good social, legal and physical infrastructure for business to flourish. Under such philosophy, expenditure on economic services and on social welfare has been kept at a relative low level of around 5% and 6% of total public expenditure respectively. On the other hand, tax rates on Profits Tax and Salaries Tax are kept at a relatively low level in order to attract foreign investment. Progressive tax rate schedules are neutralized by adopting a standard rate clause which renders the Salaries Tax effectively into a proportional tax system. Vertical tax equity could not be achieved under a proportional tax system. However, only horizontal equity is treated as one of the objectives of the Hong Kong tax system.[19]

This conservative fiscal policy, however successful it may seem in the past, could not meet the socio-economic and political challenges of the 1990s. The business community urges the Hong Kong government to pump resources to improve productivity and competitiveness of both manufacturing and service sectors. The current $200–500 million spent on R & D is totally inadequate to have any significant impact on the economy. R & D is crucial both for the survival of manufacturing and service industries. When a survey on firms' R & D was conducted recently by the Industry Department, only a few firms responded. The rate of response was so embarrassingly low that it did not provide any useful information of statistical significance for reference in formulating public policy on subsidizing R & D. The cruel reality is that R & D is neglected also by the private sector. It is the responsibility of the Hong Kong government to seriously promote R & D. If the Hong Kong government does not endorse the recommendation that total private and public spendings on R & D at least be equivalent to 1.0% of GDP, it must give valid reasons and must submit its alternative proposal. The R & D is perhaps the most important issue in engineering economic restructuring in Hong Kong.

Another social issue that requires public funding support is the setting up of a mandatory retirement scheme. Hong Kong has long been discussing the establishment of a retirement scheme since 1967, but remains undecided and uncommitted due to strong objection either from the Hong Kong government or from the business community. In October 1992, in responding to repeated demands from the Legislative Council, the Hong

Kong government finally drafted a consultative paper on "A Community-Wide Retirement Protection System" (CWRPS). The CWRPS is employment-related, requiring contributions both from employers and employees. The characteristics of the CWRPS are similar to a typical central provident fund except that the CWRPS is managed by the private sector, i.e. fund managers, and does not have any financial guarantee from the Hong Kong government. The general public is sceptical of the financial stability of the CWRPS, a justifiable concern given the fact that mismanagement of pension funds is not uncommon even in the mature financial markets. Both the general public and the business community demand for the Hong Kong government's financial guarantee for the CWRPS.

After a long delay, the government finally decided to reject not only the request for financial guarantee, but also the whole CWRPS, in mid-December 1993. Surprisingly, the Hong Kong government announced to adopt a "pay-as-you-go" social insurance scheme for retirement protection. The consultative paper on "Old Age Pension Scheme" (OPS) requires both employers and employees to contribute 1.5% of salaries income monthly to the scheme. The Hong Kong government's existing spending on social security is to be transferred to the scheme. Those aged 65 and above is entitled to receive $2,300 pension monthly. The Hong Kong government also uses $10 billion to set up a special fund to implement the scheme. There were hot debates among different sectors of the society on the desirability of intergenerational redistribution of the OPS. As far as public funding support is concerned, the Hong Kong government is criticized of not giving sufficient resources to the scheme because the Hong Kong government's contribution in terms of annual spending on social security as percentage of total public expenditure declines as time goes by. Some labour organizations asked the Hong Kong government to contribute monthly as much as the total sum of employers' and employees' contributions. The Hong Kong government rejected such request, arguing that using general tax revenues to make contributions, other than those promised social security spending, will make the tax system redistributive, an objective which has never been pursued in Hong Kong.

The switch from the CWRPS to the OPS is a drastic change of philosophy in funding on income support for retirement. The choice of which should be based on in-depth discussions and analysis on their merits and defects. It happened that the Hong Kong government just decided unilaterally on this important matter. One compelling reason, as more and more would tend to agree, is to reduce the Hong Kong government's financial obligation. At the time of writing, the Hong Kong government is still waiting for the result of the Sino-British Joint Liaison Group's discussion on the OPS. It seems that the Chinese side is even more conservative on SAR government's future funding commitment. There are indications that the Hong Kong government may switch back to the CWRPS. The reality is that both sides must come up with an acceptable solution, be it before or after 1997, which promises more public funding on income support on retirement.

After the announcement of building a new airport at Chek Lap Kok in October 1989, the priority of public spending, as expected, is given to the ten core projects of the new airport. A majority of these projects is financed by annual capital expenditure of financial budgets. Starting from 1990–1991 Budget, the share of capital spending on new airport projects to total capital expenditure was around 30%, and the proportion of capital expenditure to total public expenditure also rose. The normal public works projects are somehow crowded out by these new airport projects. Legislative Councillors succeeded in 1992 to persuade the Financial Secretary to set the ceiling that capital spending on new airport projects should not exceed 25% of total capital expenditure. Similarly, the growth of recurrent expenditure is residualized so as to satisfy the guideline that total public expenditure growth should not exceed the trend growth of the economy. This explains why when social and economic environments are justified for expansion in social welfare and economic services spending, the actual share of these two items remains rather stable at their levels of the 1980s. It is ridiculous to observe massive build-up of fiscal reserves amid cutting of social services expenditure.

The financial transition, including assets and liabilities, between the present Hong Kong government and the future SAR government is a very thorny business because it has not been spelled out in the Joint Declaration. When the Chinese delegation negotiated with the Hong Kong government on the viability of the new airport proposal in 1990, the issue at stake was the amount of fiscal reserves that must be set aside to, and the amount of public bonds that will have to be redeemed by, the future SAR government. The divergence between ask and offer of the two sides was so great that the negotiation came to a deadlock until it was broken by secret diplomacy in Beijing in July 1991. The 1991 Memorandum of Understanding (MOU) on the construction of Hong Kong's new airport was signed, specifying among other things that at least $25 billion fiscal reserves must be handed to the future SAR government on 1 July 1997, and that not more than $5 billion public bonds is to be redeemed by the future SAR government. The MOU is in fact a supplement to the Joint Declaration on transference of financial assets and liabilities between the two governments. The negotiation on the financial arrangement on building the new airport started immediately after the signing of the MOU. This is even more difficult because it involves private sector participation, efficiency and rates of return, and government financial injection and obligation. It took more than three years to conclude and the Agreed Minutes on Financial Arrangement was signed in November 1994.

During the long period of negotiation with the Chinese side, fiscal policy in Hong Kong became even more conservative. Growth of public expenditure was carefully controlled. Policy on fees charging on government services was revised, trading funds were set up for those government services that could be operated on commercial basis, and subsidies on social services were substantially reduced. Indirect taxes such as "Rates" were increased sharply to maintain the stable 60%:40% ratio between direct and indirect taxes. All these policy changes are controversial, but have been tactfully implementing, on grounds of using resources more efficiently so as to have more resources available for the new airport construction. It would not be unfounded to argue that fiscal policy in the transition period is short term-oriented, not beyond the 1997 sovereignty boundary, focusing primarily on building the new airport and on accumulating fiscal reserves. Long-term development in social and economic areas becomes second importance, if not neglected, in the Hong Kong government's agenda for the 1990s.

SAR: CONSERVATIVE FISCAL CONSTITUTION OF THE BASIC LAW

The Joint Declaration and the Basic Law guarantee that, after China's resumption of sovereignty, Hong Kong will maintain its existing capitalist economic system and lifestyle for 50 years. The Basic Law is a "mini-constitution" governing the SAR, specifying constitutional and institutional frameworks for the operation of the SAR. Chapter V (Economy) of the Basic Law follows the same approach except that two policy articles on fiscal policy are included. Constitutional scholars and economists have long been engaging in serious debates on the appropriateness of inclusion of policy articles in the Basic Law. Some public finance economists advocate for including the "Balance Budget Clause" in the Basic Law so as to solve the skyrocketing public debt and budget deficit problem. Some argue that such inclusion would build in rigidity in budgeting, which may be counter-productive. Similar arguments repeated during the drafting process of the Basic Law. Eventually the following Articles 107 and 108 on fiscal policy were adopted:

> The Hong Kong Special Administrative Region shall follow the principle of keeping expenditure within the limits of revenues in drawing up its budget, and strive to achieve a fiscal balance, avoid deficits and keep the budget commensurate with the growth rate of its gross domestic product.[20]

> The Hong Kong Special Administrative Region shall practise an independent taxation system. The Hong Kong Special Administrative Region shall, taking the low tax policy previously pursued in Hong Kong as reference, enact laws on its own concerning types of taxes, tax rates, tax reductions, allowances and exemptions, and other matters of taxation.[21]

Article 107 has been labelled as a "Balanced Budget Article" while Article 108 is called "Low Tax Policy Article." The spirit of Articles 107 and 108 is not much different from the financial management rules stipulated in the Colonial Regulations. They both aim to establish and preserve the financial viability and stability of the Hong Kong government and the future SAR government. Articles 107 and 108 effectively maintain the status quo of the existing fiscal policy as much as possible. Economic stabilization and income redistribution functions of fiscal policy are to play at most only a minimal role in the future. These two Articles may be more flexible than their Colonial Regulations counterpart, but they may not be flexible enough to accommodate Hong Kong's social and economic development in the 1990s and beyond. The conservative connotation of these two Articles aroused much criticism during the drafting process of the Articles. The controversy focused on the role of fiscal policy in industrial upgrading and income redistribution. In particular, the business community was very much concerned about the potential damaging effect on the economy of a more democratic political legislature pressing for higher and progressive tax rate schedule to pay for expansion of social welfare programmes. They argued that controlling public expenditure growth and maintaining a low tax rate policy could safeguard against drastic change in Hong Kong's fiscal system, and would contain indirectly the political influence of the grassroots democrats on fiscal policy. The Chinese authority endorsed this philosophy, apparently satisfying with its desirable effect on political conservatism.

Although the Basic Law is applicable only in the future SAR, the Chinese authority has repeatedly asked the Hong Kong government to observe and adhere to Articles 107 and 108 in drafting financial budgets in the transition period. The officials of Hong Kong and Macau Affairs Office of China's State Council, and those of the Hong Kong Branch of Xinhua News Agency have commented that the financial budgets in the past three years violated the principle of "living within our means."[22] The Hong Kong government was accused of introducing European-type welfare state into Hong Kong and was warned not to impose immense financial burden for the future SAR government.[23] These criticisms are unfounded, arising partly from technical difficulties in interpreting terms such as "living within our means," "strive for," etc. of Article 107 and the magnitude of "lowness" of Article 108, and partly from philosophical difference in defining "social security," "welfare state," "free lunch," and so on. It is ironic to observe that officials of socialist China apply the extreme position of ultra-conservatism of capitalist society to monitor and assess Hong Kong affairs. Tsang Shu-ki's observation is quite illuminating. He says that:

> Their [The Chinese] stance has apparently become minimalist: the less change in Hong Kong, the better. In reality, of course, Hong Kong is changing all the time. The real question is whether the direction of the emerging changes is desirable. Ruling out *a prior* preventive and rectifying measures is myopic.[24]

The Hong Kong government does not necessarily dislike China's criticism, though for different reasons. It adds weight to Hong Kong government's insistence to keep public expenditure growth within the trend growth of GDP. It also assists the Hong Kong government to rationalize the prevailing fiscal policy and to guard off any demand for reform. It would not be unreasonable to predict that if the present conservative fiscal policy were maintained for the remaining years before 1997, income disparity and manufacturing hollowing will be worsened.

It seems that the future SAR government should be concern much about inheriting a society which is being plagued with increasing social tension and deteriorating economic prospect. Regrettably, fiscal conservatism, a dominating contributory factor to this provoking scenario, has been enthusiastically endorsing and promoting during the transition period by the Chinese authority. Articles 107 and 108 give fiscal conservatism a constitutional status, prohibiting the future SAR government and the legislature to deviate much from prevailing fiscal system and policy. Hoping for the future SAR executive-led government to adopt active fiscal policy in promoting growth and equity may later turn out to be extravagant, if not wishful, thinking. Whether China will maintain its minimalist stance on SAR government's role hinges on its understanding of the growth potentials and problems of the Hong Kong economy, and the government's role in promoting economic growth and equity. After all, we need creative, responsible and committed leaders to deliver the promises of "stability and prosperity" of the innovative "one country, two systems" political design.

Notes

1. G. Shen, "Hong Kong Should Understand the Timing of Business Cycle," *Hong Kong Economic Journal* (in Chinese), 30 November 1983.
2. "The Growth Potential of the Hong Kong Economy and Its Inflation Implication," *Hang Seng Economic Monthly* (September 1990).
3 Ibid.
4. The OECD has recently predicted the growth of Asian economies for the next few years. The average real growth rate for 1994–1995 for the NIEs are as follows: Singapore 8.0%, South Korea 7.6%, Taiwan 6.2% and Hong Kong 5.4%. Hong Kong scores the lowest among the "four little dragons." See *Hong Kong Economic Journal*, 21 December 1994.
5. T. Wong, "A Comparative Study of the Industrial Policy of Hong Kong and Singapore in the 1980s," in *Industrial and Trade Development in Hong Kong*, edited by E. Chan, M. Ngaw and T. Wong (Hong Kong: Centre of Asian Studies, the University of Hong Kong, 1991).
6. *Second Progress Review of Hong Kong 21: A Ten Year Vision and Agenda for Hong Kong's Economy*, (Hong Kong: Steering Committee, Business and Professionals Federation of Hong Kong, 8 July 1992).
7. *Building Prosperity: A Five-Part Economic Strategy for Hong Kong's Future* (Hong Kong: The Hong Kong Economic Survey Ltd., September 1989).
8. *Task for the 1990s: Implementing Hong Kong's Strategy for Building Prosperity* (Hong Kong: The Hong Kong Economic Survey Ltd., June 1990).
9. *Hong Kong 21: A Ten Year Vision and Agenda for Hong Kong's Economy*

(Hong Kong: Business and Professionals Federation of Hong Kong, May 1993).

10. C. Kao, and K. Yong (eds.), *Technology Road Maps for Hong Kong* (Hong Kong: Office of Industrial and Business Development, The Chinese University of Hong Kong, 1991).

11. See *Hong Kong Economic Journal*, 12 and 23 December 1994.

12. Lee Wah-ming proposed to establish a "Fair Trade Commission" to formulate and oversee the competitive policy in Hong Kong in a motion debate on 17 February 1993 in the Legislative Council. The Motion was marginally defeated by one vote. It was amended by the Councillor from the business constituency to neutralize its effect on business.

13. See *Hang Seng Economic Monthly*, June 1993.

14. Y. C. Jao, "The Future Prospect of Hong Kong as Regional Financial and Operating Centre" (paper presented at the Conference on Transition to 1997 and Taiwan–Hong Kong Relationship held in Hong Kong, 28–29 October 1994), p. 19.

15. R. Wong, P. Liu, and A. Sin (eds.), *Inflation in Hong Kong: Patterns, Causes and Policies* (Hong Kong: Business and Professionals Federation of Hong Kong, October 1991), pp. 60–77.

16. Tsang Shu-ki, "Inflation," in *The Other Hong Kong Report 1992*, edited by Joseph Y. S. Cheng and Paul C. K. Kwong (Hong Kong: The Chinese University Press, 1992), pp. 425–45.

17. See George Shen, "China–Hong Kong Integration," in *The Other Hong Kong Report 1994*, edited by Donald H. McMillen and Man Si-wai (Hong Kong: The Chinese University Press, 1994), pp. 477–81.

18. S. Tang, "Comment on Policy Commitment of Secretary for the Treasury, Governor's Address 1994," *Hong Kong Economic Journal Monthly* (in Chinese) (November 1994), pp. 16–21.

19. Ibid.

20. *The Basic Law of the Hong Kong Special Administrative Region of the People's Republic of China*, Article 107.

21. Ibid., Article 108.

22. S. Tang, *Hong Kong Public Finance in the Transition Period* (in Chinese) (Hong Kong: Joint Publishing (HK) Co. Ltd., 1992), pp. 352–65.

23. N. Zhou, "The Importance of Maintaining Hong Kong's Economic System" (speech delivered at Hong Kong Management Association's Annual Fellowship Dinner, 16 November 1994).

24. Tsang Shu-ki, "The Economy," in *The Other Hong Kong Report 1994*, edited by Donald H. McMillen and Man Si-wai (Hong Kong: The Chinese University Press, 1994), p. 147.

8

Banking, Monetary Affairs and Developments of Financial Markets

Lui Yu-hon

INTRODUCTION

There are only about 800 days from now to 1 July 1997 on which China will resume the exercise of sovereignty over Hong Kong. After that day, Hong Kong will no longer be a colony under the British administration and instead become a Special Administrative Region (SAR) under the Central People's Government. In this transition period, people are extremely concerned about the stability and prosperity of the economy.

In the past decade, Hong Kong experienced a major structural change in its economy. In the early 1980s, Hong Kong was still an industrialized economy but now in the 1990s, Hong Kong has successfully shifted to be a service-oriented economy. As a service-oriented economy, the role of monetary and financial systems are particularly important. On the one hand, the financial sector accounts for a high percentage (about 16%) of total jobs in the economy and about one quarter of its gross domestic product (GDP). On the other hand, the systems facilitate the allocation of resources for the economy and strengthen its link with other economies. Undoubtedly, to a great extent, the stability and prosperity of Hong Kong economy depends on the functioning of its monetary and financial systems.

The importance of the monetary and financial systems triggers considerable attention on whether Hong Kong can maintain its status as an international financial centre in the run-up to 1997 and beyond. This importance has indeed been perceived by both the Chinese and the British governments. In Section VII of Annex I of the Sino-British Joint Declaration concerning the monetary and financial systems, the first paragraph specifies that:

The Hong Kong Special Administrative Region shall retain the status of an international financial centre. The monetary and financial systems previously practised in Hong Kong, including the systems of regulation and supervision of deposit taking institutions and financial markets, shall be maintained.

In addition, Article 109 of the Basic Law states that:

The Government of the Hong Kong Special Administrative Region shall provide an appropriate economic and legal environment for the maintenance of the status of Hong Kong as an international financial centre.

These indicate the two governments' concern over the future status of Hong Kong's financial systems.

Nevertheless, being an international financial centre is not a matter for declaration by sovereign states. Instead, it is a matter for recognition by global financial community. As recognition is related to confidence, the more relevant issues are how to enhance international confidence on our policies and capability in the transition period and beyond? And what, if anything, do we need to do?

Many people have a prudent and conservative thinking of maintaining the monetary and financial systems previously practised in the territory as a means to maintaining our status as an international financial centre. This standstill approach may not be a good option as financial environment is dynamic and rapidly changing. As a Chinese idiom puts it, "advance or left behind." What should be maintained is the good spirit of our systems and not the status quo. In this connection, a forward-looking and pro-active approach seems to be more appropriate to Hong Kong's current situation.

This chapter examines the challenges in banking, monetary affairs and financial markets in the territory's transition from a colony to an SAR. The recent developments in respective areas will be examined, problems ahead discussed and solutions suggested.

BANKING SYSTEM

To any financial centres, banking system is perhaps the most important foundation because of its three interacting functions:[1]

1. Provide transaction services and correspondingly administer the payments system,

2. Play the role as administrators of the credit decision-making process and providers of backup liquidity to the economy, and

3. Take the position as transmitters of monetary policy to the economy.

Hong Kong's banking sector has a long history. The first bank appeared in 1845, just one year after Hong Kong was ceded to the British government. Since then there were more banks setting up in the territory. Nevertheless, banking in the early days was simple and mainly focused on financing businesses and individuals based in Hong Kong. Only until about two decades ago did the banking industry start to become more internationalized, more sophisticated and experience significant growth.

In 1975, Hong Kong had 74 banks and the total customer deposits and total assets of the whole banking system were just HK$36.34 billion and HK$65.60 billion respectively. As at the end of 1994, the total deposits and total assets increased to HK$1,941.71 billion and HK$7,332.37 billion respectively. Their corresponding compounded annual growth rates for the period were as high as 23% and 28%. Now we have 180 licensed banks, of which 149 are overseas incorporated, coming from 27 countries. Of the world's top 100 banks ranked by assets, about 80 have a presence in Hong Kong. Over 72% of the banking sector's balance sheet is in foreign currencies.

Many factors can explain this impressive performance. Among other things, these include good business infrastructure (in terms of credible legal and judiciary systems, simple and low tax framework, efficient transport and telecommunication links, and high education standard of the workforce etc.), good business efficiency and the government's *laissez-faire* policy.[2] The attraction of Mainland China as a potential market, following its economic reform and open door policy, has also induced many international banks to have establishment here. In addition, the emergence of the Asia-Pacific region both as an economic zone on its own and as an engine of growth for the developed world, has also attracted many overseas banks to establish here in pursuit of the financing business for their customers.

Undoubtedly, the banking system is well-established in the territory but it must be mindful that past success does not necessarily guarantee a promising future. Hong Kong cannot afford to be complacent. To maintain our competitive edge, efforts on certain aspects must continue to meet future challenges.

❏ *Maintenance of High Supervisory Standards*

First and foremost is the maintenance of high supervisory standards. Since Hong Kong is a small open economy, traditionally it is easily to be affected by overseas disturbances. In the approaches to 1997, there is still uncertainty ahead and some disturbances would be inevitable. To ensure the safety and stability of the banking system, an effective banking supervision system is a must. Indeed, Hong Kong has seen much banking upheavals in the past decades. One of the major common factors behind the past banking crises is that supervisory standards were not high enough to detect and monitor risk. This is sufficient to indicate the importance of an effective supervisory system.

Fortunately, the regulatory authority could learn the lessons from the past experience. After the banking crisis in the mid-1980s, the regulatory authority has been making great efforts in improving the standards. Through amending the Banking Ordinance and issuing guidelines and circulars, several areas have been significantly improved to reduce the systemic risks in the banking system. The major works that have been done in recent years include:

1. imposing requirements on the ownership and management of authorized institutions;
2. using new techniques (such as off-site reviews and prudential meetings with senior management) to enhance the effectiveness and efficiency of the supervisory process;
3. cooperating with banks' internal and external auditors in strengthening banks' internal control and risk management;
4. implementing the Basle framework on capital adequacy and off-balance-sheet activities;
5. following international supervisory practice by issuing guidelines on regulating foreign exchange risk, money laundering and risk management of financial derivatives activities and so on;
6. improving banks' asset quality by
   i.   revising the approach to supervision of liquidity,
   ii. tightening the limits for credit exposures covered by the letter of comfort,
   iii. supervising large exposures to reduce concentration risk,
   iv. monitoring the adequacy of provisions made by institutions for country risk,

    v. implementing a loan classification system,

    vi. monitoring residential mortgage lending and so on.

In addition, to ensure a high degree of professionalism and continuity in monetary management and banking supervision in the lead-up to 1997 and beyond, the Offices of the Exchange Fund and the Commissioner of Banking were merged to become the Hong Kong Monetary Authority (HKMA) on 1 April 1993. With the setting up of the HKMA, it is believed that more expertise and professionalism may be available to further improve the regulatory standards.

From the recent background against which Hong Kong's supervisory system develops, it is apparent that the territory is moving in the right direction and the supervisory standards are being upgraded to internationally recognized level. If there is no U-turn of policy, there are reasons to be optimistic about the future of banking supervision. Nevertheless, in the future development of our supervisory standards, some points must be kept in mind:

1. Be open-minded and up-to-date as financial markets are ever-changing and dynamic.
2. Strengthen ties with international banking supervisors and keep Hong Kong in the mainstream of world supervisory practice in order to consolidate Hong Kong as a banking centre with sound supervision.
3. Regulate but avoid over-regulation. The job of bank supervisors is not to tell the banks how to run their business but to provide a level playing-field, with an effective supervisory framework that would encourage initiative and innovation.

❏ *Enhancement of Fair Competition*

Besides supervisory standards, another noteworthy point is the fair competition and transparency of Hong Kong's banking market. Although the government has been advocating a "free market" policy on bank licensing, its policy on the operations of the banking market is not as free as it claims.

The Clearing Role of the HSBC

The most prominent example is the role played by the largest note-issuing bank, the Hong Kong and Shanghai Banking Corporation (HSBC). The

HSBC is a private profit-making commercial bank with a long presence in Hong Kong. Owing to the territory's peculiar historical circumstances and institutional structure, a significant range of central banking functions has been the preserve of the HSBC. The HSBC, as a quasi-central bank, has enjoyed many privileges. Although most of its central banking functions have now been handed over since the implementation of the New Accounting Arrangements on 18 July 1988 and following the establishment of the HKMA, the HSBC still enjoys certain powers and privileges. For example, it still shares with the other two note-issuing banks on a permanent rotating basis the Chairmanship and Vice-Chairmanship of the Hong Kong Association of Banks (HKAB). It is also the Management Bank of the Clearing House of the HKAB.

The HSBC's quasi-central bank status and other privileges have attracted criticisms from its competitors and scholars. In particular, the HSBC's ability to access confidential information on other banks through its clearing role has been a source of irritation to other HKAB members. For a commercial bank to take care of central banking functions, it inevitably creates the problem of conflict of interest, favouritism and induces concentration of power. Indeed, such arrangement is quite inconsistent with the government's free market philosophy. If Hong Kong wants to maintain a competitive banking environment and does not want to ruin its image of free competition in the lead-up to the 1997 hand-over, further action on phasing out the HSBC's clearing role is necessary. A more appropriate arrangement would be having all banks clearing through the HKMA.

Interest Rate Deregulation

Another example of unfair competition in the local banking market is the interest rate regulation by the HKAB. To avoid the recurrence of a feverish "interest rate war" which led to a banking crisis in the early 1960s, an Interest Rate Agreement (IRA) was introduced by the HKAB in 1964. This agreement allowed the HKAB to set rules regarding the maximum interest rates on Hong Kong dollar deposits of less than $500,000 having a maturity below 15 months.

The regulation of deposit interest rates has aroused heated debate. The arguments for maintaining the IRA are mainly on the grounds of currency stability and bank stability. Proponents (mainly the HKAB and the regulators) argue that the IRA can be used as a monetary tool to stabilize the linked rate and as a measure to guard against emergency or risky investments by banks arising from the cutthroat competition in deposits.

These arguments have been critically refuted by advocates of deregulation (e.g. the Consumer Council). They point out that the IRA which applies only to small Hong Kong dollar deposits is itself no longer an effective monetary tool since the introduction of the 1988 New Accounting Arrangements and the subsequent monetary restructuring. In addition, the key factor to bank stability is effective and vigilant supervision rather than anti-competitive restrictions.

Indeed the existence of the IRA poses several major problems. First, the IRA restricts price competition in the deposit markets. This produces favouritism to those local banks with a large branch network in competing for deposits and creates unfair competition in the industry. These can be evidenced by the phenomenon of high concentration of Hong Kong dollar deposits on few big banks. Second, for the sake of self-interest, deposit rates are generally set by banks at an unreasonably low level. In almost all time, deposit rates are below inflation. With a negative real interest rate, it results in some macroeconomic problems such as discouraging the desire of savings, bringing about inflationary pressure to the economy, distorting resource allocation in the economy, and inducing switch of Hong Kong dollar deposits to foreign currency deposits, thus putting pressure on the linked rate. Finally, the negative real interest rate is also inequitable to small depositors because only small deposits are being regulated.

In response to repetitive lobbying by the IRA's opponents, the government eventually accepts the recommendations of the Consumer Council and proceeds with deregulation of time deposits governed by the IRA. Starting from October 1994, the IRA would be removed in four stages. So far two stages have been implemented, with the first on 1 October 1994 and the second on 3 January 1995. At the time of writing, only deposits with a maturity of 7 days or less are still subject to the interest rate cap. As expected, after partial deregulation, there is a rise in the deposit rates and a general shift of deposits from IRA-governed deposits to deregulated deposits, both within individual bank and among the banks themselves.

Although a timetable has been set for the deregulation which is now in process, resistance still remains. As the abolition of the IRA induces competition which inevitably would push up banks' funding costs and remove the favouritism enjoyed by some large banks, those banks with vested interest are extremely reluctant to see it completely removed. In mid-March

1995, the HKAB raises its old concern that deregulation of the very short-term deposits and particularly 24-hour call deposits will have a destabilizing effect on the deposit structure of individual banks. This concern is quickly echoed by the conservative HKMA. Without any public consultation, the HKMA announced to defer the implementation of stage 3 from 1 April to 1 October 1995 on the grounds that: (1) significant deposit migration has been detected and is likely to cause instability in the banking system; and (2) the distortion of statistics for January by some other factors makes data less reliable for judging the effect of deregulation.

The deferment came as a great surprise to the public. Although on the one hand the deferment may be taken as an indication of the regulator's prudence (if not conservatism), it also raises many queries on the other hand, for example:

1. Is the HKMA's decision made by itself or influenced by the HKAB? Does the HKMA concern only about banks' interest or also take into account the public depositors' interest?

2. What, and how accurate, is the HKMA's original estimation of the effect of deregulation on banks' behaviour and deposit structure? How significant is the actual deposit migration out of its expectation?

3. Why does significant deposit migration from some banks to another take place? Does this mean that some banks are not so competitive as other? If so, why is it necessary to delay the deregulation process to help these banks at the expense of small depositors?

4. If deregulation of small Hong Kong dollar deposit rates may result in deposit migration which could jeopardize the stability, why is there no instability caused by competition in the unregulated deposits (e.g. large amount Hong Kong dollar deposits, foreign currency deposits) which has existed for quite a long time?

5. If the timetable of deregulation can suddenly be changed regardless of the fact that it is agreed by both the HKMA and the HKAB, how credible will the two parties' future promises be?

To a regulator, impartiality and being responsible to the public are the most basic doctrine. "Too frequent policy reversal" or "saying one thing but doing another" will certainly damage its credibility and affect the effectiveness of its operations. The regulators should learn their lesson from the handling of BCCHK (Bank of Credit and Commerce Hong Kong) event and be mindful not to repeat the wrongdoing again. To avoid negative suspicion and the accusation of unfair competition, the HKMA should take a more impartial approach to speed up the removal of any unfair and anti-competition restrictions.

❏ *Improvement of Transparency*

In many cases, suspicion results from insufficient disclosure of information. One way to reduce or avoid suspicion is to enhance market transparency. This can be done by increasing the transparency of both the regulators' and the banks' operations. Since the setting up of the HKMA, both aspects show significant progress. As Hong Kong's central bank, the HKMA follows international central banks' practices to make clear "open, fair and transparent" as its philosophy of operations. To enhance the transparency of its operations, the HKMA adopts the following measures:[3]

1. To conduct its money market operations openly and announce them regularly on market screens.
2. To brief frequently the press, interested parties, international specialists and Legislative Council panels on its activities.
3. To produce a quarterly bulletin since November 1994.
4. To consult extensively with the banking community and other professional bodies before taking some actions.

As regard increasing the transparency of banks' operations, the HKMA has been working closely with the banking industry, the Stock Exchange of Hong Kong (SEHK) and the Securities and Futures Commission (SFC). Based on the recommendations jointly developed with these parties, the HKMA issued a *Best Practice Guide on Financial Disclosure by Authorized Institutions* on 28 September 1994. This guide requires banks to provide greater transparency on actual profitability, the nature and quality of earnings, the cost structure, the nature and quality of assets, the sources of funding and inner reserves. It is applicable to all locally incorporated authorized institutions in respect of the annual accounts for their financial years ending on or after 31 December 1994.

The disclosure guide represents a big step towards improving the transparency of Hong Kong banks' performance and financial strength. Its implementation may bring Hong Kong's standard of disclosure closer to that of other major financial centres and improve the perception of local banking system by the international financial community. This will benefit not only the whole banking system but also individual institutions which, with more information disclosed, may tap into the international capital markets in a cost-effective manner.

In short, the move in improving transparency is quite satisfactory but should still be going further. For instance, the disclosure guide should be made as a statutory document to ensure adequate disclosure of financial information in the annual audited accounts of all authorized institutions. In addition, further disclosure on balance sheet inner reserves, segmental analysis, off-balance sheet exposures, and maturity profile of assets etc. is also necessary. These would be another important job for the HKMA in the coming years.

❏ *Development of Payment System*

The above moves are necessary to maintain the integrity of Hong Kong's banking system but may not be sufficient. To ensure banking stability, one more urgent thing that needs to be done is to control payment system risks by developing a Real Time Gross Settlement (RTGS) system.

Hong Kong's present payment system was established in 1981. It is run by the HKAB's Clearing House and since inception the HSBC has been appointed by the HKAB to manage the Clearing House. Licensed banks are required to maintain their clearing accounts with the Management Bank or any other nine settlement banks.[4] The nine settlement banks also clear their transactions with the HSBC. Since 17 July 1988, the New Accounting Arrangements requires the Management Bank to maintain an account with the Exchange Fund in which the balance must not be less than the net clearing balance of the rest of the banking system.

Although the present set-up have been run very efficiently, it is still subject to the criticism of favouritism to the HSBC.[5] More importantly, the existing system has only next-day finality of settlement. As there is a time-lag between payment and finality of settlement, this exposes the banking system to several payment risks such as liquidity risk, market risk and systemic risk. To control these payment risks and eradicate the subsequent potential threat, Hong Kong must follow the latest international standards to develop a RTGS system. With this system, payments may be settled continuously on an individual order basis (without netting debits with credits) across the books of the central bank. In other words, finality of settlement is achieved irrevocably and instantaneously on a real time basis as and when a payment order is initiated. This would definitely reduce payment risks and thus be beneficial to our competitiveness as an international financial centre.

One point worth noting is the urgency of the development of RTGS. As perceived by the HKMA, Hong Kong's current system is now left behind most major financial centres which are already on RTGS or are moving quickly towards it. The international consensus is to implement RTGS as soon as possible and develop a global link-up of payment systems in the not distant future. In addition, the People's Bank of China is also setting up a national automated payment system with RTGS which is expected to be available by late 1996. If Hong Kong cannot improve its payment system by that time, it would face intense competition from other financial centres and miss the possibility of the global link-up.

As an important step to secure Hong Kong as an international centre in financial transactions, making RTGS a reality is indispensable and must be on the top agenda. By taking up the job and running the accounts for final settlement, the HKMA will not only enhance Hong Kong's competitive edge, but also greatly reinforce its central banking functions, both in improving its regulation of banks and in providing intra-day liquidity to the system. The central bank will be able to gain access to information on banks' fund movements which will in turn facilitate the regulation of the banks.

MONETARY AFFAIRS

An effective and efficient banking system is crucial to consolidate Hong Kong's position as an international financial centre but it is not the only condition to meet. Another important part of a financial centre is monetary management: how to determine a monetary objective and how to conduct monetary policy to achieve it?

❏ *Monetary Objective*

Generally, the prime objective of monetary policy is to maintain the stability of domestic currency which may be measured in terms of the internal value (the price level) of the currency or its external value (the exchange rate). With internal and/or external currency stability, it would create a stable environment for achieving other macroeconomic objectives (e.g. economic growth, high employment etc.). To achieve the objective of currency stability, central banks need to manipulate the availability and the price of money by implementing monetary policy measures such as open market operations, reserve requirements, discount window and moral suasion.

In Hong Kong, the macro-monetary policy objective is defined as stability in the external value of the Hong Kong dollar, i.e. the maintenance of exchange rate stability within the framework of the linked rate system. Starting from October 1983, the exchange rate of the Hong Kong dollar has been fixed at 7.80 to the U.S. dollar through the note-issuing mechanism. To issue Hong Kong dollar notes, note-issuing banks are required by law to submit U.S. dollar at the fixed rate to the Exchange Fund in return for its Certificates of Indebtedness as backing for the banknotes they issue. As such, Hong Kong dollar banknotes are backed by U.S. dollar held in the Exchange Fund.

The linked rate system evolved under a unique political and historical circumstance. It was originated in 1983 as a defensive measure to tackle the problem of continuing depreciation of Hong Kong dollar induced by the commencement of the Sino-British negotiations on the issue of sovereignty over Hong Kong. Given its accidental nature, people have been cautious about its sustainability since its inception. In many times when there are problems in economic conditions (e.g. high inflation and soaring property prices), the linked system often became a target for blame and numerous suggestions would appear to alter or to replace the current system.

Should the linked rate system be maintained through the transition period in 1997 and beyond? This is still a hot topic for debate even the system has been in operation for more than eleven years. Opponents of the system indicate that its major inherent weakness is inflexibility in monetary management. With a fixed exchange rate to the U.S. dollar, Hong Kong loses its monetary independence to adjust its domestic economy. In addition, its currency and economy depend on very much the performance of the U.S. dollar and the U.S. economy. When the U.S. dollar gets stronger, the Hong Kong dollar also get firmer and vice versa. The performance of the U.S. dollar has a direct effect on our local economy, and so does the impact of the U.S. government policy and its economic and political cycle.

The advocates refute this by arguing that Hong Kong is just a small open economy and inevitably influenced by external disturbances (in particular those from its major trading partners like the U.S.). With external factors often play a dominant role, it is impractical to expect that Hong Kong can have an independent monetary policy. Indeed, nowadays global economies have been increasingly integrated and international financial markets are more interdependent. Hong Kong is also in the middle of political transition. To a great extent, exchange rate stability may minimize the adverse impact of external shocks on domestic prices, output and employment.

The track record of the system seems to provide evidence in support of its value to the economy. Since adopting the linked rate system in 1983, Hong Kong economy has prospered both in terms of high per capita GDP growth (over 5%) and low unemployment (about 2%). In this period, the system has also demonstrated its vitality in weathering many disturbances (such as the October crash of 1987, the Gulf War, the June 4 incident in 1989, the BCCI [Bank of Credit and Commerce International] fiasco in 1991, the ERM [Exchange Rate Mechanism] crisis of 1992 and so on). The fluctuation of market rates never exceeded 1% in either direction. These prove that the linked system is beneficial to the prosperity and stability of the local economy.

Furthermore, the linked rate system also provides a clear and singular objective for monetary management, i.e. exchange rate stability. This is important because the objective is not only appropriate for Hong Kong's circumstances in view of an externally oriented economy in political transition, but also simple to understand and easy to operate. As a widely accepted principle in monetary management, a single clearly defined monetary policy objective, if consistently adhered to, would strengthen credibility of the policy and therefore facilitate the effectiveness and efficiency of its implementation.

The linked rate system has been in operation with a proven record of success for more than eleven years. After this long period of time, it is well accepted and understood by people from all walks of life. The public has believed in the government's commitment to the link and the link's ability to withstand shocks. The whole economy has adjusted to the link. These confidence, familiarity and adaptability lay a very good foundation for a policy objective to be implemented. In the light of these favourable conditions, it appears that maintaining exchange rate stability within the linked rate system is a good choice as Hong Kong's monetary objective and would contribute to a smooth transfer of sovereignty over Hong Kong.

❑ *Monetary Management*

Exchange rate stability provides a clear objective for our monetary management. Monetary development and measures has been directed towards maintaining the external value of the currency. On 1 April 1993, the HKMA was set up to be in charge of the following functions:[6]

1. To maintain currency stability, within the framework of the linked exchange rate system, through sound management of the Exchange Fund, monetary policy operations and other means deemed appropriate;

2. To ensure the safety and stability of the banking system through the regulation of banking business and the business of taking deposits, and the supervision of authorized institutions; and

3. To promote the efficiency, integrity and development of the financial system, particularly payment and settlement arrangements.

The establishment of the HKMA provides an institutional safeguard for the continuation of the linked system and ensures a high degree of professionalism and continuity in monetary management. To achieve the objective of exchange rate stability, the HKMA have also taken several measures to develop a mechanism to influence the availability and the price of money, or more precisely the level of interbank liquidity and the level of interbank interest rates. Some prominent examples are the introduction of the Liquidity Adjustment Facility (LAF) in June 1992, the extension of the Exchange Fund bill programme to 3-year and 5-year notes in October 1993 and September 1994 respectively, the widening of the scope of eligible securities for discounting under the LAF since 1994, and so on. These measures, together with the New Accounting Arrangements introduced in 1988, provide an effective framework for managing interbank liquidity.

Now the HKMA has many tools available to vary the level of interbank liquidity to ensure that money market conditions are consistent with the maintenance of exchange stability under the lined exchange rate system. These include:[7]

1. direct borrowing and lending of Hong Kong dollar in the interbank market,

2. sale and purchase of foreign currencies against Hong Kong dollar,

3. issue, sale or purchase of Exchange Fund Bills and Notes,

4. transfer of funds between the Treasury and the Exchange Fund.

To sum up, now Hong Kong has developed an effective system and mechanism for monetary management that is robust enough to withstand shocks and to meet future challenges. The development and availability of many monetary armouries increases the public confidence which is the cornerstone of any stable and sound financial system. This provides a favourable condition for the smooth transition in the approach to 1997. Looking ahead, the territory still needs the exchange rate stability as its monetary objectives. The government should keep the linked rate system and maintain discipline on policy. In addition, developing a good monetary relationship and cooperation with China, and minimizing the scope for political interference in monetary management would be beneficial to our monetary management.

DEVELOPMENTS OF FINANCIAL MARKETS

Financial markets are an important component of a financial system. They refer to the mechanism in which financial transactions are concluded and funds are channelled from one party to another. With financial markets, surplus funds can avoid to be left idle and can be invested for profitable use. Firms in need for funds for operations may also raise capital in financial markets. Efficient financial markets are essential to satisfy the supply of and demand for loanable funds and assure effective use of resources in an international financial centre.

❏ *Stock Market*

To gain recognition as an international financial centre, Hong Kong cannot neglect the development of its financial markets. The territory has long history in some of its financial markets. The oldest and also better-established market is the stock market which appeared as early as 1891. After more than a century of development, now the stock market which is operated by the SEHK is recognized as one of the leading markets in the world and attracting wide international interest.[8]

The factors attributed to the stock market's success are many (e.g. sound accounting system, no capital gain tax, etc.).[9] But the prerequisite is the market's openness to foreign investors. The absence of capital control and discrimination policies against foreigners provide an open environment to attract foreign investors. In fact, these are also the territory's competitive edge over its neighbouring countries.

Another competitive edge is the introduction of H shares in the local market. The listing of H shares provides a channel for Mainland enterprises to raise capital in Hong Kong and for foreign investors to invest in Mainland China. This further consolidates Hong Kong's position as a bridge for attracting foreign capital to China. Moreover, in the past few years, the local stock market has been undergoing a series of reform measures (such as the establishment of the SFC, the implementation of the central clearing and settlement and automatching, and the revision of the regulatory framework and so on) to promote market integrity and enhance investors protection. With these developments, Hong Kong has more edges to compete with other stock markets.

To prepare for the challenges in face of 1997, Hong Kong must make ongoing efforts to protect investors and market integrity. Illegal trading activities (e.g. rat trading, front running and insider trading) should be further eradicated and unethical practices prevented. More communication and cooperation with China's regulatory authorities would be useful in increasing the transparency of those companies with strong China background and reducing the loopholes for unethical trading. In addition, the SEHK should continue to expand its competitive edge of China factor. Increasing the number of China's state enterprises listed in Hong Kong and enlarging the scope of their instruments (e.g. bonds) listed would certainly benefit the territory's roles as a gateway to China for the world and as a channel for China-incorporated enterprises to access to international markets. Nevertheless, in this process, it must be mindful that quality is still the most important and should not be sacrificed for quantity.

❏ *Interbank and Foreign Exchange Markets*

Besides the stock market, another two well-developed markets in Hong Kong are interbank market and foreign exchange market. The interbank market is a market for short-term unsecured loans between deposit-taking institutions. It enables participating banks to adjust their asset portfolios and balance their funding positions, thus enhancing the efficiency of their fund management. As a market facilitating the exchange of one currency for another, the foreign exchange market strengthens the link between domestic and foreign financial markets. In addition, these two markets also provide channels for the HKMA to conduct monetary operations in pursuit of the objective of exchange rate stability.

Generally, the two markets have performed quite satisfactorily in the past decades. Now the average daily turnover of the Hong Kong dollar interbank market is above HK$80 billion, about one-third of which are the transactions with banks outside Hong Kong. Though there is no statistics about the foreign currency components of the interbank market, the size of this Hong Kong dollar component indicates its importance to the banks both in Hong Kong and overseas. Moreover, according to a global survey conducted in April 1992, Hong Kong's foreign exchange market also had an average daily net turnover of US$61 billion and was ranked the sixth largest market in the world.

As with the territory's banking system and other established markets, there are many factors behind the success of these two markets. In addition to those factors mentioned earlier (such as a well-established financial infrastructure, excellent communication, the government's positive non-interventionism, etc.), three specific factors are worth noting: an advantageous time zone, no capital control and a banking centre. The time zone is a natural factor which cannot be changed. As long as the other two factors can be maintained, the future development of these two markets appears to be optimistic.

❑ *The Hong Kong Dollar Debt Market*

It is undoubtable that the three established markets mentioned above have been contributing to the recognition of Hong Kong as an international financial centre and would continue to do so in the future. Nevertheless, there is more concern about how to develop other financial markets and make the territory to be more broad based (in terms of the variety of financial products) in order to keep Hong Kong in line with other major financial centres.

One focus of such concern is on the Hong Kong dollar debt market. Until fairly recently, Hong Kong's debt market was not well developed because of the lack of government securities as a benchmark, the lack of a local clearing system, some regulatory problems on minimum denomination requirement and on tax, and so on. The situation started to reverse in the 1990s as a result of a change in the government's attitude.

In order to introduce high-quality paper that would help manage domestic liquidity and to generate a benchmark yield curve for Hong Kong dollar debt paper, the Exchange Fund launched its maiden issue of the 91-day bills in March 1990. Afterwards the maturity profile of the issues have been significantly enhanced. In addition to 91-day maturity, now there are also 182-day and 364-day Exchange Fund Bills, and 2-year, 3-year and 5-year Exchange Fund Notes, all together providing a Hong Kong dollar benchmark yield curve for the debt market. At the end of 1994, the outstanding bills and notes amounted to HK$53.8 billion. The daily turnover on average is over HK$20 billion. As reflected by these statistics, there is no doubt that the Exchange Fund bills and notes market, besides the interbank market, becomes another very liquid market for monetary operations and for banks to manage their liquidity.

The government's support for the market development can be seen not only from launching the Exchange Fund bills and notes programme, but also from its other measures. On 8 June 1992, the LAF was introduced to facilitate banks to manage their liquidity. Under the LAF, banks are allowed to use the Exchange Fund bills and notes as securities for entering into Sale and Repurchase Agreement (Repo) with the then Exchange Fund and its successor, the HKMA. In March 1994, the scope of eligible securities for Repo under the LAF have been widened to cover instruments issued by supranational institutions (e.g. World Bank and Asian Development Bank), by banks with a credit rating of A3 or higher from Moody's, and by corporations rated at A2 or higher. The expansion of eligible securities further stimulates banks' demand for Hong Kong dollar debt papers, which in turn stimulates more local large companies to seek international ratings and to issue more papers.

In addition, the HKMA also operates a Central Moneymarkets Unit (CMU) for clearing the Exchange Fund bills and notes. This computerized book-entry clearing service was further extended to other Hong Kong dollar debt paper in January 1994.

The government's active support is also matched by other conditions. For instance, in July 1994, the SEHK simplified the rules of listing debt instruments. This reflects the SEHK's initiatives in developing Hong Kong as a centre of listed debt securities and bringing the rules more in line with that of international requirements. In 1995, the two international rating agencies, Moody's Investors Service and Standard & Poor's, come to set up an office in Hong Kong. It would promote the recent trend of more blue chip companies seeking a credit rating for gaining access to the debt market.

It is obvious that the Hong Kong dollar debt market has been developed very rapidly in recent years and the foundations have been laid for more Hong Kong dollar debt issuance and for more international participation in the Hong Kong market. Further developments should focus on deepening and broadening the debt market through the following ways:

1. Widen the issuer profile by attracting more local, mainland and overseas issuers to issue debt papers.
2. Extend the maturity profile by issuing the Exchange Fund notes of longer maturity, say ten years, to develop a comprehensive yield curve.
3. Develop a liquid market for asset-backed securities by providing an effective operating framework.
4. Enlarge the base of investors to non-financial institutions and individuals.
5. Develop an active secondary market for good-quality papers other than those eligible securities.

❏ *Derivatives Market*

Another rapidly growing market in recent years is the derivatives market. Derivatives are bilateral contracts or payments exchange agreements whose value derive from the value of an underlying asset or underlying reference rate or index. If properly used, derivatives can offer the advantages of lowering funding costs, diversifying funding sources, enhancing yields, broadening the range of investment alternatives and being a means of protection or hedging against sharp price movements.

In Hong Kong, the derivatives market had a late start in development and is small in size as compared with other major financial centres like New York, London and Tokyo. Nevertheless, its recent development is surprisingly rapid.

For exchange-traded derivatives, the first instrument is the Hang Seng Index (HSI) futures introduced in May 1986. Then came with Hong Kong dollar interest rate futures in February 1990, HSI options in March 1993 and stock futures in March 1995. Coming up in the near future includes stock options, one-day rolling currency futures and currency options. In terms of turnover, HSI futures is the most active product and its average daily turnover is about 22,000 contracts, reflecting a notional value of HK$9.35 billion.

Not only the exchange-traded derivatives are growing in variety and in turnover, but also are the derivatives in the "over-the-counter" (OTC) market. Though there is still no comprehensive statistics published for this market, its activities can be reflected by a survey conducted for the banking sector by the HKMA in 1994. Several points are revealed in the survey. First, the OTC derivatives market is highly concentrated. Only one or two of the local banks and some of the branches of foreign banks are big players. Second, the OTC derivatives are largely foreign exchange and interest rate-related. Third, as at the end of September 1994, the notional amount of these derivatives is over HK$15 trillion, more than double the total assets (about HK$7 trillion) of the local banking system.

Though using notional principal as a measure of activity in derivatives is subject to the problem of double-counting and does not necessarily measure the risk exposures associated with derivatives,[10] it can to a certain extent reveal how significant the market development is. The fast development in the derivatives market is not specific to Hong Kong but is a global phenomenon. It arouses wide attention and concerns on the risks involved, in particular those of supervisory authorities.[11] Because OTC derivatives are customized transactions, they often assemble risks in complex ways. As Yam points out,[12]

> the growing complexity of derivative instruments has made the risks involved, though of familiar nature, difficult to measure, monitor and therefore manage. The rapid development of financial engineering backed by the increasing use of sophisticated statistical models for pricing and valuation purposes is creating a widening knowledge gap on derivatives products and their risks.

The knowledge gap is not just between the originating financial institutions and their customers, but also between the institutions and the regulators. With this knowledge gap, it presents a potential threat to the stability of this market and its participating institutions, in particular banks. The challenge for regulators is how to promote safe and proper use of derivatives for the financial markets to be able to reap the benefits of these powerful inventions without giving rise to excessive and unnecessary risks. A balanced approach must be taken to protect both financial institutions and the ultimate users of the product without stifling market innovation.

By the concerted efforts of regulatory bodies (such as the Basle Committee, the Group of Thirty and the International Organization of Securities Commissions [IOSCO], etc.), progress is being made in developing a framework for managing the risks of derivatives. Some consensus have been obtained on the use of the following framework for risk management:

1. Proper risk management systems set up by financial institutions for derivatives business,
2. Sufficient capital held by participating financial institutions against the risks in derivatives activities,
3. Recognition of risk-reducing arrangements such as bilateral netting,
4. Adequate reporting and public disclosure by financial institutions of their involvement in derivatives business.

In response to the challenges posed by the rapid development of derivatives, the HKMA follows the international approaches to set up the local regulatory framework. It adopts in full the supervisory approach proposed on the Basle Committee and published the *Risk Management Guidelines for Derivatives* in December 1994. A further guideline on the operational aspect is expected to issue this year.

The prompt actions taken by the HKMA to follow in line with the best practices adopted in other major financial centres is encouraging. Nevertheless, given the individuality and complexity of derivatives transaction, the supervision is definitely a tough task. The four approaches mentioned above just provide a clear direction for further concrete actions. More still need to be done to obtain effective regulation that can protect both financial institutions and the ultimate users of the product without stifling market development.

CONCLUSION

It is a great concern whether Hong Kong will continue to be an international financial centre in its transition to 1997 and beyond, as this is crucial to the stability and prosperity of the territory's future economy.

This chapter discussed the issue by exploring the recent developments and future challenges in banking, monetary affairs and financial markets. It is encouraging that in many aspects, the recent developments have laid a foundation for the territory to meet the future challenges. Basically, the territory has developed an effective framework and mechanism in the functioning of the monetary and financial systems, and also gained global confidence in its policies and capability. To maintain our status as an international financial centre in the years ahead, it is necessary to keep and enhance our merits while removing our weaknesses. In this connection, the following principles must be implemented:

1. Adopt free market policy.
2. Allow no party to have favouritism and privileges.
3. Avoid over-regulation.
4. Be accountable to the public.
5. Be forward-looking and take innovative and professional approach in market development.
6. Follow the highest international standards in supervision.
7. Increase operational transparency.
8. Keep financial systems and markets from political interference.

NOTES

1. J. F. Sinkey, *Commercial Bank Financial Management* (Maxwell: Macmillan, 1992), p. 19.
2. The factors mentioned are also those behind the territory's success as an international financial centre.
3. Hong Kong Monetary Authority, *Annual Report 1993*, p. 13.
4. The other nine settlement banks are Bank of China, Bank of East Asia, Belgian Bank, Citibank, Overseas Chinese Banking Corporation, Security Pacific Asian Bank, Shanghai Commercial Bank, Standard Chartered Bank, and Wing On Bank.
5. See the discussion in the section on "the clearing role of the HSBC."
6. See Note 3, p. 11.
7. Monetary Management Department, "Management of Interbank Liquidity," *Quarterly Bulletin*, Issue No. 1 (Hong Kong: Hong Kong Monetary Authority, November 1994), p. 2.
8. As at the end of 1994, Hong Kong had 529 listed companies with a market capitalization of HK$2,085 billion. Its average daily turnover in 1994 was HK$4.364 billion. In terms of market capitalization, it was ranked the eighth largest international stock exchange.
9. See also the factors mentioned in the section on banking system for the impressive performance in the system.
10. Notional principal outstanding cannot be used as a measure of risk exposure (either credit or market risk) for three main reasons. First, it fails to account for offsetting exposures. Second, it fails to account for the differing sensitivities of the values of different contracts to changes in the value of the underlying as

transactions of various maturities are simply added together. Finally, it does not consider the different risk profiles of different types of derivatives.

11. As with the case of other financial instruments, the risks relating to derivatives transactions include credit risk, market risk, liquidity risk, operational risk and legal risk.

12. J. Yam, "Derivatives: Market Development and Risk Management," *Quarterly Bulletin*, Issue No. 2 (Hong Kong: Hong Kong Monetary Authority, February 1995), p. 32.

9

Trade and Industry: 1997 and Beyond*

Leonard K. Cheng

PAST TRENDS AND CURRENT POSITION

Three major external factors have affected the development of Hong Kong since the 1980s and will continue to exert their influences in the foreseeable future. First, despite protectionist threats that come and go, the world trading system has become increasingly more open. Second, economic growth in East and Southeast Asia has continued to exceed that in the rest of the world since the 1980s. Third, China's open door policy has led to increasingly deeper integration of its economy with the world economy.

Combining the above external factors with its geographical location and knowledge of the world market and international business, Hong Kong has not only resumed its traditional entrepôt functions in serving China and the neighbouring region, but also developed into a regional financial centre and a hub for multinational companies. Thus, in the future, imports and re-exports can be expected to expand further and the demand for business and professional services will also greatly increase.

As Hong Kong is economically integrated with South China, in particular with the Guangdong province, through foreign direct investment, it has lost much of its assembly and manufacturing activities to the latter, but has gained in activities such as applied research, design, and marketing.

* I would like to thank Abble Chu for her capable research assistance. Financial assistance provided by the Hong Kong University of Science and Technology through Grant RI92/93.BM01 is gratefully acknowledged.

Given that the factories set up by Hong Kong investors across the border tend to specialize in the intermediate steps of assembly and processing, it is not surprising that a good portion of Hong Kong's imports, domestic exports, and re-exports are related to outward processing in South China.

❑ *External Trade*

Hong Kong's external trade since 1985 is described by the aggregate statistics contained in Tables 1 and 2.[1] The figures in Table 1 represent values of trade expressed in current dollars whereas the figures in Table 2 measure the real volumes of trade.

The trade figures contained in Table 1 reveal a number of patterns and trends. First, through the entire period, exports and imports were roughly equal and grew at similar rates. Second, the growth rate of total trade exhibited short-term fluctuations: it reached a peak in 1987, declined thereafter, picked up again in 1991, but then fell again in the last three years. Third, the growth rate of domestic exports slowed down significantly after 1988, and in 1993 it experienced an absolute decline. Given that the growth rate was substantially below the rate of inflation since 1989, the real value of domestic exports started to decline in that year. Fourth, the slack in domestic exports was made up by expansion in re-exports. Domestic exports exceeded re-exports until 1987, but by 1993 the value of re-exports was close to 3.7 times that of domestic exports, and the ratio for 1994 estimated on the basis of available statistics is 4.27. As a result, changes in re-exports have come to dominate changes in total exports. The annual growth rate of re-exports since 1987 has been at least close to 20%, but that in 1994 will be substantially smaller.

Table 2 shows changes in the volume ("quantum") of external trade over the same period as in Table 1. The difference between changes in "quantum" in Table 2 and changes in "value" in Table 1 is accounted for by changes in the "unit value" (i.e. aggregate price index) of exports and imports. Despite the non-constancy of the growth rate of the unit values, the growth and decline as depicted by Table 2 are qualitatively similar to those depicted by Table 1.

Table 3 provides information about Hong Kong's external trade related to outward processing by its firms in China. The share of imports related to outward processing has increased steadily from 58.1% in 1989 to 76.2% in 1994. By comparison, the share of domestic exports to China varied more

Table 1: Hong Kong's External Trade (Million Dollars)

Year	Imports	Domestic exports	Re-exports	Total trade
1985	231,420	129,882	105,270	466,572
1986	275,954.55 (19.24)	153,983.44 (18.56)	122,546.37 (16.41)	552,484.36 (18.41)
1987	377,947.78 (36.96)	195,254.03 (26.80)	182,780.42 (49.15)	755,982.23 (36.83)
1988	498,797.94 (31.98)	217,663.88 (11.48)	275,405.29 (50.68)	991,867.11 (31.20)
1989	562,781.34 (12.83)	224,104.02 (2.96)	346,405.47 (25.78)	1,133,290.83 (14.26)
1990	642,530.41 (14.17)	225,875.47 (0.79)	413,998.66 (19.51)	1,282,404.54 (13.16)
1991	778,981.95 (21.24)	231,045.28 (2.29)	534,840.85 (29.19)	1,544,868.08 (20.47)
1992	955,294.97 (22.63)	234,123.30 (1.33)	690,829.42 (29.17)	1,880,247.69 (21.71)
1993	1,072,597.37 (12.28)	223,026.59 (−4.74)	823,223.72 (19.16)	2,118,847.68 (12.69)
1994	791,868.50 (17.00)	140,299.57 (−0.20)	599,688.32 (12.00)	1,531,856.39 —

Notes: (1) Figures in parentheses are % changes over previous year.

(2) The 1994 trade value figures are based on trade statistics up to July 1994. The percentage changes reported for 1994 are based on changes in trade in the first eleven months of the year compared with the same period in 1993. These figures were released by the Census and Statistics Department and reported in *Hong Kong Economic Journal*, 30 December 1994.

Sources: *Hong Kong Monthly Digest of Statistics*, various issues.

narrowly within the range of 72–79% and that of re-exports to China fluctuated between 40.4% and 50.3%.

The shares of domestic exports by commodity groups are reported in Table 4. The shares of clothing, textiles, metals, and jewellery have been rather stable throughout the period. That of plastics clearly has gone up,

Table 2: Trade Index of Hong Kong's External Trade (1990 = 100)

Year	Imports	Domestic exports	Re-exports
1985	43.49	65.4	29.99
1986	49.38 (13.54)	75.93 (16.10)	34.19 (14.00)
1987	65.03 (31.69)	92.12 (21.32)	49.88 (45.90)
1988	82.38 (26.68)	100.42 (9.00)	72.70 (45.75)
1989	89.71 (8.90)	100.53 (0.11)	86.20 (18.57)
1990	100 (11.47)	100 (−0.53)	100 (16.01)
1991	118.98 (18.98)	100.48 (0.48)	126.38 (26.38)
1992	145.50 (22.29)	100.60 (0.12)	162.40 (28.50)
1993	164.10 (12.78)	96.10(− 4.47)	194.30 (19.64)
1994	177.13 (7.94)	87.24 (−9.22)	206.60 (6.33)

Notes: (1) Figures in parentheses are % changes over previous year.
       (2) The 1994 figures are based on trade statistics up to July 1994.
Sources: *Hong Kong Monthly Digest of Statistics*, various issues.

Table 3: Shares (%) of Trade Related to Outward Processing in China

	1989	1990	1991	1992	1993	1994[*]
Imports from China	58.1	61.8	67.6	72.1	73.8	76.2
Domestic exports to China	76.0	79.0	76.5	74.3	74.0	72.0
Re-exports to China	43.6	50.3	48.2	46.2	42.1	40.4
Total exports to China	53.0	58.8	55.5	52.4	47.9	45.3

* The 1994 figures are based on trade statistics up to the second quarter of 1994.
Sources: *Hong Kong Monthly Digest of Statistics*, various issues.

while those of watches and clocks, baby carriages, and household electrical and non-electrical equipment have gone down. Finally, both telecommunications equipment and automatic data-processing machines exhibit fluctuations without any clear trends.

The ten biggest markets for Hong Kong's domestic exports in 1993 and their respective market shares since 1986 are given in Table 5. The identity of the top three markets (namely China, the United States [U.S.], and

Table 4: Shares (%) of Domestic Exports by Principal Commodity Groups

	1986	1987	1988	1989	1990	1991	1992[#]	1993	1994[*]
Articles of apparel and clothing accessories	33.87	33.45	30.92	32.07	31.95	32.82	32.96	32.22	31.95
Textile yarn, fabrics, made-up articles and related products	7.11	8.20	7.14	7.50	7.48	7.63	7.36	7.25	6.96
Plastics in primary and non-primary forms	0.39	0.69	1.20	1.60	2.02	2.13	1.99	2.06	2.29
Manufactures of metals	2.26	2.31	2.60	2.37	2.00	2.13	2.05	2.08	2.16
Watches and clocks	7.35	6.86	7.62	7.29	8.11	6.86	6.61	5.90	5.58
Jewellery, goldsmiths and silversmiths' wares	2.35	2.62	2.86	2.94	3.05	2.83	2.16	2.38	2.32
Automatic data-processing machines and units thereof	0.83	0.96	1.71	1.76	1.62	1.65	1.44	0.66	0.67
Household-type electrical and non-electrical equipment	3.16	2.90	2.52	1.90	1.49	1.39	0.82	0.67	0.58
Telecommunications equipment	3.82	4.10	5.10	5.28	5.61	4.97	4.69	5.42	5.15
Baby carriages, toys, games and sporting goods	7.63	6.47	4.70	3.19	2.41	2.12	1.78	1.50	1.26

Since 1992, the commodity grouping has been based on SITC R3.
* The 1994 figures are based on trade statistics up to August 1994.
Sources: *Hong Kong Monthly Digest of Statistics*, various issues.

Table 5: Market Shares (%) for Domestic Exports

	1986	1987	1988	1989	1990	1991	1992	1993	1994[*]
China	11.70	14.27	17.48	19.31	21.02	23.55	26.46	28.41	28.17
U.S.	41.71	37.29	33.48	32.20	29.38	27.21	27.59	27.03	26.66
W. Germany	7.20	7.65	7.46	7.03	7.97	8.36	6.82	6.26	5.90
Singapore	1.81	1.99	2.40	2.59	3.45	3.81	4.43	5.09	5.59
U.K.	6.44	6.61	7.13	6.53	5.97	5.93	5.36	4.83	4.66
Japan	4.03	4.86	5.25	5.81	5.35	5.05	4.70	4.34	4.61
Taiwan	1.08	1.22	1.59	1.99	2.53	2.63	2.78	2.81	2.67
Canada	3.17	2.90	2.75	2.81	2.38	2.17	2.14	2.12	1.93
The Netherlands	1.82	2.06	2.26	2.12	2.20	2.27	2.08	2.03	2.22
France	1.71	1.94	1.92	1.62	1.61	1.61	1.35	1.21	1.23

* The 1994 figures are based on trade statistics up to August 1994.
Sources: *Hong Kong Monthly Digest of Statistics*, various issues.

Germany) has remained unchanged throughout the period. As a reflection of the dynamism of the Asian developing economies, the market shares of China, Singapore, and Taiwan all showed steady increases, while that of Japan was relatively stable. The shares of the North American and European markets, with the exception of the Netherlands, all experienced declines.

Since 1993, China has replaced the U.S. as the biggest market for Hong Kong's domestic exports. However, if domestic exports related to outward processing in China are netted out, then China's shares in 1993 and 1994 were 7.39% and 7.89% respectively, a distant second to the U.S.

The major sources of Hong Kong's imports and their respective shares since 1986 are given in Table 6. The four top sources, in descending order, were China, Japan, Taiwan, and the U.S.

The major sources of imports for re-exports are given in Table 7. Both the identity and ranking of sources are similar to that of Table 6, which is not surprising because imports for re-exports were included in Table 6.

The major markets for Hong Kong's re-exports are given in Table 8. As can be seen, the major markets for Hong Kong's re-exports are identical to those for Hong Kong's domestic exports. However, the ranking of these markets differs somewhat from that of Table 5.

Table 6: Shares (%) of Imports by Source

	1986	1987	1988	1989	1990	1991	1992	1993	1994*
China	29.58	31.05	31.20	34.95	36.75	37.66	37.09	37.49	37.31
Japan	20.44	19.03	18.65	16.56	16.09	16.35	17.40	16.60	15.72
Taiwan	8.69	8.82	8.89	9.17	9.04	9.58	9.11	8.76	8.58
U.S.	8.41	8.53	8.29	8.22	8.06	7.55	7.39	7.40	7.24
S. Korea	3.98	4.49	5.26	4.52	4.38	4.49	4.62	4.50	4.69
Singapore	3.94	3.80	3.70	3.95	4.07	4.05	4.09	4.46	4.89
W. Germany	2.99	2.77	2.68	2.45	2.31	2.14	2.29	2.32	2.28
U.K.	3.39	3.10	2.59	2.30	2.20	2.12	2.01	2.00	1.99
Italy	1.60	1.63	1.61	1.76	1.69	1.51	1.55	1.67	1.85

* The 1994 figures are based on trade statistics up to August 1994.
Sources:*Hong Kong Monthly Digest of Statistics*, various issues.

Table 7: Shares (%) of Re-exports by Source

	1986	1987	1988	1989	1990	1991	1992	1993	1994*
China	42.10	46.10	47.76	54.35	58.07	59.02	58.45	57.58	56.98
Japan	15.16	13.46	13.69	11.26	10.21	10.70	12.30	13.36	13.27
Taiwan	7.08	6.94	7.70	7.78	7.31	7.80	7.88	7.85	7.68
U.S.	8.50	7.43	6.95	6.44	5.92	4.97	4.65	4.55	4.67
S. Korea	2.93	3.39	4.74	3.26	2.80	2.81	2.81	2.63	2.90
W. Germany	2.07	1.66	1.55	1.43	1.33	1.27	1.32	1.73	1.70
Singapore	0.88	0.86	0.99	1.45	1.14	1.16	1.20	1.44	1.60
U.K.	1.57	1.35	1.18	1.07	1.12	1.09	1.07	1.02	1.00
France	1.20	1.16	1.14	1.07	1.09	0.99	0.93	0.90	0.94

* The 1994 figures are based on trade statistics up to August 1994.
Sources: *Hong Kong Monthly Digest of Statistics*, various issues.

In re-exports, both by source and by destination, China is by far Hong Kong's largest trading partner. It has supplied more than 50% of Hong Kong's re-exports since 1989 and absorbed over 30% of Hong Kong's re-exports since 1986 except during the most recent contraction of the Chinese economy, namely 1989–1991.

Table 8: Shares (%) of Re-exports by Destination

	1986	1987	1988	1989	1990	1991	1992	1993	1994[*]
China	33.37	32.92	34.46	29.88	26.79	28.67	30.70	33.35	34.52
U.S.	18.25	17.76	17.97	20.79	21.20	20.72	21.50	21.91	22.14
Japan	5.45	5.35	6.32	6.43	5.89	5.53	5.42	5.36	5.48
W. Germany	2.30	3.15	3.26	3.90	5.65	6.00	4.79	4.96	4.46
U.K.	2.03	2.34	2.33	2.57	2.92	2.74	2.98	2.98	2.87
Taiwan	4.85	5.30	5.13	4.76	5.13	4.63	3.79	2.66	2.38
Singapore	4.29	3.55	3.16	3.18	3.04	2.26	2.01	2.08	2.08
S. Korea	4.77	4.91	4.27	3.83	3.14	2.74	1.97	1.89	1.82
France	0.71	0.99	1.12	1.31	1.55	1.69	1.60	1.56	1.46

* The 1994 figures are based on trade statistics up to August 1994.
Sources: *Hong Kong Monthly Digest of Statistics*, various issues.

The eight largest suppliers of Hong Kong's retained imports, i.e. imports retained for domestic consumption and input utilization rather than for re-exports, are given in Table 9. The figures provided in the table are calculated by assuming of a 25% re-exports mark-up for Chinese goods and 15% mark-up for goods supplied by other sources, following the suggestion of Sung Yun-wing.[2] Without allowing for any re-exports mark-up, the retained imports from China would have been negative since 1990, and had a 15% mark-up been used, the retained imports from China would have been negative in 1993 and 1994.[3]

The share of retained imports from Japan was the largest and remained above 20% from 1986 to 1993. In contrast, China's share was almost identical to that of Japan in 1986 and 1987, but continued to decline thereafter and reached a low of 5.89% in 1993 and ranked only sixth. The share of the U.S. increased slowly and was ranked after Japan beginning in 1992; that of Singapore also increased and by August 1994 it ranked third after the U.S. South Korea also experienced an increase in Hong Kong's market share, but all the other major suppliers had relatively stable shares. As pointed out by Sung Yun-wing, when Hong Kong became increasingly more affluent, Chinese goods were gradually pushed aside by products from the developed countries and other Asian newly industrializing economies.

Table 9: Shares (%) of Retained Imports by Source

	1986	1987	1988	1989	1990	1991	1992	1993	1994[*]
Japan	23.26	22.46	22.43	21.59	22.25	23.12	24.12	21.15	18.78
U.S.	8.18	9.08	9.20	9.77	10.19	10.63	11.15	12.03	11.19
Taiwan	9.50	9.92	9.65	10.25	10.61	11.41	10.37	9.69	9.47
Singapore	5.75	5.78	5.99	6.50	7.36	7.78	8.34	9.63	10.33
S. Korea	4.53	5.15	5.55	5.70	6.03	6.52	7.13	7.53	7.49
China	23.33	22.21	18.78	16.77	14.64	12.15	8.19	5.89	7.49
U.K.	4.44	4.26	3.76	3.55	3.37	3.42	3.34	3.62	3.59
W. Germany	3.50	3.49	3.59	3.45	3.35	3.19	3.65	3.21	3.13

* The 1994 figures are based on trade statistics up to August 1994.
Sources: *Hong Kong Monthly Digest of Statistics*, various issues.

❑ *Industry*

Apart from non-tradables such as public utilities, restaurant and catering, and personal services, Hong Kong's production is highly dependent on the world market's demand and supply. The bulk of Hong Kong's manufactured goods are for exports. When other areas become more competitive in the production of certain goods or in the performance of certain functions, the relevant productive activities in Hong Kong decline. By the same token, when new opportunities arise that can be efficiently exploited with its capabilities, Hong Kong's productive activities increase.

The manufacturing sector continued to decline, first in relative terms but eventually in absolute size as measured by output and employment. The number of persons employed by the manufacturing sector fell from its height of 892,140 in 1980, rebounded to 867,947 in 1987, but thereafter began a process of unprecedented decline. The employment in manufacturing decreased to 483,628 in 1993 and to 443,464 by June 1994. As a fraction of the labour force, it declined from 41.8% in 1986 without interruption to 21.3% in 1993 and to 19% by June 1994.

The employment shares of the major manufacturing industries are given in Table 10. Out of eleven manufacturing industries, only printing and machinery experienced increases in levels of employment and relative employment shares. For the remaining industries with declining employment

Table 10: Shares (%) of Employment in Selected Manufacturing Industries

	1986	1987	1988	1989	1990	1991	1992	1993	1994*
Food	0.86	0.87	0.80	0.80	0.80	0.86	0.84	0.81	0.80
Wearing apparel	12.73	12.05	11.19	10.48	9.17	7.98	6.82	5.63	4.42
Textiles	5.62	5.56	5.27	5.01	4.39	4.14	3.59	3.15	3.14
Paper and paper products	0.69	0.72	0.75	0.73	0.67	0.59	0.53	0.43	0.38
Printing, publishing and allied industries	1.55	1.53	1.62	1.56	1.64	1.71	1.80	1.77	1.74
Plastics products	4.24	3.64	3.17	2.62	2.25	1.75	1.40	1.07	0.86
Fabricated metal products	3.01	2.84	2.70	2.41	2.25	1.92	1.70	1.46	1.31
Machinery, equipments, apparatus, parts and components[#]	6.74	7.07	6.62	5.99	5.07	4.30	4.03	3.62	3.09
Transport equipment	0.62	0.62	0.55	0.58	0.57	0.57	0.61	0.60	0.55
Scientific, measuring & controlling equipment, and photographic & optical goods	1.88	1.79	1.67	1.50	1.44	1.21	1.02	0.84	0.74
Other manufacturing industries	1.51	1.60	1.52	1.42	1.21	1.10	1.03	0.95	0.84
Total manufacturing	41.82	40.50	37.84	34.96	31.31	27.72	24.79	21.29	18.97

* The 1994 figures are based on employment statistics up to June 1994.

From 1986 to 1991, this category was broken into two industries, namely: (1) machinery, except electrical, and (2) electrical machinery, apparatus, appliances and supplies. From 1992 onwards, this category was broken into five industries, namely: (1) office, accounting and computing machinery; (2) radio, television & communication equipment and apparatus; (3) electronic parts and components; (4) electrical appliances & houseware and electronic toys, and (5) machinery, equipments, apparatus, parts and components, not elsewhere classified.

Sources: *Quarterly Report of Employment, Vacancies and Payroll Statistics,* various issues.

shares, food and transport equipment were more stable whereas plastics and apparel experienced relatively large declines.

The contraction of the manufacturing sector was in stark contrast with the expansion of the service sector. Total employment in the service sector increased from 1,121,455 in 1986 gradually but steadily to 1,824,821 by June 1994. In relative terms, the sector accounted for 54% of total employment in 1986 but 78% in 1994!

A breakdown of the employment shares of four major types of services is given in Table 11. The first three types of services, which are more directly related to Hong Kong's entrepôt activities as well as financial and international business services, experienced faster growth than the fourth type (namely community, social and personal services), which is clearly closely related to local consumption. This trend can be expected to continue unless there is a disproportionate increase in publicly financed social services.

Theoretically it is possible that economic integration with South China may lead to an increase in demand for manufacturing-related services such as applied research and development (R & D), design, prototype development,

Table 11: Shares (%) of Employment in the Service Sector

Year	Wholesale, retail and import/export trades, restaurants and hotels	Transport, storage and communication	Financing, insurance, real estate and business services	Community, social and personal services
1986	29.96	4.77	9.39	10.07
1987	30.69	4.94	9.90	10.04
1988	32.16	5.22	10.64	10.16
1989	34.19	5.57	11.25	10.44
1990	36.29	5.81	12.10	10.92
1991	38.41	5.91	13.03	11.78
1992	40.12	6.39	13.79	11.76
1993	41.77	6.78	14.88	12.26
1994[*]	44.22	6.77	15.02	12.03

* The 1994 figures are based on employment statistics up to June 1994.

Sources: *Quarterly Report of Employment, Vacancies and Payroll Statistics*, various issues.

packaging, marketing and finance, i.e. upstream production activities and downstream marketing activities. While there are anecdotal evidence that this is happening, it is impossible to assess the situation quantitatively without relevant statistical data. It would be useful for the Industry Department to collect these data in order to have a more complete picture of the manufacturing sector that has undergone and will continue to undergo structural transformation.

PRESENT AND FUTURE ENVIRONMENT FOR WORLD TRADE

After more than seven years of negotiation, the Uruguay Round of multilateral trade negotiation finally bore fruit by the end of 1993: The "Final Act," which among other agreements included the creation of the World Trade Organization (WTO) to succeed the General Agreement on Tariffs and Trade (GATT) in 1995. This favourable development has set stage for a liberal world trade environment for at least another decade. The trading system will not only promote freer trade in goods and services, but also bring discipline to international investment to the extent that they are related to world trade. Moreover, the Organization for Economic Cooperation and Development (OECD) has started work to propose a multilateral investment agreement.

Hong Kong has been a contracting party of GATT since April 1986 and will thus be a founding member of the WTO. It will remain a separate customs territory in spite of reversion of sovereignty to China after 1997. As one of the world's staunchest free-trader and an economy that thrives on trade, Hong Kong has much to gain from a liberal trading system.

However, not everything is rosy. Under the Multi-Fibre Arrangement (MFA), Hong Kong has been and still is enjoying the quota benefits that are related to its past competitive position. Since the MFA is scheduled to be phased out over a ten-year period under the Uruguay Round agreements, the production of these products will eventually gravitate towards areas that enjoy a competitive advantage in these products now and in the future. One such area is China, so the production of clothing and textile products is expected to shift from Hong Kong to China more quickly than in the past.

Even before the quotas are completely phased out, Hong Kong may also lose from a change in origin rules by the U.S., i.e. from identifying the origin of production as the location where fabrics are cut to identifying it as the location at which they are stitched. It is possible that some of Hong Kong's quotas would become redundant before they are completely eliminated.

Given that Hong Kong's economy is now deeply integrated with China's, especially through direct investment in South China, Hong Kong's economic fortune is intertwined with that of the Chinese economy. No doubt China will be increasingly integrated with the world economy, but the road of integration certainly would be bumpy. After the U.S. decision in 1994 to de-link China's most-favoured-nation (MFN) status from the latter's human rights record, the prospect for long-term economic cooperation between the two countries looked much brighter. However, by the end of 1994, their positions about conditions under which China would be admitted to GATT or the succeeding WTO still were far apart.

According to World Bank calculations, China moved up to become the seventh largest economy in the world in 1993. In addition, China ranks about the eleventh largest trader in the world and its trade volume is fast increasing. It is, therefore, difficult to imagine that China would remain outside the WTO for too long. It is true that there is no guarantee that China's trade relationship with other countries will be smooth because of WTO membership. However, trade conflicts can be resolved within the dispute settlement procedures and mechanism provided by the WTO, rather than with the fiery and often scary ritual of imminent trade wars. As a trading post for China and the rest of the world, Hong Kong would benefit from the increased certainty and stability that come with China's admission to the WTO.

The Asia-Pacific Economic Cooperation (APEC) Forum is quickly gaining status. It is now widely regarded as one of three major trade groupings, the other two being the European Union (EU) and the North American Free Trade Area (NAFTA). As a latecomer in regional economic grouping and being more diverse in economic, cultural, and religious background, APEC is much looser in structure than the other two.

In their meeting in Bogor, Indonesia, in November 1994, leaders of the APEC economies made a declaration of common resolve. In the declaration, they committed themselves to the goal of free and open trade and investment no later than 2010 for developed economies and no later than 2020 for developing economies. While the specific details of trade and investment liberalization have yet to be spelt out in APEC's future meetings, it is quite safe to predict that liberalization will take place.

First, the member economies have already made commitments to liberalize trade under the Uruguay Round agreements. Second, trade and investment liberalization is politically easier when an economy is expanding, and the Asian developing economies are among the most dynamic in the world. The real question is to what extent the APEC economies can "accelerate the implementation of the Uruguay Round commitments" and continue the "process of unilateral trade and investment liberalization."[4]

It seems that Taiwan's direct trade links with the Mainland is only a matter of time. The short-term impact is obviously negative, but its impact on Hong Kong's long-run economic vitality could be negligible if China's foreign trade continues to expand and if Hong Kong's capabilities adapt to meet the needs of the new environment. In terms of impact on Hong Kong, direct trade links between Taiwan and the Mainland is similar to the development of coastal cities in China which may substitute for some of the entrepôt functions currently performed by Hong Kong.

PRESENT AND FUTURE DOMESTIC CAPABILITIES

The external factors suggest that Hong Kong has a bright economic future, provided that its domestic capabilities can effectively make use of the outstanding opportunities.

Irrespective of its economic benefits and drawbacks, the "linked-rate" exchange rate system would almost with certainty remain unchanged immediately past 1997 for stability reasons. By eliminating any exchange rate risk, the present exchange rate system is most conducive to international trade and investment, although it might have other undesirable economic consequences.

Hong Kong's physical capabilities on the whole seem to be adequate for the tasks it is performing, and wherever it is lacking, there are plans to build new and additional facilities. The latter include the new airport at Chek Lap Kok, additional container terminals, and improved road and rail links locally as well as with China. In addition, telecommunication is also fast developing.

As important as the physical infrastructure are Hong Kong's institutions, including the relatively clean and efficient civil service, the predictable legal system, and the prevailing business ethos. It is not clear whether the change of sovereignty would unleash an increase in corruption that would over time corrode these institutions, but the quality of the institutions must remain intact if Hong Kong is to maintain its unique status relative to other Chinese coastal cities. How to put in place a democratic political system that is acceptable to Beijing but strong enough institutionally to prevent serious corruption is a challenge for Hong Kong.

Physical infrastructure and institutions do not mean much unless the people of Hong Kong have the requisite skills and knowledge that are needed to exploit the emerging opportunities. Human capital is the key to the provision of business and professional services that meet international standards and to the generation of new technologies on which future manufacturing (not necessarily assembly) activities will depend. While Hong Kong's entrepreneurship and its firms' and workers' adaptability are important strengths, the workers' relatively low skill levels and insufficient R & D by firms are well-known weaknesses. Additional investment in higher education and technological capabilities is being made, but the effort must continue.

Hong Kong's comparative advantage has clearly shifted away from simple manufacturing and assembly functions towards services, but it does not therefore follow that Hong Kong should abandon manufacturing activities altogether. Quite the contrary, as economic integration with China continues, Hong Kong may very well link up with China's R & D resources and capability to design, produce, and market technology- and knowledge-intensive products. Once developed, an R & D infrastructure may become one of Hong Kong's sources of comparative advantage, and technological innovations will benefit Hong Kong's manufacturing as well as service sectors.

HONG KONG'S ECONOMIC FUTURE

Since the transport and communication facilities of the major Chinese coastal cities will take time to develop, Hong Kong can expect to handle an increasing volume (but probably a declining fraction) of China's exports and imports beyond the end of this century. The expansion of re-exports will be accompanied by a contraction of domestic exports. Existing manufacturing activities such as textiles and clothing, along with other simple manufacturing industries, will decline. The manufacturing activities to be retained by Hong Kong increasingly will be technology-, knowledge-, and capital-intensive, and many of them will be upstream production activities.

Overall, the loss in traditional manufacturing activities will be partially offset by an increase in new manufacturing activities. Employment in the service industries will continue to increase in absolute numbers and relative to that in manufacturing.

There has been a lot of discussions on Hong Kong's future role as a Special Administrative Region (SAR) of China. It is perhaps hard to keep these discussions from becoming self-centred, and spelling out the city's vision and aspiration can be useful in itself. However, it may be counter-productive to take on some self-appointed roles such as integrating the Asian economies and integrating the economy of South China. In the final analysis, Hong Kong's future will depend on what it has to offer to China and to the world as well as how well it exploits opportunities as they emerge, but not what its citizens believe they "deserve" under an SAR.

Besides its geographical location and physical infrastructure, which may lose their absolute competitive edge a decade or so later as other Chinese coastal cities develop, Hong Kong's greatest comparative advantage lies in its familiarity with both Chinese and foreign cultures, values, institutions and business practices. Obviously, to serve as China's main intermediary in its economic and business dealings with the rest of the world, it should strive to improve its understanding of China, including the ability of its citizens to speak Putonghua fluently. However, it should continue to maintain and strengthen its ties to foreign countries and to emphasize the importance of English as a working language. After all, Hong Kong cannot be expected to be more Chinese than other Chinese cities, and without the familiarity with foreign practices and world markets, its value to China may be confined to its own geographical location and physical facilities.

There is some concern that Hong Kong may become a second-class Shanghai if China's were to follow a biased policy in favour of Shanghai and against Hong Kong, including hostile containment and dismemberment of Hong Kong's current functions, i.e. distribution of these functions to other Chinese coastal cities. Unless Beijing sees Hong Kong as a serious political threat, this doomsday scenario is highly unlikely, for it would have repeated the same mistake made in the case of post-liberation Shanghai.

Suspicion of and hostility towards Shanghai, the former capitalist paradise, were partly responsible for the policy that effectively turned the most important international commercial centre in the Far East into a dull and worn-out industrial city. Given that China's open door policy is a key element of the country's economic reform, China understands the vital role played by Hong Kong both as an intermediary of foreign trade and investment and as a window to learn about international business and legal practices. However, nobody should doubt Beijing's resolve to ignore Hong Kong's economic benefits if the latter presents itself as a serious political threat to the central government.

Thus, in its effort to put in place a democratic governmental structure, Hong Kong should play its cards carefully. Sovereign states such as Finland have restrained themselves in order not to offend Russia or the former Soviet Union. And the influence on small countries by major powers has not been confined to countries with totalitarian governments. One needs to look no further than the relationship between the U.S. and the "banana republics" of Latin America. Throughout history, only major powers can afford to blunder in foreign policies without suffering disastrous consequences. Small nations, in contrast, must learn to steer their way skilfully. There should be no illusion about the relationship between China and the future SAR, and the democrats who advocate head-on confrontation with China may be leading Hong Kong on to a very dangerous path.

After 1997, the Hong Kong SAR should seek representation in the Chinese government to protect its interest. The purpose of representation is not to lobby for special favour from the central government, as its strategic position and head-start (first-mover) advantages would be powerful aids in its competition against potential challengers from the region. Instead, its representatives should seek to prevent policies that would be detrimental to Hong Kong's long-run future by articulating the usefulness of Hong Kong to China's overall development and the complementarity between Hong Kong and other Chinese cities such as Shanghai. For instance, in financial services, it is possible for Shanghai to be the national centre while Hong Kong concentrates on international operations. From this perspective, the threat of Singapore to Hong Kong is more direct and immediate than Shanghai.

CONCERNS ABOUT STRUCTURAL TRANSFORMATION AND ARGUMENTS FOR GOVERNMENT INTERVENTION

Recently, there has been some expression of concerns about Hong Kong's "hollowing out" and "Manhattanization" as if both are undesirable and active industrial and income redistribution policies are needed to reverse the trend.[5] The concern about "hollowing out" has to do with the shifting of industrial production from Hong Kong to China and the concern about "Manhattanization" is related to the expansion of the financial sector and high-paying professional services. Both reflect the same phenomenon, namely, Hong Kong's transformation from an industrial city into one that is dominated by services.

Can the shift of industries out of Hong Kong be stopped, and at what costs? Hong Kong is not the only economy that has seen the shift of labour-intensive, land-intensive, and pollution-prone industries to less developed areas. So far, few economies (including Japan, the U.S., Taiwan, South Korea, etc.) have succeeded in stopping the trend, and the reason is simple: these economies have lost comparative advantages in those industries. If the economies are net importers of the products, then trade barriers may be thrown up to protect the domestic industries (and domestic consumers be forced to pay for the costs in the form of higher prices). If the economies are net exporters, as in the case of Hong Kong, then export subsidies and production subsidies can be used. Both tariff and non-tariff trade barriers, however, are against GATT rules and are sure to invite retaliation by other countries.

For regions that have lost their competitiveness in labour-intensive industries but have not simultaneously developed competitiveness in other industries such as financial services, say South Carolina in the U.S., they must be envious of Hong Kong's good fortune that the decline of its manufacturing sector is being offset by a booming service sector that can pay even higher salaries. Clearly, the skills needed for different industries are not identical, and retraining is necessary for adjusting to changes in the economic structure. History has taught us that countries that were reluctant to adjust to changes in comparative advantages ended up paying high prices for their short-term expediency. For a small economy such as Hong Kong, the cost of not making the necessary adjustment will not only be substantial, but also be felt rather quickly.

In short, any attempt to artificially strike a "balance" between manu-facturing and service that is not based on Hong Kong's comparative advantages would be futile and unsustainable. The suggestion that Hong Kong should strike this balance in anticipation of a slowdown of China's economy, and thus a decrease in the latter's demand for Hong Kong's services, has as much merit as the argument that Hong Kong should be careful in producing wigs because the demand for wigs is only short-lived. But if the producers are aware of the uncertainty of demand, would they not be taking the necessary caution? What is the role of the government besides broadcasting its forecast about the likely paths of the Chinese economy and their implications for Hong Kong business?

Lest the analogy goes too far, let me remark that, unlike the demand for wigs, the demand for Hong Kong's business and professional services would be long-lasting. The cyclical fluctuations in their demand is no different from those in demand for Hong Kong's traditional manufactured exports.

The concern about "Manhattanization" has to do with income distribution. In a fast-changing economy, the booming financial sector is a boon to the entire economy. But those who for whatever reasons (say age and education) fail to make the necessary adjustment and to exploit new opportunities will lose compared with the status quo. To some commentators, a large-scale income redistribution in the form of social welfare payments and progressive taxes are the answer.

It is ironic but true that two groups of people with rather different political orientations have the same inclination to urge the SAR government to pursue active industrial and income redistribution policies. As Hong Kong is going to lose its status as a British colony, the urge to ask the government to "do something" appears to be strong.

The first group consists of pro-China "think-tank" members, including those who are based in China. They are traditionally suspicious and critical of the economic policies followed by the British–Hong Kong government on the grounds that the policies were not for the good of the Hong Kong economy. So, when the British are finally dislodged from the position of power, a different set of policies should be pursued. What they ought to recognize is that the successful policies followed in Hong Kong are not entirely British, just like markets are not the monopoly of capitalist economies, an idea of Deng Xiaoping that theoretically underpins China's economic reform. Indeed, for many years Britain had followed entirely different economic policies at home, and those policies eventually turned Britain into Europe's "sick man."

The second group consists of democratic political parties in Hong Kong, which in general are in favour of expanding social welfare and instituting progressive income taxes. For them, the British government has been pursuing an economic policy that is too conservative, and has not used enough means available to the government to improve the well-being of the middle and lower classes. The transfer of sovereignty is a good opportunity to change the rules of the game in order to build a kinder and more equitable society.

Handing out other people's money is a characteristic of Western democracy. In an increasingly politicized environment, Hong Kong's politicians would be led to promise additional publicly provided benefits to gain votes. The experience of the Western countries is that economic success led to generous welfare payments and sizeable income redistribution, which over the long run damaged individual incentives to work and to take risk and led to proliferation of costly social services and government wastes, which in turn led to economic hardship and eventually voter disillusion with the politicians. In some cases, correction of abuses was done relatively quickly. But in others the economies got stuck in a hole and continued to experience stagnation while voters were divided according to their vested interests in the status quo. Does Hong Kong need to go through this cycle to learn its lesson?

Rejecting the views and policy stances of the above two groups does not imply that the government should do nothing. To be sure, the Hong Kong government is not doing nothing at the present. One may debate about the adequacy of certain policies, but it is definitely moving in the right direction in terms of investing in Hong Kong's future capabilities, including physical infrastructure, human capital, managerial and technological capabilities.[6] Investment in education, training, and retraining would be superior to giving out subsidies to promote the manufacturing sector relative to the service sector.

A rejection of Western European socialist welfare systems, which have already seen the dates of reckoning, does not imply that Hong Kong cannot provide additional assistance to those who are truly in need of assistance. However, as critics of the government's proposed Old Age Pension Scheme have pointed out, social welfare must be based on need and should never become entitlements.

In summary, the concerns about the manufacturing-service mix and the welfare of the poor can be addressed by investing in human capital and technological capabilities, and by adopting an improved welfare system for the truly needy.

NOTES

1. For an analysis of Hong Kong's trade and industry from 1980 to 1990, see Ho Yin-ping, "Trade and Industry," in *The Other Hong Kong Report 1991*, edited by Sung Yun-wing and Lee Ming-kwan (Hong Kong: The Chinese University Press, 1991), pp. 169–209.

2. Sung Yun-wing, "Trade and Industry," in *The Other Hong Kong Report 1992*, edited by Joseph Y. S. Cheng and Paul C. K. Kwong (Hong Kong: The Chinese University Press, 1992), p. 183.

3. Our calculation for 1991 has yielded $336 billion of total retained imports, which is identical to that obtained by Sung Yun-wing. However, for some reasons, our share figures for the same year differ from his.

4. Point 5 of the "APEC Economic Leaders' Declaration of Common Resolve," Bogor, Indonesia, 15 November 1994.

5. See, for examples, Ai Fang, "Hong Kong's Economy after 1997," *Hong Kong Economic Journal* (in Chinese), 15 November 1994, and Tsang Shu-ki, "The Economy," in *The Other Hong Kong Report 1994*, edited by Donald H. McMillen and Man Si-wai (Hong Kong: The Chinese University Press, 1994), pp. 125–48.

6. For an argument that direct investment in China is not a substitute for Hong Kong's human capital and technological and managerial capabilities, see Leonard K. Cheng, "Strategies for Rapid Economic Development: The Case of Hong Kong," *Contemporary Economic Policy*, XIII (January 1995), in press.

10

Labour and Employment

Ng Sek-hong

Introduction

Hong Kong is now on its threshold of political transition into a Special Administrative Region (SAR) of China when its reversion from the British rule to China's sovereignty is imminent, as by 1997. The impact of the transition process since the signing of the Sino-British Joint Declaration in 1984 has been generic (and, occasionally, dramatic) in affecting literally every walk of life in this territory. It is the purpose of this chapter to survey briefly how the labour sector has been adjusting its parameters, including employment, labour legislation, trade unionism and industrial relations, etc., in the currency of such an impetuous process during the last ten years. Hopefully, such a cursory note about Hong Kong's labour in transition would serve a pointer to the mapping of the future terrain of the workplace beyond 1997.

A Pluralistic Labour Market?

What has been witnessed in this territory since the mid-1980s is a creeping yet steady process of structural transformation in the economy — itself inherent in the territory's own metamorphosis into the higher realm of "post-industrialism" but evidently compounded by the China factor and the pre-1997 political syndrome in Hong Kong. The dynamics of industrial restructuring, together with the associated shifts in the socio-demographic context of economic activities and lifestyles here, have in turn drastically transformed the configuration of the territory's labour market. These processes have, for instance, created new groups of "labour aristocracy," while reducing others into a deprived or even impoverished position of "marginalization" and "de-skilling." However, the growing advents of the "marketplace" ethos (and the intensified creed for the gains in flexibility hence implied), paralleled by the internationalization of the territory's capital and labour markets, as well as its increasingly close integration with the Chinese economy, have worked together, over these recent years, to differentiate its labour force into an even more diversified and pluralistic one than before in terms of its age, sex, skill and ethnic-cultural mix. The ramifications of a more heterogeneous and stratified workforce emerging from this decade-long process of the territory's transition have been, *inter alia*, the questioning of the adequacy of those existing regulatory institutions for safeguarding labour's standards in employment and maintaining industrial harmony at the workplace, let alone the thorny issue of updating and enhancing the skill capabilities of the workforce in order to cope with the rapidly shifting demands of the market-cum-technology imperatives. These challenges bring into the picture, therefore, the respective roles of labour law, the labour movement and the labour administration (plus its array of government agencies). However, before exploring the prospective scope of their future agenda in accommodating with these emergent challenges and pressures in the labour arena, it is useful to have a quick glimpse of the shifting contours of the labour market and its likely trends up to and beyond 1997.

The syndrome of the economy's industrial restructuring is manifest, in the first instance, in the consistent redistribution of the territory's labour force from the secondary industries to the tertiary service sector. The former's percentage share in the employed workforce declined from 47% in 1971 to 41% in 1981 and further to 28% in 1991. Accompanying such a relative advance in service employment was a parallel and sustained increase in the contribution of the tertiary industries to the gross domestic product (GDP), from 60% in 1970 to 65% in 1982 and 69.4% in 1990.[1]

The changing pattern of labour demand which the above restructuring processes imply is a key and fundamental factor giving rise to the subsequent adjustments in the character and composition of the labour force. The repercussions emanating from these shifts, to which the territory's labour force has responded with its characteristic feature of flexibility and fluidity, are several-fold, as outlined in the following discussion.

❑ *Marginalization of Production Skills*

The first feature has been the relative impoverishment and marginalization
of the industrial workers with conventional production skills due to the
gradual withering away of their demands on the shop-floor. The dampened
requirements for these skilled workmen and semi-skilled operatives who
were in short supply when the territory's manufacturing activities were in
its heyday were in part the result of their substitution by automation and
improved technology (where production in plants has moved upstream
technologically to more sophisticated products and processes of production) in the workplace. However, the chief reason remained the "pull" of the
China factor in having induced the large-scale emigration of factories
originally operating in Hong Kong northwards across the border to the
Mainland (especially South China), where labour and land for industrial
purposes were available in greater abundance and much cheaper prices.

In other words, it has been argued that the scale of Hong Kong
industrial capital has in fact not succumbed significantly because of an
endogenous restructuring process of the economy. Rather, by a *de facto*
strategy of spatial diversification (and decantation), it has successfully
maintained or even enlarged its scope and size of operations by deploying
land and labour in China in place of those (formerly) from Hong Kong.
Nevertheless, the implications for the territory's labour have been conspicuous and irreversible: the closure, removal and curtailed operations of
the bulk of manufacturing plants in Hong Kong have rendered obsolescent
a sizeable and increasing number of production workers displaced from
the (sunset) industries. As a result, the twin problems of unemployment
and underemployment have been on the rise. In this connection, a recent
small-scale local study in skill shortage commissioned under the APEC
(Asia-Pacific Economic Cooperation) auspices has summarized these
impacts on the local labour market with such an observation:

> In summary, the paradox of the intervention of the "China" factor in the
> restructuring of the Hong Kong's economy into a tertiary one is that it has
> enabled Hong Kong industrial capital to survive, sustain or even expand
> further by extending its operations across the border. In terms of the manpower
> syndrome, however, its imprints are evident to the extent that (i) the Hong
> Kong-based industry is still able to maintain a huge, industrial army, estimated
> at two to three million, of Chinese labour; and (ii) the physical withdrawal of
> these activities from the Hong Kong venue has not only reversed the earlier

picture of serious local shortage but also dislodged locally an increasing number of industrial workers into unemployment or underemployment.[2]

This study elucidated corroborative evidence for the argument that the skill shortage syndrome in the territory's secondary manufacturing sector has been drastically transformed, as a result of the closer economic integration between China and Hong Kong, especially in face of the stampede of the latter's (manufacturing) industry northwards to the Mainland. The investigator in his report confirmed the suspicion articulated in the labour sector that manpower shortage in industry has largely subsided:

> It was represented to us, for instance, in this APEC Study, that most of the respondent firms in the sample were no longer menaced by the shortage of industrial labour which was both widespread and incessant in the late 80s, precipitating bottlenecks and idle capacities on assembly-lines, and generally impeding productivity efficiencies and market competitiveness because of high wage costs and rampant vacancy gaps. These shortages were now generally alleviated — either after the firms have themselves adjusted in transferring their labour-intensive work processes to China or indirectly, because of, even for those manufacturing works (like the textile dyeing mills) which have opted to stay back in Hong Kong, the easing of the entire skill market which caters to the manufacturing sector and betrays now signs of "fatigue" due to ebbing demands from factories.[3]

What has compounded the "Balkanization" of these manufacturing skills, as a growing reserve of industrial workers are trapped now in an underemployed or unemployed status yet constrained in their abilities to transfer to a second alternative career despite the availability of nominal "retraining" assistance from the government, has been a simultaneous proliferation in the intake and admission of imported workers from outside Hong Kong. Ironically, the government, which used to be lukewarm about relaxing its hitherto strict control of imported labour of general and lesser skills into the territory, reversed such a policy stance in the late 1980s under the vociferous lobby of the industrial employers complaining about the inadequate supply of semi-skilled workers, which has become allegedly prohibitive, since the middle of the last decade, and threatened to "pull out" of their Hong Kong production base at a faster pace.

Therefore, there is an implicit logic to the theory suggesting that the local manufacturing workers have inadvertently instigated the massive recruitment by their employers of imported labour as well as the consistent relocation of their works northwards to China, thereby contributing to the emasculation of industrial labour's own market position and its reduction into a "secondary market" syndrome. The spiral of their adverse market adjustments subsequently ensued, towards the end of the 1980s, when their acute shortage began to develop and surface, touching off in sequel a chained process of "free market" adjustments in "pricing themselves out the market." Such a "market" paradox has therefore led to the appearance of a new "subclass" of Hong Kong's labour — made up of both the displaced industrial workers as well as their counterparts in the "imported labour" groups. A cursory profile of the foreign and imported workers in Hong Kong, becoming increasingly diversified in their composition, is useful for understanding the new phenomenon of "marginalization" in the labour force.

❑ *Proliferation of Foreign and Alien Workers*

At present, Hong Kong accommodates a spectrum of several streams of foreign workers across its manpower hierarchy. This feature — the territory's labour force assimilating a growing segment of alien workers — emanates from a variety of sources identifiable in its labour history:

1. a liberal admission policy, confined largely to the apex of the territory's manpower structure, which has been applied consistently to those "expatriate" employers who possess skills, knowledge or experience of value to but not readily available yet in Hong Kong. During 1993, for instance, 17,202 overseas professional and other persons with technical expertise or administrative and managerial skills from over 35 countries were admitted for employment in Hong Kong under such auspices;

2. a regulated procedure of recruiting foreign nationals, since 1973, to enter Hong Kong for employment as "domestic helpers" in local families and households. In 1993, there were 120,604 foreign domestic helpers in Hong Kong, the majority of whom (about 87%) were from the Philippines;

3. a controlled enrolment of imported workers, under the labour importation schemes initiated in 1989 and 1990, which enabled the government to approve the recruitment of altogether 15,418 workers from overseas, including technicians, craftsmen, supervisors

and experienced operatives, to work here under a two-year contract. In 1992, all these special labour importation schemes, apart from those relating to the new airport and associated projects, were consolidated into a General Scheme which expanded the scale of labour importation, subject to a ceiling of 25,000 in total at any given time. Thereafter, the 1992 scheme has also made the mandatory two-year contract for an imported worker renewable for not more than twice, while the employer responsible for the recruitment is now also liable to pay a levy, to be used for retraining those local workers adversely affected by the structural transformation of the economy;

4. a special intake of "professional" personnel recruited from the Mainland, catering essentially to the graduate employment market and intended to support the intensifying Sino-Hong Kong trade and economic relations. The initial batch of intake, announced last year, was subject to a quota of a thousand recruits in number, which was to be reviewed in due course; and

5. in addition to the existent quota of 2,000 imported construction workers designated for the airport-related infrastructural projects, the government's decision, just ceded in November 1994, of drastically expanding the quota size of such an intake specific to the new airport work to not more than 27,000, i.e. enlarging it to a scale even surpassing that for the General Importation Scheme.

Such a growing variety and number of workers imported from outside Hong Kong have, inevitably, added to the fluidity of the local labour market. Also compounding the diversity of the territory's labour force and contributing to its transient character has been an internal process of socio-demographic metamorphosis which emanates from the 1997 syndrome. The impending "change-over" of sovereignty has triggered off, during the last ten years' experiences of its political transition, a sustained exodus of emigrants from Hong Kong. Such an emigration crisis not only engenders the immediate problem of "brain drain" but also precipitates the subsequent issue of the "returning emigrants," let alone the detrimental impact of the skill outflow upon the pace of localization in the territory's professional and managerial echelons. Paradoxically, the manpower and skill gaps left by the "brain drain" episode of this dimension have, in part, been met by the "internationalization" of the labour market in the upper reach of the professional/managerial occupations. As a recent critique of Hong Kong society reflects, the internal segmentation of the territory's working population has yielded a "hybrid" feature of diversified types of both the committed, semi-committed and non-committed in the labour force:

> (i) the emigrants on their move, (ii) the prospective emigrants planning to move, (iii) the "commuting" emigrants who shuffle between destinations, (iv) the "returning" emigrants, (v) those locals in Hong Kong who are able to advance socially upwards because of the openings left vacant by the emigrants, (vi) those locals already in possession of overseas passports without the need of leaving Hong Kong to fulfil the "residential" requirements, (vii) those who are not attracted by the thesis of emigration and opt to maintain their present "citizenship" status and identity, in spite of the 1997 political transition, (viii) expatriates who are pulled by the widened opportunities available in Hong Kong, because of the gaps caused to localization of professional and managerial jobs by the present emigration outflow, and (ix) the inflow of immigrants arriving recently from China.[4]

❑ *A New Industrial Proletariat in the Making?*

At the beginning of the present decade, an authoritative review of local labouring conditions has noted the existence in Hong Kong of a relatively deprived labouring mass, located in the so-called "secondary market" of the underprivileged, inasmuch as:

> ... there was certainly a lower mass — about a third of all workers — who had generally low earnings, little security of engagement and negligible welfare provision by its employers. And this low stratum of employment was occupied mainly (but by no means exclusively) by less-skilled workers, mostly (though again not exclusively) in manufacturing; but was predominantly to be found in small, HK-Cantonese enterprises.... In the decade between our surveys of the mid-70s and mid-80s,... not merely had the characteristics of the upper and lower strata become much more definite,... (but) what we now call the "under-privileged" stratum had extended to include semi-skilled workers at large, as well as older women employees, and seems more definitely identified with smaller firms.[5]

It is suspected, therefore, as the territory moves close towards and beyond 1997, that a new industrial proletariat is in the process of crystallizing. It is in part based upon this "lower mass" of those engaged in manufacturing who are, however, increasingly marginalized because of

(1) their skill obsolescence and job dislocation from the factories which have transferred their production across the border; and (2) their labour market vulnerability in making mid-career transfer to the more prosperous service sector, except for peripheral and insecure hiring, due to such constraints as age, sex and their dubious abilities to adapt and acquire new trade skills. In part, such a relatively deprived and impoverished "labouring mass," located in the "secondary" labour market for their disadvantaged employment conditions and inabilities to move out of such a "trapped" position because of their skill rigidities and other "side-bet" constraints, is also replenished now from such marginal categories as the recent immigrants arriving from China, the diverse groups of imported guest workers, as well as the "housewife"-cum-homeworkers participating part-time in the "waged" labour market.

Exposed to the whim of the market and its associated vicissitudes (by virtue of either their own inherent market disadvantages or institutionally prescribed constraints due to restrictive rules, customs and practices), these peripheral workers are prone to involve themselves in incessant grievances at work against their employers which are, however, often beyond effective articulation in the workplace for want of their organized representation. Apart from the characteristically "lukewarm" attitude of these workers towards "trade unionism," a major cause contributing to their relative inarticulateness has been cited in the feeble provision in the average workplace in Hong Kong of any satisfactory or dependable (i.e. "trust-worthy") joint arrangements for handling workers' grievances and complaints which arise from the shop-floor. Such a problematic nature of grievance representation, afflicting labour-management relations in Hong Kong's enterprises, has been elucidated by Turner and his associates when they wrote at the beginning of the 1990s that:

> Effectively, in spite of the unions' heightened public status, private sector labour relations at the workplace level remain employer-dominated.... Thus, the combined evidence of the increased number of spontaneous trade disputes, of the extraordinary and continuing rise in officially-handled grievance claims, and of our own survey in grievances at work, suggests a considerable body of workplace discontents which finds only a limited satisfaction in public or employer policies — and a negligible expression through trade unionism.[6]

Those labouring groups which these authors viewed to be most vulnerable to work alienation and radicalization — with their implied propensity to developing in future into a deprived, frustrated, and "refractory" labouring mass — constituted, *inter alia*, those "some two-fifths of new entrants to the labour market over this period (between the mid-1970s and mid-1980s)" who "came from an exceptional intake of new Chinese immigrants, mostly into the less-skilled occupations,"[7] as well as those less-skilled or semi-skilled workers, including the older employees, mostly in manufacturing and "predominantly to be found in small, HK-Cantonese enterprises."[8] The situation is likely to deteriorate now and in future, with a plausible risk of truncating the labour force into a "we-they" dichotomy between these disadvantaged and the privileged "labour aristocracy" "concentrated in public employment and the white-collar workers of large firms of like origin,"[9] when these petty industrial workers are further depressed by the widespread and impoverishing plight of job dislocation, skill redundancies and experiences of adjustment handicaps in retraining and career transfer due to the economy's restructuring. Contributing also to such a terrain of rising "pauperism" among the ranks of these urban workers is the creeping addition of the externally recruited foreign guest labour whose segregated conditions, in spite of the officially sanctioned guarantee of their parity *vis-à-vis* their local counterparts in terms and conditions such as wages, help sustain and amplify a state of "dualism" in hiring for an increasing number of workplaces.

POSSIBILITIES OF REFORMS AND CHANGES IN THE LABOUR ADMINISTRATION

❏ *Its Past Posture*

The advents of such a proliferating mass trapped in the relatively depressed secondary layer of the territory's labour economy, compounded by the workforce's continued fluidity due to the international flow of the expatriates, imported guest workers, outgoing and returning emigrants as well as recent arrivals of Mainland immigrants, all point to perturbing signs that the territory's provisions of regulatory institutions could be heavily strained in safeguarding labour standards and prescribing a satisfactory body of the "rules of the game" for capital and labour at the workplace. Even the Gini Coefficient, which is a statistical device adopted worldwide for comparing the inequality or otherwise of different distributions of income, has been conspicuous for its sluggish or non-existent improvements over the last decade to suggest hardly any tangible narrowing in the territory's income disparities between the rich and the poor.[10] The paradox of labour's impoverishment, against the background of the territory's present buoyant prosperity and affluence, has been again noted in such a salient analysis by Turner and his associates:

> The data for a declining share of labour in total income, and an increase of inequality in general, over the period between our two studies is detailed in Ch. II.... But it does seem fairly clear that no pronounced shift to labour, of the kind that other countries have experienced in the process of economic growth, occurred in HK despite the rapidity of its movement to an advanced level.[11]

Virtually, the labour administration has been historically instrumental, in the context of the territory's postwar social development, in serving as a key lever for uplifting labour's conditions and protecting them from the vicissitudes of "industrial capital." Indeed, the image of the government as the custodian of labour protection and betterment has been enshrined since the late 1960s and early 1970s by virtue of a "reformist" agenda of enlightened labour legislation (often in emulation of the corresponding International Labour Conventions instruments) which it has consistently pursued as a sequel to the civil disturbance of 1967. The background to its inception was probably complex, rooted in such factors as:

> In the first place, it probably reflects a mild, paternalistic consciousness on the part of the governing elite of the needs for social and labour reforms. Secondly, it epitomizes an official response to increasingly vociferous expectations for better quality of life from within, as signalled by the 1966–67 upheavals and the ensuing myriad of social protests. Third, the agenda of reforms could also be intended as an answer to social critics overseas, notably, the lobby of British trade unionists, and as an effort to harmonize local labour standards with the International Labour Conventions comparable provisions in other neighbouring countries.[12]

Hitherto, in this territory, the role of a prudently interventionist administration in prescribing a "statutory floor of rights" at employment by way of legal enactment has been greeted with approval form the "grassroots" labouring mass, among whom a traditional psychology of reliance "has already developed in administrative and legalistic protection"[13] — perpetuated largely in face of the sustained industrial feebleness of the labour movement and of its dubious representativeness *via-à-vis* the general labour force, as evidenced in "the uncertain willingness and ability of the major union groups to participate in formal collective bargaining, and the apparent general scepticism among employers of that process as a viable route to improvement...."[14] For these reasons, an endemic atmosphere of "legalism" has been pervasive in the labour sector, where statutory legislation has been conspicuous as the standard-bearer for prescribing, updating and improving norms of employment at work:

> Whether explanation is to be found in the traditional Chinese deference to official decrees, or in the way they help employers take certain employment conditions out of competition, or in an inarticulate labour force unable to mobilize its collective power, there prevails an apparent cult of "legal regimentalism" — the belief that the parties will adopt these statutory norms as direct and imperative, rather than take them as the floor upon which better terms are to be built. Thus, the practice of voluntarism ... has perpetuated a vacuum and has, apparently, created its own dialectics. Namely, these are the parties' expectations upon the Government to regulate for mandatory standards of employment and to intervene to determine their levels, in view of an otherwise bizarre or even "normless" market situation that is vulnerable to excessive uncertainty.[15]

❑ *Where the Labour Administration Is Destined to Be?*

Given the ameliorative importance of the labour administration, it is logical to explore the future prospect of such an official role in balancing the future relations between capital and labour in this territory after 1997, especially in face of the present and impending transition of its labour market as documented earlier. *Prima facia*, the continuity of the legal and administrative systems as guaranteed under the Joint Declaration and the Basic Law seems to attest to the faith that both the employers and the employees in Hong Kong can continue to adhere to official arrangements and provisions as the principles of regulating their future standards and mutual relations. However, a closer scrutiny of the recent stance adopted by the labour administration suggests that such an expectation could be over-optimistic or even illusionary, in the absence of introducing to the existing system certain future adjustments or correctives as will be commensurate with the evolving socio-economic contexts.

To begin with, several features of recent development in the government's orientation to the labour and employment sector are worth noting in view of the growing imperative of the economy's management and stabilization at the macro level. First, it appears that the administration's labour policy, as it approaches towards the close of the last decade, has become increasingly less recognizable by simply inspecting alone what the government's legislative intentions are when passing new labour legislation. Instead, workers and their unions are now affected importantly by official decisions in the associated areas of manpower, employment and wages, which are primarily instruments of the government's wider economic policies in dealing, technocratically, with such issues as inflation, growth and productivity. Coinciding with the extension of the administration into these activities of economic management has been the concomitant stagnation of the official programme of labour legislation, a feature which is suggested by these developments documented in the following:

> ... it appears that as major items of labour legislation were gradually enacted and introduced to the statute book, the local agenda of legal enactment may be slowly exhausted of any further innovative proposals of significance. In so far as the mildly reformist strategy of labour law here has been to "limit the intervention of the law to those marginal areas ... the logic is apparent for the Government to concentrate labour reforms by law upon the erection of a statutory floor of workers' rights as equivalent to our neighbouring societies.... However, the building of such a basic net of substantive benefits and protection at employment was by and large completed towards the mid '80s ... unsurprisingly, there was a visible drop in the number of new enactments adding to the inventory of the territory's labour law since the late '80s ... And where they are, these initiatives are largely limited to the servicing and streamlining of existing statutory instruments like the Employment Ordinance.[16]

What has emerged from these coincidence and contradictions is, therefore, the effacing yet enlarging inroad of the official lever into the private sector's labour and wage markets, which a reluctant administration has sought to justify as a prudent package of anti-inflation package aimed to stabilize an increasingly complex city economy and to cradle its steady growth. At the same time, there has also been a visible shift to the use of administrative devices, in favour of relying principally upon legislative intervention to set mandatory yet invariable standards as it was in the past, in enabling the government to regulate with a wider measure of discretion and flexibility selected activities in private employment — noticeably, in the admission of foreign domestic helpers and of guest workers under the General Labour Importation Scheme, as well as the conditions governing their entries. Anyway, especially novelistic in such adjustments of the government's economic-cum-labour policies is its apparent departure from its sacrosanct philosophy upheld until the turn of the decade, namely that of abstaining from the free interplay of supply and demand in the labour economy by leaving private wage and employment levels basically untempered.[17] When the previous Governor, Lord Wilson, attempted to assuage the Hong Kong people's shock and resurrect their shattered morale, in the aftermath of the 1989 Beijing upheavals, with a laudably resolved policy agenda presented in his October annual address before the Legislative Council (Legco), he signalled such a new horizon in the labour domain by:

1. articulating an appeal for voluntary wage restraint in the private sector, chiefly by moral suasion but also vicariously, through the indirect administrative device of containing civil service pay rise to within acceptable levels of "non-inflationary" range; and
2. announcing the admission, in reversal of a former steadfast policy stance to the contrary, of a massive intake of foreign workers into the local labour market under the newly introduced "import labour" scheme.[18]

However, the appearance of such an augmented scope of the government's activities in the employment sector is not entirely non-problematic. In the first instance, such policy decisions transcending both employment and economic goals have appeared largely fragmental up to the present, looking more of a "stop-gap" nature and lacking any long-term insights or logic of coherent planning in orientation. This scepticism is attested by the initial and prolonged "indecision" of the government in its staggering position towards such issues of concern as inflation and "import labour," which have surfaced in the platform of the employers' lobby for several years before being addressed by the administration with, at the beginning, a characteristically "self-effacing" posture. Again it was echoed a while later, in the policy reversal by the government on its previous decisions not to introduce any territory-wide arrangements on retirement and provident provisions, when it decided in principle to introduce mandatory retirement benefits three years ago — seemingly as a compensatory deal to appease organized labour's agitational opposition to the "import labour" General Scheme.

The second reason of concern over the changing official stance is the "shifting of boundaries between economic and labour policies." It appears that the "current labour policy has had much of its earlier content distilled," inasmuch as it is increasingly drained of the initial flavour of its "legalistic agenda of the 1960s and 1970s," giving way instead to its fragmented approach which is "now widely diffused and intermingled with economic, education, social security, and welfare policies in a 'mixed bag'."[19]

Thirdly, such an emasculation of the territory's labour policies, to the extent that they are often now utilized as partial instruments serving primarily the government's wider objectives in economic management and stabilization, has also impinged upon and, somehow, compromised the authenticity of the "tripartite" nature of interest representation which used to feature the joint participation of the government, workers, and employers, and the collective organizations of the latter two, in the formulation of labour policy under the institutional auspices of the (predominantly) elected Labour Advisory Board. The growing incapacity of the Board is probably endemic to its tradition of a relatively circumscribed role as a consultative organ contained under the jurisdiction of the Labour Department, as given in the original model of the 1920s which was adopted throughout the dependent territories of the British Commonwealth:

> For one thing, the activities and structure of the Labour Advisory Board are still much fashioned after its pre-war model dating back to the 1920s.... A noticeable feature is its dependency upon the prerogative of the Commissioner for Labour to set its agenda and, therefore, to prescribe effectively its scope of jurisdiction. Perhaps, such feebleness is historic.
>
> In Hong Kong, it appears that the Labour Advisory Board has been instrumental in initiating labour legislation. Yet, as already noted, these activities have receded in their relative importance recently. As it stands, official deliberations on the present principal issues of the labour agenda — namely, import labour and compulsory retirement arrangements — seem to have taken place mainly outside the consultative domain of the Labour Advisory Board.... The detachment of the policy conception processes on these two key issues from the Board's prerogative, justified apparently on the ground that they are not strictly labour matter *per se*, has further accentuated widespread disenchantment within the labour movement with the efficacy of such a consultative organ. The dissatisfaction of the unions and their demands

for a major institutional overhaul of the Board's role have thus intensified and became quite audible.[20]

In this context, it is hence imperative "for the Government to revamp and streamline its present machinery of consultation in labour and associated policies in order to enhance the flexibility and capability of such 'tripartite' organs as the Labour Advisory Board in deliberating and advising the administration on legislative and other public policy decisions which may transcend the labour sector."[21] In particular, the existing machinery of the Board should be restructured extensively, so that "it can, while retaining its basically 'tripartite' composition, enjoy an augmented authority to advise the Government on an extended labour agenda which should embrace not only labour protection and legislation but also wages and incomes (or even prices), labour-management relations, employment and manpower, training and productivity, import labour and other anti-inflation prescriptions, etc."[22] What is even more strategic and thorny, however, is the future task for it to explore a new and better harmonized linkage it has with the Legco, in view of "the now apparently loose, duplicating and 'anachronistic' relationship" between the two.[23]

The strengthening of the functional integration between the Legco in the upper tier and of the Board below it (in a way somewhat analogous to the present link between the Transport Advisory Board and the Executive Council) is perhaps a logical corollary to the emergent syndrome of such current developments as (1) the "politicization" of labour issues, the debates about which in the legislature have turned more "polarized" (for instance, on "import labour," "retirement securitym," etc.) so that it would be quite strategic for a token of preliminary consensus to be negotiated in the "tripartite" Labour Advisory Board, before the Legco's deliberations on any labour issues, especially those involving a conflict of interest between the employer and the employee; (2) the increasing need for the Labour Advisory Board, as noted earlier already, to be consulted on a number of nominally "non-labour" public policy matters canvassed in the Legco, for reason of their salient implications for labour and employment; and (3) the essentially elected character of both the Legco and the employee representatives in the Board which suggests, institutionally speaking, a dualistic avenue for articulating Hong Kong workers' interests in the formulation of labour-related public policies, as well as a possible normative infrastructure upon which they might aspire to consolidate, in due course, a social and industrial partnership with the government and the employers. However, while the question lingers imminent row as whether the government should initiate "a comprehensive review of existing advisory/policy-making institutions and arrangements" so as to achieve a wider participation "which can ensure the efficacy of future public policy in meeting the needs of the populace,"[24] it is evident that a key role is also incumbent upon the territory's labour movement, especially given its electoral capacity in determining the workers' delegates on the Labour Advisory Board and those on the "labour constituencies" in the Legco.

A LABOUR MOVEMENT POISED FOR INDUSTRIAL PARTNERSHIP AND POLITICIZATION?

It has been noted, in an earlier review about the territory and its labour in transition, such a reference to the paradoxical nature in the union movement for its simultaneous propensities to "de-politicize" as well as to "politicize":

> Ironically, the distillation of the vanguard image of the local labour movement that emanates from the politico-ideological polemics between Communist China and Nationalist Taiwan has not emasculated or diminished the "political" activity of trade unions in Hong Kong. Instead, with the gradual transition of the "civil service" type of colonial administration to a popularly elected government for the territory, the effective role of trade unions as the representative organizations and spokesmen of the labour sector is likely to be enhanced. The "participant" status of the unions in electoral politics has been given recognition in the official White Paper, published in 1984, entitled *The Future Development of Representative Government in Hong Kong*. Specifically,... together with other so-called "functional constituencies,"... organized labour has been enshrined in a strategic partnership ... within this reformed framework of Hong Kong's present and future political institution.[25]

The option of "union incorporation" which the above implies, enabling the labour organizations to develop "their 'ministerial' capacity, this time as the standard-bearer of labour 'politicking' in the domestic arena of electoral politics,"[26] is patently attractive in its appeals. First, it helps redeem the trade unions from "their former character as 'a locally specific combination of friendly society and socio-political organization,' now that their obsession with adversarial Chinese politics is waning ..."[27] Second, it provides for organized labour a lever of quick inroad to social power and industrial influence to the extent that, in this Hong Kong context, "the political method of 'legal enactment' may eventually offer a more viable and pertinent avenue than voluntary collective bargaining for securing the improvement of employees' conditions."[28] Primarily, this is because the union movement in Hong Kong has a characteristically feeble aptitude for wrestling voluntary recognition from private employers for the right to bargain collectively — let alone the appealing possibility of enabling labour unions to bypass the plightful agony of "chronic industrial warfare and the risks of perpetuated labour-management antagonism" if they were, instead, to consolidate an autonomous institution of adversarial collective bargaining of the Western tradition, which, however, "might prove too expensive for Hong Kong," given its neurotic concern for internal stability.[29]

There were signs, albeit implicit, during the last ten years since the signing of the Joint Declaration, that organized labour in the territory has been forging slowly a type of "social partnership" with the government and employers in the public domain of policy and law-making. Politically, in addition to the two seats designated for the labour constituency in the Legco, "popular trade union leaders were able to win two directly elected seats in the Council as well as retain control of the teachers' and nurses' seats on the respective functional constituencies" in the 1991 election.[30] At the same time, two of the leading trade union centres, the Hong Kong Federation of Trade Unions (FTU) and the Hong Kong Confederation of Trade Unions (CTU), appear to have each evolved a quasi-allied relationship with two of the most powerful "political parties" in Hong Kong. These are, respectively, the United Democrats of Hong Kong (now merged with Meeting Point as the Democratic Party) and the Democratic Alliance for Betterment of Hong Kong.

What has served more conspicuous as the litmus test on the tenacity of such a social partnership is, however, a chain of episodes besetting the Hong Kong economy, around the turn of the decade, with that "growth" syndrome of an acute labour shortage and the incessant inflation spiral. The government conceded to the employers' restless lobby in approving the large-scale admission of foreign workers into the territory as a "stop-gap" anti-inflation measure to dampen the "heated" skill market, evidently departing from its established policy stance of disapproving any recruitment of imported workers, and patently in defiance of labour's agitational protests. Paradoxically, the qualms of the embattled union movement, acting concertedly across its segmented factions, were audible enough in spurring a reluctant administration to make its overturn on a seemingly compensatory deal for the territory's working class — in a piece of labour policy innovation which is "reminiscent of a 'social contract' popular in Western Europe and the United States in the 1960s and 1970s."[31] The euphoria greeting the government's initiative to institutionalize retirement protection for the workforce on a territory-wide level was noticeable, as narrated in such terms:

> This was a proposal to introduce to the territory a mandatory system of statute-backed retirement benefits. Thus, as an article of faith of the official commitment to its "responsibility to the workforce," the government switched from its previous policy stance of non-regulation of "central providence" by declaring, in 1991, a decision to legislate on the compulsory provision of pension schemes by employers. Such an official decision was applauded in the labour sector and the community at large, as a positive stride towards enhancing the confidence and stability of the working strata.... These provisions will have the additional effects of harmonizing with the stipulations of the Basic Law on labour welfare.[32]

However, there is yet scepticism over such optimism in heralding the labour movement's efficacy to play a standard-bearer role in any future stable "partnership" with the government and private employers for a number of reasons. First, the status of labour in such type of "social contract" is always that of a junior partner to the state and capital — even in nations having evolved a well-structured framework of "state corporatism" such as Singapore. Second, in the Hong Kong context, doubts have been often raised on the representativeness of the union movement in acting as the authentic spokesman for the grassroots employees on the shop-floor, given its historic nature of development as the agents of the "labour aristocracy," rather than of the relatively unorganized labouring mass whose growing market vulnerability has been briefly surveyed in an earlier section of this chapter.[33] Third, in so far as the labour movement has retained its essentially "pluralistic" and divided character of internal fragmentation in spite of its political ascendancy, it is likely for such a sustained property of "multi-unionism" to continue to emasculate its internal solidarity and by implication, its creditability to pose as a united voice of labour. A divided labour movement provides, in addition, a laudable defence for many employers to maintain their steadfast position of evading or resisting the extension of voluntary recognition to the relevant trade unions for collective bargaining purposes.[34] The fourth constraint is perhaps most stifling, as it pertains to an issue of principle, in terms of the need to demarcate and to conserve the jurisdiction of trade unions as industrial combinations, and not as quasi-"grassroots organizations" to perform the mere role of politicized "corporatist" institutions. The following critique, written almost ten years ago when the labour movement was on the threshold of entering its newly designated political "realm," is still by and large applicable today:

> (it) engenders an imminent risk of inducing these trade union associations to evolve into quasi-political parties. The desirability of such a development is questionable, inasmuch as the performance of these voluntary bodies will no longer be measured by what they might have accomplished for their membership as specific interest groupings, but by how successful they are in canvassing electoral support and campaigning for an elected seat in the Legislative Council. By so doing ... the trade unions will be tempted to distort the use of their funds and resources in such a manner as to compromise the initial purpose of their association. What claims precedence on the union's platform ceases to be the commitment to "deliver the goods" wanted by their membership, but instead becomes the question of how best to appeal to the voters....
>
> As designated participants in the democratic process of the "establishment," trade unions may increasingly come to feel the crunch of being held responsible for various policy decisions of the government, especially for the unpopular ones for which they will find it more difficult to disclaim a share of the liability engendered.... Conflicts will be endemic if trade unions, which are intrinsically sectional-interest associations, attempt to act like politicians or political parties in addressing political issues from a community-wide perspective. A vivid illustration of this is the perennial debate on the official regulation or protection of strikes, as well as the sponsorship of collective bargaining.[35]

THE FUTURE AGENDA

To the extent the local labour movement is handicapped in its representative role to articulate fully the interests of the labouring mass (especially for the disadvantaged, marginalized and often unorganized groups), the government will probably remain a principal source of leverage for ameliorating industrial grievances and injustices in this territory after 1997, where labour and capital are to be sustained in "that type of paradoxical mutual relationship" as given by the "imperative nature" of the free market,[36] to be conserved here because "Hong Kong's previous capitalist system and life-style shall remain unchanged for 50 years" under the guarantee of the Joint Declaration and the Basic Law.[37] However, such a prospect, intrinsically uncertain due to the process of the political change-over itself, is obscure in face of the increasingly staggering or even inconsistent stance which now characterizes the labour administration. A cursory look at the present and future agenda of labour and related legislation may provide a glimpse of these impending doubts and ambivalence in the labour arena.

Prima facia, it appears that the territory's programme of labour legis-lation has become exhausted in its stamina after its noticeable rigour in the 1970s and 1980s — in harmonizing with comparable provisions in its neighbouring societies as well as selected salient international norms laid down under the International Labour Conventions (in particular, for the newly industrializing economies). Having accomplished by and large a statutory floor of protective employment rights, the agenda of new labour enactments has retreated conspicuously, as from the turn of the decade onwards, to the relatively peripheral concern of "servicing and streamlining of existing statutory instruments like the Employment Ordinance."[38] It stops short, for instance, at the more fundamental propositions of legis-lating on (1) minimum wage; (2) unfair dismissal; (3) strike protection; (4) workplace representation; and (5) collective bargaining arrangements. Virtually, the only item having been given the official pledge of a sub-stantial commitment on its legislative intention is in the area of retirement protection. However, in view of the polarized controversies centred upon the government's far-reaching suggestion to convert the proposal into a quasi-social security blueprint under the guise of an "old age pension," it looks as if the entire initiative has been grounded, with a grim prospect for it to materialize into a territory-wide arrangement on "provident" provisions before 1997.

Such a legislative paucity does not imply, however, the purge entirely of any government activity in nurturing other prospective enactments having important repercussions on labour and employment in Hong Kong. These initiatives are, instead, highly visible under the purview of its task to eradicate sex discrimination and accomplishing (the appearance of) equal opportunities in the workplace — given the currency of a local popular movement to propagate, upgrade and institutionalize human rights in the territory, as epitomized earlier by the passing of the Bill of Rights Ordinance in 1991. Internationally, such a comprehensive set of legislation now in the pipeline will also help in pegging Hong Kong to a worldwide league on the recognition of the benchmarking United Nations instrument, the Convention on the Elimination of All Forms of Discrimination Against Women (CEDAW). However, as hinted in the preluding 1993 government's consultative document entitled *Green Paper on Equal Opportunities for Women and Men*, this laudable endeavour to ratify the principle of women's rights and gender equality has implied the imminent introduction to Hong Kong of a cumbersome equal pay legislation, as well as the creation of a laborious litigation machinery and elaborate procedures for recovering rights in abuse or dispute. If pursued unwittingly, these new arrangements are liable to envisage rupturing effects, in so far as they will have modified significantly the territory's repute as a bastion of "free-enterprise capitalism." The following critique is exemplary:

> Equal pay legislation and its associated regulatory framework would entail a certain degree of government intervention into the operation of individual employers and the labour market. This could induce rigidities into what has been a highly competitive and self-adjusting market. To meet the statutory requirements, employers might be required to develop a formal system of recruitment and promotion procedures. The size of the business establishments in Hong Kong is relatively small. These establishments may find it onerous and costly to comply with the legislation. Furthermore, employers may fall under pressure to sacrifice certain remuneration principles such as bonuses for individual outstanding employees in order to avoid claims of sex discrimination. Employers may need to engage extra personnel staff to ensure that all hiring and promotion policies and procedures are in compliance with the equal pay legislation.[39]

These new inventories on sex equality provisions are hence likely to be expensive if they are to be enforced strenuously at the workplace, let alone the hidden implication that a stampede of civil litigations for remedies or recompense of damages may be touched off as a result. Further scepticism has been cast with the observation that notwithstanding such provisions already in place in the industrially advanced West, "sex differentials in income have been resistant to change in several economies."[40]

Virtually, any benefits otherwise accruing from this elaborate set of prospective legislation on right vindication to the working class women can be notoriously immaterial, inasmuch as for many of them, it appears that "the subject of sex inequality or discrimination is not problematic, since it is barely relevant to their main concerns about general social deprivations."[41] What they yearn for are, instead, fundamental improvements in their employment protection (such as for contingencies to cover lay-offs, short-hours, job security, retirement support, as well as for fairer deals in wages and other supplementary benefits) or betterment in life chances *vis-à-vis* the more privileged groups in the labour aristocracy, instead of having to campaign against their blue-collar male counterparts who could be equally captives of their own competitive disabilities in the deprived "secondary" tier of the labour market. In other words, apart from enabling Hong Kong to claim, rhetorically, that it has entered a new "realm of the estate" in having ratified certain key features of the commonplace institutional package on human rights, the proposed sex equality provisions are seemingly oriented *not* towards the bulk "rank-and-file" members of the labour force as their principal beneficiaries. Rather, as it appears, they are more biased in favour of the relatively aristocratic "middle-class" women professionals, who are demonstrably more sensitized to the issue of "gender-based" disparities at the workplace.[42]

Therefore, the new set of labour law purporting to buttress these so-called "equalities" in employment can look grossly superficial and luxurious in terms of its social cost-effectiveness, if its regulatory ambits, while expensive in outlays, were to entail just a marginal impact upon those who are most in need of officially sanctioned protection at the "grassroots" level of the manpower hierarchy. This is not to deny the ultimate importance for the government to sponsor the attainment of better work life qualities in human rights among members of the general labour force, especially in terms of promoting gender equality and improving Hong Kong's international image in this trendy aspect . However, as the process of its gestation evolved, the importance of such legislation could have been inflated politically — yet with little or just nominal appeal to the "working class" interests of the less advantaged groups in the labour market.

There is hence a drifting danger that the administration's priorities in legislating on labour and employment matters have been unwittingly distorted and misplaced. The hiatus is even less explicable when the urgency for the government to improve its existing inventory of protective and regulatory labour law, in particular for those relating to individual employment rights and collective labour-management relations, has not only persisted but also intensified in face of the growing complexity and diversity in the general workforce, which have been outlined earlier in this chapter. However, the administration's attitude in presenting again a vigorous agenda of labour legislation, equivalent to that of the 1970s, to address these issues has been lukewarm and sluggish, or even obscure and indecisive. For reasons which have been noted in the foregoing, an official complacency with the erection of an embryonic statutory framework on a floor of employment standards, largely accomplished through the assiduous legislative activities of the 1970s and 1980s, seems to have, instead, prevailed.

The contradictions now identifiable in the arena of the labour administration between official policy decisions and what could have been done in helping advance employment standards and industrial relations in the day-to-day conduct of workplace activities imply, therefore, a glaring gap of both legislative and institutional imbalances and inadequacies which the future SAR government may have to inherit and face in the field of employment relations after 1997. There is, for instance, a lingering impasse due to the indecision of the present public policy designers as to the choice of the appropriate legislative options in order to first, revamp the jurisdiction and efficiency of the Labour Tribunal as a quasi-labour court of simplified procedures and second, restructure the present mechanism of official intervention into labour disputes so as to improve its authority and creditability while maintaining intact its essentially "voluntaristic" character. An offshoot of the latter problem is hence the persisting ambivalence of the law about the protection of the strikers and their employers in a work stoppage, in spite of the general guarantee provided on the right to strike under the Basic Law and the Bill of Rights Ordinance.[43] In 1993, the government was nearly in the mood of being prepared to move a modest statutory package of overhauling the existing legal framework governing industrial conflicts in the territory, probably as a sequel to the 17-day strike of the flight attendants at the Cathay Pacific Airways earlier in the year.[44] However, this initiative stopped short at the gate of the Legco, as it hardly went beyond the ritual of appearing as an internal (government) review document submitted for perusal to the Legco, whose follow-up actions on the proposals canvassed therein have been, so far, conspicuous for their absence.

Even such a cursory blueprint for possible labour law reforms hinted in the above-mentioned document is noticeable for its "conservative" feebleness in having reiterated the government's non-committal stance to buttress, at law, a wholesome framework of the employee's protection, such as what could be analogous to the celebrated system of "unfair dismissal" protection in Britain. Instead, by suggesting merely piecemeal amendments of a "stop-gap" nature which make only marginal reference to unfair dismissal legislation in its proposed enhancement of the anti-union discrimination legislation, the government's 1993 review document has incited "considerable disenchantment among those who expected an enlightened overhaul of Hong Kong's body of legislative norms governing industrial conflict, inasmuch as its prescriptions have denied categorically any intention on the part of the labour administration to consider introducing a protective framework such as that enshrined under the British concept of unfair dismissal."[45] In fact, whether now or in future, statutory innovations along such a line of prescription in the British legacy are clearly desirable in strengthening the territory's institutional safeguards on "job security" — given the vulnerability of an increasingly "Balkanized" working mass threatened by trade/skill obsolescence and unstable work supply in the "secondary" labour market, let alone the relative ineffectiveness of the workers' own collective organized power in defending their job interests, which has been a weakness endemic to the comparatively aristocratic yet industrially docile labour movement.

Equally important is the search for appropriate procedural legislation to sanction the creation of some workable arrangements to regularize labour-management dialogue (including, especially, the provision of jointly administered procedures for worker representation and grievance handling) at the level of the individual enterprise, if industrial relations stability is to be better sustained in the workplace. Earlier reference has already been made to "a consistent and creeping growth of disaffection among the vulnerable groups of the migrant and imported workers, as well as in pockets of other types of marginal labour (e.g. temporary, casual or part-time workers) who are mostly clustered in the relatively disadvantaged secondary labour market...."[46] There is hence a latent risk for these grievances, if left unaddressed and to intensify in culmination, to escalate and explode into agitational unrest of industrial militancy or workplace radicalization. The answer of its aversion, it follows, probably rests in "prescribing for Hong Kong workers, at least at the enterprise level, their rights of representation, of consultation and of access to information disclosed by their employers on matters of mutual concern."[47] Given the characteristic apathy of the government to invest proactively in this area other than its nominal efforts in promoting the voluntary practice of joint consultation in the private sector, which has yet achieved little or negligible impact since 1967,[48] the onus of orchestrating a more determined effort on this task will perhaps be incumbent upon the future SAR administration after 1997.

It hardly needs reiterating that the territory's institutional infrastructure still remains notoriously underdeveloped, for the conspicuous absence of a territory-wide mandatory minimum wage law and of a comprehensive retirement protection arrangement (especially where private provision of superannuation for the retired and aged has been the exception rather than the rule in the small-firm industry here). In spite of its spectacular industrial advances, the Hong Kong economy is still widely abhorred for its non-availability of any decent "wage supplement" facilities to pockets of low-paid and underemployed workers and their families, who are staggering around the "poverty line" in their earnings. The eventual answer, as few would have disputed, will reside with the prospect of Hong Kong in consolidating for its people either a central provident fund or, as what the government suggests now in its revised recommendation, an old-age pension scheme. However, given the cumbersome experiences which have already been consumed in the prolonged and oscillating process of government's initial writing, rewriting and extended consultation on this subject-matter, there is little ground for optimism that the Hong Kong labour force will be equipped decently with a viable system of insurance to cover contingencies like retirement and old age security before the end of this century.

What could be primary to the concern of the future SAR government in its labour administration, if construing from the above analysis, is hence the much desired expectation for it to avoid the same pathos of fragmented and ill-coordinated activities of official intervention into the labour and employment sector, which seems to have beset the labour administration in the current transitional years since the turn of the decade. However, it is also evident that the key to the rediscovery of a more streamlined and rationalized labour policy will depend, *inter alia*, upon how successful the Labour Advisory Board, as a time-honoured institution of "tripartite" participation and labour-management consensus building, can be reformed and strengthened from its heavily emasculated position at present, so that it is able to represent a wholesome forum for the joint setting of policy priority among the three principal parties concerned, in a coherent and comprehensive fashion, in order that the variety of policy tasks still outstanding on the territory's labour reform agenda can be handled in future with tact, confidence and determination.

NOTES

1. See Labour Department, Hong Kong government, *Labour and Employment in Hong Kong* (Hong Kong: cyclostyled, July 1992), paras. 1.2.6 and 1.2.7, p. 2.
2. Ng Sek-hong, "Hong Kong: A Profile of Its Labour Force" (unpublished report submitted to the APEC Project on Assessing Skills Shortages in APEC Countries, Hong Kong, cyclostyled, September 1994), p. 16.
3. Ibid.
4. Ng Sek-hong, and Cheng Soo-may, "The Affluent Migrants as a 'Class' Phenomenon: The Hong Kong Case," in *Inequalities and Development: Social Stratification in Chinese Societies*, edited by Lau Siu-kai, Lee Ming-kwan, Wan Po-san and Wong Siu-lun (Hong Kong: Hong Kong Institute of Asia-Pacific Studies, The Chinese University of Hong Kong, 1994).
5. H. A. Turner, Patricia Fosh, and Ng Sek-hong, *Between Two Societies: Hong Kong Labour in Transition* (Hong Kong: Centre of Asian Studies, University of Hong Kong, 1991), p. 92.
6. Ibid., pp. 76–77.
7. Ibid., pp 93–94.
8. Ibid., p. 92.
9. Ibid., p. 92. There is yet a broad intervening "medial" stratum, making up about 40–50% of the labour force, which includes "most white-collar employees outside the public or social service sector and the large 'Western' firms or financial institutions," as well as "much of the commercial sector otherwise, including a variety of 'other outland' firms (Japanese, P.R.C., etc.)."
10. The Gini Coefficient (which should display a value of 0.00 where all incomes in the entity were shared in absolute equality, or of 99.99 if one person were in monopoly of the whole population's revenues) has increased from 0.43 in the mid-1970s to 0.46 by the mid-1980s, reversing an earlier trend of its slow secular decline. Recently, after the turn of the decade, the Gini Coefficient has increased even further, now to 0.48. See the statement in 1992 made by the then Secretary for Economic Services, Anson Chan, before the Legislative Council, as reported in the *South China Morning Post*, 27 February 1992. On the earlier movements of the Gini Coefficient, see Note 5, p. 32.
11. See Note 5, p. 97.
12. Ng Sek-hong, "Labour Administration and 'Voluntarism': The Hong Kong Case," *Journal of Industrial Relations* (June 1982), p. 277.
13. H. A. Turner, *et al.*, *The Last Colony: But Whose?* (Cambridge: Cambridge University Press, 1980), p. 163.
14. Ibid.
15. See Note 12, p. 276.

16. Ng Sek-hong, "Labour Law and Policies: Retrospect and Prospects," in *Hong Kong in Transition* (Hong Kong: One Country Two Systems Economic Research Institute, 1992), pp. 216–17.

17. Thus, the legislative reforms in labour law over the last two decades since the late 1960s have been confined to the orthodoxy of ensuring painstakingly "that whatever moderate degree of state intervention that may be, it does not imply rupture with the traditional voluntarist framework" — which is hence, in essence, by "leaving the key issues of general wages and work hours basically unregulated." The hallmark of such an official aloofness has been its hitherto refusal to legislate on a territory-wide minimum wage floor, except for the pockets of foreign domestic helpers and imported general workers whose wages are regulated administratively by virtue of contractual norms which the government prescribes. See Note 12, pp. 279 and 276.

18. The "interventionist" ramifications of the "import labour" dosage for the home labour market are rather apparent — namely, in augmenting labour supply in the private economy and hence dampening the upward tendencies of local wages otherwise sustained by labour shortage. However, the official rationale was, understandably, to help contain inflation (which has become excessive and harassing) and to conserve the economy's productivity and competitiveness (lest it would be impeded by prohibitive labour costs and bottlenecks).

19. Ng Sek-hong, "Labour Administration and Tripartitism in Hong Kong: Past and Future," *The Asian Journal of Public Administration*, Vol. 15, No. 1 (June 1993), p. 75.

20. Ibid., pp. 76–77.

21. See Note 16, p. 222.

22. Ibid., p. 221.

23. Ibid., p. 221.

24. See Note 19, p. 72.

25. Ng Sek-hong, "Labour," in *Hong Kong in Transition*, edited by Joseph Y. S. Cheng (Hong Kong: Oxford University Press, 1986).

26. Ibid., p. 281.

27. Ibid., p. 281.

28. Ibid., p. 281.

29. Ibid., p. 293.

30. Ng Sek-hong, David A. Levin, and Teresa Wong, "Hong Kong in the 1990s: A Postscript," in *The Business Environment in Hong Kong*, edited by David Lethbridge (2nd ed., 6th impression; Hong Kong: Oxford University Press, 1993), p. 260.

31. Ibid., p. 262.

32. Ibid., p. 262.

33. Such an interpretation was first canvassed, in the late 1970s, by Turner and his

associates in their landmark inquiry into the territory's labour and labour relations:

> Thus, the most active of Hong Kong's union groups and its largest, the civil servants and the left-wing alliance, are both in a large degree organizations of a labour aristocracy.... In the upshot, the lower mass of manufacturing and commercial workers remains unrepresented industrially. And on broader social matters, not even these two groups act as effective spokesmen of labour's "interests." (See Note 13, p. 157.)

This critical observation about Hong Kong's organized labour was upheld by the same group of authors in their "re-visit" study ten years afterwards when they noted, in 1991, such a continuity that:

> ... there are effectively two powerful concentrations of employee organization: one in the administration's own employment and associated social services, the other in transport and communications.... Occupationally, these are now fairly well established in what we earlier called the upper and middle strata of HK's employment structure. They constitute, in effect, a labour aristocracy among HK employees. (See Note 5, pp. 99–100.)

34. At present, a "tripod" division of power seems to characterize the internal split of the labour movement, featuring the two veteran organizations — the left-wing Hong Kong Federation of Trade Unions (FTU), and its right-wing counterpart, the Hong Kong and Kowloon Trades Union Council (TUC) — as well as the third and newly constituted Hong Kong Confederation of Trade Unions (CTU), which draws its affiliates largely from the white-collar occupations in the civil service and the public-subvented sector. On the whole, it is not prospective for these separate union centres to cooperate beyond their present mutual linkages of nominal dialogue or, at best, occasional harmonization on *ad hoc* issues such as to present a concerted front against labour importation. See Ng Sek-hong, "In Place of Strife: The Future of Trade Unionism," *The Employment Report*, Vol. 2, No. 5 (1994), pp. 39–40.

35. See Note 25, pp. 283–85.

36. Ibid., p. 291.

37. *A Draft Agreement between the Government of the United Kingdom of Great Britain and Northern Ireland and the Government of the People's Republic of China on the Future of Hong Kong* (Hong Kong: Government Printer, 1984), p. 14, Annex I, para. I. Also see Note 25, p. 290.

38. See Note 16, p. 217.

39. Ng Sek-hong, "Employment and Human Rights in Hong Kong: Some Recent Developments," *Hong Kong Law Journal*, Vol. 24, Part I, pp. 123–24.

40. See Note 5, p. 96.

41. See Note 39, p. 114.

42. It has been observed, in this connection, that in Hong Kong "where female factory workers are concentrated in clusters of seemingly low-status women jobs, their sensitivity to sexual discrimination is masked by class feelings of 'relative deprivation'." See Ng Sek-hong, "Perception of Sex Discrimination in Employment and the 'Class' Context," *British Journal of Sociology*, Vol. 37, No. 3 (September 1986), p. 330.

43. For a critique, see, for instance, Ng Sek-hong, "Trade Union Organization and Labour Legislation," in *Human Rights in Hong Kong*, edited by Raymond Wacks (Hong Kong: Oxford University Press, 1992), pp. 457–60. Also see Note 39, pp. 131–34.

44. See, for instance, Note 39, pp. 132–34. Also see "In Place of Strife: The Future of Trade Unionism" (Note 34), p. 48.

45. See Note 39, p. 134.

46. See "In Place of Strife: The Future of Trade Unionism" (Note 34), p. 47.

47. Ibid.

48. For a succinct review of the relative docility of the private sector in practising the British-inspired system of joint consultative committees, in spite of an official zeal to propagate such a notion among the reluctant Hong Kong employers, see, for instance, Ng Sek-hong, "Workplace Industrial Relations in Hong Kong," in *The Development of Sound Labour Relations* (Bangkok: International Labour Organization, 1991), pp. 38–42.

11

Urban and Regional Planning*

Ng Mee-kam

INTRODUCTION

Hong Kong has come a long way from "a barren island with hardly a house upon it"[1] in the 1840s to a vibrant city housing close to six million people within an area of 1,070 square kilometres. While the government had played an important role in determining the principal laying-out and use of land since the inception of the colony, enforcement actions were absent and subsequent development was to a great extent accomplished by the private sector.[2] In fact, before the Second World War, spatial development was largely driven by market forces.

The eventful years of economic and urban development in Hong Kong after the establishment of the People's Republic of China in 1949 and the consequent need for urban planning have been well-documented.[3] Today, the Planning Department, taking policy directives from the high-level Chief Secretary Committee,[4] and the Planning, Environment and Lands Branch, is responsible for all types of planning at the territorial, subregional and district levels.

Together with the efforts of other planning-related departments such as the Transport and Housing Departments, land use planning and related projects in Hong Kong are daunting.

* This research is supported by the Urban and Environmental Studies Trust Fund, Centre of Urban Planning and Environmental Management, University of Hong Kong.

1. At the strategic level, we have the Territorial Development Strategy, first completed in 1984 and currently under review as a result of rapid changes in the regional and local context; the Port and Airport Development Strategy and its core projects, after much controversy and negotiating with the Chinese government, are under rigorous construction; and have a set of planning standards and guidelines for the provision of various land uses and facilities.

2. At the subregional level, development strategies for the five sub-regions (including the Metroplan for the main urban area) help to translate strategic goals of territorial development into more specific planning objectives.

3. At the district level, both the statutory and departmental plans allocate land uses within the framework set by higher-level plans. To better direct planning and development, the Town Planning Ordinance has been under comprehensive review since 1991 and a White Bill is expected to be published for further consultation in 1995.

4. Nine new towns — Tsuen Wan, Sha Tin, Tuen Mun, Tai Po, Yuen Long, Fanling/Sheung Shui, Tseung Kwan O, Tin Shui Wai and North Lantau (Tung Chung and Tai Ho) — are in various stages of planning and development.

5. About three million people — half the population — now live in subsidized public housing in some 874,000 flats in 286 estates throughout Hong Kong. Some 2.6 million people live in 688,000 rental units while some 500,000 people live in purchased flats.[5]

6. The Second Comprehensive Transport Study was updated in 1993 to facilitate the planning of the territorial transport network up to the year 2011.[6] Contrary to cities like Taipei where modes of public transport are confined to buses and taxis only, Hong Kong is served by a network of railways (heavy rail, mass transit, light rail and trams), ferries, bus (franchised buses, minibuses) and non-franchised bus operators and taxis.

7. The port of Hong Kong is one of the busiest in the world. In 1993, it handled 9.2 million TEUs (20-foot equivalent units). About 63% (or 5.8 million TEUs) were handled at the Kwai Chung Container Port, and another 30% (or 2.8 million TEUs) were handled by mid-stream operators.[7] Some 165,000 ocean-going and river trade vessels arrive in Hong Kong annually, handling over 100 million

tonnes of cargo and over 20 million international passengers, most of whom are carried on the world's largest fleet of high-speed ferries.[8]

8. In 1993, Kai Tak was the second and third busiest airport in the world in terms of the international cargo handled (1.14 million tonnes, valued at HK$390,096 million) and the number of passengers (24.5 million) respectively.

9. The need for sustainable economic and urban development has also been recognized in recent years. *The Hong Kong Environment: A Green Challenge for the Community*, a second review of the 1989 White Paper *Pollution in Hong Kong — A Time to Act*, represents the government's endeavour to remedy environmental issues which were long-neglected in the last decades of rapid economic growth.

While these achievements are impressive, land use planning in Hong Kong is neither perfect nor problem-free. In fact, many people have criticized various aspects of the land use planning mechanisms while others have done some crystal-gazing into the future development and planning issues of the territory.[9] This chapter attempts to do both. With the onset of economic and political transitions in the 1980s, land use planning in Hong Kong has been facing many uncertainties. A strategic planning framework will be adopted to analyse the types of uncertainty. Then an environmental scanning, basically a SWOT (Strengths, Weaknesses, Opportunities, Threats) analysis[10] will be carried out to assess Hong Kong's ability to handle these uncertain situations. Strategic planning issues will be identified, the government's current responses will be reviewed, and recommendations will be put forward for planners in the territory to consider.

PLANNING UNDER UNCERTAINTIES

To borrow from Friend and Hickling,[11] three types of uncertainty can be identified in the planning process (Figure 1):

1. Uncertainties about the working environment (UE);
2. Uncertainties about guiding values (UV); and
3. Uncertainties about related decisions (UR).

While uncertainties about the working environment will require more technical research and analysis, uncertainties about guiding values need the clarification of planning goals and perspectives by decision-makers and affected parties. Uncertainties about related decisions, however, demands some form of coordination, negotiation or planning exercise that will allow the current decision problem to be explored alongside others within a broader, more synoptic problem focus (Figure 2).[12]

These three types of uncertainty will be used to analyse the current planning context in Hong Kong.

❑ *UE: Uncertainties about the Working Environment*

The economy of Hong Kong has been undergoing a restructuring process for about two decades. Push factors such as escalating land and labour costs in the territory, and pull factors like the availability of cheap land and manpower resources across the border since China's adoption of the open door policy in 1978, have led to a deindustrialization process in Hong Kong. The contribution of the manufacturing sector to the gross domestic product (GDP) has dropped from its highest point of 31% in 1970 to 15.2% in 1991. By contrast, the booming tertiary sector accounted for three quarters of the total GDP in 1992.[13]

Hong Kong is now one of the world's leading financial centres, being the fourth largest in terms of the volume of external banking transactions, the sixth largest in terms of foreign exchange transactions and the seventh largest in terms of stock market capitalization.[14] There are 515 banks and deposit-taking companies in the territory. Of the world's top 100 banks, 83 have established a presence in Hong Kong, 79 of which operate with a full banking licence.[15] By 1993, 624 overseas companies had established their regional headquarters in Hong Kong.

The growing internationalization of Hong Kong's economy is also reflected its trade figures. From 1982 to 1993, Hong Kong's total trade with Asia increased by 664% in value terms. Domestic exports grew by 475%, and with growing economic integration with China, re-exports surged 1,033%.[16] In fact, between 1979 and 1992, some three-fifths of all direct foreign investments (DFIs) in China were made by Hong Kong entrepreneurs and in Guangdong province, 80% of DFIs were from Hong Kong.[17]

As a result of the deindustrialization process and the internationalization of Hong Kong's economy, a major restructuring of the built environment is necessary in order for Hong Kong to meet new economic needs.

Figure 1: Three Types of Uncertainty in Decision-Making

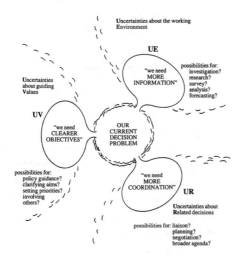

Figure 2: Extending the Problem Focus

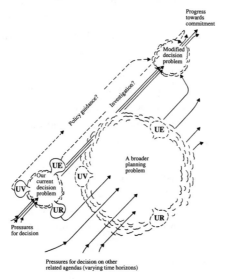

Source: For Figures 1 and 2, refer to J. Friend and A. Hickling, *Planning under Pressure: The Strategic Choice Approach* (Oxford: Pergamon Press, 1987), Figures 3 and 5, reprinted by permission of Butterworth-Heinemann Ltd. and the author.

While the forces that shape the outcome of the economic restructuring process have yet to be fully understood, there are new uncertainties regarding what the guiding values should be in the course of reshaping the city.

❑ *UV: Uncertainties about Guiding Values*

As argued elsewhere,[18] before the transition period in the 1980s, when the political future of Hong Kong was not a contested issue between Britain and China, the administration-led polity and the politically apathetic community had allowed planning to be done behind closed doors very "efficiently" and "rationally," according to criteria defined by the government of Hong Kong in the name of public interest. Whether the government, as the biggest landlord in the territory, had vested interests in the planning stage, or whether the development process was biased towards the interests of the property developers, was seldom questioned by the lay public.

Should such conditions still prevail in the transition period, the task of restructuring the physical space to meet emerging economic needs would be a much easier one. However, the growth of a young political community, and the high-profile existence of China in Hong Kong after the signing of the Sino-British Joint Declaration in 1984, have challenged the traditionally closed planning system, the basic philosophy of which is to facilitate economic growth and development.

The general lay public, especially the young political organizations and the green groups, have become more vocal and argue that planning, besides facilitating economic growth, should also meet environmental and social needs. They argue that genuine citizen participation should be part of the planning process. Such ideas, of course, are strongly objected to by the development-oriented economic sector, which has all along enjoyed a large degree of development rights. Their strong reactions to the Comprehensive Review of the Town Planning Ordinance, which aims to introduce more citizen participation in the planning process and allow planners greater power to control development, is a case in point.

The once autonomous government is also constrained by the imminent presence of the China factor in the territory. The controversies over the Port and Airport Development Strategy (PADS)[19] and financial arrangements for the airport core projects,[20] and the still continuing tug-of-war over the mode of land disposal at Container Terminal No. 9 in Tsing Yi Island, illustrate that the government can no longer apply its own values alone in the planning process. At least the future sovereign power of Hong Kong–China has to be consulted and its agreement solicited, before any development that straddles 1997 can proceed.

The uncertainties about guiding values are compounded by uncertainties about related decisions which, again, have much to do with planning and development in China.

❏ *UR: Uncertainties about Related Decisions*

Since 1978, the open door policy in China has opened up new horizons for the labour-intensive and low value-added industries in Hong Kong. The "exodus" of these industries to southern China, and in particular the Pearl River Delta in order to tap the cheap land and labour resources, has created many problems, both within Hong Kong and in the broader region. It has been estimated that around 25,000 factories, employing three to four million workers in the Pearl River Delta region, are engaged in outward processing for Hong Kong companies.[21] This in turn has generated a large volume of "outward-processing trade" between China and Hong Kong. In 1993, Hong Kong's total trade with China amounted to HK$740.1 billion, with domestic exports amounting to HK$63.4 billion and re-exports HK$274.6 billion.

As a result, the local container port in Hong Kong has now become a regional port and there is an accelerated demand for new berths and port backup services. The uncontrolled conversion of rural land into dumping ground, storage sites and "container country" prompted the 1991 amendment of the Town Planning Ordinance to extend planning and development control to the New Territories. Tackling traffic bottlenecks at the border areas also has become an urgent task with the growth of outward-processing activities in the Pearl River Delta.

At the same time, localities in southern China have become more ambitious in the light of the open door policy. In order to establish themselves in the region and participate actively in the world economy, they have various plans for building their infrastructures. For instance, at least 10 uncoordinated ports (Guangzhou/Huangpu, Zhanjiang, Shantou, Chiwan, Mawan, Shekou, Yantian, Jiuzhou, Lianhuashan and Foshan) in the Pearl River Delta are open to international shipping. In addition, there will be at least four international airports (Hong Kong, Macau, Shenzhen and Guangzhou) in the region. Coordination among local Chinese authorities in the construction of road networks, power plants, etc. has been poor.

Hence, there is an urgent need for strategic planning at the regional level in order to rationalize and economize investments. A rational and politically acceptable regional division of labour is also imperative to strengthen the region's competitiveness in the world economy. However, overcoming the administrative barriers to achieve coordinated planning and development is very difficult in the Pearl River Delta, which has two Special Administrative Regions (Hong Kong in 1997 and Macau in 1999), two Special Economic Zones (Shenzhen and Zhuhai), the Provincial Capital (Guangzhou), and Pearl River Delta Economic Open Zone. While Hong Kong as a small city-state has little experience in regional planning, high politics will definitely introduce more uncertainties in any endeavour towards regional cooperation and planning.

❏ *Summary*

Planners in the 1990s are entrusted with the challenge to restructure local and regional space not only to meet new and yet-to-be fully understood economic needs, but also other competing interests. While economic interests still loom large in land use planning, environmental and social concerns can no longer be neglected given the trend of democratization in Hong Kong. Political considerations (the China factor) have also influenced land use planning. Not only are planners less sure about what the guiding values in the planning process should be; the need to understand the regional dynamics, and yet the difficulties in obtaining accurate information from the Chinese authorities, let alone formal dialogue and cooperation with them, have also introduced many uncertainties in any attempt to plan for the territory in the last years of the transition period.

The situation is similar to Figure 2. In tackling uncertainties in related decision areas, it is found that uncertainties about the planning environment, values and related decisions in southern China have to be understood before local planning issues can be dealt with properly.

In the following section, a SWOT analysis is carried out to assess how well Hong Kong can handle these uncertainties.

STRENGTHS, WEAKNESSES, OPPORTUNITIES, THREATS (SWOT) ANALYSIS

A SWOT analysis is a useful tool for scanning the internal and external environment of an organization. According to Wechsler and Backoff,[22] an organization should assess its internal strengths and weaknesses through a critical examination of its own resources such as strength of leadership, information flow, sources of funding, etc.; the existing strategy; and the performance of the organization in terms of its history, initiative, and attitudes towards change, and so on. In scanning the external environment, the organization should try to identify opportunities and threats at different geographical levels (international, national, regional and local), in various aspects (demographic, economic, technological, cultural, political, etc.), and through the understanding of the preferences of different stakeholders. While the following discussion will be guided by this theoretical framework, it should be remembered that different stakeholders may have completely different perceptions and interpretations of strengths, weaknesses, opportunities or threats. The following is just one way of interpreting Hong Kong's strategic environment. In fact, a conclusive understanding of any strategic planning context can only be legitimized in a democratic political arena.

❑ *Strengths*

The annual real GDP growth in the territory between 1983 and 1993 averaged 6.4%, and its per capita GDP in 1992 was second in Asia among the non-oil-producing economies. These figures suggest that Hong Kong's strength lies in its ability to facilitate and enhance capital accumulation. Many factors contribute to such spectacular economic achievements.

Unlike other Chinese communities[23] where rule of law seems to be alien to its traditional culture, Hong Kong, after more than a century of British colonial influence, has a much higher respect for law and order, which is vital for the running of a capitalist society. Over the years, both the private and public sectors have learnt many useful lessons and accumulated valuable experience in planning and managing various aspects of compact urban development in the small territory of Hong Kong. The policy framework has been set and modified by the relatively clean and efficient administration, to provide a proper infrastructure to facilitate the evolving needs of the economy. When necessary, quasi-public corporations are set up to tackle various development issues. Examples are the Housing Authority, the Land Development Corporation, the Mass Transit Railway Corporation and the Kowloon–Canton Railway Corporation. For those private utilities businesses which affect the livelihood of the general public, regulations are in place to monitor their performances.[24] The container ports and tunnels, etc. are run by the private sector. Although many grassroots organizations have criticized various aspects of these arrangements, it cannot be denied that Hong Kong has witnessed highly successful urban development through public and private partnership.

Hong Kong is practically an open economy, which guarantees the freedom of capital movement. The city is linked with the rest of the world by an efficient transportation and communication network. There are also excellent social and physical infrastructure and service facilities.

Of course, these are all due to the existence of many brilliant brains in the territory. The entrepreneurial private sector needs no elaboration. Private developers have been the "community builders" since the birth of the colony. With an efficient communication system, established legal provisions and codes of practice, the bilingual (fluent in both Chinese and English) professionals such as architects, lawyers, engineers and planners, etc. have ensured that the planning, construction and management of the city are of high professional standards. Highly qualified technicians and labourers have also contributed to a high standard of city development. The provision and management of an excellent infrastructure by both the private and public sectors have also been facilitated by the existence of a sound and yet dynamic financial sector.

The territory's long-established connections with the international market have strengthened its world status, especially after the opening up of the huge China market immediately north of its border.

One may argue that Hong Kong's strength lies in its economics. However, in recent years, this bias towards money-making has been counterbalanced by growing environmental concerns. Also, the democratization of the polity and the birth of a political community have led to a reconsideration of development goals. Some business persons may consider this to be detrimental to rapid economic growth and hence a weakness of Hong Kong's strategic environment. However, if genuine development is to benefit the community in an all-round way, it should not be biased towards economic growth. The recognition of this point should be counted as a strength of our society.

Since the government is the biggest landlord, a great "developer" and the planning authority in the territory, it should be able to satisfy environmental and social needs if it has the political will to do so. This was demonstrated by the setting up of an *ad hoc* interdepartmental Task Force on Land Supply and Property Prices that was formed to tackle the problem of escalating property prices.

❏ *Weaknesses*

In face of economic and political transition, we have begun to realize the effect of one-sided emphasis on economic growth. While our institutions and expertise are very efficient and effective in facilitating economic development, we have little experience in planning for social and other needs. Many of the strategic plans such as the Port and Airport Development Strategy or even the Metroplan, have focused on financial implications rather than their (re)distributional effects on the general public.

While strategic planning in other contexts means the translation of sectoral policies into spatial terms to coordinate investment, the proclaimed "positive non-intervention" economic policy in the territory sets the limit for effective land use planning. If the government is not prepared to adopt a vision for economic growth and development, land use planners can only play a passive role in satisfying the needs of the market forces.

In fact, the government has a poor record in facilitating the technological upgrading of industries or curbing speculative activities in the property market. According to *Ming Pao*,[25] the six biggest developers in the territory have a land bank of 9.3 square kilometres, close to 1% of the total land area in Hong Kong. While the Housing Authority has been quite successful in redeveloping its own housing estates, and a quasi-public Land Development Corporation was set up in 1988 to facilitate redevelopment, a comprehensive urban renewal policy (which inevitably has to involve the private sector) is still absent in Hong Kong. A lack of political will to redefine the role of the government in the face of economic and political transition is obvious.

Besides the lack of experience and political will to meet needs other than economic ones, Hong Kong also lacks experience in regional planning and development, which have become urgent as a result of the economic integration of China and Hong Kong.

Furthermore, the strongly executive-led administration is not accountable to the general public and has been very reluctant to listen to different voices or solicit their collective wisdom, even in the face of so many uncertainties. So as 1997 approaches, the "brain drain" has become a serious problem, reflecting a lack of confidence and commitment by the middle class due to the uncertain political future.

The scarce land resources in Hong Kong demand a scrupulous land use planning process to achieve economic growth, environmental sustainability, social equity and general satisfaction. It has been argued by many planning theorists that this can only be achieved with the legitimate participation of various stakeholders in the planning and decision-making process. The weakness of the planning system in Hong Kong is that participation of all affected parties is out of the question, given the yet-to-be democratized executive-led polity. Today, high politics and the prominence of the China factor have also tarnished the performance of the administration. Tied by the traditional "positive non-intervention" economic policy, the government's vested interests in land-related development, and a closed planning system with little formal dialogue with the general public or China, land use planners today can only afford an "incremental or muddling through" type of reactive planning.

❑ *Opportunities*

Hong Kong's role as the gateway to an expanding world market, China, is an opportunity unmatched by its counterparts in the rapidly growing Pacific region. More importantly, southern China is keen to absorb market practices, and develop market-oriented attitudes. It also has the political and institutional freedom to devise a facilitating environment for the invisible hand to operate. This will definitely provide ample opportunity for both the public and private sectors in Hong Kong to offer their valuable experience in the planning, construction and management of a built environment conducive to capital accumulation.[26] Given the fact that Hong Kong has developed a better institutional (legal or otherwise) framework to carry out planning and development compared to Taiwan or China, with political will, Hong Kong should be able to play a very important role in furthering and realizing the "greater China community" concept.

In addition, as there are now more than 3,000 Mainland Chinese companies operating in Hong Kong, investing some HK$15–20 billion dollars,[27] the transfer of experience in running an international city can take place within Hong Kong.

In terms of land resources, the building of Chek Lap Kok airport on Lantau Island and the launching of airport core projects (for instance, 62 hectares of land will be available for development along the airport railway[28]) as well as the removal of Kai Tak Airport, have opened up new spatial opportunities for better planning within the territory. This will help to achieve Metroplan's aim of thinning out population in the metropolitan area.

❏ *Threats*

Political uncertainty is probably the greatest threat for the territory. While the "one country, two systems" concept guarantees great autonomy in Hong Kong, there is the constant fear that China will choose to interfere in the running of Hong Kong after 1997, as witnessed in the controversies over the airport and container port projects,[29] and the establishment of the Preliminary Working Committee and its proposal for the setting up of a provisional legislature in 1997. Also, law and order is not well-respected and corruption is rampant in China. Institutions in China have been weak in controlling development, arresting environmental degradation, improving transportation, encouraging training and education, and providing up-to-standard infrastructure. With the approach of 1997, many people in Hong Kong have chosen "exits" rather than "voices," to avoid seeing the degeneration of the built environment and hence the vitality of Hong Kong. Also, the threat that people from China will "flood" into Hong Kong after 1997 exists and if this happens, the sustainability of Hong Kong as an already densely populated city will be questioned.

The lack of appropriate coordination and the keen competition from various local authorities in southern China may, in the long run, diminish the competitiveness of the region, especially in the face of the rapid development of other mega-urban regions within China (Xiamen, Shanghai, Shandong) and in Asia (the southern Growth Triangle centred around Singapore, Bangkok in Thailand or even Indonesia).

On the economic front, since industrialists in Hong Kong have invested heavily in China, China's position in the world economy is very important to Hong Kong. For instance, if the United States denied China's most-favoured-nation (MFN) status, around two-thirds of China's exports to the United States, many of which originate in Hong Kong-owned factories in southern China, would be cut off.[30] According to recent estimates by the Hong Kong government, the loss of China's MFN status would cost Hong Kong up to 70,000 jobs and up to three percentage points of Hong Kong's annual GDP growth.[31]

❏ *Strategic Planning Issues*

Theoretically, the SWOT analysis should allow us to appreciate better our external and internal environment, so that strategies can be devised to "build on strengths, overcome weaknesses, exploit opportunities and blunt threats."[32] From the above analysis, three strategic planning issues can be identified.

1. Existing strengths, in terms of effectuating the planning, design, financing, construction and management of sophisticated city development by public-private partnerships, should be fully utilized in order to restructure the built environment to suit evolving development needs.

2. In order to overcome weaknesses of the land use planning system in accommodating all-round development needs, efforts should be made to satisfy economic as well as social and environmental needs.

3. To overcome our lack of regional planning expertise, and to exploit opportunities in the expanding China market as well as blunt uncertain political threats, there should be vision and genuine efforts to develop Hong Kong and southern China as an even more competitive mega-urban region in Pacific Asia. This logically will require a rethink of the economic development philosophy and strategy in the territory.

The following section will review what the government has done to tackle these issues. Some comments will be made on the government's actions so far, and finally, recommendations to overcome different types of uncertainty related to the three strategic planning issues identified will be put forward.

STRATEGIC PLANNING ISSUES: ACTIONS, CRITIQUE, AND SUGGESTIONS

❏ *Government Actions*

Interestingly, while there are subtle differences, the issues identified above are not markedly different from those specified in the Territorial Development Strategy (TDS) review which, as the top tier of plans in Hong Kong, is designed to spell out the strategic goals of territorial development:

The primary goal of the TDS review is to establish a broad, long term land use-transport-environmental planning framework within which the necessary land and infrastructure can be provided, having regard to resource availability, to enable Hong Kong to continue to grow as a regional and an international city and become a better place in which to live and work.[33]

While this goal and the six principal objectives of the TDS review[34] have been extensively endorsed by the general public,[35] how they are generated is not specified in the review. The first objective: "[to] enhance the role of Hong Kong as an international city and a regional centre for business, finance, information, tourism, entrepôt activities and manufacturing," is related to the third strategic planning issue identified. Objectives two to five argue that land use and infrastructure provision should aim to meet various sectoral needs in order to facilitate the convenient movement of people and goods within a conserved and good-quality environment. These are related to the second strategic issue identified. Objective six, which stresses the importance of public-private partnerships to satisfy changing demand within resource constraints, is also similar to the first strategic planning issue identified.

In the following, we shall proceed to review what the government has done so far in relation to the strategic planning issues identified in the previous section on SWOT analysis. Table 1 is a list of planning-related policies, plans, studies or actions undertaken by the government.[36]

Restructuring the Local Built Environment

Of the three strategic planning issues, it seems that the government has done a lot on planning how to reshape the local built environment as a result of the economic restructuring processes. The pendulum of spatial development in Hong Kong has swung from decentralization (new town development) in the 1970s to recentralization of the main urban areas (the 1984 TDS) in the 1980s. Today, both the metropolitan area (Metroplan) and the western part of the territory are the focus of spatial development. In fact, as a result of the economic integration between Hong Kong and the Pearl River Delta, the North West New Territories (NWNT) has become the "gateway" to China within Hong Kong. With the announcement of the PADS in 1989 and the airport core projects, it has already been predicted that the gravity of economic activities will shift westward.

The Updating of the Second Comprehensive Transport Study, the Freight Transport Study and the Rail Development Study have all

Table 1:   Selected Planning-related Policies, Plans, Studies or Actions
           Undertaken by the Government

Restructuring the built environment

Land use planning

Hong Kong Planning Standards and Guidelines
Constantly under review. Available for sale and reference, not consultation or comments.

Territorial Development Strategy Review

1991	Foundation Study for Business Park Development Final Report
Nov. 1991	Foundation for Recreation Land Strategy
Dec. 1991	Foundation Study for Industrial Land Development Strategy
1992	Hong Kong Science Park Study Stage One
Oct. 1992	Foundation Study for an Office Land Development Strategy
*1993	Territorial Development Strategy Review — Development Options: A Consultative Digest
1993	Foundation Study for Lantau Port and Western Harbour Study
*July 1993	Territorial Development Strategy Review: Foundation Report
*July 1993	Territorial Development Strategy Review: Environmental Baseline Conditions
Nov. 1993	Study on the Restructuring of Obsolete Industrial Area (ROBINA)
*Sept. 1994	Territorial Development Strategy Review: Report on Public Consultation
Ongoing	Foundation Study for Rural Land Use Strategy Review
Ongoing	Tourism Study
Ongoing	Hong Kong Science Park Study Stage Two

Port and Airport Development Strategy and Core Projects

Oct. 1989	Port and Airport Development Strategy
July 1991	Memorandum of Understanding
1993/94	Port Development Strategy Review
Nov. 1994	An "agreed minute"

Sub-Regional Development Strategy

An Interim Recommended Strategy on the NWNT, SWNT Development Strategies
– pending the finalization of the TDS review

NENT Development Strategy Review
– commenced September 1993

SENT Development Strategy Review
– will commence in due course

Metroplan
*April 1988	Metroplan: The Aims
*1990	Metroplan: The Initial Options
*Nov. 1991	The Selected Strategy: An Overview

The Town Planning Ordinance

1991	Town Planning (Amendment) Ordinance
*July 1991	Comprehensive Review of the Town Planning Ordinance: Consultative Document

Table 1 (cont'd)

Satisfying all-round developmental needs

Transport	
May 1989	Hong Kong: Second Comprehensive Transport Study
*May 1989	Green Paper on Transport Policy in Hong Kong
Jan. 1990	Moving into the 21st Century — The White Paper on Transport Policy in Hong Kong
*Oct. 1992	Taxi Policy Review
July 1993	Updating of Second Comprehensive Transport Study Final Report
1993	Freight Transport Study
*April 1993	Railway Development Study
Dec. 1994	Railway Development Study unveiled to the Legislative Council

Environment	
1989	White Paper: Pollution in Hong Kong — A Time to Act
1989	Long Term Sewage Treatment Plan (currently under review)
*July 1993	Territorial Development Strategy Review: Environmental Baseline Conditions
Dec. 1993	Second White Paper Review of the Environment: The Hong Kong Environment: A Green Challenge for the Community

Housing	
1987	Long Term Housing Strategy
1988	Land Development Corporation
*1993	Mid-Term Review of the Long Term Housing Strategy
June 1994	Final Report of the Mid-Term Review of the Long Term Housing Strategy
June 1994	Report of the Task Force on Land Supply and Property Prices

Enhancing regional development

July 1990	Hong Kong–Guangdong Environmental Protection Liaison Group (first meeting)
Since 1990	Hong Kong Trade Development Council has focused on penetrating China's market and facilitating direct foreign investment projects from rest of the world to China
1993	Study of Development Trends in Guangdong Province: Part I
Dec. 1994	Study of Development Trends in Guangdong Province: Part II
Jan. 1995	First meeting of the cross-border Infrastructure Coordinating Committee (ICC)
Forming	An applied research centre which draws together the expertise of tertiary institutions in Hong Kong and the Chinese Academy of Sciences

* Published for general public consultation and reference. However, it should be noted that it is an administrative practice for many of the stated plans, legislation or policies to have some kind of public consultation via the District Boards or other relevant organizations.

recognized the importance of transport links to the border area and the strategic location of NWNT, and hence the need for transport infrastructure development.

This point is further stressed in "Points of Principle" in the TDS review,[37]

> ... there will be a further strong gravitational pull of development along a SE–NW axis in Hong Kong connecting up with a corridor of growth along the east bank of the Pearl River. These forces of change will require substantial upfront investment in infrastructure and ... new strategic development at suitable locations along ... E–W on Lantau and SE–NW around Yuen Long South, Kam Tin and Lo Wu. The fulcrum of these two axes will be Tsuen Wan–Kwai Tsing, which can be expected to become a focal point for new investment in a range of private sector-led activities. [see Figure 3]

Satisfying All-round Development Needs

If we compare the principal goal of the 1984 TDS with the one stated in the TDS review, we can see that the government has paid more attention to environmental concerns and the regional development context. The 1984 TDS was:

> ... to produce a long-term land use/transportation strategy for Hong Kong to cater to a derived target population and associated socio-economic activities in a manner which will produce the highest quality environment within constraints set by resource availability and the time frame within which the needs of the target population have to be met.

While the PADS was drawn up behind closed doors and hence caused grave concern for the Chinese government and the general lay public,[38] consultative documents on Metroplan, the TDS review and the Comprehensive Review of the Town Planning Ordinance have been published in order to solicit comments and ideas from the general public (Table 1). In particular, the Planning Department has published a *Report on Public Consultation on the TDS Review*. These practices will definitely contribute to the clarification of complicated planning goals and objectives as defined by the administration.

Enhancing Regional Development

As can be seen from Table 1, the government's approach to enhancing

Figure 3: Potential Areas for Strategic Urban Development in TDS Review

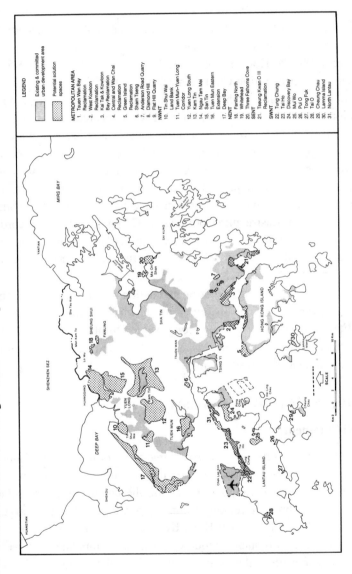

Source: Planning Department, *Territorial Development Strategy Review: Foundation Report* (Hong Kong: Government Printer, July 1993), Figure 6.2, reprinted by permission of the Planning Department, Hong Kong Government.

development in the region is to reshape Hong Kong internally so that it can serve its hinterland. In order to understand the hinterland thoroughly so that Hong Kong can better serve the wider region, the Study of Development Trends in Guangdong Province was commissioned in 1992. However, actions beyond a better understanding of the hinterland through study and analysis are *ad hoc* and not coordinated.

Since 1990, the Hong Kong Trade Development Council (HKTDC) has focused on penetrating China's market and facilitating direct foreign investments to China.[39] The Hong Kong–Guangdong Environmental Protection Liaison Group was set up in 1990. It was reported in the *1994 Policy Address Progress Report* that close contacts have been maintained in respect of major infrastructure projects such as the Shenzhen River Regulation Project, the Strategic Sewage Disposal Scheme, the Fill Management Study, and a $2 billion project to expand the supply of water from Guangdong. Recently, both governments have endorsed the establishment of a cross-border Infrastructure Coordinating Committee (ICC). According to the *1994 Policy Address Progress Report*, an applied research centre will also be established to draw together the expertise of Hong Kong's tertiary institutes and the Chinese Academy of Sciences.

The lack of more formal coordinated action can be understood, since Britain is eager to maintain its autonomy in running Hong Kong before 1997. Furthermore, even if Hong Kong wanted to plan with the Chinese authorities, institutional barriers arising from the complicated local political economies are not easy to surmount.

❑ Critique of Government Actions

Overall Comment

In the previous sections, we discussed three types of uncertainty found in Hong Kong's planning context: uncertainties about the economic restructuring process, guiding values in reshaping the urban fabric, and related decisions in the broader region (China in particular). We also argued, through a SWOT analysis, that Hong Kong's strength lies in its ability to construct a built environment conducive to capital accumulation. However, it is weak in meeting other social, environmental or regional development needs. The territory also faces political uncertainties in the future. With its growing economic integration with China, sound economic growth in the territory will depend on healthy development in southern China.

From the review of government actions, it can be argued that the government is most competent in overcoming uncertainties about the planning environment through voluminous studies. The government is less enthusiastic about changing the guiding values which reshape the urban fabric. While they are a breakthrough in Hong Kong's planning history, the recent public consultation exercises resemble publicity activities to "propagate" the administration's value judgements, rather than genuine dialogue between the administration and the general public in order to sort out a set of compromised goals and objectives. Furthermore, for political reasons, the government has restrained from tackling uncertainties in related decision areas.

Because of this approach, the essence derived from the recent spatial development strategies is not very different from previous ones. The prime objective still lies where Hong Kong has been strongest: facilitating economic growth. Hence, the following critique will focus on the government's failure to overcome its weaknesses: satisfying all-round development needs and enhancing regional development and planning.

Publicity or Public Consultation?

Theoretically, a spatial strategy should be able to coordinate investment with physical development for the implementation of specific sectoral policies. In other words, the product of spatial planning is closely related to the specific goals and objectives of different socio-economic sectors. Hence, the opportunity to question the spatial plan itself is not adequate. The average citizen should also have the chance to comment on the specific goals and objectives of various sectoral policies. For instance, the chance to comment on the quality, quantity and whereabouts of industrial locations is not adequate. People should also be given the opportunity to ask questions such as: Should the government do more to help the upgrading of the industrial sector, since the Hong Kong's outward-processing activities in the Pearl River Delta would not be sustainable if China could not renew its MFN status?

However, both the TDS review and the Metroplan only allow comments on the spatial plans. Details of foundation studies of the TDS review (on different sectors) are not available for public scrutiny (Table 1). The general public has to accept the baseline taken by the administration which, very often, is the status quo. However, as argued previously, the economic and political transition since the 1980s has introduced many uncertainties in Hong Kong's planning environment and it is questionable if we should assume that the status quo will go on beyond the twenty-first century. The values embedded in the Foundation Studies are defined by the administration and the general public is not invited to comment on those values. Furthermore, without access to the detailed reports, it is almost impossible for the lay public to give penetrating comments. With the trend of democratization, it can be expected that this monopoly of the agenda, goal setting and planning information by the administration in the planning process will be increasingly challenged by various political organizations.

While the government has emphasized environmental concerns in the current TDS review, other values such as social concerns are an obvious omission, as reflected in the contents of the Foundation Studies (Table 1). Although the government produced a *White Paper on Social Welfare into the 1990s and Beyond* in 1991 and a *Green Paper on Equal Opportunities and Full Participation: A Better Tomorrow for All*, strategic planners seem to have nothing to say about how the built environment can help realize the goals and objectives stated in these documents. The administration argues that the "TDS review is not a social policy document."[40] Yet, the TDS review has claimed as its goal to make Hong Kong "a better place to live and work" and has also specified in its objective two that "land use and infrastructure needs arising from ... major socio-economic activities" are to be satisfied.

The lack of discussion about social concerns at the strategic level has grave implications. Spatial implications of social policies, very often, are more obvious to the general public at the micro or district level. However, for many social policies to succeed, the support of spatial planning policies is necessary. The *Hong Kong Planning Standards and Guidelines*, for instance, is widely used for formulating development strategies, preparing town plans, drawing up planning briefings or scrutinizing development proposals. However, these non-statutory standards and guidelines have never been reviewed with public involvement. The justification and rationale for setting up this document remain unknown to the average citizen. Yet it provides standards and guidelines to determine the quality of the place in which we live and work.

Also, when the government decided to build the core airport projects, the average citizen did not know what trade-offs would be for Hong Kong to carry out these mega-projects. The Metroplan, a subregional development strategy to guide the restructuring of the main urban area, aims to thin out the population in the metropolitan area and the administration claims that "[the] majority of the policies needed to achieve main Metroplan objectives already exist." However, the government does not have a comprehensive urban renewal policy. In addition, the strategic plans have not dealt with the impact on those living in new towns when the focus of development returns to the metropolitan area and the virgin land in the western part of the territory. As NWNT and especially Tsuen Wan and Kwai Tsing are under great development pressure to serve regional or even international economic needs in the near future, the quality of life for the existing residents has been affected. What measures has the government proposed to balance the "life space" versus "economic space"[41] issues?

In other words, despite the various public consultation exercises, the government has not done much to overcome its weaknesses in achieving all-round development needs. Publicizing extracts of strategic studies seems to serve mainly to propagate the government's method of physical planning. Although this comment may not apply to the Comprehensive Review of the Town Planning Ordinance, which tries to introduce more citizen participation in the planning process, it should be noted that the Ordinance only deals with two out of four types of district plans. In its formulation, the statutory district plans have to be bounded by the policy framework within the upper tiers' strategic plans. If the average citizen does not have much power in influencing broader policy issues and strategic plans, they may not have much policy support in demanding changes at the district level, even though they are given wider participation rights.

Regional Planning or Hong Kong-centred Planning within a Region?

Available information shows that the government, due to understandable political reasons, is not particularly enthusiastic in overcoming its lack of experience in tackling regional development and planning. Although a Study of Development Trends in Guangdong Province has been done, this again is not available for the scrutiny of the general public. Nevertheless, the government's understanding of the Pearl River Delta and its perceived implications can be found in a small paper distributed by the Planning Department at a conference on "Hong Kong as a Regional Hub" held in

1994. While it is stated in the paper that "[within] the Pearl River Delta itself, it would seem that the principal needs in the medium term will be the expansion of power supplies, the extension and upgrading of road and rail networks, the expansion of port and airport facilities, the rationalization of urban development patterns and wider implementation of environmental protection measures,"[42] the government stops short of suggesting that given Hong Kong's strength and valuable experiences in these matters, it should therefore have a much more important role to play in effectuating these developments.

Instead, the government argues that "Hong Kong needs to consider the complementary provision of infrastructure within the territory to help facilitate such changes."[43] Yet this may not be a desirable or viable strategy in the long run. Unlike other great cities in Asia, where low value-added and labour-intensive productive activities are relocated outside the countries, those in Hong Kong are relocated to its immediate hinterland. Like the southern Growth Triangle in Singapore and the contiguous state of Johore Bahru in Malaysia, the proximity between Hong Kong and the Pearl River Delta means that Hong Kong too has to face many of the consequent environmental, social and transport problems generated by the relocated economic activities. And more importantly, informal contacts or advisory bodies alone, no matter how valuable, cannot resolve these issues effectively.

Furthermore, if Hong Kong really wants to serve the Pearl River Delta and the inner provinces of China, strategic physical or telecommunication connections with various points of production having forward and backward economic linkages are essential. This would require planning not just for additional strategic transport links between Hong Kong and the Pearl River Delta, but also for strategic production sites in southern China.

❏ *Suggested Actions*

Table 2 summarizes the actions suggested to tackle the three types of uncertainties related to the three strategic planning issues. As discussed above, the government has, in fact, done a lot to understand the restructuring of the economy and its spatial impacts. Also various strategic plans have been devised to reshape the urban fabric in order to serve new economic needs. However, it seems that the administration lacks the political will to break away from its previous economic philosophy of "positive non-interventionism." This in turn has reinforced the status quo of various sectoral development strategies which, in the long run, may not keep pace with the changing needs of society as a result of economic and political transitions. Also, the region as a whole may have to pay a high price if regional planning continues to be neglected amid rapid economic integration of the regional economies. In other words, the government, in devising its strategic actions, has built on strengths. Yet the strategies cannot overcome weaknesses, and offer little scope to exploit opportunities or blunt threats.

It will be argued that the government can in fact contribute a lot more towards clarifying the guiding values of development. To facilitate the restructuring of the regional built environment and to enhance regional development, it is suggested that the government set up an independent Institute of Regional Development and Planning in order to prepare the groundwork for the private sector and the future Special Administrative Region (SAR), to play a more prominent role in regional development and planning.

A Critical Review of Sectoral and Spatial Development Policies

With the gradual democratization of the political system and the opening up of the government, it is believed that top-down high-handed planning and policy-making can no longer satisfy the competing interests of the community. In fact, the involvement of the lay public in the planning and decision-making process is essential to ensure their subsequent support at the implementation stage. Only consolidated support can give greater legitimacy to planning proposals and help to blunt political uncertainties. It is therefore suggested that the government should schedule a timetable for the systematic review, with genuine citizen participation, of the various sectoral policies. In order to put the public in a better perspective and hence make the review a fruitful exercise, intersectoral and spatial impacts should also be specified in the review process.

Hong Kong has been very successful in creating a built environment conducive to economic success. It is time for us to adopt a bolder vision to make our city a better place to inhabit. Hence, social and environmental concerns should also be important considerations in spatial planning. If Hong Kong can succeed in striking a balance between these competing demands, the experience will definitely be very useful for other cities or countries.

Table 2: Suggested Actions to Build on Strengths, Overcome Uncertainties and Weaknesses, Exploit Opportunities and Blunt Threats

Strategic planning issues	UE (Uncertainties in planning environment)	UV (Uncertainties in guiding values)	UR (Uncertainties in related decisions)
Satisfying all-round development needs (A critical review of the sectoral development policies with genuine citizen participation)	– Critical review of individual sectoral policies. – Assess intersectoral impacts and trade-offs, and the spatial implications of adopting specific goals and objectives for different sectoral policies.	– Interactive public consultation such as public briefings, hearings and discussions, to solicit the general public's opinions on the goals and objectives of sectoral policies and their intersectoral impact and spatial implications. – Selective consultation with the neighbouring authorities may be useful.	*Before 1997* – If we accept the argument that only China can represent the future SAR government before 1997, China should also be invited to comment on the policies. *After 1997* – The "one country, two systems" concept should allow self-determination of local affairs by the people of Hong Kong.
Enhancing regional development and planning (The government should set up an Institute of Regional	*Facilitating the restructuring of the built environment* – Comparative research on the economic restructuring processes and their impact on Hong Kong and southern China. – Comparative research on the governance of local urban development in the region.	– Consultation with private developers who may invest in China's infrastructure development to see how the government can facilitate their investment. – Consultation with Hong Kong investors in China.	– Formal and informal contacts with various players in China in order to clarify various issues concerning uncertainties in the planning environment and the guiding values.

| Development and Planning to pave way for more proactive regional development planning by both the private sector and the future SAR) | – Comparative research on planning, construction, and management of city development by both the private and public sectors in Hong Kong and southern China.
– Assess possible role of public and private sectors in effectuating spatial changes in the region.

Laying the groundwork to enhance regional development
– Development in the Asia Pacific rim and implications on regional development in Hong Kong and southern China.
– Database on Hong Kong and Southern China: regional accounts (income and expenditure information on production, consumption and investment), inter-industry relationships, and employment situation, demographics, infrastructure development, direct foreign investment, resource inventory, regional disparities, human resources, technological development, housing conditions, land resources, etc.
– History of regional development and planning.
– Institutions and policies related to regional development and planning in China.
– Major players in regional development and planning.
– Land suitability analysis.
– Scenarios of regional divison of labour. | – Perhaps a consultation network has to be set up, especially among the various governments, professional groups, academics, civil organizations (or its equivalent in China, if any).
– Experiences in other countries may be studied to improve the consultation channels and procedures.

Most work can be done by the academics and private sector and the government may play a facilitating role through information provision and policy support, etc.
– In the long run, no co-ordinated regional development can take place without a more proactive role played by the local governments. If formal establishment is not possible before 1997, informal contacts should be made with a view to forming a long-term working relationship.
– Liaison with other Asian governments to know about their development strategies and policies for reference. |

Establishment of an Institute of Regional Development and Planning

Given the existing political situation, it may defy many people's imagination at this stage to visualize coordinated planning and development by the various local authorities in the rapidly developing mega-urban region in southern China. While this may not be possible in the near future, it is suggested that groundwork which will eventually lead to such a development can be laid now. An Institute of Regional Development and Planning (an organization perhaps not unlike the Korean Research Institute of Human Settlements[44]) can be set up to undertake basic research and liaison work.

The Institute should be responsible for two interrelated tasks: to serve as an information centre to facilitate the restructuring of the regional built environment, and to lay the groundwork to enhance regional development and planning.

To facilitate restructuring of the built environment, the valuable experiences of the public and private sectors in Hong Kong in running the city can be systematically researched. The legal framework for planning and development, the experience of establishing new towns, reclamation planning, managing various aspects of metropolitan development such as fiscal policy, budgeting, human resources planning, running port and airport and different utilities, etc. should be well documented for public reference. The dissemination of this knowledge should be very useful for the developing cities in southern China. In addition, a more systematic collection of information concerning various aspects of urban development, planning, governance, etc. of cities in China will be very useful for potential Hong Kong investors in China. This knowledge should enable them to make a more intelligent evaluation of the investment environment in China and hence make better market decisions.

The Institute need not conduct all these research projects or studies. In fact, many academics in various tertiary institutions have already been working on these issues.[45] What the government needs to do is to allocate funding for the systematic organization of information, further research, dissemination of research results and support of formal and informal contacts between academics and professional groups in Hong Kong and southern China. The Institute would serve as the prominent place for displaying these collective research results for the general public's reference.

In terms of gathering relevant information on the region to enhance regional development planning, Table 2 lists a number of activities that the Institute may engage in. The Institute, besides gathering hard data on regional development and planning, can also help disseminate knowledge and collect feedback on this data from various sources in the region. The Institute should also attempt to work out different scenarios of development in the region, suggest possible regional division of labour and develop strategies for urban and rural areas. It can also undertake active comparative research to synthesize lessons of regional development and planning in other countries. Of course, these tasks will be futile if the planned strategies are not implemented. Perhaps one of the top items on the agenda for the SAR after 1997 will be the institutionalization of regional planning in southern China.

CONCLUSION

Land use planners in Hong Kong have been facing new and formidable challenges since the transition period in the 1980s. On the one hand, they need to make sense of the economic restructuring process in order to reshape the existing urban fabric to serve the evolving needs of the economies in the region. On the other hand, because of the democratization process, they also have to understand and serve the growing environmental and social concerns. It is now imperative for planners to strike a balance between these competing demands in the land use planning process.

The economic and political integration between Hong Kong and China also opens up new dimensions for the work of planners. Good planning becomes almost impossible if the China factor is not considered. With the rapid development of the Asian regional division of labour, Hong Kong and southern China as a whole is facing keen competition from other mega-urban regions. While the region still has the cutting edge over the other new newly industrializing economies such as Bangkok in Thailand or Jabotabek in Indonesia, its continued competitive advantage has to be cultivated by the bilateral efforts of both the private and public sectors in Hong Kong and southern China. Regional development planning, therefore, should have a lot to offer to make the region a better place for life and livelihood.[46]

This may not be a palatable solution to those who fear the encroachment by Chinese authorities on the territory's autonomy, or those who have absolute faith in market forces to take care of resource allocation. However, history has shown that political differences can only be resolved through dialogue, cooperation, negotiation and compromise, not by isolation. In fact, isolation is no longer possible or desirable given the intensity of economic integration. Economic development to date has also suggested that if not coordinated or planned, economic growth will take place at the expense of the natural and social environment, the cost of which may extend to many subsequent generations. In the wake of Hong Kong's reversion to Chinese rule in 1997 and the approach of the twenty-first century, perhaps it is time for the small city of Hong Kong to think bigger in terms of strategic urban and regional development.

NOTES

1. A comment made by Lord Palmerston, the then British Foreign Secretary in 1841. In fact, he was not satisfied with the cession of Hong Kong and did not believe Hong Kong would become a mart of trade. See G. B. Endacott, *A History of Hong Kong* (2nd ed.; Hong Kong: Oxford University Press, 1964), p. 18.

2. R. Bristow, *Land-use Planning in Hong Kong: History, Policies and Procedures* (Hong Kong: Oxford University Press, 1984), pp. 57–58.

3. See, for example, R. Bristow, *Land-use Planning in Hong Kong: History, Policies and Procedures* (Hong Kong: Oxford University Press, 1984); M. Castells, "The Shek Kip Mei Syndrome: Public Housing and Economic Development in Hong Kong," in *Centre of Urban Studies and Urban Planning Working Paper No. 15* (Hong Kong: Centre of Urban Studies and Urban Planning, The University of Hong Kong, 1986); K. S. Pun, "Past and Future Development of Urban Planning in Hong Kong," *Planning and Development*, Vol. 5, No. 1 (1989), pp. 7–13; B. Taylor, and R.Y.W. Kwok, "From Export Center to World City: Planning for the Transformation of Hong Kong," *Journal of the American Planning Institute* (summer 1989), pp. 309–22.

4. Before 1995, the overall land development and planning policy framework was set by the Land Development Policy Committee chaired by the Chief Secretary. Since 1995, this function has been incorporated into one of the subcommittees under the Chief Secretary Committee.

5. Hong Kong Government, *Hong Kong 1994* (Hong Kong: Government Printer, 1994), p. 187.

6. Ibid., p. 235.

7. Ibid., p. 247.

8. Ibid., p. 246.

9. See, for example, A. R. Cuthbert, "Hong Kong 1997: The Transition to Socialism — Ideology, Discourse and Urban Space," *Environment and*

Planning B: Society and Space, Vol. 5, No. 1 (March 1987), pp. 123–50; A. R. Cuthbert, "For a Few Dollars More: Urban Planning and the Legitimation Process in Hong Kong," *International Journal of Urban and Regional Research*, Vol. 15, No. 4 (December 1991), pp. 575–93; M. K. Ng, "Strategic Planning in Hong Kong: Lessons from TDS (Territorial Development Strategy) and PADS (Port and Airport Development Strategy)," *Town Planning Review*, Vol. 64, No. 3 (1993), pp. 287–311; A.G.O. Yeh, "Urban Development of Hong Kong in the 21st Century: Opportunities and Challenges," in *Pacific Asia in the 21st Century: Geographical and Development Perspectives*, edited by Yeung Yue-man (Hong Kong: The Chinese University Press, 1993), pp. 69–103.

10. A. M. Pflaum, and T. J. Delmont, "External Scanning — A Tool for Planners," *Journal of the American Planning Association*, Vol. 53, No. 1 (Winter 1987), pp. 58–68.

11. J. Friend, and A. Hickling, *Planning under Pressure: The Strategic Choice Approach* (Oxford: Pergamon Press, 1987), p. 11.

12. Ibid., pp. 10–11.

13. According to the *Revised Estimates of Gross Domestic Product 1961 to First Quarter 1994* (pp. 40–41) published by the Census and Statistics Department in Hong Kong in August 1994, the contributions to GDP of wholesale, retail and import/export trades, restaurants and hotels; transport storage and communication; financing, insurance, real estate and other business services; and community, social and personal services are 26.2%, 9.7%, 24.5% and 1.2% respectively.

14. "Overview of Current Hub Functions" (paper distributed at the Conference on Hong Kong as a Regional Hub organized by the Hong Kong Institute of Planners at CGO Conference Hall, Hong Kong, 30 September 1994).

15. According to "Overview of Current Hub Functions" (Note 14), there is also a strong presence of the world's other major financial institutions in Hong Kong: 226 overseas securities and commodity trading companies; 124 overseas insurers; and 862 unit trusts and mutual funds. See also Y. P. Ho, and Y. Y. Kueh, "Whither Hong Kong in an Open-Door, Reforming Chinese Economy?" *The Pacific Review*, Vol. 6, No. 4 (1993), p. 336.

16. See Note 14, p. 2.

17. See "Whither Hong Kong in an Open-Door, Reforming Chinese Economy?" (Note 15), p. 336.

18. M. K. Ng, "The Changing Politics in Hong Kong: Whither the Role of Planners," *Planning and Development*, Vol. 8, No. 2 (1992), pp. 2–12.

19. M. K. Ng, "A Case Study of the Port and Airport Development Strategy (PADS) in Hong Kong," *American Institute of Certified Planners' Casebook 7, American Planning Association* (Summer 1993).

20. D.K.Y. Chu, "Transportation," in *The Other Hong Kong Report 1992*, edited by Joseph Y. S. Cheng and Paul C. K. Kwong (Hong Kong: The Chinese University Press, 1992), pp. 351–64.

21. Same as Note 17, p. 344.

22. B. Wechsler, and R. W. Backoff, "The Dynamics of Strategy in Public Organizations," *Journal of the American Planning Association*, Vol. 53, No. 1 (Winter 1987), p. 36.

23. Singapore, with a dominant Chinese population, also has a clean and efficient government with high respect for law and order. However, Hong Kong is a much more liberal society than Singapore in terms of freedom of speech and expression.

24. For instance, the China Light and Power Company Ltd., Eastern Energy Ltd. and Peninsula Electric Power Company Ltd., China Motor Bus Company Ltd., Hong Kong Air Cargo Terminals Ltd., Hong Kong Air Terminal Services Ltd., Hong Kong Telephone Company Ltd., Kowloon Motor Bus Company (1933) Ltd., etc. are regulated by the government through Schemes of Control by the government.

25. *Ming Pao*, 11 December 1994, p. G1.

26. For instance, the Hong Kong-based Hopewell Group, through joint-venture arrangements with the Guangdong General Power Company, had completed the Shajiao A and B plants providing 1.9 million kilowatts. Shajiao C plant is now under construction to provide an additional 0.66 million kilowatts. See Planning Department, "Development Trends in the Pearl River Delta: Background Notes" (paper distributed at the Conference on Hong Kong as a Regional Hub organized by the Hong Kong Institute of Planners at CGO Conference Hall, Hong Kong, 30 September 1994).

27. Same as Note 17, p. 348.

28. Five sites along the airport railway have been identified for property development: Hong Kong Central (3.18 ha), Kowloon (13.96 ha), Tai Kok Tsui (16.97 ha), Tsing Yi (5.4 ha), and Tung Chung (22.48 ha). It was estimated by the government that the premium payable could be close to HK\$100 billion. See B. Porter, "Agreement Brings \$100 Billion Property Bonanza Step Closer," *South China Morning Post*, 5 November 1994.

29. For a summary of the controversies over the financing of the airport core projects, please see "Airport Special," *South China Morning Post*, 5 November 1994; "The Eventful Development of the Airport in Hong Kong," *Ming Pao*, 4 November 1994, p. G10 (in Chinese); "Disposal of Land along the Airport Railway to Be Discussed by the Sino-British Land Commission," *Hong Kong Economic Journal*, 4 November 1994, p. 3 (in Chinese).

30. Same as Note 17, p. 347.

31. Ibid.

32. P. C. Nutt, and R. W. Backoff, "A Strategic Management Process for Public and Third-Sector Organizations," *Journal of the American Planning Association*, Vol. 53, No. 1 (Winter 1987), p. 49.

33. Planning Department, *The Territorial Development Strategy Review — Development Options: A Consultative Digest* (Hong Kong: Government Printer, 1993), p. 3.

34. Ibid.

35. Planning Department, *Territorial Development Strategy Review: Report on Public Consultation* (Hong Kong: Government Printer, September 1994), pp. 1–3.

36. It should be noted that the list is by no means exhaustive. Since many government studies and activities are carried out behind closed doors, it is difficult to know thoroughly what the government has or has not done. For details about the environment, housing and transport sectors, readers may want to refer to relevant chapters in this book.

37. See Note 33, p. 9.

38. M. K. Ng, "Strategic Planning in Hong Kong: Lessons from TDS (Territorial Development Strategy) and PADS (Port and Airport Development Strategy)," *Town Planning Review*, Vol. 64, No. 3 (1993), pp. 287–311. Also see Note 19.

39. C. Tuan, and C. S. Wong, "Evolution of Foreign Direct Investment Patterns and Management of TNCs in Hong Kong," *Regional Development Dialogue*, Vol. 14, No. 4 (Winter 1993), p. 128.

40. See Note 35, p. 154.

41. J. Friedmann, *Life Space and Economic Space: Essays in Third World Planning* (New Brunswick, U.S., and Oxford, U.K.: Transaction Books, 1988).

42. See "Development Trends in the Pearl River Delta: Background Notes" (Note 26), p. 8.

43. Ibid.

44. The Korean Research Institute of Human Settlements is a non-profit-making and independent research organization established to carry out, *inter alia*, the following:

   – to improve the knowledge and understanding of the conditions and problems of the nation's landed resources and their interactions with people;

   – to assist the government in formulating long-range development plans and strategies, and to make policy recommendations on related matters;

   – to cooperate with academic circles in solving theoretical and practical problems concerning critical human settlement issues;

   – to develop and maintain a data bank containing up-to-date information and statistics on the nation's land resources for use by the government, scholars, and the general public;

– to exchange and disseminate significant research findings at home and abroad as they relate to human settlement management and planning.

The activities of the Institute are financed by annual appropriation from the government, grants from public and private organizations and income from endowment (quoted from *KRIHS*, the Korea Research Institute for Human Settlements, 1994).

45. See, for example, Y. M. Yeung, and D.K.Y. Chu (eds.), *Guangdong: Survey of a Province Undergoing Rapid Change* (Hong Kong: The Chinese University Press, 1994).

46. See Note 41, p. 102.

12

Planning and Management of Hong Kong's Border

Anthony G. O. Yeh

The designation of Hong Kong as a Special Administrative Region (SAR) by China in the signing of the Sino-British Joint Declaration in 1984 that guarantees "one country, two systems" for 50 years after July 1997 is the recognition of the importance to maintain prosperity and stability of Hong Kong. The Basic Law of the Hong Kong SAR prepared and enacted by the National People's Congress (NPC) in April 1990 was to protect the autonomy in domestic affairs of Hong Kong after it becomes an SAR in July 1997. The Hong Kong SAR will be governed by an authority mainly consisted of local inhabitants. It will possess its own executive, legislative and independent judicial power, including its own court of appeal. China will assume responsibility for Hong Kong's defence and foreign affairs, while the local government will be in charge of public order. Hong Kong will continue to decide its own economic and trade policies and maintain its existing capitalistic system.

The maintenance of local autonomy undoubtedly is very important for the prosperity and stability of Hong Kong. But prosperity and stability cannot be achieved if the border of Hong Kong cannot be maintained. There are 1.2 billion of people across the border of Hong Kong. Because of the big differences in income and living standards, there is a strong desire of people across the border to come to Hong Kong. The influx of a small percentage of these 1.2 billion of people to Hong Kong will cause great problems to the housing, education, welfare, employment, and transport system in the territory, overturning its prosperity and stability.

The border of Hong Kong is covered under Article 116 of the Basic

Law which specifies that the Hong Kong SAR shall be a separate customs territory. It is also covered under Article 22 of the Basic Law which specifies that departments of the Central People's Government as well as provinces, autonomous regions and municipalities directly under the central government shall not interfere in the affairs of the Hong Kong SAR. People from other parts of China must apply for approval for entry into the Hong Kong SAR. But is this adequate to maintain the border of Hong Kong?

It may be the central government's desire to protect the border of Hong Kong as reflected in the Basic Law, but it relies on good management, tight control of the border, and cooperation of the neighbouring provinces in order to achieve this. The possibility of large influx of people from China is not without grounds. Casual discussions with people in China, particularly the younger generation in the Pearl River Delta region, will testify this. They all indicate that they will march to Hong Kong to have a taste of prosperity after Britain returns Hong Kong to China in 1997. This chapter attempts to discuss the importance of the border in maintaining the prosperity and stability of Hong Kong after it becomes an SAR. It will also explore some of the planning and management issues of the border area.

IMPORTANCE OF HONG KONG'S BORDER

Broadly speaking, the border of Hong Kong covers the air, land, and sea. The flow of goods and people to Hong Kong by air is more easily controlled than by land and sea because of the need of expensive air carriers to enter into Hong Kong. The entry of goods and people to Hong Kong by sea and land is very difficult to control.

Border relationship between Hong Kong and China has changed a lot in the post-Mao period which emphasizes economic development by the adoption of economic reform and open door policy in 1978. Prior to 1978, particularly during the Cultural Revolution in 1966–1976, the border relationship is very tensed. The flow of goods and people was tightly controlled, especially by China. However, since 1978, the border relationship has changed from confrontation to cooperation. There is increasing flow of goods, capitals, and people from both sides. The flow of capital from Hong Kong to China has contributed greatly to the recent rapid economic development of China, especially the nearby Pearl River Delta area. Hong Kong ranks first in the source of foreign direct investment (over 60%) to China.[1] The proportion is even higher in the Guangdong province, with over 87% of it from Hong Kong. To facilitate Hong Kong people to travel to and invest in China, a special Home Visit Permit (*huixiang zheng*) is issued to Hong Kong residents with Chinese origin. This allows them to go to China as many times as they want without the need to apply for a visa. As a result, the number of people going from Hong Kong to China has grown tremendously since 1978.

The control of people coming to Hong Kong has always been tight. The occasional relaxation of the border control has caused much disruption to Hong Kong's development. The high living standard in Hong Kong has been achieved through spectacular economic development on the one hand and low population growth rate on the other. Since the early 1990s, Hong Kong's per capita income is higher than that of the United Kingdom. This is achieved through high economic growth but low population increase in the last twenty years since the 1970s. Any sudden major increase in immigration will lower its living standard.

Natural increase in Hong Kong's population is under controlled with a falling birth rate and a stable death rate. The major component of its population growth is from immigration. Hong Kong's population growth is often inflated by sudden influx of migrants from China (Figure 1). China has been a predominant source of legal and illegal immigrants of Hong Kong.[2]

Although immigration from China has been generally under control since the establishment of the People's Republic of China in 1949, there have been occasional tides of migrants from China as a result of its changing political climate. The population of Hong Kong has increased sharply from 0.6 million in 1945 to 2 million in 1951, an increase of 40% per annum. It was estimated that over one million people migrated to Hong Kong from China between 1949 and 1950 because of the change of regime. This led to the widespread of squatters and poor housing conditions in Hong Kong. Relaxation of the border control by the Chinese government and the failure of the Great Leap Forward in China resulted in over 70,000 people crossing the border to Hong Kong in the early 1960s.

The recent tide of immigration occurred after the downfall of the "Gang of Four" in 1976, which led to much freer population movement in and out of China. Pressure of immigration was further exacerbated by Hong Kong's philanthropic "touch base" policy which allowed illegal immigrants from China to stay in Hong Kong if they were able to reach the urban area.[3]

Figure 1: Natural Increase and Net Migration, 1946–1994

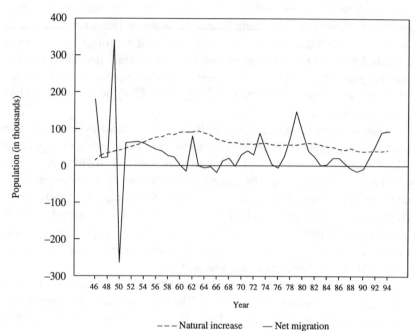

Year

– – – Natural increase   —— Net migration

Source: Census and Statistics Department.

The number of captured illegal immigrants increased sharply from 1,800 in 1977 to 82,000 in 1978 and a record high of 89,000 in 1979. Although the "touch base" policy was abandoned in October 1980 and a policy of immediate repatriation of illegal Chinese immigrants was adopted to discourage further illegal immigrants from China, Hong Kong experienced a sudden sharp increase in population in the 1980s due to this tide of illegal immigration. In 1979 alone, there were 170,000 legal and illegal immigrants from China, who caused a 3.5% increase in population, a growth rate that is much higher than the average annual growth rate of 1.6%.

The sudden increase in population undoubtedly has increased the supply of skilled and semi-skilled labour, but it had upset the plans for the provision of social facilities, especially public housing. This can be reflected, to some extent, by the increase of squatter population from 300,000 in 1978 to 750,000 in 1980.[4] Such an unpredicted wave of immigration was given by the Governor in 1981 as one of the reasons for failing to achieve the objective of improving housing conditions in Hong Kong.[5] Fortunately, the influx of illegal immigrants from China is now largely under control with the cooperation of China. After 1997, the number of legal migrants allowed to enter into Hong Kong can be carried out through the granting of entry visa that can be discussed between the SAR government and the central government. But illegal immigration is most difficult to control without the cooperation of the central government and nearby provinces. To maintain its prosperity and stability, it is important for Hong Kong to be able to maintain its border and control the number of immigrants, both legal and illegal, into the territory.

BORDER SCENARIOS

The designation of Hong Kong as an SAR for 50 years is a temporary measure to deal with the great discrepancies in the economic and political systems, income, and living standards between Hong Kong and China. In the long run, Hong Kong has to become part of China. At that time, the border of Hong Kong will become a city boundary, like other city boundaries which do not have any borders. Until this happens, the border of Hong Kong has still to be kept, otherwise the whole purpose of designating Hong Kong as an SAR will be defeated.

Although the control of people from China entering into Hong Kong is protected by the Basic Law, it does not say how permeable is the border. A number of border scenarios have been discussed in Shenzhen, the Special Economic Zone (SEZ) abutting the border of Hong Kong. The SEZ of Shenzhen was designated in 1979, soon after the adoption of economic reform and open door policy in 1978.[6] It is the fastest growing SEZ and city in China because of its locational advantage of being right next door of Hong Kong, the largest source of foreign investment to China. It has developed from a small border town of less than 70,000 people in 1978 to a large city of over 1.5 million in 1994. Apart from the border between Hong Kong and Shenzhen, a second border has been established at the northern part of the Shenzhen SEZ to control the flow of people from entering into the SEZ. People from other parts of China has to obtain a border pass before they can enter into Shenzhen. Shenzhen sees the advantage of being more integrated with Hong Kong. A number of border scenarios have been discussed and they can be grouped into three main categories:

1. *Status quo* — The border between Shenzhen and Hong Kong remains at it is with little changes.

2. *Increasingly permeable border between Hong Kong and Shenzhen* — The border between Hong Kong and Shenzhen still exist but it will be more relaxed than present. People from Hong Kong will be allowed to go to Shenzhen freely without the need of going through the immigration and customs counter. They only need to use their Home Visit Permits when they go outside Shenzhen to other parts of China. Flow of people from Shenzhen is still controlled and they need to obtain a pass to come to Hong Kong but this pass will be more easily obtained than present. Similar to people, goods crossing the border will be monitored but not checked. However, they have to go through customs if they go outside Shenzhen to other parts of China.

3. *Abolishment of the border between Hong Kong and Shenzhen* — This scenario is more drastic than the first two. The Shenzhen SEZ will be merged with Hong Kong to form one large SAR. Although it is understood that the boundary of Hong Kong is the existing border (that is south of the Shenzhen River, comprising land that were ceded and leased to Britain in the nineteenth century), it is not explicitly stated in the Basic Law. Under this scenario, the territory of Hong Kong will be expanded and merged with the Shenzhen SEZ, pushing its border from the Shenzhen River north to the northern second border of the SEZ. People of Hong Kong and Shenzhen will become citizens of the same SAR and can move and live freely from one place to another.

   This scenario is the most unlikely one in the immediate future because of the great discrepancies in lifestyles as well as public services and facilities between the two cities. If this happens, the public services and facilities of Hong Kong which are planned mainly to cater for the needs of its people will not be able to cope with the sudden addition of the 1.5 million or more population from Shenzhen. Although there is a border at the northern part of Shenzhen, the 85 km border is too long to keep. With the great discrepancies in living standards and income between Hong Kong and the rest of China, it is not difficult to envisage what will happen if Hong Kong integrates with Shenzhen and uses the northern second border of Shenzhen as its border. Millions of people from other parts of China will flood through this long border to Hong Kong. Many large cities in China are having difficulties in controlling the influx of floating population.[7] Shenzhen is no exception. It is estimated that the floating population in Shenzhen is of similar size to its permanent and temporary population. However, apart from the possibility of abolishing the SAR in total, this may be one of the possible scenarios when the SAR status of Hong Kong is subject to review at the time the 50-year status quo period after 1997 is about to expire.

The three scenarios have different implications to the planning of the border area. Scenarios 1 and 2 permit the relatively free flow of people and vehicles from Hong Kong to Shenzhen but restricted the flow of people and vehicles the other way round. The main difference between scenarios 1 and 2 is the degree of permeability in regard to the flow of Hong Kong people to Shenzhen. Because of the need to control illegal immigrations from China through Shenzhen, a buffer zone with little development is needed to facilitate the patrolling of the border. Border service areas are also needed for cross-border vehicles to provide services to them while they are waiting to go through the border. Under scenario 3, there will be no border between Hong Kong and Shenzhen and people and goods can go freely from one place to another. Neither border patrol nor border service areas are needed because the border will no longer be there. As a result, there is no need for a border buffer area and more development can take place at the existing border area.

The status quo, an increasingly permeable border between Hong Kong and Shenzhen, or something in between is the most likely scenario of the border of Hong Kong when it becomes an SAR in 1997. It may take a very long time before the border between Hong Kong and Shenzhen will be abolished. A more permeable border between Hong Kong and China is expected even Hong Kong would not become an SAR in 1997 because of the increasing economic interactions between the two places.

As experienced in North America and Europe, the relaxation of border control and "vanishing border" is the outcome of economic rather than political needs.[8] The borders between Canada and the United States, the United States and Mexico, and many countries in Europe are very relaxed, allowing relatively free flow of goods and people. The main concern is the stopping of criminals and smuggling. The most extreme form is the

Schengen Agreement in Europe which threw open the internal borders of Belgium, France, Germany, Luxembourg, the Netherlands, Portugal, and Spain in March 1995. The vanishing border is a worldwide phenomenon in the era of transnational capitalism, international division of labour, and development of global cities. Hong Kong and China is affected and benefited from these trends of economic development. Many Hong Kong industries are benefiting from the cheap labour and land in the Pearl River Delta. At the same time, the Pearl River Delta is benefiting from the capital, technology, management skills, and entrepreneurship of Hong Kong. Many people in Hong Kong are also buying houses and property in the Pearl River Delta. The border of Hong Kong may not go into a position as extreme as the Schengen Agreement in Europe, but it will be more permeable than before because of the needs of the people and the economy for more cross-border traffic of people and goods. The increase in cross-border traffic will inevitably affect the transport and land use planning system in Hong Kong.

CROSS-BORDER TRAFFIC

Even without the sovereignty transition in 1997, Hong Kong's ties with China are expected to increase if China continues its open door policy. The economic relationship between Hong Kong and China has increased tremendously since the signing of the Joint Declaration in 1984. China's adoption of an open door economic policy since 1978 has led to rapid increase in economic links between the two places. Since 1985, China has become Hong Kong's largest trading partner. Merchandise trade between the two places has grown by 39% per annum in 1978 and 1988.[9] China is now the largest market and second largest market for Hong Kong's re-exports and domestic exports respectively. China is also the largest supplier of goods to Hong Kong. Hong Kong also overtook Japan in 1987 to become China's largest trading partner, accounting for 27% of China's overall external trade. Since 1979, China has been Hong Kong's largest re-export market as well as the largest source of goods re-exported through Hong Kong. In 1988, nearly 80% of Hong Kong's re-exports were related to China either as a market or a source of supply. Besides merchandise trade, various forms of invisible trade between Hong Kong and China also increased. These included tourism and travel services, transport services, financial services, and professional and other business services.[10]

Hong Kong is the most important source of foreign investment in China. Many Hong Kong manufacturers have established compensation trade and outward-processing arrangements with Chinese enterprises, especially those in the Pearl River Delta region and the Shenzhen SEZ. The growing economic relations between Hong Kong and China have added a new dimension to Hong Kong's economic growth.

The major form of foreign participation and investment in manufacturing in China is in the form of outward-processing which takes advantage of the cheap labour of China. Partners in China provide the plant, labour, water, electricity and other basic facilities, whereas foreign investors supply the machinery, materials, product design, and are responsible for marketing. The Pearl River Delta has significantly changed Hong Kong's traditional subcontracting relationship between small, medium and large factories. There is a new spatial division of labour between Hong Kong and the Pearl River Delta.[11] The subcontracting and outward-processing to China is increasing sharply. Table 1 shows the sharp increase in outward-processing to China between 1988 to 1993 in terms of domestic exports and re-exports. The nearby areas of Hong Kong in the Pearl River Delta has urbanized very rapidly as a result of foreign investment and outward-processing activities of Hong Kong. A large megalopolis is emerging in the Delta. What is happening there is similar to the experience in other border areas, such as the United States–Mexico border[12] and the Growth Triangle of Johor–Singapore–Riau.[13] Such a development of transnational urbanized

Table 1: Values of Hong Kong's Outward-processing Activities in China (HK$ million)

Year	Domestic export trade	Re-export trade
1988	7,921	10,725
1989	31,962	44,906
1990	36,418	55,496
1991	40,369	73,562
1992	44,271	97,368
1993	45,141	115,037

Source: Census and Statistics Department, *Hong Kong Annual Digest of Statistics* (1994).

areas along national borders is the outcome of the era of global cities where there is a frequent movement of population, industry, and capital to international boundary regions.[14] Urbanization over the border is an extension of the functional role of the urban system where the investment originates.[15]

Hong Kong is providing a hub function to China. It is resuming the function of an entrepôt. Re-exports to and from China have increased sharply since 1990 (Figure 2). Apart from providing transhipment services by the world's second largest and highly efficient container port in Kwai Chung, Hong Kong also has an efficient banking system to handle letters of credit for China. Such economic ties with China have increasing impact on urban development in Hong Kong, which is evident in the recent

Figure 2: Export and Import between Hong Kong and China

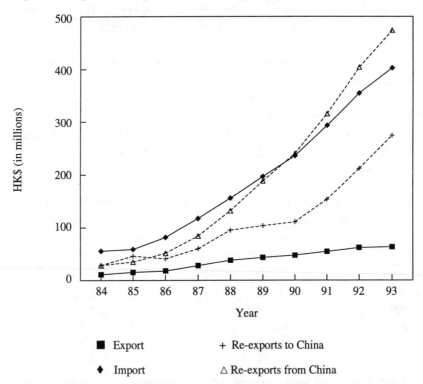

Sources: *Hong Kong Monthly Statistics, Hong Kong Trade Statistics.*

construction of the new China Ferry Terminal and headquarters of the Bank of China, and the expansion of the Kwai Chung container port. Chinese capital is playing an increasingly important part in property and infrastructure development in Hong Kong.

Communication technology is often regarded as space-extending and allow individuals and firms to function within a geographically larger set of boundaries.[16] Communication technology has helped to decentralize economic activities and population away from the city centre of Western cities. The improvement in telecommunication in the Pearl River Delta, the increase in economic ties between Hong Kong and the Delta, and the big difference in house price have made many Hong Kong people to buy houses there. Some even live in Shenzhen and commute to work in Hong Kong. In 1992, 69,561 housing units were being marketed in Hong Kong and about 30,000 of them were sold in Hong Kong.[17] This is a huge amount compared to the 26,222 domestic units completed in Hong Kong in the same year.[18]

The amount of cross-border traffic has increased tremendously since 1983 when the investment from Hong Kong to the Pearl River Delta began to take off. Travellers crossing the Lo Wu border has increased from less than 10 million in 1983 to 40 million in 1994 (Figure 3) Vehicles crossing the border also increased from 0.7 million in 1983 to 8 million in 1994 (Figure 4). The unanticipated 10 times increase in cross-border vehicular traffic has caused much traffic problems in Hong Kong. The Tuen Mun Highway and the Tolo Highway that were designed in the late 1970s were not for the purpose of handling such a large volume of cross-border traffic. As a result, traffic congestion often occurs in these two highways that link the new towns in the New Territories with the city centre.

To prevent illegal immigration, a long fence has been constructed along the border. The border used to be patrolled by the army, but patrol work has been shifted to the police in three phases from 1990 to 1992. There are at present four border checkpoints — Sha Tau Kok, Man Kam To, Lo Wu, and Lok Ma Chau (Huanggang). Lo Wu is the largest checkpoint, which is for train passengers and goods, whereas checkpoints at Sha Tau Kok, Man Kam To and Lok Ma Chau (Huanggang) are for vehicles. The Lok Ma Chau (Huanggang) checkpoint is a relatively new one opened in 1989. Border licences are given to vehicles which can only use the designated checkpoint on the licence. Some vehicles using Man Kam To were diverted to Lok Ma Chau (Huanggang) after its opening. It is the largest vehicle checkpoint and since November 1994 provides 24-hour service. As this checkpoint is close

Figure 3: Cross-border Passengers

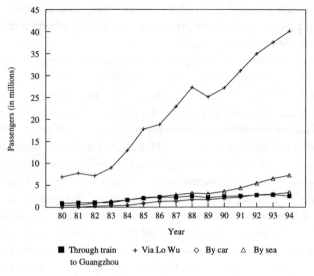

Source: Immigration Department.

Figure 4: Cross-border Vehicles

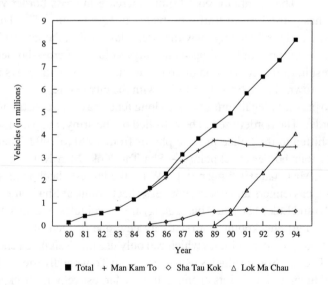

Source: Immigration Department.

Table 2: Distribution of Cross-border Passenger Trips

	From Hong Kong to	To Hong Kong from
Shenzhen SEZ	54.67%	53.30%
Other areas of Shenzhen	14.98%	16.91%
Pearl River Delta	27.82%	27.19%
Other areas of Guangdong and China	2.53%	2.60%
Total	100.00%	100.00%

Source: Alan W. G. Wong, "Cross Border Traffic," in *Border Town Development and Planning — Hong Kong and Shenzhen*, edited by A.G.O. Yeh and Sun Huasheng (Hong Kong: Centre of Urban Planning and Environmental Management, forthcoming).

to the new city centre of Futian, to minimize noise pollution, vehicles originating from or going to areas outside Shenzhen, such as Guangzhou and Dongguan, are only allowed to use the checkpoint after midnight.

As Shenzhen is a border town, much of the traffic going through the border and the city is external traffic. It is estimated that over 55% of the cross-border passenger trips are passing through the Shenzhen SEZ to other places in the Pearl River Delta (Table 2).[19] The increasing role of Hong Kong as an entrepôt has led to a major increase in cross-border freight traffic. There is not enough bypasses to divert cross-border traffic that needs to go to places outside the SEZ away from the city centre, thus causing traffic congestion in the city centre.

Most of the cross-border trip is related to business. Some 60% of the passenger trips from Hong Kong are business trips.[20] Cross-border traffic is highly asymmetrical. Hong Kong controls very tightly the flow of people and vehicles from Shenzhen, whereas Shenzhen does not have much control over the flow of people and vehicles from Hong Kong. Although Shenzhen uses a quota system for issuing cross-border vehicle licences, the quota is quite large. Hong Kong people can go freely into Shenzhen if they have valid Home Visit Permits and Chinese driving licences, and there are Chinese registration plates on their vehicles. Because of this, only around 6% of the cross-border passengers are from China, the rest being from Hong Kong.[21]

Passengers have little choice on transport modes to the border crossings. Train is the only mode from Hong Kong to Lo Wu. However, a variety of choices like trains, buses, cars, minibuses, and taxis is available after they cross the border to Shenzhen. Vehicles are the only mode of transport for the Sha Tau Kok, Man Kam To and Lok Ma Chau (Huanggang) checkpoints.

PLANNING OF BORDER AREA

The need for a more permeable border between Hong Kong, Shenzhen and Guangdong was considered an important factor for Hong Kong to be economically successful in the future. A thorough review of policies and practices related to border traffic should be carried out with input from Hong Kong businesses and institutions. Also, a separate unit responsible for cross-border affairs was considered necessary to create a commercially unobstructed border for maintaining high economic growth in Hong Kong.[22]

There were a lot of uncertainties when Hong Kong was preparing its Territorial Development Strategy (TDS) in the early 1980s.[23] The political future of Hong Kong and its economic relations with the Pearl River Delta were the major uncertainties. The preparation of the TDS started in 1980 and finished in 1984.[24] Britain at that time was negotiating with China on the political future of Hong Kong and China was experimenting with the setting up of SEZs in promoting economic development. Whether the SEZs would be successful and what would be the impact on Hong Kong were the concerns of Hong Kong people. Economic relations between Hong Kong and the Pearl River Delta did not pick up until 1984 after the TDS was prepared (see Figures 3 and 4). Because of this, cross-border traffic and relations were not given much emphasis in the TDS. The TDS mainly dealt with the internal transport and land use interactions of Hong Kong, but gave little attention to cross-border traffic and its likely impact on the transport and land use of Hong Kong.

The TDS was prepared in view of the shortcomings of piecemeal planning and development in the 1970s. The Land Development Policy Committee in 1980 considered it necessary to formulate a comprehensive long-term development strategy for Hong Kong in the 1990s and up to 2001. The TDS was not only concerned with meeting the population requirements for land, services and facilities, but also paid regards to sustaining the growth of key economic activities in Hong Kong.[25] The decision to formulate the TDS was in part attributable to the recognition of the lack of coordination between urban development and transport provision, especially in the case of new towns where transport is still inadequately provided. The TDS took four years to prepare and was completed in 1984. The objective was to determine the long-term development potential of the five subregions in Hong Kong and consequently recommend a preferred development strategy on subregional basis.

In the TDS study, the future location of Hong Kong's international airport was recognized as a significant factor affecting the future development pattern of the territory. While a number of development options concerning future airport location were proposed and considered, doubts were cast over the possibility of relocating the existing airport in view of the uncertain political future of Hong Kong in 1984, a time when Britain was negotiating with China on the future of Hong Kong. As a result, two alternative long-term growth patterns based on the existing airport location at Kai Tak were produced. Both options saw a need for major improvements and extensions of the existing planned highways and rail systems. Each represented an end-state plan for the year 2001 and beyond, and fundamental changes in basic assumptions might be necessary. In view of the uncertainties of Hong Kong's political and economic future, a common-component approach was used to identify in the two-option common projects where detailed planning and associated works could be started soon in order to sustain the momentum of urban development. This led to the preparation of the Metroplan[26] after the decision to relocate the airport to Chek Lap Kok in 1989.

Since the adoption of the TDS in 1984, there has been a sharp increase in economic relations with China, and as a result major increase in cross-border traffic (see Figures 3 and 4). The government decided to have a major review of the strategy in 1990 soon after it realized that the future of Hong Kong's economy relied on its integration with China, particularly with the Pearl River Delta. A consultation paper, *Territorial Development Strategy Review — Development Options*, was published in 1993 for public consultation.[27] The review was needed because the location of the key infrastructure of the port and airport which was not determined in the TDS of 1984 has been determined. In 1989, the Port and Airport Development Strategy (PADS) decided to relocate the airport from Kai Tak to Chek Lap Kok and to expand the port facilities on North Lantau and in the Western

Harbour Area. The review was also needed because of the major increase in economic interactions and cross-border traffic between Hong Kong and the Pearl River Delta after 1984. There has been a sharp increase in truck traffic between Hong Kong and Shenzhen. A long-term planning framework for the provision of land and infrastructure that takes into consideration the increase in cross-border traffic is needed.[28]

The recognition of the importance in the linkage with the Pearl River Delta has been fully acknowledged in the review of the TDS. It is one of the two major principles in the formulation of the TDS, the other being the direction of growth within the territory which is also affected by the linkage with the Pearl River Delta. The development scenarios are also closely related to the interactions and development of the Pearl River Delta. Scenario A assumes the Pearl River Delta region as Hong Kong's primary economic hinterland while Scenario B includes both the Delta and the inner provinces of China as the economic hinterland.

Under Scenario A, two further sub-scenarios were developed — steady growth (AI) and high growth (AII). Both sub-scenarios assume growth in Hong Kong and the Pearl River Delta, the only difference is the degree of reliance of the Delta on Hong Kong. The steady growth scenario (AI) assumes that there would be considerable growth in the Pearl River Delta but the relationship between Hong Kong and the Delta would be more as equal partners. The high growth scenario (AII) assumes that Hong Kong will be a primary centre of development in the Delta. It will be the key trading outlet, entrepôt and financial centre of the region.

Scenario B assumes that Hong Kong's economic ties will go beyond the Pearl River Delta and reaches the inner provinces of China, providing entrepôt services, and acting as a major trading outlet and source of foreign investment. This scenario is considered as the extra high growth scenario by adding 20% allowance over the high land use and transport demand in Scenario AII (high growth).

From these scenarios, a range of land use and infrastructure require-ments will be established. Cross-border transport demands range from relatively low in Scenario AI to extra high in Scenario B. The increase in cross-border traffic will not only affect the border but also the internal traffic as well. New internal transport networks and cross-border linkages are proposed based on the updated findings of transport studies, such as the Railway Development Study. Route Y which would link the proposed Lantau port facilities via Tuen Mun Road southern bypass, Tuen Mun West to Ma Wan area in Shenzhen is considered under Scenarios AII and B. Route Y was first recommended under the updating of the Second Comprehensive Transport Study (CTS-2).

❑ *Proposals of Cross-border Transport Links*

To anticipate future increase in cross-border traffic, each side along the border is proposing new transport linkages (Figure 5).

Proposals from Hong Kong

Route Y that will link the proposed Lantau port facilities via Tuen Mun Road southern bypass, Tuen Mun West to Ma Wan area in Shenzhen is considered under the High Growth and Extra High Growth Scenarios of the TDS. Under the Railway Development Strategy,[29] the Western Corridor railway would provide a new arterial link to the border. It will provide a port rail line to the container port at Kwai Chung, a long-distance passenger service to China, and a subregional passenger rail link between the Northwest New Territories and the urban area. The new railway is considered important for the future development of the container port of Hong Kong which would carry standard containers directly to the container port without intermediate handling. This can help to reduce pressure on the road system caused by freight traffic. It can also diverted some of the passenger using the congested and reaching its capacity checkpoint at Lo Wu to a proposed border crossing at Lok Ma Chau. This will relieve the existing congested Lo Wu terminal and provide easier access to Huanggang and the Futian new city centre. The Western Corridor railway is one of the priority area of the Railway Development Strategy and it is hoped to be completed in 2001.

Proposals from Shenzhen

To meet future traffic demand, Shenzhen is at the same time preparing its own transport plan which consider what is advantageous to itself. A Shenzhen–Hong Kong Western Corridor Project was proposed. The project consisted of two parts — the Shenzhen–Hong Kong Highway and the Shenzhen–Hong Kong Railway. The Shenzhen–Hong Kong Highway requires the construction of the Deep (Shenzhen) Bay Bridge, connecting Yuen Long with Dongjiao and then linking to the proposed Airport

Figure 5: Cross-border Transport Links

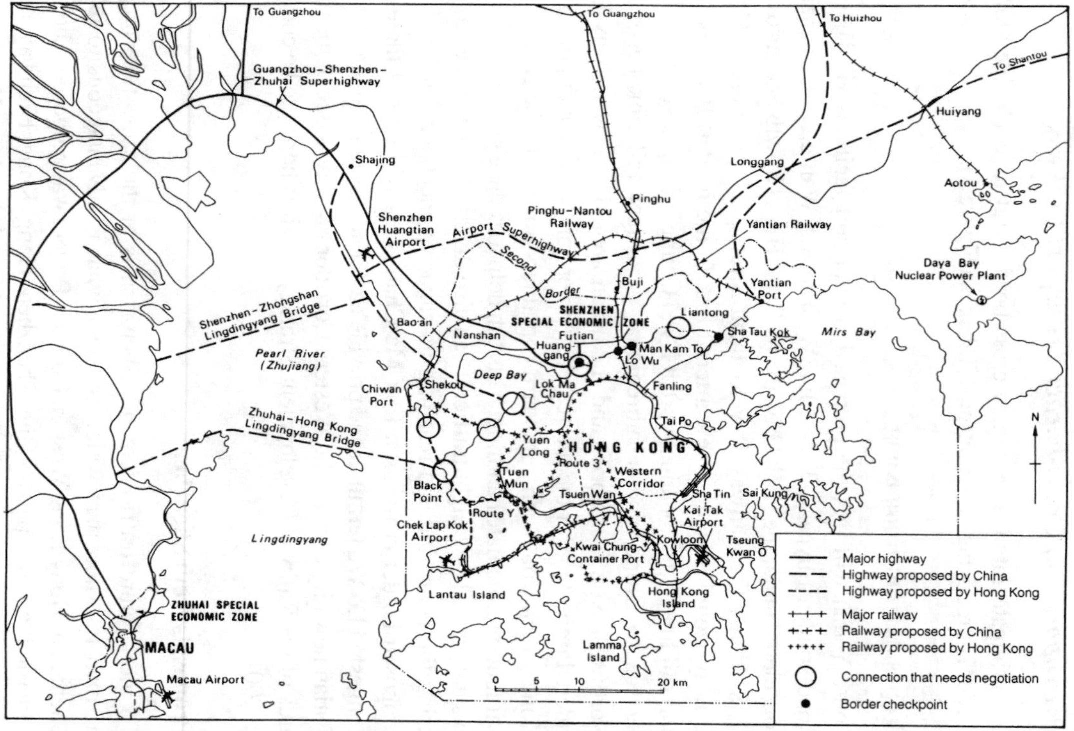

Superhighway, the Shenzhen Airport, and the Guangzhou–Shenzhen–Zhuhai Superhighway. The second project is the Shenzhen–Hong Kong Railway which requires the construction of the Deep (Shenzhen) Bay Railway Bridge connecting Tuen Mun with Shekou, and linking with the Pinghu–Nantou Railway which links up with the Guangzhou–Shenzhen Railway. The connection points of the road and railway bridges are very different from what the Hong Kong side has envisaged. The need of the Shenzhen–Hong Kong Western Corridor Project is understandable because Shenzhen would like to divert traffic away from Lok Ma Chau which is right in front of its new city centre at Futian. They hope to have a city centre less congested than Lo Wu which is the major transport hub. It strongly oppose the proposal of the Hong Kong government of using Lok Ma Chau as the second railway connection point for freight transport.

There is also a plan to relieve the congestion of the road checkpoint in Man Kam To by opening up a new road checkpoint at Liantong.

Proposal from Zhuhai

To cut short the distance by road between Zhuhai, Hong Kong and Shenzhen, the Zhuhai–Hong Kong Lingdingyang Bridge has been proposed by the Zhuhai government for a long time since the early 1990s. It is a long bridge that will connect Jinding Town in Zhuhai, Qi'ao Island, Inner Lingding Island, and Black Point near Tuen Mun in Hong Kong. The total length of the six-traffic-lane bridge is 40 km. It will cut short the need to go round the Humen Bridge connecting the Guangzhou–Shenzhen–Zhuhai Superhighway with the Eastern Guangzhou–Zhuhai Highway. This bridge will help the development of Zhuhai, especially the Zhuhai Airport and Gaolan Port. However, the proposal may cause severe traffic congestion at the Hong Kong side by traffic passing through Hong Kong to Shenzhen.

There are many disagreements with the proposals by the three sides. The disagreements are mainly on: (1) whether there is a need for the connection; (2) whether the other side can absorb the traffic created by the new crossing; (3) timing of the completion date of the new crossing; and (4) nature of the crossing, whether it should be road or rail.

A border liaison channel at an operational level for government departments in border matters, such as the immigration, customs, and police departments, has been established since the early 1980s. Such channel only deals with day-to-day operation of the border, such as the border opening hours, number of counters to be added during peak period in Christmas, the Chinese New Year, and Easter holidays. It cannot deal with the very complicated and political issues of new cross-border crossings and infrastructure. A Sino-British Infrastructure Coordinating Committee proposed by China was set up in December 1994. It will identify and set priority of discussion on issues concerning the development of air, sea, and land facilities straddling the border. Some of the immediate issues are: the plan by Zhuhai to build a bridge linking it with Tuen Mun; the plan by Shenzhen to build two bridges across the Deep Bay; coordinating the use of air space by the new airports in Shenzhen, Hong Kong, Macau, and Zhuhai; and solving problems of proposed new cross-border rail links.

The Committee is not a decision-making organization but a formal channel for exchange of views and information and for seeking common view on the coordination of cross-border infrastructure to and from Hong Kong. Membership of the British side includes the Secretary for Planning, Environment and Lands, Secretary for Transport, Secretary for Economic Services, Director of Planning, Director of Highways, Deputy Secretary for Constitutional Affairs, and Assistant Political Adviser. Members of its China counterpart include Head of the Economic Department of the Hong Kong and Macau Affairs Office, Deputy Head of the Economic Affairs Department of the Xinhua (New China) News Agency, and officials in charge of state planning, aviation, energy resources, railway, and transport coordination. The Committee is further divided into four expert panels that deal with railway, roads and bridges, air traffic control, and marine channels. The setting up of this Committee is a major breakthrough in the planning of border area between Hong Kong, Shenzhen, and Zhuhai.

BORDER MANAGEMENT

The management of the border mainly concerns how to avoid traffic queues at the border. Long queues at the border will impede the flow and interactions between Hong Kong and China. Traffic queues will also create traffic congestion at both sides of the border.

The use of information technology can speed up the processing of people, goods, and vehicles crossing the border. The processing of cross-border passengers has increased tremendously since the establishment of the Shenzhen SEZ. The Chinese immigration counter has been using bar-code scanner to speed up the processing of the Home Visit Permit of Hong Kong residents in the mid-1980s. Special VIP and businessmen counters have been set up to separate investors from travellers, reflecting the emphasis on attracting foreign investments by the Shenzhen SEZ. Similar to many international border checkpoints, green and red passages have been set up to speed up the custom checking procedure. Travellers who carry duty items have to go through the red passage for customs declaration and checking, while those without duty items have to go through the X-ray and are subject to random checking.

Although no VIP and businessmen counters are set up at the Hong Kong side of the border, there are separate counters for Hong Kong residents for whom only simplified immigration procedure is required and non-Hong Kong residents who need to go through the normal immigration procedure. Hong Kong residents only need to show their Hong Kong Identity Card without being required to fill in the departure and arrival forms, while other travellers have to show their travel documents and fill in the forms. Random checking is carried out by the Customs Officers of the Customs and Excise Department. An optical character recognition reader is recently installed to process the Hong Kong Identity Card in September 1994. Time taken to process an Identity Card is reduced by 4 seconds and a machine-readable passport by 20 seconds after the installation of the reader. The number of people going through the immigration checkpoint has increased tremendously. The Lo Wu border is one of the busiest border in the world. In 1992, it handles over 34 million travellers, an average of 98,000 a day. Long queues occur during public holidays and weekends, especially during Christmas and the Chinese New Year. An average of 120,000 persons per day passed through the border in the 1994 Christmas and the 1995 Chinese New Year.

The immigration and customs procedure is different between Hong Kong and China. In Hong Kong, departing travellers do not have to go through the customs, but just the immigration counters. They only have to go through the customs when they enter Hong Kong. Travellers, however, have to go through both when they enter or leave China.

The setting up of more border checkpoints is one of the solutions in making the border checkpoints less crowded and people crossing the border more comfortable. However, the simplification and speeding up of the checking procedure are also needed. There is a limit on what high technology can do in speeding up the immigration process. The simplification of the border crossing arrangement can further shorten the time that needs to go through the border.

One method is the processing of travellers only at the point of entry and not at the point of exit. Travellers are allowed to leave freely, with random immigration and customs checks. But they need to go through the immigration and customs at the entry point. Such practice is very common in the border between Canada and the United States. Both sides will share information of the travellers and each will help the other in checking for illegal and duty goods and suspected criminals. This arrangement requires the willingness of both sides to share information of the people and goods going through the border. It also requires the cooperation of the other side to help to stop people and goods that are not allowed to leave. This requires a high level of cooperation and trust between the two places. Another method is to have a combined counter in which travellers after passing the immigration and customs of one side will go to the counter of another side to be checked by the other party immediately, without the need to queue up again. This will save some time in queuing but the time saved will not be as much as the entry-only checking.

The choice of the checking procedure will also depend on which border scenario is being implemented in the future. If an increasingly permeable border between Hong Kong and Shenzhen is being adopted, there is only the need for the setting up of the Hong Kong departure and arrival counters for travellers from China and non-Hong Kong residents.

Longer opening hours, such as 24-hour operation of the border, may be of little help in relieving the pressure of the passenger checkpoints such as Lo Wu, because the number of passengers fall sharply after 9:00 p.m. Nevertheless, it may be of better help for freight traffic because the time that certain types of vehicles are allowed to go through the checkpoints can be controlled. Longer opening hours together with simplified customs procedures, combined checking, and the setting up of inter-departmental border liaison group will improve cross-border freight traffic.[30] In the consideration of opening the checkpoints for longer opening hours, studies have to be taken on the impact of noise pollution on areas close to the checkpoints.

The speeding up of the immigration and customs procedure also needs to be coordinated with good connecting transport system, otherwise congestion will be transferred from the immigration and customs counters to the bus and train stations outside the border checkpoints.

Cross-border ferry crossing has not been fully utilized yet. The problem is finding sites for ferry piers at the Hong Kong side. The demand for ferry is very high because of the high demand of Hong Kong people going to other places in the Pearl River Delta. At present, the Macau Ferry Terminal and the China Ferry Terminal have to deal with ferry traffic to many destinations in the Pearl River Delta. There is a need to have more ferry connections to alleviate the demand for land travel, thus relieving the pressure on the land transport network. It will involve not only the finding of more sites for ferry piers, but also finding operators for these ferry routes.

CONCLUSION

The planning and management of the border area of Hong Kong needs to resolve the conflicts between a tight border for the control of illegal immigrants into Hong Kong and a loose border to facilitate economic interactions between Hong Kong and the Pearl River Delta.

The border of Hong Kong is important to its prosperity and stability before and after 1997. The operation of "one country, two systems" will be *de facto* broken down if Hong Kong cannot keep its border and maintain a stable population. Any sudden rise in population, especially large influx of immigrants, will upset the living standard as well as all the land use and transport planning, and public facilities provision in Hong Kong.

The concern of larger-than-expected growth is not without grounds. First, the working population of the original consultation document of the TDS is 6.5 million in 2011 under steady growth and 6.9 million under extra high growth scenarios based on the population projection of the Census and Statistics Department.[31] This population projection has been considered as too low. In 1994, the population has increased to 6.06 million which has surpassed the forecast population of 5.82 million for the same year. It has even surpassed the 6.04 million population forecast for the year 2000. Many respondents of the TDS public consultation expressed the concern for the low projected population in preparing the TDS. There will be inadequate land provision to meet the needs of Hong Kong if this low estimation is used. As a result, the target population for 2011 has been increased to 7.5 million.[32]

Second, immigration from China can be better controlled before 1997, but it will be more difficult after that time. There are concerned over the number of legal and illegal immigrants. The number of legal immigrants in theory are relatively easy to be controlled because the future Hong

Kong SAR can control the number in entering into Hong Kong each year, although there may be increasing pressure from the central government to increase the quota from China. Even this, however, may be a problem because of technical difficulties in controlling legal migrants. Article 24 of the Basic Law states that children of permanent residents of Hong Kong born outside Hong Kong can have the right of abode in the Hong Kong SAR. In 1994, 8,000 babies were born from Chinese visitors with two-way exit permit. The increasing marriage of Hong Kong residents in China will also increase this number of babies born outside Hong Kong. The number of legal migrants from these sources will upset Hong Kong's land use, transport, and public facilities planning. Another major concern is the large influx of illegal immigrants going through the border, such as those that have occurred in 1949, 1962 and 1978. The maintenance of the border is important to the prosperity and stability of Hong Kong.

It is most unlikely that Hong Kong will merge with Shenzhen in the near future. A border will exist between the two places. In the planning of the border area, there is a need for a wide buffer zone between the border and the built-up areas to facilitate border patrol and avoid traffic congestion caused by cross-border traffic. Border service areas with hotels, restaurants, car parks, open storage, and gas stations are needed to serve the needs of cross-border vehicular traffic. Experience in the Shenzhen SEZ shows the problem of having the built-up areas too close to the border. Less than 55% of the cross-border traffic that goes through the transport network of the Shenzhen SEZ are from or to the SEZ. Since the transport system has to cater for the needs of the large volume of through traffic, it cause traffic congestion to its road networks. This should be avoided in the planning of the border area of Hong Kong.

A tight border with good border patrol is not adequate to prevent illegal immigrants from entering into Hong Kong. A large number of them could not be intercepted at the border and manage to enter into Hong Kong. In 1991, 24,089 illegal immigrants from China were intercepted and only 7,841 of them were arrested at the border.[33] The continuation of the existing policy of immediate repatriation of illegal immigrants is needed after 1997.

With increasing economic ties between Hong Kong and the Pearl River Delta, there is a need for more border crossings to relieve the pressure of the existing border crossings. The setting up of the Sino-British Infrastructure Coordinating Committee is a major advancement in such coordination work. The coordination of city planning in transfrontier metropolises is often a matter of foreign policy.[34] This Committee can function well before 1997 as discussion can be held between China and Britain at the foreign affairs level, similar to the status of the Sino-British Joint Liaison Group which is set up for the implementation of the Joint Declaration and for discussing matters related to the smooth transfer of government in 1997. These groups will cease to exist when Hong Kong becomes an SAR. According to Annex I of the Joint Declaration, the Joint Liaison Group will cease to function on 1 January 2000. Will there be a coordinating body that will replace the roles and functions of the Sino-British Infrastructure Coordinating Committee in coordinating cross-border infrastructure development and what form will it take? Cross-border negotiations at that time will no longer be foreign affairs but domestic affairs. Apart from the need to discuss about cross-border links, the need for better coordination in infrastructure development and environmental management is also evident in the Pearl River Delta. There are some redundancies in the development of new airports in Hong Kong, Shenzhen, Macau, and Zhuhai within a small radius of 25 km. These airports are expensive because they all planned for international flights. Better region-wide coordination and planning will help to reduce redundancies and utilize regional resources better.

The attitudes towards the border from the two sides are different. China is such a large country, they can absorb the people and vehicles from Hong Kong. Their concern is more on the smuggling of duty goods and publications that are contradictory to their political ideology into its land. On the contrary, Hong Kong is less concerned with the smuggling of goods, except for narcotics and weapons, because it is a duty-free port. It is more concerned with the inflow of people and vehicles from China. Since Hong Kong is such a small place and China is so large, just a small fraction of the latter's population and vehicles going into Hong Kong will cause severe problems to its transport, housing, and public facilities. Although at present people and vehicles from Hong Kong are welcomed in Shenzhen because they bring investment and business there, there is a limit that Shenzhen can absorb without causing diseconomies. Diseconomies, such as traffic congestion and pollution, are already evident in Shenzhen. Forward planning in Shenzhen to deal with the anticipated cross-border traffic between Hong Kong and Shenzhen is needed. In discussing border crossing, Hong Kong should not simply press for the need and convenience of itself, but should also keep in mind the traffic problems that it has generated for Shenzhen and try to help the planners there to solve those traffic problems related to cross-border traffic.

Based on the principle of cooperation and coordination, it seems that the proposed rail link by Shenzhen via the proposed Deep (Shenzhen) Bay Railway Bridge is a better choice because it can help to connect the Shekou and Chiwan ports with the container port in Hong Kong. It can also divert some of the freights from the two Beijing-to-Hong Kong (Beijing–Guangzhou–Kowloon and Beijing–Jiujiang–Kowloon) railways from the congested Lo Wu crossing via the Pinghu–Nantou Railway. This can avoid having a railway cutting through the new city centre at Futian. The Lok Ma Chau border terminus of Hong Kong's Western Corridor railway can be used for passengers only where they can cross the border to Futian. This can help to relieve the pressure of the existing Lo Wu border.

As for the road connection, it seems that the Route Y proposed by Hong Kong is preferable. If the Zhuhai and Shenzhen proposals are both adopted, there will be two border crossings, one connecting to Zhuhai and the other to Shenzhen. The Zhuhai–Hong Kong Lingdingyang Bridge will only be linked to Hong Kong. Vehicles going from Zhuhai to Shenzhen and vice versa will have to pass through Hong Kong, leading to traffic congestion here. The Route Y proposal could avoid this by enabling Zhuhai and Shenzhen to be connected with each other directly using Hong Kong as a bridge. Zhuhai–Shenzhen traffic can therefore bypass Hong Kong. This connection will facilitate the east-west traffic at the southern side of the Pearl River Delta that is much needed with the opening of the Gaolan Port in Zhuhai in the early 2000s. This can also obliterate the need to build another expensive bridge crossing the southern side of the Pearl River Delta via the proposed Shenzhen–Zhongshan Lingdingyang Bridge. This bridge can help to connect the nearby ports and airports together. The construction of these two connection points will help Shenzhen to use them as bypasses for traffic that does not have to go into the Shenzhen SEZ. The road networks in Hong Kong, especially those around Yuen Long and Tuen Mun areas which are already very congested, have to be adjusted to accommodate these new border crossings. The combination of the Deep Bay's road and railway bridges could be considered to minimize construction cost as well as the environmental and transport impacts of having two bridges across the Deep Bay.

With increase in economic linkages between Hong Kong and China, it is inevitable that there will be more cross-border crossings and traffic in

Northwest New Territories because the Pearl River Delta is at the western side of Hong Kong and the major infrastructure of the new container port and the Chek Lap Kok airport are all located at the western side. More development, especially office development, is expected to take place in areas around Yuen Long and Tuen Mun which are close to these cross-border transport hubs.

Apart from the construction of new land crossings, more ferry crossings should be encouraged to be developed because it can help to alleviate the pressure on the land crossings. Better border management, such as computerization, use of high technology (such as smart card[35]), simplification of the immigration and customs procedure, can also help to make the crossing of the border more convenient and comfortable. An efficient and convenient railway and public transport system that can take people to cross the border is also needed.

In the planning of border areas, it is also necessary to take negative externalities into consideration. The problem of negative externalities is emerging to be a major problem of the Pearl River Delta. Algae and red tides are increasing in the Delta because of cross-border pollution.[36] A Strategic Sewage Disposal Scheme (SSDS) has been proposed in Hong Kong to deal with the disposal of its sewage by discharging semi-treated sewage through tunnel sewer to the South China Sea at the south of Lamma Island.[37] This proposal has received very strong objections from China because it is dumping Hong Kong's waste into its water. Environmentalists in Hong Kong are concerned with the blowing of fumes and pollution by the prevailing winds into Hong Kong from a proposed 2,640 megawatt Eastern Shenzhen coal-fired power plant at the eastern shore of the Mirs Bay directly across Hong Kong. In the planning for Hong Kong, planners should take their neighbours into consideration. The same should apply for planners across the border. It is through cooperation and understanding that the border can be developed to mutual benefits. An example of such cooperation is the recent joint Shenzhen River Regulation Project to realign, widen, and deepen the Shenzhen River which at the border between Hong Kong and Shenzhen. The main objective of the project is to protect the bordering areas of the Shenzhen River from flooding. When this project is completed, both sides with benefit.

Hong Kong and Macau will be better integrated into the Pearl River Delta when they become China's SARs at the end of the century.[38] With competition among the cities and counties in the Pearl River Delta, it is anticipated that more cross jurisdiction problems will occur in the future. There is an urgent need to set up an inter-local government body to formulate and implement region-wide policies and plans. Although the Sino-British Infrastructure Coordinating Committee will be abolished after July 1997, it will provide very good experience on how cross-border conflicts can be resolved and how cross-border cooperation can be achieved in the region. The setting up of inter-local government body, such as the Council of Governments (COG) in the United States, should be actively pursued to deal with cross jurisdiction infrastructure development and negative externalities, and to promote inter-local government cooperation in dealing with these matters. The COG in the United States comprises of representatives from adjoining cities and counties for the formulation of area-wide policies and plans.[39] It is an inter-local government organization that provides an area-wide mechanism to study, discuss, and determine the best method to deal with cross jurisdiction problems and other common problems within the boundary of the COG. A high-level regional agency is needed to be established in the Pearl River Delta after Hong Kong and Macau become China's SARs. Coordination of regional development and cooperation will be a domestic rather than foreign affair. Existing fragmented channels in dealing with cross-border matters should be consolidated under one agency.[40]

The future of the border in Hong Kong very much depends on the future economic and political development in Hong Kong and China. Take aside the difference in political ideology, Hong Kong needs a border that can protect it from the large influx of people and vehicles from China. Otherwise, it will be very crowded and congested and all its planning and development efforts in the last twenty years will become fruitless.

Notes

1. A.G.O. Yeh, and Xu Xueqiang, "Integration of the Chinese Urban System with Pacific Asia under the Open Policy," in *Emerging World Cities in Pacific Asia: Growth and Adjustment to Global Restructuring*, edited by Lo Fu-chen and Yeung Yue-man (Tokyo: United Nations University Press, forthcoming). Also see D. R. Phillips, and Anthony G. O. Yeh, "Foreign Investment and Trade — Impact on Spatial Structure of the Economy," in *The Geography of Contemporary China: The Impact of Deng Xiaoping's Decade*, edited by T. Cannon and A. Jenkins (London: Routledge, 1990), pp. 224–48.

2. R. Skeldon, "Hong Kong and Its Hinterland: A Case of International Rural-to-Urban Migration," *Asian Geographer*, Vol. 5, No. 1 (1986), pp. 1–24.

3. Terry T. Lui, "Undocumented Migration in Hong Kong," *International Migration*, Vol. 21, No. 2 (1983), pp. 260–76.

4. Hong Kong Housing Authority, *Annual Report 1980–81*, (Hong Kong: Hong Kong Housing Authority, 1981).

5. Peter K. W. Fong, and Anthony G. O. Yeh, "Hong Kong," in *Housing Policy and Practice in Asia*, edited by Ha Seong-kyu (London: Croom Helm, 1987), pp. 12–47.

6. K. Y. Wong, and D.K.Y. Chu (eds.), *Modernization in China: The Case of the Shenzhen Special Economic Zone* (Hong Kong: Oxford University Press, 1985). Also see Y. C. Jao, and C. K. Leung (eds.), *China's Special Economic Zones: Policies, Problems and Prospects* (Hong Kong: Oxford University Press, 1989).

7. The definition of floating population in China is different from transient and temporary population. Floating population are those who enter a city either legally or illegally without permanent or temporary residency in that city.

8. Niles Hansen, "European Transboundary Cooperation and Its Relevance to the United States–Mexico Border," *Journal of American Planning Association*, Vol. 49, No. 3 (1983), pp. 236–343.

9. Hong Kong Government, *Hong Kong 1990: A Review of 1989* (Hong Kong: Government Printer, 1990).

10. Lau Pui-king, "Economic Relations between Hong Kong and China," in *Hong Kong in Transition*, edited by Joseph Y. S. Cheng (Hong Kong: Oxford University Press, 1986), pp. 235–67.

11. V.F.S. Sit, "Hong Kong's New Industrial Partnership with the Pearl River Delta," *Asian Geographer*, Vol. 8, Nos. 1 and 2 (1989), pp. 103–15.

12. See Note 8. Also see Lawrence A. Herzog, "Cross-national Urban Structure in the Era of Global Cities: The U.S.–Mexico Transfrontier Metropolis," *Urban Studies*, Vol. 28, No. 4 (1991), pp. 519–33.

13. Lee Tsao-yuen (ed.), *Growth Triangle: The Johor–Singapore–Riau Experience* (Singapore: Institute of Southeast Asian Studies, 1991).

14. See "Cross-national Urban Structure in the Era of Global Cities: The U.S.–Mexico Transfrontier Metropolis" (Note 12).

15. Luis Suarez-Villa, "Urban Growth and Manufacturing Change in the United States–Mexico Borderlands: A Conceptual Framework and an Empirical Analysis," *The Annals of Regional Science*, Vol. 19, No. 3 (1985), pp. 54–108.

16. J. F. Brotchie, "Technological Change and Urban Form," *Environment and Planning A*, Vol. 16 (1984), pp. 583–96. Also see A. Kellerman, "Telecommunications and the Geography of Metropolitan Areas," *Progress in Human Geography*, Vol. 8, No. 2 (1984), pp. 222–46.

17. *Ming Pao*, 4 January 1993.

18. Rating and Valuation Department, *Hong Kong Property Review* (Hong Kong: Rating and Valuation Department, Hong Kong Government, 1993).

19. Alan W. G. Wong, "Cross Border Traffic," in *Border Town Development and Planning — Hong Kong and Shenzhen*, edited by A.G.O. Yeh and Sun Huasheng (Hong Kong: Centre of Urban Planning and Environmental Management, forthcoming).

20. Ibid.

21. Ibid.

22. Business and Professionals Federation of Hong Kong, *Hong Kong 21 — A Ten Year Vision and Agenda for Hong Kong's Economy* (Hong Kong: Business and Professionals Federation of Hong Kong, 1993).

23. Anthony G. O. Yeh, "Planning for Uncertainty — Hong Kong's Urban Development in the 1990s," *Built Environment*, Vol. 11, No. 4 (1985), pp. 252–67.

24. Hong Kong Government, *Planning for Growth* (Hong Kong: Government Printer, 1985).

25. Ibid.

26. Metroplan is not a strategic plan for the metropolitan area of Hong Kong. The definition of metropolitan area in the TDS is different from the common usage in other parts of the world which is the city and its surrounding commuting areas. It only covers the Hong Kong Island, Kowloon, New Kowloon and Kwai Chung–Tsuen Wan and not the whole territory of Hong Kong. Because of this, although the name "Metroplan" suggests that it is a plan for the metropolitan area of Hong Kong, it is indeed not. The "Metroplan" is only one of the subregional plans of the five major subregions of the TDS.

27. Planning Department, *Territorial Development Strategy Review — Development Options* (Hong Kong: Planning Department, Hong Kong Government, 1993); Planning Department, *Territorial Development Strategy Review — Foundation Report* (Hong Kong: Planning Department, Hong Kong Government, 1993).

28. See *Territorial Development Strategy Review — Development Options* (Note 27).

29. Transport Branch, *Railway Development Study — Public Consultation Document* (Hong Kong: Transport Branch, Hong Kong Government, 1993); Transport Branch, *Railway Development Strategy* (Hong Kong: Transport Branch, Hong Kong Government, 1994).

30. One Country Two Systems Economic Research Institute, *The Problems of Road Freight Traffic between Hong Kong and Shenzhen* (Hong Kong: One Country Two Systems Economic Research Institute, 1994) [in Chinese].

31. See *Territorial Development Strategy Review — Foundation Report* (Note 27).

32. Planning Department, *Territorial Development Strategy Review: Report on Public Consultation — Executive Summary* (Hong Kong: Planning Department, Hong Kong Government, 1994).

33. Hong Kong Government, *Hong Kong 1992: A Review of 1991* (Hong Kong: Government Printer, 1992).

34. Same as Note 14.

35. A smart card system has been used in the Singapore–Johore Bahru border to speed up immigration procedures by doing away with the filling of immigration forms and long queues. Instead of going through the immigration every time and getting the passport stamped, the traveller can be issued a smart card that can go through a reader that record arrivals and departures (see Note 13). The card is issued based on a valid multiple-entry business visa and is for non-Malaysian only to facilitate them to work or live across the border.

36. Betty Ho, "Cross-Border Pollution," in *Border Town Development and Planning — Hong Kong and Shenzhen*, edited by A.G.O. Yeh and Sun Huasheng (Hong Kong: Centre of Urban Planning and Environmental Management, forthcoming).

37. Planning, Environment and Lands Branch, *Saving Our Environment: First Review of Progress on the 1989 White Paper on Pollution in Hong Kong — A Time to Act* (Hong Kong: Planning, Environment and Lands Branch, Hong Kong Government, 1991); Planning, Environment and Lands Branch, *The Hong Kong Environment: A Green Challenge for the Community* (Hong Kong: Planning, Environment and Lands Branch, Hong Kong Government, 1993).

38. Macau will become an SAR in December 1999.

39. John C. Bollens, and Henry J. Schmandt, *The Metropolis: Its People, Politics, and Economic Life* (Fourth Edition; New York: Harper and Row, 1982).

40. There are at present a number of committees that deal with cross-border affairs. The main ones are the Hong Kong–Guangdong Environmental Protection Liaison Group set up in July 1990 and the Sino-British Infrastructure Coordinating Committee set up in December 1994.

13

Housing for Millions: The Challenge Ahead

Peter K. W. Fong

INTRODUCTION

In the early 1950s, there was insufficient decent housing to meet the need of the massive influx of immigrants from China and the rapidly growing population. High cost placed housing beyond the affordability of low-income households, and there was a shortage of developable urban land. The Hong Kong government responded to these problems by building high-rise, high-density low-cost public housing for those who were in genuine need of shelter. Prior to 1954, the government's involvement in housing was minimal. However, after a series of squatter fires, particularly with the huge one in Shek Kip Mei on the Christmas Eve of 1953, the government started to construct large-scale emergency resettlement housing. These fragmented public housing programmes by various agencies, such as the Resettlement Department, the former Housing Authority, and the Public Works Department, lasted almost two decades. The government gradually recognized the need for a comprehensive approach and an integrated housing agency. In 1973, it established a new Housing Authority (HA) and launched a ten-year public housing programme. Throughout the decade of the 1980s and the early 1990s, public housing policies changed significantly in response to the changing socio-economic and political environments in Hong Kong.[1]

Over the last four decades, the government played a very significant role in providing and managing low-cost housing for low-income members of the community who could not afford accommodations in the private housing market. By the end of March 1994, close to 3 million people (i.e. about half of Hong Kong's total population) lived in 150 public rental housing (PRH) and 120 Home Ownership Scheme (HOS) and Private Sector Participation Scheme (PSPS) estates. Hong Kong's achievement in housing is impressive by any international standard. Few countries, with the exception of Singapore, can measure up to what Hong Kong has accomplished in the last forty years. Despite this remarkable accomplishment, there are still complaints from some sectors of the community about housing provision and management. Has the housing problem been solved? What do people really want in housing? How does the change in the socio-economic and political environments as well as the change of sovereignty from a British colony to a Special Administrative Region (SAR) of China affect the formulation of public policies on housing? This chapter attempts to examine the issues in public housing provision and management as a result of changing environment. It starts with a review of public housing development in the last decade. After identifying and analysing the causes of the problems in housing provision, some strategies for tackling these problems are suggested. Finally, this chapter concludes with a glimpse into the future of how the challenge in housing for millions could be met in the post-colony years.

A REVIEW OF HOUSING DEVELOPMENT, 1984–1994

❑ *Population and Housing Stock*

The population of Hong Kong grew steadily from 5.3 million in 1984 to 5.9 million in 1994. The number of people living in public permanent housing also increased from 2.3 million to 2.9 million during the same period (Table 1). On the contrary, the number of people residing in public temporary housing decreased significantly from 122,000 to 65,000 while the corresponding figures in the private temporary housing were cut from 325,000 to 118,000. These figures show that there were some significant improvements in reducing the number of people living in unsatisfactory conditions associated with temporary housing.

The overall housing stock in Hong Kong increased from 1.26 million to 1.84 million units over the decade from 1984 to 1994 (Table 2). The PRH stock grew from 503,000 flats in 1984 to 647,000 in 1994. The increase was much greater for HOS/PSPS flats (from 35,000 in 1984 to 184,000 in 1994). The private permanent housing stock also expanded significantly

Table 1: Land Population (in thousands)

Type of housing	First quarter of					
	1984		1989		1994	
Public permanent	2,332	(43.8%)	2,595	(46.3%)	2,940	(49.7%)
Private permanent	2,545	(47.8%)	2,634	(47.0%)	2,792	(47.2%)
Public temporary	122	(2.3%)	112	(2.0%)	65	(1.1%)
Private temporary	325	(6.1%)	263	(4.7%)	118	(2.0%)
Total	5,324	(100%)	5,604	(100%)	5,915	(100%)

Source: Hong Kong Housing Authority, *Housing in Figures,* 1994.

Table 2: Stock of Permanent Residential Flats (in thousands)

Type of residential flats	First quarter of		
	1984	1989	1994
Public housing	568	716	863
Housing Authority (HA) rental	503	590	647
HOS/PSPS	35	95	184
Housing Society (HS) rental	30	31	32
Private housing	694	845	980
Total	1,262	1,561	1,843

Source: Same as Table 1.

from 694,000 units to 980,000 units. Although there were fewer flats in public housing (863,000) compared with private housing (980,000), the population in public housing was higher because the average household size in public housing (3.8) was larger than that in private housing (3.2) in 1994 (Table 3).

Table 4 indicates that the owner-occupation rates increased dramatically in public permanent housing from 6% to 22% over the decade while the rate for private housing increased markedly from 56% in 1984 to 70% in 1989 yet grew more slowly to 72% by 1994. The overall owner-occupation rate grew from 33% in 1984 to 44% in 1989 and 48% in 1994. The significant increase of home ownership rate in the late 1980s was

Table 3: Household Size

Type of housing	First quarter of		
	1984	1989	1994
Public permanent	4.4	4.0	3.8
Private permanent	3.5	3.3	3.2
Public temporary	3.4	3.0	2.6
Private temporary	3.4	3.2	3.0
Overall average	3.8	3.6	3.5

Source: Same as Table 1.

Table 4: Owner-occupation Rate

	First quarter of		
	1984	1989	1994
Public permanent housing	6%	14%	22%
Private permanent housing	56%	70%	72%
All permanent housing	33%	44%	48%

Source: Same as Table 1.

mainly attributed to the low and stable housing price, while the very slow growth of home ownership rate in the early 1990s was because of the sharp increase in housing prices in the private sector (Figure 1). For example, the average private housing price on Hong Kong Island increased from $13.900 per sq. m. in 1988 to $46,821 per sq. m. in 1993 (Table 5).

The aspiration to own homes is best illustrated by the number of applications for HOS/PSPS. The number of applications by "green form" (sitting PRH tenants) increased from 9,772 in 1983–1984 to 63,685 in 1993–1994 whereas the "white form" (general public) applications were even higher, from 30,457 in 1983–1984 to 157,638 in 1993–1994 (Table 6). The oversubscription rate was as high as 23.3 times for "white form" applications in 1993–1994.

Figure 1: Indices of Movements in Prices and Rentals of
Residential Property

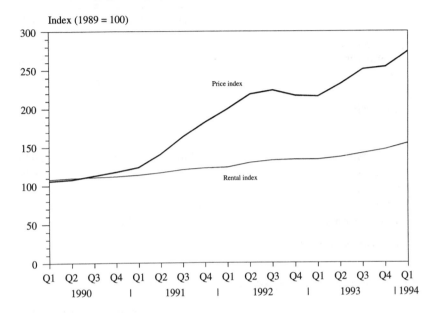

Index (1989 = 100)

Source: Planning, Environment and Lands Branch, *Report of the Task Force on Land Supply and Property Prices* (Hong Kong: Hong Kong Government, June 1994).

❑ *Living Conditions and Affordability*

Over the last decade, the overall living conditions in public housing have been improved steadily. The median internal floor area per person was increased from 6 sq. m. in 1984 to 8 sq. m. in 1994. The proportion of households living in overcrowded conditions has been reduced significantly from about 20% in 1984 to 3.4% in 1994 even with higher standards set for overcrowding in 1994. Overcrowding is defined as households with occupation density of less than 3.25 sq. m. per person in 1984 but 4.5 sq. m. in 1994.

Rents have been relatively low in public housing estates. They are only about 15–25% of market rent. Although rent has been increased from about $10 per sq. m. in 1984 to $30 per sq. m. in 1994 for estates on Hong Kong

Table 5: Housing Price (HK$/sq. m.)

	Average price/Saleable floor area		
	1983	1988	1993
Hong Kong Island			
HOS/PSPS	4,290	—	22,286
Private housing	8,171	13,920	46,821
Kowloon			
HOS/PSPS	—	—	—
Private housing	7,155	12,324	37,410
New Kowloon			
HOS/PSPS	5,170	8,800	22,080
Private housing	6,824	12,593	38,929
New Territories			
HOS/PSPS	3,890	6,740	16,330
Private housing	N.A.	11,793	36,803

Source: Same as Table 1.

Table 6: HOS/PSPS Applications

	1983–1984	1988–1989	1993–1994
Green form			
No. of applications	9,772	92,992	63,685
Oversubscription rate (times)	3.4	9.9	8.1
White form			
No. of applications	30,457	116,457	157,638
Oversubscription rate (times)	7.3	19.4	23.3

Source: Same as Table 1.

Island, the median rent-to-income ratio is still very low at 8.3% in 1994 (Table 7). The corresponding figures for private sector housing were much higher at $218 per sq. m. and 23.4% in 1994 respectively (Table 8). Sale prices for HOS/PSPS flats were also much cheaper than the private sector flats. These prices are about 45–70% of market price. The fact that there were heavy subsidization of these flats was one of the reasons for the high oversubscription rate of 23 times the number of flats offered (Tables 5 and 6).

Table 7: Living Conditions and Rent in HA Rental Flats

	First quarter of		
	1984	1989	1994
Proportion of households living in overcrowded conditions (%)	19.8	7.9	3.4
Median internal floor area per person (sq. m.)	6.0	7.0	8.0
Average monthly rent per sq. m. of internal floor area (HK$/sq. m.)			
Hong Kong Island	10.2	18.0	30.2
Kowloon	11.6	18.9	28.5
New Kowloon	9.3	16.4	29.1
New Territories	10.5	18.2	28.6
Median rent-to-income ratio (%)	N.A.	7.3	8.3

Source: Same as Table 1.

Table 8: Rental in Private Housing

	First quarter of		
	1984	1989	1994
Average monthly rent per sq. m. of saleable floor area (HK$/sq. m.)			
Hong Kong Island	65.4	120.5	218.2
Kowloon	68.6	111.7	197.2
New Kowloon	61.2	114.2	164.0
New Territories	49.5	98.0	130.6
Median rent-to-income ratio (%)	N.A.	16.3	23.4

Source: Same as Table 1.

As a result of rising household incomes and the general trend of the increasing aspiration for home ownership, the HA adjusted the production mix between rental and HOS/PSPS flats. The proportion was changed from 3:1 in 1984 to 1:1 in 1994. As shown in Table 9, the production of HOS/PSPS flats has increased from 10,117 in 1984 to 24,743 in 1994. The

Table 9: Housing Production

Number of	1983–1984	1988–1989	1993–1994
HA rental flats	28,564	39,518	19,848
HS rental flats	5	850	426
HOS/PSPS flats	10,117	10,946	24,743
Private flats	24,076	30,163	32,605
Total	62,762	81,477	77,622

Source: Same as Table 1.

Table 10: Public Housing Production Programme

	1994–1995 to 1996–1997	1997–1998 to 2000–2001
HA rental flats	58,318	92,456
HOS/PSPS flats	36,784	93,328

Source: Same as Table 1.

projected production programme for 1997–1998 to 2000–2001 for rental and HOS/PSPS flats are 92,456 and 93,328 respectively (Table 10).

Despite the growing demand for home ownership, there is still a substantial demand for PRH. The number of applicants on the waiting list remained high at 150,000 in 1994. At an allocation rate of about 15,000 flats to those on the waiting list each year, it might take another five years to clear this backlog even if only half of those on the waiting list are eventually eligible at the time of allocation (Table 11).

Presently, the average waiting time for a household to be allocated a public rental flat is about six years. As the monthly income limit for applicants is adjusted upward annually, the number of eligible households for public housing will not be reduced significantly in the near future. The HA has to strike a balance between allocating the new flats for sale or rent to meet the different demands.

CHANGING ENVIRONMENTS

In the last few decades, the socio-economic and political environments

Table 11: HA Rental Housing Allocation

	1983–1984	1988–1989	1993–1994
Categories of allocation			
Waiting list	13,000	10,000	17,000
Clearance	8,000	5,000	5,000
Redevelopment	6,000	8,000	12,000
Others*	7,000	9,000	6,000
Total	34,000	32,000	40,000
No. of applicants	162,000	139,000	150,000
Monthly income limit for 4-person household	HK$4,200	HK$5,400	HK$11,400

* Include emergency, compassionate, junior civil servants and pensioners, reuse of temporary housing areas, major repairs and transfer and relief of overcrowding.
Source: Same as Table 1.

in Hong Kong have undergone some significant changes. The following changes have impacts on public housing policies.

❑ Political and Social Environment

Hong Kong has been moving progressively towards a more representative government which allows greater citizen participation in public policies since the introduction of the District Administration Scheme in 1982. The signing of the Sino-British Joint Declaration in 1984, the election of non-official members to the Legislative Council (Legco) in 1985, the introduction of Public Sector Reform in 1989, the June 4 incident in 1989, the promulgation of the Basic Law of the Hong Kong SAR of the People's Republic of China (P.R.C.) on 4 April 1990, the formation of political parties and the first direct election of Legco members in September 1991, the arrival of the new Governor Chris Patten in July 1992, the breakdown of Sino-British negotiation on the 1994–1995 election arrangement in early 1994, and the passage of the Governor's Political Reform Bill in June 1994, all have significant impacts on public Policy Formulation.

After the passage of the Political Reform Bill, all appointed seats on both the District Boards and the Urban and Regional Councils were abolished. The traditional input from appointed professional and business sector members were replaced mostly by more politically and socially active members. At the same time, channels for citizen participation were also increased. Many community activists and politicians paid more attention to local residents in public housing estates as they represented half of the total population of Hong Kong. Most politicians who ran for seats on the three-tier Boards and Councils have incorporated the interests of public housing residents in their election platforms in order to gain voter support in their constituencies. Housing policies became a political issue and were the subject of keen concern and heated debates in various forums. Some pressure groups and political parties even went further by organizing petitions, demonstrations and protests when their demands were not met through the normal policy-making mechanism. In the run-up to 1997, the voice of the lower-income groups, particularly public housing residents, will become louder as a result of the recent political reform. However, this current trend may be altered if China goes ahead with its threat to disband the newly established three-tier political system and revert to the pre-reform system. In any case, housing policies will become more political in the coming years as the percentage of people living in public housing increases every year.

❑ *Economic Environment*

Hong Kong has been transformed from a manufacturing centre in the late 1960s and 1970s into a trade and financial centre in the 1980s and early 1990s. The deindustrialization proceeded rapidly particularly in the last few years. In 1984, the manufacturing industry employed 960,000 workers, but a decade later in 1994, the workforce in manufacturing was reduced by half to 460,000 persons. The workforce in wholesale/retail, import/export trades, restaurants and hotels increased from 550,000 to one million while those engaged in financing, insurance, real estate and business services jumped from 130,000 to 350,000 over the same period.[2] Given the extremely low unemployment rate in recent years (average from 1.1% to 2.0% between 1989 and 1994), most workers managed to switch from one sector to another without difficulties. Household income also grew steadily for the decade and was higher than the price increase from 1984 to 1990. This generated a substantial demand for home ownership and better quality housing. However, the prices of residential flats have been rising ahead of household income since 1990. It led to a large number of households being priced out of the private residential property market. Their incomes were above the income eligibility limit for HOS. The growing size of the middle-income households did exert pressure on the government to provide assistance in coping with the high cost of home ownership.

PROBLEMS AND ISSUES IN HOUSING PROVISION

The demand for housing reflected the changes in the socio-economic and political environments in Hong Kong over the last decade. The changes in the political system allowed people to have more say in which government policies are formulated. Public Sector Reform made government departments more open, more accountable and more efficient in delivering services to the public. Political and social awareness enabled many lower-income households to articulate their rights and needs more clearly. Economic growth and the restructuring of the economy from secondary manufacturing industries to tertiary finance and trade service industries have led to increases in household income and the emergence of middle-income class with aspiration for home ownership.

All the above changes did have major impacts on housing provision and management. Demands on the quality and quantity of housing rose steadily over the years. These demands for better housing were reflected through various channels such as the media, the government advisory boards and councils as well as in political and social actions. In response to these growing pressures in housing provision and management, the government organizations responsible for these matters have to find ways and means to address these issues efficiently, effectively and equitably. The following sections examine some of the problems faced by the government and the HA in recent years.

❏ *Inadequate Supply*

In response to the changing needs and aspirations of the population in the mid-1980s, the HA announced its Long Term Housing Strategy (LTHS) in April 1987 and forecast that about 960,000 new housing units would be needed to satisfy the demand by 2001. However, in the 1993 Mid-Term Review of demand and supply of housing under the LTHS, it was found that there was inadequate supply to meet the projected demand. A shortfall of

16,600 rental flats was estimated between the period 1994–1999. This shortage of flats will prolong the waiting time for those on the waiting list because they are accorded a lower priority compared to other committed categories. The estimated supply is only about 34,000 flats per year between 1994–1995 to 1997–1998, about 10,000 flats below the average production of 44,000 flats per year between 1985–1986 to 1992–1993 (Table 12). The shortage is particularly acute for one-person and two-person units.

The main factor contributing to the low production is insufficient land supply. In general, sites for public housing are allocated by the government at no cost to the HA. The HA has to compete with other departments and in particular private developers for valuable sites. Since land sales generate large sum of revenue for the government, it is not easy for the government to forgo the potential land sale revenue by allocating more sites for public housing development instead of selling them to private developers. Revenue from land auctions amounted to $15.8 billion and $15.6 billion for the government in 1993–1994 and 1994–1995 respectively.[3] There has been a constant shortage of serviced sites for public housing development, particularly for the coming four years, resulting in a low level of production forecast for 1994–1998 (Table 12). How to increase production in the coming years remains a major problem for the HA.

Table 12: Programmed Public Housing Production

Year	Public rental		Public sales		Total	
	No.	%	No.	%	No.	%
1993–1994	23,900	49	25,300	51	49,200	100
1994–1995	23,700	69	10,800	31	34,500	100
1995–1996	15,800	47	17,700	53	33,500	100
1996–1997	17,800	50	18,000	50	35,800	100
1997–1998	17,900	55	14,400	45	32,300	100
1998–1999	20,900	44	26,300	56	47,200	100
1999–2000	30,800	55	25,100	45	55,900	100
2000–2001	22,800	41	32,600	59	55,400	100

Source: Hong Kong Housing Authority, *A Report on the Mid-Term Review of the LTHS*, October 1993.

❏ *Competing Priorities of Housing Allocation*

In response to growing aspirations for home ownership, the HA changed
the production mix between PRH and HOS/PSPS flats from 3:1 to 1:1 in
recent years. This change reduced the number of rental flats available for
allocation. As a result of the low projected production in the coming four
years, the allocation of available flats to different categories becomes more
difficult. Under the existing allocation policy, priority is given to tenants
affected by the Comprehensive Redevelopment Programme (CRP) and
squatter and Temporary Housing Area (THA) clearees. Although at least
14,000 flats are set aside for the waiting list applicants, there are still over
150,000 on the list, with more than 1,000 new applications added to the
list every month. The average total demand for rental flats from various
categories outnumbers the forecast average supply for allocation in the
next five years. How these limited resources should be allocated to various
categories and who should have higher priorities over the other groups pose
difficult questions for the HA.

❏ *Slow Mobility of PRH Tenants to Home Ownership*

To increase the home ownership rate is one of the government's objectives
in housing. The new Governor, Chris Patten, set the overall home ownership rate at 60% by 1997 in his first policy address in 1992. About 15% of
the 60% would come from the public sector since the rate in the private
sector had already exceeded 70%. However, the actual rate of increase in
the public sector was much lower than expected. The overall rate only
increased from 44% in 1989 to 48% in 1994 (Table 4). In 1993, a more
realistic projection was forecast at 54% by 1997 by the HA.

There were several factors attributing to this slower growth. First of all,
the government decided not to launch the Sale of Flats to Sitting Tenants
Scheme (SFSTS) because there were not sufficient subscriptions to the
Scheme. This, in effect, reduced about 1.4% of the ownership rate in the
public sector.

Second, a high percentage of redevelopment tenants and clearees consistently indicated a strong preference for rental flats even though many of
them could well afford to buy. Table 13 shows that there were only 4–9%
of clearees opting for HOS/PSPS upon relocation.

Third, the failure of the Home Purchase Loan Scheme (HPLS) had also

Table 13: Percentage of Clearees Opted for HOS/PSPS

Year	THA/Squatter area	PRH redevelopment	Total
1990–1991	9	10	9
1991–1992	1	7	4
1992–1993	1	10	8

Source: Same as Table 12.

Table 14: Operation of the HPLS

Year	Loan amount (HK$)	Annual quota	Quota consumed	PRH flats recovered
1988–1989	70,000	2,500	557	501
1989–1990	110,000	6,000	3,022	1,627
1990–1991	130,000	3,000	2,935	1,610
1991–1992	130,000	3,500	1,042	508
1992–1993	150,000	1,500	269	129
1993–1994	200,000	1,000	701	225
Total		17,500	8,526	4,600

Sources: See Table 12. Also refer to the 1993–1994 annual report of the Housing
          Authority.

significantly reduced the growth of ownership rates. The HPLS, introduced
in 1988 as part of the LTHS, assumed that 102,500 private sector flats
would be taken up via the scheme between 1988 and 2001. However,
the response to the HPLS was very poor for several reasons. The rising
property prices, the tightening up of the mortgage lending ratio, and the
high conveyancing, legal charges and stamp duties made the HPLS less
attractive. Despite annual increases of the loan amount, the annual quota
has always been under-utilized. Only 8,526 — less than half of the total
quota of 17,500 — were taken up during the period between 1988 and 1994
(Table 14). Hence, the original target take-up of 102,500 private sector flats
for the whole strategy period was reduced significantly by 85% to just
15,800 in the 1993 LTHS review. A serious review of the HPLS is needed
to see how it can compete with other forms of housing subsidies in relation
to the changing socio-economic circumstances and community aspirations.

❏ *Private Property Ownership by PRH Tenants*

Since actual rents for public housing tenants only represent 15–25% of market rent, a large number of households made use of their accumulated savings on rent to purchase private properties. In a survey conducted in July 1993, it was revealed that about 13% or 74,000 out of 580,000 PRH households owned private domestic properties. Another survey on tenants in North Point Estate showed that 18% tenants owned private domestic properties in the urban area alone, not to mention in other parts of the territory or even overseas. A separate analysis of 2,000 actual transactions in the private property market showed that 24% of these purchases were made by PRH tenants in the period between October 1992 and March 1993. All these survey results reflect the prevalence of private property ownership by PRH tenants. It raises a serious social equity issue over the use of limited public housing resources on those who are not in genuine need. There is concern whether some of the PRH tenants who owned private domestic properties should continue to receive heavy housing subsidies while there are still over 150,000 households on the waiting list for public housing. Allowing property owners who are not in genuine housing need to remain in PRH is obviously contrary to the objective of providing subsidized housing only to those in need. How this complicated issue should be tackled requires careful studies given the large number of people involved and the likely social and political repercussions should drastic actions be taken. It may be necessary to seek a balanced option which could redress social equity without causing social instability.

❏ *Estate Management and Maintenance*

The HA has been producing a large quantity of flats annually. However, as socio-economic conditions have changed significantly in recent decades, the expectations of the general public on the quality of flats have also changed. Unlike the situation in the 1950s when most people were very grateful to be allocated tiny resettlement cubicles even without any internal facilities such as kitchen, water-tap or toilets, people nowadays demand a much higher standard of accommodation in public housing. Residents care very much about the quality of design, production, and management and maintenance of the housing estates. In recent years, there were security and safety problems with the design of some of the housing blocks which led to the occurrence of certain crimes and accidents. There were also complaints about the poor finishing of flats due to the use of inferior building materials and workmanship. The completion of a large number of flats required additional professional management and maintenance staff which are not easy to hire and assemble in the tight labour market situation that prevails in Hong Kong. The training of these professional and technical personnel usually takes several years. Against the zero growth policy in the civil service, there is a concern over the endless addition of staff to manage the growing public housing stock. Moreover, the increasing public account-ability, openness, and introduction of performance pledges under Public Sector Reform also generate more responsibilities for the management and front-line staff. How to cope with the pressing and increasing demands from the public with limited manpower resources warrants serious con-sideration by the HA.

MACRO-STRATEGIES FOR GOALS AND ORGANIZATIONS

After identifying some of the main issues and problems in housing provision in the past few years, we now proceed to develop some strategies in tackling these issues and problems during the transition and post-1997 years. We might have to tackle both the macro and micro issues resulting from the rapidly changing socio-economic and political environments. We first address the broad goals and objectives of the new housing policies and then tackle the specific problems discussed earlier in this chapter.

❏ *Goals and Priorities*

Hong Kong's public housing programme began with the goal of providing emergency and basic low-cost rental accommodations to victims of natural disasters and the very poor during the 1950s and 1960s. It evolved gradually in the 1970s to adopt the goal of providing all households with adequate housing[4] at an affordable rent or price as soon as possible. It moved slowly from the original emphasis solely on quantity to quality. In 1987, the goals were further broadened in the LTHS to incorporate the promotion of home ownership by constructing more flats for sale and subsidizing the lower-middle-income households to purchase private sector flats. In the early 1990s, the goals of the LTHS were further translated into specific operational objectives and publicly pledged targets.[5] They are:

1. substantial clearance of the waiting list backlog by 1997;
2. achieving an overall home ownership rate close to 60% by 1997;
3. clearance of all urban squatters on government land by 1996; and
4. making rehousing offers to all existing THA residents by 1997.

Three of the above objectives (i.e. objectives 1, 3 and 4) are by no means beyond challenge since they target households in need of assistance for adequate permanent housing. They are also in line with the aim of achieving efficient and equitable use of resources by ensuring that a household's benefit from the housing subsidy is in relation to need. However, the objective of achieving 60% home ownership rate by 1997 is not very convincing. There is no strong rationale, urgency nor significance for achieving the 60% rate by 1997.

A more appropriate strategy regarding the goal of public housing policies should focus on providing assistance in obtaining adequate affordable housing to households who could not satisfy their housing needs in the private property market. As shown in the model for housing provision in Hong Kong (Figure 2), the public sector's role should focus on assisting the very low-income to lower-middle-income households who are priced out of the private housing market. The lowest-income group at the bottom rung of the ladder, particularly the one to two-person households still residing in dangerously overcrowded bed-spaces in private housing, should receive the highest priority in rehousing. Priorities and the amount of housing subsidies for other income groups moving up the ladder as their incomes increase should decrease proportionally until they reach a certain income limit set by the government. Those above this line should satisfy their housing needs either through buying or renting in the private housing market. The choices of owning or renting should be left to individual households and market forces with no predetermined ratio between owners and renters. The principle of progressive vertical equity should be observed in public housing policies.[6] With the objective and priority of helping those with the greatest housing needs first, housing resources should be allocated accordingly.

❑ *Roles of Housing Organizations*

The Hong Kong government's basic approach in housing development is to provide sufficient land, supporting infrastructure and a financial environment which induces private sector investment in property development.

Figure 2: A Model for Housing Provision in Hong Kong

Supplier	Housing type	Household type
High quality		High income
Private developers	Private housing	Owners/Tenants > HOS & SCH income limit
Housing Society Private developers	Sandwich class housing (SCH)	Owners < SCH income limit > HOS income limit
Housing Authority Private developers	HOS/PSPS HPLS	Owners < HOS income limit
Housing Authority	$1\frac{1}{2}$ to 2 × rent	Better-off tenants
Housing Authority Housing Society	Public rental housing	Tenants < Waiting list income
Housing Authority Private sector	THA, squatter and substandard housing	Waiting list applicants, new immigrants and elderlies
Low quality		Low income

Assisted housing for those who cannot afford private housing is mainly provided through the HA and the Housing Society (HS). Only recently, at the end of 1994, the government re-established the Housing Branch to tackle the problem when residential property prices had risen beyond the reach of the average household. The following sections will examine these three housing organizations and suggest what roles they should play in tackling the housing problems and issues in the coming years. Table 15 summarizes the roles played by the three housing organizations.

Housing Branch

The Housing Branch was established in late 1994 to take over the responsibilities for developing policies and strategies for the provision of both

Table 15: Roles of Housing Organizations

Organization	Role	Housing type
Housing Branch	Policy-maker/Coordinator	Public housing Private housing
Housing Society	Provider/Loan administrator Provider/Administrator	Sandwich class housing Public rental housing
Housing Authority	Provider/Administrator Loan administrator Provider/Administrator Provider/Administrator	HOS/PSPS HPLS Public rental housing THA and squatter housing

public and private housing and for coordinating the implementation of the government's housing policies and programmes. Some of these responsibilities were formerly vested with the government's Planning, Environment and Lands Branch which has a much wider scope of responsibilities. The new Housing Branch will focus on housing-related issues with an aim of providing adequate supply of housing at affordable rents or prices to meet the demand in both public and private sectors.

Being directly under the Government Secretariat, the Housing Branch should take up an active role in providing adequate land for residential development by speeding up infrastructure development. The Branch should be in a much better position to work with other government branches and departments in accelerating the infrastructure and land development process which neither the HA nor the HS could perform effectively. On the private sector side, the Branch should play the role of a regulator and monitor of the private property market. It should facilitate the adequate provision of land for private residential development as a means of stabilizing residential property prices.

Housing Society

The HS, as an independent non-profit organization, had a total of 32,000 rental flats and 7,000 sale flats under the urban improvement scheme in 1994. The HS was entrusted by the government in 1993 to operate the Sandwich Class Housing Scheme (SCHS). The Scheme aims to assist households that are neither eligible for public housing nor able to afford buying their own homes in the private property market. The income limit was set between $20,000 and $44,000 per month. The interim scheme started with a capital of $2 billion from public funds to provide low-interest loans for up to 4,000 eligible families to purchase flats in the private sector. The first phase of the interim scheme was launched in August 1993, the second phase in April 1994, and the third phase in October 1994. Under this interim scheme, successful applicants may borrow up to 25% of the flat price or $550,000, whichever is the less. The main scheme aims to produce 10,000 flats for sale to the sandwich class at affordable prices. These flats will be completed before 1997. The first batch of about 1,000 flats is expected to be completed in 1995.[7]

Apart from the newly entrusted SCHS, the HS has been managing a relatively small number of rental housing estates and some sale flats. The growth in the production of rental flats is limited. Therefore, the HS should focus its role in administering the SCHS and, to a lesser extent, continue its efforts in the urban improvement and the flat-for-sale schemes by looking for opportunities in urban redevelopment. Its rental housing units should be used as relieving flats in the urban improvement scheme.

Housing Authority

The HA is the largest developer and estate management agent in Hong Kong. As shown earlier in Table 2, it had a stock of 184,000 HOS/PSPS and 647,000 rental flats in 1994. It should continue to play the role of providing affordable adequate housing for those in need. As pointed out earlier, its primary role should be on meeting the needs of the very poor. It should also allocate its resources in a decreasing order for those with increasing household income. It should also try to upgrade its management and improve the quality of the living environment in its housing estates in response to the changing requirements of its tenants.

MICRO-STRATEGIES FOR PROBLEM-SOLVING

After tackling the macro issues on objectives and roles of the housing organizations, we can now address the specific problems and issues which the HA encountered in recent years. Once a policy is formulated after careful consideration on various technical, financial, administrative, political and social aspects, the HA should adopt a proactive and aggressive public relations strategy in the consultation process with politicians and community groups. Since the socio-political environment has changed significantly in recent years, the traditional reactive ways of dealing with the public have to be turned around. Certain marketing strategies employed in the private sector may be useful in promoting a policy to residents. The use of pilot scheme to test the reaction to a certain policy is a good way in gauging community support and refining a policy. The following sections address some of the problems and issues raised earlier in this chapter.

❑ *Increase Supply of Flats*

The production of housing units is a lengthy process. It involves the identification of sites, planning and design, infrastructural and site preparation, building construction, and fitting out. The whole process takes five to seven years. Providing more land and accelerating the development process are the two key factors for increasing the housing supply. Table 16 shows that there was an increase of the overall supply of land for residential development in between 1990 and 1995. The new Housing Branch is also working on bringing forward the land production programme and associated infrastructural development works. In order to boost supply, the

Table 16: Land Disposals for Residential Development

	1990–1991	1991–1992	1992–1993	1993–1994	1994–1995
CR/R1/R2	12.55	20.04	18.25	15.71	19.43
R3/R4	2.94	3.42	2.08	2.65	5.95
HOS/PSPS	17.65	13.51	1.87	14.79	19.10
SCH	N.A.	N.A.	N.A.	1.80	5.74
HKHS	0.51	0.02	1.43	3.17	3.59
Total	33.65	36.99	35.63	41.12	53.81

Notes: CR = Commercial residential development
R1/R2 = High and medium-high-density residential development
R3/R4 = Medium-low and low-density residential development
HKHS = Hong Kong Housing Society

Source: Same as Figure 1.

HA may have to push hard for a larger share of available sites in competition with other potential users, particularly the private sector. The Housing Branch might be able to work with relevant government departments to expand the transport and infrastructural capacities to accommodate more residential development.

Internally, the HA should continue to explore ways of reducing the planning and design lead time by streamlining pre-contract procedures, shortening piling and building contract periods and allowing the submission of alternative tenders for shorter construction period.[8]

In addition, the HA should also try to maximize the development potential of infill sites in existing and future estates by optimizing site densities and greater use of podium design to meet open space requirements. With a combination of the above efforts, housing supply should increase accordingly.

❑ *Priorities in Housing Allocation*

Priorities in allocating limited housing resources should directly relate to the objectives of public housing policies. As suggested earlier, the highest priority should be given to those with the greatest housing need. Those living in substandard and overcrowded bed-spaces in private flats and squatter settlements, particularly the one to two-person elderly households, should have the highest priorities. Following this, priorities should go to the waiting list applicants and then those affected by clearance and redevelopment. Improving the living conditions of tenants in older PRH estates is important but it should not be overemphasized. Therefore, the comprehensive redevelopment programme of existing rental estates should be flexible enough to allow deferment on justifiable operational grounds.

Regarding the production ratio between rental and ownership flats, the policy should not be biased towards home ownership. The number of sale flats produced should not exceed those for rent. Although the growth in the home ownership rate is slow, it does not cause real hardship or problem for anyone. The low percentage of clearees from THA/squatter area and PRH redevelopment opted for HOS/PSPS should be accepted since most of these households make their tenure choice based on their affordability. Actually, HOS/PSPS flats should be used as a means of inducing better-off PRH tenants to vacate their rental flats for those who are in greater need of housing assistance. The HOS/PSPS allocation quota at 67:33

between green form and white form applicants should be maintained as this will make available more vacant rental flats in existing rental estates for reallocation. As for the HPLS, the loan amount should be increased in relation to changing economic and property market conditions. It should be regarded as a small-scale supplementary programme to assist those who have some difficulties in the private property market.

❑ *Private Property Ownership by PRH Tenants*

As several survey results indicated general support for taking action against property owners still occupying heavily subsidized PRH flats, the HA should introduce control measures in tackling this issue. The principle of "one house for one household" should be introduced to impose property restriction on all PRH tenants based upon the policy of relating housing subsidies to need. However, in order to minimize adverse impact and maintain social and political stability, alternative options and grace periods for affected tenants before new restriction is imposed should be provided. Sitting tenants should be given a period of 18 to 24 months to disposed of their properties in order to keep their tenancy. After the lapse of the grace period, those who choose to stay in their PRH flats would have to pay market rents.

In addition, the names of other family members who own private properties should be deleted from the tenancy register and should not be allowed to inherit PRH flats. However, exemption should be granted on compassionate grounds, i.e. tenants over the age of 60 owning one property as the main source of income. All new tenants admitted after the implementation of the new policy would not be permitted to own private domestic properties throughout their tenancy. Their eligibility for PRH would be subject to regular review. They should be informed before admission to the PRH flats that their tenancy will be terminated once they own private domestic properties. In order to ensure that limited public housing resources are used properly, it is necessary to step up enforcement actions against abuse in PRH estates, such as non-occupancy or subletting. Special enforcement teams from the Housing Department should be tasked to initiate inspection of suspect units. Neighbouring tenants should be encouraged to report any abuse and awards should be offered to reports on substantiated cases.[9] Enforcement efforts not only ensure that scarce housing resources are not wasted, but also recover flats for those waiting to be rehoused. The measures suggested here would redress social equity without causing too much adverse effect if they are implemented carefully.

❏ *Better Estate Management*

The HA has been exploring various means in improving its housing production and management. Its Construction Branch, now renamed Works Group, was certified in August 1993 with the quality management system under ISO 9001. More than fifty companies on the HA's List of Building Contractors had also acquired certification in 1994. With these quality improvement efforts, the HA should continue to ensure that the standards and quality do not just appear on papers and manuals. They should be reflected in the actual finish products and services.

In order to restrain the endless increase of staff for estate management and maintenance, serious consideration should be taken in the privatization and contracting out of most of the management functions in PRH estates. These functions include cleansing, maintenance and improvement, security, rent collection, tenancy enforcement and car parking. As the management of some of the HOS estates had already been undertaken by private property management agents, the practice should be extended to the management of PRH estates. Strategies to ensure a smooth transition and a successful implementation should be devised. The roles and responsibilities of all parties involved — the HA as the landlord, the property management agents and the tenants — should be clearly defined. Tenants should be involved in the whole process of contracting out at the very beginning in drafting the contract. An incremental approach of starting with a pilot scheme in a new rental housing estate should minimize the frequency of problems. It can be extended to other new rental estates in different phases. There should be a public relations strategy to gain public support. The objective of the scheme, that is to improve the quality of service of management in PRH estates, should be clearly explained to all concerned parties, including the tenants, pressure groups, Legislative Councillors and the Housing Department staff. The public relations exercise should stress the following:[10]

1. Housing Department will retain overall management responsibilities.
2. There will be more responsive and efficient housing management services to tenants.

3. Housing Department's subsidies to management costs will continue and there will be no rent increase because of the property management agent arrangement.
4. There will be no staff redundancy in the Housing Department.

The privatization and contracting out of some management functions in the management of PRH estates could achieve the objective of quality improvement if careful implementation strategies are devised. Ultimately, it can also help to restrain the growth of staff in estate management in the Housing Department.

Conclusion

The Hong Kong government has achieved quite a lot in terms of providing adequate housing for those in need of assistance. It should continue to focus on the work which it has done relatively well over the last four decades. As the socio-economic and political environments change rapidly during the transition period, it should modify its policies accordingly and set realistic goals and objectives in allocating its housing resources. Should the government adopt some of the strategies suggested here in this chapter, most of the problems and issues in housing provision in the immediate post-colony years could be eased, if not completely resolved.

Notes

1. Peter K. W. Fong, and Chan Chik, *Home of Yesterday* (Hong Kong: Joint Publishing Co., 1993).
2. Hong Kong Government, *Hong Kong 1985* and *Hong Kong 1994*.
3. *Ming Pao*, 31 March 1995.
4. "Adequate housing" is defined by the Hong Kong government as:
    i. built of permanent materials;
    ii. self-contained (an unit with own entrance, kitchen, bathroom/flush toilet, pipe water and electricity supply);
    iii. occupied on an unshared basis except in case of very small (one-person) households;
    iv. not overcrowded; and
    v. at a rent or price within household's means.
5. Hong Kong Housing Authority, *Final Report on the Mid-Term Review of the LTHS*, June 1994

6. Lau Kwok-yu, "Public Housing," in *The Other Hong Kong Report 1994*, edited by Donald H. McMillen and Man Si-wai (Hong Kong: The Chinese University Press, 1994), p. 282.

7. Planning, Environment and Lands Branch, *Report of the Task Force on Land Supply and Property Prices* (Hong Kong: Hong Kong Government, June 1994).

8. Same as Note 5.

9. Senior Staff Course Centre, *Group Project Report on Ownership of Private Domestic Properties by PRH Tenants*, SSC 23, March 1995.

10. Senior Staff Course Centre, *Group Project Report on a Feasibility Study Report of the Privatization of the Management of PRH Estates*, SSC 21, June 1994.

14

The Environment

Man Si-wai

Some cultures make good plumbing; some others, good space-rockets. (J. R. Ravetz, *The Merger of Knowledge with Power*, p. 199.)

... [T]he best defenders of the forest have been forest-dwelling communities; and any conservation strategy that excludes them will be counter-productive. (Quoted from Vandana Shiva's review on the book *Who Will Save the Forest*.)

Your father is working on night shift monitoring meters [at Daya Bay]. He loves you. He also loves me. But he loves the nuclear island more. (Lyrics of *Daya Bay Lullaby*, which was broadcast on China Central Television in August 1994.)

THE ENVIRONMENTAL PROBLEMATIC

To say that the environment of Hong Kong is unique and the approach Hong Kong takes towards environment-related issues will undergo unique changes in the switch-over of sovereignty in 1997 is far from a cliché, the reason being that "the environment" is neither a specific set of physical or ecological conditions that can be objectively specified or delimited, nor is it a fixed set of problems the "solutions" of which can be evaluated by some definite criteria of adequacy. Put simply, the environment is more a "problematic" interweaving different levels of discussions which take place in a community. Why the community is the appropriate locus with reference to which deliberations on various kinds of environmental choices could be knitted into some meaningful discourse is not difficult to explain. There is in fact no single list of factors (such as flora and fauna, climate, population, human needs,... etc.) which "naturally" constitutes an environmental problematic, at least not until subjective meaning, which has been debated in a "public forum," is pertained to these factors. That is, unless people begin to put forward their ideas, idiosyncrasies, values and aspirations so as to effectuate mutual understanding and negotiations, they do not share a subject of discourse which can be called "an environment." Furthermore, though members participating in this public forum may not agree among themselves at the end of the day, they will still share a commitment to the problematic, and become empowered in having taken an active role in creating the problematic. Coming back to the transition to Chinese rule, the unique Hong Kong community and an environmental problematic negotiated in it will definitely be confronted, in the years to come, with explicit or tacit requests for redefinition with reference to a stronger Chinese identity. As for the extent of this impact on the environmental problematic and, more importantly, the public forum which underpins it, that remains to be seen.

Meanwhile, the formation of the existing environmental agenda of Hong Kong is, unfortunately, administered mostly in disregard of the more critical aspect of the political, social, economic, and cultural debates that have been going on in the community. Even the multifacetedness of the topic has been overlooked. More specifically, the environmental agenda has often, if not always, been delimited to match the archetypal image of Hong Kong as a place where its people are efficient, profit-maximizing, ruthlessly individualistic in the market but only to serve the goal of fulfilling familial duties at the end of the day. This Hong Kong archetype is expected to perpetuate in the future, given that the honourable duty of "continuing to lay golden eggs" has been unequivocally bestowed upon the place by the Chinese officials ever since the early 1980s. In the rest of this introduction, I shall account for three "overarching principles" that Hong Kong will continually, or increasingly, be subjected to in the articulation of its environmental agenda.

First, "Hong Kong is a modern economy and is an economic miracle, just like the other Little Dragons. Yet it cannot survive unless the magnificent rate of growth it enjoyed in the past is sustained well into the future." Under this theme, for Hong Kong to set higher standard for pollution control, or try experiencing the "luxury" of keeping a piece of unexploited countryside within its territory is therefore suicidal. It will mean slowing down the pace of development, and that is absolutely out of the question. The Planning Branch of Hong Kong has always put forward blueprints for infrastructural development for Hong Kong based on an extra high rate of growth scenario. The "Territorial Development Strategy" reports which map out the infrastructural development up to 2011 are filled with large-scale reclamation projects, extensive and intensive development of the northwest of the New Territories, new rail and road links across the border, and massive port development.[1] This is of course the most environmentally damaging option for Hong Kong.

Second, "to reintegrate into the Greater China and play a useful part in the latter's recent leap into market economy and prosperity is a role assigned to Hong Kong, now and even more so after 1997." Being the most important entrepôt in the Pearl River Delta region, a fast-developing economic zone, Hong Kong should not plan for its future (including its environmental future) by simply focusing on the limits and capacities within its boundary. For example, there may not be a need to preserve a piece of green of its own, because with the whole of Hong Kong turns metropolitan there still will be a "garden" for its people to enjoy if they care to travel further north. This suggestion, in effect, has sidelined all ecological and cultural concerns related to local environmental issues. Furthermore, any such concerns may be deemed contradictory to the vision of "anti-localism," an apparent theme of the post-1997 ideological campaign in Hong Kong. In other words, judged against the nation-building agenda set down by the Chinese central authority, the significance of the Mai Po Reserve, for instance, will definitely shrink, despite its present crucial ecological significance as the only relatively well-preserved wetland for birds staying in or on seasonal migration past South China.

Third, "Hong Kong is a relatively free place in terms of political and civil liberties; it can only preserve these freedoms if China recognizes its significance as the spearhead of its economic development programmes and would not interfere with its day-to-day running of business." A corollary of this claim is that there is a need to perpetuate a pattern of development defined by international power relations and a value system based on market ideology. If this pattern of development requires Hong Kong to relocate all polluting and hazardous industries among underprivileged sectors of the society (within or outside the Hong Kong territory), so be it. The contenders of this theme will find no difficulty in assenting to local and global "environmental arrangements" in consequence of this pattern of development.

Despite the fact that these overarching principles are and also likely to be in the future supported by dominating parties in environmental agenda-setting, there are however other levels of enigmas more pertinent to the environmental discourse which have not been totally sidelined in the community. They are captured in discourses on indigenous culture and identity, civil society versus national (state) interest, global hegemony, and the philosophical approach to the nature-human linkage. Not surprisingly, the ultimate contention embedded in the associated enigmas can be summarized as a revolt against different kinds of domination which lead to the demolition of the public forum so crucial to a judicious formulation of the environmental problematic. This is of course why we have made the claim in the beginning of this chapter that the community, which by nature can accommodate and represent a diversity of perspectives on subjects that are value-connected, is the most appropriate context for launching the environmental discourse.

Contrariwise, special interest groups such as the Heung Yee Kuk and the Automobile Association, which represent those with *de facto* power to determine, respectively, land use in the New Territories and traffic policy of Hong Kong, are formed on basis of fixed and restricted agendas of interest protection and enhancement. They would not operate at the level of the community to develop interactive relation with other sectors which have alternative aspirations and perspectives. Instead, they prefer to work with the government in putting their impact on matters environmental and otherwise. Unfortunately, in Hong Kong, that has been the way for environmental agenda-setting. The government, which exercises state control after engaging in negotiation with the special interest groups, has largely neglected to accommodate the aspirations and needs as articulated and mediated in the public forum. The concentration on the command-and-control approach in environmental protection, and its subsequent failure on many accounts, therefore, come as no surprise.[2] Equally unsurprising is the indication in survey findings that people generally agree that there are environmental problems to be tackled, and yet demonstrate a lack of commitment to bear out their concern by actions that are supposed to be environmentally friendly.[3] The reason I think lies very much in the feeling of alienation towards much of the environmental agenda as well as the so-called environmental obligations for the citizens, which have been articulated without the people's participation.

In this section, we have briefly summarized the nature of the environmental problematic by underscoring its anti-domination theme, which can only be fully explored, at the theoretical and praxis levels, with reference to the public forum of a community. In this way we have poised to argue for the need for people's repositioning at different levels (political, social, economic, and cultural) so as to address the environmental challenge in any real sense. More precisely, the three overarching principles (of unlimited growth, nationalism, and libertarianism), and the monolithic image of the Hong Kong milieu that matches them, have to be put under careful scrutiny with reference to a framework of critique which encompasses anti-domination at the political, economic, social and cultural levels. In the following sections, I shall give a preliminary survey of some aspects of the current situation in light of this framework.

BACKGROUND : VOICES OF THE HONG KONG COMMUNITY

At present, the direction and pace of, and priorities related to "environmental protection" in Hong Kong can be read between voluminous environmental ordinances initiated by the Environmental Protection Department (EPD) and subsequently passed in the Executive and Legislative Councils, with inputs from the consultative body — Advisory Council on the Environment (ACE) (previously known as the Environmental Pollution Advisory Committee [EPCOM]). The environmental ordinances are then enforced by various government departments including the EPD itself, the Police Department and the Urban Services Department. Operating within the executive-led political structure, the EPD is regarded as the single most important unit as far as policy-making is concerned. Yet as a department in a large bureaucratic structure, the EPD is extremely limited in its jurisdiction. Most of the time, the administration adopts policies in total disregard of the targets and goals laid down by the department. Only recently has the EPD complained that the Transport Branch had drafted the traffic plan to curb the territory's growing traffic problem without consulting it, and that the drafted plan gave no special consideration to environmental protection. The Urban Council, Urban Services Department and the Recreation and Culture Branch, which are responsible for the rebuilding of the Hong Kong Stadium, also generated scandal in planning the Stadium to be used for housing popular concerts which the EPD had long anticipated to be creating noise pollution which far exceeds the allowable level in that area, which is residential. Also, starting from November 1994, container trucks have been on a roll round-the-clock from Lok Ma

Chau to the container ports in Kwai Chung. Again, the extension of opening hours at the border, which has caused all the irritations to the residents living near the traffic route, was never a subject of consultation with the EPD. All in all, the administration has been less than accountable in its decisions relating to environmental protection. Moreover, it is not even an open government in the sense that information as regards the decisions and decision procedures is not open to the public. Only in 1994 has it rejected the private member's bill of Christine Loh, a Legislative Councillor, which aimed at giving a legal framework to citizens' right to information regarding government operations. Without the legal framework, however, not even the ACE members, who are supposed to give advice on matters relating to the environment, are guaranteed accessibility to information on the (government-)selected topics on which they are consulted on.

It is obvious that government policy on environmental issues always gears at soliciting support of the special interest groups. For example, the Heung Yee Kuk is a target for canvassing support, especially over land use in the New Territories. When the government finally announced in 1994 its plan to clean up those land in the New Territories which was turned into dumping grounds for wrecked cars and unused containers (the conversion of farmland into other uses without government approval has been illegal since 1991, when the Town Planning Ordinance was revised after many years of delay), the vice-chairman of the Kuk vowed to ignore the task force of the government, unless compensation is tendered. The deadlock has not to date been broken, and environmental deterioration in the New Territories continues. Yet whether the Kuk's position reflects the interest of those who still till their farm in the New Territories is very doubtful, given that farmers are those who have suffered most as a result of the conversion of land use, which is believed to be at least partially responsible for causing the disastrous floods in recent years.

In order to understand the limit of the current structure of environmental decision, which is represented by a series of co-opting of selected sectors of the society, I shall in the next two sections discuss the process and consequences of government coalescence with three specific kinds of grouping in its environmental decision-making. They are the Green Groups, the business sector (especially big corporations which try to build up a green image), and environmental experts. As the resulting pattern of coalescence might well exist beyond 1997, given that the Special Administrative Region (SAR) government is never meant to be an open and accountable one (at least in the legal sense), it is therefore worth the effort to examine the orientations, frames of reference, and limitations of these groupings so as to assess the future environmental decisions in Hong Kong. Yet before that, it is necessary to investigate the structural as well as ideological backdrop against which these groupings have risen to eminence as regards environmental decisions. It is interesting to note that the maturation of the Hong Kong community has in fact nurtured the conditions which the Green Groups and environmental experts come to thrive on, as well as created the need for business to acquire a green image. Yet, will the community become the hand which is bitten by those it has fed? Will the bent towards conservatism, which typifies politics and the social atmosphere of the transition period and the years ahead, be seen as a chance by these groupings to join the dominating ruling power to further alienate the community in environmental decisions and stifle the public forum for environmental discourse? To answer these questions, one has to back up a bit to examine how these groupings have been handling the environmental agenda in recent years, in their capacity as representatives to channel "the community's views" into the government structure and other social outposts. It would be extremely ironical and sad, however, for these representatives, especially those who used to be active or seen as such in grassroots mobilization, to have begun working in directions that eventually could dampen the strength of the community as well as the environmental cause which is defined in its context.

The fast growth and maturation of the Hong Kong community started more than two decades ago, just as participation of the local-born or local-educated citizens in social movements began. Unlike their parents who found Hong Kong merely a safe haven to escape political turmoils and economic hardship in Mainland China and who marked out Hong Kong as playing only a minimal part in charting their identity, the younger generation began asserting their rights as citizens here while challenging the dominant ideology (the *laissez-faire* policy) and the execution of state control (political authoritarianism), both having served to underpin the concentration of power and resources ultimately in the hands of a small clique of business elites. On the other hand, the economic success of Hong Kong in recent decades helped create conditions for the younger generation to enjoy considerable individual autonomy. All these form the backdrop against which emerged the strong urge for self-expression and a corresponding social mobilization process. As a result, a public forum has come out and the contours of a community that can be uniquely called Hong Kong's have found their appearance.

The community of Hong Kong has since developed cultural elements definitely in contradistinction to those of the "Greater China." Among other things, they consist of a critical or sometimes even defiant attitude towards government policies which are considered detrimental to their living environment and, more precisely, to the living conditions of the grassroots sector and the general welfare of the place these people call home. Also, expecting responses from the government, be they deemed satisfactory or not by the community, is also part of the Hong Kong culture. The saga of popular protest against the planning for a nuclear power plant at Daya Bay (just across the border in China) in 1986 epitomizes these parts of the Hong Kong political culture. When people's discontent was stonewalled and even reprimanded as "ignorant and anti-science" by the Chinese officials and technocrats, as well as facilitators of the project here in Hong Kong — those Hong Kong government-appointed legislators and self-proclaimed experts on nuclear technology eager to promote the project which involves local and British business interest as well as the Chinese nationalistic sentiments, the community was disgusted. A conspiratorial hypothesis of golden handshake between the British and the Chinese governments was postulated, forerunning a series of popular protests against the two governments' sweetheart deals over the constitutional arrangements for Hong Kong in the transition period.

In sum, it seems obvious that with the public increasingly aware of their identity being intertwined with the Hong Kong narrative they help to construct, important parts of the narrative (such as the environmental problematic) also become essential elements of their identity too. In fact, different social and civil groups emerging in the past two decades have, in a way, laid the foundation for the Daya Bay protest movement. Mobilization among different social sectors, especially the grassroots sector, to fight for better living conditions had started before the Daya Bay issue boiled over. Concern over the living conditions of squatter areas, and the founding of concerned groups for environment in Tsing Yi and Kennedy Town respectively, for example, represent efforts and mobilizations in that direction.[4] At the same time, local environmental groups (later called Green Groups) slowly began to move into the limelight to inject into the public forum a more general concern for conservation, especially of the natural environment of Hong Kong. In fact, the first environmental group of Hong Kong is the Conservancy Association, which in the late 1960s and the 1970s was the only watchdog of government mishandling of the natural environment as well as a conscientious organizer of educational programmes on environmental protection for school children. As far as the larger social context is concerned, the maintaining of Hong Kong's status as an open city with respect to ideas from abroad, be they articulated by overseas environmental non-governmental organizations (NGOs) and other civic and social NGOs, or otherwise, has allowed the community's perspectives to be continually enriched. These new idea inputs range from those of a more philosophical nature (e.g. celebrating nature as human-kind's common heritage in contradistinction to seeing it as an object of exploitation) to debates in social and institutional studies which underpin different tactics and strategies of the environmental movement (e.g. "direct action" as practised by Greenpeace in contradistinction to a "support of government's technological-fix approach" which is often promoted by state technocrats).

It is in reaction to the general trend of grassroots social mobilization that a more advanced stage of colonial rule has been developed, in order that government's control on agenda-setting (for environmental issues and otherwise) can be maintained. On the other hand, with the impending change of sovereignty and the community becoming more reflective on its possibility to maintain a public forum, chances do exist for a repositioning for more participation in environmental decision-making. Nevertheless, the three forces which the current government co-opts in environmental decision-making may well retain their privileged position in future. Their existing status and orientations deserve some detailed investigations.

THE GREEN GROUPS: WHEN GREENER PASTURES ARE OFFERED ...

The development of local environmental NGOs (so-called Green Groups) in recent years, especially with regard to their relationship with the govern-ment and the community, is indeed intricate and yet revealing. One can say that it more or less follows the trend of the local middle class (members of these groups mainly come from this sector) being co-opted into the decision-making process. Their involvement is even intensive. As a leading member of one of the groups put it, these groups face the problem of "the

draining of manpower by participating in government advisory committees."[5] This partially causes the groups to become increasingly loose in their
ties with the community. Not surprisingly, in the second review of the 1989
White Paper published by the government, *The Hong Kong Environment:
A Green Challenge for the Community*, "joining the green groups" is
recommended as a positive action young people can take to protect the
environment; elsewhere in the document, the government is full of praise
for these groups. Yet, behind all these cordial remarks, just how does the
government perceive the role of these groups to be? In the most recent
issue of the annual official report of the EPA, *Environment Hong Kong
1994*, a table listing the nature, aims and activities of the local Green
Groups is included (see Table 1). Except for the relatively new and small
group of Green Lantau Association, none of these groups is represented
as taking policy-monitoring as its aim or target of its activities. This more
or less provides some insight as to how and why the government has been
associated with the Green Groups. These groups are indicatively portrayed
as sponsors of environmental education and healthy lifestyle campaigns.

One may contend that the educational programmes run by these groups
can, after all, still be critical and community-oriented in nature, since
education can take anti-domination as its central theme. However, that
has not been the case in local environmental education endeavours. To
the contrary, evidence shows that the social, economic, political and
institutional factors underpinning the exploitation of the environment
was scarcely, if ever, revealed to and shared with the public in these
programmes.[6] (I shall cite a couple of examples in the following paragraph
for illustration.) As for the environmental and related policies that the
Green Groups have been consulted on, seldom have they been turned into
issues that the community in turn is mobilized to get acquainted with, not
even at the "knowledge level" (*vis-à-vis* the praxis level).

One example is the way proliferation of golf courses has been handled
by the Green Groups. Even though they may lodge their objection to
individual proposals submitted to the government, in no instance have they
placed the proliferation issue in a public forum. Incidentally, the pro-golf
camp has already begun their campaigns to "educate" the public and
familiarize young people with the golf culture. For example, in "donating"
the first public golf courses, now under construction in Kau Sai Chau, the
Jockey Club had even co-opted the Secretary for Recreation and Culture
who then pronounced in a Legislative Council session that Hong Kong

needs many more golf courses to meet the demand of young golfers. Currently, a whole string of courses and driving ranges planned by private developers or the Golf Association of Hong Kong are pending approval (see Figure 1). In the mean time, 1995 will see the opening of the Jack Nicklaus Golf Academy in Wan Chai. As for the Green Groups' response, it has concentrated on submitting arguments to counter the developers' environmental impact assessments (EIAs), unaware of the pitfalls hidden in these EIA debate exercises. (I shall discuss these in detail in the next section.) Only when they fail to effectuate a change of heart of the government regarding the more recent approval of the development project in Nam Sang Wai (an ecologically crucial area which serves to sustain the vitality of the Mai Po Reserve), which consists of golf courses construction among other things, did they for the first time launch a small signature campaign soliciting citizens' support for protecting the wetlands of Hong Kong.

Another environmental theme which has never been explored in the

Figure 1: Golf's Future in Hong Kong

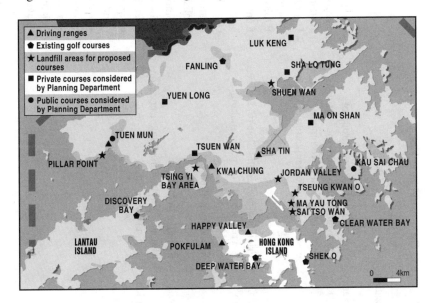

Source: *Sunday Morning Post*, 20 November 1994, reprinted by permission of South China Morning Post Publishers Limited.

Table 1: Green Groups in Hong Kong

Organization	Nature	Objectives and activities	Enquiry Tel. No.
Conservancy Association	– Founded in 1968 by a group of environmentally conscious activists. – The earliest non-government environmental organization in Hong Kong.	– Cares about ecological well-being and protecting the environment so as to make planet Earth a habitat for sustainable living. – Undertakes scientific research and study, promotional campaigns and educational projects. – Publishes *Green Alert* magazine.	2728 6800
Friends of the Earth	– Friends of the Earth (Charity) Limited is a registered non-profit-making organization. – Founded in 1983.	– Runs various educational programmes for schools, business and public. – Organizes projects and campaigns to raise public awareness to improve the quality of life in Hong Kong. – Publishes newsletter and quarterly magazine *One Earth*.	2528 5588
Green Peng Chau Association	– Founded in 1991. – Slogan: "Environmental conservation is part of your life."	– Promotes public awareness and education, and actively involves in environmental protection programmes. – Over the past 2 years: • organized a community paper recycling programme and exhibition; • held competition, jumble sales, children exchange markets and collected clothes for refugees; • visited Produce Green, Mai Po Marsh and Lions Club Nature Education Centre; and • gave talks in natural medicine and a natural way towards better health.	2982 0828

Organization	Description	Phone
Green Power	– Founded in 1988 by a core group of scientists, academics, artists, clergymen, doctors, government officials, executives, journalists, economists and other professionals.	2314 2662
	– Promotes a lifestyle compatible with the requirements of the nature.	
	– Publishes a monthly bulletin *Green Fields*.	
	– Involves in promoting environmental protection and "green" living in Hong Kong, especially among the local Chinese population.	
	– Organized a local 1993 "Clean Up the World Campaign."	
Green Lantau Association	– Established in 1989 to oppose plans for the building of a power station in the Lantau Country Parks.	2985 5099
	– Involves in the monitoring of Port and Airport Development Strategy with the aim to achieve a reduced impact of airport projects on Lantau's unspoilt environment.	
	– Works towards improving refuse collection, upgrading sewage treatment and controlling illegal dumping.	
	– Cooperates on territory-wide issues with other green groups.	
World Wide Fund For Nature Hong Kong	– Inaugurated in 1981 by the international President of WWF, His Royal Highness The Duke of Edinburgh.	2526 1011
	– To stop and eventually reverse the accelerating degradation of the planet's natural environment.	
	– To help build a future in which human lives in harmony with nature.	
	– Actively works for the protection of Hong Kong's threatened environment by lobbying the government to implement conservation policies, and managing WWF wetland projects.	
	– Conducts conservation research projects.	

Source: *Environment Hong Kong 1994* (Hong Kong: Environmental Protection Department, 1994), pp. 165–66.

Green Groups' environmental education programmes is the even more pressing problem of the destruction of Hong Kong sea waters by government's and private developers' projects. The dredging and dumping of toxic mud as well as reclamation works have, in ruining the water, also caused a lot of hardship to the fisherfolks. However, this inhumane and hegemonic (crushing all "unmodern" lifestyles) side of environmental destruction has never been represented in the Green Groups' education programmes. Naturally, no fisherfolks have ever been enlisted to co-sponsor their educational programmes so as to help the public in focusing the problem more clearly and to instill an element of "empowerment" in the programmes themselves.

The failure to relate environmental issues to values and choices of the community in educational programmes run by the Green Groups may, on the one hand, be explained by the groups' inclination to seek sponsorship for these programmes among multi-national corporations (MNCs), busi-ness-dominated organizations, and the semi-governmental organization of Environmental Campaign Committee (ECC).[7] Another reason has to do with their eagerness to build up a "professional" image by organizing activities for a more exclusive circle of audience (e.g. a Chinese Environmental Law course for the business people, or environmental conferences for specialists). This image may of course help them eventually in their applications for government funding. All in all, control through sponsorship that these Green Groups are subjected to is expected to perpetuate, unless they resolve to attain financial independence in the future. It is also no coincidence that the extremely depoliticized and personalized theme of the ECC is re-echoed over and over in the environmental education programmes run by these groups. By the way, the catch-phrase of the ECC public education cam-paigns is "environmental protection starts with you and me," but who is to follow our steps — the MNCs? the government? Who is to monitor their performance at the social, political, economic and institutional levels? Without attempting to seek answers for these questions, the Green Groups have been totally devoted to the personalized theme in their educational endeavours, which have in fact been quite successful in terms of capturing public attention and helping to circumscribe the scope of discourse for the environmental problematic of Hong Kong in the past few years.

The personalized theme is, moreover, in congruence with the natural sentiment of the middle class-dominated Green Groups. The heavy con-centration of activities of Green Power on sharing vegetarian menus and expensive eco-touring plans, for example, fits in well with the middle-class concerns of weight-watching, stress-beating, cancer prevention, and so on. Summer schools organized by the same group demand strong participation of the parents, thus again limiting participants to children of the middle-class families. As for educational activities involving mass participation, often the "environment" theme was overshadowed by the public relation gimmicks or carnival features of the events. For example, the Green Expo organized by Friends of the Earth (HK) [FoE(HK)] in 1994 served to present more of an image of industry-government-Green Groups cooperation over environmental issues than to alert the public to the environmental theme. There were products on display or promoted at the Expo which did not even remotely relate to the environmental theme.[8]

Other events organized hardly paid any attention to the public's right to be involved in environmental decisions. An example is the "Clean Up the World" campaigns organized by Green Power, which highlighted the need for the public to be inculcated with the habit of reducing the amount of garbage they throw away during visits to the Country Parks and disposing of garbage in proper places in the Parks. At the same time, there was complete silence over the enormous damage that the government has over the years been inflicting on the Country Parks. Citizens' right to hold the government accountable for its bad policies towards the environment (including turning some parkland into a rubbish tip and permitting transmission lines — and possibly also highways — to run through another Park) was never mentioned. The lopsidedness of the handling of the subject illustrates quite vividly how the community's right to participation at the environmental policy level has no place in these educational programmes. Another example is the campaign for collecting used paper in schools for recycling, which has never included an explanation to the students concerned that what they collect might not end up in any recycling plants. The reason is that with no government policy to promote recycling and use of recycled paper (so as to provide an economic incentive for producing recycled paper locally), there is at present only one local plant which produces recycled paper. Similar plants in the neighbouring areas (mainly in China) which may process used paper collected in Hong Kong, on the other hand, are often very polluting. All these crucial issues are, however, missing from the "curriculum" of the environmental education programme on paper recycling.

The personalization and depoliticization (to exclude discussions on community participation) of the environmental agenda as represented in the programmes organized by the Green Groups could result in another form of damage, namely the marginalization of the public, especially the grassroots sector, in terms of environmental conceptualization and praxis. The under-privileged and underrepresented, who come to find themselves powerless regarding environmental deterioration which they experience or have been the victims of, could become impoverished "morally" in being conveyed the idea that the environmental cause is totally irrelevant to them. They will be further alienated "morally" in being excluded from the "moral minority" group which has the economic affluence to afford a green lifestyle (by purchasing expensive imported recycled paper or going on eco-tours, for example). The damage, nevertheless, can be mitigated if not totally eliminated if environmental campaigns take the alternative direction of involving the community in the fight for the right to environmental agenda-setting and decisions. Empowerment would then become the main theme of the educational programmes.

The Green Groups would, under this alternative scheme, be utilizing their comparative advantage in information gathering and facilitating en-vironmental movements and educational endeavours which emphasize the empowerment theme by coordinating and liaising among various social groups and sectors. Yet, a review of the record of past endeavours of the Green Groups reveals that they have been very detached from various kinds of social mobilization, especially in recent years. There has been minimal effort made to share with the community the full complexity of choices and constraints embedded in environmental debates and decisions. While in terms of legal and technological expertise, which hinges very much on a solid financial base, the Green Groups have only limited resources to spare (the recent episode of the World Wide Fund for Nature (HK) [WWF(HK)]'s experts being outgunned by the developer's team in testify-ing before the Appeal Committee of the Town Planning Board on the development of Nam Sang Wai is a classic example[9]), nevertheless the human resources they can tap can be almost unlimited if their work is geared more to community empowerment and grassroots mobilization. Unfortunately, that has not been the line that these groups toe.

Yet, why all this abstinence from community empowerment and social mobilization? The views of two prominent figures in local Green Groups may give us a hint. On a television public affairs talk show (the 1994 Chinese New Year Day session of "Newstease"), Wan Shek-lun, a green activist who has been championing for the environmental cause for many years, in response to the host's question of whether he thinks environmental movement should be staged in protest of the Daya Bay Nuclear Power Plant as well as other nuclear power plants planned to be built in the vicinity of Hong Kong, indicated clearly that he found engaging in environmental movements futile because "the public's environmental awareness is too low." Another leading figure in the local environmental arena, Simon Chau, was even more forthright when he, in the summer of 1994, expressed regret over his involvement in the "anti-Daya Bay project campaign" in 1986. He was particularly concerned that such movements may be interpreted as anti-Chinese government.[10] On other occasions, Chau poised to define the role of local Green Groups as working "within the establishment," i.e. in cooperation with the government, high-flyers and celebrities to promote green lifestyle, while condemning those suggesting more radical approaches such as "direct action" as "publicity-seeking."[11]

Although not everyone of the Green Groups agrees with Chau or Wan, there is however a conspicuous trend that the government (in conjunction with big corporations) have been quite successful in persuading the Green Groups to work mainly within the framework set in accordance with the current decision-making structure. This trend, on the one hand, impoverishes the community in that despite (unlike what Wan claims) people's growing concern for the environment,[12] they are not supplied with conceptual, informational, and organizational support to the effect that the community's perspectives can be more clearly articulated, negotiated, and implemented. On the other hand, the Green Groups, in cutting off ties with the community, are in fact disempowering themselves too in terms of losing opportunities to be enriched by ideas which reflect the full complexity of the environmental problematic. For instance, grievances relating to hardship in livelihood or loss of the community's heritage by fisherfolks, divers who enjoy the underwater scenery, farmers whose fields are overwhelmed by severe flooding due to intensive construction works in the New Territories and across the border, residents who live in areas marked for redevelopment,... etc. have not been invited to participate in formulating the environmental agenda so as to enrich the fabric of the discourse; and their grievances are not redressed with reference to their environmental right and aspirations.

By concentrating on conveying their environmental policy perspective through the consultative channel operated by the government, the Green

Groups have not gone very far even in the limited areas covered by their own agenda. The underlying reasons can be crystallized into the following three types of constraint not uncommonly found in consultative politics. First, the agenda items and amount of information concerning these items that are released to members of the consultative body (e.g. the ACE) are government-controlled. Without a legal guarantee to freedom of information, little improvement can be expected in the future. Second, the composition of the consultative body is determined by the government. For instance, the representatives of the Green Groups, though having won their battle to gain the present status to attend as representatives of their groups instead of as individuals, have little hope of becoming the majority voice in the ACE. Their view will continue to be sidelined by business interest and government policy orientations (cf. Table 2). Third, being representatives of their groups, they also suffer from the image problem of being not really publicly accountable, given that these groups are not particularly responsive to the public's views and perspectives. The risk of being branded as "unrepresentative" by the government in the event of sounding out of dissenting opinions is forever present.

With these three kinds of constraint, there is little wonder that the representation of the Green Groups at the ACE has borne little impact on the final decisions of the government. The Kau Sai Chau golf course project, which had previously been endorsed by the ACE, was later challenged individually by FoE(HK) when Jockey Club, which had initiated the project, refused to sign a guarantee for full implementation of what is recommended in the EIA and for the protection of the area from further degradation and development. So, was the project endorsed unanimously in the ACE in the first place? Were there dissenting arguments presented by representatives of the Green Groups? If so, how were the difference in opinions resolved?... The public would never know.

Also, the lack of transparency and accountability of the consultative machinery as a whole is demonstrated in the public's being kept in the dark as to what position the Green Groups have regarding the Strategic Sewage Disposal Scheme (SSDS). As a matter of fact, the Hong Kong government had already committed funds and started laying the groundwork (i.e. Phase One) for the scheme when the public for the first time was seriously alerted to the controversial aspects of the scheme by the Chinese government. The two governments have since locked horn over the scheme. There was also the notorious incident of the WWF(HK)'s supporting the Nam Sang Wai development project when it was first submitted, a position which they eventually backed down from. Despite all these blunders which may call into question the credibility and representativeness of the Green Groups, the government has, in the mean time, expressed its full confidence in the competence of these groups in their capacity as government advisers. In *The Hong Kong Environment: A Green Challenge for the Community*, this confidence is reaffirmed in the paragraph on "Green Groups" (10.51), which contains the following remark:

> ... In many ways, the green groups act as the conscience of the community reminding it that there is more to be done and urging more action.... Until the general public takes environmental concerns as seriously as it takes other everyday issues, the green groups will be acting on behalf of us all in bringing problems to the attention of the government and in highlighting deficiencies in public policy and its implementation. In recognition of this role, government meets with the green groups to discuss environmental issues and to take account of their proposals.

The consultative machinery has, throughout recent decades of the British rule in Hong Kong, been functioning to co-opt potential or existing political forces to the administration's ruling apparatus. In more recent years, the targets of co-opting include civil and social groups emerging into prominence through extensive social mobilization. This is meant to dilute the hostility or political frustration of these groups, and could be seen as efforts made to install a safety valve to release tensions which might have been built up in the society. Assigning a formal platform to the Green Groups in the consultative machinery is one of these co-opting moves. The move has so far borne a considerable depoliticization impact on the Green Groups, a result that the future SAR government, in fearing of "Hong Kong becoming a political city," is likely to perpetuate. The alienation of the community in environmental debates and decisions, which is also the result of the current depoliticization of the Green Groups, will therefore continue to serve the end of homogenization of the society's views. To re-establish their relevance to a vigorous environmental discourse which is to take place at the community level, Green Groups have to reinstate linkage with various local NGOs (e.g. those focusing on transport, housing, welfare, consumer rights, and civil rights) as well as transnational NGOs working for the environment and other human right causes. In this way, they can be resensitized to domination at various levels and refocus

Table 2: Environmental Pollution Advisory Committee (now known as Advisory Council on the Environment) Membership List (as at December 1993)

Professor Wang Gungwu, CBE (Chairman)
Vice Chancellor, University of Hong Kong
Room 1042, Knowles Building,
Pokfulam Road,
Hong Kong
Tel: 2859 2100
Fax: 2858 9435 / 2858 2549

The Hon. Mrs. Peggy Lam Pei Yu-dja, MBE, OBE, JP
G/F, Southorn Centre,
2 O'Brien Road,
Wan Chai,
Hong Kong
Tel: 2838 6633   Fax: 2838 6911

Dr. the Hon. Samuel Wong Ping-wai, MBE, JP
Associated Consulting Engineers
4/F, 88 Hing Fat Street,
Causeway Bay,
Hong Kong
Tel: 2806 0288   Fax: 2806 1010

Mr. Henry S. S. Chiu
Hong Kong Productivity Council
HKPC Building,
78 Tat Chee Avenue,
Kowloon
Tel: 2788 5000 / 2788 5913
Fax: 2788 5900

Mr. Chan Kwok-wai, JP
Managing Director
Universal Pharmaceutical Labs. Ltd.
Unit 1–4, Eastern Centre, 1/F,
1065 King's Road,
North Point,
Hong Kong
Tel: 2562 8131   Fax: 2565 7913

Mr. Lam Kwok-cheong
Woo & Woo Solicitors and Notaries
Room 1102, Gloucester Tower,
Pedder Street, Landmark,
Hong Kong
Tel: 2526 0556   Fax: 2810 4546

Mr. David DaSilva, MBE
Manager of Projects and Products Development
Hong Kong Petrochemical Co. Ltd.
Room 1901–7, Shui On Centre,
8 Harbour Road, Wan Chai,
Hong Kong
Tel: 2802 4860   Fax: 2824 0282

Mr. Joseph Lau Man-wai
Executive Director
Kong Sun Dyeing Works Ltd.
Long Life Industrial Building,
15 Ko Fai Road, Yau Tong Bay,
Kowloon
Tel: 2349 6231   Fax: 2772 7110

Dr. Leung Yee
Director, Centre for Environmental Studies
Reader, Department of Geography
The Chinese University of Hong Kong,
Sha Tin, New Territories
Tel: 2609 6473   Fax: 2603 5006

The Hon. Albert Chan Wai-yip
Block B, 2/F, Kapok Mansion,
123 Castle Peak Road, Tsuen Wan,
New Territories
c/o Legco Building,
8 Jackson Road, Central,
Hong Kong
Tel: 2411 3107   Fax: 2415 7070

Mr. John Chan Koon-chung
8/F, New World Tower 1,
16–18 Queen's Road Central,
Hong Kong
Tel: 2840 2888   Fax: 2801 4410

Mr. Fung Shiu-wing
The Methodist Centre, Basement,
22 Hennessy Road, Wan Chai,
Hong Kong
Tel: 2527 2025   Fax: 2865 4966

Mr. George Cardona
HSBC Holdings plc,
Level 34,
1 Queen's Road Central,
Hong Kong
Tel: 2822 1166   Fax: 2868 0244

Mr. M.J.D. Rushworth
Sales Director
Crown Motors Ltd.
1063 King's Road,
Quarry Bay,
Hong Kong
Tel: 2562 2226 / 2880 1330
Fax: 2811 1060

The Hon. Christine Loh Kung-wai
8/F, New World Tower 1,
16–18 Queen's Road Central,
Hong Kong
Tel: 2840 2676   Fax: 2801 4420

Mr. William C.W. Hui (Secretary)
*Principal Assistant Secretary
  (Environment) 1,
Planning, Environment and Lands
  Branch*
Environment Division,
20/F, Murray Building,
Garden Road,
Hong Kong
Tel: 2848 2551   Fax: 2845 3489

Source: *Environment Hong Kong 1994* (Hong Kong: Environmental Protection Department, 1994), p. 116.

the environmental concern against a broader, more egalitarian and humanistic, and realistic context of discourse. To break through the current limited horizon is also important for the Green Groups to maintain the state of health of their organizations, as their current high profile in the government consultative structure can in future easily become more and more a nominal trait when inputs of other sectors (notably business and the environmental experts) to government's environmental policy become increasingly substantial.

Before going on to examine business' and the environmental experts' impact on environmental decisions, let me briefly cite the position of FoE(HK) on an overseas environmentally-related conflict to support my previous comment about the need for local Green Groups to upgrade their environmental understanding. Recently, when a member of FoE(HK) challenged the group's acceptance of funding from Shell Oil Company, which was considered by Greenpeace to be associated with the atrocities committed by the Nigerian government, FoE(HK) has the following response.[13] It found Shell Oil not having a good environmental record as far as its oil extraction projects in Nigeria are concerned. Yet, it also found the conflict between the Ogoni people and the Nigerian government over the right of control of the area where oil was extracted (and for that matter also the government atrocities that resulted from the conflict) not a matter of Shell Oil's responsibility. Even though one might agree that it is debatable whether FoE(HK) should receive Shell Oil sponsorship even if the company's Nigerian venture is deemed unethical, their viewpoint cited above is still too narrow and anti-community in approach to be acceptable. This is because it has left outside the picture the very fact that the investment of the MNC could not have materialized in the first place without the full blessing of the government, so any conflict arising from local people's complaint of government violation of their right in endorsing the project cannot be considered unrelated to the conduct of the MNC. Furthermore, being a Green Group, FoE(HK) is inconsistent to think that the ripping off of a community by the concerted effort of a MNC and a state power (in the name of progress and modernization), which is every bit hegemonic in nature, is unproblematic. Environmental concern without taking into account the people's welfare and right to live in an ecologically sustainable and egalitarian society sounds very self-defeating.

JUMPING ON THE BANDWAGON

To any ruling regime, views arising from the community which are divergent from the official way of delineating environmental problems and their solutions can be potentially subversive. In Hong Kong, the incumbent sovereign power, compared to the existing ruling regime, has to cope with the additional hang-up of fearing that the non-unanimity of opinion could have a conspiratorial origin, namely the British. In short, the present and future rulers will, at different stages and to different extent, be guarding the environmental agenda against dissenting voices of the community. To ensure that this is possible, not only will the government concerned be co-opting potentially dissenting groupings such as the Green Groups to the establishment, it also has to create other groupings of "environmental leaders" out of sectors or classes in the society which it trusts, so that any remaining dissenting voices from the community can be diluted. These are ways to "legitimize" the government line in an age of pluralism, particularly when democracy is not regarded as an overarching principle in the society.

The creation of environmental leadership under the existing sovereign power generally follows the pattern of including the most powerful interest group (namely the business sector) and the more recent comer to the limelight whose authority is recognized in the legal-rational framework of modernity (namely the environmental experts). I shall briefly account for the respective roles of these groupings which have just made their presence on the environmental bandwagon. The problems with restricting environmental discussions and decisions to this exclusive club will also be explored.

❏ *The Business Sector*

There are three main roles the business sector plays in the current environmental scene of Hong Kong. The first role is consultative. For a long time in the colonial history of Hong Kong, a large representation in the Executive and Legislative Councils has been given to them, thus making them key players in environmental decisions throughout this period. As for membership in the ACE (formerly known as EPCOM), business representation has also been strong since the start. One interesting observation to make is that only recently, when air pollution resulting from road traffic became an area of concern in the community, has the consultative body started to include a member with an automobile industry background! This is simply a recent phenomenon in congruence with the long history of strong influence of the automobile industry on government policies. For example, private vehicles, which make up about 60% of Hong Kong's registered vehicles, have increased by the rate of 11% each year for many years. And the government's recent resolution to tackle the problem was only motivated by the need to prevent traffic gridlock which would, according to its prediction, result in huge economic losses in future. At the same time, the shift to unleaded gasoline is only very slowly implemented. Moreover, the traffic planning is completely negligent of environmental impacts. New towns like Ma On Shan, Tseung Kwan O, and Tuen Mun are linked to the main traffic only by motorways, even though overseas experience has clearly demonstrated that more mileage of motorways always generates growth of private car demand, and more pollution subsequently. The construction of mass transit systems leading to these places has only recently started to appear in the agenda. In the mean time, road projects still dominate the scene (cf. Figure 2). There is also no indication that the government will include environmental concern in its agenda for cross-border negotiation on traffic arrangement either.

The other role recently assumed by the business sector in association with the environment is the apparently proactive role in combating environmental pollution. The government too has been keen to promote business' green image, something which can help justify its minimal control of the industry in the environmental regard and its giving high representation in its consultative machinery to this sector. For instance, the Environmental Protection Committee, an organization of the private sector for the environment, has in the beginning of 1994 been generously given a piece of crown land as a permanent site for building an Environmental Protection Centre. This might not be a bad thing if the shows put up really bear substantial positive environmental impact. Unfortunately the gap between words and deeds is often wide. For example, in a survey done by reporters of the *New Shatin*, staff members of a considerable proportion of the department stores, supermarkets, and fast food restaurants which had joined the "Reduction of Use of Plastic Bag Campaign" said they are unaware of the campaign and have never been instructed to take corresponding actions.[14] Other disappointing survey findings are presented in the FoE(HK)'s study on how big corporations participating in the 1992 "Prince of Wales Business Leaders Forum" have been performing in terms of environmental

Figure 2: Recommended Highways Projects for Hong Kong.

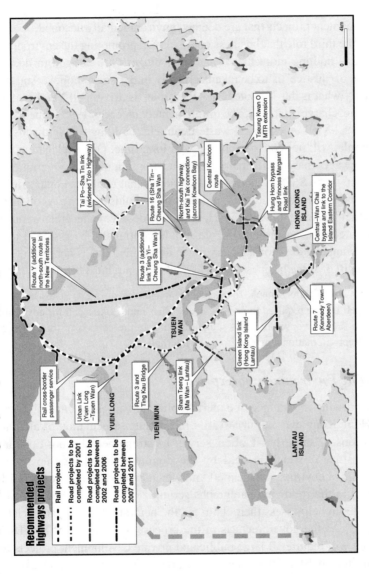

Source: *Sunday Morning Post*, 13 November 1994, reprinted by permission of South China Morning Post Publishers Limited.

duties.[15] Exactly two years after pledging to be leaders in the environmental field, many still have not appointed green managers or done any environmental audits. Some companies active in sponsoring environmental campaigns and educational activities have been equally keen in launching development projects that are deemed environmentally unsound.

The third role that business could play in promoting the environmental cause is nothing more than what other citizens are obliged to do, if the theme of "justice" is to be taken seriously in our social policy. And that is exactly what is the "Polluter Pays Principle" is driving at. Yet, besides the sewage charge that is to be implemented in early 1995, other similar charges levied on chemical waste treatment, building rubble disposal, for example, will not be forthcoming for a long time. One explanation is that the sewage charge will mainly be used for funding the government pet project — the SSDS. Another explanation is that unlike the others, it is not only targeted at the industries; ordinary households have to pay too. In sum, whether business practice in Hong Kong deserves the green reputation attributed to it, or prominent role should continually be assigned to it in environmental decisions, is very much debatable. This is not to contest the goodwill of some businesses, yet as Tolba has put most lucidly,

> ... [I]t is unreasonable to expect companies to do more unless their competitors are required to do so as well. This sounds like a call for governments to set clear environmental standards; and, in the context of traded goods in freer international market, to do so internationally.[16]

❏ *The Environmental Experts*

The growing importance of experts' opinion in environmental discussions in Hong Kong may not necessarily mean better articulation of alternative positions. Contrarily, it often serves to strengthen the position in the "mainstream" which is held by the dominant interest groups. As the epitome of environmental expert knowledge put to application is the EIAs, I shall in the following paragraphs scrutinize the actual context for EIAs in order to help assess their claim to "the neutral, objective, and scientific status." As the government is in the process of pushing for an EIA bill, which will require all large public and private development projects to be subjected to EIAs, the state of the art of the environmental experts is expected to become the major yardstick for appraising all future environmental discussions and decisions.

The social, political and value components entrenched in an EIA exercise, in multifarious ways, render it vulnerable to manipulation by the dominant force of the society. First, an EIA is often done without examining assumptions relating to its often arbitrarily drawn (i.e. not ecologically justified) boundary within which the assessment is done. The exclusion of environmental impact on Zhuhai and the neighbouring region in the planning for the SSDS is an example. For the same reason albeit with the parties switched, whether the environmental impact of the nuclear power plants planned for construction in the neighbouring areas of Guangdong is assessed with reference also to Hong Kong's ecology, or whether impact on the Mai Po Marshes at this side of the border will be considered in environmental assessments on development projects across the border, is highly contingent on the political or even cultural power relationship between the two places.

Which project or which part of a project is required to undertake EIA or, more generally, what is taken to be an appropriate "unit" for which the EIA is undertaken, is another intriguing problem that is seldom honestly addressed. Pretending that this problem does not exist means that the following kinds of loophole may bring great distortions to the assessment result. One possible loophole is the fragmentation of a bunch of projects with interrelating and mutually reinforcing impacts in the EIAs concerned so that the overall effect is discounted or the multiplying effect totally neglected. An example of this is that effects of reclamation and dredging works for different projects — the new airport, the Metropolitan extension, container terminals, to name but a few — have been assessed separately, only to give very misleading pictures on the real impact on Hong Kong sea waters. Another loophole is found in the omission of some parts of a project when the EIA is undertaken, only to have them reinserted when the project is in progress. The fuel barge to deliver aviation fuel to Sha Chau, an island northwest of Chek Lap Kok, was not included in the airport EIA exercises, nor was the reservoir for irrigating the golf courses mentioned in the Kau Sai Chau environmental assessment which was presented to the ACE.

The time frame for EIAs constitutes the third problem area. In Hong Kong where time is money, the pressure to finish an EIA as early as possible may result in cutting corners. More significantly, this also creates the problem of marginalizing those who cannot afford to hire "reputable" experts who can complete "acceptable" EIAs within a short period of time. This problem is aggravated by the lack of data in the relevant areas. (This lack of information and narrow dissemination of what little is known concerning the ecology of Hong Kong do cause significant drawbacks to environmentalists arguing for their cases.[17]) Added to this is the biased and yet common practice of putting the "burden of proof" on the environmentalists (a practice which is again not based on any "scientific" reason); as a result, to argue against any project is almost mission impossible. This is because in order to prove that there will be irreversible damage done to the environment if a project is given the green light, an environmentalist would have to produce massive amount of environmental data, not only on the ecology of the area marked out for possible development, but also on that of other areas possibly reaching as far as other countries or even continents. Right now in Hong Kong, there is a notorious case of this nature. Ecologists are frustrated to witness the perishing of the Chinese White Dolphin in the Hong Kong waters while there seems little that they can do to revert the tragedy. This is because before they can produce foolproof evidence for the uniqueness of these dolphins and for the absolute impossibility for them to "emigrate" to other waters, there is little chance that serious thought would be given on the part of the government to sanction any project that is expected to cause further degradation to the waters they now live in. The tragedy, however, lies in that the proof of the uniqueness of the species would not be "complete" without adequate data on dolphins found in the whole of East Asia being included. And that is not possible — at least not until long after the local dolphins become extinguished. On the other hand, one could argue for the uniqueness of the Hong Kong dolphins on basis of their cultural and ethical meaning to the community. In that way, the "burden of proof" will naturally be on the developers to prove that no harm is done in threatening the survival of these living natural monuments. Seen in this light, the "value" stance (biases) embedded in the current requirement as regards "burden of proof" in EIAs is quite obvious.

There is the fourth problem which demonstrates even more vividly the politico-economic bent of all EIAs. In face of the fact that experts of different camps disagree, the identification of "true" experts is crucial. However, by what criteria do we appraise the ability of experts of the same field? A strong record of success in generating reports which led to approval of the projects could be one indicator, but that is definitely not taking into account various (non-scientific) factors in environmental decision-making, and the snowballing effect in consequence of them. Also, in-group evaluation is only valid if business success (which is related to the so-called record of success) of the experts is not taken into account, and that is quite impossible in a capitalist society. Moreover, the relevance of the field of expertise is also hardly an "objective" issue. When experts from the United Kingdom (with the help of "top briefing solicitors"[18]) successfully convinced the Appeal Committee of the Town Planning Board of the feasibility of their client's development project near Mai Po, does that mean that those experts who have worked in and studied Mai Po Reserve and the nearby Deep Bay Marshland for years and testified against the project proposal have less relevant expertise concerning the impact of development works?

Finally, there is the implementation problem. Right now there is no legal framework or operational support to guarantee that measures to prevent further environmental deterioration, or compensatory measures which developers promise to take, will be undertaken. This monitoring usually will have to start on the day when the project is launched, and it may last for many years or even till long after the project is completed. We have already mentioned the case of FoE(HK)'s urge for a written statement of guarantee in these respects concerning the Kau Sai Chau golf course project being rejected by the Jockey Club.

The public should therefore caution against over-concentrating on the routinization of EIA as a solution to environmental problems, for they could be welcoming a Trojan Horse. The Green Groups must also not be persuaded into thinking that this is their chance of proving their "expertise" in the area, for they can always be outgunned by experts of "higher calibre" hired by the opposite camp. Just as we have argued, the expert-centred approach which is more and more in fashion could well be a business interest-dominated approach in disguise. With development projects fully legitimized by the expert findings (in the form of EIA reports), all alternative perspectives towards the environment could then be sidelined, at least in the environmental decision process. Open discussions at the community level, on the other hand, could also be stifled if the "expert-centred" ("scientific") paradigm, through the promotion efforts of the Green Groups and some academics, eventually comes to dominate the scene. The way dissenting views on the Daya Bay project has been choked off in the mid-1980s serves as a good reminder to the Hong Kong people of how the "expert-centred approach" can be turned into an abusive and abrasive mechanism against them.

Even more recently, when the public became alerted to safety concerns regarding the nuclear power plant — concerns which include problems relating to the ignoring of maintenance procedures, they were told by experts of the International Atomic Energy Agency that the complaint, being filed by a sacked engineer of the power plant, could be dismissed.[19] The Agency, however, has long been criticized as an "atomic club" of the United Nations which aims at promoting the "peaceful" use of nuclear energy. How then, could we expect its experts to come up with an "objective assessment" of the situation which might constitute a challenge to the credibility of one of its greatest potential customers — China — with respect to the handling of the technology? Despite experts' assurances, the number of shut-downs (13) during the first months of operation of the plant (1 February to 20 December 1994) was 10 times the average elsewhere.[20] Meanwhile, the community has been quite silent over these issues, probably a consequence of the topic now being accepted or reiterated by Green Groups, some politicians, as well as some academics as off the bounds of the Hong Kong public forum. This passivity is aggravated by the increasing dominance of the "progress" and "development" agenda as Hong Kong moves towards the SAR era. We shall explain this agenda in detail in the next section.

Two Dominant Themes for the Future?

With the environmental problematic gradually being steered away from the public forum of our community, some may turn to international conventions and treaties for inspirations and practical guidelines for local environmental movements. In fact, there has been general optimism towards countering environmental destruction through global cooperation after the Rio Earth Summit in 1992, during which a number of documents were signed by government representatives from all over the world. On the worldwide level, this optimism has since been dampened quite a bit, mainly by some governments' unwillingness to substantiate the promises they made during the Summit by action (by providing financial assistance to developing countries to upgrade their technology to meet higher environmental standards, say).[21] At the local level, most communities have not been benefiting from campaigns to promote the environmental ideals highlighted in the global meetings. For as long as the campaigns are state-led, it is likely that they would be repackaged to fit the modern state's "progressive," growth-oriented, and aggressively interventionist nation-building agenda, and it is to this that the real environmental cause would inevitably have to succumb or be subordinated.

One must therefore be careful in pushing for government initiatives at the legal and policy levels. Preventive measures must be made to guarantee that subsequent actions taken will not be at the expense of other efforts to empower and mobilize the community for the enhancement of its autonomy and diversity in environmental perspective. Without this guarantee, the so-called globalization approach, being subjected to the constraints of the state-dominated framework, will just become another pretext for the state's coalescence with the MNCs to "develop the natural resources" on a global scale, only to benefit each other at the expense of the community and the natural environment. Business will earn its profit while the state broaden its scope of control through intervening in more and more aspects of people's lives and livelihood. Hence, abstract ideals as represented in international conventions and treaties will sometimes just be the guise for circumventing the real conflicts of interest and difficult choices related to the local milieu. Putting unrealistic expectations on these ideals as guidelines for environmental movements could end up protecting vested interests which exist in the real and specific context of a society, and are possibly associated with the environmental degradation in that place too.

In scrutinizing the specific context which Hong Kong society is situated, one would not find much difficulty in identifying dominating forces in the political, social, economic, and cultural aspects that are responsible for much of the homogenization of the environmental perspective and impoverishment of the discourse. One prominent ideological and structural strait-jacket is manifested by the spell cast by the Chinese central government on Hong Kong, directing its authoritarian and capitalistic status quo to "remain unchanged for 50 years." Relatedly, Hong Kong is prescribed the role as spearhead of the Chinese modernization and development drive which, among other things, sidesteps any concern for social equality and possibly also human dignity. As a result, the environmental problematic, alongside other areas of discourse, is circumscribed by the Chinese authority's assumption of a monolithic statue for the Hong Kong community in which these discourses are staged. The statue is supposed to be exemplified by the Hong Kong people's obsession with (1) horse-racing (gambling), (2) dancing (both underscored by Deng Xiaoping in the 1980s), and (3) pornography (recently underscored by Lu Ping, director of the Hong Kong and Macau Affairs Office), and nothing else.

In the rest of this chapter, I shall concentrate on two underlying themes which are expected to outline the environmental agenda to an increasingly large extent in the future. They have much to do with Hong Kong's chance of defining its own identity, as opposed to it being prescribed the role of a ruthless exploiter of human and natural resources in the Pearl River Delta region — one who takes absolutely no interest in exploring an environmental future which allows room for human compassion and a community's pursuit of welfare, material and spiritual.

❏ *Theme One: The Development Imperative*

The Bruntland Report on Sustainable Development (*Our Common Future*) which the United Nations Environmental Programme commissioned its authors to prepare in the early 1980s came at a time when many developing countries in Africa and South America were experiencing major set-backs in their economic development. Increasingly were they overwhelmed by the burdens of foreign debts, environmental degradation, and social disintegration brought about by "development projects" sponsored by overseas funding (such as large hydroelectricity plants, the "green revolution," etc.) There was a growing awareness of the darker side of the modernization drive which is staged top-down by the government in cooperation with foreign companies. For reasons too complicated to explain here, this grim picture of modernization has not been shared by the majority of the communities in some fast-developing countries in East Asia. Furthermore, some business corporations of these countries have since become MNCs themselves, bringing wealth to those areas which started to develop at a relatively early stage. They are now playing a prominent part in taking advantage of the low labour and environmental costs charged by the late-starters in the region, such as China.

Hence, while other countries of the South have, in the run-up to the 1992 Rio Earth Summit, been revolting against the domination of the environmental agenda by countries of the North, which is represented by the commodification of nature and manpower in accordance with market price largely determined by the MNCs, Hong Kong, and more recently the Chinese government, have not faced any strong opposition regarding the commodification approach. Hong Kong, followed suit by the more developed and urbanized areas of the Pearl River Delta, in the mean time, has been taking full advantage of its relatively less-developed neighbours' lacking in environmental regulations (or the poor implementation of the regulations) to "export" to them polluting industries. And this is undertaken with the full blessing of the Chinese government, which has designated the Pearl River Delta region, with Hong Kong as the spearhead, a fast-growing economy. Under this cultural construction, Hong Kong should find the destruction of all natural and historical monuments (within its territory and otherwise) for development's sake a matter of course, only to be circumscribed by the lack of marginal profit projected. Even then, the quest for a modernized Greater China would still justify a go-ahead of the development works.

Yet, what if the Hong Kong community is not only aspired to money-making (in consequence of which they can continue to indulge in gambling, dancing, and pornographic commodities)? Do they then have to acquire a new identity by subscribing to Chinese nationalism, so that the development and construction spree will perpetuate, though the justification proffered for it will be different this time? Or, is there a third option for the Hong Kong community, which is to negotiate in a public forum the community's position with respect to mediating between development and preservation of its natural and historical monuments? The position can be a no-growth scenario, a de-development scenario, or a scenario of attaining community self-reliance through applying appropriate technology and co-ordinating with other communities to devise fair and sustainable trading policies. For the third option to be possible at all, Hong Kong will have to be bequeathed or develop for itself an autonomous public forum and an open decision-making structure. Moreover, not only must debates and decisions concerning matters of Hong Kong's own jurisdiction (such as the deliberation on whether to harvest more metropolitan land from continuous reclamations) be free, Hong Kong must also be allowed the freedom to negotiate with other places in the Pearl River Delta and beyond to dismantle the prisoners' dilemma game or zero-sum game that have been forced upon it and the other parties by market competition. For example, they could enlighten and support each other in providing eco-friendly style of tourism in the region instead of having each place to build golf courses and luxurious hotels to attract tourists, and in consequence could preserve much of the region's natural environment. Yet for this kind of coordination for policy choices to materialize, the ultimate condition is for China to stop putting Hong Kong, possibly also its neighbouring areas in Guangdong, under suspicion — Hong Kong as the "base for subversion" while its neighbours as being "spiritually contaminated" by it.

What I have demonstrated in this section is that though global vision may be relevant to environmental discussion, gross generalizations which are often associated with discussion at that level should not become a pretext for neglecting people's vistas, needs, and aspirations and avoiding challenges presented by the real-life social conflicts. In other words, the global vision found in international conventions and treaties, and local environmental protection ordinances, may all be irrelevant if basic issues such as the stance on development is not negotiated by the community in an open forum. We have of course witnessed futility of this kind when the Country Park Ordinance, Wild Animal Protection Ordinance, Town Planning Ordinance which provides for the designation of coastal pro-tection areas, Sites of Special Scientific Interest, green belts,… etc., as well as the government's signing of the (international) Ramsar Convention for protection of wetland, all failed to protect the Nam Sang Wai site from development. These laws and conventions either contain too many loopholes so that they can easily be bypassed, or they are simply not easy to administer. Either way, there is at present no unequivocal ban on develop-ment in many ecologically significant sites. The next two down the list are probably Sha Lo Tung and Tai Long Wan.

❑ *Theme Two: Marginalization of the Underprivileged and the Underrepresented in Environmental Protection*

Another specific problem to be investigated is the lack of concern for and involvement of the underprivileged and the underrepresented in policy-making in general and environmental decisions in particular. The environ-mental cause therefore can sometimes be a source of grievance in terms of jeopardizing these people's livelihood or ways of life. Overseas examples of similar nature are abundant. Campaigns to protect endangered species are mostly targeted at poachers who are hard-pressed for means of survival, often because their traditional ways of life have been demolished under modernization. At the same time, the core of the problem is overlooked when these environmental campaigns fail to target at the corrupt bureaucracies or the international crime networks which participate in trading the endangered plants, animals, or their parts. One repercussion of the ban on international ivory trade has been the loss of means of life for the local ivory craftsmen, yet they are too small in number to capture the attention of the politicians and the government.

In terms of having their own kind of trade falling into disgrace and being stigmatized as being environmentally untenable, the pig farmers in Hong Kong suffered in the same way as the ivory craftsmen, though probably to a larger degree, given the greater publicity they were exposed to. Moreover, the local pig farmers won even less sympathy because they had been offered assistance by the government in switching to a new method of treating pig dung and yet subsequently found to be failing to meet the standard. Their complaint of the impracticality of the method was cold-shouldered. Even less attention was paid to the fact that the change demanded of these farmers was not only technical but also managerial and conceptual in nature; and support in those aspects had been minimal. The subsequent marginally violent protests of the farmers and the decision of some of them to move their business to the Mainland do not really help the environmental cause. Furthermore, the whole episode shows that little, if any, consideration has been given to Hong Kong's need for diversity in the source of meat supply, given that epidemic outbreaks or radioactive contamination in the Mainland, which is our main meat supplier, cannot be totally ruled out. Connected to this short-sightedness is the lack of appreciation for the contribution of the farmers who have been providing fresh meat for the community in the past. All in all, the greatest harm in emphasizing bureaucratic control (which concentrates on law and punishment) in environmental protection has been demonstrated in this case, where farmers were not only marginalized economically, but also ethically (in being portrayed as culprits of environmental pollution). This marginalization is in fact in coherence with a very impoverished concept of the environment and an equally impoverished concept of environmental ethics, which exclude mutual respect, appreciation and cooperation, and communal understanding. As a matter of fact, there has been, in this case, no mediating of the environmental issues in terms of the community at all.

A more current row was kicked up when shipyards in Tsing Yi inflicted an unbearable level of noise pollution to the nearby residents. The whole conflict is in fact due to poor planning on the part of government bureaucrats, who approved residential blocks to be built so near to the shipyards which had already been permitted to operate in that area. Now the mistake is "rectified" by having the shipyards scheduled to move in April 1995 to a new site in Tsing Yi. Yet the new site is only 200 metres from some new luxury apartment blocks. Will the shipyards have to move again in the near future? If so, there is the possibility that the cost of all the moving exercises could be beyond the means of the owners who then would decide to close the shipyards for good. In that case, the 3,000 workers, especially the 2,000 who are unskilled and have worked in the shipyards for most of their lives, would be the main victims of the series of bureaucratic blunders. The unfortunate incident also reveals the need to address predicaments arising from competing needs of the society at the community level. Without negotiations being tendered at the community level to handle predicaments of this kind, justice cannot be expected to deliver, either at the substantial level (in avoiding victimization of the most vulnerable sector of the society) or at the procedural level (with decision-making no longer only in the hands of the dominant interest groups). In sum, under the social Darwinian structure and ideology of Hong Kong, where success in competition is the ultimate measure for all people, environmentalists should be particularly vigilant in preventing their cause from being turned into a zero-sum game in which the underprivileged and the underrepresented are most likely to lose out — in being portrayed as environmental culprits because they are at the scene of pollution or cannot afford a "green" lifestyle.

Environmental awareness does not mean pointing fingers at the most vulnerable sector of our society; in fact, it should mean more attention paid to the grievances of this sector which suffers as victims of environmental degradation. Emphasizing the global perspective to environmental issues, on the other hand, is also not meant to be a vague acknowledgement of Hong Kong's responsibility in environmental protection, while leaving unanswered the specific question of what structural and ideological factors are preventing the society from taking a more responsive part in this aspect. In fact, both topics have to be mediated with respect to a careful investigation of the power structures at the local, national, and international levels. Dominance and control imposed by these structures on the political, social, institutional, cultural, and economic contexts of environmental discourse and decision must be underscored, in order that the element of empowerment (of every individual in particular and the ecology in general) can be restored to the environmental cause. Given this understanding, proffering a global perspective would mean standing in solidarity with all those whose right to participate in the public forum for environmental discourse has been violated, mostly through marginalization imposed under the subterfuge of modernization, nation-building, or greater participation in the international market. Locally, the coalescence of the government bureaucrats (existing and future ones), the Green Groups (which represent middle-class interest), the business sector, and the environmental experts in delimiting the environmental status quo and delineating the environmental programme should be underlined and assessed. On the other hand, richness can only be restored to the environmental problematic if the latter is to be reattached to the sense of identity which the Hong Kong community mediates for itself. In the process of the mediation, the two themes which underscore the top-down approach in environmental agenda-setting in Hong Kong in the transition period ("pro-development" and "marginalization of the poor") have to be scrutinized and criticized. Finally, it is in light of all these critical discussions that one could find the chance of properly focusing and addressing questions on what roles the traditional village of Nga Tsin Wai, the Chinese White Dolphins, eco-farming, residents living near the busy Kai Tak Airport, shipyard workers, Deep Bay marshland,... etc. should play in the future environment of Hong Kong.

NOTES

1. See, for example, reports in *Ming Pao*, 30 October 1994 and *South China Morning Post*, 26 December 1994.
2. Man Si-wai, "The Environment," in *The Other Hong Kong Report 1993*, edited by Choi Po-king and Ho Lok-sang (Hong Kong: The Chinese University Press, 1993).
3. One of the more recent surveys for reference is reported in *Hong Kong United Daily News*, 30 September 1994.
4. C. Chan, and P. Hills (eds.), *Limited Gains: Grassroots Mobilization and the Environment in Hong Kong* (Hong Kong: Centre of Urban Planning and Environmental Management, The University of Hong Kong, 1993).
5. Hung Wing-tat, "The Environment," in *The Other Hong Kong Report 1994*, edited by Donald H. McMillen and Man Si-wai (Hong Kong: The Chinese University Press, 1994).
6. Man Si-wai, "A Critique on Environmental Education — The Case of Hong Kong," *Proceedings for the International Conference on Environmental Education, Guangzhou, Dec. 29–31, 1994* (FoE(HK) and Guangzhou Environmental Science Association, 1994), pp. 138–44.
7. Mostly recently, there was an Environment Fund set up to provide funding for environmental education projects and research. The $100 million fund was established with $50 million injections each from the government and the Wheelock & Co.

8. "Expo Success," *One Earth*, No. 24 (Autumn 1994), pp. 24–25.

9. "Letter to Editor" by Clive Viney, *South China Morning Post*, 25 November 1994.

10. *Eastern Express*, 18 July 1994.

11. See, for example, Simon Chau, "Absolutely Accountable to the Public — A Reply to the Protest of Dr. Man Si-wai," *Sunday Chronicle*, 7 August 1994, p. 35.

12. Cf. the rise in pollution complaint figures as a general trend in the past years as reported in various issues of *Environment Hong Kong*, published by the EPD.

13. "A Shell Game?" *One Earth*, No. 24 (Autumn 1994), pp. 36–37.

14. See the survey report in *New Shatin*, 30 October 1994, published by the Department of Journalism, The Chinese University of Hong Kong.

15. K. Griffin, "A Paler Shade of Green?" *One Earth*, No. 24 (Autumn 1994), pp. 6–11.

16. Cf. M. Gubb, *et al.*, *The "Earth Summit" Agreements: A Guide and Assessment* (London: Earthscan Publications Ltd., 1993), p. 39.

17. Cf. D. Dudgeon, and R. Corlett, *Hills and Streams: An Ecology of Hong Kong* (Hong Kong: Hong Kong University Press, 1994), p. 171.

18. See Note 9.

19. See report in *South China Morning Post*, 24 October 1994.

20. See report in *South China Morning Post*, 7 January 1995.

21. "Two Years after the Earth Summit," *Time* (7 November 1994), pp. 39–43.

15

Education: Evolving Patterns and Challenges

Lee Wing-on & Mark Bray

INTRODUCTION

The analysis in this chapter starts with a broad review of the literature on education and colonial transition. It examines experiences in other territories which have undergone colonial transition. The review of their experiences is important, as this can provide both a reference point for comparison and an indicator of what might be expected in Hong Kong. Although Hong Kong's transition is in many respects different from that of most other colonies, it also has some similarities.

The nature of Hong Kong education during the transition period has been a focus of earlier writing by the present authors, both together and separately.[1] The first section of the chapter summarizes part of this work in order to highlight some key issues. Subsequent sections build on the earlier work, not only by updating facts but also by exploring further conceptual issues. Discussion in these sections is mainly based on incidents taking place at a later stage of colonial transition in Hong Kong. Hopefully, this can provide some hindsight of the characteristics of educational development that are different from those of the earlier stage. One question concerns the extent to which the education sector has become a battleground for competing influence and ideology. Another question concerns the extent to which, depending on the outcomes of the battles, education may be a vehicle for resisting rather than for achieving social and political change.

EDUCATION AND COLONIAL TRANSITION: COMPARATIVE PERSPECTIVES

The authors' 1993 paper focused on issues of education and democratization. The paper pointed out that in general, colonial education had several characteristics. First, it was mainly elitist. Schooling was far from universal, and few primary school leavers were able to proceed to secondary schools. In most colonies, it was only when self-government began to seem fairly imminent that emphasis was given to universities and colleges.[2] In Hong Kong's case, the territory has had a university since 1911. However, the most dramatic expansion of tertiary education has occurred during the transition period.

The paper also pointed out that colonial education did not generally provide for fundamental political emancipation, and that it was never conceptualized for the purpose of placing the colonized on an equal political footing with the colonizers. The major aims of colonial education were capacity-building for colonial development and promotion of a harmonious society. Colonial authorities commonly attempted to defuse potential social conflicts through curricular manipulation, and colonial education mainly focused on improvement in the material situation. For example, British "adapted education" for Africa focused on basic skills and knowledge in health and hygiene, housing and living conditions, use of local resources for agriculture and handicrafts, and the organization of leisure time. American colonialists in the Philippines collaborated with the Filipino ruling class, and conceived of education as a human resource development plan for a dependent agricultural colony. It is not difficult to find similar comments on education in other colonies.

Colonial education was therefore ill-prepared for democratization. However, with the advent of decolonization, many colonial authorities and their local counterparts found themselves under pressure to democratize society and to use education as an instrument to do so. In this respect, development patterns in education in Hong Kong have paralleled those in other colonies.

By contrast, one factor which has made patterns in Hong Kong different from that of most other colonies has been the strong influence of its neighbour. China's role in Hong Kong affairs has long been an obvious factor not only in daily life but also in the sphere of policy-making. The advent of 1997 of course increased linkages and it has become necessary in education as well as in other sectors to view patterns and changes from the perspective of the People's Republic of China (P.R.C.) as well as from the local perspective. Lee Wing-on's 1992 paper addressed one aspect of linkages, focusing on pressure for educational excellence in China and its implications for education in Hong Kong.

Commonalities and differences between Hong Kong's experiences and those of other colonies were further explored in a 1994 paper by Bray which focused on the "remnants of empire." Among the commonalities noted in the paper was the desire by colonial powers to retain links and influence even in the post-colonial era. Again, the experience of other colonies may give a pointer what might be anticipated in Hong Kong. At the same time, one may expect considerable tension between the old and the new. Education may become both an instrument for change and a vehicle for asserting the new sovereignty. Depending on the balance of forces, however, education may also be a vehicle for resisting decolonization of attitudes and structures.

Turning to differences, the 1994 paper pointed out that the decolonization processes of the remnants of empire have in many respects diverged from those of the main body, and that this has had implications for education as well as for other sectors of the society and economy. First, by the end of the century the decolonizing powers generally accepted and even welcomed the decolonization process. Colonies had become something of an embarrassment, and the metropolitan powers sought ways to adjust the political framework as smoothly as possible.

Second, decolonization in the 1990s has operated on a much longer time scale. India, Ceylon and Burma were all decolonized within three years of the end of World War II. Decolonization of Indonesia, Vietnam, Laos, Cambodia and Libya was not far behind; and the decolonization of French West Africa was entirely accomplished within four years. By contrast, the agreement on the decolonization of Hong Kong allowed a lead time of 13 years, and that of Macau allowed a lead time of 12 years. These frameworks provided a much less hectic time scale for planning of all sectors, including education. The importance of this may be exemplified by curriculum planning. Whereas in most transitions, curriculum adjustments could only be made after the change of sovereignty, in Hong Kong it has been possible to embark on advance preparation.

A third difference is that while most colonies in the main era of decolonization moved to sovereignty, this has been less common among the smaller territories and the remnants of empire. The Marshall Islands and the Federated States of Micronesia moved not to full independence but to "sovereignty in free association" with the United States. Cook Islands moved to a similar status in free association with New Zealand. Irian Jaya and East Timor were reintegrated with Indonesia; and the arrangements for Hong Kong and Macau have been for reintegration with the P.R.C. The difference in post-colonial frameworks has had major implications for both the content of education and the mechanisms of policy-making.

CHANGES IN THE CURRICULUM

Elaborating on the point made above, this section focuses on evolution and change in school curricula. It begins with the nature and content of specific school subjects before turning to civic education which has mostly been conceived as an ingredient crossing subject boundaries. Discussion then turns to controversy over textbooks and their contents.

❑ *The Contents of School Subjects*

Among the first people to study the nature of changes in school syllabuses caused by the advent of 1997 was Paul Morris.[3] At the level of Secondary Forms 1–5, Morris analysed evolution in Economic and Public Affairs (EPA), Economics, History, Social Studies, Geography, Chinese Language, and Chinese History.

Concerning the first of these, Morris pointed out that between 1972 and 1976, EPA mainly focused on description of the institutions and processes of government in Hong Kong. The only alterations in 1976 were the removal of the term "colony" (an indication that the word was already becoming unfashionable), and addition of a topic concerned with the links between Britain and China. Greater change came in 1984, with increased focus on systems of government, especially those involving representation and consultation, and on the principles of law-making. These themes were elaborated in the 1987 syllabus.

The History syllabus also changed. Whereas previously the section of the syllabus which focused on China covered only the pre-1949 period, a change in 1988 permitted study of Chinese history up to 1970. Morris commented that the new syllabus provided pupils with "a more politicized historical framework than was previously the case, and one more relevant to Hong Kong's future."[4]

John Tan's detailed examination of the History syllabus is also instructive. He points out[5] that at the level of the Hong Kong Certificate of Education Examination (HKCEE), there was a decline of Anglocentricism with deletion of British colonial and Commonwealth history in European history. A notable difference between the 1988 syllabus and its predecessor was that the original version was only two pages long, whereas the later one had 13 pages.[6] In the syllabus of the Hong Kong Advanced Level Examination (HKALE), two major changes in Hong Kong history were made. First, Hong Kong was described as dependent on China rather than on Britain; and second, the period of Hong Kong history was lengthened. As Tan observes:

> In the 1980–83 syllabus, questions on Hong Kong history appeared under British Colonial and Commonwealth History in Paper II and Constitutional Developments in the British Commonwealth 1900–1960 in Paper III. In 1984, Hong Kong history disappeared from the syllabus. It reappears in the 1994 syllabus under "Modern Asian History" and its coverage began in the year 1800, not 1841.[7]

Tan further points out that this structure would show students that Hong Kong was part of China before British colonization. It would also undermine any implication that the modern history of Hong Kong began with the arrival of the British.

Changes also occurred in Social Studies, which is taken by secondary students in Forms 1 to 3. Prior to 1989, the syllabus comprised a selection of topics from the mainstream social science disciplines. Pupils were given a description of how the Hong Kong government worked, and of their rights and responsibilities as citizens. Very little mention was made of China. The syllabus released in 1989 contained essentially the same descriptive political orientation, but made specific reference to the 1984 Sino-British Joint Declaration and the Basic Law. Pupils were also given more information about China. In an updated version of his 1988 paper, Morris points out that:

> In encouraging pupils to draw the flag of the P.R.C., describe the development and structure of the Chinese Communist Party, study the biography of Mao Zedong, and understand the need for central planning, the revised syllabus constitutes an about-face in terms of what is viewed as acceptable content for school subjects in Hong Kong.[8]

In the late 1980s, a new subject, Government and Public Affairs (GPA), was introduced. It was first examined as an HKALE subject in 1988, and as an HKCEE subject in 1989. Unlike EPA, which mainly focused on the institutions and processes of government at a descriptive level, GPA emphasized concepts which are central to liberal Western democracies (such as the rule of law, representation, consultation and elections), and to the study of political processes in China. Morris documented the events leading to the introduction of GPA, including pressure from some Legislative Councillors who argued that all Hong Kong citizens should receive "a true democratic education."[9]

The political emphasis of GPA became more explicit in the 1996 HKALE syllabus. The 1988 syllabus had specified the aim of analysing "concepts, structures, and process involved in the study of government, political science and public affairs." However, the 1996 syllabus confined the aim to the analysis of "concepts, structures, and process involved in the study of political science." The 1996 syllabus also placed stronger emphasis on conceptual analysis, on understanding of China, on China–U.S. relations, and on Hong Kong's colonial transition (see Table 1).

Another new subject was Liberal Studies, which is part of the Hong Kong Advanced Supplementary Level Examination. This subject also includes the understanding of China and Hong Kong's colonial transition among its major aims. For example, "China Today," one of its six modules, aims to help students "to appreciate the special relationship that H.K. [Hong Kong] and China enjoy and the mutual advantages that flow from that relationship, and to understand better the contribution that H.K. is making, and can make, to China's modernization."[10] The syllabus also covers major issues in China studies, such as socialism versus capitalism, modernization of China, the legal system, and the roles of the Communist Party and the People's Liberation Army (PLA).

However, major changes did not occur in all subjects during the transition period. The Geography syllabus had already incorporated increased focus on Asia, and particularly on China, during the early 1970s, and since that time the syllabus has remained largely the same. Throughout the period, moreover, the syllabus was relatively apolitical in nature.[11] Likewise, although the Chinese Language syllabus was revised in 1991 to include contemporary texts from the P.R.C., these were distinctly apolitical and in any case were counterbalanced by inclusion of a similar number of texts from Taiwan.

❑ Civic Education

To supplement analysis of formal school subjects, it is useful to chart

Table 1: Comparison of the Demands of the 1988 and 1996
         A-level GPA Syllabuses

Aim	1988	1996
1	Understand a number of salient terms in the political vocabulary.	Same as 1988.
2	Describe and discuss the categorization of state forms, and the criteria on which they are based.	Analyse the relationship between the individual and the state.
3	Have an understanding of the differing assumptions and practices of Western pluralistic systems and Marxian systems.	Apply the various concepts and theories learned in (1) and (2) above to the understanding of Hong Kong, the P.R.C. and the U.S.
4	Compare three political systems and analyse the roles of the political actors.	Examine the government and politics of Hong Kong with special reference to its transition from a British dependent territory to a special administrative region of the P.R.C.
5	Discuss the relationship between the government and the governed with different, but specified, political systems.	Discuss the underlying philosophies, institutions, and the operation of the governments and politics of the P.R.C. and the U.S.
6	Be aware of the government and politics of Hong Kong and its relationship with other political systems.	Evaluate the similarities and differences of the governments and politics of the P.R.C. and the U.S.

Source: F. Cheung, "The Politicization of Hong Kong Secondary School Curriculum" (unpublished P.C. Ed. assignment essay, Faculty of Education, The University of Hong Kong, January 1995).

developments in civic education. Historically, civics was taught as an independent subject in vernacular schools before World War II, and was offered as an examination subject in the school-leaving certificate from 1950. With the creation of EPA in 1965, civics ceased to exist as an independent subject. Throughout the 1970s, neither the annual Education Department reports nor the various White Papers on education mentioned civics, and S. M. Lee comments that the dormancy was so deep that some people held that there had never been any civic education in Hong Kong.[12]

This situation changed markedly in the mid-1980s. One year after the signing of the Joint Declaration, the authorities issued a set of *Guidelines on Civic Education in Schools*.[13] The opening sentence referred to the 1984 *White Paper on the Further Development of Representative Government*, and the document presented ways in which schools could promote civic education through formal and informal curricula.

The introductory chapter to the Guidelines addressed several sensitive issues, including that of political indoctrination. It suggested that:

> The nature of politics is interpreted in different ways by different people at different times. Many in Hong Kong are well aware that Dr. Sun Yixian [who led the 1911 revolution in China] defined politics as the management of public affairs. If this definition is accepted, then there is no point in trying to distinguish civic education from political education since civic education must essentially be political in nature.[14]

However, the document stressed the need for free and informal discussion with balanced appraisal of evidence and views. This approach, it suggested, was "less likely to be misconstrued as indoctrination than would be the case if one person's conclusions were imposed on others."

The Guidelines were the focus of three major evaluations by the government.[15] The first stated that its findings were encouraging, because:

> an overwhelming majority of schools reported that they had found the "Guidelines" useful. These findings were further supported by the fact that many of the recommendations in the "Guidelines" had been adopted by the majority of schools.[16]

A similar picture was presented in the second report,[17] though Tang and Morris[18] criticize these two evaluations, exposing weaknesses in their methods and shallowness in their analysis. The authors suggest that the evaluations were merely exercises in *post hoc* legitimation, and their own survey of secondary school History teachers found a picture very different from that presented in the two reports.[19]

Nevertheless, there is evidence of official commitment to civic education. Starting from 1988, the Education Department Civic Education Standing Committee published the *School Civic Education Bulletin*. The bulletin is only an annual publication, and hence is not able to supply materials frequently. However, while the government basically relies on commercial publishers to produce textbooks and reading materials for the other subjects, the publication of a specific official bulletin for civic education does have significant implications.

The third survey on the implementation of civic education conducted in 1990 indicated that seminars "were held regularly to help teachers promote civic education in schools," and that special teaching packages had been produced with such themes as "Know Your Rights and Duties," and "Development of Rational Thinking Skills — Theory and Practice."[20] The government attempted to keep issues alive through inter-school civic education competitions, open forums, and exhibitions.

The introduction of Liberal Studies is also perceived as a form of providing civic education. For example, addressing the issue of Hong Kong in colonial transition in the China Today module has signified the extension of civic education to the formal curriculum in Hong Kong. According to Wan-Chan,[21] Liberal Studies serves as a formal vehicle for civic education at sixth form level. She further points out that the subject pays special attention to the promotion of political awareness:

> Political awareness, as such is not explicitly spelled out in the subject or module aims and objectives. Nevertheless, investigation of issues, such as concepts of democracy, "one country, two systems," the roles of the Communist Party, PLA and people in China, would involve political or ideological underpinnings. Political awareness would thus be a natural by-product of studying the syllabus.[22]

In line with a later shift to thinking skills in the *Civic Education Bulletin* and the emphasis on conceptual analysis in GPA, the Modern World and China Today modules of Liberal Studies aim to sensitize students to the awareness of issues in international politics and political participation in China.[23]

❑ *The Textbook Controversy*

Although the increase in political content of the curriculum has been given official approval and encouragement, the government has remained ambivalent about aspects of this content. In 1994, the Director of Education announced censure of a paragraph in a new Chinese History textbook which contained an account of the 1989 June 4 incident. According to the press, the Director of Education made this decision one day after that paragraph came to his notice, and his major justification was that no historical event within the last 20 years should be included in textbooks.[24]

The Director's statement provoked vigorous criticism. First, some history and education experts queried the grounds for excluding events that had occurred within the last 20 years. History experts pointed out that this was not an established principle, and educationalists claimed that students not only had a right to be informed about recent historical events but also should be encouraged to think through various possible perspectives in interpreting them.[25] Second, the policy was criticized as inconsistent, since many other historical events in existing Chinese History and other textbooks had not been censored. One example was the signing of the Joint Declaration which, as noted above, was even an explicit part of the Social Studies syllabus. Moreover, the press identified at least one Chinese History textbook which described the June 4 incident but had not been censored. Third, education bodies, such as the Hong Kong Professional Teachers' Union, strongly protested against administrative intervention on an academic judgement.[26] Fourth, it was pointed out that even in China, the June 4 incident had been included in a 1993 textbook, and it was therefore suggested that the Hong Kong government was over-sensitive to political issues.[27]

However, the Director's action did gain support in some quarters. At least some people felt that inclusion of recent historical events in textbooks required caution. Since it usually takes a long time for historical events to be reviewed, interpreted and judged, it was argued that it is undesirable to give students "pre-mature" judgements.[28]

Interestingly, government reactions were also split. The Chief Secretary, Anson Chan, publicly defended the decision of the Director of Education.[29] However, the Governor, Chris Patten, expressed alarm when hearing that his officials were censoring textbooks, and ordered an immediate review.[30]

This particular controversy eventually died down. However, the textbook issue remained politically sensitive, and publishers began to worry about producing textbooks not acceptable to the changing polity because this might affect their sales. A group of publishers therefore approached the Preliminary Working Committee (PWC) for the future Special Administrative Region (SAR) on the matter. The PWC responded by suggesting three criteria for approval, namely that textbooks should be (1) in line with the Basic Law, (2) supportive of the one China policy, and (3) devoid of terminology with colonial characteristics. This statement seemed to give clear guidelines, but the publishers' approach to the PWC aroused strong public reaction since their initiative was seen as actively inviting intervention and censorship, and thus a self-limitation of academic freedom.[31] The legitimacy of the PWC in setting criteria for approval was also queried, because it was not yet a formal government body.

❑ *Nationalism and Education*

The textbook controversy was related to, and helped expose, a further issue related to nationalism. In May 1994, the PWC stated the view that existing Hong Kong textbooks should not be banned after 1997. However, the PWC also expressed concern that existing textbooks were rather Hong Kong-centred, for example with China being described as a "third" country, and weak in nationalism. The PWC suggested that publishers might wish to revise this aspect of their textbooks.[32] This matter was also addressed by Weng Xinqiao, Head of the Education, Science and Technology Department of the New China News Agency. He asserted that post-1997 educational policy should be set by Hong Kong people, and expressed the view that educational policy during the transition period should be as stable as possible. However, he also suggested that nationalistic elements should be increased in textbooks.[33]

In parallel, a PWC subgroup on cultural issues announced its view on the issues of textbook and civic education as follows:[34]

1. Civic education in Hong Kong has been underemphasized, and is weak in nationalism and patriotism.
2. Following the resumption of Chinese sovereignty, civic education in Hong Kong should aim at building nationalism and patriotism, and at strengthening the teaching of the Basic Law and the concept of "one country, two systems."
3. Education in the transition period should strengthen learning in Geography and Chinese History, as well as the Basic Law.
4. Hong Kong's Education Department should facilitate the development of civic education as a formal subject in primary and secondary schools.

The government responded by pointing out that focus on China was specifically mentioned in the 1985 Civic Education Guidelines and had also increased in other parts of the curriculum. However, the government did decide, possibly with the concerns of the PWC subgroup in mind, to set up an *ad hoc* working group to review the Civic Education Guidelines.

EDUCATION AND POLITICAL ATTITUDES

Education seems to be necessarily related to politics in one way or another. During Hong Kong's period of colonial transition, a positive correlation has been observed between education and concern for democracy. Surveys conducted in 1988 and 1990[35] found that people with higher educational levels were much more likely to have an opinion on the nature of the political situation, and were much more likely to be dissatisfied with the situation at the time. The figures from the 1988 survey are summarized in Table 2. The findings do not necessarily mean that people with higher educational level all favoured increased democracy, but a significant proportion of them did so. When the respondents were asked whether they wanted the Hong Kong government to become more democratic or authoritarian, the former was obviously favoured. Some 71.2% of respondents preferred the Hong Kong government to be democratic but not really strong and powerful, while only 13.6% wanted the government to be strong and powerful but not really democratic.

However, the 1988 survey also showed that in spite of general acceptance, democracy was perceived as less important than stability and prosperity. This point may be linked to the traditional apathy of Hong Kong

Table 2: Degree of Satisfaction with the Present Political Situation, by Educational Levels of Respondents, 1988 (%)

	Dissatisfied	Average	Satisfied	Don't know
Primary education and below (n = 660)	9.7	18.2	26.4	45.8
Secondary education (n = 882)	21.2	29.6	27.3	22.0
Tertiary education (n = 169)	31.4	36.7	21.9	10.1

Source: Lau Siu-kai, Kuan Hsin-chi, and Wan Po-san, "Political Attitudes," in *Indicators of Social Development: Hong Kong 1988* (Hong Kong: Hong Kong Institute of Asia-Pacific Studies, The Chinese University of Hong Kong, 1991), p. 174.

people to political matters. When the respondents in the survey were asked to compare the importance of democratic government with stability and prosperity, 58.6% considered the latter more important, while only 17.2% thought otherwise (with 21.0% ranking them equally important).

Yet the 1988 survey[36] also demonstrated that the respondents' conception of democracy was rather different from that in Western political theory. Although in the latter, the election of representatives is the *sine qua non* of democratic government, it did not seem important to the respondents. When asked what a democratic government was, 44.2% classified a government as democratic if it was willing to consult public opinion. The second largest proportion (19.7%) regarded a government that could lead the people as democratic. Only 14.9% considered democratic government as a government elected by the people; and 8.1% even thought that a government which treated the people in a fatherly way was democratic. Apart from those who had no definite opinion on the matter, who were likely to be less educated and older, no significant difference was found among socio-economic groups. The findings may be linked to the need for civic education in schools, though it must be recalled that the 1985 Civic Education Guidelines were themselves distinctly vague on the matter of democracy.

EDUCATORS AS POLITICAL ACTORS

Another link between education and political change concerns the role of teachers as political leaders. As pointed out by Mark Ginsburg and others,[37] educators are political actors regardless of whether they are active or passive, autonomous or heteronomous *vis-à-vis* other groups, conservative or change-oriented, seeking individual or collectivist goals, and/or serving dominant or subordinate group interests. What the educators do in the "private sphere" of classrooms, laboratories, libraries, meeting rooms, and offices is a form of political action, as is "public sphere" participation or non-participation in demonstrations, lobbying, voting, and running for office. Linda Dove's study of the role of teachers during colonial transitions suggests that teachers were commonly involved in leadership roles during the pre- and immediate post-independence periods.[38] Moreover, Ginsburg and others observe that educators have been leaders of political parties as well as being over-represented (compared to other occupational groups) as active members in party organizations.[39]

In Hong Kong, a teachers' seat filled through a functional constituency was established in the Legislative Council (Legco) following the 1984 White Paper. Teachers have also become increasingly prominent in direct election to open seats. Political analysts believe that teachers could have an edge because they can make use of holiday periods to organize campaigns and canvass for support. Gerard Postiglione adds that the nature of the profession, and the knowledge among the public that teachers' salaries are not nearly as high as for other occupations that command an equal level of educational qualifications, contribute to the image of the teacher as a "dedicated politician."[40]

The "Deadline Effects"

It was pointed out above that the duration of Hong Kong's transition period, like that of many remnants of empire, greatly exceeded that of the colonies in the main era of decolonization. This has permitted a much more leisurely pace for planning.

However, it also became apparent during the 1990s that 1997 was taken as a deadline for introduction of a wide range of reforms. The closer the year 1997 approaches, the deadline effects become stronger and more visible. The argument seemed to be that uncertainty about the nature of the SAR government and its policies made it essential to have structures in place by the time of the transition. As a result, the pace of change greatly increased during the 1990s, leaving many government officers, teachers, parents and other members of the community feeling somewhat breathless.

One example of a major reform introduced with a very short timetable was the scheme for Targets and Target-Related Assessment (TTRA). Partly because of the overhasty way in which it had been conceived, the scheme attracted considerable criticism. It was then modified and renamed Target-Oriented Curriculum (TOC), though still had a very ambitious timetable.

The TTRA was first proposed in the Education Commission Report No. 4.[41] Following the government's approval, the Education Department announced an implementation schedule in 1992 (see Table 3). The Education Department offered a two-day seminar in June–July 1992 for principals of primary schools, and a three-day seminar for teachers of Primary 4 to 6. Within these two or three days, principals and teachers were supposed to master the concepts of TTRA and learn to apply them to the teaching process. The implementation schedule was published before important

Table 3: Proposed Implementation Schedule for TTRA

Key stage	Class/level	Commencement of teaching using TTRA programmes of study	First external end-of-key-stage target-related assessment (TRA)
1	Primary 1	April 1994	June 1996
	Primary 2	April 1994	
	Primary 3	April 1994	
2	Primary 4	May 1993	December 1994
	Primary 5	September 1993	
	Primary 6	September 1994	
3	Form 1	September 1995	December 1997
	Form 2	September 1996	
	Form 3	September 1997	

Source: "General Administration Circular No. 10/92, Targets and Target-Related Assessment" (Hong Kong: Education Department, 27 May 1992), cited by Choi Po-king, "Education," in *The Other Hong Kong Report 1992*, edited by Joseph Y. S. Cheng and Paul C. K. Kwong (Hong Kong: The Chinese University Press, 1992), p. 260.

details had been sorted out, including the precise nature of the targets and the implications for subjects, textbooks and funding.[42]

As might be expected, this schedule provoked strong opposition. Teachers and others pointed out that the scheme was complex and vague, that the proposed implementation was too hasty, and that it would generate considerable extra work at the school level. Recognizing the validity of these complaints, the government revised and renamed the scheme.[43] However, the implementation schedule for the new version was still very demanding (see Table 4).

The government's TOC implementation schedule gave no hint of allowance for modification following evaluation of results in the pilot schools. This implied an assumption that the piloting would be successful, and again presented evidence of haste. Public opposition to the schedule was again strong, and in January 1995, petitions signed by 6,300 primary school principals and teachers who particularly objected to commencement

Table 4: Proposed Implementation Schedule for TOC

Year	70 pilot primary schools	All other primary schools
1995–1996	Primary 1	
1996–1997	Primary 1–2	Primary 1
1997–1998	Primary 1–3	Primary 1–2
1998–1999	Primary 1–4	Primary 1–4
1999–2000	Primary 1–5	Primary 1–5
2000–2001	Primary 1–6	Primary 1–6

Source: *Wen Wei Po*, 14 January 1995.

of implementation in 1996 were submitted to the Legco. However, this time the government endorsed the timetable and refused to back down.

While the TTRA/TOC is perhaps the most obvious example of a major reform pushed through with a hasty timetable, it is not the only one. Other examples include expansion of tertiary education, for which the government already had ambitious targets that were further raised in 1989;[44] and the School Management Initiative (SMI), which was announced in 1991 and which moved rapidly to full-scale implementation.[45] These were top-down policies, the nature of which contrasted sharply with efforts to democratize the political system.

GROWTH AND DIVERSIFICATION OF THE INTERNATIONAL SCHOOLS SECTOR

In parallel with these government initiatives were developments in the private international schools sector which had not been widely predicted. The sector grew markedly in the years following 1988–1989 (see Table 5), and also changed in emphasis and shape.

One factor underlying the growth was Hong Kong's economic boom, coupled with large-scale infrastructure projects such as the tertiary education expansion and the new airport which required employment of substantial numbers of expatriates. Another factor was economic growth across the border, which attracted thousands of foreign companies to set up beachhead operations in Hong Kong.[46] A third factor was that

Table 5: Growth of the Private International Schools Sector,
          1988–1989 to 1993–1994

	Primary		Secondary	
	Schools	Pupils	Schools	Pupils
1988–1989	*	4,656	*	2,826
1989–1990	*	5,375	*	3,080
1990–1991	15	5,266	12	3,420
1991–1992	17	5,585	14	4,198
1992–1993	18	6,265	18	4,547
1993–1994	19	6,808	18	6,220

* Number of international schools not indicated separately from other institutions.
Sources: Education Department, *Enrolment Survey*, various years.

many families were preparing to emigrate to such countries as Australia, Canada and the United States, and wanted their children to embark on education in schools allied to the systems in those countries. And a fourth factor was the return of many migrants who had already secured passports but whose children had already commenced schooling in Australian or North American schools and who could no longer fit easily into local schools.[47]

Expansion in the private international schools sector was paralleled by expansion in the government-assisted schools operated by the English Schools Foundation (ESF). Admission policies to ESF schools underwent a subtle change between the early 1980s and the mid-1990s. According to a 1981 official publication:

> It is the responsibility of the ESF to provide sufficient places for English-speaking children for whom no suitable alternative educational facilities are available in the public sector in Hong Kong. Children whose knowledge of Chinese is limited but whose mother tongue is not English are not considered to be part of the primary responsibility of the ESF.[48]

However, a 1994 publicity sheet prepared by the ESF indicated that the institutions "welcome students from all nations who can be educated through the English language." Not only did this new policy permit the ESF to enlarge its catchment, it also blurred the edges of the system and made it seem less colonial. In 1993–1994, 22% of ESF pupils were "returning Chinese," and another 43% were other Asians.

The irony is that the demand for international schools increased dramatically during the twilight of the colonial era. Indeed, so great was the pressure that the government felt it desirable to consider increasing financial grants to international schools.[49] Also of significance is that some international schools had established branches in Shanghai, Guangzhou and other parts of the P.R.C. These branches sought to meet demand from the new elite in the P.R.C.

CONCLUSION

As the above discussion demonstrates, education in Hong Kong became increasingly politicized during the later period of colonial transition. This was seen in the increase of political elements, particularly those related to China, in the curriculum, and the textbook controversy. That was to be expected, and matches the experience of many other territories which have gone through colonial transition. However, comparison of Hong Kong's situation with that of the main era of decolonization shows a number of differences. One of them is the long lead time, which allowed more time for planning.

A second difference from most other colonies has been that Hong Kong's decolonization is not to independence but to reintegration with the original mother country. Even before the close of the colonial era, forces within the P.R.C. played an increasingly active role in the education system. Indeed, this raised the question whether Hong Kong's education is in fact being decolonized or recolonized. Tensions relating to the locus of control are likely to create major challenges in the future.

However, experiences in other countries have shown that education can be a vehicle for resisting change as well as for promoting it. In so far as basic structures, and the personnel who operate those structures, are likely to show strong continuity, it is far from certain that life at the classroom level will undergo any immediate and radical changes. Textbooks may change, and syllabuses may change; but it is more difficult to change the basic values of those who operate the system. In response to the recent initiatives put forward by the government, many schools seem to respond either by open protest or quiet "adoption" with lip-service but without many real changes implemented. As a matter of fact, curriculum changes and educational innovations can only be a longer-term process, and will be strongly dependent on wider forces in society.

The fact that some international schools moved during the mid-1990s to establish branches across the border also deserves further comment. Such activities have political as well as commercial implications, for the links with the P.R.C. elite may help protect the international schools in the post-1997 era. It seems likely that some members of the P.R.C. elite will want to use Hong Kong's international schools as a route to higher education in Western countries. If this is the case, then the international schools as a group may be much less vulnerable than they would otherwise be. In turn this has implications for the broader society since it implies ongoing provision for foreign nationals and a retention of diversity within the system.

A final point may be made about the pace of change. This chapter has noted that despite the long lead time, the pace of change greatly increased during the early and mid-1990s because 1997 was taken as a sort of deadline. The transition will itself, of course, require some further changes. However, it may be anticipated (and hoped) that the pace of change thereafter will become more moderate. Many administrators, teachers and parents feel that recent changes have been too rapid, and they look forward to a period of greater stability.

NOTES

1. See Mark Bray, and Lee Wing-on, "Education, Democracy and Colonial Transition: The Case of Hong Kong," *International Review of Education*, Vol. 39, No. 6 (1993); Lee Wing-on, "Pressure for Educational Excellence in China: Implications for Education in Hong Kong," in *Education and Society in Hong Kong: Toward One Country and Two Systems*, edited by G. A. Postiglione with J.Y.M. Leung (Hong Kong: Hong Kong University Press, 1992); Mark Bray, "Decolonization and Education: New Paradigms for the Remnants of Empire," *Compare*, Vol. 24, No. 1 (1994).
2. See "Education, Democracy and Colonial Transition: The Case of Hong Kong" (Note 1), p. 543.
3. Paul Morris, "The Effect on the School Curriculum of Hong Kong's Return to Chinese Sovereignty in 1997," *Journal of Curriculum Studies*, Vol. 20, No. 6 (1988).
4. Ibid., p. 514.
5. John Tan, "History of the History Curriculum under Colonialism and

Decolonization: A Comparison of Hong Kong and Macau" (M.Ed. dissertation, The University of Hong Kong, 1993), p. 146.

6. Ibid., p. 69.

7. Ibid., p. 75.

8. Paul Morris, "Preparing Pupils as Citizens of the Special Administrative Region of Hong Kong: An Analysis of Curriculum Change and Control during the Transition Period," in *Education and Society in Hong Kong: Toward One Country and Two Systems*, edited by G. A. Postiglione with J.Y.M. Leung (Hong Kong: Hong Kong University Press, 1992), p. 136.

9. See Note 3, p. 515.

10. Hong Kong Examinations Authority, *Hong Kong Advanced Level Examination: Regulations and Syllabuses* (Hong Kong: Hong Kong Examinations Authority, 1994), p. 446.

11. See Note 3, p. 518.

12. S. M. Lee, "Political Education and Civic Education — The British Perspective and the Hong Kong Perspective," *International Journal of Educational Development*, Vol. 7, No. 4 (1987), p. 243.

13. Civic Education Committee, Education Department, *Guidelines on Civic Education in Schools* (Hong Kong: Government Printer, 1985).

14. Ibid., p. 7.

15. See Education Department, *Report on the Evaluation of the Implementation of the "Guidelines on Civic Education in Schools"* (Hong Kong: Government Printer, 1986); Education Department, *Second Report on the Evaluation of the Implementation of the "Guidelines on Civic Education in Schools"* (Hong Kong: Government Printer, 1987); Education Department, *Education Department Annual Summary 1990–91* (Hong Kong: Government Printer, 1991).

16. See *Report on the Evaluation of the Implementation of the "Guidelines on Civic Education in Schools"* (Note 15), p. 26.

17. See *Second Report on the Evaluation of the Implementation of the "Guidelines on Civic Education in Schools"* (Note 15), p. 46.

18. Tang Chun-keung, and Paul Morris, "The Abuse of Educational Evaluation: A Study of the Evaluation of the Implementation of the Civic Education 'Guidelines'," *Educational Research Journal* [Hong Kong], Vol. 4 (1989).

19. Ibid., p. 48.

20. Education Department, *Education Department Annual Summary 1990–91* (Hong Kong: Government Printer, 1991), p. 17.

21. K. K. Wan-Chan, "Liberal Studies — A Viable Vehicle for Civic Education in the Sixth Form Curriculum," *Civic Education Bulletin*, Vol. 6 (1994), p. 63.

22. Ibid., p. 62.

23. F. Cheung, "The Politicization of Hong Kong Secondary School Curriculum"

(unpublished P.C. Ed. assignment essay, Faculty of Education, The University of Hong Kong, January 1995).

24. *Ming Pao*, 28 and 29 June 1994.

25. *Ming Pao*, 30 June 1994; *Overseas Chinese Daily News*, 5 July 1994.

26. *Hong Kong Commercial Daily*, 30 June 1994.

27. *Ming Pao*, 30 June 1994.

28. *Wen Wei Po*, 30 June 1994 and 15 November 1994.

29. *United Daily News*, 7 July 1994.

30. *South China Morning Post*, 4 July 1994.

31. *Sing Tao Daily*, 16 November 1994.

32. *Ta Kung Pao*, 19 May 1994.

33. *Ming Pao*, 22 September 1994; *Wen Wei Po*, 26 September 1994.

34. *Ta Kung Pao*, 13 September 1994.

35. Lau Siu-kai, Kuan Hsin-chi, and Wan Po-san, "Political Attitudes," in *Indicators of Social Development: Hong Kong 1988*, edited by Lau Siu-kai, *et al.* (Hong Kong: Hong Kong Institute of Asia-Pacific Studies, The Chinese University of Hong Kong, 1991), p. 174. Also see Lau Siu-kai, "Political Attitudes," in *Indicators of Social Development: Hong Kong 1990*, edited by Lau Siu-kai, *et al.* (Hong Kong: Hong Kong Institute of Asia-Pacific Studies, The Chinese University of Hong Kong, 1993), p. 133.

36. See Lau Siu-kai, *et al.*, "Political Attitudes" (Note 35), p. 184.

37. Mark B. Ginsburg, *et al.*, "Education/Politics," *Comparative Education Review*, Vol. 36, No. 4 (1992), p. 421.

38. Linda Dove, *Teachers and Teacher Education in Developing Countries* (London: Croom Helm, 1986), p. 31.

39. See Note 37, p. 440.

40. Gerard A. Postiglione, "The Decolonization of Hong Kong Education," in *Education and Society in Hong Kong: Toward One Country and Two Systems*, edited by G. A. Postiglione with J.Y.M. Leung (Hong Kong: Hong Kong University Press, 1992), p. 19.

41. Education Commission, *Education Commission Report No. 4: The Curriculum and Behavioural Problems in Schools* (Hong Kong: Government Printer, 1990), p. 84.

42. Choi Po-king, "Education," in *The Other Hong Kong Report 1992*, edited by Joseph Y. S. Cheng and Paul C. K. Kwong (Hong Kong: The Chinese University Press, 1992), pp. 260–61.

43. Paul Morris, *The Hong Kong School Curriculum: Development, Issues and Policies* (Hong Kong: Hong Kong University Press, 1995), p.118.

44. P. Morris, J.A.G. McClelland, and Y. M. Leung, "Higher Education in Hong Kong: The Context of and Rationale for Rapid Expansion," *Higher Education*, Vol. 27, No. 2 (1994).

45. Andrew K. C. Wong, "Achieving Effective Schools Status through the School Management Initiative?" *New Horizons*, Vol. 33 (1992). Also see Andrew K. C. Wong, "School-based Management, School Effectiveness and the School Management Initiative: Different? How Different?" in *Teacher Education and Development*, Education Paper 18, edited by A.B.M. Tsui and I. Johnson (Hong Kong: Faculty of Education, The University of Hong Kong, 1993).

46. Paul C. K. Kwong, "Internationalization of Population and Globalization of Families," in *The Other Hong Kong Report 1993*, edited by Choi Po-king and Ho Lok-sang (Hong Kong: The Chinese University Press, 1993), p. 147.

47. Mark Bray, and Pedro Ieong, "Education and Social Change: The Growth and Diversification of the International Schools Sector in Hong Kong" (paper presented at the annual conference of the Hong Kong Educational Research Association, City University of Hong Kong, 1994), pp. 3–5.

48. Education Department, *The Hong Kong Education System* (Hong Kong: Government Secretariat, 1981), p. 206.

49. See Note 47, p. 19.

16

Health Care Services

Peter P. Yuen

ABSTRACT

This chapter examines the existing health care financing and delivery system in Hong Kong, and highlights a number of potential problems as well as opportunities when the territory becomes a Special Administrative Region (SAR) of the People's Republic of China in 1997. Problems include the reluctance of the current government to make any significant changes in health care financing during the transition period, the further strain on the territory's already overused health services by Mainlanders, and the lowering of the standard of health care as a result of the influx of China's health care professionals to Hong Kong. The opportunities include an increased supply of health manpower, and the development of traditional Chinese medicine as an alternative for consumers.

INTRODUCTION

It might appear to many that health care is a policy area that would be relatively free from controversy as Hong Kong changes its status from a British colony to a Chinese SAR. Health care is basically apolitical. At present, it has no value as a source of revenue for the government (given the existing policy of charging only a nominal fee for services delivered by public health care institutions); the government has hitherto been relatively successful in keeping health care expenditure under control (hence it cannot be accused of creating a new financial burden for the future SAR government); the public appears to be quite content with the status quo; and China did not voice any opposition to the formation of the Hospital Authority in 1990 as it did with some other public corporations.

However, despite the apparent lack of controversy, a smooth transition on the financing and delivery of health services is not a foregone conclusion. The health care system in Hong Kong is likely to experience important changes as the territory undergoes the change in sovereignty. There are threats as well as opportunities, depending on how some of these matters are tackled. This chapter first reviews the strengths and weaknesses of the existing health care system. It then attempts to ascertain whether or not the strengths of the existing system can be preserved, and to evaluate the impact of the change in sovereignty on some of the long-standing problems of the existing health care system. It also highlights a number of new issues associated with the transfer of sovereignty which could have a significant impact on both consumers and providers of health care services.

The Existing Health Care System

Hong Kong has a rather unique health care financing and delivery system, based partly on a capitalistic free enterprise philosophy and partly on "socialist" principles. Health status indicators, such as infant mortality rate and life expectancy at birth, rank Hong Kong among the best in the world (see Table 1). Universal access to care is also guaranteed by the government. Furthermore, compared to many Western countries, the Hong Kong government has been relatively successful in containing the growth of health care expenditure — confining the territory's overall health care expenditure to under 6% of gross domestic product (GDP), and the public sector share of total health care expenditure to 33% (see Table 2).

However, some analysts have criticized the system as outdated and too bureaucratic.[1] Others have pointed out that the territory does not have an adequate mechanisms to formulate long-range policies for health care, and that the existing structure lacks effective mechanisms to integrate the public and private sectors, as well as the different levels of care.[2] The characteristics of the various component of the health care system are discussed in greater detail in the paragraphs below.

❏ *Out-patient Services*

Out-patient primary care is delivered predominantly by private general

Table 1: Life Expectancy at Birth and Infant Mortality Rate of
Selected Countries

Country	Male	Female	Infant mortality rate (per 1,000 births)
Hong Kong (1992)	75.1	80.7	5.3
Japan (1991)	76.1	82.1	4.6
Australia (1990)	73.9	80.0	8.2
United Kingdom (1991)	73.2	78.8	7.9
United States (1990)	72.0	78.8	9.1
W. Germany (1989)	72.6	79.0	8.3
Singapore (1988)	71.7	76.3	7.0

Sources: *OECD Health Systems* (Paris: Organization for Economic Cooperation and Development, 1993), pp. 54–55, 69; Hong Kong Government, *Hong Kong 1993* (Hong Kong: Government Printer, 1993), p. 445.

Table 2: Total Health Spending as a % of GDP and Public Sector
Share of Total Health Spending of Selected Countries

Country	Total health spending as a % of GDP	Public sector share of total health spending(%)
Hong Kong (1990–1991)	5.7	20.0
Japan (1991)	6.8	72.0
Australia (1991)	7.1	67.8
United Kingdom (1991)	6.1	83.3
United States (1991)	11.2	43.9
W. Germany (1991)	8.2	71.8
Sweden (1991)	9.0	78.0

Sources: *OECD Health Systems* (Paris: Organization for Economic Cooperation and Development, 1993), p. 18; The World Bank, *World Development Report 1993: Investing in Health* (Oxford: Oxford University Press, 1993), p. 210.

practitioners, most of whom are solo practitioners trained in Hong Kong or the United Kingdom (U.K.). They provide approximately 70% of all out-patient consultations.[3] These services are paid for through direct payment or private health insurance. The Department of Health also operates general

out-patient clinics providing approximately 15% of all out-patient consultations at a subsidized rate ($35 inclusive of medication, a fee which is
roughly 20% of the actual average cost per consultation). The remaining
15% of the out-patient visits are provided by private alternative medical
practitioners, with traditional Chinese medical practitioners being the
largest group.[4] Presently, Chinese medicine is almost totally unregulated.[5]

The majority of the working population and their families receive care
from private practitioners of Western medicine, while patients who use
services provided by the Department of Health's clinics and traditional
Chinese medical practitioners tend to be mostly elderly and persons from
lower-income groups.

The Department receives its income from the government's general
revenue, and all staff are salaried civil servants. The Department also
delivers a wide range of preventive and other primary care services including immunization, screening, health education, school dental health service,
and maternity and child health services. All of these services are free or
charged at a nominal rate to Hong Kong residents.

Critics of the services of government clinics point to long waiting
times, extremely brief consultation times, rudeness on the part of staff, and
the fact that only a small percentage open on Sundays and in the evenings.[6]
The quality of care varies widely among private practitioners, both in
Western medicine as well as in traditional medicine. Even with Western
medicine, there are virtually no post-registration quality assurance mechanisms to protect consumers. In general, however, private practitioners
tend to be more consumer-oriented than government clinics in terms of
opening hours and staff courtesy.

❑ *Hospital Services*

The bulk of specialist and in-patient care is financed and delivered by
the public sector through the Hospital Authority. The Hospital Authority,
established in 1990, owns and operates 39 institutions, which accommodate close to 90% of all hospital beds in Hong Kong. The remaining 10% or
so of the beds are found in private hospitals. Hospitals under the Hospital
Authority provide a comprehensive range of "no-frills" type secondary and
tertiary care at a heavily subsidized rate — patients pay a fixed all-inclusive
per diem fee ($60 a day) which is less than 2% of the actual average cost of
a patient day in an acute care public hospital. All Hong Kong residents are

eligible to receive care from public hospitals and clinics at the subsidized rate. Although the Hospital Authority is technically a corporation, it receives 98% of its income from the government's general revenue.[7] There is no special hypothecated health tax or national health insurance fund. Various health care financing reform options put forward by the government in a consultation document in 1993 were rejected almost unanimously by members of the public.[8]

Shortages of nurses[9] and doctors in some medical specialities have been long-standing in public hospitals.[10] Furthermore, public hospitals are often criticized for being unresponsive to the personal needs of patients, and for the long waiting lists for non-emergency cases.

Care in private hospitals is financed by direct payment or private health insurance. Less than 14% of the population is covered by private health insurance.[11] Private doctors admit patients only to private hospitals with which they have prearranged admission privileges. Many of these hospitals position themselves as up-market acute-care facilities with high-technology equipment, good hotel services and free choice of doctors.

There have been numerous allegations of patients being charged exorbitantly for surgical procedures performed by private doctors in private hospitals.[12] Technical quality also tends to vary widely among private specialists.

PROBLEMS AND OPPORTUNITIES

The questions of most concern to the public are, firstly, whether or not the future SAR government will continue the current policy of guaranteeing access to care for all; and secondly, whether or not Hong Kong would be able to maintain its relatively high standard of care and yet be able to keep cost under control. Also important is the question of whether or not the solutions to some of the long-standing problems in the system — such as nurse shortages and the lack of quality assurance in the private sector — will be affected by the change of sovereignty.

The health care system is also likely to experience a number of new problems stemming from the political change. Firstly, the question of treating and charging Mainlanders in Hong Kong public hospitals is likely to be more acute as the number of people crossing the border from the north increases after 1997. Secondly, political considerations would require the alteration of practices in the health care industry which are inconsistent with

China's resumption of sovereignty over Hong Kong, such as the blanket recognition of the professional qualifications of U.K. medical and allied health graduates. Thirdly, the Basic Law requires the future SAR government to develop traditional Chinese medicine. The current state of under-development and under-regulation of Chinese medicine will have to be changed. The paragraphs below examines these issues in greater detail.

❏ Preserving Strengths and Overcoming Weaknesses

The existing policy of access to all is extremely popular and there are no political or ideological reasons for the future SAR government to radically change this policy. Article 138 of the Basic Law allows the future government to formulate and develop its own medical and health policies. However, a number of contextual and institutional forces are likely to cause health care costs to escalate significantly in the coming years, thus creating serious financial problems for the SAR government. Factors such as the ageing of the population, the increase in population from immigration, the increased expectation of the population as a result of increased affluence, the proliferation of high-technology medicine, the loosening of expenditure control over public hospitals arising from reform initiatives, and pressure from politicians to increase expenditure are likely to drive health care expenditure upwards over the next few years.[13] The current government policy of financing public hospital services from general taxes, and guaranteeing access to all types of services for everyone might no longer be feasible in the future, especially in times of financial difficulties. Alternative financing arrangements and more effective cost-containment measures must be implemented urgently in order to maintain the quality of care and the policy of universal access.

However, the government appears to be avoiding many of the tougher problems confronting the health care system during the transition period. The 1993 consultative document *Towards Better Health* presented a number of options regarding health care financing.[14] After extensive public consultation, the government decided to pursue the more incremental and less controversial options — the registration of private health insurance and the creation of semi-private beds in public hospitals. While the two options are laudable, as they create greater choice and protection for the consumer, as well as preserving the most important features of the existing system of universal access to care, they are only workable so long as the financial situation of the Hong Kong government remains good, and extra resources are available from the government to meet additional demands. In times of financing stringency, it is highly unlikely that these two options alone would be able to generate sufficient income to sustain the quality, type and additional quantity of services demanded as the result of the above-mentioned contextual and institutional factors.

While a number of reports and documents on a number of specific health care policies have been published in recent years, no overall health policy white paper has been produced since 1974. Despite a large number of management initiatives having been launched by the Hospital Authority, the basic financing mechanisms for public hospital services have not changed significantly. Despite the fanfare over the Patients' Charter, the private market is as under-regulated as ever before, and consumer protection in health care is still grossly inadequate. Policy officials appear to be adopting a "wait and see" attitude and avoiding the more controversial questions in the run-up to 1997. This current inertia could cause serious problems for the future SAR government.

❑ *The Influx of Patients from the Mainland*

Ironic as it may sound, the health care system in capitalistic Hong Kong is far more "socialist" than the one in the People's Republic of China. In Hong Kong, all residents are eligible to receive care from the clinics and hospitals of Department of Health and the Hospital Authority at a heavily subsidized rate. Fee waivers are often granted to those who cannot afford even the nominal fee. In China, however, less than 25% of the population have some form of health insurance coverage.[15] This discrepancy in coverage could cause serious problems for Hong Kong after 1997. A brief analysis of the current health care system in the Mainland illustrates the magnitude of the problem.

In China, the afore-mentioned insured population are covered under one of the three major insurance schemes: (1) the Public Medical Insurance Scheme, which covers Party and government officials, as well as students and retired cadres; (2) the Labour Insurance Medical Care Scheme, which covers workers in state enterprises; and (3) the Cooperative Medical Care Scheme in the rural areas, operated in the past by different People's Communes. In 1990, around 26.9 million cadres and students were covered under the Public Medical Insurance Scheme, and around 111.6 million workers were covered by the Labour Insurance Medical Care Scheme. An additional 66.4 million dependants enjoyed partial coverage under the two schemes, giving a total of less than 20% of the population covered by the two schemes. In the rural areas, with the disintegration of the communes in the late 1970s, the number of medical care cooperatives have become fewer and fewer. By the mid-1980s, these cooperatives covered less than 4.2% of the population.[16] Individuals who are not covered under any one of the above schemes are required to pay for their own health care expenses. They include the majority of the peasants, the self-employed, the unemployed, migrant workers, and employees of private, foreign and jointly owned companies. In the past, fees and charges for health care services were kept well below the true cost by the State Prices Bureau. Basic health care was, in general, quite affordable even to the uninsured. However, with the introduction of market-oriented reforms, service providers have been allowed to raise their fees and charges. Accessibility to care has now becomes a serious problem. The number of uninsured in urban areas is also growing rapidly, also as a direct consequence of the reforms.

As Hong Kong becomes an SAR of China, the current discrepancies in health care coverage are likely to attract more Mainland patients seeking care to come to Hong Kong. Notwithstanding the fact that immigration from the Mainland will continue to be controlled,[17] and the policy of only granting Hong Kong residents the subsidized rate in public health care institutions, it will still be extremely difficult to deny care to those who find their way to Hong Kong, one way or another, and present themselves at a public hospital with an acute condition.

During 1992, a total of 365,000 residents from China visited Hong Kong.[18] The figure is increasing every year, and is likely to increase even more substantially after 1997. It has been reported that many female visitors from the Mainland overstay in order to give birth while in Hong Kong. There were 1,746 births of this kind in 1990, 2,750 in 1991, and over 3,000 in 1992. Most of these deliveries took place in public hospitals.[19]

The public health care system is already showing signs of stress. Average waiting times for a first appointment at the Hospital Authority's specialist out-patient clinics is three months. Average waiting times for non-urgent ear, nose and throat surgery is also three months.[20] The recorded turn-away cases at the Department of Health's General Out-patient Clinics climbed as high as 144,815 in 1989.[21]

In sum, it is unlikely that the public health care system will be able to cope with the additional demand created as a result of the sharp increase in the number of visitors, and both legal and illegal immigrants from the Mainland after 1997, especially when the majority of them will not be full-fee paying patients.

❑ *Health Care Professionals from the Mainland*

Another controversial issue is the question of the credentials of health care professionals from the Mainland. An announcement was made in October 1994 by the Cultural Subgroup of the Preliminary Working Committee (PWC) for the future SAR government that the degrees of 561 Mainland higher educational institutions should be automatically recognized in Hong Kong after 1997.[22] The announcement has been interpreted by some as the beginning of a process that would eventually allow Mainland trained doctors and other professionals to practise in Hong Kong without restriction.[23]

The issue concerning non-local graduates in the health care industry is not new, nor is it peculiar to Hong Kong. In the United States, for instance, registered doctors from one state may not be able to practise automatically in another state. In Hong Kong, it has been the traditional practice, in most cases, that any person with a professional qualification obtained in Hong Kong and the U.K. is allowed to practise without further vetting or examination. This apply to doctors, nurses, and allied health professionals.

There are examinations to enable graduates of non-Commonwealth countries to achieve registration in Hong Kong, and there are special schemes which allow them to work in certain authorized places.[24] This policy has merits and demerits. On the merit side, the policy protects local graduates from the competition of graduates from many neighbouring countries and regions, especially those from the Mainland or Taiwan; it assures a relatively high standard for the professions; and it allows graduates of non-Commonwealth countries to practise after passing a qualifying examinations equivalent to those taken by local graduates. On the demerit side, it restricts the supply of health care professionals, resulting in chronic shortages in certain professions and specialities in the public sector, and exorbitant fees charged by these professionals in the private sector; and it discriminates against graduates from non-Commonwealth countries, including those from countries with very high standards.

Article 142 of the Basic Law permits Hong Kong to maintain its own distinct professional licensing requirements. It states that:

> The Government of Hong Kong Special Administrative Region shall, on the basis of maintaining the previous systems concerning the professions, formulate provisions on its own for assessing the qualifications for practice in the various professions.... The Government of the Hong Kong Special Administrative Region shall continue to recognize the professions and the professional organizations recognized prior to the establishment of the Region.

However, it is almost certain that graduates from the U.K. will not continue to enjoy their privileged status when Hong Kong returns to China. In fact, various licensing authorities, such as the Medical Council, the Dental Council, the Nursing Board, etc. have initiated amendments to various registration ordinances, and the introduction of a universal examination for all graduates from non-local institutions wanting to practise in Hong Kong.[25] Such an approach is clearly fairer than the existing practice.

From the community's perspective, the availability of health care professionals from China to come and practise in Hong Kong could be desirable, so long as there are adequate quality assurance mechanisms in place to ensure the standard of care. As pointed out earlier, nurse shortages appear to be chronic, and the inability of the public sector to retain an adequate number of doctors in medical specialities such as anaesthesia, diagnostic radiology, pathology, and psychiatry has also been a long-standing problem.

The doctor to patient ratio in Hong Kong is still low compared to many industrialized countries (see Table 3). Allowing more health care professionals from the Mainland to practise in Hong Kong would increase the supply of health care personnel without requiring Hong Kong taxpayers to pay for their basic training. It is in the interest of Hong Kong to explore innovative ways in which Hong Kong could take advantage of the human resources available in the Mainland to alleviate the problem of shortages in certain professions/specialities, inject greater competition and consumers' choice to the system and, at the same time, safeguard quality for patients and employment opportunities for locally trained health care professionals.

❑ *Traditional Chinese Medicine*

The regulation of traditional Chinese medicine (TCM) is a development which would probably benefit the Hong Kong community as a result of the change of sovereignty. Despite the fact that there are between 4,000 to 10,000 TCM practitioners actively practising in Hong Kong, that there

Table 3: Comparative Doctor Manpower Ratios
(Doctor per 1,000 Population), 1988–1992

Country	Doctor per 1,000 population
Hong Kong	0.93
Australia	2.29
Japan	1.64
United Kingdom	1.40
United States	2.38
Singapore	1.09
Sweden	2.73

Source: The World Bank, *The World Development Report 1993* (Oxford: Oxford University Press, 1993), p. 208.

are over 1,600 retail herbal shops and over 200 wholesalers of Chinese medicine, and that over 60% of the population in Hong Kong have consulted TCM practitioners of one form or another,[26] Chinese medicine in Hong Kong is almost totally unregulated and grossly underdeveloped. There is no registration for TCM practitioners; there is no accreditation of training programmes; and there is no control over the manufacturing, sale or dispensing of herbal and other proprietary Chinese medicine, including the highly toxic ones.

Resistance to the regulation and development of Chinese medicine comes from some TCM practitioners themselves, who fear that regulation would restrict their scope of practice,[27] as well as from the Western medical profession, who has always viewed alternative medicine as a threat to their virtual monopoly in the health field.[28] This total lack of concern for consumer protection and patient safety would probably have continued. However, Article 138 of the Basic Law requires the SAR government "to develop Western and traditional Chinese medicine." The Hong Kong government now has the mandate to rectify this unsatisfactory state of affairs. A Working Party on Chinese Medicine appointed by the Secretary for Health and Welfare published a report in October 1994 for public consultation, recommending the establishment of a preparatory committee to develop the necessary legislative framework for the regulation and development of Chinese medicine. This is a positive move, which will offer not only greater consumer protection and safety, but also more choice for treatment and health promotion to Hong Kong residents.

CONCLUSION

The health care system, which has played an important role in making Hong Kong one of the healthiest societies in the world, is currently facing a number of important challenges. The above analysis shows that 1997 offers both opportunities and problems to Hong Kong's health services providers and consumers. Some of the important issues, such as TCM and the universal examinations for non-local medical practitioners, are currently being addressed by various government bodies, while it remains to be seen how the government is going to tackle some of the more complicated questions, such as treating patients from the Mainland, and health care financing in the long term. The recent policy speech by Governor Chris Patten fails to address any of these issues.[29] It appears that the future SAR government will be left with some rather sticky problems to sort out.

NOTES

1. Joel W. Hay, *Health Care in Hong Kong: An Economic Policy Assessment* (Hong Kong: The Chinese University Press, 1992), pp. 35–41.

2. See, for example, R.T.T. Young, *Health for All — The Way Ahead: Report of the Working Party on Primary Health Care* (Hong Kong: Government Printer, 1990), p. 139; P. P. Yuen, "Medical and Health," in *The Other Hong Kong Report 1992*, edited by Joseph Y. S. Cheng and Paul C. K. Kwong (Hong Kong: The Chinese University Press, 1992), pp. 284, 287.

3. R.T.T. Young, *Health for All — The Way Ahead: Report of the Working Party on Primary Health Care* (Note 2), pp. 131–32.

4. Hong Kong Government, *Towards Better Health: A Consultative Document* (Hong Kong: Government Printer, 1993), p. 9.

5. Hong Kong Government, *Report of the Working Party on Chinese Medicine* (Hong Kong: Government Printer, 1994).

6. See, for example, Huang Chen-ya, "Medical and Health," in *The Other Hong Kong Report 1991*, edited by Sung Yun-wing and Lee Ming-kwan (Hong Kong: The Chinese University Press, 1991), p. 322. Also see Note 3, p. 129.

7. See Note 4, pp. 4, 7.

8. Health and Welfare Branch, "The Summary of Public Views on Reforms Options" (document prepared for members of the Legislative Council by the Health and Welfare Branch, Hong Kong, 1994).

9. *Ming Pao*, 26 April 1994, p. D2.

10. According to a document on "Flexible Employment Terms" by the Hospital Authority Human Resources Committee (October 1994), the Hospital Authority had problems with attracting and retaining doctors from four medical specialities — Anaesthesia, Diagnostic Radiology, Pathology and Psychiatry.

11. See Note 4, p. 13.

12. See, for example, N. Maharaj, "Doctor's Fee Cruelest Cut of All," *South China Morning Post*, 11 March 1990; H. Signy, "Hospital Fee Arbitrary, Says Insurers," *South China Morning Post*, 5 June 1991.

13. For a more detailed discussion on the factors, see P. P. Yuen, "Health Care Systems Reforms in Hong Kong: The Implications of Greater Private Sector Participation," *Philippine Journal of Public Administration*, Vol. XXXVI, No. 1 (1992), pp. 64–78.

14. See Note 4, pp. 28–40.

15. Peng Ruicong, Cai Renhua, and Zhou Caimeng, *Zhongguo gaige quanshu: Yiliao weisheng tizhi gaige juan* (China's Reform Encyclopaedia: Medical and Health Systems Reform Volume) (Dalian: Dalian Press, 1992), p. 17.

16. Ibid., pp. 16–19.

17. Consultative Committee for the Basic Law, *The Basic Law of the Hong Kong Special Administrative Region of the People's Republic of China* (Hong Kong: C & C Offset Printing Co. Ltd., 1990), p. 10 (in Chinese).

18. Hong Kong Government, *Hong Kong 1993* (Hong Kong: Government Printer, 1993), p. 382.

19. Paul C. K. Kwong, "Internationalization of Population and Globalization of Families," in *The Other Hong Kong Report 1993*, edited by Choi Po-king and Ho Lok-sang (Hong Kong: The Chinese University Press, 1993), p. 169.

20. Hong Kong Government, *Progress Report: The 1994 Policy Address* (Hong Kong: Government Printer, 1994), p. 23.

21. See Note 3, p. 130.

22. Q. Wang, and Q. Chan, "HK Doctors Fear Lower Standards," *South China Morning Post*, 16 October 1994.

23. C. H. Leung, "Let's Keep It Professional," *South China Morning Post*, 16 October 1994.

24. Colonial Secretariat, *Report of the Working Party on Unregistrable Doctors*, (Hong Kong: Government Printer, April 1975).

25. K. Bishop, "Health Policy 'Sick' as Government Dithers," *South China Morning Post*, 31 December 1994.

26. Hong Kong Government, *Report of the Working Party on Chinese Medicine*, p. 5.
27. Ibid., p. 28.
28. See Note 1, p. 44.
29. Hong Kong Government, *Policy Commitments: The 1994 Policy Address* (Hong Kong: Government Printer, 1994), p. 19.

17

Social Welfare: The Way Ahead

Nelson W. S. Chow

CRITICAL ISSUES SURROUNDING SOCIAL WELFARE BEFORE AND AFTER 1997

Ever since the signing of the Sino-British Joint Declaration between the Chinese and British governments in 1984 over the future of Hong Kong, concern has been expressed regarding the roles that social welfare should play after 1997.[1] Such concern arises from the fact that social welfare services have changed so much in their scope and purposes that they could no longer be regarded simply as benevolent activities of the government to meet the needs of the poor and the indigent. In an article which I wrote in 1985, I argued that the future development of social welfare in Hong Kong must be viewed as a choice involving political, social and economic considerations.[2] In that paper, I also pointed out that despite the increasing importance given by the Hong Kong government to the provision of social welfare, especially during the governorship of Lord MacLehose, a consensus was absent among the populace on the goals which social welfare should achieve. It was obvious at the time, and still true today, that while the business community was wary of Hong Kong becoming a Western-style "welfare state," grassroots organizations leaned, on the other hand, towards the establishment of a system emphasizing social equality and justice. As it would be impossible for the various parties to come to an agreement, it would be difficult to foresee the kind of social welfare system to be developed after 1997.

Circumstances in Hong Kong have no doubt changed greatly since the signing of the Joint Declaration, especially the political and economic changes which have occurred since Chris Patten took up the governorship in July 1992. One of the most significant changes is that democratic groups, which were yet to present themselves as formidable political forces, have not only made great strides in the last few years in gaining the support of the public, but also become the most influential group in the "corridors of power." The rise of the "democrats," a term which, for some unknown reasons, refers only to members of the Democratic Party (which is the result of an amalgamation of the former United Democrats of Hong Kong and the Meeting Point) and the Association for Democracy and People's Livelihood, was definitely unexpected; their landslide victory in the first direct election of the Legislative Council (Legco) in 1991 had also caught many by surprise. While the influence of the Democratic Party is only beginning to be felt, signs show that the Hong Kong government has already changed its ways of ruling this place.

From the date when Hong Kong was ceded to the British, it has always been assumed that it is the responsibility of the Governor, as representative of the Crown, to safeguard the interests of the people living in the territory. Thus the Hong Kong government has the authority to make all the decisions affecting its people. When Chris Patten assumed his office in July 1992, he still maintained in his address that the Hong Kong government is an executive-led one.[3] Although constitutionally things seem to have remained the same, the introduction of directly and indirectly elected seats in the Legco and the stipulation in the Joint Declaration that the future executive authorities must be accountable to the legislature clearly indicate that a new style of governance is emerging which will ultimately affect the making of policies.

While it would be too early to say that a new style of governance has already emerged, signs show that the government could no longer be sure of having all its bills and budgets approved by the Legco as in the days when the Legco was regarded as no more than a "rubber stamp." Whether this change is a deliberate attempt of the British to prepare Hong Kong people for self-rule after 1997, or simply an inevitable outcome of democratization, is hard to judge. What is important is that the government could no longer adhere to the practice of what is known as the "administrative absorption of politics" and consult only people in whom it has confidence.[4] It is now the common practice of the government to put forward its policies for public consultation before planning their implementation. Government secretaries who are responsible for the various policy areas are now also expected to defend and uphold the position of the government, as in the case of the proposed Old Age Pension Scheme. In other words, the days have gone for government policies to be treated as merely administrative decisions; they must now be debated openly, taking into consideration not only the influence of the various political parties but also the value premises upon which they stand.

As a government without a legitimate mandate to rule, the Hong Kong government has generally treated ideologies as irrelevant to the making of policies. We were thus given such illogical statements as "positive non-interventionism" as the guiding principle for our economic development. Notwithstanding the numerous Green and White Papers issued by the government on various education, medical, public housing and social welfare services, few people appear to be aware of the kind of society that the government wants to create. In fact, what the government wants the people to know is that their living standard has been steadily improved with the growing prosperity of Hong Kong, and this would have not been achieved if there are adherence to any particular ideology.

Although no one can dispute this pragmatic stand, the question that needs to be asked now is: As Hong Kong becomes more and more politicized with government policies made only after the interplay of various political forces, can one still regard the influence of ideologies, especially those adopted by political parties, as being irrelevant? If yes, does it imply that the political parties represented in the Legco, and thus playing an important role in influencing, if not exactly being responsible for, the making of policies are simply schemists seeking for power who have no value stands of their own? If no, to what extent and in what ways have the ideologies of the different political parties influenced the making of government policies? The above question is particularly relevant to this discussion because the future making of social policies will hardly escape the influence of the ideologies of the political parties, with services proposed to reflect their views.

In my paper presented in 1985, I concluded with the remark that the future development of social welfare in Hong Kong would ultimately depend on the choice of the people, as I did not believe that a social welfare system contrary to the belief of the people could exist long in any place. I was also sure at that time that a Western-style "welfare state" would not emerge in Hong Kong as I believed that, ideologically, people in Hong Kong were not ready for a social welfare system largely emphasizing the role of the state. Furthermore, I did not believe that any political group at that time would hinge their future on the accomplishment of such an illusive task. In other words, a "welfare state" would unlikely materialize in Hong Kong because the majority of people would choose not to have it, and often on pragmatic grounds. Does this conclusion still stand now? Has the welfare ideology of the people in Hong Kong been modified to such an extent that we can at least expect something close to the "welfare state" to be developed? As Hong Kong becomes a Special Administrative Region (SAR) of the People's Republic of China, can people in Hong Kong look forward to better welfare protection? If a better welfare system should succeed to be established, what sort of ideology should it be based on? How should its development be linked to the social, economic and political changes which are expected to occur in Hong Kong, both before and after 1997?

In the following, I would argue that although there is no grandiose goal or ideal to be found in the policy papers on social welfare produced so far by the Hong Kong government, examples are not absent in which policies are, in one way or another, affected by the ideologies which the people hold dear. How the government gauges the choice of the people would be discussed later, but the fact that the Hong Kong government itself is not committed to a particular set of beliefs probably makes it more flexible in responding to the changes of ideas, as long as such policies do not go beyond its financial ability. Hence, I would first try to show how the ideologies of the people have in the past influenced the making of social welfare policies. I would argue that the effects have, in fact, been so prominent that an understanding of social welfare development in Hong Kong would not be complete without a discussion of the ideologies of the people. Furthermore, if what the people perceived as important had played an important role in the making of social welfare policies in the past, there are more reasons to believe that with the increasing influence of political parties, the role played by ideology would become even more conspicuous. In tracing the changes which are likely to occur among the people in their views about social welfare, as well as the stands to be taken by the various political parties, one is probably in the best position to understand the future development of social welfare in Hong Kong.

THE INTERPLAY BETWEEN IDEOLOGIES AND SOCIAL WELFARE

What part have ideologies played in the development of social welfare in Hong Kong? What kind of ideologies has the Hong Kong government adhered to in making its social welfare policies? And more recently, what sort of welfare ideologies have been expressed by the political parties? If one focuses on the years after World War II, one can easily identify three distinct periods, each with its own set of values and ideologies. These periods are: the first from 1946 to 1966; the second from 1967 to 1982; and the third from 1983 to the present. Not only have the three periods differed in the welfare ideologies upheld, but the legacies they have left behind are also exerting different influences in shaping the future development of social welfare.

❏ *Power Sharing in Social Welfare*

The twenty years immediately following the end of World War II have often been described as an emergency period in almost every aspect of development in Hong Kong. So far as social welfare is concerned, the most conspicuous development during this period is the establishment of a great number of voluntary or non-governmental welfare organizations, whose purposes were mainly to provide relief for the poor and the unfortunate. Most of these welfare organizations were linked to their parent bodies overseas; only a few were the outcome of efforts made by the local people like the *kaifong* and clansmen associations. During this emergency period, the internationally linked welfare organizations had probably done much more than the government in meeting the welfare needs of the people. The contribution of the voluntary welfare organizations was officially recognized by the White Paper on social welfare published in 1965 which stated:

> There are many religious and welfare organizations in Hong Kong, often with substantial resources, which are willing and able to provide welfare services, some of which in other countries would be provided by the public authorities.[5]

For these voluntary welfare organizations with international connections, the most common cause which had motivated their establishment was the ideals of some religious or humanitarian beliefs, while the indigenous charitable and mutual-help associations often had their philosophies based on the traditional Confucian or Buddhist notions of benevolence or common good. The 1965 White Paper on social welfare also said that "The ideal of 'fuk lei' or social service is held high by many Chinese."[6] The importance of the above welfare notions has no doubt greatly diminished and some might now find the word "fuk lei" derogative. But the influence of these notions has not completely disappeared and at least in the following two ways has continued to impact upon the development of social welfare in Hong Kong:

1. Though few would now regard social welfare as a form of charity handed out by kind-hearted philanthropists, the majority of the Chinese in Hong Kong are still unable to wipe away the traditional notions of welfare and the most they can accept is to regard it as a responsibility to be shared between the state and one's relatives and friends.

2. It is important to note that while the notions held dear by the welfare organizations established after World War II have gradually diminished in their importance, the mode of voluntary organization itself has survived and even flourished. Some voluntary organizations established in the 1950s did close or move their offices elsewhere when large-scale relief was no longer needed in Hong Kong, but more new ones were formed, with the majority of them receiving financial support from the Social Welfare Department.

In addition to the operation of the services, the non-governmental agencies have also been allowed, through the Hong Kong Council of Social Service, to participate in their planning. So the making of social welfare policies in Hong Kong is often described as the outcome of the joint efforts of the government and the non-governmental sector. The continuing influence of the non-governmental agencies, which came into being only as an emergency measure at the end of World War II, implies that in the area of social welfare, the making of policies will always be shared between the government and the non-governmental sector.

❏ *Social Justice and Equality*

After the hard time of the 1950s, Hong Kong became economically more self-sufficient with its flourishing manufacturing industry; and by the mid-1960s, dire poverty had largely disappeared. With near-to-full employment, the majority of the families in Hong Kong were able to make ends meet and some had even managed to improve their living standard. Voluntary agencies established after World War II, mainly for the purpose of bringing in overseas relief, were by the latter half of the 1960s gradually shedding much of their relief activities. But instead of closing down, as mentioned above, most of these voluntary agencies had continued their operation and taken up new roles. The special feature of the second period, from 1967 to 1982, was represented by the new roles taken up by the voluntary agencies. One and perhaps the most important of these roles developed during this period was to act as an "agent" of the government in running the services. Not all agencies, however, were content with this role and they were desirous of breaking new grounds to justify their existence. But the charitable and humanitarian ideals which had paved the ground for social welfare development in the years immediately after World War II had already, by this time, lost their attraction and further advancements must be grounded on new ideas and concepts.

The fifteen years from 1967 to 1982 is one of the turbulent periods in Hong Kong. The riots in 1966 and 1967, though caused by very different reasons, showed unmistakably that Hong Kong was far from being a harmonious society and conflicts abounded. Corruption, which is regarded as almost unavoidable in a Chinese society, had flared up so conspicuously in the late 1960s that most people were convinced that something must be done to eradicate the injustice. It was against this background that social workers were seeking for new directions in their work and a new welfare ideology began to emerge in the early 1970s. It should also be mentioned that with the establishment of professional social work training at The Chinese University of Hong Kong and The University of Hong Kong in the mid-1960s, a new brand of social workers, who tended to be more idealistic in their outlook, had begun to join the profession. The development of the "welfare states" in the West during this period had also made their impact on Hong Kong and this was shown by the fact that Fabian Socialism was the most fashionable approach taught in the social work schools of the two universities at the time.

The three central values of the Fabian Socialists, as summarized by Paul Wilding and Vic George, are: equality, freedom and fellowship.[7] Why young social workers in the 1970s were attracted to the ideals of the Fabian Socialists is not difficult to understand. The reason is: one of their professional commitments is to help develop the potentialities of the people whom they work with and "it is only in a more equal society," according to the Fabian Socialists, "that the individual has the opportunity to realize his potentialities."[8] Hong Kong in the late 1960s, as mentioned above, was a society with glaring injustice and the discontent of the young social workers was more than justified.

On the other hand, as Hong Kong developed into an industrial and commercial centre, resources were more readily available not only for guaranteeing everyone a living standard above the subsistence level, but also for promoting a more just and equal society. So the question, as understood by the young social workers, was no longer the availability or otherwise of resources but whether or not it was the wish of the government to push for a more equal society by providing the needy with the necessary social welfare services. When Lord Murray MacLehose, the first diplomat with a socialist background sent to Hong Kong, became the new Governor in 1972, he raised a lot of hope among the young social workers abiding by the Fabian Socialist ideals that the injustice and inequality of Hong Kong society would soon give way to a much fairer and equal system.

During the 1970s, the predominant ideology influencing social welfare development is obviously one emphasizing justice and equality. Social welfare policies made during this period did not necessarily set their aims at achieving these two ideals but as long as they were upheld by the majority of the social workers, they had also made a lasting impact on social welfare development. Their impact could in fact be observed in the following two ways.

First, as mentioned above, some voluntary agencies during this period were not content with the role of simply running social welfare services on behalf of the government and were determined to usher in more radical changes. As a result, some new agencies were formed and their objectives were to create greater equality and justice. Examples of these agencies included the Hong Kong Christian Industrial Committee, the Hong Kong Society for Community Organization, the Hong Kong People's Association for Public Housing, and the Ecumenical Social Service Centre in Tsuen Wan. Other than the above, a number of voluntary agencies had also experimented with new projects, mostly not funded by the government, adopting confrontational approaches which might be found unacceptable even within certain sectors of the social work community. Subsequently, the government branded these organizations as "pressure groups," since these organizations often took actions to pressurize the government to succumb to their demands. Social actions which were almost unheard of before 1967 had become common and have continued to form part of the democratization process in the 1980s. Hence, one of the significant legacies of the predominance of the socialist ideology during this period has been the emergence of a number of non-conformist organizations to act outside the orbit of the government establishment in order to press for greater equality and justice.

The second consequence of the predominant welfare ideology of this period is the realization that piecemeal improvements, based on humanitarian notions, were inadequate to resolve the emerging conflicts of Hong Kong society. After assuming his governorship for one year, Lord MacLehose announced in 1973 that education, public housing, medical and social welfare services would be treated as the four pillars in building a better society and that he intended to make drastic and long-term improvements in these areas.[9] Although the economic recession in the mid-1970s had frustrated many of the plans to achieve a fair and caring society, the fact that the government was determined to do far more than the minimum in promoting the welfare of the people did give social workers and other "social activists" the belief that changes were possible and that organized and collective efforts were necessary to bring pressure on the government.

❏ *Politics and Social Work*

The notions of social justice and equality have not actually faded away in the third period of social welfare development, from 1982 onwards, but the signing of the Joint Declaration in 1984 over the future of Hong Kong has brought new dimensions to the thinking of the social workers. In fact, even before the signing of the Joint Declaration, the development of social welfare had already become very much politicized, especially when more and more social workers have been standing for election to the District Boards and the two municipal councils. Although some social workers were a bit worried at the beginning about the close relationship between the practice of social work and politics, the increasing number of social workers becoming politicians and the influence they exerted in the District Boards and the Urban and Regional Councils convinced most members of the profession that political participation and even electioneering should be regarded as a legitimate means to achieve a better social welfare system.[10] Hence, in addition to the advocacy of social justice and equality, the notions of democratic participation and citizenship or welfare rights have also gradually become important ideologies influencing social welfare development since the mid-1980s.

Before the development of representative government in the late 1970s, Hong Kong people were known to have enjoyed maximum freedom but no democracy. With the opening up of the political system and the introduction of direct elections, albeit first at only the district level, Hong Kong people suddenly realized that they had always been denied the opportunity to participate in decisions affecting their own lives. As an important motto of the social work profession is self-determination, it is clearly a mission of the social workers to promote among the people their widest participation in matters concerning their own welfare. The quest for democracy, which stood out as the most conspicuous social phenomenon in the 1980s, has no doubt the staunch support of the social workers. In order that people might determine their own fate, groups of social service recipients, including public housing tenants, the elderly, the physically and mentally hand-icapped, the unemployed, the public assistance recipients, and mothers with young children were organized to fight for their own rights. Similar group-ings have long existed in the West but their formation in Hong Kong has become one of the most formidable political forces and has subsequently contributed to the success of social workers in political elections.[11]

Indeed, Hong Kong people have seldom been conscious of their rights as a citizen. Although the two international covenants — one covering civil and political rights and the other economic, social and cultural rights — as enshrined in the Joint Declaration have been in force in Hong Kong since the early 1970s, they have rarely been heard of by the people they were meant to protect. Hong Kong people were only made aware of their entitle-ments with the proclamation of the Joint Declaration and were slow to fully understand the implications of the two covenants.[12] Social workers, partly out of their professional conviction to safeguard the innate rights of the people, were quick to move in and lead the way to ensure that people's rights were not easily forgotten. A comparison of the attitudes of the people at the beginning and at the end of the 1980s clearly shows that most people in Hong Kong have advanced in their conception of their own rights and some would even regard the provision of social welfare as an undeniable responsibility of the government.[13]

It would not, of course, be appropriate to attribute this change in attitude entirely to the efforts of the social workers; the government itself has also played its part in educating the public about their rights through its various civic education programmes. Once the people have accepted the concept of rights, consultation and participation become an expected part of the government decision-making process. Social workers have again quickly seized the opportunity in helping the people to express their opinions and so reinforced, once more, the impression that they were fighters of people's rights.

Democratic participation and citizen rights have therefore stood out as the most prominent notions underlying the development of social welfare in the period beginning from the mid-1980s and have also helped to establish firmly the influence of the social workers in the political arena. Hence, in addition to the mission of advocating a fair and just society, social workers have now a more important role in fighting for the rights of the people. What has happened is that not only were social workers finding themselves more and more involved in political activities, but also was social welfare development so closely identified with the fight for greater democracy and citizen rights to the extent that the fate of the former is now largely dependent on the success of the latter. In other words, if social workers and their democratic allies are successful in gaining progress in their fight for greater democracy, there would probably be a greater chance for a more adequate and comprehensive social welfare system to be introduced. On the other hand, a legislature with the democrats forming the minority would imply the continuance of the status quo.

The close relationship between democratization and social welfare development is clearly demonstrated by the decision regarding the establishment of a retirement protection system in Hong Kong.[14] Before the introduction of direct election to the legislature in September 1991, the government was clearly abhorrent of any kind of contributory retirement protection scheme. The result of the election had drastically changed the stance of the government because the call for such a scheme would definitely have the approval of the majority of the members should retirement protection be debated once more in the Legco. There is no doubt that in reversing its stand the government was clearly influenced by the change in the composition of the legislature. Hence, it is not surprising to find that a substantial number of social workers hold the belief that aggressive reforms of the social welfare system would only be possible with a faster pace of democratization.

OUTLOOK FOR SOCIAL WELFARE DEVELOPMENT

Although the history of social welfare development is a brief one in Hong Kong, the above analysis indicates that even within the past half a century since the end of World War II, different ideologies have exerted their influence in different periods. These varying welfare ideologies have also produced very different impacts and they must be considered in any discussion about the future of social welfare development in Hong Kong. The identified legacies so far produced by these welfare ideologies can be summarized as follows:

1. The continuing important position occupied by non-governmental organizations in social welfare means that the making of relevant policies is not entirely left in the hands of the government; the non-governmental sector also plays a decisive role as it is often the non-governmental agencies which are actually operating the services.

2. The ideas of social justice and equality have greatly enlarged the role of the social workers. As fighters for a just and equal society, social workers are now expected to put pressure on the government not just on matters within the narrow confines of social welfare, but on all issues, whether political, economic or social in nature, which have bearings on the promotion of a fair and just society. Compared with the role of their counterparts in other countries, social workers in Hong Kong have obviously a much greater influence on society and their involvement in public issues is also unrivalled.

3. The ideas of democratic participation and citizen rights in social welfare, as advocated by social workers, have now been translated into the goals of nearly all of the newly formed political parties. The progress of social welfare is hence closely linked with the pace of democratization, and achievements in one is now dependent on those of the other.

As Hong Kong enters into a transition period, it would be difficult to say for sure what lies ahead for social welfare. So far as the social and economic factors affecting the demand for social welfare are concerned, they have already been clearly analysed in the 1991 White Paper on social welfare, which included a further ageing of the population, more marriage breakdowns, a continuing disintegration of the traditional support networks, and a general improvement in the living standard of the people. Hence, there will be an increasing need for social welfare services to support the elderly and to strengthen the family. However, as for the welfare ideologies, what have been stated in the 1991 White Paper differed little from those adopted by the government in the previous three White

Papers on social welfare.[15] In this respect, the Basic Law of the future Hong Kong SAR also fails to offer much help as what is emphasized there consists of no more than a continuation of the existing system. Article 145 of the Basic Law states that:

> On the basis of the previous social welfare system, the Government of the Hong Kong Special Administrative Region shall, on its own, formulate policies on the development and improvement of this system in the light of the economic conditions and social needs.

What one can learn from the Basic Law about the future development of social welfare is that it must be based on some practical considerations, like the need of the people and the financial capabilities of the SAR government, rather than on any abstract ideological ground.

In the paper which I presented at the 1985 Conference on the future of Hong Kong, I also examined the possibility for Hong Kong to become a "welfare state." I perceived at that time that the inclination of social workers towards social justice and equality would ultimately lead them to demand the introduction of a social welfare system akin to that of "welfare states." But my analysis in that paper was that, while financially and administratively Hong Kong was capable of adopting the "welfare state" model, ideologically it was unacceptable as the people were on the whole unprepared for having their needs met collectively. As the spirit of collectivism was yet to be accepted, I concluded in 1985 that there would be little chance for Hong Kong to become a "welfare state."

Have the people in Hong Kong forsaken their individualistic attitude now and become more ready for the collective approach? So far, there is little evidence to support an answer in one way or the other. In a "social development indicators" survey conducted in 1988, the researchers found that "52.7% of our respondents thought that welfare should only be for the very needy while 47.3% thought that it should be as a matter of right."[16] They further found that

> 40.3% of our respondents thought that government and employers should share the welfare responsibility equally, while 31.2% thought that welfare should be the sole responsibility of the employers. Only 16.6% thought that welfare should be wholly the responsibility of the government.[17]

A repetition of the survey in 1990 found that

> a substantial majority of respondents (44 per cent, N = 400) thought that the

welfare service system should go to the most needy while a significant percentage indicated that welfare should be a citizen's basic right (34 per cent).
Only a very small percentage thought that welfare should be charity (3.5 per
cent).[18]

The researchers thus concluded that "Our findings confirmed that
while the prevailing climate for welfare was still very much residual, there
is a growing number within the society who relates welfare to citizens'
rights and state responsibility."[19]

Tam and Yeung also made the similar observation in their study on the
attitude of the people in Hong Kong towards social welfare that "The
research findings indicate that the community as a whole is not as politically alienated nor as family-oriented as in the past, but is more appre-
ciative of individual rights and more receptive to collectivist welfare."[20]
They thus concluded that their findings might be "indicative of a general
support for a reluctant collectivist approach to social welfare in which
social welfare is seen as a shared responsibility of the government, the
family and the individuals themselves."[21]

There is no doubt that people in Hong Kong are increasingly looking to
the government as the provider of social welfare.[22] While the Hong Kong
government, both before and after 1997, must assume a greater responsibility in providing social welfare, it does not necessarily imply that a
system that aims at achieving social justice and equality is the wish of the
people. It means only that more and more of the people will perceive the
enjoyment of social welfare services as their entitlement. In other words,
the future development of social welfare will not merely be dependent, as in
the past, upon the demand for such services and the financial affordability
of the government, but also on such concepts as social justice and citizens
rights, which the "pressure groups" have advocated since the mid-1970s.

Article 39 of the Basic Law states that:

> ... the provisions of the International Covenant on Economic, Social and
> Cultural Rights, and the international labour conventions as applied to Hong
> Kong shall remain in force and shall be implemented through the laws of the
> Hong Kong Special Administrative Region.

Article 36 of the Basic Law also states that:

> Hong Kong residents shall have the right to social welfare in accordance with
> law. The welfare benefits and retirement security of the labour force shall be
> protected by law.

While the idea that residents of the Hong Kong SAR "shall have the right to social welfare" may not bestow upon the people entitlements to particular services, it has at least sanctioned the government's obligation to protect the welfare of its people. The questions one has to answer now are what form such protection should take and the extent to which the government should assume its responsibility. In this regard, one might take the retirement security of the labour force as an example for discussion. The government proposed the introduction of an Old Age Pension Scheme for Hong Kong in July 1994.[23] As the Basic Law states that workers shall be entitled to retirement security, the necessity of such a scheme is never a matter for dispute between the Chinese and British governments. What appears to be the disagreement is whether or not the proposal is the most appropriate arrangement that may be acceptable to the SAR government.

The time has certainly passed for social welfare to be regarded as mere charity, nor as benevolent acts of the government. Tam and Yeung suggested in their study that what would be most suitable for Hong Kong might be a form of reluctant collectivist approach which recognizes, on the one hand, the responsibility of the government, while not doing away with, on the other, the contribution of the family and the market. It should be remembered that unlike "welfare states" in the West, the welfare role of the government in Hong Kong has never been excessive, with the expenditures on social welfare normally representing about 1% of the gross domestic product, or 6% of the total government expenditure. And with this limited amount, the government has always ensured, as mentioned above, that services are provided with the cooperation of the non-governmental sector. In other words, "privatization" of social welfare services has long been a standing practice in Hong Kong, both in terms of financing and management. And this will continue after 1997 as Article 144 of the Basic Law states:

> The Government of the Hong Kong Special Administrative Region shall maintain the policy previously practised in Hong Kong in respect of subventions for non-governmental organizations in fields such as ... social welfare and social work.

There should not, therefore, be any worry or prospect that the reluctant collectivist role so far adopted by the Hong Kong government in social welfare will change after 1997.

On the other hand, while the trend is set for more and more people in

Hong Kong to regard the enjoyment of social welfare as their right and to ask for greater participation in the making of policies on these services, there is no indication that a social welfare system which lays the burden entirely on the government will develop in Hong Kong. It is stated in the Basic Law (Article 107) that:

> The Hong Kong Special Administrative Region shall follow the principle of keeping expenditure within the limits of revenues in drawing up its budget, and strive to achieve a fiscal balance, avoid deficits and keep the budget commensurate with the growth rate of its gross domestic product.

This principle will apply to the development of social welfare and it means the future SAR government of Hong Kong must retain the same kind of welfare policy as presently adopted by the British Colonial Administration. The increasing demand for democratic participation and the enlargement of citizen rights have no doubt changed very much the attitude of the people towards social welfare, but as long as the above principle is faithfully kept, there appears to be little likelihood for radical changes to occur. One can even predict, in accordance with the stipulations of the Basic Law, that social welfare in Hong Kong will remain largely residual in nature, with the government confining its help to people who, for one reason or the other, cannot have their needs satisfied through the family or the market. One should also not be misled by the increasing importance given to social welfare in recent years as it is more a result of the diminishing functions of the traditional support networks than of the rising demand for social justice and equality.

What one can conclude from the above discussion is that social welfare development in Hong Kong has never lacked an ideological basis — whether that basis is perceived to be an archaic one grounded on charity and benevolence, or a progressive one based on social justice and equality. While welfare ideologies have exerted great impacts on the way in which the common people have perceived social welfare, they have altered little the objectives to be achieved. Social welfare in Hong Kong remains until today mainly as attempts to care for the weaker members in society. What has changed is that this caring responsibility no longer falls entirely, as in the past, on family members, with the help of some charitable organizations, but is now shared with the government.

The last question which needs to be asked is whether the above conclusions will be changed as political parties in Hong Kong increased their influence. This may be difficult to predict as political parties are not perceived to have a role to play in the Basic Law, and their continuance after 1997 is therefore in doubt. Furthermore, as political parties are in their embryo in Hong Kong, they have yet to make clear their stands on social welfare. But as long as the government in Hong Kong remains an executive-led one, political parties will have little power to initiate or to change policies enacted by the government. The future for political parties to make an influence on social welfare looks, therefore, rather pessimistic and one would even question the relevance of their welfare ideologies since political parties would never have a chance to govern and hence the opportunity to put them into practice. However, as discussed above, the ideologies of the people, even if they do not have a direct impact on the kind of welfare policies implemented, do often create an environment which ultimately leads to change. The fact that the Hong Kong government is now more prepared to take up a greater responsibility in looking after the welfare of its people is, no doubt, a result of the change of the perception of the people regarding the government's welfare role. Hence, the role of the political parties should not only be assessed according to the extent to which they are able to influence the actual formulation and implementation of social welfare policies, but rather their impact on the ideologies of the people. Furthermore, it should be remembered that the social welfare system in Hong Kong has already been firmly established as one of the most important institutions; it is no longer there just to care for the weaker members, but also to help build a stable and fair society. Perceived in this way, and despite all the restrictions laid down in the Basic Law, it appears that social welfare will still have much room for further development, as it has done in the past. And the course for such future development, as Hong Kong transforms from a British colony to an SAR of the People's Republic of China, will again depend on the role it is perceived to perform.

NOTES

1. Cecilia Chan, "Social Welfare," in *The Other Hong Kong Report 1993*, edited by Choi Po-king and Ho Lok-sang (Hong Kong: The Chinese University Press, 1993), pp. 237–63.
2. Nelson W. S. Chow, "Welfare Development in Hong Kong — The Politics of Social Choice," in *Hong Kong and 1997: Strategies for the Future*, edited by

Y. C. Yao, *et al.* (Hong Kong: Centre of Asian Studies, The University of Hong Kong, 1986), pp. 475–91.

3. Nelson W. S. Chow, "Social Welfare Development in Hong Kong — An Ideological Appraisal," in *25 Years of Social and Economic Development in Hong Kong*, edited by Benjamin K. P. Leung and Teresa Y. C. Wong (Hong Kong: Centre of Asian Studies, The University of Hong Kong, 1994), pp. 321–35.

4. Ambrose Y. C. King, "Administrative Absorption of Politics in Hong Kong, Emphasis on the Grassroots Level," *Asian Survey*, Vol. 15, No. 5 (May 1975), pp. 422–39.

5. Hong Kong Government, *A White Paper on Aims and Policy for Social Welfare in Hong Kong* (Hong Kong: Government Printer, 1965), p. 8.

6. Ibid., p. 6.

7. Vic George, and Paul Wilding, *Ideology and Social Welfare* (London: Routledge and Kegan Paul, 1976).

8. Ibid., p. 64.

9. See Note 2, pp. 475–91.

10. Joe C. B. Leung, "Problems and Changes in Community Politics," in *Social Issues in Hong Kong*, edited by Benjamin K. P. Leung (Hong Kong: Oxford University Press, 1990), pp. 43–66.

11. Lau Siu-kai, "The 1985 District Board Election in Hong Kong, the Limits of Political Mobilization in a Dependent Polity," *Occasional Paper No. 8* (Hong Kong: Centre for Hong Kong Studies, The Chinese University of Hong Kong, 1985).

12. Lau Siu-kai, and Kuan Hsin-chi, *The Ethos of the Hong Kong Chinese* (Hong Kong: The Chinese University Press. 1988).

13. Lau Siu-kai, Lee Ming-kwan, Wan Po-san, and Wong Siu-lun (eds.), *Indicators of Social Development: Hong Kong 1988* (Hong Kong: Hong Kong Institute of Asia-Pacific Studies, The Chinese University of Hong Kong, 1991).

14. Secretary for Education and Manpower, *A Consultation Paper on a Community-wide Retirement Protection System* (Hong Kong: Government Printer, 1992).

15. Hong Kong Government, *A White Paper on Social Welfare into the 1990s and Beyond* (Hong Kong: Government Printer, 1991).

16. See Note 13, p. 77.

17. See Note 13, p. 80.

18. Lau Siu-kai, Lee Ming-kwan, Wan Po-san, and Wong Siu-lun (eds.) *Indicators of Social Development: Hong Kong 1990* (Hong Kong: Hong Kong Institute of Asia-Pacific Studies, The Chinese University of Hong Kong, 1993), p. 73.

19. Ibid., pp. 71–72.
20. Tony S. K. Tam, and Yeung Sum, "Community Perception of Social Welfare and Its Relations to Familism, Political Alienation, and Individual Rights: The Case of Hong Kong," *International Social Work*, Vol. 37 (1994), pp. 47–60.
21. Ibid.
22. Nelson W. S. Chow, "Social Welfare," in *The Other Hong Kong Report 1990*, edited by Richard Y. C. Wong and Joseph Y. S. Cheng (Hong Kong: The Chinese University Press, 1990), pp. 429–44.
23. Secretary for Education and Manpower, *A Consultation Paper on the Government's Proposals for an Old Age Pension Scheme* (Hong Kong: Government Printer, 1994).

18

Law and Order: Transition, Uncertainties and Vacuums?

John D. Ho

On 1 July 1997, police badges and insignia will be replaced. The Special Administrative Region (SAR) of Hong Kong, under Chinese sovereignty, will come into existence and the Basic Law will come into operation under the principle of "one country, two systems." That day is about 800 days away, as countdown clocks specially made for the purpose keep reminding the world. However, not much else can be said with equal certainty, for this is uncharted territory in Hong Kong's development. With such a fundamental change, it would have been hard to ponder all the complexities of the transition even if the Joint Liaison Group (JLG) had been able to work out the necessary details for the transfer of power. But as a result of the rift between the British and Chinese governments over the pace of democratization, the quest for "convergence" and the "through train" is no longer viable. Instead of the JLG, it is now necessary to look to pronouncements of the Preliminary Working Committee (PWC), whose existence is provided for neither by the Joint Declaration nor the Basic Law, for a glimpse into the future, and the PWC does not always speak with one voice.

For a century and a half, China and Hong Kong have developed along different lines economically, politically, legally and culturally. They have different views with regard to law and order. In Hong Kong, it is built on the concept of the rule of law, the adversarial system, due process and the presumption of innocence. In China, law is an instrument of the state, and law and order is to a large extent the manifestation of state authority and control. Whether law and order in Hong Kong will maintain its own identity separate from that of the Mainland depends on the extent to which the principle of "one country, two systems" is implemented successfully.

Not all the changes and uncertainties stem from the reversion of sovereignty alone. China's adoption of a "market economy with Chinese characteristics" means the continuation of its open door policy and economic liberalization. As a result, the two systems — those of Hong Kong and China — have been undergoing an integration on an economic level, even ahead of political reintegration. The impending reversion of sovereignty only accelerates and deepens the economic integration of the two systems, as one country.

It is the interaction of the two opposite forces — one coming from political and economic integration, and the other from the historical differences and the attempt to maintain the systems as two — that will shape the transition of Hong Kong from colony to SAR.

In this chapter, we focus on the crimes that may be on the increase in the transition: corruption, triad activities, and cross-border crimes such as drug crimes, smuggling and illegal immigration. We discuss the challenges faced by the institutional framework, in particular the judicial system and the police. We also discuss cooperation with China, which will undoubtedly have to be strengthened, and the corresponding issue of jurisdiction, which will attract more attention as political reintegration with China approaches. Finally, we examine the legal framework and the tug of war between the concern for civil liberties and the wish to strengthen the powers of the state.

CRIMES ON THE INCREASE

❏ *Corruption*

To put things in perspective, the latest police statistics show that the overall crime rate in Hong Kong is only one-eighth that of Washington, DC, one-seventh that of London, and half that of Tokyo. But few people in Hong Kong will disagree that the most worrisome crime on the economic front is corruption. While no violence may be used, it erodes the "level playing field" that is vital for the success of a capitalist market economy, and it undermines law and order by perverting the administration of justice.

While statistics show many crimes decreasing, corruption is one category of crime that is showing a dramatic increase. In 1993, reported cases of all types of corruption jumped by 44% over 1992, while reports of business corruption rose by 52%. And the upward trend is intact. Statistics available for 1994 show another 11% rise in reports on corruption until October, with 3,022 cases, compared with 2,731 in the same period the year before. In particular, in the private sector, the statistic was highest with 1,543 cases in the first 10 months of 1994, compared with 1,472 in the same period of 1993.

One reason is the undesirable side-effect of the economic integration of Hong Kong and the Mainland: increasingly, corruption involves people doing business with China. It is widely recognized that corruption on the Mainland is rampant. Many government bodies in China have gone into business, creating an unhealthy conflict of roles and mixture of power and money. Business is often done with kickbacks to officials. Although some "progressive" cities like Shenzhen, Guangzhou and Hainan have set up their own anti-graft machines, unlike Hong Kong's Independent Commission Against Corruption (ICAC), they are not independent, but under Party control. Hong Kong business people are said to pick up bad habits from the Mainland and bring them back. Surveys by the ICAC also suggest that the 1997 countdown is nourishing the so-called "fast-buck syndrome," i.e. people attempting to make as much money and as quickly as possible by any means. While there is a global trend for multi-national corporations to develop codes of conduct to cover ethical and legal problems in regard to offering and accepting advantages, insider trade, conflicts of interest and the use of privileged information, Hong Kong companies are reluctant to do so for fear that they might be disadvantaged in the competitive China environment if they had such a code.

Neither is the public sector immune to the allure of "opportunities" in China. There are reports of Hong Kong civil servants getting involved in corruption, running karaoke bars and providing vice services on the Mainland, as well as taking part in smuggling and illegal immigration, in cooperation with officials there.

Many people believe the "China factor" will grow more even more pronounced after 1997. Some 62% of respondents to a 1994 ICAC poll expected corruption to worsen after the reversion of sovereignty, up from 37% a year earlier. This suggests people are uncertain whether the SAR government will have the will and ability to fight corruption, even though the establishment in the SAR of a Commission Against Corruption which "shall function independently and be accountable to the Chief Executive" is provided for in Article 57 of the Basic Law.

❏ *Triad Activities*

Another major law and order concern is triad activities. Since the Communist revolution of 1949 on the Mainland, Hong Kong has been the world headquarters of triad societies. Unlike the Mafia, these societies are loosely knit — so much so that even their leaders may not know how many members they have at any one time. The Hong Kong police have identified more than fifty different triad societies. Many of these societies trace their roots back to secret and nationalistic societies that helped to overthrow the Qing Dynasty. It has been estimated that they pull in $200 billion a year from heroin-trafficking, smuggling of illegal immigrants, prostitution and pornography, extortion and protection-racketeering, loan-sharking and debt collection, and white-collar crime. Triad extortion has become so institutionalized in many sectors of Hong Kong society that some victims treat the payment of protection money as a regular business overhead and are reluctant to report the activity to the police. While most crimes in Hong Kong are on the decline, triad-related extortion, like corruption, is on the increase.

Like other sectors of society, the triads face uncertainty brought by the transfer of sovereignty in 1997, and they are intent on making as much money as possible before that time. But they are also hedging their bets. There are reports that they have befriended a network of Chinese provincial officials and police, which is making it increasingly easy for them to do business on the Mainland. When China's Minister of Public Security Tao Siju was reported as saying that China was happy to unite with triads provided they were patriotic and concerned with the stability and prosperity of Hong Kong, and that while China "vehemently opposed any of these organizations engaging in crimes such as murder, arson and looting,... one must also see some members or some organizations have renounced past wrongdoings and started to do good things," there was an outcry of concern in the community that triads might gain legitimate status in the SAR. A Chinese spokesman subsequently insisted that Tao was misunderstood. But that does not seem to have calmed the fears about the growing influence of triads in Hong Kong and China.

It is unlikely that the triads will forsake their base in Hong Kong after the establishment of the SAR unless they are forced to do so. Meanwhile, as tens of thousands of people emigrate from Hong Kong to other continents, the triads have followed, laying the foundation for a sophisticated intercontinental network of criminal activities and turning the "crisis" of 1997 into a golden opportunity.

❏ *Drug Crimes, Smuggling and Illegal Immigration*

Drug-related crimes are another category that is on the rise. The number of drug crime cases, including manufacturing, trafficking and possession of dangerous drugs, jumped 31.7% to 4,618 in 1994. At the same time, the number of people under the age of 21 arrested for these crimes increased 34.1% to 3,177.

The main source of heroin for Hong Kong is the Golden Triangle. To avoid police detection, traffickers take advantage of the huge volume of cross-border traffic between China and Hong Kong and drugs are increasingly smuggled into Hong Kong from Thailand via China rather than directly, as it is impossible for customs authorities to stop and search every commuter.

As a result of the economic liberalization in China, drug crimes there are also on the rise. Potentially, it is a huge and attractive market for drug dealers. Unless effective measures are taken to combat the trend, the China market for drugs will grow. Hong Kong could become a regional as well as international centre for the drug trade, with drugs sent from the Golden Triangle into the international drug market via the so-called "Chinese passage," and then Hong Kong, with its sophisticated transportation, communication and banking facilities, as a transfer post.

With the improvement of standards of living on the Mainland, Hong Kong has also gained importance as a major centre for China-bound smuggling for luxury goods. Speedboats have long been used to smuggle television sets, audio-visual equipment, cigarettes, and other expensive items into the Mainland. Ships and barges have been taking containers stuffed with cars stolen from Hong Kong. Smuggling on land is also on the rise.

While goods are smuggled northwards across the border, illegal immigrants come in the opposite direction. Many illegal immigrants take up jobs as labourers, but others work as prostitutes or take part in crimes, often involving violence and at the hire of local gangs. As Hong Kong has a far wealthier community and more lenient and tolerant legal system, the prevention of these crimes will continue to be a challenge for the SAR after 1997.

THE INSTITUTIONAL FRAMEWORK

❏ *The Judiciary*

A Court of Final Appeal will replace the Privy Council in London as the highest court of appeal in the SAR, as provided by Article 82 of the Basic Law, which says:

> The power of final adjudication of the Hong Kong Special Administrative Region shall be vested in the Court of Final Appeal of the Region, which may as required invite judges from other common law jurisdictions to sit on the Court of Final Appeal.

An agreement on the establishment of the Court of Final Appeal was reached by the JLG in 1991 and the Court was scheduled to be introduced in 1993, but its implementation has hit repeated snags. As a result of its restriction on the number of optional overseas judges to one, it met with intense opposition from the legal profession and its establishment based on the agreement was rejected in an unprecedented Legislative Council (Legco) debate in December 1991, when legislators called for more flexibility to invite foreign judges to sit on the Court.

Although the government now hopes to establish the Court by 1996, the stalemate is unlikely to be resolved any time soon. In December 1994, by a vote of 247 to 14, the Bar Association again refused to accept a bill drafted by the government based on the 1991 agreement. The Bar Council also said the bill was "unduly restrictive" over the criminal jurisdiction of the Court. Under Clause 29 of the bill, leave to appeal for criminal cases shall not be granted unless it be certified "that a point of law of general public importance is involved in the decision and it appears to the Court of Appeal or the High Court that the point is one which ought to be considered by the Court."

On the other hand, the Law Society Council voted to support the bill but an extraordinary general meeting of the Society was called by a group of liberal solicitors to consider the issue. That meeting was called off one hour after it started on the grounds that the meeting room was unable to accommodate the 800 members that showed up. Another meeting called in early 1995 voted to support the government bill. Now the bill will have to be deliberated by the Legco. Meanwhile, the United Nations (UN) has reportedly begun an inquiry into claims that the Legal Department and senior partners in Hong Kong's leading law firms pressured lawyers into supporting the bill, after a complaint was filed with the UN Commission on Human Rights by a Law Society Council member.

When asked whether the Chinese government would guarantee that the judges would remain in place after the hand-over in 1997 if the British side had set up the Court in accordance with the 1991 agreement, the vice-chairman and secretary-general of the PWC, Lu Ping, was quoted as saying:

> ... according to the relevant provisions of the Basic Law, the judges in the Court of Final Appeal, including the chief judge, will be appointed by the Chief Executive after the Chief Executive wins the endorsement of the Legislative Council on the basis of the recommendation of an independent commission. After 1997, the judges in the Court of Final Appeal will be appointed according to such procedures [as] specified by the Basic Law. Therefore, it will be the business of the SAR government to decide how to appoint the judges in the Court of Final Appeal and how to arrange their continuing service after the hand-over ...

The impasse over the establishment of the Court has raised concerns for a "judicial vacuum." While there is no question that the Privy Council will not be the final forum of appeal after the SAR comes into existence, it is anybody's guess whether the Court of Final Appeal will be in place before the transfer of sovereignty, and even if it is, how long it will take the SAR government to appoint judges to sit on the Court after the government comes into existence.

An even more fundamental question is whether there will be enough qualified people to replace retiring judges. Within the next year or two, there will be at least eight retirements from the High Court. Four additional judges will be needed if the Court of Final Appeal is to be set up in 1996. The judiciary's policy commitments have proposed the creation of two more High Court judges. In other words, for the High Court and above, the judiciary will need to recruit a total of 14 new judges. That is a large number considering that the present establishment of the High Court and Court of Appeal judges is only 33. Experienced local barristers are notoriously reluctant to give up their lucrative private practice to join the bench. With the uncertainty surrounding the "through train" for judges, it would be even harder to recruit them to fill the potential vacancies. In the current political environment, it is doubtful whether overseas recruitment will be an acceptable solution. The suggestion by the Law Society that solicitors be permitted to sit on the higher courts has met with resistance from the Bar.

The transition to SAR also dictates a change in the language to be used in court. Even whilst a colony, the problem of language used in court proceedings has often posed difficulties. Recently, a case was adjourned by a judge after finding a juror unable to understand the proceedings conducted in English. Last year a High Court judge had to discharge the jury just as the verdict was being deliberated after jurors asked for explanations in Cantonese. Although Article 9 of the Basic Law allows the use of English in the judiciary of the SAR, it is hard to imagine that English will be permitted to remain the predominant, not to mention the only (as it currently is in the District and higher courts), language. To prepare for the transfer of sovereignty, it is necessary for the judicial system and the legal profession to gear up for the use of Chinese. However, the use of the Chinese language in court proceedings must be allowed time to take root, and that requires corresponding changes in the attitude and training of judges and legal practitioners, as well as the development of an authoritative and adequate Chinese legal vocabulary. The laws of Hong Kong consist largely of the statute law and the English common law, and Article 8 of the Basic Law provides that in the SAR, "... the common law, rules of equity, ordinances, subordinate legislation and customary law shall be maintained ...." Not all existing legislation has been translated into Chinese, and it is impracticable if not impossible to translate all the common law case precedents. Compounding the problem is the current non-existence of authoritative and widely accepted Chinese equivalents to some of the legal principles, concepts and expressions.

Traditionally, judges and lawyers in Hong Kong have been trained in English. Even with the approach of the transfer of sovereignty, that situation has not changed, as most of legal teaching materials are in English. Many judges and lawyers will require intensive retraining before they can conduct court proceedings in Chinese. While it has been observed that the frequency of conducting trials in Chinese in the Magistrates' Courts has increased and junior lawyers are more willing to use Chinese in trials, the difficulties are exacerbated by the fact that only a minority of existing District and Supreme Court judges are Chinese-speaking.

❏ *The Police Force*

The manpower crisis does not exist in the judiciary alone. Like many other government departments, the police force is faced with the possible nightmare of a mass departure of the staff as 1997 approaches, leaving behind a gap or "vacuum" in leadership. While locals are concerned about political changes, expatriates are worried about the impact of localization on them.

Compounding the difficulties of the problem is that its full extent is still unclear, as many people might indicate a willingness to stay, while at the same time still keeping their options open until the last moment to make the choice. A clearer picture will probably not emerge until 1996.

Almost 60% of its 500 most senior staff are expatriates. A large number of senior expatriate police officers belong to the Association of Members of Her Majesty's Overseas Civil Service who will receive lump-sum compensation of about $1 million for the loss of sovereignty protection. They can opt to take the payout and retire early, regardless of their age, before Hong Kong reverts to Chinese rule. In the first five months of the 1994–1995 financial year, the number of early retirees has already exceeded the total number of early departures recorded for the whole of the preceding financial year. Of the remaining 200-odd locals, about 20% will reach the early retirement age of 50 by 1997. Under the government's old pension scheme, officers reaching the age of 50 can effectively retire early without having prior approval, and under the new pension scheme, staff may retire early at the age of 55.

RELATIONS WITH CHINA: COOPERATION AND JURISDICTION

The integration of Hong Kong with the Mainland means it is impossible for either China or Hong Kong to deal with the law and order problems without the help of the other. The ICAC has forged important working links with Mainland anti-corruption bodies, and a mutual assistance agreement has been established for several years, allowing both Hong Kong and China to gather evidence within the other's borders under supervision. This agreement does not give the ICAC the right to act against Hong Kong residents suspected of corruption in China, nor does it enable Chinese authorities to prosecute Mainland officials suspected of corruption in Hong Kong.

The sensitive issue of jurisdiction is inevitable in the context of transition to SAR and it was brought under the spotlight by remarks of the deputy procurator general of the Supreme People's Procurate, Liang Guoqing, that China would cooperate with the ICAC and that corrupt activities involving

Chinese enterprises were to be prosecuted and dealt with by China. In response, the ICAC insisted that China had no jurisdiction to take action against those involved in corruption in Hong Kong, although Chinese authorities were fully entitled to impose disciplinary action for illegal conduct by employees of Chinese enterprises. Liang's statement was later described as being misunderstood.

Notwithstanding the ICAC's firm position on jurisdiction for the time being, whether the line demarcating jurisdiction will remain sharp and clear when Hong Kong becomes "one country" with China remains to be seen. Meanwhile, given the economic integration between China and Hong Kong, the pressure will always exist to strengthen the cooperation with Mainland authorities against corruption. Recently, the ICAC has begun passing some of its investigations directly to Chinese authorities in cases where information is obtained in Hong Kong about corruption occurring solely on the Mainland.

Like the ICAC, the police, with an establishment of nearly 30,000 in a population of more than six million, must be prepared to cooperate with Chinese authorities in intelligence, investigation, anti-triad and drug-trafficking exercises, and in action against commercial crimes to combat an increasing trend in cross-border crime. Its gigantic immediate neighbour, the province of Guangdong, has only about 70,000 officers policing 60 million people and a 10 million-strong "floating" population, and is experiencing a deterioration in social order as a result of the economic transformation, declining morality, an increasing mobile population, and a failure to institute an effective system to maintain law and order. Last year, the province witnessed at least a 9% increase of crime.

In 1997, the SAR will join Beijing's National Central Bureau as a subsidiary partner and come under policy guidance of China instead of belonging to Interpol as a separate entity. In the mean time, to facilitate liaison with the Mainland police, two Mainland Interpol officers have already been stationed in Hong Kong.

A growing number of criminals use Hong Kong as a safe haven after they had committed crime on the Mainland. Extradition of these suspects is difficult because China and Hong Kong do not have the same legal system and there is no extradition agreement. While China's legal code allows the government to prosecute criminals for crimes committed outside the country, Mainland criminals who flee to Hong Kong can often escape punishment because the Hong Kong judiciary does not have jurisdiction over crimes committed in China. The need to speed up negotiation with Hong Kong on an extradition agreement in order to plug the legal loophole is apparent.

But human rights activists have warned that an extradition accord with China might contradict the principle of "one country, two systems" and could be abused by Beijing in demanding the return of political dissidents who have sought refuge in Hong Kong.

Upon his return from a recent official trip to China with the Police Commissioner Eddie Hui Ki-on, the Director of Criminal Investigations, Tsang Yam-pui, spoke enthusiastically of greater sharing of information, and said more Mainland police, under strict controls, could be allowed to come to Hong Kong to conduct investigations. He was also keen to see a maintenance of the operational status quo, stressing the imperative of autonomy.

He was quoted as saying:

> It needs to be a necessary procedure with worthwhile conditions so the people of Hong Kong know that the standards of proof — and the sense of fair play — will continue,... It would be very difficult to operate without such procedures. We also hope the rule of law stays. We have been given assurances many times that the Royal Hong Kong Police Force will be autonomous in all that we will be doing.... I don't see things changing for the worse in cooperation and liaison. It will only get better.

The need for an extradition agreement with China and the issue of police autonomy may become moot after the reversion of sovereignty, if Macau's current relationship with China is an indication for Hong Kong's future. While Macau's reversion to Chinese rule will not occur until two years after Hong Kong's reversion, its government prides itself with the cooperative and harmonious relationship with China. Portugal, which still administers Macau, has abolished capital punishment since the nineteenth century. During Portuguese Prime Minister Anibal Cavaco Silva's visit to China, Macau's Superior Court reversed its own decision and agreed to extradite two ethnic Chinese to the Mainland, where they were wanted for murder and fraud, and could face the death penalty. The extradition request was granted despite a Portuguese statute forbidding extradition if the person is likely to face the death penalty and the absence of an extradition treaty between China and Portugal. A guarantee that the two men would not face the death penalty if convicted of their crimes in China was allegedly given from Xinhua News Agency, but it was denied by a Xinhua vice-director the next day.

In another case, a Chinese-born Australian citizen and Hong Kong resident was taken from a Macau hotel by the Macau judiciary police, driven to the border with Zhuhai and handed over to the Chinese authorities. The case seems to have originally stemmed from a dispute over whether his company had improperly acquired a stake in a Mainland-listed firm. Although both a Guangdong appellate court and the Hong Kong Supreme Court had already ruled in his favour, the dispute was not put to rest. Imprisoned in Shenzhen without being charged, he accused the judiciary police of collaborating with Chinese police and forcing him to sign a document in Portuguese which he could not read. The judiciary police insisted that he was not arrested, but instead went to China voluntarily, although in the presence of the judiciary police, saying his case would be more easily solved there. The judiciary police also maintained that since he was not arrested, an attorney was not required, and did not inform the Legal Department until a month later.

THE LEGAL FRAMEWORK

❏ *The Bill of Rights*

As 1997 draws near, there seems to be a corresponding increase in concern for the preservation of human rights and civil liberties. The legal framework is being shaped to a large extent by the Bill of Rights Ordinance, which came into operation on 8 June 1991. It contains 22 articles taken almost verbatim from the International Covenant on Civil and Political Rights (ICCPR). An amendment to the Letters Patent had been made to ensure that no future legislature which derived its competence from the Letters Patent could validly enact any law inconsistent with the ICCPR as applied to Hong Kong. This amendment also came into effect on 8 June 1991.

According to both the Joint Declaration and the Basic Law, the ICCPR as applied to Hong Kong will remain in force after 1997.

Under the Bill of Rights Ordinance, any pre-existing legislation on 8 June 1991 must be construed, so far as its language permits, consistently with the Bill of Rights, and if it cannot be so construed, be repealed to the extent of inconsistency.

The first Court of Appeal decision on the Bill of Rights struck down some statutory presumptions which reversed the onus of proof in the Dangerous Drugs Ordinance. Since then many reverse onus presumptions have been challenged with varying degrees of success.

The Bill of Rights Ordinance has caused some governmental departments, including the ICAC and the police, to conduct internal reviews of their practices, resulting in varying degrees of change in administrative practice or internal rules. Prosecutors no longer rely on Section 25 of the Prevention of Bribery Ordinance (POBO) for fear that it would contravene the Bill of Rights. Under this Section, when it is proved that the accused in certain proceedings gave or accepted an advantage, the advantage shall be presumed to have been given and accepted as inducement or reward as alleged in the particulars of the offence unless the contrary is proved.

Another powerful Section, 10(1)(a) of POBO, previously used by the ICAC to prosecute former government lawyer Warwick Reid, was held void by a District Court judge in a recent case against a retired Lands Department surveyor and the charge was quashed, again on the grounds that the Section contravened the Bill of Rights, as it placed upon defendants the burden of proving their own innocence. Under that Section, a civil servant or a former civil servant shall be guilty of an offence if he maintains a standard of living above that which is commensurate with his present or past official emoluments, unless he gives a satisfactory explanation to the court as to how he was able to maintain such a standard of living. This Section is regarded by the ICAC as a vital weapon in its armoury as it makes it possible to prosecute civil servants suspected of corruption when it is impossible to prove that they have received specific bribes.

The District Court's decision was overturned by the Court of Appeal, and Section 10(1)(a) was reinstated. Had that not happened, the government would undoubtedly have taken its fight all the way to the highest court, be it the Privy Council or the yet-to-be-established Court of Final Appeal.

The conflict between the Bill of Rights and reverse onus presumptions stems from the difficult balance that must be struck between safeguarding the interests of the accused against false charges and the public interest in the conviction of the guilty and avoidance of unmerited acquittals. The Court of Appeal found Section 10(1)(a) dictated by necessity and went no further than necessary. If the Section was not resurrected on appeal in the current judicial system, it would find a second chance when the SAR comes into being. The PWC, widely regarded as a shadow government and predecessor of the Preparatory Committee, views the Bill of Rights Ordinance with disapproval. Its legal subgroup has been highly critical of the human rights law, saying it would undermine the government's power to rule and possibly cause social chaos. The legal subgroup has also called for the Societies Ordinance and Public Order Ordinance, which have been recently liberalized to conform with the Bill of Rights, to be restored to their original form after 1997. It is suspicious that such amendments are part of a British conspiracy to undermine Hong Kong's current system by unilaterally liberalizing the laws before the transfer of sovereignty. The subgroup has said that after the hand-over of sovereignty, the Bill of Rights should lose its power to override other laws. Some members have also called for the restoration of the death penalty.

❑ *The Organized and Serious Crimes Ordinance*

Despite the anxiety of the PWC, not all changes in the law restrict the powers of the government in the enforcement of law and order. In October 1994, the Organized and Serious Crimes Bill was passed by the Legco, although it did take two years to do so.

The Ordinance strengthens the powers of the police and Customs and Excise officers to investigate organized crime and triads. In an investigation of an "organized crime," the High Court may make an order compelling a person having relevant information to the investigation to attend an interview with an authorized officer. The person may also be compelled to bring to the interview records, documents or objects that may be relevant to the investigation and to answer questions about the items. Although the person may not be required to furnish any information or produce any material relating to items subject to legal privilege, he is not excused from furnishing information or producing any material on the basis of self-incrimination. If he refuses to comply or willingly misleads the authorities, he will face jail terms. His answers, however, may not be used against him as evidence in a subsequent trial other than to impeach his credibility and in proceedings in relation to the giving of a false statement.

The Ordinance therefore provides a powerful weapon to obtain information about organized crime from persons who may have knowledge about the offences under investigation, and to break through the "wall of silence" that frequently prevents investigators from effectively and successfully investigating organized crime. While arrests of triad foot-soldiers have been common, very few triad leaders have been arrested and successfully prosecuted because of the "wall of silence." To minimize disincentive in giving information, a coordinated witness protection system will be set up.

The Ordinance gives the High Court and District Court jurisdiction to confiscate proceeds from serious crimes. It also enables the High Court and District Court to receive information about the offender and the offence in order to impose greater sentences upon persons convicted of an offence amounting to an organized crime, triad-related offence, or other serious offences.

It also creates an offence of money-laundering in relation to indictable offences.

One major reason for the delay in the passage of the bill was the fear that it may be manipulated for the persecution of political activists. As 1997 approaches, there is increasing concern for possible abuse of government powers in breach of rights to privacy, the liberty and security of person, and a fair trial.

❑ *A "Legal Vacuum" and a "Haven for Criminals"?*

The growth of Hong Kong as a financial centre means it is also becoming an important policing centre, requiring more cooperation and liaison with other countries, including the signing and maintenance of extradition arrangements.

Currently, Hong Kong has about 90 extradition agreements. But these agreements are among a range of international treaties and agreements covering vital international relations ranging from civil aviation to international arbitration that will lapse when sovereignty is transferred in 1997, unless they are renewed with the blessing of China. Only four treaties, with the Netherlands, Australia, Canada and Malaysia, now exist that would straddle 1997.

A government lawyer has warned that if the extradition treaties are not in force in 1997, there will be a gap in the law — a "legal vacuum," and the SAR will not be able to return foreign criminals to where they come from. Similarly, the chairman of the Legco's legal affairs panel, independent legislator Simon Ip Sik-on, has warned that Hong Kong could become a "haven for criminals" if not enough extradition treaties were signed with other countries. Chinese officials, however, do not seem to share the urgency. One has accused the British side of being alarmist.

CONCLUSION

The transition of Hong Kong as colony to SAR witnesses the interplay between the two opposing forces inherent in the concept of "one country, two systems." The two systems are recognized to be different, and they will be allowed to stay different for 50 years. Yet they will become one country, and no longer can one operate without considering implications for the other.

With regard to law and order, the conflict over the appropriate balance between civil liberties and state power will manifest itself time and again. There are many in Hong Kong who worry about losing the liberties and freedoms they have enjoyed, so much so that they are willing to take measures to preserve them at the expense of sacrificing some state power. On the other hand, there is fear on the part of the Mainland government that Hong Kong might become a "Trojan horse" and that it will become a beachhead for subversion of the Communist regime. Conspiracy theories abound, and every attempt at liberalizing law and order measures to preserve civil liberties is viewed with suspicion and mistrust.

Yet in the final analysis China really holds all the cards. Article 23 of the Basic Law mandates the enactment of laws by the SAR

> to prohibit any act of treason, secession, sedition, subversion against the Central People's Government, or theft of state secrets, to prohibit foreign political organizations or bodies from conducting political activities in the [Special Administrative] Region, and to prohibit political organizations or bodies of the Region from establishing ties with foreign political organizations or bodies.

These laws will no doubt be given top priority in the legislative agenda of the SAR.

The Basic Law provides that the Chief Executive shall be accountable to the Central People's Government. The People's Liberation Army will be stationed in the SAR.

Under Article 18 of the Basic Law, in the event of social turmoil which endangers national unity or security and is beyond the control of the SAR government, the Standing Committee of the National People's Congress may declare a state of emergency and the Central People's Government may issue an order applying the relevant national laws in the SAR. Apparently with this Article in mind, Lu Ping was quoted as saying:

> According to the Basic Law, if Hong Kong is afflicted by a serious natural disaster or is plagued by social turmoil beyond the control of the SAR government, at the request of the SAR government and with the approval of the central government, the armed forces stationed in Hong Kong can help maintain law and order and participate in rescue action. This should be first requested by Hong Kong, and the troops stationed in Hong Kong will not take the initiative to act. As for who is to make the request, what formalities are to be gone through, who is to give approval, and in what situations the troops are to be called in, this will be considered by the PWC social and security affairs group as a major subject in the second half of [1995], and the group will work out its proposals.

There is no doubt that China has the authority and power to maintain law and order in the SAR. But that authority and power must be exercised with wisdom and restraint if Hong Kong is to be maintained as a thriving and efficient international business centre and allowed to play its role in the economic development of the motherland. The extent to which the SAR will continue to enjoy the success it has achieved as a colony will be testimony to the success of the principle of "one country, two systems." From a broader perspective, the success of the SAR will also have fundamental implications for the future reunification with Taiwan.

19

Telecommunications

John Ure

In the world of modern digital telecommunications, high speeds of exchange switching and transmission along bundles of hair-thick optical fibres, and the compression of microwave signals from base-stations and satellites, have replaced thick cables and wide spectrums of high-frequency radio-waves. This is important because it drives up the volumes of traffic the network can carry, and drives down the unit costs, and sometimes the absolute costs, of carrying it.

At the heart of these changes to the economics of telecommunications lies the revolution in micro-electronics, which has done much more than to reduce the real cost of networks. It has added intelligence to the network. Initially the intelligence was software built into the switch as firmware, but today the intelligence can be located at any nodal point in a network, including at the end-user terminal, such as a personal computer or telephone handset. The potential of this is to transform networks into as many sub-nets as there are terminals, and the commercial system of telecommunication operators into a set of subsets, each catering to its own particular market segment. This, it must be stressed, is the potential, more realizable in some markets than in others, but the trends are already well apparent worldwide as the traditional monopolies of public utility operators give way to market competition, to bypass of the public network, and to self-provisioning among different categories of users.[1]

HONG KONG TELECOMMUNICATIONS IN TRANSITION

Hong Kong took its first steps into this brave new world of telecommunications in the 1980s when customer premises equipment (CPE), paging services and then mobile cellular telephone services were opened to market competition. Downlinking from satellites directly into customer premises, and uplinking to satellites by broadcasters such as STAR TV, were also liberalized, having previously been treated as a part of the exclusive privilege of Hong Kong Telecom International (HKTI). Lobbying for these changes from important commercial interests, including the Hong Kong Telecommunications Users Group, was effective, but this lobbying was given greater poignancy by the fact that Hong Kong is in competition with Singapore to be the region's leading telecommunication hub. Hubbing refers to the use of the territory by overseas organizations as a node to originate, terminate and process voice and data traffic, and through which to transit traffic to other parts of the region. The same consideration in 1995 is allowing international companies based in Hong Kong to use satellite uplinking and downlinking to self-provide their own telecommunication traffic, a bypass of the public network.[2]

All these steps are but a transition stage. On 1 July 1995, the monopoly of the Hong Kong Telephone Company (HKTC) over the basic voice public switched telephone network (PSTN) is replaced by an open market, limited only by the number of new fixed telecommunication network services (FTNS) licences which the regulator, the Director-General of Office of the Telecommunications Authority (OFTA), is prepared to issue. Currently, and in addition to HKTC, that number is three: Hutchison Communication, Wharf Holding's New T&T Hong Kong, and New World Telephone. But even this step is but one into the transition. The technologies driving the potential of telecommunications are reconstructing the relationship between fixed-wire and wireless systems.

Although radio was originally conceived by Marconi as a method of communicating between moving ships to immobile land sites, in past decades radio was used for connecting fixed sites over long distances of land or sea, while wirelines were put in place locally to serve people moving between sites, each site having its own wireline. Today the vision is swinging back to Marconi's view. Personal communications systems (PCS), the next wireless generation of telephones, are designed to assign telephone numbers to people rather than places. Personal communications networks (PCN), a variant of PCS, are designed partly to complement the existing embedded fixed-wire networks, but also partly to substitute for them. The existing generation of digital cellular telephones, and their analogue forerunners, were most definitely designed as complements, although in countries such as China where there is a desperate shortage of a PSTN, they do become substitutes by default. However, cellular phones require to interconnect with the PSTN to carry calls to and from the network, but the PCS and PCN operators in Hong Kong will be given the right to construct their own cable network backbones.

This underscores the point that in the local loop, previously the domain of the wireline, wireless communications will edge their way in. Technologies such as cordless telephones (CT1 for the home, CT2 for the street) are transforming into more sophisticated office networks, such as DECT (the digital European cordless telephone) which replaces the fixed-line PABX (private automatic branch exchange, or office switchboard) serving an office with radio communications inside the building and between the building and the local exchange of PSTN. The distinction between a fixed wireline operator and a wireless operator will cease to be meaningful as the operators of each will need to offer the services of the other. In Hong Kong, OFTA has already stated its intention to abolish the licensing distinction, probably by the end of the decade. Only then will Hong Kong have truly made the transition to the new era of telecommunications.

HONG KONG'S TELECOMMUNICATIONS AND CHINA

Synchronous digital hierarchy (SDH) is a technology for high-speed transmission of data. Data includes everything that can be translated into binary coding, and that includes voice, sound and image. Speed, or b/s (bits per second) is equivalent to traffic volume. In November 1994, China's first SDH network was opened linking Guangzhou, Dongguan, Huizhou, Shenzhen to Hong Kong, with a speed of 2.488 Gb/s. This link supplements an analogue microwave system and two existing optical fibre cables, and instantly upped the equivalent number of voice circuits between Hong Kong and southern China from 12,480 to 22,290.

China's rate of telecommunication development is substantial, close to 20% annual growth in exchange capacity; unfortunately only 60% of that capacity is connected up to subscribers, a problem typical of low-income developing countries. By late 1994, China was reporting an exchange capacity of 48 million circuits, but there were under two subscribers per 100 inhabitants.[3] The national target for year 2000 is 140 million circuits exchange capacity, of which 114 million will be provided by the Provincial Telecommunication Administrations (PTAs), which come under the Ministry of Posts and Telecommunications (MPT). The remaining circuits are those anticipated by the MPT to be provided by other organizations, including the two new entrants given authority by the State Council in 1993 and 1994, the Jitong Corporation and the Liantong (or Unicom — United Communications) Corporation. Teledensity is planned to reach between 30–40 mainlines per 100 inhabitants in the major cities, and 6–8 per 100 countrywide.

In addition, China is building out long-distance optical fibre trunk lines between all major cities, an extensive network of satellites and earth stations to provide nationwide telecommunications and television coverage, microwave coverage for trunking across less populated areas, high-speed digital data networks for the cities and a medium-speed communication network for national data links.[4] Inevitably, these developments are uneven between the thrusting economies of the coastal provinces in the south and east, and the poorer central and western areas. This shows up most starkly in the figures for cellular mobile phones. By the end of 1994, there were probably not less than one million in use in China, 500,000 of them in Guangdong province, which in November 1994 also pioneered China's digital GSM (Group Speciale Mobile) system. Roaming between Hong Kong and Guangdong using the analogue TACS (Total Access Communications System) can now be extended to GSM. Roaming is also extensive between the two territories using pagers.

The year 1994 also saw Guangdong's network exchange capacity overhaul Hong Kong's, but again the connection rate, even in Shenzhen on Hong Kong's border, is less than 60%. Network congestion in Guangdong, as elsewhere in China, reduces the successful call ratio (SCR) to below 60%, and during busy hour often to below 30%. Nevertheless, a direct beneficiary of China's network development has been HKTI. China traffic now accounts for 50% of HKTI's IDD traffic volume and over 30% of IDD revenues. The next closest is U.S. traffic which accounts for 11% of IDD revenue. Over recent years, China–Hong Kong traffic has been growing at an annual rate of around 30%, although the rate fell during 1994, apparently due to a 50% hike in international call charges in China imposed in January and September 1994 for foreign companies and local residents respectively to compensate for the abolition of FEC (Foreign Exchange Certificates) and the cumulative decline in the exchange value of the Renminbi. About 80% of this traffic is between Hong Kong and China's southern province of Guangdong, with most of it terminating in Shenzhen.

The rapid changes taking place in the telecommunications sector in China and Hong Kong in many ways complement each other. For example, in both cases policy towards monopoly and competition has shifted decisively in favour of the latter. However, for China, telecommunications remains an issue hovering between being a security concern on the one hand, that is as a source of state information and control, and on the other being an industry which is simultaneously an essential infrastructure, a dynamic source of economic growth in its own right, and a catalyst for other information technology sectors, from computers and databases to information services to cable TV and videotex services. For the average Chinese citizen, a telephone remains a much sought-after item, while a personal computer or facsimile machine remains beyond reach. By contrast, for Hong Kong citizens, telecommunication customer facilities and services have become less utility items and more like commodities sold in supermarkets, available at affordable prices to whoever wants them.

China still prohibits any foreign direct investment in public or private telecommunication network management, but encourages foreign funding of network construction, and at least at provincial level seems flexible about the financial arrangements to repay the foreign partner. Especially in the area of mobile cellular telephone, paging and trunk radio networks, numerous Hong Kong and other Asian-based companies have entered agreements to build local networks, supply equipment such as base stations and handsets, and offer consultancy services covering items such as network management, customer billing, maintenance and repair.

These deals are arranged with organizations in China which have access to radio spectrum and a potential customer base. For example, a state enterprise, such as a steel mill or large manufacturing plant, may employ thousands of workers who are potential customers of a private paging network, while a port authority or a local public security bureau responsible for emergency services will require extensive trunk radio systems. The People's Liberation Army (PLA) is another major operator of mobile radio services with radio spectrum available to it, and Hong Kong-based companies, such as Champion Technologies, ABC Communications and Star Paging, and equipment suppliers such as S. Megga, and Tricom and others, have entered a number of supplier contracts.

The financial arrangements vary according to circumstances, but may involve a joint venture or joint agreement to finance, supply and build the network while the Chinese-side partner is the network operator. Rates of return, paid out of network revenues, can be structured in a variety of ways. If the non-Chinese partner is committed for the long term, investment returns can be designed to increase the value of the network, or they can be designed to produce "equity-like returns."[5] (These can be upwards of 50% for new ventures in telecommunications.) Alternatively, or additionally, they can be designed to accumulate in value until such time as the law permits them to be converted into equity. Another way, which is now used extensively by local Chinese investors, for example state enterprises with access to cash, is the leaseback arrangement, whereby the private investor purchases equipment, such as a switch, and leases it to the network operator, usually a provincial telecommunications authority (PTA). At the lease-end the ownership of the equipment transfers to the PTA.

Hong Kong companies directly benefit from the massive expansion of telecommunication networks in China. The Hong Kong Telecom Association (HKTA), which represents most of the territory's telecommunication equipment manufacturers and equipment suppliers, lists over 60 members in its *1993 Official Guide to Telecommunications in Hong Kong*. Exports of telecommunication equipment, parts and accessories from Hong Kong rose from HK$3,900 million in 1983 to HK$12,095 million in 1993, but of this rise the proportion going to China rose from HK$705 million (18%) to HK$9,601 million (79%). Re-exports of the same rose from HK$872 million in 1983 to HK$34,088 million in 1993, with the proportion destined for China rising from HK$14 million (1.6%) to HK$16,606 million (49%).

Hong Kong has not developed a telecommunications manufacturing base to the same extent as other "little dragon" economies, notably South Korea and Taiwan, but the 1992 Survey of Industrial Production[6] lists 157 establishments in Hong Kong as manufacturing radio, television and communication equipment and apparatus, employing 7,361 persons and with annual gross sales of nearly HK$9 billion. Most of the actual manufacturing takes place in China, while Hong Kong specializes in management, research and design, principally for niche markets, such as Chinese-character set alpha-numeric pagers, network connector devices, switchboards, terminal equipment, and so on. Hong Kong operators also specialize in service innovations, such as financial information, secretarial and messaging services, and transactions technologies which are well-adapted to the changing business and social requirements of Chinese customers. For an economy like Hong Kong's, which relies upon high adaptability to rapidly changing world and regional market conditions, a vibrant telecommunication equipment supply sector has a significant role to play in the territory's future prosperity.

HONG KONG AS TELECOMMUNICATIONS HUB

Hong Kong is in fiery competition with another dragon, namely Singapore, and this is one of the drivers of Hong Kong's policies towards telecommunications and related information services, such as broadcasting. The regional competitive advantages which good telecommunications bring Hong Kong cut both ways. Without effective and efficient telecommunications, Hong Kong would soon lose its position as a financial and banking centre, and as a hub for regional headquarters and offices of international companies. These are vital to Hong Kong's open economy. But modern telecommunications facilities — high-speed digital exchanges for the integration of data, image and voice switching, and high-speed transmission routes over satellite and through optical fibre submarine cables — also allow multi-national corporations to shift many of their business functions, such as data processing, customer accounts, design, boardroom meetings, and so on, away from any particular location, especially one considered to be unstable or politically high-risk.

Without an open telecommunications environment, Hong Kong would soon lose its position as a financial and banking centre, and as a hub for regional headquarters and offices of international companies. In the past this was not necessarily so. A monopoly carrier was able to provide, in Hong Kong and Singapore alike, a reliable, high-quality service at regionally competitive tariffs. Today the technology offers major corporate users opportunities to bypass the public networks, and would-be service providers an increasing number of opportunities to provide innovative services, ranging from alternative carriage to network management and integration of corporate customers computer networks to wireless services and highly specialized niche market services. International companies are requiring more because although their unit telecommunications costs are falling, their total volume usage of telecommunications is rising. This is in part a function of their greater reliance upon computer-generated data, in part an elastic substitution effect of falling relative costs of telecommunications,[7] and in part a function of the locational division of business functions within the multi-national corporation.[8]

These international companies, and their hubbing activities, are vital to

Hong Kong's open economy. According to a survey conducted by the Industry Department,[9] there are more than 7,000 overseas companies in Hong Kong, and during the three consecutive five-year periods since 1980, the average annual number of regional headquarters being set up in Hong Kong rose from 20 to 44 to 53. The two primary reasons for choosing Hong Kong were given by respondents as the banking and financial facilities (94.6%) and infrastructure (91.9%). The survey — 2,993 questionnaires were returned — revealed nearly 2,000 regional operations run from Hong Kong, including over 700 regional headquarters. According to Hong Kong Telecom (HKT), over 450 international companies use Hong Kong to hub their regional telecommunications traffic, and at least 50 of these have regional headquarters in the territory. Petrazzini[10] adds that approximately 70% of U.S. firms with Asian headquarters centralize their operations in Hong Kong.

Hong Kong's Telecommunications Policy

For 70 years, Hong Kong's domestic fixed-wire PSTN has been run by the HKTC as a private, but regulated, monopoly. Since 1984, HKTC has been a subsidiary of the British company Cable and Wireless plc, which also owns HKTI. Both have become subsidiaries of the holding company HKT, along with HKTC's subsidiary CSL which provides competitive services, such as mobile telephones, pagers and data services. The ground for shifting from HKTC's monopoly to competition was prepared by replacing rate of return regulation, which traded off profit stability for higher prices, with price-cap regulation which trades off price stability for higher profits.[11] The former system worked well because rapid technological change in basic network infrastructure rapidly reduced costs, so higher nominal prices still meant lower real prices. Since many of those technological gains have now been realized, the latter system only works well if other cost-cutting measures are effected.

Hence HKT is under constant pressure to reduce staff and other costs, or spread them across new business areas.[12] HKT has adopted both approaches, including forming a joint venture (Great Eastern Telecommunications Ltd.) with its parent company to explore regional investment opportunities, with China at the top of the agenda. The 1994 appointment of Linus Cheung as Chief Executive Officer of HKT was widely seen as significant in this regard. Not only is he the first Chinese to hold the top position, but coming from Cathay Pacific he is the first top executive to be appointed from outside the group, and indeed outside the industry. This "localization" is a significant shift for a company that traditionally has been run by British engineers or accountants.

Under the rate-of-return regime, HKT was required to separately account for its franchised PSTN (HKTC), its exclusively licensed international (HKTI) and its competitive (CSL) services, but from 1995 HKT will want to integrate HKTC and CSL as far as possible to reduce duplicated costs and maximize business synergies. This is likely to bring HKT into conflict with the OFTA and the new entrants. The OFTA will be on the lookout for predatory pricing and hidden cross-subsidies, while the new entrants will complain that HKT's competitive business units unfairly have exclusive knowledge of customer records and of the network. Since the establishment of the OFTA in July 1993, the Director-General in his role (under the Telecommunication Ordinance) as the Telecommunications Authority (TA) has stressed a pro-competitive policy commitment. The most contentious issue at stake is the future of HKTI's exclusive international licence.[13]

Ahead of schedule, the licence was renewed by the Hong Kong government in 1981 for 25 years as a gift to Mrs. Thatcher and her Conservative government in Britain, at a time when her government had chosen Cable and Wireless to be the first state enterprise to be privatized. However, technology has moved so far since then that most new services, such as private satellite transmissions, and high-speed digital data circuits, have easily been interpreted to fall beyond the scope of the licence. Since 1991, Hong Kong has progressively liberalized the IVANS (international value-added network services) market, and by the end of 1994, thirty licences to operate IVANS had been issued. Much now turns on the interpretation of the licence to determine how far the remaining exclusively applies to "basic" services and network "facilities." For example, the OFTA has interpreted store-and-forward fax as non-basic, and is extending this to store-and-forward voice. Another example involves foreign-based companies with voice-messaging and switching facilities in Hong Kong, who are being allowed to operate a free 800-number service to North America from where they reroute international calls to the country of destination, in effect bypassing HKTI's outbound network. (HKTI continues to receive the incoming accounting rate settlement payments where call-back is involved, but loses the collection of the local IDD charges.)

The OFTA is proving effective both in continuing the policy, adopted in the days when the TA was the Postmaster General, of opening up the radio communications markets, that is cellular mobile telephony, CT2 and paging, as far as the market will bear, and in preparing the ground for the day when the distinctions between wire and wireless in Hong Kong will become meaningless. That is, for the day when the choice of technologies will be determined by user requirements rather than operator preferences. But related issues, such as the technology convergence between telecommunications, computer networking and television networking, are less clear-cut from a regulatory point of view.

Telecommunications comes under the Economic Services Branch (ESB) of the government — to whom the OFTA reports — but broadcasting and narrowcasting policy falls under the Recreation and Culture Branch (RCB), while content comes under the aegis of the Television and Entertainment Licensing Authority (TELA). Issues such as pornography and defamation over networked computers is governed by the general laws of the territory, as would similar material on a CD-ROM and on a video, unless it were screened for public broadcast. But how to treat Video-on-Demand (VOD) over a telephone line? Since HKT is making trials of VOD, Wharf Cable, which holds the territory's cable TV franchise on an exclusive basis until October 1996, wants VOD to be constrained by the exclusivity period and subject to the same oversight restrictions as its own programme content. But if VOD is deemed to be a telecommunication service, exclusivity does not apply. The OFTA and the RCB seem to have different views on this matter. Further, since VOD would be available on a point-to-point rather than a point-to-multipoint basis, it could be treated more in the category of a video rented from a shop than as a video broadcast, and thereby not be subject to the same content oversight by the TELA.

These types of issues can only proliferate as multi-media applications come along, but fundamental to these changes is the restructuring of the telecommunications industry. Hong Kong is leaving an era which stretched from the late 1960s to the early 1990s, during which universal service on demand was accomplished, and the network fully digitalized. This success does not just place Hong Kong at the forefront of Asian networks, it also offers opportunities for market entry which previously did not exist.

Market entry depends critically upon one of two conditions. Either a new entrant can provide a service, or a bundle of services, on a stand-lone basis more efficiently than the incumbent operator, or regulation guarantees an economic rate of return on investment for the new entrant. The traditional competitive advantages of the incumbent operator arise from economies of scale and of scope. The former spread overheads, such as administration costs, depreciation, and building and maintenance costs, over the entire embedded network and its customers, something a new entrant serving only a fraction of the market cannot match. The latter spread the costs of the network over a wider range of products and services. Ironically, digitalization has increased the range of such services which an incumbent can offer,[14] and in that sense has strengthened the hand of the incumbent operator.

From the customer's viewpoint, being on a large rather than a small network offers economies of scale in terms of calls that can be made and received, and being on a digitalized network offers scale economies in terms of getting many additional services, such as teleshopping, call forwarding, and so on,[15] for zero or low incremental cost. But if a customer is to have choice — and without choice a customer has no market power to express preferences — new entrants require the right to interconnect their small networks and limited services to customers over the incumbent's network. The rationale for doing so does not lie in a "right of choice" as such, but in the premise that there may be selected areas of service, made possible by the technological revolution in micro-electronics, and made realizable through the inventive activities of entrepreneurs, which can be more efficiently (lower cost) or more productively (quality of service) offered by new entrants than by the incumbent. The underlying challenge is the question: why should the incumbent be best at everything? Of course, the underlying answer is: if the incumbent is best at everything, then monopoly is natural.

It is the undermining of the idea that telecommunications is a natural monopoly that lies at the heart of the radical policy changes which have swept through telecommunications authorities the world over. However it is not a foregone argument. There remain substantial reasons for viewing many elements of long-distance telecommunications which use optical fibre cables for high-speed transmission of data and high volumes of voice traffic as close to natural monopolies.[16] But the point is mute for Hong Kong which is too small to have any long-distance traffic. The real question for Hong Kong is whether it is too small to sustain any effective competition in telecommunications, and the real answer is that, if we set aside for a moment the China market, the potential for Hong Kong's market to grow in new directions depends upon the stimulation of demand through product and service innovation. That, in turn, requires more bandwidth to be available to innovators, and that shifts the question from insufficient demand to insufficient spectrum. However, the bottom line for the three new FTNS licencees will be the share they can win away from HKTC of international traffic delivered to, and received from, HKTI's gateway. For outgoing traffic they will earn just over 8% of outgoing IDD call charges, and for the delivery of incoming traffic they will earn 41% of "international" settlements from Guangdong province, Shenzhen and Macau, and 59% from the rest of the world. By passing on some of this revenue to customers — that is, lowering IDD call charges — the three new FTNS licencees may win additional customers, at least up to the point where HKTC calculates that a response is financially and strategically justified.

Hong Kong and China after 1997[17]

How things may work out after 1997 can only be speculated, but it is possible to identify issues which are likely to be influential. It needs to be stressed that if the authorities in a small city-state like Hong Kong have had difficulties in coming to grips with the implications of the technological and commercial transformation of the industry, the Chinese authorities have even greater problems. Generally, they are less exposed to the knowledge and experience of the leading OECD (Organization for Economic Cooperation and Development) economies, and so lack many of the human resources required to initiate and see through policy and regulatory changes. Issues like state enterprise reform and the introduction of modern methods of cost-accounting, business planning, pricing policy and market research, are in their infancy. In addition, China has to tackle simultaneously the basic problems of low levels of development and achieving universal service, and the challenge of upgrading its leading trade, manufacturing and service centres to meet world-class standards.

It follows, therefore, that China has more to learn from Hong Kong than Hong Kong does from China in the area of telecommunications. How China transfers that knowledge from Hong Kong will be one of the most interesting questions after 1997. It need not be a zero-sum game, but there is a fear that it could become so. To consider the alternatives, it will help to sketch out three possible scenarios, and consider the implications and likelihood of each.

Scenario One: Nothing changes. The OFTA remains the regulator under the Special Administrative Region (SAR), the industry continues to be governed by the Telephone and Telecommunication Ordinances, the three new fixed-wireline licences come into operation, as do all the other licences the OFTA may consider approving in areas such as radio mobile communications and value-added networks and network services. Company ownerships remain unchanged and the status of Hong Kong as an independent telecommunications authority in the world continues.

Scenario Two: Everything changes. Despite the Joint Liaison Group (JLG) having approved the three new FTNS licences, China either revokes them or imposes severe restrictions on their future scope, and the MPT, with State Council approval, declares that basic services must be a state monopoly, or may be provided only by Chinese-designated companies, and uses China International Trust and Investment Corporation (CITIC) as a vehicle to make Cable & Wireless plc an offer for HKT it cannot refuse. The regulation of the international telecommunication networks and services effectively passes into the hands of a Hong Kong office of the MPT.

Scenario Three: Some things change, most importantly the status of traffic between Hong Kong and China, along with two-way investment between the Hong Kong SAR and other provinces of China, especially Guangdong province. In particular, the Guangdong Bureau of Posts and Telecommunications seeks to build upon the economic integration of Hong Kong and Guangdong province by breaking down the regulatory barriers between the two territories. In the much longer term, this could lead to either a "free trade telecoms area" (the benign option) or a Guangdong take-over of Hong Kong's telecommunications riches. Looked at from another perspective, it could mean Guangdong promoting its provincial interests in relation to Hong Kong to the detriment of the influence of the MPT in Beijing.

❏ *Scenario One*

On the assumption that 1997 brings no appreciable changes to telecommunications policy, or the way it is administered, we can say that Hong Kong will remain a separately administered telecommunications authority, and the FTNS licences for Hutchison, New World and Wharf will go ahead unhindered. The OFTA has introduced a fresh and welcome degree of transparency into policy discussion through the issuing of thoughtful and well-presented discussion papers which have sought, and received, public comment, and has established an advisory/consultative committee structure which has been widely welcomed by the industry, and could well be taken as a lesson for other parts of government in Hong Kong. If this process of a more open society survives and continues beyond 1997, then Hong Kong can become an experimental base for the information society from which China itself can learn many valuable lessons. This is clearly the ideal relationship: Hong Kong as a mirror in which China can reflect on how to do things successfully in the field of information technology and telecommunications.

Of course Hong Kong has been playing this role in various ways since China adopted the open door policy. Hong Kong has been, and continues to be, China's international telecommunications gateway, as the earlier discussion of traffic volumes illustrated. Cooperation between Hong Kong and the rest of China is clearly mutually beneficial, such as the agreement between HKT and the MPT to provide one-stop shopping for leased circuits between the two territories. Hong Kong remains the region's leading communication hub, spurred on by keen competition from Singapore, and despite uncertainties about 1997, it seems that Hong Kong is the preferred base for regional headquarters, other things being equal. But uncertainty about continuity and stability has undoubtedly led to contingency planning by international companies, and the removal of business operations, such as sensitive databanks, to overseas locations is likely.

Some have already been moved. This, of course, is made possible by Hong Kong's international telecommunication facilities, and will actually add to traffic flow, which highlights an important point. Unlike other industries which relocate to the loss of the economy they are leaving, telecommunications-related activities network across economic locations and enhance their competitive advantages. These wide-area locational economies will play an increasingly important role in Asia, and here lies the key to Hong Kong's future involvement with the regional economies of China.

But the model relationship is not a straightforward "integrationist" one where Hong Kong and Shenzhen merge rapidly into a single economic unit and Hong Kong becomes more like southern China as southern China becomes more like Hong Kong, the two meeting somewhere in the middle. On the contrary, Hong Kong's competitive advantage, to itself and to the rest of China, lies precisely in the fact that it is not like southern China and that it straddles two very different economic realms, the realm of a reformist China which is looking outwards to a world market in which it is still very poorly equipped to compete, and the realm of advanced post-industrial economies which are looking for risk-reduced entry into the China market.

So, under the first scenario, Hong Kong is seen expanding its own internal telecommunication markets for mobile and personal communications, for interactive home services such as VOD and cable TV combined with telephony, and business value-added networks being spurred by competition from both domestic new entrants and growing pressure from the world alliances of international telecommunications carriers which are now forming to capture international corporate business.

In relations with the Mainland, the driver will remain the rate of network growth in China, which is obviously long-term related to China's economic development. As both Chinese and foreign companies multiply, and their business grows, the demand for data communications and network information services as well as basic services will begin to take off, but the larger the plane the longer the runway, so it will take time. The danger of foreshortening development forecasts could yet lead to some very unwise investments. The really significant development within this scenario is the possibility of policy changes in China towards foreign direct investment (FDI) in the ownership and management of networks and network services.[18]

What is the likelihood of scenario one? On paper it is by far the most likely, but like most issues concerned with the transfer of sovereignty in 1997 there is uncertainty attached to it. One danger is that many items of business that need to be sorted out through the JLG before 1997 will be left hanging in the air, and then the rules of the game could become very flexible. Of course, flexibility is not always a bad thing, especially if it reflects the underlying transformations in technologies, market situations, world trading agreements, and crucially the shifting balance of interests between stakeholders, whom we may identify as including users in different segments of the market, the carriers and their stakeholders, the public interest in having an information economy and information society, the regulator and the state. It is to be hoped that regulatory flexibility after 1997 will continue to be the result of good judgement exercised by an independent regulator.

❏ *Scenario Two*

The second scenario need not be presented in Machiavellian terms. Rather it can be approached from looking at the issue from the Chinese side, and making an argument along the following lines: the interpretation of "one country, two systems" is well understood in general terms, such as leaving property rights as a system unchanged, but in working it out in practice there have to be some guiding principles. The first principle should be Hong Kong's contribution to the People's Republic of China, not Hong Kong in isolation. So detailed interventions in the economic and industrial structure can be justified so long as the essentially capitalist nature of Hong Kong is maintained. By "capitalist" I understand this to mean, in the Hong Kong context, a system of property rights rather than the role of markets. In this respect, it is interesting to note in passing that one of the structures underpinning the success of Hong Kong is a quasi-socialist state (or Crown) ownership of land. Landlease sales finance social expenditure while keeping down personal and company taxation. The Chinese would not be hard-pressed to come up with arguments for other forms of intervention which nevertheless maintained the essential structure of property rights.

One speculation, and it has no more status than that, has been that the State Council will use CITIC to take over HKT, perhaps offering Cable & Wireless minority shareholder status to pay lip-service to property rights, and will protect the monopoly rent for Telecom by revoking new FTNS licences. This would not be feasible in the mobile communications market since existing players clearly have entrenched property rights, but the issuing of future licences could, of course, be restricted either to Telecom or to other Chinese companies considered suitable.

In a word, this scenario is improbable. First, it goes against China's own internal development. The State Council has come out in favour of what we might term "controlled competition" for telecommunication networks in China. It has backed the creation of the MEI's (Ministry of Electronics Industries) Jitong Corporation for the construction of nation-wide information networks, the so-called Golden Projects, and it has given approval for the creation of the Liantong Corporation (Unicom) to run long-distance, local loop and cellular networks.

Second, China has clearly recognized at the highest levels that its need for an efficient information economy requires, as a matter of urgency, the widest possible mobilization of funds for network construction. We noted earlier the SDH development in Guangdong, which is to be replicated in other leading provinces and municipal cities. Guangdong is also pioneering an ATM (Asynchronous Transfer Mode) high-speed data switch for broadband services, such as cable TV and video-conferencing, in a particularly· interesting joint venture with an American consortium, SCM/Brooks, which is putting up the finance and apparently is to have some involvement in the operation of the project once its working. The MPT, having opened the packet-switched Chinapac network is now undertaking a national digital data network. The State Planning Commission and the State Information Centre are planning a national satellite-based information network, and so on. The emphasis is upon diversity, to attract funding, and flexibility with regard to provincial initiatives, but within a framework which maintains Chinese control.

So the proposition that China, or the MPT, will swoop into Hong Kong on 1 July 1997 to "take over" the telecommunications industry seems inconsistent with the direction of China's policy on the Mainland. Of course, Hong Kong will be exceptional in having foreign-owned companies running the networks, but that is part of the "one country, two systems" concept, and is not incompatible with China's needs. It is also important to distinguish between the ministerial interests of the MPT and the political and macro-economic interests of the State Council. The MPT has to balance the revenues it currently enjoys from Hong Kong traffic to the Mainland, with the damage that would be done to Hong Kong as a hub should a take-over occur. The State Council has an interest in keeping Hong Kong as a spur to the diffusion of information technology on the Mainland. Only if political interests are directly affected would the State Council adopt a different attitude.

Finally, on the role of CITIC as a stalking horse for a China take-over, of course anything is possible, but is it probable? CITIC has invested heavily in infrastructure in Hong Kong, which is a strategic investment both from the financial point of view (its all blue-chip) and from an economic point of view since there are obvious synergies with China trade. But CITIC is not an entrepreneurial company.[19] It has stuck to investments, and even reduced its holdings of HKT stock from 20% to 14.5% in January 1994 when profit-taking looked like a smart option. With China looking to become a member of the World Trade Organization, it would hardly seem beneficial to China to provoke a trade-in-services issue in such a strategic world industry.

❑ *Scenario Three*

In this scenario, the Guangdong Bureau of Posts and Telecommunications (GBPT) leverages the Guangdong provincial government into embracing Hong Kong's lucrative telecommunications market. Traffic between Hong Kong and Guangdong is redefined as either intra-provincial long distance, or failing that, inter-provincial trunk. Either way tariffs fall,[20] which is politically very popular, and Guangdong and not the MPT in Beijing initially receives the revenue of incoming traffic — although this is subsequently redistributed through the MPT — which is politically even more popular with local government. Furthermore, mobile roaming becomes automatic, and to ease the commercial arrangements the GBPT buys heavily into HKT, or alternatively into a competitor, and possibly offers HKT, or a competitor, or both, a quid pro quo in Guangdong. (For GBPT we could just as easily substitute one or two other organizations, such as a business arm of the PLA or the MEI.)

This is the start of a transition period in which the regulatory barriers to cross-border traffic dissolve. The HKTI licence is allowed to run its course to 2006, but is undermined by the redefinition of China traffic as non-international. The impact upon HKTI's revenue growth could be more than offset by a strategy of acquisition of Mainland operators under relaxed foreign investment laws which permit minority holdings and joint ventures, starting with value-added networks and radio communications systems covering mobile cellular, vsats (very small aperture terminals) and radio local loop. In the horse-trading and manoeuvring implied by this scenario, the regional hubbing business of HKT remains its strong card for China, and the new SAR Chief Executive is therefore likely to provide vigorous support for Hong Kong interests, demanding reciprocity for any redefinitions of traffic and services.

This scenario is almost inevitable somewhere down the tract because as the level and quality of the Guangdong network improves, the demands by similar customers for the same level of provision at the same level of prices will become irresistible. Bypass in one form or another will force these changes, and maintaining separate regulatory regimes will become an anachronism. So the time factor is one dimension. The pace of development will be uneven across Guangdong, but the leading areas will drive the issue, so the other dimension is the geography of development. The closer to Hong Kong, for example along the Pearl River Delta, the faster will come the transition.

But the idea that Guangdong will rapidly overtake Hong Kong as the hub for southern China, with the implication that Guangdong will suck the life out of Hong Kong's telecommunications industry, does not ring true. Hubbing requires a level of quality and reliability of service and human resources, not just technology, that goes beyond network numbers. There is no reason why Guangdong should not achieve the required levels in, perhaps, 15–20 years, but by then who knows by how much the information economy will have become a more distributed network of networks? Will this still leave a role for regional hubbing? Perhaps not.

THE FUTURE OF TELECOMMUNICATIONS IN HONG KONG

The trends in telecommunication technologies and patterns of network evolution Asia will follow tomorrow are to be found in the U.S. today. This is not to say what works in the U.S. will be simply transplanted to Asia. On the contrary, the nature of local and regional markets in Asia are diverse and different from those of North America. For instance, ideogrammatic scripts like Chinese and Japanese present many problems for the standardization of computer software, and therefore for the use of E-mail and EDI (electronic data interchange), but are easily handled by "scribble-and-send" methods, such as facsimile and palm-top electronic organizers. But the underlying economic realities will be much the same across the global market-place.

Intelligent nodes and terminals and distributed computing power will create opportunities for business and social users alike to create their own virtual networks, and the costs of doing so will encourage increasing levels of bypass of more expensive systems. The critical issues will pass from the direct regulation of prices and profits to policing a regime of open access networks which allows users, and operators, to plug into any public network, be it telecommunications, cable TV, Internet, or whatever, and pay a price which is non-discriminatory between the user and what the service providers charge themselves. On this basis market entry will become increasingly common, opening up a host of specialist information and communications services.

Of particular importance will be the size and scope of China's information requirements in the years to come, and Hong Kong is uniquely well-positioned both to serve the China market directly and to act as an information gateway between China and the rest of the world. As a gateway, Hong Kong can provide a secure, efficient and cost-effective hub for data-storage, retrieval and processing and for information relay. As a regional centre of international companies, and as a base for an increasing number of influential Asian service companies, Hong Kong also has the prospect of developing further its acquired advantages in activities which increasingly use electronic communications such as banking and financial services; management, business and property services; research and design; software production and distribution; education and health technologies; entertainment and information services; and so on. But underpinning all these technologically based advantages is the human resource advantage that Hong Kong has acquired for itself: knowing how to apply and manage these technologies in the market-place, and for social benefit. There will be no shortage of opportunity in China for Hong Kong's skills. This is the potential, but the time-frame for its realization depends upon how economic relations between Hong Kong and the Mainland develop post-1997.

In the immediate future, Hong Kong must position itself by encouraging the transition it has embarked upon in telecommunications. In practice, this means (1) regulating the terms and conditions for the new fixed wireline entrants, and (2) preparing the ground for abolishing the wireline-wireless distinction. The OFTA has already defined the terms of entry for the new FTNS licencees by taking direct control of the numbering plan and by introducing new rules governing revenue-sharing for the origination and termination of international calls by both the new FTNS licence holders and the cellular mobile telephone operators. Guaranteeing equal access by all telephone service operators to numbers for their subscribers is a basic condition for fair competition, otherwise inertia and/or inconvenience would deter many existing subscribers from changing their service providers. Yet to come is a satisfactory means of administering and paying for a network numbering system which can provide personal numbering, as opposed to terminal (mobile) or locational (immobile) numbering, which is also portable across competing networks. As a first step, each FTNS licensed operator will be able to offer personal numbering as a value-added service across their own network.

The revenue-sharing arrangements between new FTNS operators, mobile cellular operators, and HKTI could prove to be a contentious area, especially if the new entrants find it difficult to win market share from HKT. Current arrangements provide for operators terminating incoming calls from HKTI to receive HK$0.62 for calls from Guangdong province, Shenzhen and Macau, and HK$12.12 for calls from the rest of the world. For outgoing IDD calls delivered to HKTI, service operators will be able to claim a weighted average of 8.19% of HKTI's IDD call charge. But these operators will receive less than the share HKTC receives from HKTI, the difference being a subsidy towards HKTC's universal service obligation. According to the OFTA[21] in 1991–1992, this was the equivalent of 45 cents per minute of international traffic, or almost HK$1.2 billion. Calculating this figure presupposes a number of accounting assumptions regarding the allocation of costs between services, and if more public light can be brought to bear upon the true costs of providing social obligations, this will be important information for service providers, customers, regulators, legislators and public bodies such as the Consumer Council when decisions have to be made about the future rebalancing of tariffs between local and long-distance international calls, and between so-called basic and value-added services.

In a digital world, the distinction between basic and value-added services only exists as a regulatory fiction for protecting the monopoly of the PSTN operator. Hong Kong has moved beyond that stage, but the immediate challenge for the new entrants will be to make a market for their services, whether defined as basic voice or value-added. The representative company in Hong Kong is not the multi-national corporation with its sophisticated telecommunications requirements, but a small or medium-sized enterprise (SME), employing less than 200 staff, usually less than 50, frequently less than 10. These companies have a high rate of attrition, are especially vulnerable to trade fluctuations, and frequently move premises due to the two-year cycle of rent-fixing in Hong Kong. SME's survive on their adaptability, which involves minimizing their fixed, and sunk, capital commitments. They provide a thriving market for mobile telecommunications, a potential market for portable office automation, and a limited market for information and data services provided over networked PCS.

In this respect, two challenges face Hong Kong. First, the introduction of a territory-wide EDI network for trading companies seeking documentation from government departments. Progress in Hong Kong seems painfully slow, yet EDI could be a powerful catalyst for the spread of an electronic communications culture among Hong Kong's smaller businesses. The other side of this coin is the role of government, which also seems to be painfully slow in adopting information technology to go on-line with the public. Looking ahead, there is no reason why, for example, the post office should not introduce an EDI system of its own to replace paper and envelops and time-wasting queues at its offices. The spread of electronic mailboxes should be only a matter of years away.

The second challenge is that of so-called multi-media products and services. In the U.S., the Information SuperHighway is projected as the universal network to bring broadband services, such as VOD, teleconferencing, and many others, to everyone's home or office. For the foreseeable future, Hong Kong will develop these services slowly due both to the lack of an adequate universal broadband infrastructure, and to a limited market. The markets will emerge as the information society emerges, which implies cultural and social changes. The information society will emerge as service providers experiment with alternative technologies and information services. Hong Kong's challenge, therefore, will be to complete the transition to a telecommunity in which equal access to public networks is universal, thereby encouraging experimentation by innovators. Worldwide, these development are irreversible, and if the post-1997 era for Hong Kong and China also permits this development, then times will indeed be interesting.

Notes

1. The most comprehensive, and readable, mapping of these changes is to be found in P. W. Huber, *The Geodesic Network: 1987 Report on Competition in the Telephone Industry* (Washington, DC: U.S. Department of Justice, Antitrust Division, 1987), and its sequel, P. W. Huber, M. K. Kellog, and J. Thorne, *The Geodesic Network II: 1993 Report on Competition in the Telephone Industry* (Washington, DC: The Geodesic Company, 1994).

2. See *Position Paper: Hong Kong's Telecommunications Policy* (Hong Kong Government: Economic Services Branch, Government Secretariat, January 1994) for the broad outlines of policy.

3. By contrast, Hong Kong has 3 million telephone mainlines, or 50 for every 100 inhabitants, the highest percentage, or "teledensity," in Asia outside Japan. Of these, 1.8 million were residential lines catering for 1.6 million households, around 90% of which have telephones, an average of 1.3 lines per household. As a saturation level this sounds rather high, suggesting maybe half-a-million or so business lines are registered as residential to avoid higher monthly rentals.

4. For details of China's telecommunications policies and development, see the China Special Issue of *Telecommunications Policy*, Vol. 18, No. 3 (April

1994). For China and Hong Kong, also see J. Ure (ed.), *Telecommunications in Asia: Policy, Planning and Development* (Hong Kong: Hong Kong University Press, 1995).

5. Following an announcement earlier in the year between Cable and Wireless and China's MPT to form a submarine cable-laying joint venture, in November 1994, Hong Kong Telecom announced two contracts, one with the MPT and the other with the Beijing PTA, to help finance and build an optical fibre cable link between Beijing and Shenzhen, and a GSM cellular system in China's capital city. The financial arrangements of the latter have been described as involving "equity-like returns." See *Asia-Pacific Telecommunications — An Industry in Transition* (Hong Kong: Salomon Brothers, December 1994), p. 20.

6. See *Annual Digest of Statistics* (Hong Kong: Census and Statistics Department, 1994).

7. For example, video-conferencing is cheaper than flying staff around the world to a central location. Sending product designs and orders by EDI (electronic data interchange) is faster and cheaper than by a courier service, as E-mail is faster and cheaper than post, fax and possibly a phone call.

8. An absorbing review of the locational aspects of the information economy is found in M. Castells, *The Informational City* (Oxford, U.K., and Cambridge, U.S.: Blackwell, 1989). A model of the information economy, which relates an increasing demand for electronic communications to an increasing world division of internal corporate labour, and the consequential requirements for commercial and industrial coordination, is discussed by L. Gille, "Growth and Telecommunications," in *Information, Telecommunications and Development* (Geneva: International Telecommunications Union, 1986).

9. Industry Department, *Report on the 1994 Survey of Regional Representation by Overseas Companies in Hong Kong* (Hong Kong: Hong Kong Government, 1994).

10. B. Petrazzini, "Hong Kong's Telecom Market," *Transnational Data and Communications Report* (July–August 1994).

11. The distinction between a profits-cap and a price-cap is not quite so clear-cut. In setting the price-cap the regulator is required to take a view of likely future productivity gains, and in this way indirectly imposes a profits-cap. For a discussion of the issues, see M. Beesley, and S. Littlechild, "The Regulation of Privatized Monopolies in the UK," *Rand Journal of Economics*, Vol. 20, No. 3 (1988).

12. Maintaining HKT's contribution to its parent company, Cable and Wireless, may be considered a further pressure. Between two-thirds and three-quarters of the group's world earnings and profits derive from HKT.

13. For the text of the licence, together with a critical review of the monopoly, see

M. Mueller, *International Telecommunications in Hong Kong: The Case for Liberalization* (Hong Kong: The Chinese University Press, 1992).

14. Digitalization reduces all telecommunications traffic, be it sound or image, to "data" in binary notation, and thereby allows, with the right switching, transmission and terminal equipment, sound and image to be combined in all sorts of ways, opening up a potential for a multitude of multi-media products and services.

15. For example, booking cinema tickets, paying utility bills, checking airline timetables, polling information over the facsimile machine.

16. For example, Huber *et al.* (see Note 1) argue that in the U.S. only excessively favourable terms of revenue-sharing, insisted upon by the Federal Communications Commission (FCC) keep MCI and U.S. Sprint as long-distance competitors to AT&T. For an incumbent operator, ineffective competition is better than both effective competition and none. "AT&T is now buying protection." (p. 1.13)

17. The following section is based on a paper "Hong Kong and China: Telecommunications after 1997," delivered to the IIR Hong Kong Telecommunications and Network Competition Conference at Furama Hotel in Hong Kong, 28–30 September 1994.

18. Elsewhere I have argued that China has ways of funding its telecommunications expansion plans which do not hinge upon FDI, but much more depend upon human resources and technology transfer issues. See J. Ure (ed.), *Telecommunications in Asia: Policy, Planning and Development* (Hong Kong: Hong Kong University Press, 1995). Also see J. Ure, "Breaking the Bottleneck in Telecom Nets," *South China Morning Post*, 6 October 1994.

19. According to Minister Wang of the State Enterprise and Trade Commission, after state enterprise reform: "State investment bodies will enjoy only the rights of shareholders and will not perform administrative functions." *China Daily*, 20 December 1994, p. 4 (quoting an article in the State Council's *Economic Daily*).

20. International tariffs in part reflect to accounting rate system used between international administrations to compensate each other for the termination of calls. The accounting rate establishes a per minute charge, for example US$1, and the settlement rate determines the split between administrations, usually 50:50, for example US50 cents per minute for a delivered call. If traffic volumes (incoming and outgoing) between two administrations exactly balance, then their payments cancel out. The telephone company charges its customer a collection rate (the IDD tariff) for making the call, which normally covers the net settlement cost for traffic on that particular route. If Hong Kong–China traffic were not treated as international, the accounting rate system would no longer apply, and IDD rates could reflect that accordingly.

But since the settlement rate is 33.3:66.7 in China's favour, the MPT would be reluctant to give it up.

21. *Guidance Note for the Submission of Proposals for the Operation of Fixed Telecommunication Network Services in Hong Kong* (Hong Kong: Office of the Telecommunications Authority, 1993), Annex C, p. 1.

20

Freedom of the Media

Li Yuet-wah

Hong Kong has always been described as a place enjoying a high degree of freedom, in particular freedom of the press, but little democracy. However, a close examination of the situation would find the foundation of press freedom in Hong Kong under the British colonial rule is actually very fragile. The following illustration may best explain how free the press in Hong Kong really is.

Armed with the draconian powers available in the statute books, the present colonial administration is like a gunman pointing a loaded pistol at the media, his finger on the trigger. Yet at the same time, he guarantees that he will never really pull the trigger and cause heavy casualties among journalists.

While there is no guarantee that the post-1997 gunman will not pull the trigger and cause those heavy casualties, the guarantee from the pre-1997 administration is also no longer trustworthy. A classic example was the prosecution of three senior *Ming Pao* journalists by the Independent Commission Against Corruption (ICAC) for violating a press-gag provision in the Prevention of Bribery Ordinance (POBO). The details and implications of the case will be examined later in this chapter. However, it is worth noting that this case clearly demonstrates that if a particular power exists, then the government — however tolerant it may be — may use it against the media.

Freedom of the press is one of the cornerstones for the success of Hong Kong as an international business centre. Whether there will be press freedom after 1997 is a question Hong Kong journalists ask themselves from time to time and are frequently asked by people concerned about freedom of the press in recent years. We have no crystal ball to help us make a prediction about the future.

However, many journalists do worry that the present degree of press freedom will be compromised after 1997. This sentiment is not exclusive to journalists. The Hong Kong Journalists Association (HKJA) and Radio Television Hong Kong (RTHK) have been sponsoring a series of public opinion surveys since June 1994 to monitor media performance and freedom of speech in Hong Kong in the run-up to 1997. These surveys reveal a constant pattern of pessimism among the general public about the future of press freedom in Hong Kong.

The first survey was conducted in June 1994. Of the 538 respondents surveyed, 46% felt that press freedom had increased over the past three years, while 31% felt it had decreased. Their views on the future, on the other hand, were bleak. Some 60% thought there would be a decline in press freedom in the coming three years, while only 11% thought there would be an increase.

The second survey was conducted six months later. While the result was similar to that of the first survey, the trend seemed to be even more pessimistic. Only 6% of the 521 respondents of the second survey thought press freedom would increase in the coming three years.

A separate public opinion poll revealed the same pattern of pessimism. The poll, aimed at establishing a "freedom index" in Hong Kong, was jointly conducted by RTHK and three other institutions in September 1993.[1]

Of the 587 respondents aged 15 or above, 94.7% considered Hong Kong to be a free society but did not think the current degree of freedom would last, while 34.2% expected that the territory would have less freedom in the next three to four years, and as many as 56.5% expected less freedom in the territory after 1997.

Regarding freedom of speech and of the press, 81.8% of the respondents saw no constraints on the discussion about society, politics and current affairs and felt they were free to speak; nearly 65% said generally speaking the local newspapers, TV and broadcasting stations could report and comment on various issues without restraint.

Meanwhile, 70% expected less freedom of the press in the territory after 1997 and only 7.2% believed there would be more freedom after 1997.

This opinion polls reflect the importance that Hong Kong people attach to freedom, but it also illustrates the worries they have over the degree of freedom in the future, especially freedom of the press in the territory.

There is no doubt that China is the major factor for worry in the future. However, it is not fair to just criticize China. Despite the frequent public pledges on various occasions made by the Hong Kong Governor, Chris Patten, and other senior government officials on the importance of freedom of the press to Hong Kong, the sincerity in implementing concrete measures to safeguard this most cherished and most fragile freedom remains questionable.

THE COLONIAL LEGACY: A FREE PRESS?

The right to freedom of expression, of which press freedom is a vital component, is always regarded as the foundation of all human rights. Yet, until the passage of the Bill of Rights Ordinance (BORO)[2] in June 1991, and the subsequent entrenchment of the International Covenant on Civil and Political Rights (ICCPR) as applied to Hong Kong in the Letters Patent, which is Hong Kong's *de facto* colonial constitution, freedom of expression had not been positively protected by law in Hong Kong. To the contrary, numerous draconian laws exist in our statute books which pose a threat to press freedom.

While maintaining these ready tools for gagging the press, the Hong Kong government has been relatively restrained in the past two decades in exercising these powers against the media. However, the colonial administration was not unknown for its hostility towards the media, an attitude dating back to the 1950s.

Ta Kung Pao, a local pro-China newspaper, was charged with publishing seditious writings in 1952. The "seditious" article, published on 5 March 1952, was a commentary from the *People's Daily* which criticized the British colonial administration's handling of patriotic Chinese in Hong Kong.

The publisher and editor of the paper were convicted and fined while the newspaper was suspended from publishing for six months under the Control of Publications (Consolidated) Ordinance.[3] Although the suspension order was later dropped, the draconian gagging tool, the Control of Publications (Consolidated) Ordinance, was only repealed in 1987, more than two decades later.

The police seizure of tapes from two broadcasting stations in 1989 was a more recent case illustrating how the draconian statutory powers were used by the authorities. On 29 September 1989, the New China News

Agency (Xinhua), the *de facto* Chinese embassy in Hong Kong, held a reception at a Chinese restaurant in the World Trade Centre in Causeway Bay to celebrate National Day of the People's Republic of China. The celebration was marred by a group of demonstrators, mainly university students and others. About 40 members of the April 5th Action Group, a coalition of the radical left, were prevented by the police from marching to the venue to join the large demonstration. The confrontation turned violent and several April 5th members were arrested for allegedly assaulting police officers. The Police Public Relations Bureau subsequently contacted the territory's two television stations, Television Broadcasts Limited (TVB) and Asia Television Limited (ATV), to "borrow" the raw video footage of the incident. When the stations refused, the police obtained a warrant from a magistrate under Section 50(7) of the Police Force Ordinance on 3 October and seized several video tapes from the two stations. Another member of the April 5th group was arrested the day after the seizure.

Although the police guaranteed that the seized tapes would not be used in court as evidence to prosecute the suspects and returned to the stations soon after the seizure, the Director of Public Prosecutions admitted that the tapes were needed by the authorities to determine if more serious charges should be laid against the suspects.

Though the application of law this time was not directed at prosecuting journalists, however, by turning journalists into "agents" of the authorities was equally damaging to freedom of the press. Such worry was amplified at the time people still clearly remembered how the Chinese government identified an innocent Chinese citizen through a television interview by a foreign television network and arrested him and put him into jail for the "crime" of talking to reporters about the June 4 massacre.

Another important case was the prosecution of the "*Ming Pao* Three" by the ICAC. They were alleged to have violated Section 30 of the POBO which bars the disclosure of anti-corruption investigations without lawful authority or reasonable excuse before an arrest is made.

ICAC officers contacted a number of news organizations after they received complaints against a controversial land auction in May 1994 to request the journalists who had been reporting the land auction to give evidence to the ICAC.

The only "crime" committed by the "*Ming Pao* Three" was to report that the ICAC was investigating the controversial land auction. No names were mentioned in the report, nor did it provide any details of the investigation, apart from the fact that the probe was taking place.

This problematic provision of the POBO was in fact the most frequently used press-gag law in recent years. Since its enactment in 1970, there were nine prosecution cases, including that of the *"Ming Pao* Three," under Section 30. Three out of the nine cases were targeted at the media. The previous two cases took place before the enactment of the BORO in 1991 and the subsequent amendment of Section 30 of the POBO in 1992. The previous version of Section 30 prohibited any disclosure of ICAC investigations without lawful authority even after the arrest was made. The defendants simply did not have any ground for defence.

The editor and the business editor of the *South China Morning Post* (*SCMP*) pleaded guilty and were fined \$15,000 and \$10,000 respectively for revealing in December 1986 an ICAC investigation against a former senior government banking official. In another case, the editor of the *Target*, a financial service bulletin, pleaded guilty and was fined \$20,000 for publishing an ICAC investigation against a Police Commercial Crime Bureau officer. The HKJA and the journalistic profession has long pointed out that Section 30 of the POBO violates Article 16 of the BORO and should be repealed.

However, such calls have fallen on deaf ears. Although the ruling of the *Ming Pao* case reinforced our viewpoint, the ICAC arrogantly insists on retaining the power.

Magistrate Hugh Sinclair ruled on 16 February 1995 that Section 30 of the POBO had been overridden by the BORO because of its inconsistency with Article 16 of the Bill. The three *Ming Pao* defendants were then granted no case to answer and discharged.

In his 21-page judgment, Sinclair said:

> The usefulness of Section 30 in facilitating investigations into Bribery Ordinance offences does not, I find, correspond to but is, on the contrary, disproportionate to a social need to combat corruption. It is a blanket restriction taking no account of particular circumstances. Accordingly I find that the provisions of Section 30 of the Prevention of Bribery Ordinance are inconsistent with BORO and do not permit of a construction such as to render it consistent.

Yet regrettably, in no respect to the magistrate's ruling, the ICAC issued a statement stating that the magistrate's decision in this case had no binding effect on other similar cases and that the ICAC should continue to respond to any breach of Section 30 in the same manner.

It is clear that there is a pressing need for the colonial administration to clean up Hong Kong's statute books before the change of sovereignty in 1997. Article 19, a London-based international centre against censorship, and the HKJA has jointly published a report entitled *Urgent Business: Hong Kong, Freedom of Expression and 1997* in January 1993, examining in great detail the threats that the repressive colonial laws posed to freedom of expression in Hong Kong. The HKJA has been campaigning for many years to amend or repeal these draconian laws.

It is clearly on our agenda that ensuring legal safeguards for this fundamental right is an "urgent business," particularly in the light of recent events happened in the media. However, for the colonial government, reform of the press-gag laws is a matter of political convenience which would change with the political needs rather than of true urgency. The government's attitude towards the issue over the past few years is a best illustration of this mentality.

The first clear policy statement by the government on this matter was given during a debate in the Legislative Council (Legco) in February 1992. Legislative Councillor Emily Lau, the former chairperson of the HKJA, moved a motion on press freedom in the Legco on 26 February 1992. The motion read "that this council recognizes the vital importance of protecting freedom of the press in Hong Kong and urges the administration to demonstrate its positive commitment to this principle by undertaking to initiate without delay the repeal of all legislation which is in breach of press freedom as protected by Article 16 of the Hong Kong Bill of Rights Ordinance 1991."

Lau further elaborated in her speech by clearly listing out the laws that were in question, including on top of her list the Emergency (Regulations) Ordinance, the Broadcasting Authority Ordinance, Television Ordinance, the Official Secrets Act, etc. Her concerns on the potential dangers that press freedom would face were echoed by many other legislators and some went further to ask the government to enact a Freedom of Information Ordinance (later called the Access to Information Ordinance) to strengthen the right of the public to information.

The response of the government was disappointing, but not surprising. Sir David Ford, the then Chief Secretary, replied in his speech that the three official members in the Legco were voting for the motion. However, it was not for the reason that they admitted that there were laws in breach of the Article 16 of the BORO and the government committed to repeal them. On the contrary, the administration believed that no laws were in breach of the BORO. Sir David Ford said in his reply:

> I want to make it very clear that we have no difficulty with this motion. The administration is committed to defending freedom of the press and freedom of speech in Hong Kong. As I have explained, our judgement is that none of the laws mentioned breach Article 16 of the Bill of Rights. And for that reason the three officials will therefore be voting in favour of this motion.

He emphasized in his speech that the administration was of the view that the laws identified by legislators were not inconsistent with Article 16 of the BORO and, nor did they infringe upon press freedom. The only "positive" achievement out of this debate was the announcement of adoption of the Official Secrets Act (OSA) 1989 later in the year to replace the even more draconian 1911 version.

In diluting the argument of legislators for the localization of the OSA, Sir David replied by stating that:

> We in the administration have taken the view that this important advance (the adoption of OSA 1989) should not be delayed. It would take far longer clearly to enact local legislation and I can see no good reason to delay action when we have a ready-made provision which is far superior to the present law.

Of course Sir David did not explain why the administration had not introduced into Hong Kong this "far superior" 1989 version to replace the 1911 OSA much earlier.

This "no-delaying" tactic of the government was not unfamiliar to people in Hong Kong. Just two years later, in rejecting the demand to enact an Access to Information Ordinance by legislators and the public, Anson Chan, the Chief Secretary, employed this "no-delaying" tactic again. She tried to convince the public that an administrative code of practice was a better means than legislation to guarantee greater public access to government information.

She was quoted saying that a code of practice was "practical and effective proposals can be introduced with minimal delay." Satirically this "no-delaying" tactic was described by the *SCMP* editorial as the "classic delaying tactic." Under the administration of Lord David Wilson, the former Governor and Sir David Ford, the former Chief Secretary, the question of reforming press-gag laws was a closed chapter. The present Governor Chris Patten seems to take a slightly more liberal stance on the matter. However, despite a number of public statements made by Patten, particularly before overseas audiences, on the importance of press freedom to Hong Kong and his commitment to enhance its protection, there is in fact not much substantial progress in the area.

Patten agreed to conduct a further review of laws during a meeting with representatives of the HKJA in August 1992. The HKJA then formally submitted to the government a list of 17 laws[4] which were incompatible with Article 16 of the BORO, or otherwise pose a threat to press freedom. Among the 17 laws, 11 related directly to press freedom, the others related to a broader area of freedom of expression.

While the administration did carry out the review, the result was far from satisfactory. In a press release issued on 17 March 1993, the government claimed that freedom of the press was secure under Hong Kong law, according to the result of the review. However, the government would propose to amend seven laws or regulations related to the media. In their words, the provisions in these laws and regulations were "either obsolete or seemed to be at odds" with the BORO.

Nevertheless, the government did not commit itself to reform those security-related laws, for example the OSA, the Emergency Regulations Ordinance and the Crimes Ordinance. For the OSA 1989, the administration was of the view that this act had only recently been placed on the statute books and it was premature for a review. The administration only committed to consider localizing the OSA before 1997. Even for this very limited scope of change, the reform process is almost a standstill. It has been two years at this writing since the preliminary result of the government review was announced, yet not a single law promised in the 1993 review has been amended.

These included relatively simple changes to the Registration of Local Newspapers Ordinance and the Prison Rules.

Out of the 17 laws the HKJA submitted to the government in August 1992, only some problematic provisions of three broadcasting laws — the Television Ordinance, the Broadcasting Authority Ordinance and the Telecommunication Ordinance were amended. The three amendments were introduced at the time the government had to provide a legal framework for the operation of Wharf Cable in the territory. Yet further liberalization of these broadcasting-related laws are needed.

Another small triumph was the scrapping of the political censorship provision in the Film Censorship Ordinance in December 1994.

However, the achievements should not be attributed to the colonial government. The abolition of the provision was put forward by Legislative Councillor Martin Lee in the form of a private member's bill. The government simply did not oppose its passage.

There are two other laws which have little progress. They are the Summary Offences Ordinance (sections on the use of loud hailers and the requirement for a police permit and assembly at night) and the Public Order Ordinance (a section on police power over public meetings and processions). Amendment bills were introduced into the Legco on 20 April 1994. They are still being studied by the Bills Committee of the Legco at this writing.

For other laws, there seems to have been continual slippage. Of particular concern are the delays in the review of security-related laws, including the OSA, the Emergency Regulations Ordinance and the Crimes Ordinance. The review of these laws was meant to have been completed in 1994. However, at this writing, the results of the review was still pending. A table compiled by the HKJA showing the "missed deadlines" in the reform of these laws is attached as an appendix at the end of this chapter for reference.

It appears that the government may lack the political will to amend many of these suspect laws, either because of resistance from within the civil service or because of fear of an adverse reaction from China.

However, the reality is that time is fast running out. There are in fact only two legislative sessions left before the hand-over in 1997, and possibly only one, if the final session is devoted to transitional matters.

There is a clear and urgent need to bring forward meaningful changes to suspect laws in the very near future to ensure that the law reform process can be completed well before 1997. The British government cannot shake off its moral responsibility if the future administration were to use these draconian laws to gag the press after 1997. It is now time for Governor Patten, as the last Governor of Hong Kong, to demonstrate his commitment to the people of Hong Kong.

PRESS FREEDOM IN THE SAR: AN OASIS OR A MIRAGE?

To a communist regime, the army and the media are the two things over which it seeks to have absolute control. There is no concept of a free press under a communist regime. All news media are generally regarded as the mouthpiece of the party. Their function is to serve the party, instead of acting as a watchdog on behalf of the people. A journalist's normal practice of gathering information would be equated with espionage, and any unfavourable reporting would be viewed as a deliberate act to damage the image of the party or the government, or to undermine its authority. Although the golden principle of "one country, two systems" is enshrined in both the Sino-British Joint Declaration and the Basic Law, a mini constitution for the Hong Kong Special Administrative Region (SAR), the free press in Hong Kong cannot be completely immune from the pressure experienced by our counterparts across the border. Events in recent years have proven that such worry is not unfounded.

The relationship between the Hong Kong press and the Chinese government has turned sour since the crack-down of the 1989 pro-democracy movement in China. It is probably true that Beijing has never forgiven the Hong Kong media for its forthright reporting of the 1989 pro-democracy protests.

In October 1989, the State Council's Hong Kong and Macau Affairs Office issued a set of seven regulations to restrain unauthorized reporting on the Mainland. The regulations basically required Hong Kong journalists to apply for approval before carrying out their journalistic duties in China. Journalists can only carry out reporting on the specific topic that had been approved. Any other reporting could be deemed as illegal. Although the implementation of the seven regulations has been relaxed over the years, the underlying deterrent effect remain unchanged. They are still the convenient tool frequently used by the Chinese authority to screen out unfavourable news organizations or individual journalists.

According to a September 1990 report in *Contemporary*,[5] a China-watch magazine, Beijing has classified the Hong Kong news organizations and journalists into four categories after the June 4 crack-down. They are:

1. left-wing newspapers controlled by the Chinese Communist Party (CCP);
2. publications which are politically neutral but which can be exploited and manipulated by the CCP and thus are the prime targets of united front tactics; these are further divided into organizations which actively court Beijing, and those that need to be coaxed;

3. publications which claim to be politically neutral or "middle-of-the-road" but are in fact pro-Taiwan. These are less easily manipulated but with extra united front work may be brought round;
4. those to be isolated and attacked.

Contemporary magazine also reported that journalists had been also classified into similar categories. While many Hong Kong journalists would not be surprised to learn about such surveillance conducted by the Chinese authorities, they were shocked by the arrest and jailing of Hong Kong journalist Xi Yang in 1994. The incident also shocked many people in Hong Kong. To many journalists, the Xi Yang case is a clear warning issued by the Chinese authorities.

Xi Yang is the second Hong Kong journalist to be detained by the Chinese authorities since 1992 on charges of spying on state secrets.

The industry was shaken when China detained a woman journalist, Leung Wai-man, of the Chinese-language newspaper *Express Daily* on 25 October 1992. She was alleged to have stolen "party and state secrets and documents." The "secrets" concerned was an advance copy of the keynote speech by Jiang Zemin, the General Secretary of the CCP, for its 14th Congress. Leung was detained for seven days before regaining her liberty but a Mainland journalist working for the New China News Agency was jailed for life for leaking Jiang's speech to Leung. His wife was given a six-year jail term.

Local journalists thought at the time that Leung's case might be an isolated incident. They held the view that with increased alertness, they could probably avoid stepping on the minefield again. However, with the second arrest came eleven months later, the signal sent out by the Chinese authorities was very clear — Hong Kong journalists had to "behave themselves," otherwise retribution was likely.

Xi Yang, who worked for many years as a journalist in China before joining the China desk of the Chinese-language newspaper *Ming Pao* in 1992, was arrested in Beijing by the State Security Bureau officers on 27 September 1993. His formal arrest was announced on 7 October along with that of Tian Ye, a deputy director of the foreign affairs department of the People's Bank of China.

Both Xi and Tian were charged under the provisions of the State Security Law. Xi was accused of "spying and stealing state financial secrets," and Tian of passing on the information to Xi. According to the official New

China News Agency, the information included unpublished interest rate changes and the bank's plans for international gold transactions.

The agency said, without elaboration, that the theft of this information had "caused serious consequences "and that both Xi and Tian had "candidly confessed" to the charges laid against them.

The journalistic profession was disturbed not only by the seriousness of the charges, but also by the way the Chinese authorities handled the case. Despite the numerous calls from both the local and international journalistic community and various groups in Hong Kong to urge the Chinese authorities to substantiate the charges against Xi and ensure that he would be tried in an open and fair manner, Xi was held incommunicado for six months after his arrest. He was allowed access only to his father, and that was only once. He was denied access to legal representation and his employer. No further details of his charges were disclosed.

Xi was tried in camera by the Beijing People's Intermediate Court on 28 March 1994. He was sentenced to 12 years' imprisonment. He will be deprived of his political rights for a further two years.

The ruling reached Xi's family verbally four days later, in the early morning of April Fool's Day. The court refused to confirm the ruling publicly until 4 April, a week after the sentence. The written judgment has never been made public, which itself is a violation of China's Criminal Proceedings Law.

Two Chinese lawyers had the courage to take on Xi's case on appeal. They argued for his innocence, on the grounds that there was inadequate evidence, a lack of clarity in the facts and improper application of the law when the intermediate court reached its verdict. They argued that Xi had not committed what the law defined as stealing, nor did he consciously try to "spy" on state secrets.

It came as no surprise when the Beijing Supreme People's Court upheld the original verdict. The harsh sentence provoked an unprecedented reaction from the journalistic profession and the community at large in Hong Kong. Hundreds of journalists joined a spontaneous march to the New China News Agency headquarters, and 1,300 of them, some from Taiwan, signed a petition letter to the Chinese leadership, regretting the conviction and heavy sentence. The general public also reacted strongly against the sentence. More than two thousand people took part in a march after Xi's appeal was rejected.

Another incident of serious concern to Hong Kong journalists has been the arrest in Beijing of Gao Yu, a Mainland journalist who has contributed articles to the *Mirror*, a pro-China magazine in Hong Kong. After being detained for more than 13 months, Gao's family was finally informed in November 1994 that she had been sentenced to six years in jail for "leaking state secrets to parties outside Mainland China." The Beijing Supreme People's Court rejected her appeal in December.

Gao was detained on 2 October 1993, two days before her scheduled departure for Hong Kong. She was due to travel on to the United States to take up a fellowship at the Columbia University Journalism School.

She was subsequently charged with revealing state secrets to people outside Mainland China. Like Xi, Gao was kept incommunicado. She was tried in camera in April 1994, but the Beijing Intermediate People's Court returned the case to the prosecutor for more evidence. There have been no developments since then.

Gao was the deputy editor of the now defunct *Economics Weekly*, which was run by Wang Juntao, a famous dissident who was sentenced to 13 years in jail, following the crushing of the 1989 pro-democracy movement. Wang was released in early 1994, apparently as part of China's efforts to secure American renewal of its most-favoured-nation (MFN) trading status. Many people see Gao's case as an example of China's "revolving door" system. One prominent dissident is released, then another is detained, to ensure there is another victim for the next round of trade concessions.

Although Gao's case was less publicized in Hong Kong, but together with the case of Xi, they cast a long shadow over press freedom in the run-up to 1997 and beyond. To journalists in Hong Kong, like Xi, Gao has become another victim of the ambiguous nature of Chinese law, in this case on state secrets.

To people in Hong Kong, Xi's case is not only about justice. It also has wider implications for the future of press freedom in Hong Kong. The underlying message is clear — Hong Kong journalists should not cross the line of what is and is not permissible in the eyes of the Chinese authorities. Yet the danger is that one can never tell for sure where the line is drawn. Together with the ambiguities involved in Chinese law, the Beijing authorities tend to interpret their laws freely, to suit a particular political need.

This worry is not unfounded or over-exaggerated. Take, for example, Hong Kong's post-1997 constitution, the Basic Law. Article 23 of that document stipulates that the post-1997 legislature must enact laws "to prohibit any act of treason, secession, sedition, subversion against the Central People's Government, or theft of state secrets." With the final interpretation of this part of the Basic Law lying firmly in the hands of the Standing Committee of China's National People's Congress — a political body — instead of the Hong Kong courts, post-1997 press freedom is in serious doubt.

Although the Chinese officials and their propaganda machinery in Hong Kong had publicly tried to assure the journalistic profession and the people in Hong Kong that press freedom is well protected by the Basic Law, but the message revealed was more worrisome than assured. While it is true that Article 27 of the Basic Law stipulates that "Hong Kong residents shall have freedom of speech, of the press and publication," and it is the first time that "freedom of speech" and "[freedom] of the press" has ever been enshrined in the constitutional documents in Hong Kong, the concept of "press freedom" seemed to be given a new kind of interpretation under the principle of "one country, two systems."

The new concept is simple: stick to your system, stay away from criticizing the other system too much. This new interpretation of press freedom was subtly revealed in an editorial in *Ta Kung Pao* on 2 June 1994. It was later echoed by Tsui Sze-man,[6] the proprietor of the pro-China *Mirror* magazine, in an commentary[7] appearing in *Wen Wei Po*, another Beijing mouthpiece in the territory.

While the press freedom report card in Hong Kong has not been encouraging over the past year, the issue of press freedom has been pushed to the forefront of the Sino-British political dispute as well. Journalists are now in a much more precarious position than in the past.

A very significant politicization of the issue was prompted by remarks made by Hong Kong's Chief Secretary, Anson Chan, in New York on 18 October 1994. She was speaking at a Hong Kong, United States business seminar.

Answering a question from the floor, Chan echoed the concerns of journalists that in recent years there had been a tendency on the part of some sections of the media to exercise self-censorship. She further reiterated that the Hong Kong government was committed to removing those draconian laws that inhibited press freedom.

To those who have been campaigning for several years to repeal those draconian laws, Chan's remarks sounded hollow. However, Chan's remarks drew immediate criticism from a Chinese official based in Hong Kong with the New China News Agency. Without naming Chan, the Agency's propaganda chief, Sun Nansheng, accused senior Hong Kong government officials of misleading outsiders into believing that Hong Kong would not have press freedom after 1997.

He questioned the motives of those who "exaggerated" the issue, as he put it. He implied that government officials wanted to incite anti-Beijing feelings and stir up mistrust over the principle of "one country, two systems," under which Hong Kong is meant to retain its separate identity after 1997.

He further warned that if the Hong Kong government wanted to amend any law to create trouble for the post-1997 administration, its plan would fail, because the future legislature would repeal any such law.

He also said self-censorship was a form of social responsibility, and a manifestation of journalistic ethics. He said news executives had the freedom to decide which articles should be included in a publication, and which should not. Two days later, the communist-controlled newspaper in Hong Kong, *Wen Wei Po*, echoed the same argument in an editorial.[8]

Both the New China News Agency propaganda chief and the editorial writer for *Wen Wei Po* tried to rationalize self-censorship as responsible media behaviour. To them, any resistance to self-censorship would be regarded as a lack of responsibility to readers, society and professional ethics.

While the arrest and detention of journalists has an obvious intimidating effect over journalists, self-censorship poses a more worrisome threat to press freedom.

A 1990 survey conducted by The Chinese University of Hong Kong[9] asked journalists about their attitude towards self-censorship. It found that 23% of about 500 respondents were apprehensive when criticizing the Chinese government. About 55% said they were not. The HKJA is, at this writing, in the process of finding out whether this trend has worsened through the series of public opinion surveys aimed at monitoring media performance and freedom of speech.

Acts of self-censorship are difficult to substantiate with hard evidence. However, the largest number of documented cases were recorded over the past two years. The following are a few examples.

1. The leading television station in Hong Kong, TVB, has so far refused to air two BBC documentaries on China, even though it

had the rights to the programmes, which it bought from the British broadcaster in the latter half of 1993. The documentaries are *Chairman Mao, the Last Emperor*, and *The Laogai*, which reports on Chinese labour camps. The reluctance of TVB to air these programmes was clearly aimed at avoiding embarrassment for China, which had in particular attacked the Mao documentary on the grounds that it had "seriously hurt the feelings of the Chinese people."

2. The management of the territory's other terrestrial broadcaster, ATV, intervened in an editorial decision in May 1994 to broadcast parts of a Spanish documentary on the Beijing massacre in June 1989, to mark the fifth anniversary of the crushing of the pro-democracy movement. Management backed down, after six senior journalists from the station's News and Public Affairs Department made a public protest. However, the journalists decided to resign, citing a loss of confidence in management.

3. In April 1994, Rupert Murdoch's satellite broadcasting station, STAR TV, dropped BBC World Service Television from its northern beam, which covers China and Hong Kong. Murdoch subsequently admitted in an interview that he had dropped the BBC in the hope of easing tensions with China. He also admitted in the same interview that the sale of his shares in a major Hong Kong newspaper group, the *SCMP*, was likewise aimed at avoiding conflict with China.

Although these examples all relate to the broadcast media, it does not mean that the print media is immune from self-censorship. It merely indicates that self-censorship in the print media is more discreet and more difficult to prove.

Self-censorship highlights another problem — the desire of media proprietors to maintain good relations with Beijing, or at least not to be seen to be anti-Beijing. As more and more media enterprises would like to extend their markets to China, the pressure on media owners for self-censorship is growing during the run-up to 1997.

Hong Kong's media has entered an era when challenges and hopes coexist. While the picture for the future of press freedom may be gloomy, it is not hopeless. To many people, particularly our counterparts in Mainland China, Hong Kong is an oasis of press freedom in the region. To remain so after 1997, and to water the surrounding desert with the free flow of information, are challenges for both the journalistic profession and society at large. There is no ready and easy solution except to keep eternal vigilance in safeguarding this basic human right.

AFTERWORD

After this writing, the government hastily introduced a number of legislative amendments to the Legco in April, May and June, hoped that they would be passed by July 1995, the end of the 1994–1995 legislative session.

These include changes to the Places of Public Entertainment Ordinance, Defamation Ordinance, Judicial Proceedings (Regulation of Reports) Ordinance, Complex Commercial Crimes Ordinance, Criminal Procedure Ordinance, Registration of Local Newspapers Ordinance, Interpretation and General Clauses Ordinance, and Emergency Regulations Ordinance.

Many of these amendments are peripheral to critical freedom of expression issues, some appear to be cosmetic.

NOTES

1. The "freedom index" poll was conducted by RTHK, the Department of Communication of Hong Kong Baptist College (now Baptist University), the Faculty of Humanities and Social Sciences of City Polytechnic of Hong Kong (now City University) and the Polling, Business Strategies and Market Research Consultants Co. Ltd.
2. Article 16 of the BORO reads:
   (1) Everyone shall have the right to hold opinions without interference.
   (2) Everyone shall have the right to freedom of expression; this right shall include freedom to seek, receive and impart information and ideas of all kinds, regardless of frontiers, either orally, in writing or in print, in the form of art, or through any other media of his choice.
   (3) The exercise of the rights provided for in paragraph (2) of this article carries with it special duties and responsibilities. It may therefore be subject to certain restrictions, but these shall only be such as are provided by law and are necessary — (a) for respect of the rights or reputations of others; or (b) for the protection of national security or of public order (ordre public), or of public health or morals.

3. 元邦建編著：《香港史略》，中流出版社，頁232。

4. The 17 laws were: Official Secrets Act, Television Ordinance, Telecommunication Ordinance, Broadcasting Authority Ordinance, Emergency Regulations Ordinance and Emergency (Principal) Regulations, Crimes Ordinance (the part on treason and sedition), Police Force Ordinance (Section 50(7) on search and seizure), Prevention of Bribery Ordinance (Section 30), Registration of Local Newspapers Ordinance, Judicial Proceedings (Regulation of Reports) Ordinance, Contempt of Court (need for a comprehensive ordinance), Film Censorship Ordinance (political censorship), Places of Public Entertainment Ordinance (prohibitions), Summary Offences Ordinance (section on the use of loud hailers), Public Order Ordinance (control of meetings and processions), Undesirable Medical Advertisements Ordinance, Defamation Ordinance (criminal libel).

5. "Structuring Policy towards Hong Kong and Macau: The Media Classified into Four Groups," *Contemporary*, 8 September 1990, p. 4. The *Contemporary* was closed down in March 1995 due to financial reasons.

6. Tsui Sze-man is a member of the Standing Committee of the People's Political Consultative Committee of the People's Republic of China and a member of the Preliminary Working Committee of the Preparatory Committee for the Hong Kong SAR.

7. Tsui Sze-man, "The Concert of Press Freedom under the One Country, Two Systems," *Wen Wei Po*, 21 June 1994, p. A10.

8. "To Comment on Anson Chan's 'Theory of Media Self-censorship'," *Wen Wei Po*, 25 October 1994, p. A2.

9. The survey on Hong Kong journalists was conducted by Dr. Joseph M. Chan, Dr. Paul S. N. Lee and Dr. Chin-chuan Lee. Dr. Chan and Dr. Paul Lee are both lecturers in Journalism and Communication at The Chinese University of Hong Kong. Dr. C. C. Lee is professor in Journalism and Mass Communication at the University of Minnesota, U.S.

Appendix

PRESS FREEDOM: A HISTORY OF MISSED DEADLINES*

Legislation	Provision	Government's position	1993 status	1994 status	1995 status
1. Emergency Regulations Ordinance	Subsidiary legislation providing powers to deal with a state of emergency or occasion of public danger. Powers include regulations providing for censorship, amending/suspending other enactments and control of essential services.	The Attorney-General's Chambers (AGC) has conducted a review of the Ordinance and the subsidiary legislation to establish in particular whether it is compatible with the Bill of Rights and to see if there is a need for more defined legislative controls upon the exercise of these powers.	Review to be completed by the end of 1993.	AGC's review completed. Security Branch advised the Legislative Council (Legco)'s Constitutional Affairs Panel at its meeting on 21 February 1994 that the Administration was working on proposals for amendment of the Ordinance and subsidiary legislation and would submit these to the Executive Council (Exco) in the next few months.	Still under review. The government has pledged to report back to the Legco by July 1995.

* As at 17 March 1995. Reprinted by permission of the Hong Kong Journalists Association.

Appendix (cont'd)

Legislation	Provision	Government's position	1993 status	1994 status	1995 status
2. Official Secrets Act 1989	The 1989 Act provides for six areas of information, where it can be shown that disclosure caused damage to the national interest. The Act will cease to apply after 1997.	Consideration is being given to the localization of the law. The government is of the view that it is more liberal than previous legislation and although not subject to the Bill of Rights it is consistent with the Bill.	In November 1993, the government expected to put proposals to the Exco in the next few months.	In May 1994, no decision on the preferred course of action or on timing had been reached by the Administration. Further consideration was required before the advice of the Exco could be sought.	As above.
3. Crimes Ordinance	Sections 2 and 9: Treason and sedition are offences under the Crimes Ordinance.	There is a need to review the provisions, as they are predicated on British sovereignty and will need adaptation before 1 July 1997. Consultation with the Chinese side will be required on any such adaptation. As treason and sedition are also specified in Article 23 of the Basic Law, they will be looked at together with other Article 23 offences.	As of November 1993, the review was pending. Expected to put proposals to the Exco in the next few months.	In May 1994, there had been no decision on the preferred course of action or timing. Further consideration is required before the advice of the Exco could be sought.	As above.

| 4. Prevention of Bribery Ordinance (POBO) | Under Section 30, it is an offence to disclose, without lawful authority or reasonable excuse, the identity of a suspect under investigation or the details of an investigation, before any arrest is made. | The Administration thinks the provision is necessary to protect the integrity of an investigation and to protect the identity and reputation of a suspect when an investigation results in no arrest or other similar action. | No change proposed. | ICAC Review Committee upheld the government's position on Section 30. | The Administration has decided to appeal against a magistrate's ruling that Section 30 of the POBO was inconsistent with the Bill of Rights. Result of the appeal is pending. |

Appendix (cont'd)

Legislation	Provision	Government's position	1993 status	1994 status	1995 status
5. Police Force Ordinance	Section 50(7): Police power of entry, search and seizure.	Section 50(7) was amended in 1992 to remove possible inconsistency with the Bill of Rights Ordinance. There is therefore no need to pursue any immediate amendment for Bill of Rights compatibility. It is doubtful whether journalistic materials should be singled out for different treatment. The Law Reform Commission (LRC) report on police powers recommended changes.	An inter-departmental working group was studying the LRC report on police powers. As of November 1993, the group had examined four out of ten chapters of the report. Hoped to finish examining the LRC recommendations and take a view as soon as possible. A public consultation exercise would then conducted.	As of May 1994, the inter-departmental working group had examined six out of the ten chapters of the report. Hoped to finish examining the LRC recommendations and take a view as soon as possible. A public consultation exercise would then be conducted.	Still under review. The government has pledged to report back to the Legco by July 1995.

6. Public Order Ordinance	Sections 6, 9, 13, 14, 17, 17D: Police power to regulate public meetings and processions to prohibit, stop, prevent holding of, and disperse public gatherings.	It may be considered as restriction on freedom of expression. A review on grounds of operational needs has been conducted. The primary objective of the review is to balance public order/safety concerns with the rights of individuals to exercise their rights of assembly and expression in public gatherings.	Currently under review on grounds of operational need and Bill of Rights considerations.	The Bill was introduced into the Legco on 20 April 1994.	Bill is being studied by a Legco Bills Committee. No time has been fixed yet for the resumption of second and third reading.
7. Summary Offences Ordinance	(a) Section 4(29): Use of loud hailer and the requirement for police permit.	Provision not necessary and will be repealed since Section 5(1)(b) of Noise Control Ordinance already makes it an offence to use a loud hailer in a public place, the noise of which is a source of annoyance to any person.	As of April 1993, the government intended to introduce amending legislation in the next few months.	The Bill was introduced into the Legco on 20 April 1994.	Bill is being studied by a Legco Bills Committee. No time has been fixed yet for the resumption of second and third reading.

Appendix (cont'd)

Legislation	Provision	Government's position	1993 status	1994 status	1995 status
	(b) Section 8(d): Offence of assembly at night without lawful excuse and failure to report such assembly.	Provision outdated and unreasonable. It will be repealed.	As of April 1993, the government's position on this section depended on enactment of amendments arising from a comprehensive review of the Ordinance. Hopefully, this would be completed by mid-1994.	A provision repealing Section 8(d) was included in the Administration of Justice (Miscellaneous Provisions) Bill, which was introduced into the Legco on 11 May 1994.	Provision repealed on 17 February 1995.

| 8. Places of Public Entertainment Ordinance | (a) Under section 8(2) of the Ordinance, the Commissioner for Television and Entertainment Licensing (CTEL) is given wide powers in regard to the issue of permits which control the content and form of public entertainment. | The Administration has reviewed the Ordinance with the objective of bringing the content of the Ordinance more in line with present-day circumstances and the needs of the community, and removing provisions which are no longer in use. The dual licensing of public entertainment events will be avoided since this is cumbersome and bureaucratic. Besides, CTEL's very wide discretion in the grant, refusal or cancellation of permits is probably inconsistent with Article 16 of the Bill of Rights Ordinance. This section will be repealed and the permit system will be abolished. The two municipal councils will become the sole authority to issue licences governing the structural and fire safety of venues for public entertainment, as well as safety of the participants. | The government intended to introduce amending legislation in the 1993–1994 Legco session. | Amendment bill will be introduced into the Legco before the end of the 1994–1995 session. | Unlikely to be introduced into the Legco in the 1994–1995 session, because there is no Legco slot. |

Appendix (cont'd)

Legislation	Provision	Government's position	1993 status	1994 status	1995 status
	(b) Regulation 174(1): Police power to close or temporarily vacate places of public entertainment.	The Administration agrees the Police should not be the guardian of public morals. At the same time, police power to stop an entertainment for public order or public safety reasons should be retained.	As above.	As above.	As above.
9. Registration of Local Newspapers Ordinance	(a) Regulation 3 of Newspapers Registration and Distribution Regulations, and Regulation 4 of the News Agencies Registration Regulations.	Unfettered discretion of Registrar in requiring particulars from applicants to register a local newspaper/news agency. Discretion to be narrowed by deleting the word "absolute." The Registrar would still be able to require additional information but only in line with Article 16(3) of the Bill of Rights.	As of April 1993, the government intended to introduce amending legislation in the 1993–1994 Legco session; in November 1993, the target date was revised to the 1994–1995 Legco session.	Amendments will be submitted to the Exco for approval in September 1994.	Subsidiary legislation will be introduced into the Legco in March/April 1995.

| (b) Regulation 14 of Newspapers Registration and Distribution Regulations: Registrar has wide discretionary power in approving documents that can be distributed with newspapers. No document (other than a document forming an integral part of a newspaper) shall be distributed in or with any newspaper without the consent of the Registrar. | This is too vague and the Administration suggests repealing it. | As above. | As above. | As above. |

Appendix (cont'd)

Legislation	Provision	Government's position	1993 status	1994 status	1995 status
10. Prison Rules	Prison Rules 76(a) and (b) restrict the disclosure of information by Correctional Services Department (CSD) staff to the public and the press. Prison Rule 239(1)(e)(ii) makes it a disciplinary offence for CSD staff to divulge information to the press and the public.	Prison Rule 76(a) will be recast to narrow its application to the effect that CSD staff must not disclose information which would affect prison security or interfere with prisoners' privacy. Prison Rules 76(b), 239(1)(e)(ii) will be deleted.	As of April 1993, the government intended to introduce amending legislation in the next few months; in November 1993, the target date was revised to January 1994.	Target date for amendment in May/June 1994.	Subsidiary legislation will be introduced into the Legco in March/April 1995.

11. Television Ordinance	(a) Regulation 4 of Television (Standards of Programmes) Regulations excludes certain material from broadcast.	Regulation is to be amended along the lines of the Film Censorship Ordinance.	Will be included with next amendments to subsidiary legislation under the Television Ordinance or in the proposed Broadcasting Bill in July 1994.	Will be included with next amendments to subsidiary legislation under the Television Ordinance or in the proposed Broadcasting Bill in February 1995.	The proposed Broadcasting Bill will not be introduced into the Legco until early in the 1995–1996 session, because its February 1995 slot has been transferred to the Control of Obscene and Indecent Articles (Amendment) Bill.

Appendix (cont'd)

Legislation	Provision	Government's position	1993 status	1994 status	1995 status
	(b) Regulation 6 of Commercial Television (Advertising) Regulations requires the approval in writing of the Director of Health before advertisements for any medical preparation can be broadcast on television.	The scope of Director of Health's discretion is unqualified, i.e. there is no indication of the criteria upon which his discretion is to be exercised. The Administration will look into the regulation in the context of the Broadcasting Bill and propose amendments to clarify what sort of medical advertisements were intended to be covered.	This will be looked into in the proposed Broadcasting Bill in July 1994.	Action will be taken in the proposed Broadcasting Bill in February 1995.	As above.

12. Telecommunication Ordinance	(a) Section 13C: It deals with prohibitions on the broadcasting of certain materials and programmes on radio. Under this provision, the Broadcasting Authority (via a licence condition) may require a licensee to "refrain from broadcasting any programme" which the Authority thinks would contravene directions issued by Governor-in-Council or any regulation under Section 130.	The power of the Broadcasting Authority is considered too broad and it seems there is no need for it when adequate powers already exist to deal with licensees who broadcast programmes which contravene directions or regulations. Section 13C will be reviewed/repealed in the context of the Broadcasting Bill.	Action will be taken in the proposed Broadcasting Bill scheduled for July 1994.	Action will be taken in the proposed Broadcasting Bill scheduled for February 1995.	The proposed Broadcasting Bill will not be introduced into the Legco until early in the 1995–1996 session, because its February 1995 slot has been transferred to the Control of Obscene and Indecent Articles (Amendment) Bill.

Appendix (cont'd)

Legislation	Provision	Government's position	1993 status	1994 status	1995 status
	(b) Section 28 makes it an offence to transmit, by telecommunica-tion, a message known to be false.	Article 36 of the Constitution of the International Telecommuni-cation Union obliges members to take the steps required to prevent the transmission or circulation of false or deceptive distress, urgency, safety or identification signals. However, current wording of Section 28 is far wider than is necessary for this particular purpose. Propose to circumscribe it in line with obligations under Constitution of the International Telecommuni-cation Union, Article 36.	An overall review of telecommunica-tion legislation, which will encompass this matter, is being conducted. Firm intention to introduce an amendment bill into the Legco in the 1994–1995 session.	An overall review of telecommunication legislation, which will encompass this matter, is being conducted. Firm intention to introduce an amendment bill into the Legco in the 1994–1995 session.	Amendment is planned for the 1995–1996 Legco session.
	(c) Section 33 provides for prohibition and interception of telecommuni-cations.	The LRC is examining existing legislation on privacy, including interception of communications. The Administration is also reviewing legislation to see if it is compatible with the Bill of Rights. It wishes to take the LRC's views into account in this review.	Action is pending LRC report, which will be available probably around early 1995.	Action is pending LRC report, which will be available probably around early 1995.	Still under review. No timetable set.

Ordinance				
13. Post Office Ordinance	(a) Section 13 provides for interception of mail.	As above.	As above.	As above.	As above.
	(b) Section 32(1)(h) prohibits people from sending by post any seditious publication.	There will be a need to review this subsection as well as Section 32(1)(g), which prohibits people from sending by post anything whose circulation is forbidden in Hong Kong or the country of destination. This review will need to take into account Bill of Rights aspects.	The review is pending. Expected to put proposals to the Exco in the next few months.	This is part of an overall review which includes the Official Secrets Act.	Still under review. No timetable set.
14. Defamation Ordinance	Under section 6, it is an offence to maliciously publish any defamatory libel.	The Administration thinks that this section is necessary "for respect of the rights or reputations of others," i.e. a permissible limitation under Article 16 of Bill of Rights.	No change proposed.	No change proposed.	To be repealed by the Administration of Justice (Miscellaneous Amendments) Bill, which will be introduced in May 1995.

Appendix (cont'd)

Legislation	Provision	Government's Position	1993 status	1994 status	1995 status
15. Judicial Proceedings (Regulation of Reports) Ordinance	Under Section 3(1)(a), it is an offence to publish, in relation to any judicial proceedings, any indecent matter or any medical, surgical, or physiological details of a revolting or offensive nature.	The Administration believes that a ban on publishing proceedings under Section 3(1)(a) can be characterized as a measure designed to protect public morality. A ban on publishing the details of matrimonial proceedings under Section 3(1)(b) can be seen as necessary to protect the parties' private lives, and to protect their reputations. Both are permissible limitations on the right to freedom of expression under the Bill of Rights.	No change proposed.	No change proposed.	Change proposed, as above.

Note: Laws 1–7 are security-related ordinances of grave concern to the HKJA; laws 6–12 are those first proposed for reform by the government in March 1993; laws 13–15 are other laws proposed for change.

21

Public Opinion in the Late Transition Period

Robert T. Y. Chung

This chapter focused on the development of pubic opinion as reflected in various opinion polls conducted in the latter half of the transition period, from 1991, to be exact.[1] If we take the year 1985 to be the beginning of transition, then 1991 was exactly at the middle of the twelve-year period in the run-up to 1997. Incidentally, it was the year when the first direct election to Hong Kong's top legislature, the Legislative Council (Legco), took place, and with it the rapid development of opinion polls.[2] At the time of writing, there were about two years before the final countdown, and Hong Kong was in the middle of its late transition period. After four years' rapid development, opinion polls have become an event of everyday life, and many opinion questions have been tracked over a long period of time. Other than constitutional changes and their related political development, the emergence of opinion polls at the second half of the transition period was probably the most significant development in the political culture of Hong Kong.

To put the development of public opinion in perspective, we will first attempt a schematization of the twelve-year transition period, and then present the findings of opinion polls under five broad headings, namely people's trust in different governments, their faith in political leaders, their support of political parties, their feeling over the constitutional disputes, and their views of future development.

A SCHEMATIZATION OF THE TRANSITION HISTORY

Rumour has it that Murray MacLehose, then Governor of Hong Kong, first raised the issue of the future of Hong Kong in his visit to Beijing between

24 March and 4 April 1979.[3] Chinese Vice-Premier Deng Xiaoping allegedly told MacLehose in private that China wanted to recover the sovereignty of Hong Kong in 1997, but asked him to convey his message to investors in Hong Kong that they should put their hearts at ease.

On 7 October 1979, the Chinese Premier Hua Guofeng, at a press conference held before his visit to Europe, said,

> At present, our relationship with both the United Kingdom and the British authority in Hong Kong is quite good. We think that, through negotiations, a satisfactory way can be sought to settle the question of Hong Kong, Kowloon and the New Territories. But I can say, no matter how the question is resolved, we would take into consideration the interests of the investors there.[4]

This was the first official statement from China that the future of Hong Kong could be settled through negotiations.

A number of development followed, the most significant being China's formulation of the concept of Special Administrative Regions (SARs) whereby existing lifestyle and socio-economic systems of the regions could remain unchanged irrespective of any change of sovereignty.[5] In various occasions, Chinese leaders also told investors not to worry about the transition of sovereignty, and that Hong Kong people will be given great autonomy to govern Hong Kong after 1997. Under this background, on 22 September 1982, the British Prime Minister Margaret Thatcher arrived Beijing for negotiations.

What happened in the following two years was not the subject of this chapter, suffice it to say that the first round of formal talks began on 12 July 1983, and the last (twenty-second) round finished on 6 September 1984. Agreement was finally reached and on 19 December 1984, Britain and China signed the Sino-British Joint Declaration on the future of Hong Kong. The Joint Declaration was ratified on 28 May 1985, and Hong Kong formally entered into a twelve-year period of transition. The period of twelve years was not chosen because of its desired length, but rather to set at rest uncertainties about the future status of Hong Kong in view of the expiry in 1997 of the lease over the New Territories.[6]

To schematize the history of Hong Kong's transition, we may divide the twelve years from 1985 to 1997 into three stages of four years, namely the early transition period, the mid-transition period, and the late transition period. Incidentally, the six-year period from 1979 to 1985 can be considered as the pre-transition period which could itself be divided into two halves: the first half being the period between 1979 and 1982 when Britain and China tested each other on possible formulations for the future of Hong Kong, and the second half being the period between 1982 and 1985 when twenty-two rounds of formal talks occurred, culminated by the ratification of the Joint Declaration. These two periods could be called the early and late pre-transition period respectively.

The division of Hong Kong's transition period between 1985 and 1997 into three periods was not simply a heuristic device; each period was marked by significant events which affected the development of public opinion (see Table 1).

❑ *Early Transition Period*

As shown in Table 1, the period between June 1985 and June 1989 can be called the early period of transition. June 1985 marked the date when the Joint Declaration officially came into effect, as well as the establishment of the Basic Law Drafting Committee under the National People's Congress, while June 1989 marked the period of uproar and unrest across the whole of China. Over a million people in Hong Kong took to the streets to protest against China's crack-down on pro-democracy movements in Beijing and other major cities. The Hong Kong Alliance in Support of Patriotic Democratic Movement in China was formed and became a focal point for anti-Beijing activities up to this date. On the public's mentality, the signing of the Joint Declaration in 1984 signified an definite schedule for the change of sovereignty, but exactly how the "one country, two systems" would work was still something to be seen. The Joint Declaration was apparently received with optimism from the general public, but they were in fact offered no choice.[7] We could therefore characterize people's general feeling at this early stage of transition to be one of reserved optimism.

In the middle of this early transition period, in May 1987, the government released a Green Paper to consult the public on a range of options for political reform,[8] the most controversial of which was whether direct elections should be introduced into the Legco election in 1988. A survey office was set up to receive submissions from the public, as well as commissioning a large opinion survey by a consultant firm. In October 1987, the survey office produced a report concluding that the public was not in favour of introducing direct elections in 1988.[9] But the methods used to

Table 1: A Schematization of Hong Kong's Transition Period

Mid-year	Periodization	Events	The public sentiment	Development of opinion polls
1979–82 Early	} Pre-transition period	1979: MacLehose visited China	Wished for maintaining the status quo	Scanty
1982–85 Late		1982: Sino-British talks began		Scanty
1985–87 Early	} Early transition period	1985: Joint Declaration ratified	Reserved optimism	Scanty
1987–89 Late		1987: Green Paper on constitutional development		Green Paper generated some polls
1989–91 Early	} Mid-transition period	1989: June 4 incident	Despair and distrust	Rallies rather than polls
1991–93 Late		1991: First Legco direct elections		Rapid development after 1991
1993–95 Early	} Late transition period	1993: Sino-British row	Settled for future	Momentum continued
1995–97 Late		1995: Second Legco direct elections		[too early to tell]
		1997: Hong Kong become an SAR under China		

aggregate the public submissions, and the research design used by the survey consultant, was widely criticized and the report was generally held to be of no value.[10] Nonetheless, in February 1988, the government released a White Paper based on the report confirming that there were not to be any changes in 1988 other than the addition of two more functional constituencies and a slight reduction of the number of appointed members.[11] The introduction of directly elected seats in the Legco was deferred to 1991.

During the four-month consultation period on the Green Paper, the survey office received a total of 131,589 written submissions, 168 opinion surveys, and 21 signature campaigns, in addition to the large survey conducted by the consultant firm. In the middle of this early transition period, therefore, the public's attention was at one point drawn to the issue of constitutional development. Opinion polls were used, and possibly engineered, to represent the public's view in addition to written submissions and other forms of expression. On the whole, however, the public appeared to have remained calm and cautiously optimistic.

❑ *Mid-transition Period*

The next stage of transition, namely the mid-transition period, marked a very different period of political development. The June 4 incident of 1989 sent a thrilling thunder across China and the whole world. Over a million people in Hong Kong were estimated to have taken to the streets in support of the pro-democracy movements in China. Television coverage of the crack-down instilled not just anger at the People's Liberation Army, but also fear in the communist regime. The assurance that China would allow the people of Hong Kong to live the way they like was wiped out in a single day. The Hong Kong Alliance in Support of Patriotic Democratic Movement in China was formed in the midst of anger and despair. The more the Chinese government denounced the Alliance as subversive, the stronger was people's feeling against the Chinese government. It was against this background that the liberals managed to secure a landslide victory in the first direct elections of the Legco held in September 1991.[12] As one scholar observed,

> It is not clear, however, that all the supporters of the Hong Kong Alliance were necessarily committed to the liberals' vision of a democratic future which, in any event, was rather vaguely stated. What united them — and what may have

been reflected in the 1991 direct elections results — was a profound distaste for the Chinese system of government, for its political values and for the implication which this had for Hong Kong.[13]

The public mood in this mid-transition period was therefore anger and unrest. In the first half of this period, between 1989 and 1991, public discontent usually took the form of mass rallies. After the direct elections of September 1991, however, with the liberals' success in gaining their entries to the top legislature, confrontations began to take place within the council chambers. Election politics also facilitated the rapid growth of opinion polls, which quickly became a popular instrument for testing the public's sentiment. In this mid-transition period, therefore, election politics and opinion polls together provided some new channels for public expression, which were taken with great scepticism by the Chinese government.

The exact time for the ending of this period and the beginning of the next was not a clear-cut one. In the middle of 1993, China and Britain were again undergoing formal talks over the constitutional development of Hong Kong. But unlike their previous talks in the early 1980s, these talks did not conclude with any agreement. On the contrary, the talks merely provided occasions for the two sides to reiterate their stands at the conference table, and to exchange accusations outside the conference room. This mid-transition period, therefore, ended in the middle of a big row over the constitutional development of Hong Kong.

From a developmental perspective, the row was in fact a natural outcome of Hong Kong people's reaction towards the June 4 incident, on the diplomatic level. We have seen how the liberals secured their landslide victory in the 1991 direct elections because of people's distaste for China's cracking down on pro-democracy movements. Britain after 1989 also readjusted its policy towards China, and by the end of 1991, saw the opportunity to stiffen its stand towards China over the development of Hong Kong. David Wilson was called back to Britain in early 1992, and a political heavyweight Chris Patten replaced him as the Governor of Hong Kong from July 1992. Sino-British relationship turned sour immediately after Chris Patten announced his package of constitutional reform in October 1992. After some heavy exchanges of rhetoric, talks were opened in April 1993 to discuss constitutional development in Hong Kong. But after seventeen rounds of talks spanning over seven months, they finally broke down in November 1993 without any agreement. From then on, Hong Kong entered its final stage of transition: the late transition period.

❑ *Late Transition Period*

After the breakdown of Sino-British talks, Patten's reform package was quickly put to the Legco. The first part of the proposals was passed on 15 December 1993, and the second part on 30 June 1994. Together they set down the system for the new wave of direct elections for 1994–1995, at all three levels of representative government. At the time of writing, the District Board elections and the municipal council elections have already taken place on 18 September 1994 and 5 March 1995 respectively; the most important elections of all, the Legco elections were due to take place on 17 September 1995. It was not yet possible to summarize the development of public opinion at the late transition period, but at least in the first half, after the breakdown of Sino-British talks, the public was preparing themselves for the final changes in the political system, before reverting to China. Likewise, the Chinese were also carving a way out of the final transition in their own way. The author believes that at the latter half of the final transition period, after the September 1995 elections, public opinion will gradually settle on the technical operation of the 1997 transition, and a direction for post-transition development will gradually take shape. On top of these, election politics and opinion polls will continue to develop, and the society would continue to become more open and cosmopolitan.

TRUST IN GOVERNMENTS

In 1985 and 1986, just after Hong Kong entered the early transition period, a research team from The Chinese University of Hong Kong conducted two surveys in the district of Kwun Tong, as a pilot study of some extensive territory-wide surveys in the years that followed.[14] On respondents' trust in different governments, the 1985 survey yielded the figures in Table 2.

Similar findings were obtained in their 1986 survey, where 76.4% of the respondents trusted the Hong Kong government, 56.6% the British government, and 31.8% the Chinese government.[15] As seen in Table 2, the rating scale used by the researchers did not have a mid-point value, and may

Table 2: People's Trust in Governments, 1985

	Hong Kong govt.	British govt.	Chinese govt.
Distrust very much	3.9%	3.5%	8.1%
Distrust	12.9%	30.9%	34.8%
Trust	68.2%	37.8%	29.7%
Trust very much	3.9%	1.7%	1.8%
Don't know/No answer	14.0%	26.1%	25.6%

Source: Lau Siu-kai, and Kuan Hsin-chi, *The Ethos of the Hong Kong Chinese* (Hong Kong: The Chinese University Press, 1988), p. 84.

Table 3: People's Trust in Governments, 1988 (n = 1,662)

	Hong Kong govt.	British govt.	Chinese govt.
Strongly distrust	0.9%	4.2%	6.7%
Distrust	17.3%	25.3%	37.1%
Average	27.5%	26.9%	23.3%
Trust	45.1%	29.0%	19.6%
Strongly trust	3.4%	1.4%	1.4%
Don't know/No answer	5.7%	13.2%	11.9%

Source: Lau Siu-kai, Kuan Hsin-chi, and Wan Po-san, "Political Attitudes," in *Indicators of Social Development: Hong Kong 1988* (Hong Kong: Hong Kong Institute of Asia-Pacific Studies, The Chinese University of Hong Kong, 1991), p. 199.

have the effect of polarizing the result. In 1988, a similar question was repeated by an expanded team of researchers in a territory-wide survey,[16] and the results are shown in Table 3.[17]

We could therefore conclude that at the early transition period, Hong Kong people tended to distrust the Chinese and British governments, but had reasonable faith in the Hong Kong government. Researchers of the 1988 survey explained Hong Kong government's legitimacy by the satisfactory performance of the bureaucracy, the lack of viable political alternatives, and habituation, but did not explain people's lack of trust in the Chinese and British governments. Whatever the reason, the pattern repeated itself at the late transition period, as shown by Table 4.

Table 4: People's Trust towards Different Governments

	1994 average			1993 average		
	Hong Kong govt.	Chinese govt.	British govt.	Hong Kong govt.	Chinese govt.	British govt.
Successful cases	6,325	6,325	6,325	7,572	7,572	7,572
Response rate	59.5%	59.5%	59.5%	56.7%	56.7%	56.7%
Raw data						
Very much	6.7%	2.2%	1.9%	8.9%	2.8%	2.8%
Just so	40.5%	17.0%	20.5%	45.8%	21.1%	24.7%
Neutral	23.3%	21.5%	23.4%	16.9%	17.3%	19.4%
Not much	19.2%	37.0%	33.5%	17.6%	34.2%	30.7%
Not at all	3.6%	13.9%	12.3%	3.8%	15.0%	12.8%
Don't know	6.8%	8.4%	8.3%	7.1%	9.6%	9.5%
Total	100.0%	100.0%	100.0%	100.0%	100.0%	100.0%
Collapsed data						
Trust	47.1%	19.2%	22.4%	54.7%	23.9%	27.6%
Neutral	23.3%	21.5%	23.4%	16.9%	17.3%	19.4%
Distrust	22.8%	50.8%	45.8%	21.4%	49.2%	43.5%
Don't know	6.8%	8.4%	8.3%	7.1%	9.6%	9.5%
Total	100.0%	100.0%	100.0%	100.0%	100.0%	100.0%
Omitting "don't know" (i.e. % of those expressing an opinion)						
Trust	50.6%	21.0%	24.4%	58.8%	26.4%	30.5%
Neutral	25.0%	23.5%	25.6%	18.2%	19.1%	21.4%
Distrust	24.5%	55.5%	50.0%	23.0%	54.4%	48.1%
Total	100.0%	100.0%	100.0%	100.0%	100.0%	100.0%

Out of the 6,325 respondents questioned by 12 monthly polls throughout 1994, 47.1% trusted the Hong Kong government, 22.4% the British government, and 19.2% the Chinese government. The 1993 figures were 54.7%, 27.6%, and 23.9% respectively. This showed a drop of trust level for all three governments from 1993, as well as from 1988, if they were comparable.

All in all, whatever the reason, people's trust in the Chinese government have remained very low throughout the period discussed, both before and after the June 4 incident of 1989. The wide gap between people's trust in the Hong Kong government and the British government also indicated that people did not perceive the colonial government as simply an agent of British sovereignty. In view of people's low level of trust towards the Chinese government, it would be very important for the future SAR government to be able to exercise its autonomy under the "one country, two systems" formulation, until people have built up enough faith in the Chinese government, otherwise the SAR government would have to suffer a legitimacy crisis which would be detrimental to both China and Hong Kong.

TRUST IN POLITICAL LEADERS

Based on their 1985 and 1986 survey findings, Lau and Kuan observed,

> The unavailability of respected and trusted political leaders has been a perennial shortfall in the political system of Hong Kong. Bureaucratic hegemony and the non-existence of a meaningful electoral process almost completely preclude the emergence of popular, not to say charismatic, leaders exercising diffuse and personal authority.[18]

Later, using their survey data collected in 1988 (after the 1987 debate on introducing direct elections to the Legco), they reported that 64.1% of the respondents claimed to trust Legco members, but only 48.0% gave positive answers to the following question: "Do you think that through the direct election of Legislative Council members, some more trustworthy political leaders can emerge?" They then reported that only 25.0% of the respondents supported the formation of political parties in Hong Kong while 50.5% opposed it.[19]

To monitor the public's support of the political leaders in the course of electoral development, since July 1991, the author has constantly conducted polls which requested respondents to rate their support of various Legco members on a 0–100 point scale.[20] Table 5 summarized the findings obtained in 1993 and 1994 for the most popular members.[21]

Recognition rates in Table 5 referred to the proportion of valid ratings for individual leaders across the entire sample, indicating their general popularity. The support ratings were in fact averages of all valid ratings, and was used to indicate the degree of support enjoyed by individual leaders. A leader must be very popular in both senses in order to top the ladder.

Generally speaking, the list was fairly stable across the two years. Six members were regularly on the list throughout the two years, namely Lau Chin-shek, Emily Lau, Martin Lee, Szeto Wah, Selina Chow, and Allen Lee, and could be regarded as the most popular Legislative Councillors. In terms of support ratings, Elsie Tu dominated the top position up to April 1994, and then dropped out of the list altogether. Emily Lau has constantly occupied either the first or second position, while Lau Chin-shek was never below the fourth position. Martin Lee, Szeto Wah, Selina Chow, and Allen Lee were the other more well-known members and usually had the highest recognition rates.

Looking at the relative ranking of the members across the two years, there were three special cases worth mentioning. The first was the disappearance of Elsie Tu in mid-1994, which symbolized a change of political values among the general population. Tu had been on the top of the list since such rating exercises started in mid-1991. She was accorded with great respect for her services to the population especially for her anti-government stand in the colonial age. Nevertheless, less and less people knew her in spite of her relatively high support ratings, and her popularity was surpassed by other new, and more radical, faces, one of them being Christine Loh, the second case of interest.

Christine Loh entered the list in April 1994 about the time Elsie Tu dropped out. Loh remained in the 5th position for four months, and then advanced to the 4th position, stayed for another four months and then further advanced to the 3rd position in December 1994, displacing Martin Lee from top three. Her sudden appearance on the list was very much due to her radical stand on the New Territories issue,[22] and she was recognized as a radical liberal.

The final case which deserved mentioning was Lau Chin-shek. Since 1992, Lau had always occupied the 3rd or 4th position of the ladder, but

Table 5: Ratings of Top Ten Legco Members, 1993–1994

	Support	Std. err.	Total sample	Raters	Recognition
POP POLL 19–20 DEC. 1994					
Lau Chin-shek	68.2	0.9	577	420	72.8%
Emily Lau	67.5	0.9	577	398	69.0%
Christine Loh	65.3	0.9	577	384	66.6%
Martin Lee	64.7	1.0	577	423	73.3%
Szeto Wah	61.6	1.0	577	412	71.4%
Fung Kin-kee	60.3	0.9	577	329	57.0%
Selina Chow	59.2	0.8	577	403	69.8%
Tam Yiu-chung	55.7	1.0	577	327	56.7%
Allen Lee	52.9	0.9	577	381	66.0%
Lau Wong-fat	51.3	1.1	577	317	54.9%
Top 5 average	*65.5*				*70.6%*
Top 10 average	*60.7*				*65.8%*
POP POLL 26–31 OCT. 1994					
Emily Lau	64.7	0.9	501	403	80.4%
Martin Lee	62.5	1.0	501	413	82.4%
Lau Chin-shek	61.0	1.0	501	385	76.8%
Christine Loh	60.0	1.0	501	361	72.1%
Szeto Wah	59.7	1.0	501	413	82.4%
Lee Wing-tat	56.0	1.0	501	332	66.3%
Fung Kin-kee	55.0	0.9	501	331	66.1%
Andrew Wong	54.6	0.9	501	344	68.7%
Selina Chow	54.5	0.9	501	384	76.6%
Allen Lee	51.6	0.9	501	400	79.8%
Top 5 average	*61.6*				*78.8%*
Top 10 average	*58.0*				*75.2%*
POP POLL 10–12 AUG. 1994					
Emily Lau	65.6	0.7	1,027	858	83.5%
Martin Lee	63.5	0.7	1,027	895	87.1%
Lau Chin-shek	62.4	0.7	1,027	802	78.1%
Christine Loh	62.3	0.7	1,027	807	78.6%
Szeto Wah	59.6	0.7	1,027	898	87.4%
Selina Chow	57.8	0.6	1,027	862	83.9%
Fung Kin-kee	56.0	0.7	1,027	704	68.5%
Allen Lee	52.4	0.6	1,027	804	78.3%
Andrew Wong	51.9	0.7	1,027	732	71.3%
Lau Wong-fat	48.1	0.7	1,027	760	74.0%
Top 5 average	*62.7*				*83.0%*
Top 10 average	*58.0*				*79.1%*

Table 5 (cont'd)

	Support	Std. err.	Total sample	Raters	Recognition
POP POLL 31 MAY to 1 JUNE 1994					
Emily Lau	63.2	0.9	538	413	76.8%
Martin Lee	61.9	0.9	538	435	80.9%
Lau Chin-shek	60.5	1.0	538	385	71.6%
Szeto Wah	57.4	1.1	538	416	77.3%
Christine Loh	57.1	1.1	538	396	73.6%
Fung Kin-kee	55.5	1.0	538	342	64.6%
Selina Chow	54.6	0.9	538	399	74.2%
Allen Lee	50.0	0.9	538	377	70.1%
Andrew Wong	49.4	1.0	538	343	63.8%
Lau Wong-fat	46.1	1.1	538	342	63.6%
Top 5 average	*60.0*				*76.0%*
Top 10 average	*55.6*				*71.6%*
POP POLL 25–27 APR. 1994					
Elsie Tu	65.8	1.0	517	327	63.2%
Emily Lau	63.3	1.1	517	390	75.4%
Martin Lee	61.9	1.1	517	415	80.3%
Lau Chin-shek	61.7	1.1	517	358	69.2%
Christine Loh	60.7	1.2	517	357	69.1%
Szeto Wah	59.2	1.1	517	400	77.4%
Selina Chow	59.0	0.8	517	381	73.7%
Allen Lee	51.4	1.0	517	362	70.0%
Andrew Wong	49.6	1.1	517	305	64.6%
Lau Wong-fat	47.4	1.0	517	342	66.2%
Top 5 average	*62.7*				*71.5%*
Top 10 average	*58.0*				*70.9%*
POP POLL 1–7 FEB. 1994					
Elsie Tu	66.3	1.0	510	366	71.8%
Emily Lau	62.4	1.0	510	391	76.7%
Martin Lee	61.9	1.0	510	437	85.7%
Lau Chin-shek	61.7	1.0	510	399	78.2%
Yeung Sum	59.8	1.2	510	317	62.2%
Szeto Wah	58.6	1.0	510	432	84.7%
Selina Chow	57.4	0.9	510	416	81.6%
Tam Yiu-chung	55.9	1.0	510	326	63.9%
Andrew Wong	54.9	1.0	510	328	64.6%
Allen Lee	52.3	1.0	510	395	77.5%
Top 5 average	*62.4*				*74.9%*
Top 10 average	*59.1*				*74.7%*

Table 5 (cont'd)

	Support	Std. err.	Total sample	Raters	Recognition
POP POLL 9–14 DEC. 1993					
Elsie Tu	62.7	1.0	531	372	70.1%
Emily Lau	62.0	1.0	531	414	78.0%
Martin Lee	61.8	1.1	531	461	86.8%
Lau Chin-shek	59.8	1.0	531	408	76.8%
Yeung Sum	58.0	1.3	531	338	63.7%
Selina Chow	57.3	0.8	531	445	83.8%
Szeto Wah	56.6	1.1	531	447	84.2%
Andrew Wong	53.0	1.0	531	354	66.7%
Tam Yiu-chung	52.9	1.1	531	343	64.6%
Allen Lee	50.2	1.0	531	421	79.3%
Top 5 average	*60.9*				*75.1%*
Top 10 average	*57.4*				*75.4%*
POP POLL 12–14 OCT. 1993					
Elsie Tu	64.1	0.9	505	363	71.9%
Emily Lau	62.9	1.0	505	415	82.2%
Lau Chin-shek	58.5	0.9	505	404	80.0%
Yeung Sum	57.1	1.0	505	369	73.1%
Andrew Wong	57.0	0.8	505	378	74.9%
Selina Chow	56.9	0.8	505	420	83.2%
Martin Lee	55.5	1.1	505	440	87.1%
Allen Lee	55.4	0.9	505	437	86.5%
Tam Yiu-chung	55.4	0.9	505	369	73.1%
Szeto Wah	53.9	1.1	505	444	87.9%
Top 5 average	*59.9*				*76.4%*
Top 10 average	*57.7*				*80.0%*
POP POLL 18 AUG. 1993					
Elsie Tu	68.6	0.9	617	453	73.4%
Emily Lau	66.4	0.9	617	474	76.8%
Lau Chin-shek	64.1	0.8	617	492	79.7%
Martin Lee	61.9	0.9	617	524	84.9%
Szeto Wah	60.0	0.9	617	528	85.6%
Selina Chow	59.8	0.8	617	495	80.2%
Allen Lee	58.0	0.8	617	513	83.1%
Andrew Wong	57.9	0.8	617	422	68.4%
Tam Yiu-chung	57.4	0.9	617	391	63.4%
Lau Wong-fat	54.4	0.8	617	409	66.3%
Top 5 average	*64.2*				*80.1%*
Top 10 average	*60.9*				*76.2%*

Table 5 (cont'd)

	Support	Std. err.	Total sample	Raters	Recognition
POP POLL 17–18 JUNE 1993					
Elsie Tu	70.3	0.8	574	428	74.6%
Emily Lau	67.4	0.9	574	469	81.7%
Martin Lee	65.0	1.0	574	506	88.2%
Lau Chin-shek	64.0	0.9	574	462	80.5%
Yeung Sum	62.4	1.0	574	372	64.8%
Szeto Wah	61.3	1.0	574	507	88.3%
Allen Lee	60.1	0.9	574	493	85.9%
Andrew Wong	60.0	0.8	574	413	72.0%
Selina Chow	56.6	0.8	574	449	78.2%
Lau Wong-fat	54.5	1.0	574	388	67.6%
Top 5 average	*65.8*				*77.9%*
Top 10 average	*62.2*				*78.2%*
POP POLL 15–16 APR. 1993					
Elsie Tu	66.9	1.0	548	408	74.5%
Emily Lau	65.8	1.1	548	413	75.4%
Martin Lee	63.6	1.1	548	457	83.4%
Lau Chin-shek	62.8	1.0	548	410	74.8%
Yeung Sum	60.7	1.1	548	340	62.0%
Szeto Wah	59.6	1.1	548	452	82.5%
Fung Kin-kee	59.2	1.0	548	359	65.5%
Andrew Wong	56.9	1.0	548	385	70.3%
Allen Lee	52.6	1.1	548	434	79.2%
Selina Chow	51.1	1.0	548	424	77.4%
Top 5 average	*63.9*				*74.0%*
Top 10 average	*59.9*				*74.5%*
POP POLL 8–10 FEB. 1993					
Elsie Tu	65.7	0.8	610	502	82.3%
Emily Lau	62.0	0.9	610	479	78.5%
Lau Chin-shek	60.8	0.9	610	505	82.8%
Fung Kin-kee	58.7	0.8	610	406	66.6%
Martin Lee	58.1	1.0	610	545	89.3%
Szeto Wah	56.2	1.0	610	537	88.0%
Andrew Wong	56.0	0.8	610	455	74.6%
Tam Yiu-chung	54.4	0.9	610	403	66.1%
Selina Chow	54.0	0.8	610	486	79.7%
Allen Lee	52.3	0.8	610	521	85.4%
Top 5 average	*61.0*				*79.9%*
Top 10 average	*57.8*				*79.3%*

Note: All data are weighted by sex of valid raters.

suddenly in December 1994, after his announcement to resign from the Legco in protest against the government's withdrawal of the Employment (Amendment) Bill, he leapt to the top of the list for the first time, with a high score of 68.2. A poll conducted by the author on 16 December 1994 (two days after his announcement) found that his rating once reached 72.2. This showed that his surge in popularity at the end of the year was directly related to his resignation. Confrontation rather than consensus politics paid again.

Putting aside individual cases, the average support rating of the top five Legco members was usually between 60 and 65 points, while that of the top ten was usually between 55 and 60 points. The average recognition rate of the top five was normally between 70% to 80%, which was quite high. Compared to Lau Siu-kai and Kuan Hsin-chi's observation in 1988 that the unavailability of respected and trusted political leaders has been a perennial shortfall in the political system of Hong Kong, the situation has certainly changed when Hong Kong reached the late transition period, after direct election was introduced to the Legco. Nevertheless, people's view towards political parties may not have changed very much.

Support of Political Parties

Table 6 summarized the popularity ratings of major political groups in 1993 and 1994, in the same way as Table 5 for Legislative Councillors, only that top five ratings were given instead of top ten. The main reason was simply because there were not many groups in existence.

The average support rating of the top five political groups as reported in Table 6 was usually around 55 points, which was about 5 to 10 points less than the top five Legco members. The average recognition rate for the top five groups was normally between 50% and 60%, which was about 20% less than that of the top five Legco members. We could therefore conclude that the people of Hong Kong were much more acquainted with political leaders than political groups. Across the table, as 22 out of the 60 recognition ratings reported took on values below the 50% benchmark, over one-third of the support ratings were not very meaningful.[23]

Another evidence supporting this observation was that among the most popular Legislative Councillors reported in Table 5, those normally occupying the top positions, like Elsie Tu, Emily Lau, and the fast-emerging Christine Loh, were not members of any political party, and other

Table 6: Ratings of Top Five Political Groups, 1993–1994

	Support	Std. err.	Total sample	Raters	Recognition
POP POLL 19–20 DEC. 1994					
DP	62.8	1.0	577	327	56.7%
FTU	58.8	1.0	577	300	52.0%
ADPL	58.5	1.0	577	271	47.0%
LP	56.4	1.0	577	341	59.1%
DABHK	55.3	1.0	577	280	48.5%
Top 5 average	*58.4*				*52.7%*
POP POLL 26–31 OCT. 1994					
DP	59.2	1.1	501	323	64.5%
ADPL	56.5	0.9	501	283	56.5%
DABHK	54.9	0.9	501	326	65.1%
LP	53.8	1.0	501	344	68.7%
LDFHK	50.4	1.1	501	208	41.5%
Top 5 average	*55.0*				*59.2%*
POP POLL 10–12 AUG. 1994					
UDHK	59.7	1.0	602	436	72.4%
FTU	56.3	1.0	602	337	56.0%
MP	54.1	0.9	602	358	59.5%
ADPL	53.3	1.0	602	322	53.5%
LP	52.5	0.9	602	398	66.1%
Top 5 average	*55.2*				*61.5%*
POP POLL 22–23 JUNE 1994					
UDHK	59.8	1.1	602	380	63.1%
MP	54.8	1.0	602	312	51.8%
ADPL	52.5	1.0	602	291	48.3%
LP	52.3	1.1	602	350	58.1%
DABHK	51.1	1.1	602	289	48.0%
Top 5 average	*54.1*				*53.9%*
POP POLL 25–27 APR. 1994					
UDHK	61.2	1.2	517	332	64.2%
FTU	58.6	1.6	517	237	45.8%
MP	58.5	0.9	517	239	46.2%
LP	55.4	1.0	517	286	55.3%
DABHK	51.8	1.1	517	239	46.2%
Top 5 average	*57.1*				*51.6%*

Table 6 (cont'd)

	Support	Std. err.	Total sample	Raters	Recognition
POP POLL 24–28 FEB. 1994					
UDHK	58.2	1.2	524	328	62.6%
FTU	53.9	1.4	524	204	38.9%
MP	52.8	1.2	524	219	41.8%
LP	50.1	1.2	524	291	55.5%
DABHK	49.3	1.3	524	186	35.5%
Top 5 average	*52.9*				*46.9%*
POP POLL 28–30 DEC. 1993					
UDHK	60.9	1.2	502	345	68.7%
MP	56.1	1.0	502	257	51.2%
LP	54.3	1.0	502	327	65.1%
FTU	52.2	1.2	502	255	50.8%
DABHK	48.7	1.3	502	237	47.2%
Top 5 average	*54.4*				*56.6%*
POP POLL 3–8 NOV. 1993					
UDHK	58.2	1.2	494	332	67.2%
MP	57.0	1.0	494	238	48.2%
LP	55.8	1.1	494	306	61.9%
FTU	54.6	1.1	494	229	46.4%
LDF	51.3	1.3	494	218	44.1%
Top 5 average	*55.4*				*53.6%*
POP POLL 25–26 AUG. 1993					
UDHK	60.8	1.1	513	374	72.9%
MP	53.9	1.1	513	258	50.3%
FTU	53.7	1.1	513	280	54.6%
LP	52.5	1.1	513	311	60.6%
LDF	51.0	1.2	513	242	47.2%
Top 5 average	*54.4*				*57.1%*
POP POLL 29–30 JUNE 1993					
UDHK	56.1	1.1	509	411	80.7%
ADPL	53.9	1.2	509	212	41.7%
MP	53.4	1.0	509	266	52.3%
LP	50.9	1.1	509	330	64.8%
DABHK	46.2	1.2	509	263	51.7%
Top 5 average	*52.1*				*58.2%*

Table 6 (cont'd)

	Support	Std. err.	Total sample	Raters	Recognition
POP POLL 27–28 APR. 1993					
UDHK	55.0	0.8	622	444	71.4%
FTU	51.2	0.9	622	339	54.5%
MP	50.0	0.8	622	294	47.3%
CRC	49.5	0.8	622	415	66.7%
DABHK	47.3	0.9	622	278	44.7%
Top 5 average	*50.6*				*56.9%*
POP POLL 23–24 FEB. 1993					
UDHK	55.8	0.9	631	491	77.8%
ADPL	51.4	1.1	631	269	42.6%
MP	51.2	1.1	631	305	48.3%
CRC	49.6	0.9	631	442	70.0%
DABHK	45.9	1.2	631	289	45.8%
Top 5 average	*50.8*				*56.9%*

Abbreviations:	ADPL	=	Hong Kong Association for Democracy and People's Livelihood
	CRC	=	Cooperative Resources Centre
	DABHK	=	Democratic Alliance for Betterment of Hong Kong
	DP	=	Democratic Party
	FTU	=	Hong Kong Federation of Trade Unions
	LDFHK	=	The Liberal Democratic Federation of Hong Kong
	LP	=	Liberal Party
	MP	=	Meeting Point
	UDHK	=	United Democrats of Hong Kong

Note: All data are weighted by sex of valid raters.

independent members like Andrew Wong and Lau Wong-fat were also regularly among the top ten.

This said, it was still a hard fact that the United Democrats of Hong Kong (UDHK), and later its successor, the Democratic Party (DP), remained to be the most popular political group throughout the period. The group remained at the top of the list throughout 1993 and 1994, both in terms of recognition and support. Its recognition rating never fell below 50%, and the only other group which managed to maintain this level of popularity was the Liberal Party (LP), and its predecessor, the Cooperative

Resources Centre, but the latter group enjoyed a much lower level of support from the public. Looking down the lists, names like the Hong Kong Federation of Trade Unions, the Hong Kong Association for Democracy and People's Livelihood, the Democratic Alliance for Betterment of Hong Kong, the Liberal Democratic Federation, and Meeting Point (MP) appeared. These groups did not called themselves "parties" and this raised the question of whether they could be regarded as "political parties." In fact, groups which called themselves "parties" like the LP and the DP may not in themselves be real parties, in the strictest sense of the word. Theoretically, the primary function of political parties was to compete for power. Hong Kong being a British colony before 1997, and an SAR under China after 1997, offered no opportunity for political parties to rule.[24] Political parties in the Hong Kong context, therefore, could at most be political groups which have gained considerable *influence* in the running of Hong Kong. Nevertheless, probably as an effort to promote the sturdy image of the groups, many political groups in Hong Kong have claimed themselves to be political parties, some have literally named themselves as such.

Before 1991, the use of such a name was itself not wise. As Lau and Kuan observed, "The term 'political party' conjures up images of confrontation, factions, totalitarianism, corruption, political plots, ideological indoctrination, closed political arenas and adversarial politics."[25] In their 1985 survey, only 34.8% of the respondents agreed that "the emergence of political parties will make the political system of Hong Kong better."[26] In their 1988 survey, the researchers reported that only 25.0% of the respondents supported the formation of political parties in Hong Kong while 50.5% opposed it.[27] The abhorrence of political parties seemed to linger on, the researchers concluded.

About a decade after Lau and Kuan conducted their first research, survey findings gathered in 1993 and 1994 seemed to confirm that political parties were still far from being well-known, not to say the extent of party affiliation. However, with the gradual development of electoral politics in Hong Kong, the recognition rates of political parties were bound to rise in due course. In fact, the relatively lower ratings registered in Table 6 may partly be explained by the relatively short history of some political groups, as well as the dynamics of recent changes. For example, the merging of the UDHK and MP into the DP in October 1994 structurally wiped out MP from the table, and pushed up a less popular group into the top five. Moreover, people needed time to get to know the new DP, and a drop in its recognition rate was very natural. A similar development was observed in the early history of the LP in 1993.

The Row over Constitutional Development

As pointed out in the first section of this chapter, the big row over Hong Kong's constitutional development, which marked the beginning of the late transition period, was in fact an outcome of the June 4 incident. The chain of events following June 4, including the landslide victory enjoyed by the liberals in the 1991 direct election, and then the appointment of Chris Patten as Governor of Hong Kong in 1992, all led to the occurrence of the dispute. There was no doubt that Patten was a political heavyweight and was the most influential person affecting the development of Hong Kong in the late transition period.

Since Patten was designated the last Governor of Hong Kong in April 1992, the author has been tracking his popularity on a 0–100 point scale described before on a regular basis.[28] Table 7 tabulated Patten's support ratings across the entire period from the announcement of his appointment in April 1992, through his swearing into office on 9 July 1992, up to the end of 1994, on a monthly basis.[29] Figure 1 presented the change graphically. One major observation was his steep rise in popularity in the first six months after his appointment, due to his success in public relations, and in his meetings with the public. His support rating reached as high as 65.5 points on the day he delivered his first policy speech on 7 October 1992, fluctuated a while, and then plunged to about 55 points in December 1992. That plunge was almost as sharp as the ascent three months earlier, indicating that the support he had gained from the people was far from solid, and was quickly lost in face of China's fierce attack.

Perhaps he had over-read people's enthusiasm, perhaps he had miscalculated China's reaction. In any case, he never fully recovered from the plunge; up to the end of 1994, his support ratings normally fluctuated between the narrow range of 55 to 60 points, which was far behind the ratings enjoyed by the most popular Legco members.

Immediately after Patten delivered his first policy address in October 1992, when he proposed a series of dramatic constitutional changes, Sino-British relationship turned sour. After some heavy rounds of rhetoric exchange, talks were finally opened in April 1993, but after seventeen rounds of unproductive talks, they finally broke down in November 1993,

Table 7: Monthly Ratings of Chris Patten
(From April 1992 to December 1994)

Month	Number of raters	Rating
April 1992	622	53.3
May 1992	1,002	56.1
June 1992	574	58.2
July 1992	—	60.7
August 1992	662	63.1
September 1992	—	63.6
October 1992	4,282	64.1
November 1992	1,908	61.6
December 1992	3,552	55.7
January 1993	2,328	58.0
February 1993	2,639	57.3
March 1993	3,093	58.0
April 1993	2,135	56.2
May 1993	2,286	58.2
June 1993	2,443	58.6
July 1993	1,823	58.6
August 1993	1,945	58.8
September 1993	2,267	57.6
October 1993	3,983	59.5
November 1993	2,152	57.6
December 1993	1,533	57.2
January 1994	473	55.6
February 1994	1,003	55.3
March 1994	419	54.9
April 1994	877	55.2
May 1994	936	55.0
June 1994	993	55.6
July 1994	433	57.9
August 1994	1,472	57.9
September 1994	446	57.0
October 1994	2,805	55.5
November 1994	483	55.1
December 1994	938	54.8

Total: 52,507

Note: The monthly ratings were obtained by averaging specific ratings obtained in separate polls during the month, except the ratings of July and September 1992 which were calculated by interpolation. The number of raters referred to the total number accumulated during that month.

Figure 1: Monthly Ratings of Chris Patten

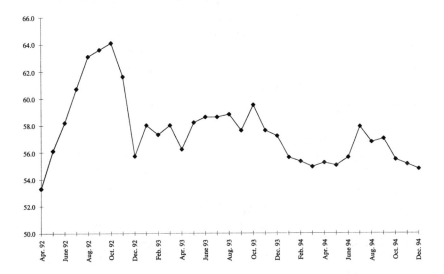

and Patten's reform proposals were quickly put to the Legco. The first part of the proposals was passed on 15 December 1993, and the second part on 30 June 1994. Together they set down the system for the new wave of direct elections for 1994–1995, at all three levels of representative government.

In spite of the tense debates on the diplomatic level, the people of Hong Kong was on the whole quite ignorant of the content of the reform proposals, according to a series of tracking polls conducted by the author between December 1992 and September 1993. At the end of September 1993, 64% of the respondents to a survey replied that they did not understand the first part of Patten's proposals,[30] which was tabled at the Legco about two months later. The second part of the reform package was even worse. On 24 June 1994, about a week before the second and more controversial part of the reform package was tabled at the Legco, 89% of the respondents to a poll conducted by the author replied that they did not understand the content of the proposal, nor the counter-proposals being vigorously debated. People had apparently lost interest in constitutional reforms. The final outcome of the Legco vote, in support of the original proposals, could hardly claimed to have received people's blessing.

One reason for the public's general ignorance was due to insufficient public discussions on the content of the proposals. Between July and December 1993, the public's attention was mainly drawn to the progress of the talks, the general principles, and issues like "through train." After the talks broke down in November 1993, the public's attention was drawn to the reasons for their failure, and then to party politics before the passing of the reform bills. Very little effort was made by the government and the political parties to educate the public on the content of the proposals and counter-proposals.[31]

The other reason for the public's ignorance, and in fact, growing apathy, was probably because of their sense of powerlessness at what was going on behind closed doors. Opinion polls conducted by the author between June and November 1993 consistently showed that over half, sometimes as high as four-fifths, of Hong Kong people were dissatisfied with the progress of the talks, about 60% did not like the talks being kept secret, over two-thirds did not accept any secret agreement between Britain and China, and 35–45% did not think that Hong Kong people's wishes would be taken care of by both parties. Nevertheless, people remained optimistic about the outcome of the talks — until the last two months.

Table 8 and Figure 2[32] showed that Hong Kong people received the opening of the talks with very high spirit. On 28 April 1993, when the second round of talks began, 63% of the respondents felt optimistic that agreement could be reached, against 9% who felt pessimistic. As the talks

Table 8: People's Optimism about the Outcome of Sino-British Talks

Date of poll	Optimistic	Half-half	Pessimistic	Total
10 March 1993	40.0%	23.1%	36.8%	100%
14 April 1993	46.2%	37.5%	16.3%	100%
28 April 1993	62.7%	28.6%	8.7%	100%
9–10 June 1993	57.6%	22.1%	20.3%	100%
6–7 July 1993	44.8%	36.1%	19.1%	100%
22–23 July 1993	47.5%	26.7%	25.8%	100%
8–9 September 1993	37.0%	30.5%	32.5%	100%
12–14 October 1993	29.4%	25.6%	45.0%	100%
15–16 November 1993	32.5%	31.4%	36.1%	100%

Figure 2: Optimism about Sino-British Talks

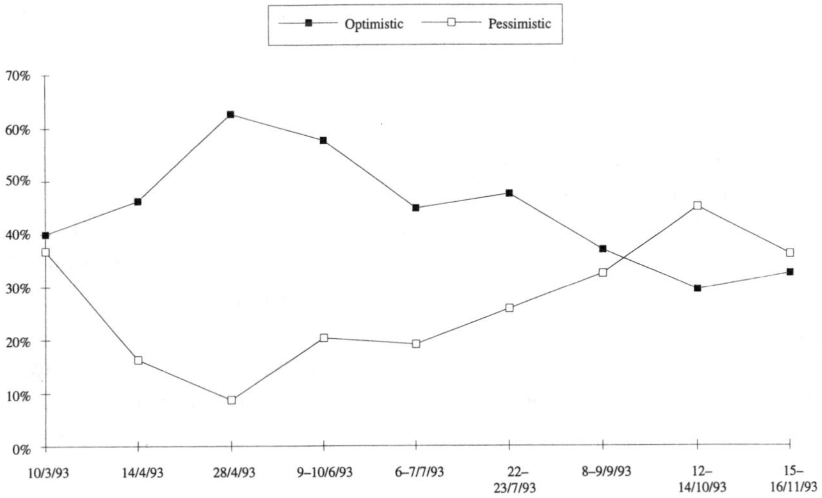

Note: The horizontal scale is spaced according to poll-time, not calendar time.

dragged on, however, people's optimism faded, until pessimism finally took over in October 1993. But even after the "indefinite suspension" of the talks in late November 1993, more people believed in the reopening of the talks than otherwise. A poll conducted as late as 17 December 1993, after Patten tabled his reform package at the Legco, registered 49% of the respondents still optimistic about the reopening of the talks, as against 30% who felt pessimistic. This, on the one hand, demonstrated the tough spirit of Hong Kong people, but, on the other hand, signalled how disappointed Hong Kong people must have been in the final event.

When the talks reached deadlock, in October 1993, 62% blamed *both* Britain and China for not reaching agreement, as against 15% or so who blamed either government. This shows that Hong Kong people were generally pragmatic in outlook: they were more interested in the final result than the pros and cons of the argument, it was probably because of this that they did not have faith in either the Chinese or the British government. Tracking polls reported in the early part of this chapter have shown that Hong Kong people generally distrusted both governments. Their performance at the negotiation table once again disappointed the people.

LOOKING AHEAD INTO THE FUTURE

At the time of writing, Patten's political reform proposals have already become law, the District Board and municipal council direct elections have already taken place on 18 September 1994 and 5 March 1995 respectively. The final and most important elections of Hong Kong's colonial history, the Legco elections of 17 September 1995, were due to take place. Against this background, it may well be time that we shifted our attention from the pre-1997 issues to the more important post-1997 problems. Let us start from the most sensitive issue: the June 4 incident and the future of the Hong Kong Alliance in Support of Patriotic Democratic Movement in China.

The Alliance was formed in 1989 in the midst of the June 4 turmoil. Ever since then, it was denounced as a subversive organization by China, and was very unlikely to have a bright future under the future SAR government. In the course of the Sino-British negotiation over the constitutional development of Hong Kong, China has proclaimed that all leaders of the Alliance would not be allowed to sit on any "through train" straddling 1997.[33] However, the more the Chinese government denounced the Alliance as subversive, the stronger was people's feeling against the Chinese government. We have seen how the liberals managed to secure a landslide victory in the 1991 direct elections of the Legco because of people's distaste for the Chinese government. Whether this would happen again in September 1995 would be a critical test to the Alliance and the Chinese government.

From 1992 onwards, the author has conducted opinion polls tracking people's feeling of the June 4 incident and their support for the Alliance around May each year. The latest survey in 1994 showed that the support rating of the Alliance on a scale ranging from 0–100 has dropped from 59.5 in May 1992 to 54.1 in May 1993, and then became 54.3 in May 1994, while its recognition rate has dropped from 86% in 1992 to 73% in 1993, and then 69% in 1994.[34] This indicated that people's support towards the Alliance has become stabilized in 1994, but their knowledge of the Alliance has gradually decreased. The author did not have ratings of the Alliance before 1991, but judging from the million or so people who had taken to the streets in 1989, the Alliance must have had very high ratings then.

Looking back into 1989, 77% of the respondents still thought that China had taken the wrong action in suppressing the Beijing students, but

14% said the students were wrong in themselves. As on human rights conditions in China, 49% felt that conditions had improved since 1989, another 38% felt that conditions would become better by 1997. This reflected some degree of optimism towards China's future development, but a persistent feeling that the Chinese government was wrong in 1989. This explained why only 12% of the respondents thought that the Alliance should be disbanded, while 49% said it should not. It thus seemed that one important task of the Chinese government over the resumption of Hong Kong's sovereignty would be to resolve the "June 4 complex" of the Hong Kong people, if it would like to gain their trust.

As 1997 drew near, it was also very important to test whether people actually had faith in the "one country, two systems" formulation. Table 9 summarized the findings of ten surveys conducted by the author in 1993 and 1994 over this problem. It was found that a consistent 44% of the respondents did not believe the "one country, two systems" formulation would work, as against 38% who thought it would. The Chinese government, therefore, would need to give more assurance to the Hong Kong people that it would genuinely honour its promise to respect Hong Kong's autonomy, by word and by deed.

Table 9: Hong Kong People's Confidence in the "One Country, Two Systems" Formulation

	1994 average	1993 average
Successful cases	3,146	2,159
Response rate	55.3%	57.5%
Confident	37.7%	38.6%
Not confident	43.8%	44.2%
Don't know	18.4%	17.2%
Total	100.0%	100.0%

Before straddling 1997, the author has also tracked people's general satisfaction over Hong Kong's current conditions, as well as their area of major concern. Tables 10 and 11 summarized the findings of 13 opinion polls conducted in 1993 and 1994.

Table 10: People's Most Concerned Problems

	1994 average	1993 average
Successful cases	3,305	4,058
Response rate	57.2%	56.2%
Raw data		
Political problems	18.4%	19.5%
Economic problems	35.9%	32.1%
Social problems	33.1%	28.7%
Don't know	10.3%	17.1%
Other answers	2.4%	2.6%
Total	100.0%	100.0%

Table 10 showed that Hong Kong people were mainly concerned with Hong Kong's economic conditions, followed by social, and then political conditions. Fortunately, their degree of satisfaction also followed that order. Table 11 showed that over 60% of the respondents were satisfied with Hong Kong's current economic condition, over 55% with the social condition, but only about one-third over the political condition, and 1994 appeared to be a better year than 1993. It therefore followed that more effort has to be paid by the Hong Kong and Chinese governments to smooth out the political conditions of Hong Kong, especially over the problem of convergence and constitutional arrangement.

One very important lingering question at the time of writing was the selection of the First Chief Executive of the SAR government. A poll conducted by the author between the end of December 1994 and the middle of January 1995 found that a candidate's personality, executive experience, and acceptance by the Hong Kong people were considered to be the three most important criteria, while acceptance by the Chinese government and the civil servants were thought to be of less importance.[35]

As on the desired background of the prospective Chief Executive, 42% of the respondents said politicians were most desirable, followed by civil servants (15%) and professionals (13%). Asked for specific names, 92% of the respondents could not name any ideal candidate, and even when prompted with ten names frequently tipped by the media, 31% of the respondents did not wish to choose any. This shows that although the

Table 11: People's Satisfaction of the Social, Economic and Political Conditions

	1994 average			1993 average		
	Soc. condition	Econ. condition	Pol. condition	Soc. condition	Econ. condition	Pol. condition
Successful cases	3,305	3,305	3,305	4,058	4,058	4,058
Response rate	57.2%	57.2%	57.2%	56.2%	56.2%	56.2%
Raw data						
Very satisfied	4.9%	6.8%	2.4%	3.9%	5.1%	2.2%
Just satisfied	53.7%	59.1%	32.3%	52.2%	57.2%	30.7%
Neutral	13.8%	10.0%	14.4%	13.1%	9.6%	12.2%
Just dissatisfied	22.1%	18.9%	28.5%	24.4%	19.8%	29.4%
Very dissatisfied	2.9%	2.3%	5.2%	3.0%	3.3%	6.9%
Don't know	2.7%	2.9%	17.3%	3.4%	5.0%	18.6%
Total	100.0%	100.0%	100.0%	100.0%	100.0%	100.0%
Collapsed data						
Satisfied	58.6%	66.0%	34.7%	56.2%	62.3%	32.9%
Neutral	13.8%	10.0%	14.4%	13.1%	9.6%	12.2%
Dissatisfied	24.9%	21.1%	33.7%	27.4%	23.1%	36.4%
Don't know	2.7%	2.9%	17.3%	3.4%	5.0%	18.6%
Total	100.0%	100.0%	100.0%	100.0%	100.0%	100.0%
Omitting "don't know" (i.e. % of those expressing an opinion)						
Satisfied	60.2%	67.9%	41.9%	58.1%	65.5%	40.5%
Neutral	14.2%	10.3%	17.4%	13.5%	10.1%	14.9%
Dissatisfied	25.6%	21.7%	40.7%	28.4%	24.3%	44.7%
Total	100.0%	100.0%	100.0%	100.0%	100.0%	100.0%

people of Hong Kong apparently have a fairly concrete idea of what to expect from the First Chief Executive, they were still far from having made up their mind as to who was the best. As on the timing for selecting the First Chief Executive, 13% hoped it could be done as soon as possible, 40% (accumulative) opted for any time before early 1996, and 56% opted for any time before mid-1996. If we add the 10% who said it did not matter, we could conclude that 50% of the respondents would not object to having the Chief Executive chosen by early 1996. The appointment of the Chief Executive would definitely be an important benchmark in Hong Kong's transition. Whether it would bring more conflict or harmony to Hong Kong remained to be seen.

We have seen that Hong Kong people were still not yet confident of the "one country, two systems" formulation, but in two years' time, it would be a hard fact that Hong Kong became a part of China. It would therefore not be too early to start tracking the population's opinion on national issues, like the Taiwan and Tibet problems. Tables 12 to 15 summarized the findings of ten surveys conducted by the author in 1993 and 1994 over such questions.[36]

Tables 12 and 13 tested respondents' feeling towards possible independence of Taiwan and Tibet. It was found that roughly one-third of the respondents agreed to Taiwan's independence, but about half objected to it. One-quarter agreed to Tibet's independence, but about half objected. On Taiwan's rejoining the United Nations, Table 14 showed that about half agreed, and one-quarter disagreed. As to whether China and Taiwan could finally unite, Table 15 showed that 47% of the respondents of the 1994 surveys felt pessimistic, as against 35% who felt optimistic, which was a

Table 12: People's View on Possible Independence of Taiwan

	1994 average	1993 average
Successful cases	3,146	2,159
Response rate	55.3%	57.5%
Agreed	34.2%	32.1%
Disagreed	48.7%	52.1%
Don't know	17.1%	15.8%
Total	100.0%	100.0%

Table 13: People's View on Possible Independence of Tibet

	1994 average	1993 average
Successful cases	3,146	2,159
Response rate	55.3%	57.5%
Agreed	22.2%	24.0%
Disagreed	48.0%	51.4%
Don't know	29.8%	24.6%
Total	100.0%	100.0%

Table 14: People's View on Whether Taiwan Should Rejoin the United Nations

	1994 average	1993 average
Successful cases	3,146	2,159
Response rate	55.3%	57.5%
Agreed	48.1%	52.1%
Disagreed	28.6%	26.0%
Don't know	23.5%	21.9%
Total	100.0%	100.0%

Table 15: People's Confidence in the Reunification of China and Taiwan

	1994 average	1993 average
Successful cases	3,146	2,159
Response rate	55.3%	57.5%
Agreed	34.9%	41.6%
Disagreed	46.7%	41.7%
Don't know	18.4%	16.7%
Total	100.0%	100.0%

drop of about 7% from the 1993 figure, and should be taken seriously. Although the Taiwan problem was far from being a pressing problem for the Hong Kong people, it carries important symbolic meaning for both the Chinese government, the Hong Kong people, and the entire Chinese nation. Whether the "one country, two systems" formulation would work in Hong Kong or not would set a very important example for the future development of the entire nation. Hong Kong people should, of course, have a say.

FINAL REMARKS

It was almost impossible to summarize all the opinion polls conducted during Hong Kong's transition period. Even the reporting of opinion polls conducted by the author would take up much more space than the present chapter. The author has, therefore, concentrated on a number of themes which were thought to be more relevant to Hong Kong people's mentality facing the transition from a British colony to an SAR under China. As opinion polls have only become popular since 1991, which incidentally bisected Hong Kong's transition period from 1985 to 1997, and there were still two more years before 1997, this chapter has mainly concentrated on opinion poll findings between 1991 and 1995 in general, and 1993 and 1994 in particular. Efforts have been made to draw reference to the historical root of current opinion development, as well as to throw some light on its future development. At a time when both the people of Hong Kong and the Chinese government were carving a way for Hong Kong's final transition, some kind of historical and futuristic treatise may provide a useful perspective on top of a structural and cross-sectional view of the public opinion.

NOTES

1. Opinion poll discussed in this chapter mainly, but not exclusively, referred to those conducted by the author under the Public Opinion Programme (POP) of the Social Sciences Research Centre (SSRC) of The University of Hong Kong. Other polls were rarely used because:
   i. their occurrence were less frequent, and
   ii. their research methods were very often not reported.
   For methodological details of the POP Polls reported, like sampling method,

response rates, and exact wordings of the questions, readers may refer to the full reports published by the SSRC.

2. The author traced the development of opinion polls in Hong Kong, with particular reference to the 1991 development in his article "Public Opinion" in *The Other Hong Kong Report 1993*, edited by Choi Po-king and Ho Lok-sang (Hong Kong: The Chinese University Press, 1993), pp. 401–23.

3. Joseph Y. S. Cheng, *Hong Kong: In Search of a Future* (Hong Kong: Oxford University Press, 1984), pp. 28, 245. Also see Ian Scott, *Political Change and the Crisis of Legitimacy in Hong Kong* (Hong Kong: Oxford University Press, 1989), p. 18.

4. See *Hong Kong: In Search of a Future* (Note 3), p. 246 (Note 3).

5. The concept was officially raised by Ye Jianying, Chairman of the Standing Committee of the National People's Congress, on 30 September 1981 as an offer to Taiwan for peaceful reunification. A nine-point plan was offered, and the concept was embedded in the third point. The concept of establishing Special Administrative Regions to facilitate the reunification of China was formally written into Article 31 of the *Chinese Constitution* promulgated on 4 December 1982. Many commentators were of the view that the concept was created mainly for the reunification of Taiwan, rather than for Hong Kong and Macau. The "one country, two systems" formulation subsequently adopted for Hong Kong's development was simply an outgrow of the formula for Taiwan.

6. Yash Pal Ghai, "The Constitutional Framework for the Transition of Hong Kong," in *Hong Kong in Transition 1992* (Hong Kong: One Country Two Systems Economic Research Institute, 1993), pp. 293–325.

7. An Assessment Office manned by local civil servants was set up to consult Hong Kong people's acceptability of the Draft Agreement on the future of Hong Kong between October and November 1984. Ian Scott described the background for setting up the Office, and said, "[Hong Kong people's] endorsement of the proposals was at best lukewarm and it did not escape many of those who did respond, and possibly most of those who did not, that this was an agreement which was being imposed by the British and Chinese governments on the people of Hong Kong" (see *Political Change and the Crisis of Legitimacy in Hong Kong* [Note 3], p. 2).

8. *Green Paper: The 1987 Review of Developments in Representative Government* (Hong Kong: Government Printer, May 1987).

9. *Public Response to Green Paper: The 1987 Review of Developments in Representative Government: Report of the Survey Office* (Hong Kong: Government Printer, October 1987).

10. There were two main points in dispute. Firstly, the survey office did not distinguish individual submissions from preprinted cyclostyled submissions, the effect of which was to over-represent those opposed to direct elections. Of

60,706 submissions against direct elections, 50,175 came on cyclostyled forms, 22,722 of which being from the Hong Kong Federation of Trade Unions. Of the 35,129 submissions in favour of direct elections, only 1,313 were on cyclostyled forms. Furthermore, 220,000 signatures collected by the liberals were also excluded from calculation. On the second front, the questionnaire designed by the consultant firm, AGB McNair Hong Kong Limited, was criticized for not providing a clear choice for direct elections in 1988. On the whole, the government was criticized for having deliberately engineered the result, and ignored the opinions of the majority. See *Political Change and the Crisis of Legitimacy in Hong Kong* (Note 3), pp. 30–31, 284–98.

11. *White Paper: The Development of Representative Government: The Way Forward* (Hong Kong: Government Printer, February 1988).

12. The liberals won 16 out of the 18 directly elected seats, and obtained 58.2% of the popular vote. See Ian Scott, "An Overview of the Hong Kong Legislative Council Elections of 1991," in *Votes Without Power: The Hong Kong Legislative Council Elections 1991*, edited by Rowena Kwok, Joan Leung and Ian Scott (Hong Kong: Hong Kong University Press, 1992), p. 5.

13. See "An Overview of the Hong Kong Legislative Council Elections of 1991" (Note 12), pp. 17–18.

14. Lau Siu-kai, and Kuan Hsin-chi, *The Ethos of the Hong Kong Chinese* (Hong Kong: The Chinese University Press, 1988). The methodology of the surveys were reported in its Appendix (pp. 213–14). A total of 767 and 539 residents living in Kwun Tong were interviewed in the 1985 and 1986 surveys respectively.

15. See *The Ethos of the Hong Kong Chinese* (Note 14), p. 84.

16. Lau Siu-kai, Lee Ming-kwan, Wan Po-san, and Wong Siu-lun (eds.), *Indicators of Social Development: Hong Kong 1988* (Hong Kong: Hong Kong Institute of Asia-Pacific Studies, The Chinese University of Hong Kong, 1991). The survey composed of one set of core questions and four different modules, each focusing on different topics and took on different sample sizes. Political attitudes discussed in this chapter is based on Module D of the survey, which had a valid sample size of 649 respondents.

17. Lau Siu-kai, Kuan Hsin-chi, and Wan Po-san, "Political Attitudes," in Lau Siu-kai, Lee Ming-kwan, Wan Po-san and Wong Siu-lun (eds.), *Indicators of Social Development: Hong Kong 1988* (Note 16), p. 199.

18. See Note 14, pp. 103, 105.

19. See Note 17, pp. 184–86.

20. 0 indicated absolute no support, 100 indicated absolute support, and 50 indicated neutral. This 101 point scale with 50 as mid-point can be simplified as a 0–10 point scale with 5 as mid-point. Conversion between the two scales required the shifting of one decimal place.

21. Some of these findings have been reported by the author in *The Other Hong Kong Report 1993* (Note 2), and *The Other Hong Kong Report 1994*, edited by Donald H. McMillen and Man Si-wai (Hong Kong: The Chinese University Press, 1994), under chapters on "Public Opinion."

22. Christine Loh argued that all indigenous women in the New Territories should have an equal right to inherit lands as did their male counterpart. This created an uproar across the male-dominated village communities, and Loh was accused of destroying the spirit of village life.

23. The author has always maintained that when the recognition rate of a political figure or group fell below 50%, that is, less than half of the respondents to a survey gave a definite rating to the person or group, the final average rating should only be used as a casual reference and not for serious comparison. Strictly speaking, therefore, the 22 entries in Table 6 with recognition rates below 50% should be taken away for valid comparison.

24. Perhaps only the Chinese Communist Party (CCP) fit under this definition, but exactly how CCP would operate under, or over, the future SAR government still remained to be seen.

25. See *The Ethos of the Hong Kong Chinese* (Note 14), p. 78.

26. A total of 36.9% of the respondents did not form an opinion, and the researchers concluded that "the topic of political parties is still a very controversial subject to the Hong Kong Chinese and they have difficulty in arriving at an established opinion on it. See *The Ethos of the Hong Kong Chinese* (Note 14), p. 79.

27. See Note 17, p. 185.

28. Between 7 and 23 October 1993, Patten's popularity was tracked on a daily basis for over half a month, and then on a weekly basis up to the end of 1993. From 1994 onwards, his popularity was tracked on a monthly basis.

29. Recognition rates were not shown, as they remained very stable at over 90% level.

30. But there was general support for the expansion of functional constituencies, increasing directly elected seats in the District Boards and the municipal councils, and some other specific proposals, upon prompting and probing.

31. Some parties adopted the Chinese line of thinking that Patten's proposals contradicted the Basic Law and the Joint Declaration, and therefore should not be discussed at all.

32. These table and figure have already been reported by the author in *The Other Hong Kong Report 1994* (Note 21), pp. 110–11.

33. It meant that all leaders of the Alliance, if elected into the Legco in the run-up to 1997, would not be allowed to sit on the First Legislative Assembly of the SAR. It subsequently turned out that, with the final breakdown of the Sino-British talks, there would not be "through train" for *any* Legco member.

34. POP Poll 17–20 May 1994 conducted by the author, and reported by various news media on 4 June 1994. Previous years' figures were also summarized in the poll report.

35. The poll captured 1,080 respondents over two separate samples of about equal size. On the desired quality of the First Chief Executive, the following table summarized the findings:

Attributes prompted	Very important	Important + very important
Candidate's personality	70.4%	87.7%
Executive experience	66.2%	85.9%
Acceptance by the Hong Kong people	57.7%	86.5%
Acceptance by the Chinese government	36.0%	68.6%
Acceptance by the civil servants	24.7%	65.7%

36. The polls were the same as those reported in Table 9.

22

Culture

Stephen M. H. Sze

THE SIGNIFICANCE OF CULTURE

The idea of culture is adopted from Raymond Williams, understood in a broadly social sense, as "a description of a particular way of life, which expresses certain meanings and values not only in art and learning but also in institutions and ordinary behaviour."[1] He goes further to clarify the theory and analysis of culture as follows:

> I would then define the theory of culture as the study of relationships between elements in a whole way of life. The analysis of culture is the attempt to discover the nature of the organization which is the complex of these relationships. Analysis of particular works or institutions is, in this context, culture analysis of their essential kind of organization, the relationships which works or institutions embody as parts of the organization as whole. A keyword, in such analysis, is pattern: it is with the discovery of patterns of a characteristic kind that any useful cultural analysis begins, and it is with the relationships between these patterns, which sometimes reveal unexpected identities and correspondences in hitherto separately considered activities, sometimes again reveal discontinuities of an unexpected kind, that general cultural analysis is concerned.[2]

However, the analysis is confined within areas of information, entertainment, consumer culture and forms of everyday life manifested as recorded culture "in either print, film, artefacts or, most recently, electronic media."[3] How these areas are related to the existence or formation of attitudes, values and beliefs is the foremost concern of this chapter. The other concern is to analyse the relation between culture and the society of policy-makers and recipients, because their cultural practice reflects not only the whole way of life and conflict,[4] it is also socially significant and its success or failure may imply social integration or disintegration.

THE MODE OF BRITISH COLONIAL CULTURE IN HONG KONG

British colonialism is best characterized by its cultural non-interventionism as compared with the French. In the history of Hong Kong since the 1840s, British colonists have not tried to graft the British way of life upon the masses in Hong Kong. The result is a remarkable cultural segregation between the elite colonial minority and the Chinese majority. The traditional Chinese way of life of the common people has been retained, which is best manifested in the preservation of the traditional Chinese customs and cultural entertainment. As a matter of fact, even the Westernization that took place after World War II with the progress of material affluence was more a result of American than British cultural influence. Hollywood films, U.S. popular music and sports, and even the fast food culture that took root since the 1970s are all American importations.

Recently, the Japanese cultural influx among the younger generation is another interesting cultural phenomenon. The most typical case is popular music. Formerly from the 1950s to the 1970s, many popular songs, mainly sung in Mandarin, borrowed their melody from U.S. popular songs. From the late 1980s till now, Japanese popular song melodies are continuously borrowed to match with Chinese texts to form local popular songs.

In comparison, the British way of life is of no importance in Hong Kong. With the dawning of material affluence upon Hong Kong since the late 1970s, indigenous forms of mass culture emerged. Good indicators of the predominance or at least the greater popularity of indigenous culture can be observed in the press, radio and TV media. Newspapers, radio and TV channels in Chinese language outnumber and enjoy much wider audienceship than those in English language. Local TV productions account for over 90% of the whole volume of productions in the Chinese Channels of broadcast TV, a phenomenal achievement. Locally produced popular songs and feature films are much better received than foreign productions. All these indicate the rise of an indigenous form of cultural interest, although it is more entertainment-oriented.

Cultural Transition of a Society from Scarcity to Affluence in Hong Kong

The intensive proliferation of cultural life of the masses has a lot to do with several aspects of the socio-economic development of Hong Kong in recent years. There is, first of all, great increase in the working population of Hong Kong (see Table 1). There has been a trend of accompanying reduction of working hours (see Table 2). The increase of household income has also been startling (see Table 3).

Table 1. Economically Active Population (over 15 years of age)

Year	Female	Male
1981	885,415	1,618,389
1986	1,037,437	1,716,411
1991	1,068,731	1,742,271
1992	1,026,500	1,766,500

Sources: Census and Statistics Department, *Hong Kong 1991 Population Census, Main Report*, p. 85; *Hong Kong Annual Digest of Statistics*, 1993 edition, p. 29.

Table 2. Number of Working Hours per Week

Year	No. of working hours/week	
	Female	Male
1976	48	51
1981	47	50
1986	45	48

Source: Census and Statistics Department, *Hong Kong 1986 By-Census, Main Report*, Vol. 1, p. 39.

With the sharp increase in the working population (especially more women having been mobilized into the workforce), the reduction of working hours (also more so when women are concerned), and the tremendous increase of household income as a result of higher productivity and greater

Table 3. Household Income per Month

Year	Household income/month (value of 1991 in HK$)
1981	2,955
1986	5,160
1991	9,964

Source: Census and Statistics Department, *Hong Kong 1991 Population Census, Main Report*, p. 63.

involvement of the family members, the outcome is the unprecedented material affluence of Hong Kong society. These factors have contributed to a cultural change in several ways. In fact, as early as 1984, a research showed that the social values of Hong Kong had encountered a transition from a materialistic to a post-materialistic mode, "from giving top priority to physical sustenance and safety towards heavier emphasis on belonging, self-expression, and the quality of life."[5] The 475 adult residents of Hong Kong who were interviewed expressed greater concern for "more say in government," "more say on job," "freedom of speech," "less impersonal society" and even "cultural growth" than "fight against prices," "fight against crime," "economic growth" and even a "stable economy."[6]

THE COMMERCIALISM IN THE CULTURAL PRIVATE SECTOR

The affluence of Hong Kong society is manifested by high mass consumption oriented towards luxury goods and service, intensive media exposure and proliferation of entertainment as well as information.

❑ Advertising and Consumer Culture

The most important indicator of this kind of culture is the advertising expenditure in media. Table 4 shows the trend from 1984 to 1991, while Table 5 illustrates the greater increase in advertising expenditure in recent years.

From 1982 to 1992, the average growth rate of advertising expenditure is 18.3%. To sustain this high rate of growth, the market requires an equally flourishing rate of expansion. Within this high growth rate in advertising

Table 4: Advertising Expenditure in Media in Hong Kong, 1984–1991 (HK$ million)

	1984	1985	1986	1987	1988	1989	1990	1991
All media	2,355.0	2,871.2	3,376.3	3,898.9	4,711.0	5,531.7	6,719.0	7,569.2
Television								
ATV Home	206.6	284.4	289.1	268.4	294.8	339.6	514.6	611.2
TVB Jade	1,083.6	1,286.8	1,500.4	1,759.7	2,067.9	2,196.6	2,488.6	2,829.6
Total Chinese	*1,290.1*	*1,571.2*	*1,789.5*	*2,028.1*	*2,362.7*	*2,536.2*	*3,003.2*	*3,440.8*
ATV World	40.3	61.1	62.8	73.7	73.6	69.2	90.5	123.7
TVB Pearl	87.0	95.3	116.6	137.6	171.7	187.8	197.3	215.3
Total English	*127.3*	*156.3*	*179.3*	*211.3*	*245.3*	*257.0*	*287.8*	*339.0*
Total	1,417.5	1,727.5	1,968.8	2,239.4	2,608.0	2,793.2	3,291.0	3,779.8
Radio	108.3	105.9	101.5	96.8	132.2	207.6	295.8	353.1
Print								
Newspapers	536.9	675.1	864.2	1,019.0	1,237.9	1,587.3	1,927.8	2,139.5
Magazines	236.3	276.8	325.9	401.5	543.2	715.3	904.1	964.2
Total	773.2	951.9	1,190.2	1,420.4	1,781.0	2,302.6	2,831.8	3,103.8
MTR	36.6	52.4	77.0	89.2	115.2	141.6	196.7	227.6
Cinema	12.8	25.4	29.3	44.4	65.6	75.5	87.2	87.3
Others	6.7	8.1	9.5	8.6	8.9	11.2	16.5	17.6

Source: Hong Kong Adex 1984–1991.

Table 5. Advertising Expenditure in Media in Hong Kong, 1991–1993

Year	TV advertising expenditure (HK$ billion)	Total advertising expenditure (HK$ billion)
1991	3.78	7.6
1992	4.34	9.2
1993	4.97	11.0

Source: SRG Research Services

expenditure, the performance of the TV medium is losing weight while that of newspapers and others are increasing in weight. From 1986 to 1992, TV advertising expenditure increased in money terms, but its proportion to the total expenditure decreased from 58% to 47%. At the same time, the proportion of newspapers increased from 26% to 31%, and that of magazines from 10% to 12%.

It is also interesting to examine the advertising categories in recent years shown in Table 6.

"Leisure" here stands for travel and accommodation for people in Hong Kong who arrange tours overseas or in Mainland China. This is, in fact, one of the fastest growing service industries in Hong Kong. Real estate have become the second largest category of advertising expenditure as a result of the opening of TV advertising market for local and Mainland Chinese real estate developers and the booming for real estate markets in the two places. Looking at the figures, one can observe the general trend of the remarkable increase of expenditure on luxury goods and services reflected by the domination of these categories in the advertising market. Real estate should not be considered as necessary goods, because the price of real estate far exceeded the affordability of the general public, and these have become a luxurious item of speculation by 1993 and 1994.

A recent research sponsored by *Overseas Chinese Daily News* (formerly named *Wah Kiu Yat Po* and now having been closed down) reflected the high brand name consciousness of the general public in Hong Kong. Out of the 100 most popular brand marks, 87 are international ones and 13 local. Neither Mainland Chinese nor Taiwanese brand marks are on the list. In categories of automobiles, electrical appliances and photo-appliances, Japanese, European and U.S. brand marks reign supreme. European and

Table 6. Advertising Categories

	Rank		1992		1993		Per cent increase
	1993	1992	HK$m	%	HK$m	%	
Leisure	1	1	1,450.0	15.7	1,614.0	14.6	11.3
Real estate	2	2	1,103.2	11.9	1,597.9	14.5	44.8
Retail	3	3	862.5	9.3	954.3	8.7	10.6
Toiletries	4	4	598.6	6.5	671.7	6.1	12.2
Personal items	5	5	584.4	6.3	643.5	5.8	10.1
Foodstuffs	6	7	550.2	5.9	640.1	5.8	16.3
Industrial/office equipment	7	8	476.2	5.1	609.2	5.5	27.9
Electrical appliances	8	6	551.9	6.0	581.2	5.3	5.3
Finance and banking	9	9	409.1	4.4	572.1	5.2	39.8
Miscellaneous	10	14	326.1	3.5	486.9	4.4	49.3
All categories			9,260.5	100.0	11,018.3	100.0	19.0

Source: *Media*, 18 February 1994.

U.S. brand marks dominated the market of sports articles and high fashion.[7] In short, the popularity of designer fashions, accessories, cosmetics and toiletries, hairstyling shops, sports articles and equipment, and finally tourism indicate the luxurious lifestyle of Hong Kong nowadays.

❏ *Media Culture*

Among the different forms of popular culture, TV is still the most popular one. Every evening, broadcast TV still attracts more than two million people. Despite the advent of STAR TV and Cable TV, broadcast TV still enjoys supremacy. One interesting phenomenon was the success of the TV series *Pao, the Judge* (包青天) imported from Taiwan. It reached as many as 1.9 million people on the average every evening from 9 August 1993 to 21 May 1994 at TVB Jade. As a matter of fact, Taiwanese TV series have never been so popular before in Hong Kong, the reason being its inferior production technicality — too much low-key lighting and the tempo too slow — when compared with that of Hong Kong. The *Pao* series was successful because of not only the editing done to streamline the plot with good quality of synchronization, but also the freshness of the series in comparison with the situation comedies that have turned into clichés without good plots and even good lines. Furthermore, some critics even attributed the success to a plausible ideological context: the people of Hong Kong have become so demoralized and helpless in face of the political transition that the image of Judge Pao, a person of strong character (even at times, authoritarian), can act as a kind of wish-fulfilment for the masses as a benevolent patriarch or saviour.

The success of this series was followed immediately by the relative success of another Taiwanese sword-fight series *Heaven Sword vs. Dragon Sabre* (倚天屠龍記), which ranked fifth among the whole list of series broadcasted in 1994. Another locally produced sword-fight series *The Legend of the Condor Heroes 1994* (re-make) (九四射雕英雄傳) ranked third. *The Fate of the Last Empire* (清宮氣數錄), a historical drama, ranked second in 1994, and *Fate of the Clairvoyante* (再見亦是老婆) ranked fourth. This last series earned appreciable success, and became the talk of the town because of its tackling the problem of ex-marital sex, divorce and the reorientation of the way of life of a jilted wife. These problems have become more common and are no taboo of discussion. The message of the series was very conservative in the sense that the housewife attained higher self-consciousness after being jilted by keeping fit, becoming more beautiful by better style of dressing and make-up. The moralism was reflected by her faithfulness to her husband and the repentance of the latter at the end.

The popularity of the different genres of TV series reveals the way of reception of TV audience. Despite the fact that these successful genres are quite different from each other in type, they have some traits in common. They are mixed genres with certain common fundamental denominators: *Pao, the Judge*, *The Fate of the Last Empire*, *The Legend of the Condor Heroes 1994* and *Heaven Sword vs. Dragon Sabre* contain melodramatic elements, suspense, sword and fist fights, to provide for sensuous gratifications. *Fate of the Clairvoyante* contains melodramatic elements, gags and romances. All these reflects the populistic form of TV entertainment in Hong Kong ever since its advent.[8] Nevertheless, TV audience are fickle and their attention span has become shorter and shorter. The strategy so far is to revolve around the common lowest denominator of the different genres in succession.

Film culture in Hong Kong has also undergone a process of crisis. The total box office of locally produced films in 1994 has dropped below \$1 billion to only \$957 million, while the total box office becomes stagnant at \$1.3 billion, despite the annual dramatic increase of ticket prices. In 1993, the film that topped box office was *Jurassic Park* (over \$60 million), and in 1994, it was *Speed* (over \$40 million), thus breaking the predominance of local productions over foreign films in Hong Kong for over a decade. There is the accusal driven at young directors saying that foreign films are made merely for the winning of international prices, instead of catering for the entertainment needs of the general public. Many critics counter-argued that the local film production had degenerated into fixed formulae of big star system, mixed genres of the lowest denominators — either kung fu, action films or nonsensical comedies, in which gun, sword or fist fights, gags and melodramatic elements intermixed to provide audience with sensuous gratifications all-round. The film industry in Hong Kong has been too reliant upon a small number of big film stars to get good box office. These big stars have begun to lose their lustre and popularity without successors, and their wages have reached an exorbitant level that moderate budgets cannot afford to engage them. The result is a great dilemma: film producers must either run the risk of engaging these big stars and cut down other expenses to produce a qualitatively poor film, or they dispense with these big stars but run the risk of not being attractive enough, despite better production quality. The result is great polarization of the box office of locally produced films. At one end, there are a few successful super budget films that can cash up to \$30 million or more; at the other end, there are a lot more films with revenues below \$6 million. The number of films that can gather \$10–20 million are decreasing.[9] Like other production industries, film production also move into Mainland China, and the speed is quite fast despite the strict conditions of cooperation and censorship.

Another similar phenomenon of mass culture is that of popular music. A research on popular music carried out by the *Hong Kong Policy Viewers* showed that the award-winning popular songs of Hong Kong from 1984 to 1993 numbered 138, of which 102 are love songs. The top four production companies produced 113 songs out of the 138. The state of oligopoly leads to the conservative policy of producing overwhelmingly love songs to guarantee profit. Furthermore, the popularity of the songs depends more and more upon the idols. From 1984 to 1989, the top three singers procured an average of 37.8% of the award-winning songs, while from 1990 to 1993, the top three singers procured an average of 51.8%.[10] Thus, the popularity and success are more and more concentrated upon fewer idols and their affiliated production companies.

Beginning from the 1990s, there is also a gradual fusion of the popular song culture between Mainland China, Taiwan and Hong Kong. The ascending popularity of Mandarin popular songs sung by local popular singers can be attributed not only to the greater market demand of these songs, but also to the ease of identity of local singers with the Mainland culture, which was rather difficult from the 1970s to the early 1980s when Hong Kong became affluent and looked down on Mainland culture and society. The fusion is not one-sided, for the younger generation in Mainland China are also familiar with and fond of Cantonese popular songs of Hong Kong as well. The syncretism of Cantonese, English, Mandarin and other languages in song texts have also become more common than before, although orthodox critics regard this trend as vulgarization and cultural disintegration. This development is the remains of a cosmopolitan cultural snobbery found in the mass culture of Hong Kong.

THE CULTURAL AGENDA OF THE GOVERNMENT

The role of the government in cultural matters are threefold: (1) to regulate the free market against monopoly and irregularities; (2) to support those cultural activities that are necessary to maintain a good cultural identity and development; and (3) to lay down basic norms for cultural practice to safeguard freedom of speech and public decency at the same time. Measuring by the above criteria, the performance of the Recreation and Culture Branch (RCB) of the Hong Kong government is highly inadequate. The policy of the RCB has been very passive especially in dealing with TV broadcasting. Since the launching of Cable TV in late 1993, the general public as well as a great number of Legislative Councillors have supported the introduction of Public Access TV and the Government Channel, reserved for RTHK (Radio Television Hong Kong) productions. It is deemed that the former can guarantee communal communication and creativity, while the latter can balance off the detrimental effect of commercial TV programmes. The decision-making process has been continuously delayed without adequate explanation.

Admittedly, the RCB has been supporting serious performing arts activities through the Council for the Performing Arts and the Music Office. The estimated support for the former in 1994–1995 is $40 million, as compared with \$36.68 million in 1993–1994, and an average of \$35 million per annum from 1990–1993. However, there is a great discrepancy between those groups officially funded and those funded only by project. The former are more traditional and ordained as the mainstream, while more progressive and avant-garde groups are discriminated in a way. Furthermore, in matters of mass culture like popular music, film, and printed materials, the government adopts the *laissez-faire* policy.

Only RTHK performs as a keen competitor in the radio scene and as a weak compensator in the TV scene. It is hoped that the establishment of the Arts Development Council can ameliorate the grievances and develop a more comprehensive arts and cultural policy to embrace high art and mass culture as a whole.

With regard to the role of the government as the watchdog of social decency in media, it is seen in the social awareness level of the abuse of legislation loopholes by certain media owners. The flooding in the streets of advertising posters of category III films in the summer of 1993 led to wide protests from different social pressure groups, in the purpose of urging the government to introduce censorship to these posters before they are put up for public display. The trend of publishing pornographic comics (class II, indecent printed material, only to be purchased by and circulated among people above 18) in the form and packaging for young lovers or those in love in the summer of 1994, which can be easily mistaken for class I (suitable for all ages) and contain scenes of loose sexual morality, alarmed the general public as well as media critics and educators. The government was forced to react by drafting new laws to make class II materials more distinguishable, with contact address of publishers, and to enforce more strongly the law against selling these materials to the underage. All these tumults reflected the passive role of the government in defending public decency and protecting minors in matters of pornography and violence in printed media. There exists an opinion in the RCB that the government should act in this aspect only in accordance with public opinion. This is ridiculous because public opinion is often too diffused to be tapped, and in matters of pornography, the public tends to be too moralistic and overreact. Even if there is a well-formed public opinion, it is also the duty of the government to judge and to implement a good policy. Thus, the government should be able to investigate and rationally decide upon the baseline of social decency, safeguard the rights of the people to be informed and entertained, and also to be protected against abuses, offence and harm.

If the commercial media culture in Hong Kong is often unscrupulous in matters of violence and pornography when profit is concerned, it is very compliant in political matter. This is best manifested in the joining of seven stations (4 TV and 3 radio stations) to broadcast the programme of the National Day of the People's Republic of China upon the request of the New China News Agency (NCNA). Yet, the audience rating was discouraging and the general reception rather poor. This showed the antipathy of Hong Kong population against too much political zeal. It may be right to say that the cultural mind of Hong Kong people is apolitical, hedonistic and rather pragmatic.

NEW DEVELOPMENTS IN FACE OF 1997: TOWARDS A "CULTURAL CHINA"?

In face of 1997, China has become a more important source of cultural influence to Hong Kong than ever before. A scholarly critic pointed out three characteristics of recent development. First, Mainland Chinese become more and more accepted in the media of Hong Kong. They were formerly conveniently stereotyped as or associated with whores, armed robbers, persons of ridicule and comic figures. Now their images are less stereotyped and more decent and congenial in the media as entertainers. Second, there are more and more programmes related to Mainland China, as guidance for tourism, objects of quiz and other entertainments. Third, owing to cheaper production costs in Mainland China, joint film and TV productions of Hong Kong or Taiwan with China become more and more common. The screening of productions from these regions are also increasing in a fast pace. *Pao, the Judge*, a Taiwanese production, for instance, was screened also in Mainland China before it was screened in Hong Kong.[11]

The creation of a cultural China is nowhere more vehement than in the field of satellite TV. As many as 4 locally based consortia scramble for opening the Mainland Chinese TV market with some 16 other foreign giant corporations. The China Entertainment Television Broadcasting Ltd. is a typical example. The owner, Robert Chua, wants to "tailor" his programmes especially for Mainland China, whereby there will not be any sex and violence, and most important of all, no news programme, which is deemed even more dangerous by the Chinese censors. If this is the necessary orientation for the development of a cultural China, then the result will be a negative utopia of entertainment and no critical social consciousness. The cultural status quo of Hong Kong is already no cause for enthusiasm, but there is really a danger of further degeneration into this kind of negative utopia after 1997.

CONCLUSION: POSSIBLE AND REMOTE CULTURAL CRISIS IN (HONG KONG) SAR AND REMEDIES

❏ *The Hedonism, Social Apathy and Possessive Individualism of the General Public*

Culture in Hong Kong is polarized into the elite forms of high culture and the vulgar forms of mass culture. Although the elite forms of high culture have gained greater popularity than before, the success is too moderate when considering the amount of financial support from the government. Naturally, these cultural forms require support, or else they will die out. However, the result is providing free cultural dinner to the elite or snobs in the middle and upper social strata, while the general mass is left to the mercy of the commercial cultural enterprises or oligopoly with their vulgarity and hedonism. This kind of polarization has social roots. It is due to the total lack of artistic and cultural components on the one hand, and media component on the other, in the curricula of the primary and secondary schools, or even in tertiary education, that the general public is ignorant of the meaning and significance of high art on the one hand, and of the vulgarity and manipulation of mass culture on the other.

In face of this cultural polarization, there is hardly any room for cultural consciousness and identity of an authentic nature. Admittedly, there is a long existent elite culture of classical music, art film, artistic performances and even traditional Chinese cultural performance of all kinds. The last form has enjoyed great expansion recently due to the more frequent visits and performances of Mainland artistic groups. This forms a part of the cultural awareness in the sense of inheriting the past excellence in culture. There is, however, little development of a cultural awareness and identity of an indigenous kind, to express in cultural form the form of life, its significance and value in the context of Hong Kong. On the contrary, elite art is better understood as mimicry, and a despisement of the provincialism of what is indigenous. In matters of mass culture, it is the reverse — a provincialism loomed large, as if it were the very label of the Hong Kong way of life, not so much liberal but libertine. There is also a strong sense of arrogance and chauvinism, with which even the fusion of the forms of mass culture into a cultural China is also infused, because the technicality, packaging and image design of Hong Kong productions are all deemed more advanced and superior, as much as the stars are more versatile — in fact, it is due to media parasitism or symbiosis that TV, popular music and film stars are the same batch of people, exploiting their success in one by grafting conveniently upon all to save promotion of new talents and secure the earning of quick cash. Hedonism and egoism are mistaken as a form of individual freedom, vulgarism is adopted as a way of tongue in cheek reaction against the orthodoxy or excellence of traditional culture.

There is one common characteristic between the high and mass culture of Hong Kong. This was labelled as "possessive individualism":

> Possessive individualism is revealed in high culture as personal distinction and accomplishment. Being educated in high culture is a personal good, a way to earn a decent living, an honour to be able to entertain the leisure class. High culture has become a symbol of class distinction, because no people from the masses can afford the leisure nor possess the intellectual ability to accomplish high culture. High culture is something that one can be proud of and a cause for the leisure class to be arrogant about themselves.
>
> At the other extreme in mass culture, one sees the general masses inebriated by the entertainment and consumption offered. More mass entertainment means less awareness of the social reality of great discrepancy of power, status and social opportunities. More consumption means a tighter yoke to the status quo of the establishment, more hard work in blind obedience, and more harm done to the environment through the production of social waste....[12]

❑ *The Role of the State*

The impending cultural crisis is that of reverting from *laissez-faire* in mass culture, and policy in favour of the cultural elite, to that of total control and prescription. This is the worst possible culture nightmare that can be anticipated. Undeniably, the long apolitical and commercial forms of mass culture, as well as the fostered high culture as mimicry alike, have not benefited the cultural and social awareness and identity of the different social strata. Yet, total cultural control and complete determination of the agenda can be just as undesirable. How to steer between these two reefs is of primary importance. The policy is to provide room for the further development of both commercial mass culture and high culture whenever possible, and determine the basic code of social decency, balance off the commercial and hedonistic by providing programmes of better taste and higher quality whenever necessary. This can maintain cultural pluralism without undermining the private and commercial sector on the one hand, and promote better taste, higher critical consciousness and more consolidated social and cultural identity on the other.

In fact, not only RTHK is considered to be rendering great service to the community, some critics with visions deem the necessity of promoting better film and popular music culture by the government through the setting up of funds to support better productions. Of course, it is the responsibility of independent commissions of experts to judge whatever is good, and not the government. This kind of practice is common in many countries with over-commercialized mass culture. To work against the predominance of Hollywood film culture, Germany and Taiwan (the latter also has to counter Hong Kong influence in commercial cinema) are typical examples that guarantee quality national film production through public funding. The result so far is encouraging. On the other side of the pendulum, one can see the loosening of the grip of political and ideological control upon film production in Mainland China, not only because too much control or protection have brought about a great deterioration in quality and competitiveness, and hence the loss of popularity, but also because the economic burden for the state is too great to shoulder.

Social awareness and cultural identity are not values that can be achieved within a short time. As long as our education system is still examination-oriented, the question of artistic values and good taste never belong to the curricula; as long as the general public is not yet aware of their rights in media and as consumers, nor have they the necessary media literacy to be critical of mass media, there will be little prospect of improvement. Thus, there is the need of the education system and the media to act in unison under succinct supervision to promote media literacy, higher and more critical cultural awareness, and finally to incur greater consciousness of the rights of the citizens to be well informed, critically educated and decently entertained.

Notes

1. Raymond Williams, "The Analysis of Culture," in *Culture, Ideology and Social Process*, edited by Tony Bennett, *et al*. (London: Open University, 1981), p. 43.
2. Ibid., p. 47.
3. Diana Crane (ed.), *The Sociology of Culture* (Oxford: Blackwell, 1994), p. 3.
4. Dick Hebdige, "From Culture to Hegemony," in *The Cultural Studies Reader*, edited by Simon During (London: Routledge, 1993), p. 362. Here D. Hebdige contrasted the descriptive understanding of culture as "a theory of relations between elements in a whole way of life" by R. Williams with that of a conflict model of culture as "the study of relationships in a whole way to conflict" of E. P. Thompson. Actually, harmony and conflict in culture coexist in a complex for which merits detailed analyses.
5. Ronald Inglehart, *Culture Shift in Advanced Industrial Society* (New Jersey: Princeton University Press, 1990), p. 66.
6. Ibid., p. 154.
7. *Overseas Chinese Daily News*, special feature, 28 November 1994.
8. From "1994 TVB Jade Dramas Ratings Performance," Marketing Research and Information, 25 January 1995. The author have to express his thanks to Mr. Siu Wai-hung, Head of Programme Development of TVB, for his supply of the required data and advice on the interpretation of the materials.
9. *City Entertainment* (電影雙週刊), Issue 410 (29 December 1994–11 January 1995), pp. 29–32.
10. Please refer to "Hegemony and Popular Culture — A Content Analysis of Gold Songs," *Hong Kong Policy Viewers* (November 1994), pp. 28–29, especially the two tables.
11. Please refer to the article by Ma Kit-wai on "The Creation of the New Plan of Cultural China by the Film and TV Media" (影視媒介創劃「文化中國」新版圖), *Hong Kong Economic Journal*, 19 August 1994.
12. Stephen M. H. Sze, "Cultural Life in Hong Kong," in *The Other Hong Kong Report 1992*, edited by Joseph Y. S. Cheng and Paul C. K. Kwong (Hong Kong: The Chinese University Press, 1992), p. 461.

Index

Legend: † place names